LINCOLN
and the
WAR DEMOCRATS

The Grand Erosion
of Conservative Tradition

Christopher Dell

Rutherford • Madison • Teaneck
Fairleigh Dickinson University Press
London: Associated University Presses

© 1975 by Associated University Presses, Inc.

Associated University Presses, Inc.
Cranbury, New Jersey 08512

Associated University Presses
108 New Bond Street
London W1Y OQX, England

Library of Congress Cataloging in Publication Data

Dell, Christopher, 1927-
  Lincoln and the War Democrats.

  Bibliography: p.
  Includes index.
  1. United States—Politics and government—Civil War, 1861-1865. 2. Democratic Party. 3. Lincoln, Abraham, Pres. U. S., 1809-1865. I. Title.
E459.D33   320.9'73'07   73-21227
ISBN 0-8386-1466-3

*Dedicated
with Profound Appreciation
to
my father, the late Floyd Dell,
and
my wife, Kathleen Kane Dell.*

*Without Floyd's help this work would never
have begun; without Kate's help it would
never have been finished.*

Contents

Introduction

Abraham Lincoln was the Pied Piper of Civil War politics who lured unwary Democrats with Conservative phraseology and Radical intent. At his urging, enough voters left the Democratic party between 1860 and 1865 to weaken the framework of Conservative American tradition, and bring it down in shambles. By talking and acting as he did, he saw to the creation of a mighty force—the so-called "War Democracy"—which agreed to fight against its own instincts and prejudice, at the expense of men and theories and principles it had been worshipping for many years. And as spiritual father of the wartime Union party, Lincoln saw to the destruction of "Democratic Regularity"—the staunch and firm defender of slave property rights—until the flag of Conservatism trailed in the dust and the Democratic party was exposed as the fanatical protector of the cotton interests and the Judas of Jeffersonian idealism.

In keeping with Conservative purposes, a great many Democrats opposed the Lincoln policies of 1861–1865, demanding peace at any price. They recognized Lincoln for what he was—the butcher of Conservative tradition—and on that basis refused to help him with his war. Against them stood a host of War Democrats, who joined with Lincoln in the battle for American survival.

The War Democrats were highly important to the Union cause. There are grounds for contending that without their assistance the federal government would have been powerless to restore the Union by force of arms. Credit for the nonpartisan support rendered the federal authorities at this

9

juncture must of course go mainly to the War Democrats themselves. But a measure of credit must also go to Lincoln, who secured the following of thousands upon thousands of non-Republicans in 1861, and held much of it, against terrible odds, through four long years of Civil War.

The coalition of Lincoln and the War Democrats was neither natural nor comfortable. The Democratic party of 1861 was strong and proud, and during the sixty years since Thomas Jefferson assumed the presidency, at the turn of the century, non-Democrats had occupied the White House for only two short terms. The Republican victory of 1860 was regarded by Democratic observers as an unfortunate fluke, and there were few of them who saw in Lincoln a man who could guide the country through a prolonged period of crisis. He seemed in this context as an interim president, between James Buchanan and the next Democrat, to be elected in 1864. The Democrats had foolishly divided in 1860 and Lincoln had sneaked in as a result; but he was not going to be there long before normalcy returned. Or so it was believed by Democrats in general in 1861.

On this basis, the War Democrats lined up at Lincoln's side when the Civil War began, expecting a brief encounter and a smashing early victory: They were mistaken in their optimism, in company with many other Unionists, and as time wore on they found themselves fighting for the very life of the republic; seemingly in the forefront all the way.

The War Democrats, at the outset of the war, regarded the Republican party, *per se,* as radical and revolutionary on the subject of the Negro race issue and its subsidiary issue, chattel slavery. They regarded Lincoln as a visionary, having vague, unspecified connections with certain radical elements incessantly plotting slave uprisings, wholesale emancipation, and amalgamation of the races. They believed that Lincoln's party had brought on the Civil War, to a large extent, by assuming an intransigent position and refusing to compromise with anybody. They did not like Lincoln and did not trust him, and he agreed to trust them only because he had no other choice. Nor, for that matter, had the War Democrats any choice. What was established between Lincoln and the War Democrats was at best a compulsory, nervous, neurotic partnership which seemingly had every reason to collapse at every hint of crisis. And yet, miraculously, the partnership prevailed and continued to prevail in the face of extraordinary pressures.

The War Democrats sought to sway the policies of Lincoln, without significant effect. In time, with the dramatic shifting of popular opinion in the loyal states, many Democrats who had once endorsed the Union cause decided to abandon it; but others held on, despite radical political developments of many kinds. At the close of the war the term "War Democrat" was well known and hailed as a badge of honor. Publications on the subject of the Civil War as late as the 1890s used the term frequently. In time, however, it fell into disfavor. Historians, seeking shortcuts and easy explanations, chose to emphasize not the War Democrats but their opposites, the Peace Democrats, who professed to represent more accurately the Democratic faith. Once accepted on a wide scale, this notion began to undermine the memory of the War Democrats, who have faded from historical recognition with increasing rapidity since the last influential survivors of their group passed away. It is my intention to recall the glory of the War Democrats and to emphasize their importance to the country at a dreadful hour when without their aid the country might well have been shot to oblivion.

LINCOLN
and the
WAR DEMOCRATS

1

The Importance of the War Democrats

1 ...IN THE FREE STATES

It is often observed that immediately following the Confederate seizure of Ft. Sumter, in April, 1861, the North became "united to the man," in behalf of the Union. Manifestations of pro-southern sentiment in the North, widespread before the Sumter attack, vanished overnight, as did also every trace of quarreling and bickering between the several northern political factions. Within a matter of hours a pro-war spirit was said to have captured the entire northern political community, excepting only a handful of malcontents. The dramatic story of northern unity in time of crisis was widely published in the northern press of 1861, repeated with alarm in the southern press, and subsequently reported by scores of Civil War historians as though it were the gospel.[1] It is, however, a story in conflict with the facts.

When the Civil War began there already existed in the free states and in the loyal border slave states a sizable "Peace" faction, ardently opposed to the adoption of federal policies looking to forceful suppression of the Confederate cause. The Peace faction appeared for the first time shortly following secession of South Carolina from the Union (December 20, 1860)[2] and exerted a powerful influence in conservative circles from that moment until the close of the war. In the Antebellum period, leaders of the Peace faction included every non-Republican of consequence in the free states and in the

15

border slave states, excepting only the Secessionists and a sprinkling of especially ardent Unionists, some of whom were proto-War Democrats. The two 1860 Democratic presidential candidates—Stephen A. Douglas and John C. Breckinridge—were Antebellum Peace leaders. So were John Bell, presidential candidate on the 1860 Constitutional Union ticket, and his chief lieutenant, Senator John J. Crittenden of Kentucky. So were many devoted followers of Democratic President James Buchanan who himself seemed bent upon an executive policy dedicated to peace at almost any price, throughout the course of the Secession controversy.[3]

Until the Confederate attack on Ft. Sumter, it was widely believed among Conservative Unionists that Secession was merely a political maneuver; that as soon as certain assurances and guarantees were provided the South by the Lincoln administration, Secession would be forgotten and the Union sustained. It was widely believed that under no conditions would Secessionists consider firing on the American flag.[4] The Antebellum declarations and policies of many Conservative Unionists were founded on these mistaken beliefs. Immediately following the Sumter attack the Peace cause lost many thousands of Conservative Unionists, dismayed and disillusioned by what they regarded as a personal betrayal on the part of the pro-slavery faction in the slave states. And yet the Peace cause did not die, by any means.

When the first War Congress assembled July 4, 1861, the members elected from the free states on the Democratic ticket were divided into two factions: the War Democrats and the Peace Democrats. Throughout the special session (July–August, 1861) the War faction outnumbered the Peace faction three to one. When the following session convened, in December, 1861, the War faction was divided in half, fifty percent of its members adopting a position in favor of the war on certain specific conditions. The new faction, hereinafter called the Conditional War Democrats or "Conditionals," voted sometimes for war, sometimes for peace, serving as the balance of power within the Democratic organization.[5]

As the war progressed, the relative strength of the Democratic factions would change, from time to time, in Congress and within the rank and file of the northern Democracy. One thing remained constant, however. There was always disunity in the free states, on a grand scale; enough disunity, in fact, to provide the leaders of the Peace faction with a strong sense of self-confidence, from the very beginning of the war. They knew that the 1860 Republican majority in the free states was over 400,000—a formidable margin insofar as elections are concerned. On the other hand, the Lincoln ticket was endorsed in 1860 by only 57 percent of the voters in the free states, and that is not a very impressive statistic measured in terms of wartime requirements.

As of April, 1861, the Lincoln administration had sufficient support in the North to guarantee a sustained war effort, but only for a limited period of time. If the war should go badly for the Union cause, northern morale was certain to suffer and the Peace faction was certain of attracting additional Democratic support. A threat existed from the outset: that if ever the northern Democracy should once again unite for Peace, the federal war policy was doomed. That is, the Republicans could not win the war without help from the War Democrats. So reasoned the Peace Democrats and, for that matter, so reasoned the Republicans and the War Democrats themselves.

As a result of this reasoning there was *always,* in the free states, from Sumter to Appomattox, a raging battle between the War and Peace factions for control of the Democratic vote. Upon the victory of the War Democrats in this battle hung the fate of the Union—or so it was believed by many people at the time, in every political faction, North and South.

2 ...IN THE BORDER SLAVE STATES

It is often observed that the loyal border slave states were more or less dragooned into the war on the ·Union side; that a majority of the people in these states were in favor of Secession or Neutrality and that the only way they could be held to the Union was at the point of northern bayonets.[6] There is, however, no substantial evidence supporting this belief and a good deal of evidence casting doubt upon it.[7] The border slave states of Missouri, Kentucky, Maryland, Delaware, and West Virginia had some Disunion spirit, but not enough to seriously affect state policy one way or the other.

War Democrats had much to do with promoting and sustaining Unionist sentiment in every loyal border slave state. Although outnumbered within the Union party structure by border-state Whigs, Know Nothings, and "Americans," they were showered with honors and treated as a major partner. In border slave states carried by the Unionists, three War Democrats became members of the U.S. Senate,[8] 14 served in the House of Representatives,[9] and four served as Governor,[10] while countless others were elected to lesser state executive positions and as members of the several legislatures. Clearly, in the loyal border slave states as in the free states, the Union movement operated with the understanding that the backing of the War Democracy was essential to success.

3 ...IN THE UNION PARTY

It is often observed that the wartime Union party in the loyal states was merely "the Republican party under a different name."[11] The statement occasionally is accompanied by the admission that a few Democrats sometimes were placed on the wartime Union party ticket, to give the misleading impression that there really existed a genuine nonpartisan coalition. But all this was a sham, we are told, for in fact the Union party was not really nonpartisan, at all; merely "the Republican party under a different name." So say the critics of the Union party.

Actually, it was quite the other way around. There is no doubt that the Union party became a genuine nonpartisan coalition in almost every state in which it appeared. All the facts bear this out, as will be shown. It is interesting to note that the birthplace of the Union party movement was the loyal border slave states, which of all the loyal states were the ones with the weakest Republican organizations. The first merger of Republicans, War Democrats, and Union Whigs took place in January, 1861, in Missouri, where the Union Whigs appeared to be the strongest, the War Democrats the next strongest, and the Republicans the weakest.[12] Shortly afterwards, Douglas and Bell Unionists in Kentucky fused beneath the Union party banner.[13] Nor is there any basis for regarding the Union party in Missouri and Kentucky as "the Republican party under a different name." It was precisely what it purported to be: a Unionist coalition. In the other loyal border slave states the story was similar. The Union party of Maryland was originally the Unionist branch of the Democratic party, which broke away when Secessionist Democrats were nominated for office in the spring election campaign of 1861. Coalition was promptly established with the Union Whigs, Union "Americans," "Know Nothings," and Republicans. At this stage the Republicans were justifiably regarded as an altogether insignificant factor in Maryland politics.[14] The Union party coalitions organized in Kentucky, Delaware, and Western Virginia also were unquestionably genuine. And in Kentucky, Delaware, and Western Virginia, as in Missouri and Maryland, the Republican party was of slight political consequence when the Union party was formed.[15]

As the Union party movement spread north, the coalition of Republicans and non-Republican Unionists began to lean heavily on Republicans for leadership in many states where the Republicans were the dominant faction (in the same way that non-Republicans were selected for leadership in the loyal border slave states, where they had the largest popular following). Even this tendency was not pursued to its logical extreme, however. War Democrats were nominated to office on the Union party ticket in the free states far in excess of their "vote-getting" ability, if such ability can be estimated strictly in terms of partisan appeal. "Rock-ribbed" Republican Maine elected a War Democrat to the governorship in 1862. So did Republican Kansas. In Ohio the Union party nominated nothing but War Democrats for governor throughout the course of the war. Of Oregon, California, and Rhode Island it could be said that the Union party was really "the Democratic party under a different name," so numerous were the War Democrats in the upper echelons of the party organizations. [16]

During four years of Civil War, leadership of some of the Democratic state organizations changed hands several times. The pattern of the struggle was not identical in every state. In general, however, the War faction was dominant within the party from April 1861 until the Confederate victory at Second Bull Run, in September, 1862. The 1862 elections results were widely regarded as a sweeping victory for the Peace Democrats. Actually they were nothing of the kind (as will be shown), but the popular misconception to this effect had great political impact. Encouraged by the alleged "victory at the polls" and the Union defeat at Fredericksburg, immediately following the 1862 election campaign, the Peace faction took the field in force, with an open propaganda assault against the Union cause. Many War Democrats deserted the Democratic party at this juncture, in favor of the Union and Republican parties. Some switched back again following the elections of 1863, in which the Peace faction was humiliated and driven to cover. Others, disenchanted by intraparty discord, abandoned the Democratic organization for the remainder of the war, and some for the remainder of their lives.

4 . . .IN THE DISSEMINATION OF RADICAL DOCTRINE AND THE BREAKDOWN OF THE PRO-SLAVERY CAUSE

It is often observed that President Lincoln threw much of his influence to the Consservative side during the Civil War, working to appease the pro-slavery Unionists, of whom the War Democrats constituted the majority. In fact, however, the Conservative policies of the President extended only through the first year of the war, after which he moved steadily in a Radical direction, coaxing the War Democrats to follow his lead. That is not to say that Lincoln spoke or wrote in the style of a Radical, because his tone and manner always were Conservative. But the course of his policy was clearly Radical from 1862 to 1865, and the War Democrats who followed him the closest became, in many instances, the leading Radicals of the postwar Reconstruction period.[17]

There has seldom in history been so important an alliance as Lincoln and the War Democrats, nor one seemingly less likely of success. But the combination worked, not only destroying the Confederacy and the slavery institution, but charting the course American politics were to follow from the close of the war to the coming of the Roosevelt New Deal.[18]

NOTES

1. "The North is united to the man. . . ." Madison Weekly *Wisconsin Patriot.* April 27, 1861; ". . .all differences heretofore existing are forgotten; everybody is for the country and for the Union." Centreville *Indiana True Republican.* April 25, 1861; ". . .loyalty to the Union is the universal sentiment of the Northern people." New York *Times.* May 10, 1861.
   ". . .in the twinkling of an eye, as it were, when the Nation's flag was fired upon, in Charleston harbor, all bitterness seemed to disappear and Democrats and Republicans, leaders and writers came together, almost as one, every heart full of love for country, every man ready to defend the country and its honor, even to the extent of offering his life." Henry C. Campbell, *Wisconsin in Three Centuries, 1634–1905,* 4 vols. (New York, Century History: 1906), III:225.
   "During the Civil War, most Northern Democrats loyally supported the Lincoln administration, and were known as the 'War Democrats.' " James Truslow Adams, ed., *Dictionary of American History,* 5 vols. (New York: Scribner's, 1951, II:137.
2. Howard C. Perkins, ed., *Northern Editorials on Secession,* 2 vols. (New York: D. Appleton-Century, 1942), passim.
3. Allan Nevins, *Ordeal of the Union,* 2 vols. (New York: Scribner's, 1947; Kenneth M. Stampp, *And the War Came; the North and the Secession Crisis, 1860–1861* (Baton Rouge: Louisiana State University Press, 1950).
4. See chapter 3.
5. A breakdown of the voting records of the several Democratic Congressmen during the war years appears in Appendix 1, explaining which were War Democrats, which were Peace Democrats, and which were Conditional War Democrats. The basis for the designations also is provided in Appendix 1.
6. E. Merton Coulter, *The Civil War and Readjustment in Kentucky* (Chapel Hill: University of North Carolina Press, 1926), p. 17, declares of Kentucky that "between the North and the South the finer feelings of sentiment bound the state to the latter." Although admitting that the Unionists in Kentucky had the edge over the Disunionists, in 1861, James Randall also says that the people of Kentucky revealed not "the slightests impulse to fight the South," and a distinct "slowness. . .to accept the fact of war, the lingering feeling that war was not inescapable and that conciliatory efforts should still be tried." James G. Randall, *Civil War and Reconstruction* (Boston: Heath, 1937, 1953), p. 321.
7. During the Secession period, state conventions were assembled in Missouri, Kentucky, and Virginia, to decide about the matter of Secession. In Missouri and Kentucky the conventions declared for the Union, and in Virginia the delegates from all the western counties did the same. During the war the state of

Missouri was to supply almost as many troops to the Union cause as Connecticut, New Hampshire, and Rhode Island combined, and by October 1861 more Kentuckians had signed up to fight for the Union than the total number of Kentucky volunteers in the Confederate army during the full course of the war. Maryland and Delaware did not hold state conventions in 1861, and Maryland was subjected to the Baltimore riots of that year. But the Union party of Maryland carried every wartime election on a pro-Lincoln platform, and three times as many Marylanders volunteered for service with the Union army than the number that fought for the Confederacy. Charles R Anderson. *Fighting by Southern Federals. (New York: Neale, 1912), p. 33; Harold R. Manakee. Maryland in the Civil War.* (Baltimore: Maryland Historical Society, 1961), p. 108.

8. Border slave-state Democrats elected to the U.S. Senate as Unionists were: John B. Henderson of Missouri, Reverdy Johnson of Maryland, and John S. Carlile of Virginia.

9. Border slave-state Democrats elected to the House of Representatives on the Union ticket included: John A.J. Creswell, John W. Crisfield, and Francis Thomas of Maryland; Joseph W. McClurg, Benjamin F. Loan, and John W. Noell of Missouri; Lucian Anderson, Brutus J. Clay, Green Clay Smith, and Charles A. Wickliffe of Kentucky; John S. Carlile of Virginia; William G. Brown of Virginia and West Virginia; George W. Bridges and Andrew J. Clements of Tennessee. All of these supported Douglas in 1860 excepting Crisfield of Maryland, who supported Breckinridge, and Clay of Kentucky, who supported Bell. Clay became a Democrat in 1864 following service in the Union party organization from 1861 to 1863. Although elected as a War Democrat to the Senate in 1861, Carlile of Virginia abandoned the Union cause midway in the war.

10. War Democrats who joined the Union party and served as governors of the loyal border slave states during the war included: William Cannon, Delaware; Willard P. Hall, Missouri; James F. Robinson, Kentucky; Thomas E. Bramlette, Kentucky. Cannon and Robinson supported Breckinridge in 1860; Hall supported Dougas; Bramlette supported Bell but became a Democrat in 1864 following service in the Union party organization from 1861 to 1863.

11. "The Republican party took the name Union party in order to make agreeable the new alliance, though the camouflage only partially succeeded in its purposes. The War Democrats generally maintained their party organization and resisted the temptations of fusion." Elbert J. Benton, "The movement for peace without a victory during the Civil War," *Collections* (Cleveland: Western Reserve Historical Society, 1918), p. 7.

"The Union party in that state (Ohio) was essentially the Republican party." James G. Randall, *Lincoln the President,* 4 vols. (New York: Dodd, Mead, 1952), III:273.

"The Republican party had taken the guise of a Union party. . . ." Robert S. Holzman, *Stormy Ben Butler* (New York: Macmillan, 1954), p. 264.

In reference to the War Democrats: they "acted at elections in the main with the Republicans, voting the Union ticket, *as it was called* in most states." (Italics added.) James Ford Rhodes, *History of the Civil War, 1861–1865,* edited and with an introduction by E.B. Long. (New York: Ungar, 1961), p. 351.

In reference to the Union party of Wisconsin in 1862: "To catch unwary Democrats, . . . the Republicans wisely called their state session a Union convention." Frank L. Klement, *Wisconsin in the Civil War* (Madison: State Historical Society of Wisconsin for Wisconsin Civil War Centennial Commission, 1963), p. 76; See also Frank L. Klement, *Lincoln's Critics in Wisconsin: Address at Annual Meeting of the Lincoln Fellowship of Wisconsin* (Madison, February 14, 1955), p. 7: "Prominent Republicans talked of bipartisanship and the dropping of rival party labels in behalf of one to be called the 'Union party.' That Republican maneuver gained much support from prominent Democrats in the first years of war. Before long Democrats recognized it as a political strategems and wanted no more traps 'where (the) Republican cat was well concealed under the Union meal.' ''

The following misstatement concerning the Union party movement appears in James G. Randall, *Lincoln the President,* III:273: "It was not as if the Republican party had been abandoned, . . .or as if a new political body, neutral in the party sense, had been created. One could not say that a Democratic-Republican organization, with dual party machinery working toward a strictly bipartisan effect, and with equal importance for both Democrats and Republicans under the combined name of 'Union,' had been brought into practical existence.'' On the contrary, all these things *could correctly be said* about the Union party, point for point, word for word.

See also Kenneth M. Stampp, *Indiana Politics during the Civil War* (Indianapolis: Indiana Historical Bureau, 1949), pp. 94–95; George Fort Milton, *Eve of Conflict; Stephen A. Douglas and the Needless War* (Boston: Houghton, Mifflin, 1934), p. 169.

12. In the 1860 presidential campaign the Douglas ticket received 58,801 votes in Missouri; the Bell ticket, 58,372; Breckinridge, 31,317; and Lincoln, 17,028. *Tribune Almanac.* 1861. Assuming that a large majority of secessionists in Missouri were Democrats (which was the popular assumption in Missouri at the time) the Bell forces could be regarded as the largest element in the Unionist coalition.

13. E. Tarrant. *The Wild Riders of the First Kentucky Cavalry.* Louisville, 1894. p. 36.

14. In the 1860 presidential campaign the Republican vote in Maryland amounted to about three percent of the total vote. *Tribune Almanac.* 1861.

15. The 1860 Republican vote constituted about thirty percent of the total cast in Delaware, but all of it came from Wilmington. Elsewhere in Delaware the Republicans were powerless. In western Virginia, the 1860 Republican vote amounted to less than five percent of the total. In Kentucky, less than one percent. Ibid, 1861.

16. Addressing the Senate in 1858, Senator James H. Hammond of South Carolina declared: "I do not speak of California and Oregon as anti-Southern States; there is no antagonism between the South and these countries and never will be.'' *Congressional Globe* (35th Congress, 1st session), p. 70.

17. See chapter 9.

18. See chapter 4.

2

Lincoln and Conservative Tradition: 1832–1861

Lincoln was not yet cold in his grave when the Conservative political forces moved to claim him as their own. Having warred against Conservative purposes from 1832 to 1865, he was suddenly in death acclaimed the saint of Conservative tradition, which extraordinary contention has persisted to the present day. In essence, the contention is based upon the fact that the Republican party of 1860 and the Union party of 1864 were both divided in two camps, one Radical, the other Conservative, and in both cases Lincoln was regarded as Conservative by the Radical leaders. There is no disputing this. But the claims of the Conservatives of 1865 associated Lincoln, however vaguely and unclearly, with another kind of Conservatism advocated only by the Democratic party; and that was not a reasonable association. It was, in fact, absurd. For Lincoln was the agent of political reform, having rallied the anti-slavery Conservatives and Radicals in a wartime coalition favoring twin goals: perpetuation of the Union and universal Emancipation. And this cannot be said to resemble in the slightest detail the true ''Conservative'' nature of the wartime Democratic party. For the Regular Democrats of 1861 were not reformers in any sense whatever.

They might have intended to be. They may have nourished reform notions in their hearts. They might have espoused reform in the past and some were later to become reformers in the postwar period. But from 1861 to 1865 they were all the agents of reaction and the *Antebellum status quo,* the friends and protectors of Negro slavery, and the critics and defamers of the President. Having fought for slavery down to the wire, they were by 1865 identified with aristocratic principle alone. Over a four-year period, they had been quoting, repeatedly, from the Bill of Rights, the Magna Charta, and the writings of Jefferson, Madison, Washington, and Paine, with one object only in mind: to save the cause of Negro slavery. As opponents of Lincoln and the anti-slavery cause they had insisted, in the name of Conservatism, that the war be fought in such a way that slavery be spared from destruction; and if it could not be spared, many of them had frankly observed, the Union might better be dissolved. That was the tone of true Conservatism, enunciated by the leaders of the Democratic party of 1865. It would later be contended by the Democratic leaders and their defenders in the historical profession, that the Democratic party was already aiming its attack against the "anti-Lincoln Radicals," in 1865; that the Democratic leaders understood that Lincoln was closer to them than he was to the Radicals, and that they had, in a last-minute burst of recognition, come to see him for what he was: a full-fledged Conservative. There is no evidence of such a last-minute conversion, however. The chief target of Democratic party propaganda, up to the final moment of Lincoln's life, was Lincoln himself. Not Thaddeus Stevens. Not Wendell Phillips. Not Charles Sumner. But Lincoln himself. *He* was the chief villain, in the eyes of the Conservatives, and with good reason; for it was he who wrecked the grand old network of Conservative tradition that had run the country from 1776 to 1865. No wonder they hated and despised his name. No wonder they cursed him as a "fool," "an imbecile," "hell's vice-agent on earth," and as a "fungus from the corrupt womb of bigotry."[1] Yet, the moment he was dead, they clutched him to their hearts, proclaiming and serenading his Conservative intentions.

Actually, the only extent to which Abraham Lincoln was truly Conservative on the major issues of 1832 to 1865 was the fact that he lagged behind the leaders of the anti-slavery Radical faction in recommending Radical reform. By following such a course he earned the enmity of the Radicals, which caused him great trouble on occasion. Yet the very same tendency won for him the confidence and close collaboration of many scores of anti-slavery Conservatives traditionally hostile to Radical designs. That was Lincoln's special political tendency and/or maneuver, and he was brilliant in the matter of carrying it off. Having acquired the following of many Democrats in wartime with a Conservative anti-slavery lullaby, he would periodically change his tune to satisfy the Radical Republicans; then back again to the Conservatives, and so on. To that extent he was not a clear-cut Radical. Yet to call him a "Conservative," plain and simple, is non-sensical, because whenever he was finished working on an issue he invari-ably occupied a Radical position—if not the most Radical, surely Radical enough to startle all posterity.

In order to understand the actual Conservative response to Lincoln throughout the closing phase of his career, it is necessary only to read the commentary of the Democratic party press, which cursed him out at every opportunity. The moment before he was assassinated, he was condemned by one Democratic editor as an "impudent and lying . . . ignoramus." Yet, the very next moment, advised of the assassination, the same editor de-clared, in somber tones: "It is generally believed that he had fully settled upon a (postwar Reconstruction) policy which would speedily end our civil strife, and give rest to our bleeding land."[2] (That is, a postwar policy in keeping with the Conservative precepts of the Democratic party).

We must begin the study of Abraham Lincoln and the War Democrats with a clear understanding that Lincoln was not in any real sense a Con-servative on the slavery question any more than he was an outspoken Rad-ical. He was unique, and he was above all else, a very clever politician. To regard him as a Conservative grandfather-figure is a serious mistake.

*   *   *

The only Antebellum tie between Lincoln and the War Democrats was the libertarian philosophy of Thomas Jefferson. Although Jefferson was the founder of the Democratic party, which Lincoln invariably opposed, Lin-coln was, nonetheless, a Jeffersonian disciple. To make the matter clear, he wrote a letter for publication April 13, 1859, the anniversary of Jefferson's birth, explaining his position. As he saw it, the latter day Democrats had utterly deserted the principles of Jefferson by taking up the cause of Negro slavery, which Jefferson abhorred.[3] At Columbus, Ohio, in September, 1859, Lincoln delivered a speech along the same line, seeking the support of disenchanted Democrats.[4]

At that moment the Democratic party was divided between the suppor-ters of President James Buchanan, favoring the extension of slavery into the territories, and the supporters of Senator Stephen A. Douglas of Il-linois, promoter and publicist of the "Popular Sovereignty" principle, permitting the existence of slavery wherever it could gather majority sup-port. It was Jefferson who, in 1784, had recommended federal legislation forbidding the extension of slavery into *any* of the territories. And yet, seventy-six years later, the only party standing on the anti-Extension plat-form was under attack from all sides by supposed Jeffersonians. As a Republican leader, Lincoln was appealing for Democratic converts, in behalf of Jeffersonian principle.

Many northern Democrats endorsed the appeal, and in the 1860 Presidential election the Republican ticket secured enough votes in previously Democratic districts to carry the day.[5] As the Repbulican presidential candidate, Lincoln received majorities or pluralities in 17 of the 18 free states, and thereby was elected. But the Democratic faithful were wholly unconvinced, rejecting his claim to the mantle of Jefferson. In their opinion, Lincoln was a dangerous radical, and worse than many others because he claimed to be Conservative while all the time urging the country along the road to Disunion and revolution.[6]

The accusation had much truth in it. Lincoln was Conservative on the slavery question only when there was no opportunity of being anything else without danger of reaping immediate disaster. Under any other circumstances he invariably was ready to abandon the Conservative cause, as in the case of the "House Divided" speech of 1858, his refusal to back away from the "nigger-lover" charges of Stephen A. Douglas in the 1858 Debates, and his firm endorsement of the radical Jeffersonian credo "All men are created equal," against the anti-Negro jeers of Judge John Pettit and other Negrophobes.[7] There were in Illinois some Radical Republicans of the deepest dye, bordering on Abolitionist, among them Owen Lovejoy and Isaac N. Arnold. Both were Lincoln-men from first to last. Lincoln could mosey his way along, year-in, year-out, professing and implying Conservative beliefs. But the Radicals of Illinois knew better. In the Lincoln-Douglas Debates, Owen Lovejoy was up there on the platform at Lincoln's side, and the Radicals understood.[8] If Lovejoy believed in him, then Lincoln was not a true Conservative, no matter how often he might say he was.

There was a tendency among Conservative Republicans of the 1850s to regard Lincoln's great rival, Stephen A. Douglas, as a cut above many other Democrats—largely as a result of his stand against President Buchanan and the Lecompton Constitution. But the Radical Republicans had no use whatever for Douglas, whom they regarded as a conscienceless, proslavery rascal and a gross opportunist. In this respect Lincoln was clearly aligned with the Radicals. His contempt for Douglas was of colossal proportions and he made no bones about it, either privately or publicly. Whenever Douglas suffered any kind of comeuppance, Lincoln was overjoyed.[9] Douglas, on the other hand, was inclined to portray Lincoln to the public as a misguided idealist in league with revolutionary elements. The mutual antagonism of Lincoln and Douglas, surpassing that of any national leaders since Hamilton and Burr, typified the growing hostility of interparty politics that would become by 1860 a kind of mania, preventing the followers of Douglas and the followers of Lincoln from working in harmony for any cause at all. There was something about the slavery question that had a way of overcoming the old post-election traditions of "forgive and forget."

The appearance in 1853 of the anti-Catholic, anti-foreign Know Nothing party (soon to be renamed the American party) momentarily returned to the pro-slavery Democratic leadership the sense of fighting for the underdog. When the Republican party was organized in 1854 as an anti-slavery protest against Douglas and the highly controversial Kansas-Nebraska Act, Democratic leaders described the new organization as anti-constitutional in the manner of the Abolitionists, anti-Catholic in the manner of the Know Nothings and the American party, and anti-agrarian in the manner of the Federalists. As strong constitutionalists, believers in religious toleration, and friends of the farmer in the war against the bankers and the manufacturers, many thousands of Democrats took their stand against the Republicans in 1854, irrespective of the slavery controversy, and by 1861 they had not changed their minds. Regardless of what was happening down South, they were sworn to opposing the Federalist, Abolitionist, Know Nothing, commercial purposes of the Republican cause, and that was that.

Democratic response to the dramatic Republican victory in the 1860 campaign reflected this reaction on a broad scale. Democratic speakers and editors in large number, North and South, announced against the victors, implying or flatly declaring nonrecognition of their legal rights. Democrats in general simply could not conceive of actually accepting the election of Abraham Lincoln. They were shocked and humiliated and ready to urge the South to rebel. Thus encouraged, the government of South Carolina rumbled into action, and on December 20, 1860, the state seceded from the Union.

Chaos was upon the country. A President-elect, not yet sworn into office, was in the process of being repudiated, while all about him his political opponents stood back, refusing aid and comfort to his cause and, in effect, granting aid and comfort to his enemies and the enemies of the country. In this moment, and for many moments to come, from the date of South Carolina's act of Secession to the actual outbreak of the Civil War, April 14, 1861—a mighty force was to make itself known in the free states and in the several slave states which ultimately agreed to fight for the Union in company with the North. The force in question was the Antebellum Peace movement, which sought to stifle the organization of the Union cause, and to persuade the Unionists of the land that they could not, under the terms of the federal Constitution, legally coerce the forces of Secession in the interest of national unity. By mid-March, 1861, almost every Democrat in the free states was on record as a member of the Antebellum Peace cause.

Starting late and faltering, halfhearted and timid, without tradition or precedent to act upon, a small number of Democrats would band together, against the force of overwhelming Democratic sentiment, to work against the Antebellum Peace cause. Some were Douglas men and some had campaigned for Breckinridge. But all were opposed to Secession and all were ready to say so, to the great relief of Abraham Lincoln, President-elect. He could see a war coming and he knew he could not win it without Democratic support. The proto-War Democrats were harbingers of hope for a President without much reason for hope of any other kind, as of December, 1860.

NOTES

1. Frank L. Klement, *Wisconsin in the Civil War,* p. 50; Frank L. Klement, *Lincoln's Critics in Wisconsin,* p. 15.
2. *The Old Guard,* vol. III (May 1865), no. 5: pp. 237, 240.
3. "Letter to H.L. Pierce and Others," April 6, 1859, Roy P. Basler, ed., *The Collected Works of Abraham Lincoln,* 8 vols. (New Brunswick, 1953) III:375.
4. Ibid., III:416.
5. In 1856 the Republican national ticket failed to carry Pennsylvania, Illinois, Indiana, and California. In 1860 all of these voted for Lincoln. *Evening Journal Almanac,* 1861, p. 126.
6. At Greenville, Illinois, September 13, 1858, Senator Stephen A. Douglas of Illinois denied that Lincoln was conservative about slavery or about the Negro race issue. On the contrary, said Douglas, Lincoln was an Abolitionist, an Amalgamationist, and a believer in equal rights for Negroes. Roy P. Basler, ed., op. cit. III:96.
   In the 1860 presidential election campaign, one of the outstanding Democratic spokesman was William L. Yancey of Alabama. If Lincoln were elected, said Yancey, slave-stealing by Abolitionists and anti-slavery raids by northerners into the South was certain to become a regular occurrence. Emerson D. Fite, *The Presidential Campaign of 1860* (New York: Macmillan, 1911), pp. 230–31.
   Other Democrats belittled the significance of Lincoln's self-declared conservatism, believing that regardless of his personal opinions, he had to follow Republican party policy which, they insisted, was decided by Radicals and Abolitionists. See Washington (D.C.) *Constitution,* September 6, 1860.
7. For the Lincoln-Douglas exchange on the merits of the Negro see Ray P. Basler, ed., III:96, 375, 410. The contention that "All men are created equal"—set forth by Jefferson as a "self-evident" truth in 1776, was reclassified in 1854 as a "self-evident lie" by Democrat John Pettit, Chief Justice of the Territorial Supreme Court of Kansas. A great many Democrats were believed to concur in this opinion and Conservative Republicans were afraid of coming to Jefferson's defense. George W. Julian, *The Life of Joshua R. Giddings* (Chicago: McClurg, 1892), pp. 372–74; Charles A. Church, *History of the Republican Party in Illinois, 1854–1912, with a Review of the Aggressions of the Slave Power* (Rockford: Wilson, 1912). p. 67. Insofar as this controversy was concerned, Lincoln had to be counted on the Radical side, for he apparently believed that the people of the free states accepted the views of Jefferson in preference to those of Judge Pettit. Instead of playing

down his sympathy for Jeffersonian philosophy in this regard, he played it up whenever possible, with frequent references to the opposite notions of the Judge. E.g., Roy P. Basler, ed., II:275 (October 16, 1854); III:301 (October 15, 1858). The second of these citations refers to Lincoln's speech at Alton, Illinois, in the midst of his debates with Douglas, when once again he took the position that "all men are created equal," which position was embarrassing to his Conservative supporters. Joshua R. Giddings, a Radical leader at the 1860 Republican National Convention, proposed inclusion of the phrase in the 1860 party platform and was voted down by the convention majority. Attempting to leave the convention hall, Giddings was dissuaded and proceeded to reintroduce his motion, supported on this occasion with a ringing speech in its behalf. The delegates thereupon reversed themselves, voting to include in the platform Giddings' and Lincoln's favorite political phrase, "All men are created equal." George W. Julian, pp. 372–74.

8. Allen Johnson and Dumas Malone, eds., *Dictionary of American Biography*, 20 vols. (New York: Scribner's, 1930), XI: pp. 435–36.

9. In a letter to Congressman John T. Stuart, written in 1840, Lincoln described with evident delight a physical encounter between Douglas and Allen Francis, editor of the Springfield *Illinois Journal*, in which Douglas came off rather badly. According to Lincoln's account, "Douglas, having chosen to consider himself insulted by something in the *Journal*, undertook to cane Francis (its editor) in the street. Francis caught him by the hair and jammed him back against a market-cart, where the affair ended by Francis being pulled away." Rufus R. Wilson, ed., *Uncollected Works of Abraham Lincoln* (Elmira: Primavera, 1947), p. 506.

In a speech at Bloomington, Illinois, May 29, 1856, Lincoln referred irreverently to "This man Douglas, who misrepresents his constituents and who has exercised his highest talents in that direction." Advised that Douglas was reported to have abandoned all interest in a certain political race, Lincoln observed that "the report does not come in a very authentic form, so far as I can learn—though, by the way, speaking of authenticity, you know that if we heard Douglas say that he had abandoned the contest, it would not be very authentic." During the Lincoln-Douglas debates of 1858, Lincoln said, at Clinton, Illinois: "Douglas will tell a lie to 10,000 people one day, even though he knows he may have to deny it to 5,000 the next." Archer H. Shaw, ed., *Lincoln Encyclopedia*, pp. 82–86.

3

The Proto-War Democrats
Reject Conservative Tradition:
December 3, 1860 – April 13, 1861

The Antebellum Peace cause had many advantages over the combined force of the several Unionist factions opposing its designs. Of these, the most obvious and most spectacular was the presence in the White House of the ''lame-duck'' President James Buchanan, who accepted as gospel many of the States' Rights arguments of the Peace Democracy. Another spectacular advantage was the presence in the Buchanan cabinet, when the Secession crisis began, of several Peace Democrats favoring a policy of unobstructed Secession and Disunion. Less well recognized but even more vital to the interests of the Antebellum Peace cause was its overwhelming unity of hate.

The Republicans and Democrats of 1854–1861 had established a new level of inter-party discord—unparalleled in American history—culminating in the furious acts and declarations of the Secession crisis. Underlying all the verbiage attending the dispute was the race issue, the Democrats classifying the Republicans as lovers of the Negro, Republicans denying the allegation whenever possible. According to Democratic rhetoric, every living Republican was willing—in the manner of Old John Brown—to kill off civilized white southerners for the sake of uncivilized black savages and a long-nosed sense of Puritan superiority. On this basis the Republican party was pronounced a menace to the Union and to peace and prosperity. Enraged at the charge, the Republicans retaliated with a declaration of their own—that Democrats in general were wedded to the slavery institution, for which they would be willing to wreck the Union any time the southern Democratic leadership decided that was best.

Addressing a Democratic crowd on election night, in response to news of the Republican success, Isaiah Rynders of Tammany Hall expressed the view of many thousands of his kind, declaring, "It's me who hates. Yes, I hate the whole abolition (Republican) party. I don't want anything from them. . . . I believe that the carrying out of their principles, if it has not done so today, will destroy all the unity, force, and effect of the government under which we live. I despise the dirty rascals . . . . I'd like to hang 'em all up, by God! Wouldn't you?"

A major feature of every Democratic campaign against the Republicans was a strong emphasis on the race issue and repeated use of the word "nigger" by many Democratic editors and orators. The word was regarded as vital by Democratic propagandists, as a weapon in the war against Republican anti-slavery demands, and was utilized in place of argument whenever the basis for argument appeared lacking. Seizing upon the Radical opinions of Republican leader Horace Greeley, editor of the New York *Tribune,* whom he described as "nigger all over, nigger in his heart, nigger in his principles," Rynders warned that the Republicans might well be willing to "trample upon our interests for the love they bear the nigger." If civil war were to come about as a result of the Republican victory, said Rynders, he "would as soon fight the fanatics at the North as the fire-eaters of the South."[1]

Many nothern Democrats would have much the same to say in the four-month period preceding the outbreak of the war. Hatred for the Republican party, as opposed to love for the Union, was clearly the overriding tendency of northern Democrats in general throughout the course of the Secession controversy. Nor were the Republicans immune to this kind of super-partisanship. Advised of a steamboat accident on Lake Michigan involving the death of a large number Irish Democrats from Chicago, a Chicago Republican leader of the Secession period would later admit to receiving the news with a sense of cold-blooded satisfaction, because it promised a better chance of Republican victory in the coming municipal elections.[2]

Such was the political spirit of the times, and when Secession began very few of the Unionist members of the rival parties could bring themselves to alter course. Agreeing that Secession was wrong, they were far too angry with each other to allow themselves the luxury of working together in the interest of the Union. Although denouncing the Secessionists, they also were prone to denouncing one another, as accomplices to the Disunion disaster.

Congressional efforts at halting the progress of Secession proved wholly ineffective, although they did make famous the name of John J. Crittenden, Senator from Kentucky, as author of the "Crittenden Compromise." They also ruined the standing of Thomas Corwin, Republican Congressman from Ohio and author of the "Corwin Compromise." A mixture of Henry Clay's Missouri Compromise and the Popular Sovereignty principles of Douglas (plus a federal payment for runaway slaves and a ban against Emancipation in the District of Columbia), the Crittenden Compromise became—in the Secession period—the symbol of reconciliation to non-Republicans in general, excepting only the Secessionists who chose to ignore it. The Virginia Peace Conference of February 4—27, 1861, labored long on its own compromise plan, which came out sounding very much like Crittenden's. But the Radical Republicans had no use for the Crittenden Compromise, declaring hard against it; and Lincoln—for all his vaunted Conservatism—sided with the Radicals. He did endorse the Corwin Compromise, including the promise to protect the slavery institution in those states where it was legal in 1861—and the measure was promptly passed. But the war destroyed the Corwin Compromise and a Radical shift in Republican opinion, with the outbreak of the war, led to the disgrace of Corwin and his Conservative inclinations.

Of major importance to the progress of the Antebellum Peace cause was the attitude of Stephen A. Douglas, who in 1860 had railed against Secession and threatened the execution of Secessionists. Once Lincoln was elected, Douglas had suddenly abandoned his bellicose Unionism. The man who, in October 1860, was willing to hang every rebel as "high as Haman," could never be counted on to make a similar remark throughout the whole Secession crisis. Instead, together with John Bell and a large majority of Bell and Douglas Unionists throughout the free and border slave states, Douglas had little to say, between December 20, 1860 and April 14, 1861, that was not designed to hinder and embarrass Lincoln and his party. From time to time, the Secessionists would so grossly offend Unionists in general with anti-Union rhetoric, that Douglas would rise to the occasion and speak in protest. Mainly, however, he spent his time waiting, watching, and carping. He had some things to say in criticism of Buchanan and Lincoln, and of Republicans in general, but nothing to offer in the way of a constructive proposal of his own, and even less to say against Secession. In the manner of many others, he was counting on the Crittenden Compromise. By standing back in this manner, and by denying cooperation to the new administration, Douglas became an appendage to the Antebellum Peace cause, and his followers flowed into the Peace camp by thousands and thousands.

*   *   *

Of all the sections in the country that were later to endorse the Union cause, the Antebellum Peace men performed to best advantage in New York City, northern New Jersey, the southern counties of Ohio, Illinois, and Indiana, the states and territories of the Far West, and the border slave states. In New York City and northern New Jersey the major factor in the case appeared economic, northern commerce relying largely on the production of southern cotton. The border slave states were full of slaveholders, with fond feelings for their fellow slaveholders to the South, while Ohio, Illinois, Indiana, and the states and territories of the Far West had many southerners only recently arrived, and the children of southerners, with standard southern opinions of every kind. The people in all the areas in question were inclined to vote in the manner of southerners, and usually were represented locally and in Congress by Conservative pro-slavery men who, in time of crisis, could always be expected to think in southern terms. The prime spokesman for Secession among the commercial interests of the Northeast was Mayor Fernando Wood of New York City, a former Abolitionist turned arch-Conservative. At the height of the national disturbance attending the breakup of the Union the Mayor became famous for a speech delivered to the Common Council recommending the secession of New York City. The proposal rendered him the "lion of the town." Democratic Congressman John Cochrane of New York City toured the East as far south as Richmond, Virginia, preaching the word of Wood, and former Senator Daniel S. Dickinson of New York toured northern New York and New England, endorsing Wood's position in one city after another, before enthusiastic crowds. At the Pennsylvania Democratic State Convention of February 1861, Breckinridge leader Francis Hughes appeared, with a complex proposal for secession of Pennsylvania, along the same lines as those proposed by Wood.[3]

In the Old Northwest the Antebellum Peace cause rallied to the leadership of Congressmen Clement L. Vallandigham of Ohio and John A. Logan of Illinois, and former Congressman Robert Dale Owen of Indiana, more recently U.S. Minister to Naples. All were brilliant orators and all were resolutely opposed to coercing the forces of Secession. According to their interpretation of the Constitution, the Secession cause had the law on its side, and there was nothing the federal authorities could legally do but recognize the fact of Disunion. Another leading western Democrat was David Tod, candidate for Governor of Ohio, 1844 and 1846, and one of several chairmen at the 1860 Baltimore National Convention. Addressing the Ohio Democratic Convention of January 1861, Tod declared that two hundred thousand Ohio Democrats stood ready to resist the federal authority in the event of any attempt to "coerce" the southern states into retaining their allegiance to the Union.[4] Vallandigham, Logan, Owen, and Tod were Douglas men. So long as Douglas remained identified with the Peace cause, the Democrats of the Old Northwest were identified to a similar extent.

Miles away from the scene of conflict in Charleston harbor, the Far West reacted excitedly to the Secession crisis, as did also the Democrats of the Far West. There was a longstanding feud between pro-slavery and anti-slavery Democrats of the Pacific Coast. Although Democrats there outnumbered Republicans by almost two-to-one, the intra-party feud had broken the Democratic organization in half. In the 1860 campaign, the Douglas ticket polled 38.5 thousand votes in California, the Breckinridge ticket, 34.3 thousand.[5] During the Secession crisis the Breckinridge (or "Chivalry") Democracy of California was for Peace—officially. Unofficially, its leadership was vitally involved in plans for the peaceful secession of California, Oregon, and the territories of Washington and New Mexico.[6] Senator Joseph Lane of Oregon and the two California Senators, William M. Gwin and Milton S. Latham, were the most prominent leaders of the West Coast Secession cause. Lane was the Vice Presidential candidate on the 1860 Breckinridge ticket. On the Senate floor, April 16, 1860, Latham threatened the secession of California,[7] and Gwin had boasted privately of his intention to arrange for the transfer of a "friend" to take command of federal troops in California. The friend arrived on January 15, 1861, in the person of General Albert Sidney Johnston, a southerner and a Secessionist.[8] Equally hostile to the Union cause were General David E. Twiggs and Colonel William W. Loring, commanders of federal forces in Texas and New Mexico. In consequence of these factors and of open appeals by local Secessionist leaders, West Coast politics bordered on a state of hysteria throughout the first four months of 1861.[9] Governor John G. Downey of California (Douglas) and Governor John Whiteaker of Oregon (Breckinridge) did nothing to discourage the Secessionists.

In the border slave states the Peace cause was generally crowded out by the Secession cause. Only after Secession had failed, as in Delaware, Maryland, Kentucky and Missouri, did the Peace leaders play a significant part. With the failure of Secession, the Secessionists joined the Peace men, urging opposition to the federal authorities in their endeavor to coerce those states taking leave of the Union.

Against the vast array of Antebellum Peace Democrats of considerable reputation, the smaller proto-War Democracy could have accomplished very much only in alliance with Republicans, and no such alliance was forthcoming. There were some, however, who managed in the absence of a Unionist alliance to act against Secession on an independent basis, paving the way for creation of a wartime coalition. Among the most important persons in this category were three Breckinridge leaders, Jeremiah S. Black of Pennsylvania, John A. Dix of New York, and Andrew Johnson of Tennessee; and three Douglas leaders, John W. Forney of Pennsylvania, Nathaniel Paschall of Missouri, and John A. McClernand of Illinois. Every member of the group was a well known critic of the Republican party, the President-elect, and the anti-slavery cause.

As members of the Breckinridge Democracy, Black, Dix, and Johnson all had spoken publicly about the possibility of Secession, throughout the presidential canvass, working hand-in-hand with bonafide Secessionists. But none of them had sensed that actual Secession and Disunion were right around the corner. So far as they were concerned, Secession talk was nothing more than propaganda, designed to frighten the Conservatives away from Lincoln and Douglas in the North and away from Bell in the South. When they found they had miscalculated and had in fact been working for genuine Secession, they were furious, and went to work at once against the forces of Disunion.

As a member of the Buchanan cabinet—first as Attorney General, later as Secretary of State—Black was largely responsible for stiffening the spine of President Buchanan who, throughout the full course of Secession, appeared constantly ready to surrender at the drop of a hat. As author of the legal opinion made famous in Buchanan's 1860 Address to Congress, that the federal government could *not* coerce a state into performing its duties, although it *could* require enforcement of the federal laws, Black was thereafter regarded in Republican circles as a nitwit and/or Secessionist. But peculiar legal phraseology was not Black's only contribution to the Secession crisis. When Howell Cobb, the Secessionist Secretary of the Treasury, protested against Buchanan's call for the "enforcement of the laws," Black demanded Cobb's resignation and Buchanan agreed to the demand. When state-appointed "commissioners" from South Carolina arrived in Washington to negotiate the surrender of the federal forts in Charleston harbor, Black opposed their recognition and the President refused to receive them.

Upon becoming Secretary of State in mid-December, immediately following the resignation of Lewis Cass and immediately preceding the secession of South Carolina, Black came out in favor of a strong Unionist policy in every issue of consequence, from the defense of Fts. Moultrie and Sumter to the provisioning of Sumter, a vigorous response to the Confederate attack on the *Star of the West,* and genuine preparations for military defense of Washington, D.C. In the waning days of the Buchanan administration, Black was nominated for a place on the U.S. Supreme Court, but the nomination was rejected on the strength of Republican and Douglas votes combined. Clearly, there was little public knowledge of Black's true response to the Secession crisis. The actual record nonetheless is clear. He was a formidable and motivating force among the proto-War Democrats of 1861.[10]

John A. Dix joined the cabinet as Secretary of the Treasury January 11, 1861, succeeding Howell Cobb of Georgia. He instantly established himself as Black's ally, becoming famous overnight for a telegram dispatched to a customs officer at a southern port, urging the shooting of Secessionists actively engaged in pulling down the American flag.[11] Upon his arrival in Washington, Dix took a room at the White House and sat up late with the President arguing the Unionist position every night for six weeks.[12] A letter from Dix to Major Anderson at Ft. Sumter condemned the actions of southern army and navy officers who resigned their commissions to "go South." Action of this nature, said Dix, was an exhibition of "cowardice and treachery" and "evidence of degeneracy."[13] Another letter, from Dix to his predecessor, Cobb of Georgia, clearly expressed the attitude of his kind, the northern Unionist allies of "Southern Rights." "We have fought your battles," Dix protested, "without regard to the political consequences to ourselves. It is neither chivalrous nor brave to draw off because the common adversary has gained a momentary advantage, and leave us to continue the contest . . . without the support we have given to you."[14]

Of all the slave-state Unionists engaged in the Secession controversy, the most spectacular was U.S. Senator Andrew Johnson of Tennessee. Condemning Secessionist demands and rejecting threats and insults of unprecedented nature, Tennessee Unionists had held their own for several dramatic weeks in 1861. On February 9, while the Virginia Peace Conference was still in session, the people of Tennessee had voted down the calling of a state convention 69,675 to 57,798.[15] Johnson received considerable credit for the vote. He was one of the most colorful and energetic of the Unionist speakers in the state, and consequently one of the most beloved and most hated. His boldness and pugnacity rendered all other Unionist campaigners mild in comparison.

Returning to Washington, Johnson was severely criticized by Southern Rights Senators. Accused of working in collusion with the arch-Radical, Senator Benjamin Wade of Ohio, he declared in a Senate speech delivered in February: "I do not inquire what a man's antecedents have been when there is a great struggle to preserve the existence of the Government. . . . If Senator Wade . . . is willing to come up to this great work, . . . I am his ally and he is mine."[16] Infuriated by Johnson's position, Senator Louis T. Wigfall of Texas denounced him as a man who for years had done "everything he could to ingratiate himself . . . with the very worst class of the northern populace."[17]

Returning to Tennessee, in March, Johnson was overwhelmed by circumstances. When Sumter was attacked and returned fire, Secessionists raised the cry of "coercion" and the Tennessee Unionists divided. As in all the border slave states, the Tennessee Peace faction appealed for Neutrality and many Tennessee Unionists endorsed the appeal. On May 1, the legislature authorized the Governor to enter into a military league with the Confederate government, and in short time the state was full of Confederate troops. Andrew Johnson left quickly to avoid arrest, traveling north by train. Wherever he was recognized by Tennessee Secessionists he was jeered and threatened. In one instance he was required to beat back an angry mob at pistol point.[18]

*   *   *

Of the proto-War Democrats in the Douglas faction, the most spectacular were editors John W. Forney of the Philadelphia *Press* and Nathaniel Paschall of the St. Louis *Missouri Republican.* Both were on record from an early date against conciliation and compromise—a very unusual position among Democratic editors of the Secession period. Generally speaking, the only Unionists ready for a military showdown were extremely Radical Republicans. But Forney and Paschall were inclined at this time to operate in the spirit of the ultra-Radicals. Their policies enraged the Peace Democrats of Pennsylvania and Missouri, especially the Breckinridge wing, which had regarded them both as dangers to the party and the Union since the beginning of the Lecompton controversy in 1857 when they had broken with Buchanan.[19]

Forney was scornful of Buchanan's denial that the federal government had the right to "coerce" a state. He ridiculed the argument advanced by the Peace faction that southern cotton was "king" and that the North could not survive without it. When Republican Senator Wilmot of Pennsylvania refused to agree to southern demands advanced at the Virginia Peace Conference, Forney commended him and criticized the other Pennsylvania delegates for voting against him. During the Secession crisis, most Democrats advocated the calling of a national peace convention. Forney was opposed to the idea until Lincoln endorsed it in his Inaugural Address, whereupon Forney changed his mind.[20]

As leader of the Douglas forces in Missouri, Paschall had demanded that the state party leaders come out for Douglas in the national campaign, despite the fact that Claiborne F. Jackson, the candidate for Governor, and a majority of the candidates for Congress and state executive offices were well known anti-Douglas men. Should the party ignore his wishes in the matter, Paschall declared, he would place an independent Douglas ticket in the field, on his own. So great was the power of the *Missouri Republican* that the party leaders yielded to Paschall's wishes.[21] Jackson was elected Governor as a Douglas-man in August and Missouri went for Douglas in November.

The Secession crisis ended the forced marriage of Paschall and Governor Jackson, Secessionists rallying to Jackson, Unionists to Paschall. In January 1861, the nucleus of the first of the Union party coalitions in the loyal states gathered at St. Louis, in answer to an appeal sent out by Paschall. Organization was needed to elect a Unionist majority to the impending state convention, and the subsequent work of the Unionists was well executed. On February 18, 1861, the people of Missouri elected an almost solid bloc of Unionist delegates, defeating every Breckinridge candidate under consideration. The result was wholly unexpected.[22] The convention met February 21 at Jefferson City, but quickly transferred its business to the Unionist stronghold of St. Louis where Secession was beaten down in vigorous debate. On March 22 the convention adjourned. The response of the Missouri Unionists, in large part organized and urged along by a proto-War Democrat, rendered Missouri the first of the slave-states actively loyal to the Union.

In Washington, the Secession period was devoted to a great deal of haggling in Congress between the several factions, and with the notable absence, for several days, of anything resembling strong pro-Union talk by any Democrats in either house. When it became clear that Senator Douglas was not going to assume leadership of the non-Republican Unionists in Congress, the role fell to Congressman John A. McClernand of Illinois. Although nothing in the nature of a great political spokesman nor a first-class organizer, and not even very well known outside of Illinois, McClernand made up in spirit and determination what he lacked in other respects. He *was* an ardent Unionist, and he proved to be the outstanding proto-War Democrat in Congress during the Secession period. When the Congress reconvened in December 1860 he had intended to play a conservative role, proposing the creation of a federal police force to implement the Fugitive Slave Law, and a fine for any free state in which a fugitive was apprehended. The measure was submitted to the House Committee of Thirty-Three.[23] But the picture of McClernand the Conservative was altered on December 31, when Mississippi Congressman William Barksdale proclaimed on the floor of the House his readiness for an immediate settlement with the North. A New York *Times* account declared that, "Several Republicans and Northern Democrats responded spiritedly, 'Let's have it, then!' Mr. McClernand of Illinois shook his finger at Barksdale and (Thomas C.) Hindman of Arkansas, vocifering *(sic)* loudly, 'Come on! Come on! Now we are ready to meet you, and settle it quickly.' Great confusion prevailed. . . .''[24]

Two weeks later McClernand delivered a strong speech against Secession, occupying seven pages in the *Congressional Globe*. Secession was unconstitutional, he said. Douglas had previously observed that the Old Northwest could not survive without recourse to a free Mississippi River. McClernand repeated the idea. Douglas had ridiculed Buchanan for his reference to "coercion" of a state. McClernand used the point against the Peace cause rather than against Buchanan. He called the talk about coercion "a clamor got up, if not to make us all traitors, at least to frighten us out of our propriety." He called Secession "revolution" and "worse even than Red Republicanism! . . . worse than the Red Communists of France.''[25]

*   *   *   *   *

There was little in the way of consistency demonstrated by the Unionist leaders of any of the loyal-state factions during the Secession crisis. A majority of Republicans and non-Republican Unionists shifted back and forth between angry threats and offers of conciliation. The Peace forces, on the other hand, were steadily in favor of a noncoercive course, regardless of the consequences to the Union. At one point, Democratic Congressman Vallandigham of Ohio—the leading Peace man in the House—electrified Washington by voicing the demand for freedom of the Mississippi, which was essential to the Old Northwest; ". . . and if we cannot secure (from the Confederacy) a maritime boundary upon other terms," he said, "we will cleave our way to the seacoast with the sword.''[26] All Vallandigham was talking about, however, was a treaty guaranteeing northern navigation rights through independent Confederate territory. His reference to the sword was colorful but unimportant. He was still for Peace at any price, no matter what he said about rivers or weapons or rights of any kind.

The long continued resistence of the proto-War Democrats to alliance with Republicans—in the face of the national dismemberment they so abhorred—not only reflected the strong political prejudice of the small farmers and artisans of the Jacksonian school, but that of many northerners of wealth and commercial importance. For notwithstanding all the wartime Democratic campaign propaganda to the contrary, the Republican party of the Civil War years was not the stronghold of the commercial and banking interests. That distinction belonged, as it had since the collapse of the Whigs in 1854, to the Democratic party.[27] Northern businessmen had always been the bitter foes of Disunion, which they had sought to prevent by a policy of placating the Disunionists. In working for Douglas and Breck-inridge in 1860 they were following the standard commercial line, in the interest of the pro-slavery cause.

Typical of the northern businessman's reaction to the Secession crisis was the initial response of Democratic Governor William Sprague of Rhode Island. An outstanding leader in the dry-goods manufacturing indus-try and one of the richest men of commerce in New England, Sprague had ousted a Republican state administration in 1860, running with the backing of all the non-Republican factions in his state plus a dissident Conservative Republican faction largely comprised of businessmen. Sprague devoted much time and money to the Douglas campaign and when Douglas lost, turned at once to berating the incoming Republicans. At his recommenda-tion the Rhode Island Personal Liberty Law was repealed by the state legislature.[28] As of mid-February 1861, Governor Sprague of Rhode Is-land, the "Cotton King of New England," was totally aligned to the cause of compromise, conciliation, and Peace. He truly represented the spirit of multitudes of Democratic businessmen throughout the North.

$$* \qquad * \qquad *$$

Repeatedly it seemed that Senator Douglas of Illinois was on the verge of joining, full force, in the operations of the proto-War Democrats. But he never did for more than a moment, invariably retreating thereafter to the ranks of the observers. On January 3 he took the Senate floor to blame the condition of the country on his three great enemies: President Buchanan, the Republican party, and the Southern Rights Democracy. The President's Annual Address was incomprehensible, he said, seeming to contradict it-self at every turn. But Douglas provided no clarity himself. As a West-erner, he was deeply disturbed about the fate of the Mississippi River in the event of Disunion. The Great West could never consent to be walled up, without free access to the Mississippi. But he had no plan or policy to recommend, and concluded his remarks simply by denouncing the Republicans.[29]

Douglas believed, in the manner of many others, that the Crittenden Compromise was a logical solution to the national dilemma. So long as the Crittenden Compromise was under serious consideration he had compara-tively little to say, and when he did speak up, his remarks were inconsis-tent. Although critical of Secessionists as such, on more than one occa-sion, he swung about on March 15, arguing that South Carolina was enti-tled to Ft. Sumter and Florida was entitled to Ft. Pickens, and that "An-derson and his gallant band should be instantly withdrawn."[30]

In company with those previously listed, certain Democrats less well known took the opportunity to move against the Antebellum Peace cause. One of these was Major David Hunter of the Regular Army, an Indian fighter of distinction, a native of Washington, D.C., and for several years previously a businessman operating out of Chicago. Formerly a Whig, Hunter had transferred his allegiance to the Democrats by 1860,[31] but his sentiments were altogether hostile to Secession. While stationed at Ft. Leavenworth, Kansas, during the 1860 campaign, he became disturbed about the views of many of his southern colleagues, who saw in Lincoln an Abolitionist worthy of assassination. Fearing for the safety of the President-elect, Hunter wrote him warning of an attempt on his life, and received in reply an invitation to serve as bodyguard, on the presidential journey from Springfield, Illinois, to Washington. The honor was at once accepted.[32]

In keeping with the same possibility of a threat against his life, Lincoln was alleged to have entered Washington incommunicado, at the close of his trip from Illinois, wearing a Scotch cap and a long military coat. Appearing initially in the New York *Tribune,* the Incommunicado story was frequently reprinted, rendering Lincoln the object of ridicule in almost every Democratic paper in the land. Exceptional was the reaction of the Philadelphia *Press* whose editor, John W. Forney, came to Lincoln's defense, denying the truth of the *Tribune* story.[33] Upon visiting the House of Representatives in Washington for the first time, Lincoln went first to the Democratic side of the chamber, where he was subjected to the cold contempt of the Democratic leaders, none of whom came forward to welcome his arrival. Embarrassed by the scene, Democratic Congressman Daniel E. Sickles of New York jumped to his feet and made his way to Lincoln's side, offering his hand in behalf of the proto-War Democracy.[34] Lincoln had a long memory and he would keep in mind the nonpartisan behavior of Democrats Hunter, Forney, and Sickles in the tumultuous period ahead.

*   *   *

One of the first American officials to openly protest against the rebellion was Judge David A. Smalley of the U.S. Court of the District of Vermont (a Douglas man and Chairman of the Democratic National Committee from 1856 to 1860). Serving temporarily on the bench of the U.S. Circuit Court for the Southern District of New York, in February 1861, Judge Smalley presided at the trial of certain New York City gunsmiths accused of selling arms and ammunition to the state of Georgia, which had severed all connections with the Union. In the process of charging the jury, the Judge declared that civil war existed in certain portions of the country; that post offices, customs houses, and forts were being seized and the American flag fired upon, and that all the acts in question amounted to high treason. The fact that they were committed under the pretended authority of conventions and legislatures did not affect their criminal character, since no man nor any body of men could throw off allegiance to government in that way. Concluding his remarks, Judge Smalley observed that the promotion of unconstitutional programs by one faction (e.g., the Abolitionists) was not ample justification for rebellion and civil war on the part of another.[35]

Editors Forney of the Philadelphia *Press* and Paschall of the St. Louis *Republican* were joined in the expression of the proto-War Democrat philosophy by three well-known editors in the Old Northwest: Joseph W. Gray of the Cleveland *Plain Dealer,* George W. Manypenny of the Columbus *Ohio Statesman,* and James W. Sheehan of the Chicago *Post,* all of whom were Douglas men.[36] Another Douglas Democrat eager for the battle in advance of the Sumter attack was Lewis Wallace of Indiana, for several years a leader of the Douglas faction in his state. Wallace was a lawyer, and the Democratic candidate for U.S. Senator in 1861. Throughout the Lecompton controversy he had served as a major Douglas supporter in a state controlled by the Buchanan Democracy. At the Indiana Democratic State Convention of January 1860, the Douglas faction defeated the Buchanan faction, naming the state ticket and drawing up the platform. Although Indiana went Republican in the 1860 election, the Douglas faction retained control of the Democratic party in the state.[37] Wallace commanded a military company at his home town in central Indiana. When the southern states began seceding from the Union several new companies appeared in Wallace's neighborhood, drilling openly with muskets, and all of them favored the Secession cause. Wallace was highly disturbed. He went at once to Indianapolis to confer with Republican Governor Morton. In the event of civil war, Wallace said, he was with the Governor and with the Union.[38]

In Washington, cabinet members Jeremiah S. Black and John A. Dix were assisted in their pro-Union activities by Edwin M. Stanton of Pennsylvania, Joseph Holt of Kentucky, and Horatio King of Maine. Stanton replaced Black as U.S. Attorney General when Black became Secretary of State. Like Black, Stanton and King were for Breckinridge. An ardent opponent of the "Southern Rights" philosophy, Holt was the only cabinet member to favor Douglas in the recent national campaign. (He was the son-in-law of former Governor Charles A. Wickliffe of Kentucky, Chairman of the Douglas National Executive Committee.)[39] When Holt was transferred from the Post Office Department to the War Department, King became Postmaster General. All three men threw their influence against the constitutional arguments of the Secessionist cabinet members. As previously, Black was the leader of the Unionists, although on one occasion, according to a widely circulated story, Stanton delivered the angriest and noisiest anti-Secession statement uttered by a cabinet member during the whole Secession period. To surrender Sumter, Stanton reportedly declared, would be a crime the equal of Benedict Arnold's, and anyone assisting in such a crime would deserve the fate of Major André. Stanton was sufficiently concerned about the need for a nonpartisan coalition to call upon Republican congressional leaders for consultation and advice. Since public knowledge of the meetings would certainly have damaged the political standing of both Stanton and his Republican visitors, they were therefore carried out in secret.[40] Upon succeeding John B. Floyd as Secretary of War, January 1, 1861, Joseph Holt revealed at once a strong contempt for the tender feelings of certain of his southern brethren. With his approval, additional troops were ushered into Washington, and at his insistence Major P. G. T. Beauregard of Louisiana (a known Secessionist) resigned as Commandment of the U.S. Military Academy.[41] Ignoring the constitutional jargon of Secession in his dealings with an agent of the Governor of South Carolina, Holt announced that he simply was unable to agree to the request of South Carolina to "buy Ft. Sumter," which statement infuriated the government of South Carolina.[42]

*   *   *

In Congress, McClernand of Illinois was joined, periodically, in his Unionist declarations, by several other proto-War Democrats less consistent but equally disturbed. One was McClernand's close friend and lame-duck colleague, Isaac N. Morris of Illinois. Another was lame-duck Garnett B. Adrain of New Jersey. A Douglas-man opposed to the New Jersey Democratic machine controlled by the Buchanan faction, Adrain was elected on the "Opposition" ticket in 1858 with Republican and Douglas support combined. On January 7, 1861 he proposed a resolution praising Major Anderson for his course in Charleston harbor, and the Peace faction declared against it. Requested to withdraw the resolution, Adrain refused, and the resolution carried, 124 to 56, eleven Democrats voting in the majority.[43] Eight days later Adrain delivered a speech of considerable length, defending Lincoln as a Conservative Unionist. The South, he said, was heading straight for political destruction.[44]

On January 9 President Buchanan's Secession policy fell under congressional scrutiny as the result of a House resolution which was passed, 133 to 62, twelve Democrats voting in the majority.[45] McClernand's longest and most effective Unionist speech was delivered in the House on January 14, after which Samuel S. Cox, a Douglas leader from Ohio, made another of the same kind.[46] On the same day, Congressman John W. Noell of Missouri (Douglas) wrote home, exhorting his constituents to stand by the

Union at all costs.[47] Sherard Clemens of Virginia (Douglas) delivered a ringing pro-Union speech January 22, and was heartily congratulated by three other Douglas Democrats: Cox of Ohio, John Cochrane of New York, and Philip B. Fouke of Illinois.[48] When Peace Democrat George H. Pendleton of Ohio (Douglas) made a long speech comparing the Confederate cause to the American Revolutionary cause,[49] War Democrat William Howard of Ohio (Douglas) replied, denouncing Pendleton for his bad judgment in making such a statement. The Patriots of '76 had real grievances, said Howard. The rebels of '61 had no grievances worth speaking of.[50]

Less oratorical but equally vigorous was the performance of Congressman Daniel E. Sickles, for several years the outstanding Democratic spokesman in the New York delegation. (A close friend of President Buchanan, Sickles was the Democratic nominee for U.S. Senator against Republican Preston King in the New York senatorial election of 1857.[51] Although a Breckinridge supporter, he had played no part in the 1860 election campaign, having apparently ruined his political career by killing his wife's lover in broad daylight. He was subsequently acquitted on a murder charge but was not renominated for Congress in 1860.)[52] When the *Star of the West* was fired on, Sickles came out emphatically for "coercion" of the South, working closely with Attorney General Stanton (who had served as defense counsel in the Sickles murder trial.) Hoping to convince Buchanan in the wisdom of holding out against Confederate demands, Sickles and Stanton arranged a plan to broadcast telegrams to northern Democratic politicians, asking them to stage parades, fire salutes, and wire messages to Washington in honor of Major Anderson and Buchanan's refusal to yield.[53]

Another eastern Democratic leader active in the Union cause during the Secession crisis was Benjamin F. Butler, candidate for Governor of Massachusetts on the 1860 Breckinridge ticket. In the balloting for president at the Charleston Convention, Butler had caused a sensation by voting 57 times for Senator Jefferson Davis of Mississippi.[54] Angered by Secession, in the manner of *all* Breckinridge Unionists, he came to Washington to recommend strong measures to President Buchanan. First off, he suggested the Confederate Commissioners be arrested and tried for treason.[55] The advice was ignored. In conversation with the same Commissioners, Butler said that if he could have his way, they would all be tried, and if convicted he would see them hanged.[56] There was nothing unique about Benjamin F. Butler of Massachusetts. He was a Breckinridge Unionist who had come to believe he had been misused by false friends. The only unusual aspect of his behavior was that he became angry about the matter in advance of many others.

On the West Coast, without official leadership and without party unity, Unionists organized on a nonpartisan basis in response to the Secession threat. The most dramatic organizer was Republican Senator Edward D. Baker of Oregon, who stumped the Coast, speaking brilliantly for Union to the inspiration of thousands. He found support not only in Republican journals, but in certain Democratic journals, too, including the Marysville (California) *Democrat* and the Salem *Oregon Statesman*. The editor of the *Democrat* was George C. Gorham;[57] the editor of the *Statesman* was Asahel Bush.[58] Both were supporters of Stephen A. Douglas. Because Douglas Democrats comprised a large element in both the California and Oregon state legislatures, the views of both were highly influential. Another West Coast Douglas leader vitally involved in the anti-Secession struggle was former Congressman James A. McDougall, who branded Buchanan a "traitor," and praised the Republican President-elect, whom he had known years before in Illinois. Of Lincoln, he said, "I know him well. . . . I know him to be an upright, true man, a lover of his country, a sincere patriot. . . . He is my President . . . and I say it is the duty of all true patriots to sustain him, and through him the Constitution and the Union, in the day of fiercest trial."[59]

Several proto-War Democrats went to work for the Union in foreign parts. At the Hague, American Minister Henry C. Murphy drew up an elaborate exposition of the relationship between the federal government and the states, showing the supremacy of the federal. During the war the paper often was reprinted in diplomatic correspondence.[60] American Minister Joseph A. Wright attempted to persuade the Imperial Government of Prussia to release a proclamation disapproving the act of Secession, but failed in the attempt.[61] Edward J. Mallett, American Consul General to Italy, denounced Secession with such effect that President Lincoln kept him on following the Republican ascendency.[62] Canada, which had not as yet emotionally recovered from the American invasion of 1812, was highly in favor of Secession and hostile to the Union cause. Jacob W. Moore, American Consul at Windsor, advertised his Unionism at every opportunity and made a great display of raising the American flag, which greatly disturbed the pro-Confederate majority.[63]

In discussing the proto-War Democrats, it must be noted that a last-minute convert to the cause was a most important one: Senator Stephen A. Douglas of Illinois. Having withheld support from Lincoln from the day of his election through the day he was inaugurated, March 4, 1861, Douglas was so shocked and disturbed, initially, by the tone of the Inaugural Address, that he considered openly attacking it (or so we are advised by more than one of Douglas' associates). Then, overnight and without warning, he became Lincoln's champion in the Senate, during the final dramatic days of the Sumter crisis. On two occasions, when Secessionist Senators criticized the President for remarks contained in the Inaugural Address, Douglas delivered rejoinders defending him as a man of peace and reason.[64]

The position adopted by Douglas in this moment, on the brink of civil war, cannot be regarded as anything but one of major importance. Although perhaps the last person of prominence to join the small, select gathering of proto-War Democrats, in 1861, Stephen A. Douglas was unquestionably the one who made the difference.

NOTES

1. New York Herald, November 7, 1860.
2. Frederick F. Cook, *Bygone Days in Chicago* (Chicago: McClurg, 1910), p. 6.
3. For Cochrane's activity see Allan Johnson and Dumas Malone, eds., IV:253. Some other New York City leaders coming out in favor of Secession of the City included: U.S. Marshall Isaiah Rynders, shipping merchant John M. Browrer, Congressman Daniel E. Sickles, and James Brooks, editor of the New York *Express*. Rynders was for Douglas; Browrer, and Sickles were for Breckinridge; Brooks was for Bell. Philip S. Foner, *Business and Slavery* (Chapel Hill: University of North Carolina Press, 1941), pp. 290, 293; *Congressional Globe* (36th Congress, 2nd session), p. 40; New York *Express*, quoted in New York *Times*, December 6, 1860.
4. In a speech delivered in New York City, December 20, 1860, Dickinson assured the audience that "our Southern brothers will reason with us when we will reason with them. . . .The South have not offended us. . . .But their slaves have been run off in numbers by an underground railroad, and insult and injury returned for a constitutional duty. . . .If we would remain a united people we must treat the Southern States as we treated them on the inauguration of the government—as political equals." Quoted *in* DeAlva S. Alexander, *A Political History of the State of New York,* 3 vols. (New York: Holt, 1906–1909), III:3–4.
5. Edward C. Smith, *The Borderland in the Civil War* (New York: Macmillan, 1927), p. 136.
6. *Evening Journal Almanac,* 1861.
7. Congressman John C. Burch of California, a Breckinridge Democrat, was reported as saying that all the senators, representatives, and delegates from California, Oregon, Washington, and Arizona favored secession of the Far West. Elijah R. Kennedy, *The Contest for California in 1861* (Boston: Houghton, Mifflin, 1912), p. 72.
8. Referring to the prediction, in December, 1860, Latham said that his opinion on that occasion was, "to say the least, premature." In the intervening period he had come to believe that "This Union has no more loyal subjects than the people of California." *Congressional Globe* (36th Congress, 2nd session), p. 27.
9. Elisha R. Kennedy, p. 80. Democrat Henry W. Halleck of San Francisco, Commanding General of the California State Militia, was not concerned about the matter because in his opinion there were not enough Secessionists in California to send a column after. William B. Hesseltine, *Lincoln and the War Governors* (New York: Knopf, 1955), p. 22, fn. But many believed otherwise. The Bear Flag, a symbol of Californian independence from Mex-

ico, was revived as the symbol of independence from the Union, and California Unionists were alarmed at the profusion of such flags throughout the state.

10. William N. Brigance, *Jeremiah Sullivan Black, a Defender of the Constitution and the Ten Commandments* (Philadelphia: University of Pennsylvania Press, 1934), pp. 86–116.

11. Allen Johnson and Dumas Malone, eds., V:326.

12. Benjamin P. Thomas, *Stanton. The Life and Times of Lincoln's Secretary of War* (New York: Knopf, 1962), p. 106.

13. Morgan Dix, *Memoirs of John Adams Dix,* 2 vols. (New York: Harper, 1883), II:7.

14. Kenneth M. Stampp, *And the War Came,* p. 211.

15. Clifton R. Hall, *Andrew Johnson, Military Governor of Tennessee* (Princeton: Princeton University Press, 1919), p. 5.

16. *Congressional Globe* (36th Congress, 2nd session), p. 768.

17. Ibid. (36th Congress, 2nd session) p. 790.

18. Clifton R. Hall, p. 27.

19. Conservative Democrats had been reading Forney out of the Democratic party ever since 1857, in which year he supported Douglas against Buchanan during the Lecompton controversy. In 1858 Forney worked against the renomination of J. Glancy Jones, a Buchanan Democrat, and Jones was not renominated. The man who beat him—Douglas Democrat John Schwartz—was later elected over a Republican. In the Speakership contest of 1859–1860, Schwartz voted against the Radical Republican candidate, Galusha A. Grow, but ultimately swung over to support the Conservative Whig, William Pennington, who was elected. Benjamin A. Fryer, *Congressional History of Berks County* (Reading: Historical Society of Berks County, 1939), p. 153. Buchanan Democrats declared that Schwartz had, by this vote, entered the Republican party. Schwartz denied the charge and remained seated on the Democratic side of the House. On February 3, 1860 Schwartz nominated Forney for Clerk of the House. Buchanan Democrats said the nomination, "by a Republican," rendered Forney a Republican.

During the Anti-Lecompton struggles in Pennsylvania, Forney had worked in conjunction with Republicans on certain occasions and had a number of Republican leaders in his debt. One of these was Horace Greeley of the New York *Tribune,* who contacted certain Republican Congressmen, in 1859, urging that they vote for the election of Forney as Clerk of the House of Representatives, which post he was seeking. "I consider Forney *entitled* to the Clerkship," Greeley wrote to Schuyler Colfax of Indiana, "no matter how he may behave hereafter. I go for paying debts as we go along." Greeley to Colfax, November 2, 1859. Richard H. Luthin, *The First Lincoln Campaign* (Cambridge: Harvard University Press, 1944), p. 123. Forney was elected Clerk of the House with the assistance of Republican votes. Buchanan Democrats declared that here again was evidence of Forney's Republican connections.

During the 1860 campaign Forney organized the Douglas Democrats in Pennsylvania and worked furiously against any kind of fusion with the Breckinridge faction. Judge George W. Woodward of the Supreme Court of Pennsylvania wrote to Jeremiah S. Black, U.S. Attorney General, during the campaign, to say that Forney was no longer really a Democrat and by supporting Douglas merely was working for the election of Lincoln. Stanton Ling Davis, *Pennsylvania Politics, 1860–1863* (Ph.D. diss., Western Reserve University, 1935), p. 135, n.

When the Republican-dominated "People's party" captured control of the Pennsylvania legislature, in 1860, the Democrats lost the opportunity of naming a successor to Democratic Senator William Bigler of Pennsylvania. Forney therefore declared in favor of Congressman John Hickman, a recent convert to Republican principles, who had deserted the Democratic party in 1859. Of all the leading Pennsylvania Republicans, Hickman clearly was the most conservative, and on that basis appealed to Forney's political prejudice. Insofar as the Breckinridge faction was concerned, however, here again was proof that Forney was a clear-cut Republican. According to the Philadelphia *Pennsylvanian,* he no longer "took the trouble to wear a mask," and by supporting Hickman, was admitting his Republican associations. Elwyn B. Robinson, "The Press: President Lincoln's Philadelphia organ," *Pennsylvania Magazine* vol. LXV, no. 1 (January 1941):158.

20. Philadelphia *Press,* January 15, 1861; January 25, 1861; March 25, 1861; Charles B. Going, *David Wilmot, Free Soiler* (New York: D. Appleton, 1924), p. 569–70.

21. William Hyde and Howard L. Conard, *Encyclopedia of the History of St. Louis,* 4 vols. (Southern History, 1899), p. 1702.

22. Walter B. Stevens, *Missouri, the Center State, 1821–1915,* 2 vols. (Chicago: Clarke, 1915), I:249; Sceva B. Laughlin, "Missouri politics during the Civil War," *Missouri Historical Review* vol. XXIII, no. 1 (October 1928):591.

23. *Congressional Globe* (36th Congress, 2nd session), p. 78.

24. New York *Times,* January 1, 1861.

25. *Congressional Globe* (36th Congress, 2nd session), pp. 367–77.

26. *Ibid.* (36th Congress, 2nd session) p. 38.

27. War correspondent William Russell of the London *Times* observed: "Wherever wealth is prevelent, there you have the stronghold of the Republican party." Quoted in Chicago *Times,* June 3, 1863. Russell was inclined to be hostile to the Union cause, and his remark in this case may have been a propaganda note, aimed against the spreading popularity of the Union cause among the British labor class. In any event, the statement is incorrect.
New York City was the leading business center of the country and a majority of New York City businessmen were Democrats. Of those who were not Democrats, a great many supported the Constitutional Unionists in 1860. Comparatively few supported Lincoln. Philip S. Foner, pp. 172–202. Philadelphia went Democratic in 1860 and the business interests there were not conspicuously opposed to that result. The great names among Philadelphia financiers included several Biddles, all of whom were Democrats; Adolph Borie, the world famous importer and a Democrat; banker Andrew J. Antello, Democrat; and many others closely identified with Democratic party principles. The wealthy centers of the East were *not* the property of the Republican party but that of the Democrats and the Constitutional Unionists. In the Old Northwest, the business interests were largely to be found in Chicago, Detroit, Cleveland, Cincinnati, Milwaukee, and Indianapolis, all of which voted Republican in 1860 excepting Cincinnati and Milwaukee. But the business centers of the Frontier states and the Far West (St. Paul, Dubuque, Sacremento, and Salem, Oregon) voted Democratic. *Evening Journal Almanac,* 1861.

28. William B. Hesseltine, p. 125.

29. *Congressional Globe* (36th Congress, 2nd session), Appendix, pp. 39–41.

30. Ibid., p. 1461. Cited in James Ford Rhodes, *History of the United States,* 8 vols. (New York: Macmillan, 1920), III:220.

31. See Appendix 2.

32. *Report on the Military Services of General David Hunter, U.S.A., during the War of the Rebellion, Made to the War Department, 1873* (New York: Van Nostrand, 1873), p. 6.

33. Robert S. Harper, *Lincoln and the Press.* (New York: McGraw-Hill, 1951), pp. 89–90.

34. Edgcum Pinchon, *Dan Sickles, Hero of Gettysburg and "Yankee King of Spain"* (Garden City: Doubleday, Doran, 1945), pp. 150–51.

35. Walter H. Crockett, *Vermont, the Green Mountain State,* 5 vols. (New York: Century, 1921), III:497–98.
36. Cleveland *Plain Dealer,* Columbus *Ohio Statesman,* and Chicago *Post,* January–April 13, 1861, passim.
37. Charles Kettleborough, "Indiana on the Eve of the Civil War," Indiana Historical Society, *Publications,* vol. VI (1919):147–59.
38. Irving McKee, *"Ben Hur" Wallace, the Life of General Lew Wallace* (Berkeley: University of California Press, 1947), p. 33; James D. Horan, *Confederate Agent, a Discovery in History* (New York: Crown, 1954), p. 30.
39. H. Levin, *Lawyers and Lawmakers of Kentucky* (Chicago: Lewis, 1874), p. 252; *The Union army,* 8 vols. (Madison, Wis.: Federal, 1908), VIII:131; Allan Nevins, *Emergence of Lincoln.* (New York: Scribners, 1950), p. 279.
40. The story of the "cabinet scene," involving Stanton, Floyd, and Buchanan, was published originally in the London *Observer,* in 1862. The author of the story was Thurlow Weed, serving in England at the moment as an agent of the federal government. The story came to Weed from another federal agent, George Plumer Smith of Philadelphia, who heard it from Stanton's former law partner, Democratic General George W. McCook. In a later conversation with Smith, Stanton reportedly said that "McCook. . .has exaggerated what did occur," but that the story was nonetheless "substantially correct." George Tichnor Curtis, *Life of James Buchanan, Fifteenth President of the United States,* 2 vols. (New York: Harper & Bros., 1883), II:521; William N. Brigance, p. 75.

The story of the cabinet scene, as it appeared in the *Observer,* referred to the presence in the cabinet of John A. Dix preceding the resignation of John B. Floyd. This was a mistake on the part of Thurlow Weed, author of the story. There is also a school of thought which disbelieves the story in every detail. Authors George Tichnor Curtis and William N. Brigance are leading members of the school, which accepts as gospel the contention of Jeremiah S. Black that Stanton invariably was docile in the presence of Buchanan. According to Black's account, Stanton "did not furnish one atom of the influence which brought the President round to the answer to South Carolina." Benjamin P. Thomas, *Stanton,* p. 102. In January, 1861, following the alleged occurrence of the "cabinet scene," Buchanan wrote a letter to his niece in which he said that Stanton was not a force in the cabinet because he invariably agreed with whatever Buchanan said, on any question. George Tichnor Curtis, II:523. Author Curtis concludes from this that the "cabinet scene" never occurred. Yet Jacob Thompson, Secretary of the Interior, did not regard Stanton as a mere reflection of the presidential whim. In a letter to a fellow Secessionist, Thompson wrote that, "Old Buck, at heart, is right with us, but after Stanton came in I have seen him gradually giving way." Benjamin F. Thomas, *Stanton,* p. 102. Republican editors Henry J. Raymond of the New York *Times* and Horace White of the Chicago *Tribune* believed that Stanton was the "backbone" of the Buchanan administration. Ibid., p. 107. Republicans, looking back upon the situation following Stanton's wartime affiliation with the Lincoln administration, may have been inclined to prejudice in his behalf. Yet the reverse was also true, so far as Regular Democrats were concerned, since they had equal cause for prejudice. Following Stanton's death, Jeremiah S. Black insisted that the only source of the "cabinet scene" story was Stanton, and that all of the story was false. Chauncy F. Black, *Essays and Speeches of Jeremiah S. Black* (New York: Appleton, 1895), p. 289. At this point, however, Black was full of hate for Stanton, even in death, and wanted very much to injure his name in the sight of history; and Stanton, under the circumstances was unable to reply. Fletcher Pratt, *Stanton, Lincoln's Secretary of War* (New York: Norton, 1953), pp. 461–66.

41. William N. Brigance, p. 73.
42. Roy F. Nichols, *The Disruption of American Democracy* (New York: Macmillan, 1948), p. 459.
43. Democrats voting in the majority: McClernand, Philip B. Fouke, and John A. Logan of Illinois; Daniel E. Sickles and John Cochrane of New York; Samuel S. Cox and William Allen of Ohio; Jacob McKenty of Pennsylvania; William S. Holman of Indiana; Sherard Clemens of Virginia; and Garnett B. Adrain of New Jersey. *Congressional Globe* (36th Congress, 2nd session), pp. 280–81.
44. Ibid., pp. 393–94.
45. Democrats voting in the majority included McClernand, John A. Logan, and Philip B. Fouke of Illinois; William Allen, William Howard, and Samuel S. Cox of Ohio; John Cochrane of New York; Garnett B. Adrain of New Jersey; James W. Noell of Missouri; Sherard Clemens of Virginia; and Andrew J. Hamilton of Texas. Ibid., p. 296.
46. Ibid., p. 373.
47. Ibid., (38th Congress, 1st session.), p. 425. Story recounted by Senator John B. Henderson of Missouri.
48. Ibid., (36th Congress, 2nd session), Appendix, p. 103.
49. Ibid., Appendix, pp. 70–72.
50. Ibid., pp. 656.
51. New York Senate, *Journal,* February 3, 1857; New York Assembly, *Journal,* April 3, 1857.
52. W. Swanberg, *Sickles the Incredible* (New York: Scribner's, 1956), p. 107.
53. Ibid., p. 110. Douglas-leader Daniel Dougherty of Philadelphia cooperated fully with Stanton and Sickles in this regard. Florence E. Gibson, *The Attitude of the New York Irish toward State and National Affairs, 1848–1892.* (New York: Columbia University, 1951), p. 120.
54. Richard S. West, Jr., *Lincoln's Scapegoat General; A Life of Benjamin F. Butler, 1818–1893* (Boston: Houghton, Mifflin, 1965), p. 45.
55. Robert S. Holzman, p. 26.
56. Ibid., p. 26.
57. Elijah R. Kennedy, p. 74.
58. Walter C. Woodward. *Political Parties in Oregon, 1843–1868* (Portland: Gill, 1913), p. 192.
59. Speech delivered in April, 1861, in California; recounted by Senator McDougall, *Congressional Globe* (37th Congress, 2nd session), p. 1679.
60. S. H. Harlow and S. C. Hutchins, *Life Sketches of State Officers and Members of the Assembly of the State of New York in 1868* (Albany, 1868), p. 116.
61. Allen Johnson and Dumas Malone, eds., XX:560.
62. *Biographical Cyclopedia of Representative Men of Rhode Island* (Providence, 1881), p. 266.
63. *American Biographical History of Eminent and Self-Made Men. Michigan Volume* (Cincinnati: Western Biographical, 1878), p. 100.
64. *Congressional Globe* (37th Congress, Special Session of the Senate), pp. 1438–39, 1446.

4

The Rising of the War Democracy: 1861

On April 13, the day the Confederates began shelling Ft. Sumter, Republican leaders issued an appeal for unity in the loyal states. Conservative and Radical Republicans alike, in stating the appeal, emphasized that slavery was not involved as an issue in the war, that the only issue was Union versus Disunion. The main object of administration policy clearly was creation of a coalition involving *all* Unionists, pro-slavery and anti-slavery alike. It was generally believed that failure in this endeavor could well result in ruin for the Union cause.[1]

Democratic response to the Republican appeal was astonishing to everybody concerned. Despite weeks and weeks of threats and warnings that the Democrats of the North and the border slave-states would *not* agree to any military move against the Confederacy, thousands of them swung about smartly in response to the Republican call-to-arms. Major Anderson surrendered Ft. Sumter April 14 and the fort was evacuated the following day. President Lincoln issued a call for 75,000 volunteers to suppress the Confederate forces, and every state was assigned a quota. Of the 16 slave states only Delaware responded promptly to the call, eight others declaring for the Confederacy and seven for Neutrality.[2] In the free states, however, the initial popular response was heavily in favor of the federal war policy.

So strong, in fact, was the pro-Union reaction of the loyal states to the Confederate assault of 1861, it is customary to say that with Sumter's fall the North became "united to the man."[3] That is overstating the case, however. Actually, the Peace cause did *not* disappear April 15, 1861. The following day and every day for the next four years Peace advocates and Peace publications were in ample evidence throughout the loyal states. What *did* happen when the war began was division of the Peace forces in the loyal states and creation of a formidable Unionist coalition including Republicans, War Democrats, Union Whigs, and Union "Americans." Of the several kinds of non-Republicans in the Union camp, the War Democrats were by far the most numerous and therefore the most important.

A large majority of Democratic newspapers in the loyal states had supported Douglas for President and joined him in approving and/or condoning the Antebellum Peace campaign. As of April 12, 1861, the great bulk of the northern Douglas press was still in the process of denouncing the Lincoln administration and swearing opposition to all its possible designs, including that of war against the South. With Ft. Sumter four months under siege, the Republicans remained the primary enemy of Douglas Democrats in general.[4] The effect of the Sumter attack was an immediate reversal of editorial policy on the part of many northern Douglas newspapers, some of which began denouncing the Confederacy as early as April 13, the day the bombardment of the fort began. When Douglas declared in favor of the federal war policy two days later, a large majority of his northern followers fell quickly into line.[5]

In view of Douglas' political importance in the loyal states it can logically be argued that his patriotic appeal of April 15, 1861 was the deciding factor in the outcome of the war. Flashed across the country on the wires of the Associated Press, the "Douglas Dispatch" (as it came to be called) rallied the non-Republicans of the loyal states, urging them forward to war against the agents of Secession. Wholly revolutionary in every aspect and terribly disturbing to Democrats in general, the implications of the Douglas Dispatch ran against a hundred popular prejudices nurtured and developed by northern Democrats, at considerable trouble, since creation of the Republican party. It tore away the threat of Republican chicanery and for the first time established the picture of a Confederate foe in the eyes of many Americans vital to the Union cause.

Among the national party leaders identified in the public mind with the Antebellum Peace cause, Douglas was alone in embracing the federal war policy at once and with enthusiasm. Buchanan concurred, but very quietly.[6] When the fighting started, Kentucky and Tennessee were in the neutral camp and Breckenridge, Bell, and Crittenden had nothing to say, in keeping with policies adopted by the governors and legislatures of their respective states. While the Antebellum Peace leaders were dividing up in this manner, their many thousands of followers also were adapting to the shock of war, in many cases casting about in search of other leadership.

Although the Douglas faction would constitute the main body of the War Democracy and the Breckinridge faction the main body of the wartime Peace Democracy, there were numerous exceptions to the rule, many of whom were spectacular. And though loyal state Democrats in general abandoned overnight the Antebellum threat to fight "the fanatics of the North," in preference to fighting the Confederates, here again there were exceptions to the rule, many of whom were equally sensational. Reacting violently against the presidential call-to-arms, Secession sympathizers in Maryland severed all telegraph lines leading north from Washington, and broke up several bridges north of Baltimore, with the object of isolating the capital to Confederate advantage. Denied communication with the North, Washington geared to resist an expected attack by Confederate troops massing in strength south of the Potomac. Secretary of State Black had warned President Buchanan in January of a Confederate attempt to capture Washington, saying, "if they *can* take it and *do not* take it, they are fools."[7] When Sumter fell, this became the prevailing opinion throughout the loyal states.

In the winter of 1860–1861, the Army of the United States was dominated by high-ranking Democrats, including many southerners, most of whom elected to "go South," in preference to fighting other southerners. Of a different frame of mind was Colonel Joseph P. Taylor of Kentucky, Assistant Commissary General of the Army, who in April, 1861, was momentarily the highest-ranking War Democrat in uniform in Washington. Four other Democrats on the War Department staff were Major Don Carlos Buell and Major Irvin McDowell, both of Ohio, Captain Montgomery Meigs of Pennsylvania, and Captain Charles P. Stone of Massachusetts. All distinguished themselves in preparing the capital against what then was regarded as imminent attack. For so doing, all were instantly promoted and all but Taylor (who was much older than the rest) became for a while major military figures.[8]

Isolation of the capital from the loyal states rendered Democratic General John E. Wool the officer-in-charge of all Union military forces of consequence from the fall of Sumter, April 14, until May 13, at which time Washington regained telegraphic communication with the North. Wool was Commander of the Department of the East, with headquarters at Troy, New York, and second in overall command to Winfield Scott. (He was also a political figure of importance, having served as a member of the New York delegation to the Virginia Peace Conference.)[9] Called upon to act in the absence of directions from Washington, Wool appeared vigorous, imaginative, effective, and bold. Hurrying to New York City, he established himself as Acting General-in-Chief, advising and directing by telegraph the governors of the several loyal states in military matters of every kind. The repair of telegraph communications between Washington and the North ended the unprecedented and extraordinary performance of General Wool.[10]

In Pennsylvania, immediately following the initial troop call, Republican Governor Curtin appointed two major generals of militia, one of whom was Robert Patterson of Philadelphia, a Breckinridge leader and an absentee slavemaster, as the owner of sugar and cotton plantations in Louisiana.[11] The First Massachusetts Militia, involved in the Baltimore riots of April 19, were commanded by General Benjamin F. Butler, candidate for Governor on the 1860 Breckinridge ticket. The First Rhode Island Militia was organized by Democratic Governor William Sprague and led to Washington by General Ambrose E. Burnside, only recently a Democratic candidate for Congress. General Theodore Runyon of the First New Jersey Brigade was a Douglas elector in the 1860 campaign.

In the important matter of galvanizing Democratic New York City for a stand against Secession, the pro-southern traditions of the local business community and the popular Peace campaign of Mayor Fernando Wood (aided and abetted by the influential Democratic newspapers of New York City), none surpassed the performance of a pair of Breckinridge Democrats long identified with the pro-slavery cause—Daniel E. Sickles, lame-duck Congressman from Manhattan, and John A. Dix, Secretary of the Treasury under Buchanan. Resigning his seat in Congress at the word of Sumter's fall, Sickles caught a fast train home and went straight to city hall, where the Common Council was in session, A large majority of the Council consisted of Democratic politicians long identified with pro-southern policy, and Sickles was well-acquainted with everybody present. Asking and obtaining an audience, he addressed the Council at length, recommending unqualified "coercion" of the Confederacy. In conclusion, he introduced a resolution pledging the City to the full support of the Union cause and the immediate organization and equipment of a volunteer force in its defense. The Council in a state of enthusiasm, adopted the resolution *in toto*.[12]

As one of the outstanding leaders of the New York City business community Dix had been publicly commended, following his return from Washington in March, for his "decision and firmness" in managing the national Treasury "at a period when distrust and disorder seriously menaced the public welfare." The letter of commendation was signed by many local businessmen, a majority of whom were Breckinridge Democrats.[13] On April 19, the New York City chamber of commerce held a meeting at which a record number of its members appeared. Friends and admirers of Dix dominated the proceedings and the chamber went on record in favor of the Union cause. On April 20, Dix presided at a large, dramatic rally at Union Square, in New York City, honoring the return of

Major Anderson and his men from Ft. Sumter. Washington was still isolated from the North and great fear was held for the safety of the national government. Over fifty patriotic addresses were delivered at the rally (from three separate stands), including many by Democrats of very conservative reputation. The best was said to be that of former Congressman John Cochrane of New York City, the most sensational by Mayor Fernando Wood and former Senator Daniel S. Dickinson, all of whom were Antebellum champions of southern principles and Peace on southern terms. City businessmen contributed a million dollars for the purchase of federal government bonds. Munitions maker Peter Cooper and importer Alexander T. Stewart (both Democrats) reportedly gave ten thousand dollars apiece.[14] Under the auspices of the New York City Chamber of Commerce a separate move was inaugurated to procure stock in the federal government to the amount of eight million dollars.[15] A "Union Defense Committee" was appointed, to insure the security of the city and assist in the defense of the Union. Out of 29 committee members, 13 were Democrats, including Dix, James T. Brady and Edwards Pierrepont of Tammany Hall and John J. Cisco, Assistant U.S. Treasurer under Buchanan. Dix was chosen Chairman of the Finance Subcommittee which acted for the U.S. Treasury in the disbursement of thousands of dollars over the following two weeks.[16]

The Union Square rally had a strong effect on many observers, North and South. A great many southern newspapers and politicians had been promising that New York City would stand by the South. The Union Square rally shattered that belief.[17] Also affected was the attitude of numerous hesitant, seemingly undecided New York Democrats in both the Douglas and the Breckinridge camps. Union gatherings less grandiose but equally enthusiastic were held in every major city in the loyal states in the early days of the war, and in many smaller communities.[18]

By the close of April the Union tide was running strong in every loyal state, and yet the Peace cause continued to prevail in many Democratic districts. (The New York *Day-Book* observed that ". . . the stories about the union of the North in favor of the war, must be received with many grains of allowance.")[19] Especially healthy were the advocates of Peace in the Old Northwest, where the power of Clement L. Vallandigham was challenging the power of Stephen A. Douglas. In utter defiance of the patriotic trend, Vallandigham declared for publication: "My position in regard to this civil war, which the Lincoln administration has inaugurated, was long since taken, is well known, and *will be adhered to to the end.* I know that I am right, and that in a little while 'the sober second thought of the people'. . . will demand to know why thirty millions of people are butchering each other in civil war, and will arrest it speedily."[20]

The Vallandigham Letter stood in sharp contrast to the Douglas Dispatch, and many western Democrats now abandoned Douglas in favor of

Vallandigham. Western Breckinridge supporters looking for wartime Peace leaders found one quickly in editor Samuel Medary of the Columbus (Ohio) *Crisis,* recently established to serve the cause of Peace. (As Governor of Kansas Territory in February, 1860, Medary had vetoed a bill abolishing the right to hold slaves as property.[21] He was a dedicated proslavery man.) Without qualification, Vallandigham and Medary denounced the federal war policy. In the face of the Sumter attack they clung to the arguments of the Antebellum Peace campaign. The Civil War was inspired by Abolitionists, they said, and respectable Democrats should have nothing to do with it. In the East, the same message was drummed home daily by Benjamin Wood in the New York *News.*[22]

Vallandigham and Medary had many followers in the West, and Benjamin Wood had many in the East. They could not be ignored. The Unionist press portrayed them as exceptions to the rule; a threesome out of step with the mass of northern Democrats, alone against the great nonpartisan spirit of the loyal states. But this was only propaganda. At no time could Vallandingham, Medary, and Wood be said to stand alone. They were simply the most conspicuous of a large number of Peace Democrats who condemned the federal war policy from its inception to the conclusion of the war. It was in their opinion a glaring example of "executive usurpation" on the part of President Lincoln, illegal "coercion" of inoffensive sister states, and a cunning conspiracy to "subjugate" the South in the interest of Abolition principles. The Peace press, which was widely in evidence in the early weeks of the war, repeated these arguments at great length, and they soon became gospel to thousands upon thousands of Democratic readers.

In April 1861 Congress was out of Washington and had to be summoned by President Lincoln to meet in special session on the Fourth of July. In the meantime, the President was free to conduct the war by executive fiat. The raising of volunteers, the military arrest of civilians, the blockade of southern ports, enlargement of the navy and the Regular Army, and the removal of funds from the federal Treasury to cover initial war expenses, all were attended to without congressional authorization. Republicans and War Democrats accepted these actions as wholly necessary, under the circumstances, but the Peace Democracy saw it all very differently, sensing in Lincoln's policies the hand of a dictator at work. Many of them defended the Sumter attack, in the name of states' rights, and all of them criticized Lincoln for rejecting the avenue of diplomatic negotiations in favor of coercion. All were anxious for Congress to take up the reins of government and greatly disturbed about the long postponement of this event. Why had it been delayed until the Fourth of July? Why not some time in June? Why not May? The war was unconstitutional, the Peace Democracy declared. It was an anti-slavery assault upon the property rights of good Americans and a plot to establish a dictatorship, with Lincoln and the Republican party permanently in command.[23] On this basis, the Peace faction demanded repudiation of the presidential war policy.

Without accepting or expressing all the Peace arguments, *per se,* John Van Buren of the Albany Regency machine of New York state criticized the President for acting with undue haste and indefensible belligerence following the Sumter attack.[24] Many other Democrats held the same opinion, including a host of Minority Leaders in the several state legislatures.[25] Especially alarming to western Unionists were the vague and cloudy statements of the Douglas leadership in Illinois, straddling the issues of the moment to the fullest extent possible and keeping up the cursing of the President, in the spirit of the Van Buren Reservations. Congressman John A. Logan and State Senator Andrew J. Kuykendall, both of "Little Egypt," were delivering anti-Republican speeches in quantity throughout their district, and Congressmen William A. Richardson and James C. Robinson were following the same course in central Illinois. Editor Cyrus McCormick of the Chicago *Times* supported their position, as did also Virgil Hickox, Chairman of the Douglas State Committee, and former Governor John Reynolds. On April 15, Democrats attending a rally at Marion (the home town of Congressman Logan) announced for southern independence. Logan did not endorse the resolutions, but rumor had it that they had his deepest sympathy. Identical resolutions were agreed upon the same day by Democrats in Carbondale, Illinois.[26]

Diametrically opposed to every aspect of the Peace line, a large number of Democratic journalists entered the service of the Union cause in the early days of war. Most of these were Douglasites, including the proto-War faction. There was, however, a vigorous and vocal minority of Breckinridge Unionists, of whom the outstanding western example was John Geary of the Columbus (Ohio) *Capital City Fact.* At first report of the Sumter attack, Geary annouced against the "drunken minions of Jeff Davis and his slave Oligarchy." Speaking primarily to Breckinridge supporters, he warned that "Men who have disgraced their northern blood by sympathizing with the Southern oligarchy had better change their tune, and that speedily. None but traitors deserving the gibbet will be found sustaining the cause of the Southern rebels."[27] At a Union rally in Columbus on April 17, resolutions were voted approving the war policy of the *Capital City Fact,* as opposed to its Douglas rival, the Columbus *Ohio Statesman* (which came out only timidly in favor of the war).[28] Much the same sort of thing happened at Indianapolis, where John R. Elder of the Breckinridge *State Guard* announced in favor of the war, while the *State Sentinel,* a Douglas journal, was coming out against it. (A Unionist mob protesting *Sentinel* policy surrounded the office of the paper in the early days of the war and had to be disbursed by Indiana troops acting under orders from

Republican Governor Morton.) Elder of the *State Guard* had nothing to say against the action of the mob, preferring to emphasize the presence of so many Breckinridge leaders among the Union volunteers.[29] In Wisconsin, the Douglas Kenosha *Democrat* announced, in answer to the Sumter attack—"We said all in our power to avert the war. We believed it would be ruinous and think so still."[30] Speaking for the War Democracy of Wisconsin was a Breckinridge leader, Elias A. Calkins of the Madison *Argus and Democrat,* who came out firmly for coercion and trained his guns at once on slavery. "Though it require a war of ten years, the sacrifice of a million lives, and the entire devastation of every foot of slave territory, [Emancipation] and nothing . . . less must be the end."[31]

Before the year was out, Breckinridge would "go South" to accept a Confederate commission, and his supporters in the North would be subjected to the most extreme denunciation. Summing up the case for the Breckinridge Unionists was a declaration by Ormond Barrett of the Harrisburg (Pa.) *Patriot and Union.* Decidedly hostile to Secession, Barrett was outraged by anyone who questioned his loyalty on the basis of his Breckinridge associations. "When Mr. Breckinridge was the candidate of a portion of the Democratic party," Barrett declared, "he was emphatic and [we] believed sincere in his expression of devotion to the Union. His antecedents as well as his speeches and letters during the campaign, repelled the accusation that he was concerned in a conspiracy to overthrow the Union in the event of the election of Lincoln. . . . Northern supporters of Mr. Breckinridge were firmly persuaded in his loyalty. That they have been bitterly disappointed and basely betrayed is their misfortune and not their fault."[32]

Among the Douglas Democrats, the greatest Unionist performance of 1861 was provided by Douglas himself. While the eastern Democracy was joining the Unionist parade, following the New York rally of April 20, reports from the West continued to emphasize the operations of the Peace movement. War Democrats in the Illinois Assembly arranged with the Republican majority to pass a resolution requesting the return of Senator Douglas from Washington. Only his presence and the power of his personality could smash the Peace forces in the West, his admirers believed. Accordingly, Douglas was invited to address the Illinois legislature on the major issues of the moment. The invitation was accepted and Douglas set off for Illinois by train.[33]

The purpose of the trip at once became known and wherever the train stopped along the way, large crowds assembled and Douglas was called upon to speak. The first such speech was delivered in Ohio just across the line from Wheeling, Virginia, and hundreds of Virginians were present. Widely reported in the press, his remarks created a sensation. At Columbus and Indianapolis, Douglas spoke again, appealing for nonpartisan support of the war and a public demand for its vigorous prosecution. Upon arriving at Springfield, Illinois, he was met at the depot by Illinois Congressman John A. Logan, who upbraided him for befriending the Republicans and deserting the South. He was accused of attempting to sew up the Democratic party and present it as a gift to the Republicans. But, "By God," said Logan, "you can't deliver it."[34]

On the night of April 25, Douglas appeared in the chamber of the Illinois Assembly and gave another rousing patriotic speech. To a hall crowded with legislators and private citizens, he confessed his past mistake of "leaning too far to the southern section of the Union." He warned the audience against committing the same mistake. Solemnly, he said: "Whoever is not prepared to sacrifice party and organizations and platforms on the altar of his country, does not deserve the support or countenance of honest people."[35] The Springfield address was well received. Returning to his home in Chicago, Douglas was invited to speak again, as a gesture of nonpartisan unity, in the great Republican "Wigwam," where Lincoln had been nominated the year before. Accepting the invitation, Douglas rendered his last public address, in which he said: "There can be no neutrals in this war. Only patriots and traitors."[36]

The Douglas speaking tour had a telling effect. Mass desertions from the Peace ranks were reported in all the loyal states, especially in the West. Congressman John A. Logan, previously the loudest of the dissidents in Illinois, now declared in favor of the war. So did Illinois Congressman Richardson, State Senator Kuykendall and editor McCormick of the Chicago *Times*. Democratic Minority Leader Horace Heffren of the Indiana Assembly reversed his position, coming out for war. As a gesture of cooperation, he nominated for reelection the Republican Speaker of the previous session.[37] (To emphasize the full extent of his conversion, Heffern was soon to accept a commission in the Union Army.) William B. Woods, Democratic Minority Leader in the Ohio State Assembly also converted from Peace to War at this point, in company with Minority Leader Henry C. Deming of the Connecticut Assembly.[38] (Shortly afterward, Woods and Deming were offered and accepted military commissions.) In New York, former Governor Horatio Seymour and Minority Leader Francis Kernan of the State Assembly came out in favor of the war, with the blessings of the Albany Regency.[39]

Many southern leaders were shocked by the pro-Union stampede of northern Democrats formerly regarded as friends of the South. The Richmond (Virginia) *Examiner* declared: "We are told that the whole North is rallying as one man—Douglas, veering as ever with the popular breeze; Buchanan lifting a treacherous and time-serving voice from the icy atmosphere of [his Pennsylvania estate]; and well-fed and well-paid Fillmore, eating up all his past words of indignation for Southern injuries, and joining in the popular hue and cry against his special benefactors."[40] The Charleston (South Carolina) *Mercury* inquired: "Where are Fillmore, Van Buren, Cochrane, McKeon, Weed, Dix, Dickinson, and Barnard of New York, in the bloody crusade proposed by President Lincoln against the South? Unheard of in their dignified retirement, or hounding on the fanatic warfare, or themselves joining 'the noble army of martyrs for liberty' marching on the South."[41] The Richmond (Virginia) *Enquirer* singled out Daniel S. Dickinson of New York, "the former crack champion of Southern Rights," for special condemnation as a traitor to the South.[42]

On the strength of northern enthusiasm for the federal war policy, President Lincoln issued a second troop call, May 3, 1861. The number of additional volunteers desired was forty-two thousand to serve for three years, and all three-months' men were requested to reenlist for three years. The Peace faction protested, and Congressman Vallandigham dispatched a private circular to several Democratic leaders in the loyal states, urging the calling of a conference, to "rescue the Republic from an impending military despotism"; but the conference never took place.[43] The Peace cause, so firmly in control of non-Republican forces in the loyal states, as of April 13, 1861, had managed—in the course of two short weeks—to lose its advantage on every front. There were still Peace Democrats around in abundance, and some were very vocal. But the great mass of the northern Democracy had lined up, quickly and in the face of all promises to the contrary, side by side with Lincoln and the "Black Republicans."

Since almost 80 percent of the free-state Democrats were Douglas-men,[44] there is nothing rash in assuming that Douglas was to a large extent responsible for this development. It was the last contribution he had to make to the Union cause, and it was, perhaps, his greatest contribution. Upon returning to Chicago in May, he was contacted by Peace Democrat Virgil Hickox, Chairman of the Democratic State Central Committee of Illinois, who asked him to redeclare his position on the war for the benefit of those who could not reconcile his Antebellum Peace speeches with his wartime statements in favor of coercion. Seriously ill, physically exhausted, and wracked by rheumatism, Douglas rallied his resources to write a lengthy reply. Dated May 10, 1861, the letter constitutes his last known statement on the subject of the war. "One of the brightest chapters in the history of our country," he wrote, "will record the fact that during this eventful period the great leaders of the opposition sinking the partisan in the patriot rushed to the support of the government and became its ablest and bravest defenders. . . . If we hope to regain and perpetuate the ascendency of our party we should never forget that a man cannot be a true Democrat unless he is a loyal patriot."[45] The letter was forwarded by Douglas to his father-in-law, James Madison Cutts, in Washington, for publication in the Washington newspapers. On May 13,

Hickox wired Cutts to withhold publication. In a letter written the same day he explained that the statement might anger the Peace Democrats, at Douglas's expense. Cutts was not impressed. He was a War Democrat. He hated the Peace cause and he liked what his son-in-law had written for the press. The statement appeared in the Washington *National Intelligencer,* May 17, 1861.[46]

Failing rapidly, Douglas broke off all communication with the political world and on June 3, 1861, he was dead. The logical leader of the War Democrats was gone. New Leaders would have to be found to take his place. In death, Douglas would become the symbol of the War Democracy, at least in the eyes of half the Democratic party in the loyal states. The other half had other ideas. As a would-be Machiavelli, he had taken so many stands prior to the war, on both sides of so many issues, that he could serve as the hero of almost anyone espousing almost any reaction to the wartime situation. For every word he ever uttered against Secession, there was another, delivered on some occasion, against coercion. The followers of Douglas were to be found in great numbers within the ranks of both the War Democracy and the Peace Democracy. Members of both factions were fond of declaring that "if Douglas had lived," he surely would have espoused their cause.[47]

The fact is, however, that in the final analysis Stephen A. Douglas was a Union man. In the showdown he had appealed for a nonpartisan spirit in the interest of the Union cause. The remarkable patriotic response provided by the Democrats of the free-states cannot be attributed solely to the magic of his eloquence; but it was surely a matter of major significance. (In tribute to his services, Congress called for creation of the Douglas Brigade, comprising the 42nd Illinois and the 55th Illinois, both of which were raised in Chicago within a month of Douglas's demise.)[48]

With Congress out of session until the Fourth of July, the first legislative action of the war period was provided in the loyal states by the several state legislatures, in all of which the War Democrats battled with the Peace faction for party control. In every state, the Peace men followed the Antebellum line, blaming the Republicans for failure to compromise, urging the calling of a national Peace conference, denying the constitutional legality of a war against the South, branding Lincoln as a dictator, and decrying the beginning of a "war for subjugation." In all of this their purpose was realignment with the War Democracy, to whom they appealed from first to last, without effect.

In New Hampshire, for example, Douglas leader Walter Harriman and Breckinridge leader Robert Morrison were the leading lights at several Union rallies, and former President Pierce came out unequivocally in favor of the war.[49] Peace sentiment was apparent in the legislature in the early weeks of war, but only on a miniscule basis. At Albany, New York, a council of war called by Republican Governor Morgan included eleven state officials, four of whom were Democrats.[50] When the New York "War Bill" was presented for consideration, it was stoutly defended by Senate Minority Leader Francis B. Spinola, and passed without difficulty.[51] Thomas M. Browne, a Douglas elector, was chosen Secretary of the Indiana Senate with the full support of the Republican majority.[52] The first Peace arguments expounded in the Iowa Assembly in May were countered by a patriotic resolution offered by Democrat Racine D. Kellog, pledging "the faith, credit, and resources of the State of Iowa, both men and money" to the Union cause.[53] Responding to the nonpartisan spirit of Kellogg and numerous other Democrats in the Iowa legislature, the Republican majority relinquished control of three major committee chairmanships, all of which were filled by Democrats.[54]

In the matter of military organization, Republican governors fought among themselves for the assistance of talented Democrats in uniform. According to the best informed opinion, one of the outstanding West Point graduates of the past three decades was George B. McClellan of Pennsylvania, a veteran of the Mexican War and a highly competent military engineer, currently on the staff of the Illinois Central Railroad. In addition to his other qualifications, McClellan was a Democrat and a close friend of Stephen A. Douglas. (During the Lincoln-Douglas debates of 1858, he had served as a member of the Douglas entourage.)[55] When the war began McClellan was offered command of the militia in Ohio, Pennsylvania, and New York, all offers coming from Republican officials. He accepted the Ohio command.[56]

The first significant military action of the war, following the surrender of Ft. Sumter, occurred in Maryland and Missouri, in both of which states the War Democrats were rendered conspicuous by outstanding service to the Union. In Maryland, the leading military figure in May, 1861, was Democratic General Benjamin F. Butler, commanding the First Massachusetts Brigade. Never before involved in battle, Butler won the attention and respect of Unionists in general by seizing control of Annapolis and Baltimore, against the wishes of Secessionists and cautious Unionists fearful of armed conflict in their midst. The spirit of Secession, as expressed in the Baltimore Riots, was thoroughly stifled under his authority. In keeping with his Conservative reputation as a politician, Butler issued several public statements of a pro-slavery nature which were received with the greatest satisfaction by the Conservative branch of the northern press. Although removed from command at Baltimore, for offending the sensibilities of doctrinaire West Pointers and Radical Republicans, he was promoted to the rank of major general at the behest of President Lincoln who liked his style and regarded him as an important contributor to the Union war effort, in both the political sense and the military sense.[57]

In Missouri, the major event of April 1861 was seizure of the St. Louis arsenal by Union troops and Unionist civilians, followed by the disarming and arrest of the Secessionist state militia. When Secessionist civilians mobbed the Unionists in the process of escorting the militiamen to jail, they were fired upon and 28 were killed.[58] Following the conflict some Conservatives quit the Missouri Union cause, protesting the killing of civilians,[59] but many justified the action. One of the justifiers was editor Nathaniel Paschall of the War Democrat St. Louis *Missouri Republican.* Secessionist Governor Jackson was furious, and wrote a letter to the *Missouri State Journal* attacking Paschall and the *Missouri Republican* as "pimps and spies."[60] In the matter of mustering union volunteers in Missouri, a Democrat was selected to oversee the job in the person of Lieutenant John M. Schofield of the Regular Army, professor of physics at Washington University in St. Louis, on leave from West Point.[61] Another important military figure in early weeks of war was Democratic Congressman John S. Phelps of Missouri, who rallied a body of Union volunteers at Springfield, in the middle of Secessionist activity, and held the city—and southwest Missouri—to the Union.[62]

When the Union forces dispersed the Missouri state government, the threat of anarchy appeared. To meet the crisis, a proposal was offered by Nathaniel Paschall of the War Democrat St. Louis *Missouri Republican,* calling for return of the State Convention, recently adjourned, to serve as a governing body in the absence of officials elected for the purpose. A special election could be held later to fill the offices left vacant by departing Secessionists. Although a small minority of Unionists questioned the legality of Paschall's proposal, the large majority agreed to it, and a call went out for the return of the convention. Upon assembling, the delegates turned for leadership to two well-known Conservatives, one of whom was a War Democrat—John B. Henderson, a Douglas elector and one of the wealthiest slaveholders in the state. The other was Hamilton R. Gamble, an Old-Line Whig.[63] Henderson was soon to become a U.S. Senator and Gamble Acting Governor.

A major contributor to the Union cause in Illinois in 1861 was Democratic Congressman John A. McClernand, who served as a special envoy of Republican Governor Yates to the White House and the War Department. A similar role was filled in Indiana by Douglas leader Robert Dale Owen, until he was commissioned May 30 as state purchasing agent in the matter of military ordinance. McClernand was rivaled in Illinois by Democratic Congressman John A Logan who in May became a major troop raiser and went to war as a colonel of volunteers. Owen was rivaled in Indiana by Lewis Wallace, the leading Douglas spokesman of the 1860 state campaign, who became in April 1861 Adjutant General of Indiana, in response to an appeal from Republican Governor Morton.

A leading War Democrat in Ohio was David Tod, two-time gubernatorial candidate. Having caused a sensation three months earlier at the Democratic state convention by declaring that 200,000 Ohio Democrats stood ready to fight against coercion of the South, Tod now reversed himself, wiring Washington that 200,000 Ohio Democrats could be relied upon to help in crushing the rebellion.[64]

From the Pacific Coast came the services of several Democrats of prominence, the best known of whom (as a result of the 1860 election campaign) was Isaac I. Stevens, Territorial Delegate from Washington and Chairman of the Breckinridge National Committee. A West Point graduate and a veteran of the War with Mexico, Stevens was hopeful of obtaining a brigadier's commission and had the backing of several important politicians, both Democratic and Republican. The commission was not forthcoming, however, despite interviews with Lincoln and General McDowell, and Stevens was forced to accept a regimental command tendered by Republican Governor Morgan of New York. Other West Coast volunteers of note included Douglas district leaders Henry W. Halleck of California and Joseph Hooker of Oregon.[65]

*   *   *   *   *   *

A War Democrat involved in one of the more controversial legal developments of 1861 was General George C. Cadwalader of Pennsylvania, a participant in the case of *Ex Parte Merryman,* pitting Abraham Lincoln against the writ of *habeas corpus* and the power and prestige of Chief Justice Roger B. Taney and the U.S. Supreme Court. As arresting officer in the Merryman case, Cadwalader was called upon later to defy the authority of Chief Justice Taney, in keeping with a presidential proclamation. This he agreed to do, and as a Breckinridge man his action had considerable significance in Unionist circles. Americans who were standing forth in defense of *habeas corpus* in the early stages of the Civil War all were enemies of the federal war policy. In Lincoln's opinion they presented a serious threat to the Union cause and had to be intimidated and shattered. A hard-fisted policy of this kind could not be implemented without a certain amount of injustice, and as time passed considerable injustice was perpetrated in the name of the policy. Certain persons arrested as enemies of the Union turned out to be nothing worse than mere critics of administration officials and of the Republican and the Union parties. The policy of "arbitrary arrest" (as it came to be called) was nonetheless retained throughout the war and always was regarded by Lincoln as essential.

In many future cases as in the case of *Ex Parte Merryman,* a Democratic military man would be called upon to execute the arrest of Democratic civilians, for the sake of nonpartisan Union war policy. In this manner the policy was protected against attack over a long period by all except the Peace men, and even won the blessings of a number of Democrats of national reputation. Editor John W. Forney of the Philadelphia *Press* declared that the times required "universal confidence" in the Lincoln administration, which was not to be demonstrated by questioning the purposes of federal officials. It was true, he said, that an overwhelming majority of civilians arrested by the military were Democrats, but folly to assume that political difference was the reason for the arrest.[66] Democratic Judge Nathaniel G. Upham of New Hampshire (long identified with the most Conservative political forces in New England) published a treatise, entitled "Civil Liberty in New Hampshire," defending the military arrest of civilians.[67] Of even greater weight was the concurring argument of Douglas leader Reverdy Johnson of Maryland, U.S. Attorney General under Taylor. At the request of President Lincoln, Johnson drew up an extensive opinion, answering the arguments of Chief Justice Taney, point for point. The power to suspend *habeas corpus* was not legislative, as Taney said it was, Johnson declared. If it were, the Constitution would have said so, which it did not. Since *quasi-war* existed in the vicinity of Maryland, the problem involved in the release of suspected traitors from prison was a military matter, and the Constitution granted the President the power to decide upon the conduct of the war. If the President could not suspend the writ of *habeas corpus* in this instance, said Johnson, he would be rendered subordinate to a vast army of civil functionaries, all of whom had the power to issue the writ. It was clear, moreover, that the writ could be used in Maryland to disconcert the progress of the Union Army. In time of war, he wrote, the civil guarantee of *habeas corpus* had no place.[68]

*   *   *

Another political furor was aroused a short time later at Fortress Monroe, Virginia, when Democratic General Benjamin F. Butler enunciated the "Contraband" theory, as a means of jeopardizing the slave property rights of Confederates without threatening those of loyal slaveholders. All Unionists, Conservative and Radical, applauded the "Contraband" theory. Postmaster General Blair, a slave-state Conservative, wired Butler his congratulations and forwarded those of General Scott. Democratic papers in Massachusetts were wholly satisfied with the new policy, explaining that it was not aimed against the cause of slavery, merely the cause of the Confederacy.[69] When the Abolitionists also granted their endorsement, Butler said, in mock alarm, "I hope I am not to be held responsible for that."[70]

Announcement of the Contraband policy did not transform Butler into a Radical in the public mind, nor in his own mind. He was still a Conservative with a reverence for states' rights and human property rights, excepting only when they collided with the Union. Wholly different was the Radical transformation of one of his Democratic subordinates, Colonel William H. Allen of the First New York Infantry, who established a policy of antislavery assault against slave-holding residents in the vicinity of Fortress Monroe, arresting them in quantity. Butler intervened, releasing all the prisoners and directing Allen to cease and desist. When the order was ignored and more Virginia slaveholders were rounded up on treason charges, Allen was court-martialed, found guilty of disobeying orders, and cashiered.[71]

*   *   *

The highly advertised tendency to neutrality on the part of border slave-state Unionists was never long in evidence once the war began. Events in western Virginia led quickly from rebellion to counter-rebellion, to federal occupation of the entire area. Disturbed by the presence of a Union stronghold so near at hand, the Richmond authorities determined on a lightning stroke to seize the western counties. The stroke was deflected by Democratic Generals George B. McClellan and William S. Rosecrans in the battle of Philippi, June 3, 1861, and the Confederates retreated. Another Democrat in uniform actively engaged in the western Virginia campaign was Colonel Lewis Wallace of the 11th Indiana Infantry, who was vigorously praised for his part in the Union victory at Romney, June 11.

Of the several Democratic officers engaged in Virginia at this time, the careers of Generals McClellan and Rosecrans were brilliantly promoted by the outcome at Philippi and later victories at Rich Mountain, Carrick's Ford, and Laurel Hill. Democratic General Benjamin F. Butler—theretofore a national hero—was mortified by the absurd conclusion to the battle of Big Bethel, in eastern Virginia, after which he was relieved of command. The monumental Union catastrophe at Bull Run, July 21, 1861, damaged the career of Democratic General Ervin McDowell and terminated that of Democratic General Robert Patterson.

Despite all embarrassment suffered at Bull Run, the Union army fought well, generally speaking, and many pariticipants—including many Democratic officers—soon were accorded the blessings of promotion. Although a dreadful defeat for the Union cause, the battle was largely instrumental in bringing to the national attention the fact that Democrats were fighting for the Union.[72] As time wore on, it would develop that Democrats were actually the major factor in the Union's military arm.

NOTES

1. In calling upon the people of the loyal states to support the Union cause, in 1861, the Republican President, the Republican governors, Senators, and Congressmen, and many lesser Republican officials emphasized, exclusively, the issue of the Union. In no case has the author found reference by Republican officials engaged in whipping up the war spirit in April, 1861, to any issue other than the Union. Conspicuously absent from the urgings of even the most ardent Radical Republican was the slightest reference to slavery. Democratic support was clearly the object of all Republican troop-raisers, whose primary purpose was to set aside the slavery issue which had so disturbed the northern Democracy throughout the Antebellum Peace campaign.

2. In his message to the special war session of the Thirty-seventh Congress, President Lincoln commended Delaware for assistance rendered in the initial defense of Washington. Democratic Senator Willard Saulsbury responded with patriotic remarks, in Delaware's behalf. *Congressional Globe* (37th Congress, 1st session.), p. 90.

3. Pro-Union newspapers by the hundreds used the phrase, "united to the man," or stated the same idea with a slightly different wording. A few examples: Madison Weekly *Wisconsin Patriot,* April 27, 1861: "united to the man;" Centerville *Indiana True Republican,* April 25, 1861: ". . .all differences heretofore existing are forgotten; everybody is for the country and for the Union;" New York *Times,* May 10, 1861: ". . .loyalty to the Union is the universal sentiment of the Northern people." In reply to President Lincoln's initial troop call, many of the loyal-state governors restated this notion. Examples: Israel Washburn of Maine: "the people of Maine of all parties will rally with alacrity to the maintenance of the Government;" Samuel J. Kirkwood of Iowa: "Two days ago we had two parties in this state; today we have but one, and that for the Constitution and the Union unconditionally." William B. Hesseltine, pp. 146-47.
   Historians have taken up the same chant. For example: R. H. Stanley and George O. Hall, *Eastern Maine and the Rebellion* (Bangor: Stanley, 1887), p. 17: ". . .united to the man."; Henry C. Campbell, III:115: ". . .in the twinkling of an eye, as it were, when the nation's flag was fired upon, in Charleston Harbor, all bitterness seemed to disappear and Democrats and Republicans, leaders and writers came together almost as one, every heart full of love for country, every man ready to defend the country and its honor, even to the extent of offering his life."

4. Howard C. Perkins, ed., passim.

5. Ibid., passim.

6. Philadelphia *North American and U.S. Gazette,* April 16, 1861. It was here reported that Buchanan "participates in the expression of a determination to sustain the government." That was the full extent of the former President's tub-thumping for the Union at this particular time. It might be noted that Buchanan was furious over Republican congressional investigations, exposing the improper use of federal funds by highranking administration officials. In Buchanan's opinion, the exposés were brutally undertaken, unjustly conducted, and full of false implications. Roy F. Nichols, p. 331. In order to emphatically support the federal war policy it would be necessary to call upon his followers to work in concert with the same forces which had sought to disgrace him. As of April, 1861, he could not bring himself to do it.

7. William N. Brigance, P. 111.

8. See Appendix 2.

9. Walter H. Crockett, III:498. Widely known for his Conservative political opinions, General Wool had attracted a staff composed exculsively of southern officers. When the secession crisis came, every member of the staff res-

igned to accept a commission in the Confederate army. Le Grande B. Cannon, *Personal Reminiscences of the Rebellion* (New York, 1895), p. 21.

10. Allen Johnson and Dumas Malone, eds., XX:513–14; Lucius E. Chittenden, *Debates of the Peace Conference Convention* (New York: Appleton, 1864), p. 465; Le Grande B. Cannon, pp. 28–31.

Admirers of General Wool regarded his removal from command of the Department of the East as an act of pique on the part of General Scott, who had not enjoyed hearing of Wool's superb performance while serving as Acting General-in-Chief. Ibid., p. 23.

11. Pennsylvania Adjutant General. *Annual Report,* 1866, p. 90. Patterson had a laudable military record in the War of 1812 and the Mexican War and a political career stretching back to 1824, when he helped nominate Andrew Jackson for President at a caucus of Pennsylvania Democrats assembled in convention at Harrisburg. He was on two occasions a presidential elector on the Democratic ticket, and a leading supporter of the Compromise of 1850. Allen Johnson and Dumas Malone, eds., XIV: 306, Philadelphia Citizens, *Proceedings of the Great Union meeting. . . .*(Philadelphia, November 21, 1850).

12. Edgcum Pinchon, p. 154.

13. Philip S. Foner, *Business and Slavery* (Chapel Hill: University of North Carolina Press, 1941), p. 198.

14. Ibid., pp. 311–15.

15. Ibid., p. 308.

16. Ibid., p. 198.

17. In November, 1860, the Charleston (S.C.) *Mercury* reported a speech by Congressman Lawrence Keitt, in which it was declared there were "a million of Democrats in the North who, when the Black Republicans attempt to march upon the South, will be found a wall of fire in the front." John A. Logan. *The great conspiracy.* NY, Hart, 1886. p. 258. The statement was repeated many times by scores of Secessionist leaders in the weeks immediately preceding the war, on the basis of promises extended by so many northern Democrats. Economic motivation was expected in some quarters to be a major issue in determining the attitude of northern businessmen. The Richmond (Virginia) *Examiner* inquired, "Will the city of New York 'kiss the rod that smites her' and at the bidding of her Black Republican tyrants war upon her Southern friends and best customers? Will she sacrifice her commerce, her wealth, her population, her character, in order to strengthen the arms of her oppressors?" Richmond *Examiner,* April 15, 1861.

In reaction to the New York City Union Square rally of April 20, 1861, the Richmond *Enquirer* noted that great numbers of Conservative northern politicians, "heretofore most honored and confided in by the South, have come out unequivocally in favor of the Lincoln policy of coercing and subjugating the South." Richmond *Enquirer,* April 20, 1861. The Richmond *Examiner* declared, "We are told that the whole North is rallying as one man——Douglas, veering as ever with the popular breeze; Buchanan lifting a treacherous and time-serving voice of engouragement from the icy atmosphere of Wheatland; and a well-fed and well-paid Fillmore, eating up all his past words of indignation for Southern injuries, and joining in the popular hue-and-cry against his special benefactors. Richmond *Examiner,* April 24, 1861.

18. Democrat John A. Griswold presided over a Union rally at Troy, New York. He was a former Mayor of Troy, a candidate for Congress in 1860, and a Douglas supporter. Other Douglas Democrats prominent in the upstate New York Union rallies of April and May, 1861, were Congressman-elect Erastus Corning, president of the New York Central Railroad, New York Attorney General Lyman Tremain, State Senator Francis B. Spinola, and Assemblymen Francis Kernan and Sanford Church. Corning presided at a rally in Albany, where Tremain delivered an address. Kernan was present at a rally in

Utica, Church at one in Albion. Allen Johnson and Dumas Malone, eds., VIII:8–9; Sidney D. Brummer, *Political History of New York during the Period of the Civil War.* (New York: Columbia University, 1911), p. 143. Among the Breckinridge leaders in New York state, none exceeded former U.S. Senator Daniel S. Dickinson in the matter of patriotic rhetoric. Following the Union Square rally of April 20, he toured around, addressing Union rallies all over the state. Allen Johnson and Dumas Malone, eds., V:294–95.

Numbered among the leading participants at Union rallies staged in New England during April and May was Benjamin F. Hallett, editor of the Democratic Boston *Post.* At the "Chester Square" flag raising ceremony, held in April, Hallett shared the rostrum with Edward Everett of the Bell-Everett ticket. A Breckinridge supporter and a leading antebellum Peace man, Hallett was unqualifiedly hostile to the Confederate cause on this occasion. Edith Ellen Ware, "Political Opinion in Massachusetts during the Civil War and Reconstruction," *Columbia University Studies in History, Economics and Public Law* LXXIV, no. 2. (1916): p. 70.

A rally at Portsmouth, New Hampshire, April 17, was attended by Douglas leaders Albert Blaisdell, Daniel Marcy, and Andrew J. Beck, and Breckinridge leader Robert Morrison. Another meeting at Portsmouth the following day was chaired by Albert H. Hoyt, Democrat, and another at Gilmanton, New Hampshire, shortly afterwards, by Democrat Thomas Cogswell. The Gilmanton rally was addressed by Douglas elector George W. Stevens. Concord New Hampshire *Patriot,* May 8, 1861.

At a Union meeting in Augusta, Maine, Democrat Reuel Williams, a former U.S. Senator, was named to preside, Democrat Samuel Cony served as vice president, and Democrat James W. Bradbury, a former U.S. Senator, delivered an address. Louis C. Hatch, *Maine, A History,* centennial ed., 6 vols. (New York: American Historical Society, 1919), II:435–36. A leading participant in Union rallies throughout Vermont was Democrat Homer W. Heaton, a State's Attorney for Washington county. Henry C. Williamson, *Biographical Encyclopedia of Vermont of the Nineteenth Century* (Boston: Metropolitan, 1885), pp. 364–65.

At Chicago, a major figure in the Union rallies of April and May, 1861, was Democratic District Judge Thomas Drummond, who was joined in his endeavors on numerous occasions by several Democratic leaders from the Irish district: Philip Conley, Alderman John Comisky, T. J. Kincella, James Quirk, and P. Carraghar. (Comisky would soon be placed in charge of the recruiting office at Rock Island Freight House.) Mabel Mellvane, ed., *Reminiscences of Chicago during the Civil War* (Chicago, 1914), p. 75. In southern Illinois, the first Democrat to speak for the war was Greene B. Raum, a prominent Douglas leader, followed shortly afterward by Robert G. Ingersoll (law-partner of the better known John A. Logan, who initially opposed the war). Allen Johnson and Dumas Malone, eds., XV:392; IX:469.

At a giant Union rally in Cincinnati, Democrat Stanley Matthews declared against the Confederacy in company with Republican leader Rutherford B. Hayes. George H. Porter, *Ohio Politics during the Civil War Period* (New York: Columbia University, 1911), p. 74.

A rally in Detroit, on April 13, was addressed by Democratic leaders Charles I. Walker and George V. N. Lathrop. (Walker was a recent candidate for Supreme Court Judge, Lathrop a recent candidate for Congress.) Charles Moore, *History of Michigan,* 4 vols. (Chicago: Lewis, 1915), I:416. Another rally at Detroit, on April 20, was attended by Lewis Cass, Secretary of State under President Buchanan. Five days later, Cass presided at a Union meeting in Detroit, attended by former Governor Robert McClelland, Judge Ross Wilkins, B. F. H. Witherell, and Joseph Campau, all Democrats and all vice-presidents of the gathering. At Marshall, Michigan, on April 26, the crowd was addressed by several Democratic speakers, including D. D.

Hughes, Francis W. Shearman, and M. S. Brackett. (Shearman was the 1860 candidate for Superintendent of Schools.) Detroit *Free Press,* April 21, 26, 27, 1861. At Grand Rapids, Michigan, an indignation meeting was chaired by Democrat John Ball, formerly of the state legislature. Charles R. Tuttle, *General History of the State of Michigan* (Detroit: Tyler, 1873), p. 548. At the first Union rally held in Milwaukee, Democrat Alexander Mitchell was selected to preside. At Whitewater, Wisconsin, the Democratic Postmaster, G. G. Willaims, received the same honor. Milwaukee *Sentinel,* April 22, 1861. A Union rally in Columbus, Ohio, April 17, was attended by Judge Thomas W. Bartley (Breckinridge) and addressed by Judge W. R. Rankin (Douglas). Also in attendance at Columbus were Lyman J. Critchfield, Joseph H. Geiger, and Assemblyman Robert B. Warden, all Democrats. Columbus *Capital City Fact,* April 18, 1861. A rally at Cleveland, April 15, was presided over by Mayor F.S. Flint, a Douglas leader. Another Douglas leader, Jabez Fitch, served as Vice President and delivered a speech, in company with Radical Republican Senator Benjamin Wade and Radical Congressman Rufus Spalding. Cleveland *Plain Dealer,* April 16, 1861. (Spalding was one of the very few Congressmen to speak in favor of John Brown following his execution. Eugene H. Roseboom, p. 357.) Another Democrat attending the Cleveland rally of April 15 was Colonel J. W. Heisley, a veteran of the Mexican War. Cleveland *Plain Dealer,* April 16, 1861. A rally at Indianapolis, April 13, 1861, rendered the occasion "the greatest (the city) had yet seen; and probably it has never been surpassed in the intense interest, anxiety, and enthusiasm exhibited." A Democratic hero of the Mexican War, Ebenezer Dumont, was selected chairman of the rally, which was held at the courthouse in the presence of a packed house. John H. Holliday, "Indianapolis and the Civil War," Indianapolis Historical Society, *Publications* vol. IV, no. 9. (1911): pp. 548–49. In Berea, Ohio, an address was delivered at a Union meeting by Democratic leader Alexander McBride. Cleveland *Plain Dealer,* April 16, 1861. At. St. Paul, Minnesota, April 18, 1861, a rally attracted a large number of Democrats, including Earl S. Goodrich, the Douglas State Chairman, and James W. Taylor, an 1860 candidate for Congress on the Breckinridge ticket. Former Governor Willis A. Gorman, a Douglas elector, was also in attendance, in company with John S. Prince, the Mayor of St. Paul; banker Napoleon J.T. Dana, Ross Wilkinson, and district leader E. A. C. Hatch—all Democrats. Breckinridge leader James W. Taylor delivered an address. Christopher C. Andrews, *History of St. Paul, Minnesota* (Syracuse, 1890), p. 187. On the West Coast a great Union rally was staged in May, in San Francisco, and speeches were delivered by Democrats James A. McDougall and James Shields. McDougall was a former Congressman, Shields a former Senator from Illinois and Minnesota. Democratic Governor John G. Downey of California was invited to attend the rally, but declined. Democratic Colonel Edwin V. Sumner, Commander of the Department of the West, was a member of the audience. Jacksonville *Oregon Sentinel,* May 25, 1861.

19. New York *Day-Book,* quoted in New York *Atlas,* April 21, 1861.
20. James L. Vallandigham, *Life of Clement L. Vallandigham* (Baltimore: Turnbull, 1872).
21. Daniel W. Wilder, *Annals of Kansas* (Topeka, 1875), p. 24.
22. The Antebellum Peace press in New York City had run a daily advertisement throughout the Secession period, headlined, "Peace! Peace! Peace!" On April 21 the War Democrat New York *Atlas* protested that the *News* was still carrying the item and openly condemning the "murdering of our brethren at the South."
23. Vallandigham delivered a speech containing most of these charges on July 10, 1861, and the charges were often repeated by his many supporters in the

months that followed. *Congressional Globe* (37th Congress, 1st session), pp. 58–60.

24. Allen Johnson and Dumas Malone, eds. XIX:151.
25. Minority Leaders in the several state legislatures who occupied the same position as John Van Buren in the early days of the war, included: Henry C. Deming, Connecticut Assembly; Francis Kernan, New York Assembly; Heister Clymer, Pennsylvania Senate; William B. Woods, Ohio Assembly; Andrew J. Kuykendall, Illinois Senate; Frederick W. Horn, Wisconsin Senate; and Horace Heffren, Indiana Assembly, all of whom were so hostile to the actions of the President and the Republican party, and so uncritical of the Confederacy, as to appear in favor of Confederate victory in the war. W. A. Croffutt and John M. Morris, *The Military and Civil History of Connecticut* (New York: Ledyard Bill, 1869), p. 42; *Record of Heister Clymer and Historical Parallel between Him and Major General John W. Geary. . .* (1866), p. 2; Allen Johnson and Dumas Malone, eds., XX:505; Arthur C. Cole, p. 260; Wood Gray, p. 57; Salem *Washington Democrat,* April 18, 1861. The *Washington Democrat* was the organ of Horace Heffren, Minority Leader of the Indiana Assembly. On April 18 it carried an editorial calling for a palsy to strike the war arm of the federal authority; Kenneth M. Stampp, *Indiana Politics.* p. 75.
26. Arthur C. Cole, *The Era of the Civil War* (Springfield, Illinois: Centennial Commission, 1919), p. 260.
27. Columbus (Ohio) *Capital City Fact,* April 13, 1861.
28. Ibid., April 18, 1861.
29. Indianapolis *Indiana State Guard,* May 11, 1861.
30. Kenosha (Wisconsin) *Democrat,* April 19, 1861.
31. Madison (Wisconsin) *Argus and Democrat,* May 4, 1861.
32. Harrisburg (Pennsylvania) *Patriot and Union,* September 26, 1861.
33. Gerald M. Capers, *Stephen A. Douglas, Defender of the Union* (Boston: Little, Brown, 1959), p. 224.
34. George Fort Milton, p. 565.
35. George H. Porter, p. 87.
36. Thomas M. Eddy, *The patriotism of Illinois,* 2 vols. (Chicago, 1865), I:81, 84.
37. Wood Gray, *The Hidden Civil War. The Story of the Copperheads* (New York: Viking, 1942), p. 59. On June 28, Logan delivered a patriotic address to a regiment of thirty-day troops at Camp Yates, Illinois, urging them to reenlist. In September, 1861, he was commissioned Colonel of the Thirty-first Illinois Infantry. State Senator Kuykendall became Major of the Thirty-first. Kenneth P. Williams, *Lincoln Finds a General,* 5 vols. (New York: Macmillan, 1949–1959), III:18; *Union Army,* III:271. When the Congress convened, in July, Richardson of Illinois was at once identified with the War Democrats in the House of Representatives. *See* Appendix 1. On June 12, the Chicago *Times* declared: "The war must be fought to a victorious conclusion. If Mr. Lincoln does not do it, the people will. If this generation leaves it undone, the next will fly to arms and accomplish it." Quoted *in:* Kenneth M. Stampp, *Indiana Politics,* p. 75.
38. Heffren became Lieutenant Colonel of the 13th Indiana Infantry, in June; Deming, Colonel of the Twelfth Connecticut, in December; Woods, Major of the 76th Ohio, in February, 1862. *Union army,* III:116; I:285; II:405.
39. Seymour was involved in several troopraising ceremonies in Oneida county. Basil L. Lee, p. 111.
40. Quoted in De Alva Stanwood Alexander, III:10.
41. Ibid., III:10.
42. Ibid., III:10.
43. James L. Vallandigham, p. 152.

44. In Pennsylvania, New Jersey, and New York, "Fusion" party coalitions combined the Douglas and Breckinridge vote. Estimating Douglas' strength in each of these states as 60 percent of the Democratic total, Douglas can be credited with 1,115,000 votes in the free states, as opposed to 360,000 for Breckinridge. *Tribune Almanac, 1861.*
45. Robert W. Johannsen, *The Letters of Stephen A. Douglas* (Urbana: University of Illinois Press, 1961), p. 513.
46. Ibid., p. 513. James Madison Cutts was Second Comptroller of the Treasury under the Buchanan administration. *U.S. Official Register,* 1859, p. 15. In his letter to Cutts, dated May 13, 1861, Hickox contended that he was writing with Douglas' knowledge and approval. Whether Cutts believed the contention is not a matter of record, but the letter was published—in defiance of Hickox' wishes.
47. Examples: Congressman William S. Holman of Indiana, *Congressional Globe* 37th Congress, 1st session), p. 153; John W. Forney, *Eulogy upon Hon. Stephen A. Douglas. Delivered at the Smithsonian Institute, Washington, July 3, 1861* (Philadelphia, 1861), pp. 7–8; James M. Scovel, *Three Speeches, with an Introduction* (Camden, 1870), p. 13; Congressman Lucian Anderson of Kentucky, *Congressional Globe* (38th Congress, 1st session), p. 458; Congressman William J. Allen of Illinois, *Congressional Globe* (38th Congress, 1st session), p. 459; *The Old Guard,* vol. III (February 1865), p. 81; Congressman Henry C. Burnett of Kentucky, *Congressional Globe* (37th Congress, 1st session), pp. 73–74; Congressman Samuel S. Cox of Ohio, William A. Richardson of Illinois, John A. McClernand of Illinois, John Law of Indiana, Philip B. Fouke of Illinois, and Charles A. Wickliffe of Kentucky, *Congressional Globe* (37th Congress, 1st Session), pp. 35–37; Senators James A. McDougall of California and James W. Nesmith of Oregon, Ibid., (37th Congress, 1st session), pp. 27–29.
48. *Union army,* VIII:260; *Biographical Encyclopedia of Illinois* (Philadelphia, 1875), p. 546.
49. Amos Hadley, *Life of Walter Harriman* (Boston: Houghton, Mifflin, 1888), p. 84; Portsmouth (New Hampshire) *American Ballot,* April 25, 1861; James D. Squires, *The Granite State of the United States,* 4 vols. (New York: American History Publishing Co., 1956), p. 400.
50. The Lieutenant Governor of New York was Democrat David R. Floyd Jones, elected in 1859; other Democrats included Van Rensalaer Richmond, Engineer; William I. Skinner, Canal Commissioner; and Isaiah Blood, a Douglas elector and Minority Leader of the State Senate. *Evening Journal Almanac,* 1862; Frederick Phisterer, *The War of the Rebellion, 1861–1865* (Albany, 1912), p. 13.
51. Sidney D. Brummer, p. 142.
52. Indiana, *Senate Journal* (Special Session, 1861), p. 7.
53. Cyrenus Cole, *A History of the People of Iowa* (Cedar Rapids: Torch, 1921), p. 335.
54. Ibid., pp. 93, 99.
55. Clarence E. Macartney, *Little Mac* (Philadelphia, 1940), pp. 32–34.
56. Allen Johnson and Dumas Malone, eds., XI:581.
57. Robert S. Holzman, pp. 30–36.
58. James G. Randall, *Civil War and Reconstruction,* p. 326.
59. William E. Parrish, *Turbulent Partnership. Missouri and the Union, 1861-1865* (Columbia, Missouri, 1963), p. 24.
60. William Hyde and Howard L. Conard, eds., IV:2408.
61. See Appendix 2.
62. William Hyde and Howard L. Conard, eds., V:109.
63. Walter B. Stevens, pp. 319–20.
64. Edward C. Smith, p. 136; George H. Porter, p. 175.

65. Hazard Stevens, *The Life of Isaac Ingalls Stevens,* 2 vols. (Boston: Houghton, Mifflin, 1900), II:320. See also Appendix 2.
66. Robert S. Harper, p. 111.
67. Everett S. Stackpole, *History of New Hampshire,* 4 vols. (New York: American History Society, 1916), IV:191.
68. Bernard C. Steiner, *Life of Reverdy Johnson* (Baltimore: Remington, 1914), p. 49.
69. Edith Ellen Ware, "Political Opinion in Massachusetts," p. 91.
70. Concord (New Hampshire) *Patriot,* June 14, 1861.
71. Montpelier (Vermont) *Patriot and State Gazette,* July 6, 1861; Roy C. Basler, ed., IV:516.

5

Conservative Tradition at Bay: States' Rights under Fire in Congress, 1861

A matter of considerable consequence in the early months of war was the gathering of Congress, on the Fourth of July, for the Special War Session called by Lincoln in April. The primary purpose of the session was to ratify the earlier war measures taken by the President, to authorize expansion of the military and naval forces, and to provide for loans and taxes for support of the war.

There were 102 Republicans in the House, 47 Democrats, and 21 members elected on the "Union" ticket. In the Senate the count was 32 Republicans, 15 Democrats, and two Unionists.[1] Repudiating the conciliatory spirit of the Corwin Compromise, a sizable majority of Republican members announced in favor of Radical doctrine, in both House and Senate, denying positions of authority to Conservatives in almost every instance.[2] Although traditionally alarmed about Radical influence in the Republican party, the War Democrats suppressed their feelings on the subject through the full course of the Special War Session, in the interest of unity.

The leader of the War Democrats in the House was John A. McClernand of Illinois, previously cited as a major opponent of the Antebellum Peace cause. He was by nature a member of the Democratic pack and always before had sought the safest path, free from controversy in Democratic cir-

74

cles. On that basis, he had fought against the Free Soilers of 1848, supported the Compromise of 1850,[3] and joined the Douglas faction in 1852. When the Kansas-Nebraska Act backfired he had fallen under attack as one of its supporters, and was driven out of Congress for the moment.[4] Deserting Douglas, he campaigned for Buchanan in 1856, but when the Lecompton crisis arose and Buchanan became unpopular in Illinois, McClernand once again defected and was returned to Congress in 1860 running as a Douglas-man.[5]

In the manner of many northern Democratic politicians, he appeared to better advantage during the Secession crisis and the Civil War than ever before. A strong Unionist, he took his stand in the emergency without any of the vacillation for which he was so well known. Having tried for years to placate the Secession element, he no longer believed that possible. McClernand was ready now to support the Republican administration in the destruction of the Confederacy, hoping all the while that slavery would not be damaged in the process. A native of Kentucky and a strong Negrophobe, he could not believe that Abraham Lincoln (another native of Kentucky) really would abolish slavery even if he had the opportunity.

The leading War Democrat in the Senate was James A. McDougall of California, in many ways similar to McClernand of the House. Throughout the 1830s and the 1840s McDougall had lived in Illinois in close proximity to both Lincoln and McClernand. He was Attorney General of Illinois in 1845 and upon his removal to California was elected there to the same office four years later.[6] In the conflict over slavery in California, he had affiliated with the anti-slavery faction, under David C. Broderick, and was elected as an anti-slavery Democrat to Congress in 1852. In the manner of most anti-slavery Democrats, McDougall was far more hostile to the Negro than he was to slavery. Yet he feared and detested Secession, as an all-out Douglas-man. When the California legislature voted for a U.S. Senator in 1861 the Douglas faction held only a plurality, but McDougall had friends in the Republican party and was elected with the help of Republican votes.[7] Before setting off for Washington he made several Unionist speeches against the Secessionist and Peace campaigns already in the process of development.[8] In the same manner as Congressman McClernand, Senator McDougall was hopeful that slavery would not become an issue in the war. Against McClernand and McDougall, and heading up the Peace cause in Congress, were Congressman Vallandigham of Ohio and three Kentuckians—Congressman Henry C. Burnett and Senators John C. Breckinridge and Lazarus W. Powell, all of whom were to oppose the administration on every proposal looking to a strong war policy.

The combined voting strength of the several War factions in the House during the special session was 158, as against 20 for the Peace faction. The majority appears tremendous. But that was not the case whenever certain issues were involved. Attacks on slavery, for instance, or any move to benefit the Negro race, could be counted on to serve as a unifying force among the non-Republicans, all of whom were sure to vote the other way. Under such circumstances, the Republican lead was reduced by 53 votes.[9] Acting as a bloc and with the aid of only 17 Republicans, the non-Republicans had the power to determine House policy on all matters even remotely concerning slavery; and such developments occurred with surprising frequency. Radical control was better in the Senate, but even there it foundered frequently on the fact that the Radicals all had different notions about Radicalism, and outside of certain areas many of them were not willing to vote Radical at all.

* * *

With the coming of Secession, the word "Radical" suffered a temporary alteration in meaning. Whereas previously it had concerned only slavery, it also came to stand, during the Secession period, for those in favor of coercing the South. When the shooting started, still another change in meaning was discernable. As of May, 1861, the "Radicals" included all Unionists urging the abridgement of any constitutional guarantees, in the interest of a stronger federal authority in wartime. In both instances, Abraham Lincoln adopted the "Radical" position. The Special War Session of the Thirty-seventh Congress was largely devoted to attacks on Lincoln and this aspect of Radical policy by the Peace faction, and a united defense of Lincoln by Unionists in general and several War Democrats in particular.

* * *

On July 10 the Senate considered a joint resolution sustaining the President in all his actions prior to the convening of Congress. It also took up consideration of the Volunteers Bill. Spokesman for the Peace Democracy attacked the joint resolution in the name of further deliberation and respect for the democratic process, expressing particular concern about presidential suspension of the right to *habeas corpus*. War Democrat McDougall of California replied, in behalf of the joint resolution. He had come to Washington, he said, to endorse the preliminary action of the government. It was his hope that all bills would pass without debate. The joint resolution carried by voice vote.[10] Saulsbury of Delaware moved to amend the Volunteers Bill by reducing the number of volunteers from fifty thousand to twenty thousand, which was enough, he said, to defend the loyal states against attack from any quarter. The proposal was rejected by the Senate,

5 to 32, and the Volunteers Bill adopted, 34 to 4. Five Democrats voted with the majority in both instances.[11]

A clash occured July 10 between War and Peace Democrats in the House of Representatives. Speaking for the Peace faction, Vallandingham attacked as unconstitutional a bill providing congressional sanction for unorthodox means of collecting the federal revenue when standard methods proved impracticable. At the same time he delivered himself of the opinion that *all* Republicans were Radical and declared his contempt for the Republican Corwin Compromise. In rejecting the Crittenden Compromise, the Republicans had brought on the war he said. The several wartime proclamations of President Lincoln were clearly illegal, as were all executive policies looking to suppression of the Confederate cause. The presidential policy was nothing more, in Vallandigham's opinion, than a "daring plot to foster and promote secession and to set up a new and strong form of Government in the States which might remain in the Union."[12]

The following day Vallandigham was back again, denouncing the Army Appropriations Bill. It seemed to him astonishing that the House could be expected to accept the word of a mere cabinet member—the Secretary of War—without investigation. He counseled deliberation and delay. Burnett of Kentucky declared his intention of refusing to vote a single dollar for the war, and was called to account by War Democrat McClernand of Illinois. How was it possible, McClernand wanted to know, for a Congressman to support the Constitution "by folding his arms while the batteries of rebellion are aimed at the capital." It appeared to him, he said, that Burnett must want the Confederates to win.[13] The Republicans were accused by Burnett of bringing on the war for the explicit purpose of subjugating the South. The charge was countered by War Democrat Allen of Ohio who declared in favor of the Union cause "until the rebellion is put down."[14] Vallandigham replied with a proviso, which he wanted attached to the Volunteers Bill, establishing a perambulating peace commission of seven men to accompany "the army on its march," for the purpose of receiving and considering Peace proposals offered by the enemy.[15] War Democrat Wright of Pennsylvania opposed the proviso in strong terms. He was for peace, he said, only on the condition that the Confederates "lay down their arms . . . and surrender their leaders." Vallandigham had warned of the horrors of a "subjugated" South. Wright announced in favor of the "subjugation of traitors, in order that patriots may live and in order that the benefits of our laws and institutions may prevail. If the gentleman from Ohio calls that subjugation, I tell him I am in favor of such subjugation." When Wright finished speaking the Vallandigham proviso was rejected by the House.[16]

As matters of major significance continued to come before the Congress for debate, the War Democracy continued to meet the Peace Democracy in open combat. Anxious for recognition of southern Unionism, a plan was advanced by the Republican leadership to fill the vacant seats of Virginia's Secessionist senators with two good Unionists, without submitting the proposal to the conservative Judiciary Committee. When Peace Democrat Powell of Kentucky protested the move, his arguments were answered by War Democrat Johnson of Tennessee, speaking as the voice of southern Unionism. The senators-elect were seated, without consideration by committee. The vote was 35 to 5, four Democrats joining in the majority.[17]

A major feature of the wartime Peace campaign was the contention that peace would be readily available if only the Republicans would agree to the calling of a national peace conference. A House resolution proposing such a gathering was tabled July 15 by a vote of 92 to 51—but every Democrat present gave it his support.[18] The War Democrats in Congress were still receptive to the idea of negotiated peace and compromise across the bargaining tables, in which respect they were unalterably opposed by the Radical Republican leaders and many Conservative Republicans, including Abraham Lincoln. On many other issues, however, the War Democracy remained hand-in-glove with the administration. The Conspiracy Bill, imposing fine and/or imprisonment for persons plotting to overthrow the government, carried 123 to 7 with 27 Democrats voting in the majority.[19] A resolution offered by War Democrat McClernand of Illinois, July 15, pledging the House to vote for any sum of money and any number of men necessary to insure the speedy and effectual suppression of the rebellion carried 121 to 5, with 24 Democrats voting in the majority.[20]

The Peace Democracy was sharply criticized in the House by War Democrat Holman of Indiana, July 16, and in the Senate by War Democrat Latham of California the following day.[21] Republican compromise proposals in the Thirty-sixth Congress—scorned by Vallandigham in a recent House speech—were praised by Latham, and the failure of the Crittenden Compromise was described as the fault of the Secessionists.[22] Latham's remarks evoked wild applause in the Senate galleries. When it was over, War Democrat Rice of Minnesota arose to say that he occupied the same position as Latham and "indorsed to the fullest extent" all of Latham's opinions on this occasion.[23]

In the House, on July 18, War Democrat Thomas of Maryland engaged Peace Democrat May of Maryland in angry debate. May had been accused of holding criminal correspondence with the enemy. Cleared of the charge by the House Judiciary Committee, he arose to make a "personal explanation" which developed into a speech attacking the federal war policy in Maryland. Reference was made to "the downtrodden people of Baltimore," groaning beneath a "military tyranny" which "utterly prostrated their constitutional liberties."[24] War Democrat Thomas replied in behalf of the administration, defending the federal war policy in Maryland. He called the Baltimore riot "that most monstrous outrage" and criticized the police commissioners of Baltimore for protesting the presence of federal troops. The commissioners, said Thomas, had proven their incompetence to serve, in failing to prevent the burning of the bridges north of Baltimore and in failing to preserve order in the city. They did not even *try* to quiet the excitement, he declared. Republican General Banks, Commander of the federal force in Baltimore, was praised by Thomas as a man of reason and moderation.[25]

The Union defeat at Bull Run dismayed many Unionists, including some in Congress. The fact was not immediately apparent, however. On July 22 (the day following the battle) War Democrat McDougall of California made a Senate speech, proposing enlargement of the Regular Army. The motion was agreed to.[26] On the same day the House adopted the Crittenden Resolution, calling for suppression of the rebellion and promising to protect the existence of slavery in the South. The Crittenden Resolution was in two respects a severe blow to the Peace cause. It was a war measure conceived by a man deified in Peace circles for presenting the outstanding compromise proposal of the Secession period. It also interfered with the contention of the Peace faction that the war was an anti-slavery crusade. The pro-war section carried 121 to 2 (15 Democrats abstaining), the pro-slavery section carried 117 to 2 (38 Republicans abstaining).[27] Following the votes, two Democrats (Wright of Pennsylvania and Noble of Ohio) introduced pro-war resolutions of their own.[28]

On July 24 War Democrat Johnson of Tennessee introduced in the Senate a slightly reworded version of the Crittenden Resolution. Peace Democrat Breckinridge of Kentucky attacked both the resolution and the Republican party, which he said was responsible for the war, contrary to the wording of the resolution. Following debate, the resolution was adopted, 30 to 5, with four Democrats in the majority.[29] Senator Rice of Minnesota, a former follower of Breckinridge, took the occasion to renounce his leadership, face-to-face, saying: "War . . . has been brought on us . . . I, Democrat as I am, will give my vote and support to the Administration . . . so far as necessary war measures are concerned . . . . This is no time for us to be fiddling; it is no time for us to be swapping jackknives while the ship is sinking."[30]

Another attack on the Peace Democracy took place in the Senate, July 27, in response to all the Peace arguments advanced during the Special War Session. Certain Senators had described the President as a dictator, denying the necessity for any of his proclamations. It was he who had started the war, they said, by mobilizing the Union armies. In the same attacks, the Republicans were blamed for defeat of the Crittenden Compromise and it was openly declared that Republican policy had brought the war on purposely. Democratic Senator Johnson of Tennessee replied, ridiculing the Peace arguments, without exception. "It all goes to show, in my opinion," he said, "that our sympathies are with one government and against the other." Had the President gone against the Constitution? Johnson did not think so, even "admitting that there was a little stretch of power." Did military arrests endanger individual rights? Johnson did not think so. "I reckon it is equally important to protect a government from seizure as it is an individual." He turned his back on compromise, declaring: "Traitors and rebels are standing with arms in their hands and it is said we must go forward and compromise with them. . . . All the compromise I have to make is the compromise of the Constitution of the United States. . . . I say, Let the battle go on—it is Freedom's cause. . . . Do not talk about Republicans now; do not talk about Democrats now; do not talk about Whigs or Americans now; talk about your Country and the Constitution and the Union." He urged a vigorous war policy, even if it required that the Stars and Stripes "be bathed in a nation's blood."[31] The speech was easily the most forceful pro-war declaration delivered by a Democratic member of either house since the war began.

The services of War Democrat Senator McDougall of California were utilized by the Republicans in support of a proposal for the easier issuance of federal bonds and a court reform bill affecting Missouri and Kentucky, both of which measures were bitterly assailed by the Peace faction.[32]

Before the Special Session adjourned, an opportunity was presented in both houses for a vote on the major argument of the Peace Democracy, that the President was acting as a dictator, without color of law. Coming as it did on the heels of the Bull Run disaster, the vote reflected to the distinct disadvantage of the Union cause. When the Soldier Pay Bill passed the House and Senate, carrying a clause indemnifying the President and his agents against all law suits arising from the suspension of civil liberties in wartime, only four Democrats gave it their vote in the Senate, and only two in the House.[33]

The Special War Session finished business August 6, with the War Democrats still hostile to the administration and the Republican party, and still accepting as Gospel certain arguments advanced by the Peace faction. There was no doubt, however, concerning the patriotic purpose of the War Democrats in Congress, and of the many developments attracting Lincoln's attention during the chaotic summer of 1861, this was perhaps the most encouraging of all.

NOTES

1. The wartime "Union" party was formed in several states in response to Secession, and it was in these states that most of the special congressional elections occurred in the spring of 1861. All but a few of the elections in question were called at the direction of President Lincoln, to fill vacant congressional seats in advance of the regular elections, which were not scheduled to occur until later in the year. In Maryland, Kentucky, the western counties of Virginia, and the eastern counties of Tennessee, the special elections pitted Union party candidates against "Peace" and/or "Secession" candidates. In all but two cases the Union party was victorious and in most instances the victors were Old-Line Whigs and Americans. Exceptions to the rule included no Repbulicans but did include some Democrats: William G. Brown and John S. Carlile of Virginia, Francis Thomas and John W. Crisfield of Maryland, Charles A. Wickliffe of Kentucky, Andrew J. Clements and George W. Bridges of Tennessee. (Crisfield of Maryland supported Breckinridge in 1860, the rest supported Douglas. Carlile of Virginia served only five days in the House, resigning to take a seat in the Senate). Two more Unionists elected to Congress in the spring of 1861 were a pair of War Democrats from Pennsylvania: Hendrick B. Wright and Charles J. Biddle (replacing Republicans who had died in office.) See Appendix 1.
2. U.S. Congress, *Biographical Congressional Directory, 1774–1911* (Washington, 1913).
3. In voting for the Fugitive Slave Law of 1850, McClernand established himself as an arch-enemy of the anti-slavery forces, and his name was broadcast around the free states as one of the "Doughfaces" who had to be defeated by anti-slavery votes. See Langston Hughes and Milton Meltzer, *A Pictorial History of the Negro in America* (New York: Crown, 1963 (1956)), p. 44, for picture of an anti-slavery handbill, distributed in the North, containing all the names of free-state men voting for the Fugitive Slave Law.
4. Arthur C. Cole, *The Era of the Civil War* (Springfield: Illinois Centennial Commission, 1919), p. 126; Allen Johnson and Dumas Malone, eds., XI:587.
5. Ibid., XI:287.
6. *National Cyclopedia of American Biography*, XI:330.
7. Theodore H. Hittell, *History of California*, 4 vols. (San Francisco: Stine, 1879), IV:278—79.
8. McDougall described his conduct during the Secession crisis in a Senate speech delivered April 16, 1862. *Congressional Globe* (37th Congress, 2nd session), p. 1679.
9. See Appendix 1.
10. *Congressional Globe* (37th Congress, 1st session), p. 41.
11. Democrats voting in the majority: Johnson of Tennessee; Latham and McDougall of California; Nesmith of Oregon; and Rice of Michigan. Ibid., pp. 53–54.
12. Ibid., pp. 57–60.
13. Ibid., pp. 73, 77.
14. Ibid., p. 94.
15. Ibid., p. 97.
16. Ibid., p. 98.
17. Ibid., p. 109. Democrats voting in the majority: Johnson of Tennessee; Latham and McDougall of California; and Rice of Minnesota.
18. Ibid., p. 129.
19. Ibid., p. 130. Democrats voting in the majority: Baily, Lazear, Lehman, and Wright of Pennsylvania; Corning, Haight, Odell, Smith, Steele, Vibbard, and Ward of New York; Cox, Noble, and Nugen of Ohio; Cobb and

Steele of New Jersey; Fouke, Logan and McClernand of Illinois; Cravens, Holman, and Law of Indiana; English of Connecticut, and Browne of Rhode Island.
20. Ibid., p. 131. Democrats voting in the majority: Baily, Lazear, Lehman, and Wright of Pennsylvania; Corning, Haight, Odell, Smith, Steele, Vibbard, and Ward of New York; Cravens, Holman, and Law of Indiana; Allen, Noble, and Nugen of Ohio; Fouke, Logan, and McClernand of Illinois; Cobb and Steele of New Jersey; English of Connecticut and Browne of Rhode Island.
21. Ibid., p. 153.
22. Ibid., Appendix, pp. 19–22.
23. Ibid., p. 217.
24. Ibid., p. 197.
25. Ibid., pp. 197–202.
26. Ibid., pp. 219–20.
27. Ibid., p. 223.
28. Ibid., p. 224.
29. Ibid., p. 265; Democrats voting in the majority: Johnson of Tennessee; Latham of California; Nesmith of Oregon; and Saulsbury of Delaware.
30. Ibid., p. 242.
31. Clifton R. Hall, p. 29.
32. *Congressional Globe* (37th Congress, 1st session), pp. 397, 424–25.
33. Ibid., p. 442. Democratic Senators voting (if effect) to indemnify the President and presidential aides against all law suits arising out of the suspension of certain civil liberties through presidential proclamations: Johnson of Tennessee; Latham and McDougall of California; Rice of Minnesota. Democratic House members voting to the same effect: Cobb of New Jersey and Thomas of Maryland (Union party). Ibid., p. 449.

6

Conservative Tradition at Bay: Civil Liberties under Fire in Wartime, 1861

Following the Union disaster at Bull Run, certain Peace Democrats abandoned all reserve, announcing in favor of the Confederate cause. Typical was Marcellus Emory, editor of the Bangor (Maine) *Democrat:* "Onward the shouting myriads will pour, until again met by the unequaled and invincible genius of Davis, Beauregard, Johnston, and Lee, and the iron nerves of these noble men, who are defending their firesides and their homes, from the ruthless assaults of fanaticism and fury."[1]

In Oregon, the battle was depicted in several Democratic papers as a "banquet of blood." The Albany (Oregon) *Democrat* began referring to Union soldiers as "white niggers" and "the enemy," and calling the Confederacy "the glory of the land."[2] Similar catcalls were heard from other Democratic leaders in the loyal states[3] and Unionist editors were called upon to provide a dose of counter-propaganda. Some did a much better job than others. It can be assumed, in this regard, that President Lincoln took special note of editorials appearing July 25 in the New York *Tribune* and the Philadelphia *Press,* the two outstanding Unionist journals in the East.

The *Tribune* editorial was written by Horace Greeley, often called the

"Voice of the Republican party." Capable of providing strong leadership on occasion, Greeley also was capable of the greatest despair, especially in time of crisis. He was famous for recommending nonresistence to Secession when the movement first began. As time passed he had swung about, joining in the Radical Republican demand for coercion of the South and preservation of the Union, his optimism refortified, his will returning. It was the *Tribune* that originated the Union battlecry, "On the Richmond!" Then came Bull Run and carnage and defeat. Greeley was dismayed. He felt himself responsible for the catastrophe. His editorial of July 25 was a dismal apology. If he were "needed as a scapegoat for all the military blunders of the last month," he said, "so be it. Individuals must die that the nation may live." The night of July 25, Greeley wrote to Lincoln, advising him to keep on with the war only if he believed it still could be won. If not, it would be better to arrange an armistice for "thirty, sixty, ninety, one hundred and twenty days—better still for a year."[4]

Forney's editorial had no resemblance whatever to Greeley's. On the contrary, it damned all talk of compromise and urged the Union on to victory. "The people of the North must come to the work," said Forney, "and they must come with the sword. No more declamation; no more invective; . . . no more idle sympathy for traitors; . . . no more partisanship and treasonable resolutions by party Conventions—we must use the sword. It must be wielded by no divided energies, but with one will and one purpose."[5]

The *Tribune* had the largest national circulation of any Republican newspaper in the Union. The *Press* was developing one of the largest of any Democratic paper, with a special edition for the army and another for California.[6] Lincoln wanted the support of both, naturally, but there was something very special about Forney and the *Press*. Forney was apparently more stable than Greeley, which was a matter of considerable importance. And more than anything else at this point, Lincoln wanted Democratic support. If the war were to continue over a long period, Forney could serve as a significant member of any nonpartisan Unionist coalition to be established in Pennsylvania. (As a first step in this direction, Lincoln assisted in arranging the selection of Forney as Secretary of the Senate.)[7]

During the latter half of 1861, Forney divided his time between Philadelphia and Washington and often visited the White House, where he was always warmly received. Conversation with Lincoln during this period centered largely on the possibility of establishing another newspaper, with offices in Washington. Federal advertising was guaranteed and Forney could not resist the opportunity. In October, 1861, plans were consummated for publication of the Washington Sunday Morning *Chronicle,* which made its initial appearance in the closing weeks of the year. Preceding this event, the outstanding paper in Washington was the Old-Line Whig

National Intelligencer, which long had served as Lincoln's favorite reading matter. But times had changed, driving a wedge between Lincoln and editor James C. Welling of the *Intelligencer,* who hated Republican principles and was only barely in favor of the Union cause. From the moment the *Chronicle* started publication, it surpassed the *Intelligencer* as an instrument of Unionist designs. Sales went well and in 1862 the *Chronicle* became a daily publication. Whenever possible, Lincoln was to lend his assistance to the enterprise which proceeded to flourish on the strength of his interest. (It was said that in the course of the war the paper grossed thousands from War Department advertising alone.)[8] Peace Democrats were highly resentful of the Lincoln-Forney relationship and before long Forney was labeled in Peace circles as "Lincoln's Dog."[9]

The most notable events occuring in the later half of 1861 included the retirement of General-in-Chief Winfield Scott; appointment and removal of General John Charles Fremont as Commander of the Department of the West; resurgence of the Peace Democracy in the loyal states and the end of Kentucky Neutrality; extension of the policy of "arbitrary arrests" from the slave states to the free states; the "Trent Affair"; the military engagements at Wilson's Creek and Belmont, Missouri, and Ft. Hatteras, North Carolina; the raising of the "Army of New England" and the raising of the Irish Brigade. Another development concluding in January 1862, but taking place mainly in the final months of 1861, was a great commotion attending the resignation of Simon Cameron as Secretary of War. In all these matters War Democrats were vitally involved.

The disgrace of General Scott at Bull Run led to the appointment of Democratic General George B. McClellan as General-in-Chief of the Armies.[10] The disgrace of General Fremont at Wilson's Creek—followed by release of his Emancipation Proclamation—led to his replacement in the West by Democratic General Henry W. Halleck, a Douglas district leader from San Francisco and author of the California constitution of 1849. Halleck's appointment was designed to satisfy Conservatives, as was also his first major statement of policy—"General Order Number Two"—terminating military use of Negro contrabands in the Department of Missouri.[11] The rise to prominence of General Halleck represented one more Conservative Democratic link in the nonpartisan Union chain forged by Lincoln in the first year of war.

The outcome of the battles of Bull Run and Wilson's Creek inspired a rash of Peace demonstrations throughout the loyal states. In Connecticut for example, a "White Flag" movement developed in protest against the war. Former Governor Thomas H. Seymour was prominently identified with it. So was William W. Eaton, a member of the Breckinridge State Central Committee. So was the Bridgeport *Advertiser and Farmer.*[12] In New Jersey the first important Peace rally was held in Bergen county July

30, 1861, at Schraalenberg. It was addressed by Dr. Thomas Dunn English, a fiery critic of administration war policy.[13] In close concert with Dr. English, from an early date, were Rodman M. Price, former Governor of New Jersey, and James W. Wall, formerly Mayor of Burlington, currently on the staff of the New York *News*.[14] In Delaware, Peace advocates gathered on the Dover green a month preceding Bull Run, denouncing the Republicans. Following the battle the Peace sentiment was even more apparent, all over the state.[15]

Unionist response to the Peace demonstrations was angry and in many cases violent. In the late summer and the fall of 1861 some Peace rallies were forcibly disrupted by Unionist mobs. A disturbance occuring at Monroe, Connecticut, August 24, prevented the appearance of Peace Democrat William W. Eaton, who had been scheduled to deliver an address. A major participant in the mob action was War Democrat Phineas T. Barnum, the well-known entrepreneur. When the struggle was over, Barnum was raised on the shoulders of the mob and carried from the field in a gesture of tribute. On the same day, a crowd of soldiers invaded the office of the Peace Democrat Bridgeport *Advertiser and Farmer*.[16] Speaking in defense of the vigilante action, War Democrat Amos Kendall, (former Secretary of the Treasury,) wrote an angry letter to the *Advertiser and Farmer*, denouncing its policies, along with those of the Confederacy. He had no criticism for the actions of the mob.[17] Similar assaults carried out by civilians in the latter half of 1861 damaged the offices of many Peace journals in several of the loyal states. Some Democratic editors were compelled by threats of violence to swear allegiance to the Union, under humiliating conditions.[18]

Since the adoption of the Constitution, the right to freedom of speech had been set in abeyance repeatedly, when Conservative opinion was disturbed about any kind of anti-slavery propaganda. Wherever the pro-slavery forces held a majority there was nothing in the nature of free-speech for anti-slavery men. During the same period, however, Conservatives had been pretty well protected in the matter of expressing pro-slavery opinion. Civil War politics altered this arrangement, to the great despair of all Conservatives identified with the Peace cause. And in many cases, the voices urging on the Unionist mobs would belong not to Republicans and Abolitionists seeking revenge but to War Democrats, hoping to erase through violence any sense of association in the public mind between themselves and those who now came forward as the wartime champions of anti-Union principles.[19]

Not all War Democrats behaved in this manner, however, and many reacted completely to the contrary. It would appear, in fact, that the Unionist tendency to violence against the physical facilities of the Peace press was far more beneficial to the interests of the Peace Democracy than to those of any other faction in the loyal states. In the view of many Democrats adhering to the wartime standard of the Democratic organization, the mob assaults on Democratic newspaper offices had the appearance of a Republican plot to wreck the Democratic party by violent means. On that basis a great many Democrats became ardently opposed to the wartime suppression of *any* Democratic paper by *any means,* legal or illegal, peaceful or violent. The action of the Unionist mobs had rendered many Democrats the outspoken opponents of any form of censorship. When later the federal authorities began suppressing the more extreme Peace publications and jailing their editors, a large number of War Democrats protested the action in the name of free speech. Embarrassment on the part of the federal authorities in cases of this kind was the legacy of the Unionist mob attacks. Instead of demoralizing the Peace press the Unionist hooligans had raised it to the level of martyrdom.

Mob attacks on the offices of the Peace press also brought into being many secret Peace societies, organized in the interest of revenge and self-defense. Of these, the best known was the Knights of the Golden Circle. By the close of 1861 a large number of chapters were said to exist in the southern counties of Indiana, Iowa, Ohio, and Illinois. They were roundly denounced by many members of the War Democracy.

Providing an alternative to mob violence against anti-Union speakers and newspapers, President Lincoln intensified the policy of placing civilians under military arrest, without recourse to *habeas corpus.* Although Chief Justice Taney had declared the policy unconstitutional (in *ex parte Merryman),* Lincoln had chosen to ignore the decision and proceeded to keep on ignoring it for the remainder of the war. Doubting the loyalty of border slave state judges, he could not conceive of any other course to follow. For a few months the arresting agency was the State Department, until the responsibility was transferred to the War Department. Peace Democrats denouncing the war were frequently removed from their homes and held on charges of disloyalty, often without trial, at Ft. McHenry in Baltimore harbor, Ft. Lafayette in New York harbor, Ft. Warren in Boston harbor, the Old Capitol Prison in Washington, and several other dungeons. Few objections to the policy of arbitrary arrest of civilians were registered at first by civil libertarians. In time, however, the policy would arouse the greatest controversy.

One of the earliest notable complaints along this line was advanced by Peace Democrat Pierce Butler, a Breckinridge elector from Pennsylvania, held for 30 days without trial on a charge of accepting a Confederate commission. Upon his release, Butler brought suit for false arrest against the War Department and Simon Cameron, Secretary of War. Seeking counsel, Cameron hired the services of War Democrat Benjamin H. Brewster of Philadelphia, a friend of Butler's and a Breckinridge leader in his own right. (Having represented the pro-slavery cause in the famous

Dangerfield Slave Case of 1859,[20] Brewster was regarded as the most Conservative attorney in the state.) Legal finagling prevented Cameron's case from coming to trial, and Brewster was thereby established as a strong pro-Union man, despite his past political affiliations.

A pair of War Democrats actively engaged in the military arrest of civilians in 1861 were George B. McClellan, General-in-Chief of the Union armies, and General John A. Dix, commanding the Maryland Department. On September 18, a majority report was submitted to the Maryland State Assembly by Chairman S. Teakle Wallace of the Committee on Federal Relations, taking strong ground against the Union cause and against the doctrine of military necessity as a basis in suspension of certain civil liberties.[21] On orders from General McClellan, General Dix moved against the legislature, September 18, with the object of arresting every member favoring the report. When the action was opposed by the officers of the Assembly and the State Senate they also were arrested.[22] Two weeks later, McClellan and Dix moved again, in this instance against the authority of the Talbot County Court presided over by Democratic Judge Richard B. Carmichael, an open opponent of the war. In the process of charging a jury, Judge Carmichael had vilified the Union cause. He also had recommended the indictment of several Maryland Unionists accused of doing violence to Maryland Secessionists, and published a memorial to the legislature, expressing disloyal sentiments. When the federal troops arrived to arrest him in his courtroom Judge Carmichael resisted, but was restrained and removed to prison. He was at once proclaimed a martyr by the Peace faction and by some Conservative Unionists, including War Democrat John Crisfield, Congressman from Maryland, who protested the arrest to President Lincoln. In his reply the President endorsed the actions of Generals McClellan and Dix, and Judge Carmichael remained in prison until December 1862.[23]

Another controversial action, in August, 1861, was the arrest and imprisonment of James G. Berret, the Mayor of the District of Columbia. Under one of the first laws enacted by the wartime Congress, officials of the District were required to swear an oath of allegiance to the federal government. Denying the constitutionality of the law, Mayor Berret refused to take the oath. He was a Breckinridge Democrat in the process of serving his second term in office and was closely identified with the Peace faction. In all his wartime policies, Berret was opposed by War Democrat Richard Wallach, unsuccessful candidate for Mayor, 1858 and 1860.[24] For failing to take the oath the Mayor was arrested by the military and imprisoned at Ft. Lafayette. In his absence, War Democrat Wallach was designated Acting Mayor, on August 26, by order of the City Council. Berret was not released from custody until he promised to resign from office.[25] In this manner, War Democrat Richard Wallach became the wartime Mayor of Washington, D.C.[26]

* * *

Throughout the first five months of the war, Kentucky Unionists had fumed over the failure of Kentucky Governor Magoffin to place the state on a war footing in defense of the Union. From May 27 to June 3, Peace Democrats staged a "Border Slave State Convention" at Frankfort, Kentucky, with the object of endorsing "Kentucky Neutrality." The convention had the blessings of the Governor but failed to sway a majority of the voters. Only in the extreme western counties of the state was there any considerable Secessionist strength. Elsewhere, the Unionists prevailed, and Louisville was said to be a "city of flags" honoring the Union. Anxious to enlist in the Union cause, Kentuckians crossed the northern border in great numbers, signing up at Camp Jo Holt in Indiana, and Camp Clay near Cincinnati.[27]

Numerous War Democrats were busy whipping up the Union spirit in Kentucky. Of these, the outstanding example was Joseph Holt, Postmaster General and Secretary of War under Buchanan. Another leading Kentucky Unionist was Holt's father-in-law, Charles A. Wickliffe, Congressman and Chairman of the Douglas National Committee. The Speed brothers, Joshua F. and James, also were active in defiance of Kentucky Neutrality. (Joshua was a member of the Douglas State Executive Committee and a good friend of President Lincoln; James was a Douglas leader in Louisville.) Although most of the Breckinridge faction in Kentucky supported the Governor and Kentucky Neutrality, there were exceptions. One was State Treasurer James G. Garrard, grandson of Kentucky Governor James Garrard (a contemporary of Jefferson). Elected on the Magoffin ticket in 1859, Garrard announced early in behalf of the Union, to the Governor's distress. Assemblymen Richard T. Jacob and Robert A. Burton, Jr., and State Senators Thornton F. Marshall and James A. Prall, elected on the Breckinridge ticket, broke with the Governor and campaigned for the Union cause.[28]

Governor Morton of Indiana believed that Kentucky was ripe for the entrance of federal arms from the outset of the war, and that failure to send them would lead to a Confederate takeover. Advised of the Governor's opinion, President Lincoln paid no attention to it. Morton therefore contacted a close friend, Indiana Republican leader Thomas H. Nelson,[29] whose brother, William Nelson, was a native of Kentucky and closely in touch with the Union organization there. William was a Democrat and a Lieutenant Commander in the U.S. Navy, in charge of a squadron patrolling the Ohio river. Following consultation with his brother, at the urging of Governor Morton, Lieutenant Commander Nelson went to Washington and visited the White House, setting forth again the arguments of Governor Morton against further toleration of "Kentucky Neutrality." President Lincoln at last came around. The arming of Kentucky Unionists was accomplished with the help of Governor Morton and several Kentucky Democrats, including Lieutenant Commander Nelson, the Speed brothers, Charles A. Wickliffe and Thornton F. Marshall. Governor Magoffin of Kentucky was outraged by the move, but Lincoln assured the Governor that he only was acting in the interest of the Union men of Kentucky.[30]

On May 31, War Democrat Joseph Holt of Kentucky wrote a letter to James Speed, attacking Secession and "Kentucky Neutrality." The letter was vigorous and rabble-rousing. It was printed in pamphlet form and widely distributed through the state. On July 13, Holt appeared in Louisville to make a speech of the same nature, which was highly acclaimed.[31] (According to Rutherford B. Hayes of Ohio, Holt delivered "the best war speeches of any man in the land. They always brace my nerves and stir my heart when I read them.")[32] On July 15, Lieutenant Commander Nelson visited Lancaster, Kentucky, under authority of the War Department, and there commissioned several army officers including a pair of well-known Democratic leaders: Theophilus T. Garrard, named Colonel of the Seventh Kentucky Infantry, and Frank Wolford, Lieutenant Colonel, First Kentucky Cavalry.[33] Following Unionist victories in Kentucky's August elections, the War Department ordered the establishment of Camp Dick Robinson in central Kentucky. War Democrat Nelson supervised formation of the camp, referring all official complaints on the part of state authorities to President Lincoln, in Washington. Local Unionists applauded administration policy, denouncing "Kentucky Neutrality" as a fraud against the people. It was noted that several weeks earlier Confederate agents had set up recruiting stations all over the southern counties without official opposition of any kind. On September 5 Confederate troops landed at Hickman, Kentucky, and fortified the place. On September 18 the Kentucky legislature declared war on the Confederacy. When the Governor vetoed the declaration it was passed again over his veto, and Kentucky at last was in the war on the Union side.

The outcome of the Kentucky crisis was especially heartening to War Democrat Andrew Johnson, Senator from Tennessee, who had hopes of regaining control of the eastern portion of his state with the help of local Unionists. From the moment Tennessee declared against the Union (in May) the Unionists of East Tennessee had rejected Confederate authority, organizing secretly, ambushing patrols, and generally creating havoc. As soon as Kentucky announced for the war, Lincoln pressed upon the War Department the advantages of seizing East Tennessee, and Secretary of

War Simon Cameron thought it could be done. General McClellan was enthusiastic and one of his subordinates, Democratic General Don Carlos Buell of Ohio, was selected to lead the proposed expedition. Having won attention at Washington for his work in preparing the capital against attack in April 1861, Buell was highly regarded in Republican circles, and had no trouble in securing the command. He was not a man of dramatic action, however. Despite frantic appeals from Senator Johnson and other Unionist leaders in Tennessee, Buell took his time in preparing the planned invasion, and by the time he was ready to begin operations the Confederates had tracked down and rooted out the Unionists of East Tennessee, trapped in their mountain strongholds. The man most anguished by the bungling of the plan was Democratic Senator Johnson of Tennessee, who regarded the whole affair with loathing and classified Buell as a danger to the Union.[34] In the future, Johnson and Buell were to meet again, at which point Johnson would do what he could to ruin the man whom he believed had lost Tennessee to the Confederacy, almost single-handed.

*   *   *

Shaken by the news of defeat on virtually every front, Unionist morale was greatly improved at the close of August 1861 by word of a successful land-and-naval attack on the Confederate position at Ft. Hatteras, North Carolina. The hero of the battle was Democratic General Benjamin F. Butler. News of the victory was wildly received in the loyal states and General Butler (out of favor since his defeat at Big Bethel) was once again a hero.[35] A pair of Democrats actively engaged in reviving the fortunes of the Union, in the aftermath of Bull Run and Wilson's Creek, were Generals William S. Rosecrans of Cincinnati and Ulysses S. Grant of Galena, Illinois. Both were West Point graduates and former businessmen. Both had been adherents to the Antebellum Peace cause. (According to Douglas family tradition, Grant was ready to fight for the Confederates until argued out of doing so by Senator Douglas himself.[36] According to another account, he was undecided about Secession until swayed by the pro-Union exhortations of Douglas elector John A. Rawlins, at a Union rally in Galena.)[37]

Rosecrans was the moving force in the Union sweep through western Virginia, which redounded to the fame of his superior officer General McClellan. Under Rosecrans' full authority Union troops defeated the Confederates at Carnifax Ferry and Cheat Mountain, compelling the withdrawal of the Confederates (under General Robert E. Lee) from the western counties, in the direction of Richmond.[38] General Grant was meanwhile engaged in a minor but highly advertised land-and-naval assault on the Confederate position at Belmont, Missouri. (The Belmont raid involved a host of other War Democrats, including General John A. McClernand, Colonel John A. Logan, 31st Illinois; Colonel Henry Daugherty, 22d Illinois; Colonel Isham N. Haynie, 48th Illinois; Colonel Napoleon B. Buford, 27th Illinois; Colonel Philip B. Fouke, 30th Illinois; Colonel John Cook, Seventh Illinois, Lieutenant Colonel Andrew J. Kuykendall, 31st Illinois, and Captain John A. Rawlins, Assistant Adjutant General on the staff of General Grant.) The profusion of War Democrats engaged at Belmont was generally regarded as significant. Writing home following the battle, Captain Rawlins observed that the battle had proven "that Democrats will fight (I mean Union Democrats) for the country, Washington, and the stars and stripes."[39]

*   *   *

On October 21, many Democrats were involved in another Union disaster at Ball's Bluff, Virginia.[40] Overall commander of Union operations at Ball's Bluff was Democratic General Charles P. Stone; the field commander was Colonel Edward D. Baker, Republican Senator from Oregon, who was killed in the encounter. Union losses were appalling and the Peace press blamed everything on Baker. Of a different turn of mind was Democratic Major N. Buell Eldredge of the Seventh Michigan Infantry, a participant in the battle.[41] To his way of thinking, Baker was not the sponsor of the holocaust, merely the victim. Blame for the defeat belonged to General Stone for failing to provide a proper means of escape across the river. The opinion found its way into the Michigan newspapers and Eldredge was arrested on the orders of General Stone who ignored his demand for a court-martial. Upon obtaining his release after six weeks delay Eldredge resigned his commission and returned home.[42]

*   *   *

The two most publicized generals in the Union army, as of autumn 1861, were Democrats George B. McClellan, hailed as the redeemer of western Virginia, and Benjamin F. Butler, hero of Baltimore and Ft. Hatteras. Both were superior in matters of organization, and as Commander of the Army of the Potomac McClellan had ample opportunity to demonstrate the fact, rebuilding the shambles wrought by the Bull Run defeat. Butler was anxious to demonstrate his own abilities as an organizer and therefore recommended the formation of a new force, the "Army of New England," to be raised by himself and to consist exclusively of Democrats. The War Department agreed to the proposal and Butler set off on a recruiting trip.

As it turned out there were many obstacles. Rhode Island and New

Hampshire were currently engaged in their own troop-raising operations and had no men to spare.[43] Another problem was the fact that an army composed exclusively of Democrats was easier to talk about than to raise. Butler modified his plan, agreeing to include Republicans in the ranks. He wanted Democratic officers, however, and he wanted to select them himself.[44] Connecticut had an Irish regiment, the Ninth, commanded by Colonel Thomas W. Cahill, the Democratic Street Commissioner of New Haven. The Ninth became a part of the Army of New England.[45] Butler contacted a fellow Breckinridge Democrat, former Governor Thomas H. Seymour of Connecticut, urging him to raise a regiment of his own, but Seymour refused. Turning next to Douglas-leader Henry C. Deming of Connecticut, Butler was this time successful,[46] and a regiment was speedily organized under Deming's authority. (When approached by Butler on the subject of troop-raising, Deming was serving as Acting Speaker of the State Assembly, in the absence of Republican Speaker Brandagee who was ill.) Deming's regiment was designated the Twelfth Connecticut Infantry. A popular Hartford Democrat, Frank H. Peck, became Major of the Twelfth.[47]

In his native Massachusetts, Butler raised two regiments—the "Eastern Bay State" and the "Western Bay State," otherwise known as the 30th and 31st Massachusetts. For commanding officers, he selected Jonas H. French and Charles M. Wheldon, two of the most conservative Democrats of his acquaintance;[48] but here he ran against the prejudice of Republican Governor Andrew who refused to indorse the appointment of either man. French was especially obnoxious, in Andrew's opinion, having led a pro-slavery Boston mob against Tremont Temple in January 1861, with the object of breaking up an Abolitionist meeting. Nor could anything be done to change the Governor's mind on this question. It was said that French was popular in the Irish districts of Boston and that the Irish would gladly fight for him in battle. Many citizens contacted the Governor in his behalf, including a delegation headed by former Governor Lincoln. But Andrew would not yield and Butler was compelled in this case to surrender in his staunch defense of Conservative tradition.[49]

Traveling on, he raised another infantry regiment (the Twelfth Maine) the command of which was accorded to George F. Shepley, U.S. District Attorney for Maine under three Democratic administrations. Butler and Shepley had served together at the Charleston and Baltimore Conventions which Shepley attended as a Douglas delegate.[50] William K. Kimble, a former U.S. Marshal, became Lieutenant Colonel of the Twelfth; David R. Hastings was Major; one of the captains was Gideon Hastings. All were Democrats. All were lawyers. The Twelfth Maine was nicknamed "The Lawyer Regiment."[51] Once organized and ready for action, the Twelfth Maine engaged in a grand review, at Portland, where a stand of colors was presented by War Democrat Ether Shepley, a former U.S. Senator and former Chief Justice of the State Supreme Court.[52]

In Vermont, Butler visited the state capital while the legislature was in session and tendered command of the Eighth Vermont Infantry to Assemblyman Stephen Thomas, a Douglas Democrat and candidate for Lieutenant Governor in the 1860 campaign.[53] Thomas was 51 years old and doubted his ability to stand the strain of war. After thinking it over, however, he accepted. Douglas elector Edward M. Brown, editor of the Montpelier *Patriot and Gazette,* was named Lieutenant Colonel. Democrat Charles Dillingham (son of former Congressman Paul Dillingham) was appointed Major.[54] Butler's recruiting and organization procedures lasted into the early months of 1862. When the Union forces captured New Orleans, in April, Butler led the way, entering the city at the head of a slightly augmented version of the Army of New England.

There were many Irish contingents in the war—largely Democratic in makeup. Two of the most spectacular, in very different ways, were the Irish Brigade, commanded by General Thomas F. Meagher, and the 25th New York Infantry, commanded by Colonel James Kerrigan. Meagher was affiliated in Antebellum times with the *Irish News,* a Douglas paper. Kerrigan was a member of Mozart Hall and a Congressman-elect. Both were leading Peace men in the Secession period, and Kerrigan had even gone so far as to organize a regiment to fight for the Confederacy. When the war began both had changed their tune, but with different results. While Meagher was serving at Bull Run and urging creation of the Irish Brigade, Kerrigan and his men were causing disturbances in the Union ranks. Wherever the 25th New York was encamped riotous conditions prevailed. In December 1861 Colonel Kerrigan was court-martialed for disgraceful conduct and declared incompetent to command, whereupon he went to Washington and took his seat in Congress as an opponent of the war. Meagher (who was an Irish revolutionary) had sought the appointment of Democratic General James Shields (another Irish revolutionary and a hero of the Mexican War) as Commander of the Irish Brigade. When Shields declined the command it went instead to Meagher.[55]

*   *   *

A large number of War Democrats were involved in the drama arising from the *Trent Affair,* in the closing months of 1861. When Captain Wilkes of the *San Jacinto* towed his cargo into Boston, in November, depositing the Confederate Commissioners Mason and Slidell at Ft. Warren, the Union stood confronted with the gravest crisis, involving legal precedents and political realities of momentous nature. The likelihood of war with England was excellent, and war with England almost certainly meant Confederate victory in the Civil War. Parliament reacted furiously and in short time a British force of 8,000 troops was on its way to Canada.

Calling once again on his nonpartisan war policy, President Lincoln consulted numerous Democrats concerning the legal aspects of the *Trent Affair*. Included in the group were Lewis Cass, Secretary of State under Buchanan; Caleb Cushing, Attorney General under Pierce; and Samuel J. Tilden of Tammany Hall. Cass and Tilden agreed: That Captain Wilkes had broken international law, and that the prisoners ought to be released and permitted to proceed on their journey. Cushing disagreed, favoring outright rejection of the British demands.[56] Congressman Vallandigham, the leading Peace Democrat in the country, was not consulted by Lincoln. He nonetheless declared himself on the subject, coming out in favor of war with England.[57] General Benjamin F. Butler, one of the leading War Democrats in the country, agreed with Vallandigham. If necessary, Butler said, his Army of New England could seize Canada and hold it against the assaults of the British fleet. Earlier in the year Secretary of State Seward had recommended to President Lincoln policies designed to bring about a war with England. Seward believed that such a war would reunite the North and South, and the same argument was now advanced by Butler.[58] Lincoln had no more use for it coming from Butler than he had for it coming from Seward. In January 1862 Mason and Slidell were returned to the authority of the British government.[59]

No sooner had the furor over slavery subsided in the West, following the removal from command of Republican General Fremont, than it flared up again in the East, with the help of Democratic General John E. Wool, Commander of the Department of Virginia. At issue was the presence at Fortress Monroe, on the York peninsula, of a female Negro slave belonging to a Maryland slaveholder. The slave was employed as a cook by an Illinois regiment, and her owner wanted her returned to Maryland, under the terms of the Fugitive Slave Law. An official protest was lodged with General John A. Dix, commanding the Department of Maryland. Contacting Wool at Fortress Monroe, Dix demanded the return of the slave, and Wool rejected the demand, advising Dix to run his own department and mind his own business. Secretary of War Cameron supported Dix, but Wool became angry and refused to give the matter up. When the slaveowner arrived at Fortress Monroe to claim his property he was referred to the colonel of the regiment for whom the slave was working. The slave owner had accused the regiment of using the slave for immoral purposes and the colonel demanded an apology. Other officers did the same. The slaveowner withdrew charges and left without custody of the slave. Wool dispatched his aide-de-camp to Washington, to argue the case against the Army policy of enforcing the Fugitive Slave Law.[60] The anti-slavery action of Democratic General Wool was highly important in the breaking down of pro-slavery Union Army policies. It was overshadowed at the time, however, by another anti-slavery move more spectacular in nature- —the Annual Report of the War Department, calling for the arming of the slaves. The author of the report was Simon Cameron, the Republican Secretary of War—a recent convert to the Radical anti-slavery cause. Behind Cameron, however, stood a pair of Democratic advisors: Edwin M. Stanton, Attorney General under Buchanan, and John Cochrane, Colonel of the 65th New York Infantry, formerly a New York City Congressman, and a charter member of the pro-slavery Mozart Hall machine. In the process of discussing war matters with Secretary Cameron in Washington, Stanton had observed that the greatest possible blow against the Confederacy would be the arming of the slaves. Stanton was not the first Democrat to make such a statement, nor even the first Breckinridge Democrat.[61] He was the first to impress the idea on Cameron, however. The next was Colonel Cochrane. Called upon to speak at a patriotic rally on the outskirts of Washington, November 13, Cochrane and Cameron both delivered speeches and Cochrane created a sensation, coming out in favor of Emancipation and the arming of the slaves. Renouncing his many years service as a northern defender of pro-slavery principles, he called upon the government to cease equivocation and to "Take the slave by the hand, place a musket in it, and in God's name bid him strike for the human race."[62] It was this address, immediately preceded by the observations of Edwin M. Stanton, that goaded Cameron into stating the same argument in his Annual Report, for which action he was compelled to resign as Secretary of War, at the insistence of pro-slavery Unionists. Ironically, he was replaced in authority by Stanton, whose anti-slavery declarations had so affected his own political sensibilities as to cost him his administrative post. The appointment of Stanton was confirmed January 15, 1862.

*   *   *

In the closing weeks of the year, an unexpected political statement was issued by former President James Buchanan from his farm at Lancaster, Pennsylvania. Having held his opinions to himself for many months, he now came out wholeheartedly in behalf of the federal war policy.[63] The action confounded the Peace Democrats (who previously had regarded Buchanan as a friend) and also the Republicans and Douglas Unionists, who had cursed him as the devil incarnate from the outset of the war.

NOTES

1. R. H. Stanley and George O. Hall, p. 82.
2. Walter C. Woodward, p. 199.
3. The St. Paul (Minnesota) *Press,* August 16, 22, 1861, records the following list of Democratic newspapers that were clearly out for Peace, following the Union defeat at First Bull Run: Bridgeport (Connecticut) *Advertiser and Farmer;* Albany (New York) *Atlas and Argus;* Lockport (New York) *Adversiter;* Portland (Maine) Argus, Council Bluffs (Iowa) *Bugle,* Atchinson (Kansas) *Bulletin,* Troy (New York) *Budget,* Columbus (Ohio) *Crisis,* Chatfield (Minnesota) *Democrat,* Huntington (New Jersey) *Democrat,* Calion (Ohio) *Democrat.* Bangor (Maine) *Democrat,* Dayton (Ohio) *Empire,* Belle Plaine (Minnesota) *Enquirer,* Cincinnati *Enquirer,* Washington (Pennsylvania) *Examiner,* New York *Freeman's Journal,* Malone (New York) *Gazette,* Plainfield (New Jersey) *Gazette,* Dubuque *Herald,* Newton (New Jersey) *Herald, Iowa State Journal,* New York *Journal of Commerce,* Newark *Journal,* Warren (New York) *News,* Concord (New Hampshire) *Patriot,* Mankato (Minnesota) *Record,* Patterson (New Jersey) *Register,* Indianapolis *Sentinel,* Winona (Minnesota) *State,* Milwaukee (Wisconsin) *See Bote* (German), Concord (New Hampshire) *Standard,* Hartford *Times.*
4. New York *Tribune,* July 25, 1861.
5. Philadelphia *Press,* July 25, 1861.
6. Robert S. Harper, p. 110.
7. Forney was sworn in as Secretary of the Senate July 15, 1861. U.S. Congress. *Biographical Congressional Directory, 1774–1911,* p. 218.
8. Robert S. Harper, pp. 180–81.
9. Ibid., p. 112.
10. When the Civil War began General Scott was still a national hero, as a result of his part in the Mexican War, and there was a strong tendency to regard his word as gospel insofar as military matters were concerned. In placing the blame for the Bull Run defeat on Democratic General Robert Patterson he received the general support of the Unionist press. His removal from command, November 1, 1861, was not supposed to represent any kind of official reprimand but of course was so regarded, anyway.
   When the battle of Bull Run was debated in the House of Representatives, February 15, 1862, Republican Congressmen John Covode of Pennsylvania and Daniel W. Gooch of Massachusetts took the side of Scott, blaming everything on Patterson. Republican Congressman Francis P. Blair, Jr., of Missouri, defended Patterson, blaming Scott. Robert Patterson, *A narrative of the Campaign in the Valley of the Shenandoah, in 1861,* (Philadelphia: Campbell, 1865), pp. 79–81.
11. W. A. Neal, *An Illustrated History of the First Missouri Engineer and 25th Infantry Regiments* (Chicago, 1889), p. 27.
12. W. A. Croffutt and John M. Morris, *The Military and Civil History of Connecticut* (New York: Ledyard Bill, 1869), pp. 103, 186.
13. Charles M. Knapp, *New Jersey politics during the period of the Civil War and Reconstruction.* (New York: Columbia University Press, 1924), p. 60. Dr. English would later become famous as author of *Peck's Bad Boy.*
14. Ibid., pp. 59–63.
15. Henry C. Conrad, *History of the state of Delaware,* 3 vols. (Wilmington, 1908), I:203. Voting returns revealed that of Delaware's three counties, New Castle was in favor of the war from the start and Kent and Sussex were opposed to it from the start. Although the overall majority favored the war, the Peace faction held majorities in the two smaller counties and so controlled the legislature.
16. W. A. Croffut and John M. Morris, p. 107. Barnum was best known in 1861

as American agent for the famous singer Jenny Lind, and manager of the famous midget "General Tom Thumb." Robert S. Harper, p. 190.

17. Philadelphia *Press,* September 21, 1861.

18. Democratic newspapers mobbed by civilians in the latter half of 1861 included: Bangor (Maine) *Democrat,* August 12; Bucyrus (Ohio) *Forum,* September 8; Canton (Ohio) *Stark County Democrat,* August 22; Easton (Pennsylvania) *Sentinel,* August 19; Mauch Chunk (Pennsylvania) *Carbon Democrat,* August 31; and Terre Haute (Indiana) *Journal and Democrat,* October 21. A mob of soldiers attacked the Concord (New Hampshire) *Democratic Standard,* August 8. Robert S. Harper, pp. 189, 198, 197, 238, 119.

It has become the custom in the twentieth century, to eugolize the victims of Unionist mob violence in the loyal states during the Civil War Years, and certainly there was nothing commendable about the actions of the mobsters. On the other hand, it is indisputable that mob violence was an integral part of American political life throughout the entire nineteenth century, and the Peace Democrats who suffered from it during the Civil War were, in many cases, the very people who had favored and sponsored it in the Antebellum past. During the 1840s and 1850s there were many respectable, conservative citizens who urged on the persecution of the anti-slavery spokesmen, chased the Abolitionists out of town, shrugged off the news of Elijah Lovejoy's murder, and applauded the mob assault on William Lloyd Garrison, in Boston. In times past, mob action had generally been regarded as a kind of Conservative sport. The Civil War years reversed the trend in the loyal states. Suddenly, the leading pro-slavery Conservatives became the hares, after many years of being the hounds. That they were required to suffer the same kind of persecution during the war years as the anti-slavery leaders had suffered previously may be lamentable. But there were many lamentable things about the Civil War, and surely this is not one of the outstanding examples.

19. It is worth noting that the Peace cause struck some of the first blows, even in wartime, so far as mob action was concerned. On April 20, 1861 a mob attacked the offices of the Baltimore *Wecker,* a pro-Union German paper, compelling the editors to raise the Confederate flag. Also, in the first year of the war, a Peace mob in Hackensack, New Jersey moved against the office of the War Democrat *Bergen County Journal,* a pro-war paper, threatening to burn it to the ground. William C. Kimball, editor of the *Journal,* surrendered to the pressure and closed shop before the year was out. In Canada, where the Confederates were the favorites with the government and much of the population, a mob attacked a pro-Union paper, the St. Stephens (New Brunswick) *St. Croix Herald.* Robert S. Harper, p. 155; Federal Writers' Project, New Jersey, *Bergen County Panorama,* American Guide Series (Hackensack, 1941) p. 221.

20. Daniel Dangerfield, a runaway Negro slave and a resident of Philadelphia, was brought before a U.S. Commissioner in 1859, under the Fugitive Slave Law of 1850. Brewster served as lawyer for the slaveholder in the case. Dangerfield was freed. At another such hearing, involving another runaway, Brewster declared that slavery was "politically, morally, and socially right." Herman L. Collins, *Philadelphia, A Story of Progress,* 4 vols. (New York: Lewis, 1941), I:299;

21. *Biographical Cyclopedia of Representative Men of Maryland and the District of Columbia* (Baltimore: National Biography, 1879), p. 8.

22. Harrisburg, (Pennsylvania) *Patriot and Union,* September 19, 1861.

23. Roy P. Basler, ed., V:285–86.

24. Although formerly a Whig and now a self-proclaimed "Independent," Wallach was affiliated with the Washington Evening *Star,* owned and edited by his brother, W. D. Wallach, another former Whig. In 1860 the *Star* supported Breckinridge and Richard Wallach was generally regarded as a

Breckinridge man. Wilhelmus B. Bryan, *A History of the National Capital,* 2 vols. (New York: Macmillan, 1916), II:386, 419, 421, 430, 455, fn. For refusing to take the oath, Peace Democrat Berret was arrested by the military and jailed at Ft. Lafayette.

25. Roy P. Basler, ed., V:196.
26. At the time of his appointment, Mayor Wallach was only one of several permanent Washington residents closely identified with the War Democracy. Others included: editor W. D. Wallach of the Washington Evening *Star;* editor John A. Savage of the Washington *States and Union;* banker George W. Riggs, Financial Secretary of the Breckinridge National Committee; attorney Hugh J. Anderson, a former Governor of Maine; attorney Horatio King, Postmaster General under Buchanan; Judge James Hughes of the U.S. Court of Claims.
27. E. Merton Coulter, pp. 81–95; Thomas Speed, pp. 143, 169.
28. William C. Goodloe, *Kentucky Unionists of 1861,* read before the Society of Ex-Army and Navy Officers in Cincinnati, Ohio, April 10, 1884 (Cincinnati, 1884), p. 8; Thomas Speed, Ibid., p. 98; E. Merton Coulter, pp. 89, 93, 98; E. Tarrant, p. 76.
29. Thomas H. Nelson was a Republican candidate for Congress in 1860. He was defeated by Daniel W. Voorhees. *Tribune Almanac,* 1861.
30. E. Merton Coulter, p. 89; Kenneth M. Stampp, *Indiana Politics,* pp. 113-114; Old Line Whigs and "Americans" also were employed in the distribution of federal arms to Kentucky Unionists. Of these, the best known were Congressman-elect John J. Crittenden, James Harlan, and Garrett Davis. E. Merton Coulter, p. 89. For details on the Nelson brothers see Allen Johnson and Dumas Malone, XIII:424–26.
31. Joseph Holt, *The Fallacy of Neutrality, An Address to the People of Kentucky, Delivered at Louisville,* July 13, 1861. (New York: Gregory, 1861).
32. William H. Smith, *A Political History of Slavery,* 2 vols. (New York: 1903), II:47.
33. E Merton Coulter, pp. 93, 94, 98; Thomas Speed, *The Union Cause in Kentucky* (New York: Putnam's Sons, 1907), p. 111. Colonel Thomas Garrard was a Douglas elector. In the 1864 election campaign, Colonel Wolford would serve as a Democratic elector.
34. Clifton R. Hall, pp. 14–17.
35. Robert S. Holzman, p. 51.
36. George Fort Milton, pp. 566–67.
37. James H. Wilson, *The Life of John A. Rawlins* (New York: Neale, 1916), pp. 47–50.
38. *Union army,* VIII:152.
39. James H. Wilson, p. 66.
40. Democrats directly involved in the battle of Ball's Bluff included: Colonel Napoleon J. T. Dana, First Minnesota; Lieutenant Colonel Arthur F. Devereaux, 19th Massachusetts; Lieutenant Colonel Thomas J. Lucas, 18th Indiana; Major N. Buell Eldredge, Seventh Michigan.
41. Eldredge was formerly Clerk of the Michigan Senate, under a Democratic administration. Charles R. Tuttle, *General History of the State of Michigan,* pp. 466–67.
42. Ibid., p. 467.
43. William B. Hessltine, pp. 25–26.
44. In lining up a staff, General Butler obtained the services of Democrats Andrew J. Butler (his brother) and Benjamin F. Watson, both of Massachusetts; also William Cutting of New York. Watson served as Paymaster. He had been postmaster of Lawrence Massachusetts, under both Pierce and Buchanan. Benjamin F. Watson, "Abraham Lincoln as seen by a life-long Democrat," *The Magazine of History,* Volume 50, no. 1, extra number 197 (1935): p. 13; Robert S. Holzman, p. 55.

45. Cahill was a Democratic candidate for the New Haven Common Council in the city election of June, 1861. New Haven *Journal and Courier,* June 3, 1861. He was elected—Ibid., June 4, 1861—having served two terms previously. Thomas H. Murray, *History of the Ninth Regiment, Connecticut Volunteer Infantry* (New Haven: Price, Lee, and Adkins, 1903), p. 322. Cahill also was elected Street Commissioner in 1861. He had helped in founding the Washington-Erina Guards of New Haven, in 1849, and held the rank of captain when the Guards were disbanded in 1855 at the order of a Know Nothing city administration, serving subsequently as a captain of the Emmett Guard of New Haven. Ibid., pp. 322–23.

46. Samuel G. Buckingham, *The Life of William A. Buckingham* (Springfield: Adams, 1894), p. 143.

47. The Republican Speaker of the Connecticut Assembly, Augustus Brandegee, was stricken ill and Deming was chosen Speaker *pro tem* to serve in his absence. W. A. Croffut and John M. Morris. p. 35.

48. New Haven *Paladium,* September 29, 1864.

49. Robert S. Holzman, p. 57; *Union army,* I:183–84.

50. John G. Pearson, p. 233.

51. Ibid., p. 233.

52. Louis C. Hatch, II:pp. 352, 517.

53. Ibid., p. 517. On September 26, 1861, General Butler was the guest of honor at a Union rally in Augusta, Maine, presided over by Republican Governor Washburn. Other War Democrats in attendance included Colonel George F. Shepley of the Twelfth Maine Infantry, Colonel John Goddard of the First Maine Cavalry, and Caleb Cushing of Massachusetts, U.S. Attorney General under Pierce. Speeches were delivered by all. James W. North, *The History of Augusta (Augusta: Clapp and North, 1870), p. 726.*

54. *Biographical Encyclopaedia of Maine,* p. 181.

55. Robert G. Athearn, "Thomas Francis Meagher: an Irish Revolutionary in America," *Studies,* no. 1 (Boulder: University of Colorado Press, December 1949), Series in History, pp. 89–97.

56. Allen Johnson and Dumas Malone, eds., III:504, (Cass); Alexander C. Flick, *Samuel J. Tilden, A Study in Political Sagacity* (Port Washington, New York: Kennikat, 1963 (1939)), p. 134; Claude M. Fuess, *The Life of Caleb Cushing* (Hamden, Conn.: Archon, 1951), p. 285.

57. *Congressional Globe* (37th Congress, 2nd session), p. 101.

58. Robert T. Holzman, p. 48.

59. Congressman Samuel S. Cox of Ohio, a leader of the Conditional War faction in the House, was also a member of the Committee on Foreign Affairs, and in this capacity conferred with Lincoln several times concerning disposition of the *Trent* Affair. He was heartily in favor of the course adopted by Lincoln. Allen Johnson and Dumas Malone, IV:482.

60. Le Grand B. Cannon, pp. 53–53.

61. Editor Elias Calkins of the Madison *Wisconsin Argus and Democrat,* a Breckinridge supporter, came out in favor of Emancipation during the first month of war (May 4, 1861). Shortly after Stanton talked to Cameron, Democrat John W. Forney also announced in favor of Emancipation, under the pen name, "Occasional," in the Philadelphia *Press.* (Cited in St. Paul (Minnesota) *Press,* December 29, 1861). In November, New York Democrat George Bancroft wrote to Lincoln, declaring that "Civil War is the instrument of Divine Providence to root out social slavery; posterity will not be satisfied with the result, unless the consequences of war shall effect an increase of free states. This is the universal expectation and hope of men of all parties." Roy P. Basler, ed., V:26.

62. Upon returning to Washington, Cameron was angrily criticized by Conservative Republican Caleb B. Smith, Secretary of the Interior, who said that Cochrane deserved to be cashiered for speaking as he had, and that Cameron had

no business encouraging him. Benjamin P. Thomas, *Stanton,* p. 133.

63. Buchanan's pro-war statement terminated a longstanding friendship with Jeremiah S. Black, his former Secretary of State and close advisor. Having drawn back in the face of war, during the Sumter crisis, Buchanan was now and ever afterward a War Democrat, without qualification. Black, on the other hand, having urged Buchanan to take a stand against Secession at the risk of war, so modified his Unionism once the war began as to nullify his usefulness to the Union cause. He had been planning to write a biography of Buchanan, praising his administration, but abandoned the plan shortly following Buchanan's strong endorsement of the federal war policy. William N. Brigance, p. 124.

7

Lincoln Bows to the Conservatives: Elections of 1861

Another major event involving the War Democrats of 1861 was the election campaign of that year, in which the Democratic party had many things going in its favor, but managed to bungle virtually every one of them. As of April 23, 1860, the Democratic party was the giant, sprawling, pampered pet of American politics. The Democratic party got what it wanted, almost always. Occasionally it suffered from intra-party wrangling, as in the case of the four national crises over slavery preceding the Civil War—1820, 1850, 1854, and 1857, sometimes over other issues. Always, however, the Democratic party solved its family quarrels and rapidly regained its position at the top—until June 1860, when it once again divided at the Charleston Convention.

The appearance of the Know Nothing party in 1854 had driven the Democrats from power in several states and for a moment it had seemed as though the Know Nothings might well become the strongest party in the Union. But in the Whig tradition the Know Nothings had foundered on the slavery issue, dividing in half, North and South, and by 1856 they were no longer a force of major political significance. The Republicans organized in 1854 and almost elected Fremont in 1856. They were nonetheless dismissed by many Democrats as nothing more important than the Know Nothings. Even the election of Lincoln had failed to break the optimistic spirit of thousands upon thousands of Democrats who refused to regard the Republicans as anything more than a temporary phenomenon. Many problems plaguing the Democratic organization could be traced to the party division over the Lecompton Constitution. It was entirely possible that once the Lecompton issue was dead, the party could close ranks, bring home a few thousand strays or so in the currently Republican states, and return to national ascendency.

Democratic confidence in this regard was by no means farfetched. In the early months of 1861 the Lecompton issue was submerged in the free states by the Secession crisis, which united most of the Democracy behind the cause of Peace. Following the Ohio State Democratic Convention of January 23 the Cleveland *National Democrat* (official organ of the Breckinridge Democracy) suspended publication and the Douglas leadership declared an end to intra-party discord.[1] A Democrat was elected Mayor of Cincinnati in April with a plurality of 4,000, favoring the Crittenden Compromise. Democrats carried the spring municipal elections in Cleveland, Toledo, Sandusky, and Columbus.[2] In Illinois, Breckinridge leader John Reynolds issued an address, urging all Democrats to rally to the leadership of Douglas.[3] In the Wisconsin spring judicial elections, not one Republican was elected.[4] In New York State, a giant Peace rally assembled at the call of the Douglas State Committee, January 31, 1861, with many Breckinridge leaders in attendance.[5]

Revitalized Democratic forces attracted attention in New Hampshire where candidates for Congress and state offices in 1861 registered strong gains over the party's performance of the year before. The same trend was apparent in the Connecticut April elections, resulting in the defeat of two Republican Congressmen. A Democratic Governor of Rhode Island was reelected in April and two Rhode Island Republican Congressman were unseated.[6] The Antebellum Peace campaign had shown a strong tendency to fusion on the part of Democrats and Constitutional Unionists. The Constitutional Union vote was 240,000 in the loyal states and much of it was expected to transfer to the Democratic column in the approaching canvass. There was every indication that 1861 was going to be a "Democratic year."

When the war began the Republicans controlled 16 of the loyal states, non-Republicans seven.[7] Of the Republican states, however, only two appeared certain—Massachusetts and Vermont. The rest had strong Democratic organizations, confident and full of fight. In New York, for example, the "Albany Regency" had led the Democrats to victory as recently as 1857 and 1859, electing eight state executives to office, and winning control of the 1857 Assembly. A reversal of 741 votes would have elected a

Democratic Governor of Iowa in 1859 and a reversal of only 271 votes would have elected a Democratic Governor of Connecticut in 1860. In illinois the Republicans carried the 1858 elections with a mere plurality. New Hampshire and Maine went Republican only by the grace of a few thousand votes, as a general rule; Pennsylvania was traditionally Democratic and aroused against the Republican legislature of 1861 over the threat of a tax increase. In the Frontier States, the Democrats collected 47 percent of the vote in Kansas in 1859 and 45 percent of the vote in Minnesota. In the Old Northwest, embracing Ohio, Indiana, Illinois, Wisconsin, and Michigan, the closing of the Mississippi River placed the farmers at the mercy of the railroads, and economic suffering had immediately ensued. Bank failures followed in large number, especially in Wisconsin and Illinois. Every such misfortune redounded to the advantage of the Democrats, as the party out of power. And as the coming of the war reduced the fire and the fury of the longstanding Lecompton feud, the Democratic party was able once again to respond to the challenge of the opposition without the problems of factional discord.

Highly advantageous to the Democratic party in 1861 was the widespread expectation in the loyal states (preceding Bull Run) of a quick and sweeping victory by Union arms. The last major military operations undertaken by the federal government, against Mexico in the 1840s, had convinced most Americans that their army was invincible. They did not expect the hastily organized Army of the Confederacy to be any match for the peerless General Scott, who was regarded as another George Washington in battle when the Civil War began. Bull Run was a body-blow to all such thinking and a profound disappointment to many thousands of voters in the loyal states. As the party in power the Republicans were tied to General Scott and his failure was theirs, according to the rules of all politics from the beginning of time.

As the year wore on and other battles ensued, it also became clear that the overall Confederate military position was very strong. Union advantages in numbers were negated by the fact that the Confederates needed only to defend themselves, and the defensive army requires nowhere near the numbers of an invader. The Union Army was called upon to occupy and garrison an area of 800,000 square miles—equal almost to the size of continental Europe. The denial of a quick victory brought this problem to the fore, and the resulting distress on the part of many disillusioned warhawks in the loyal states was a distinct advantage to the Democrats, as the party out of power.

On these grounds, the Democratic leadership looked forward to the fall elections of 1861 with the utmost confidence, hopeful and expectant of a brilliant resurgence. Preventing this development, more than any other factor, was the sudden appearance of the wartime "Union party" movement, wrecking Democratic chances almost everywhere.

The Union party of the Civil War period, supporting the federal war policy, was based upon an old pro-slavery device. The word, "Union," in the political party sense, had Conservative connotations dating back to 1851. It was then that the pro-slavery Unionists of the South had defeated the Secessionists on a "Union party" platform, and the pro-slavery Unionists of the North defeated the Seward Whigs and Wilmot Democrats with "Union" coalitions.[8] The John Brown Harper's Ferry raid of 1859 was followed by scores of "Union" rallies throughout the North, sponsored by pro-slavery Conservatives seeking to reassure the South.[9] During the Secession crisis, the same pro-slavery northerners sponsored numerous "Union" rallies with the same object in mind. Invariably, the term "Union," as used in this context, meant "pro-Union, pro-slavery."[10] Anti-slavery men were never welcome at Antebellum "Union" rallies, excepting only the most Conservative. When the wartime Union party movement began it was able to draw upon the Antebellum tradition, and many non-Republicans entered the Union party with a sense of Conservative well-being.

*   *   *

In the border slave-state spring elections of 1861, the lone campaign issue was War versus Peace. In Maryland, Kentucky, Missouri, and the western counties of Virginia, traditional southern identification was expected to swing the voters to the Peace cause. To help in this regard the Peace advocates raised the specter of "New England" to frighten the voters away from the Union standard.

New England was a favorite Democratic straw man, utilized successfully for many years in South and West alike. The very mention of the words "New England" was enough to raise the hackles of the average Democratic audience in any section except New England itself. According to Democratic dogma, New England was an "Abolition stronghold," on the one hand, and the center of the "Money Power," on the other. The "eastern bankers" lived there, it was said, in company with the "eastern speculators" and the "eastern railroad interests."[11] All the charges and implications were false. New England was *not* an Abolition Stronghold. It was a Republican stronghold. In the 1860 campaign the Abolitionists had attacked the Republican platform and the Republican national ticket.[12] New England also was *not* the Money Power nor the center of the eastern bankers, speculators, and railroad interests. Democratic New York City held that distinction, and a majority of New York City's leading bankers and businessmen were Democrats.[13] The other major Peace argument in the border slave-state elections of 1861 was the battle cry of "subjugation," repeated *ad nauseum*. A vote for Union was a vote for Lincoln, "foreign bayonets," and "a despotic military government."[14]

In the free states the War faction outweighed the Peace faction in every Democratic state organization, but the departure of many War Democrats for the battlefields weakened the War Democracy at home and to an equal extent strengthened the position of the Peace Democracy.[15] Although most of the Democratic State Conventions of 1861 declared in favor of the Union cause, most of them were also in favor of a national Peace conference. Every Democratic convention emphasized the economic chaos wrought by the war and ridiculed Republican appeals for nonpartisan support, pointing to the mass removal of Democratic appointees from federal office (including many who were wholly in favor of the federal war policy).[16]

The 1861 campaign began with the Virginia vote on the Ordinance of Secession, May 23, in which the Union forces were overwhelmed in almost every section of the state. Exceptional was the outcome of the voting in the western counties where a large majority voted Union and, as a gesture of defiance, elected several candidates to represent Virginia in the federal Congress.[17] A Union party, hastily organized for the occasion, swept the western counties, routing the Secessionists in every encounter. There were no Republicans in the upper echelons of the Union party of Virginia. Francis H. Pierpont, an Old-Line Whig, was appointed Acting Governor by a Unionist convention and the loyal state legislature (composed exclusively of Union party men) elected six state executives and two U.S. Senators. Democrats were named to serve as Auditor and Treasurer, and of the two U.S. Senators elected, one was a Democrat. No one elected on this occasion was a Republican. Incumbent Congressman William G. Brown, returned to office in the May elections, was a Douglas elector. With no Republican leadership or membership in evidence, the Union party of western Virginia appeared exclusively comprised of Whigs, Americans, and Douglas Democrats.[18]

In January 1861 a Union party coalition had come into existence in Kentucky, consisting in large part of Constitutional Unionists and to a lesser extent of Douglas Democrats. In advance of the special elections (held in June, in preparation for the Special Session of Congress) a Union party slate was nominated comprising two Democrats and nine Constitutional Unionists. The Democrats were Henry C. Wickliffe, Chairman of the Douglas National Committee, and Douglas-elector Levi S. Trimble.[19] Two Union party leaders of consequence were John H. Harney and William P. Boone of Louisville. Both were members of the Douglas State Executive Committee and Harney was editor of the Louisville *Democrat*. To the surprise of many observers, the special Congressional elections in Kentucky resulted in an overwhelming Union party victory. Out of ten Congressional contests, Union candidates were successful in nine. At the extreme west end of the state Secessionist Henry C. Burnett was elected over War Democrat Levi S. Trimble. Elsewhere, the Union party prevailed and by a wide margin.[20] In August the Union party was again victorious in the regular state elections. Among the War Democrats, William P. Boone was elected to the state legislature, receiving 1,990 votes against 351 for an avowed Secessionist. War Democrat John W. Harney also was elected to the legislature, defeating a Secessionist by a vote of 1,583 to 628.[21] Peace Democrats would complain throughout the war that Kentucky was held to the Union by force. The 1861 election results, secured *without* the help of bayonets, indicated something entirely different.[22] The Kentucky legislature elected in August 1861 declared war on the Confederacy in September, denounced the Peace policies of U.S. Senators Breckinridge and Powell of Kentucky, and when Breckinridge was expelled from the Senate later in the year, a Unionist was elected by the legislature to take his place.[23]

In the Maryland special Congressional elections of June 1861 the War and Peace factions collided at every Democratic district convention, and in each instance the Peace faction prevailed. The War faction refused to endorse the party nominations and in two districts put up rival candidates of their own. Acting independently, some Old-Line Whigs, Americans, and Know Nothings nominated Unionist candidates in five other districts. As in Kentucky, the Maryland Unionists carried every district except one. War Democrats elected in this manner were former Governor Francis Thomas (Douglas) and former Congressman John W. Crisfield (Breckinridge). On the basis of the congressional victories a Union party was established in Maryland later in the summer.[24]

In all the free states the Radical Republicans opposed, in 1861—with varying degrees of success—creation of the Union party. Disturbed about the presence of so many anti-slavery Conservatives in their own ranks, they wanted no association with Democrats who were even more Conservative. As a result, the War Democracy acted independently in many of the free-state elections, aiding the Republicans only indirectly. So it was in Maine where the actions of the War Democrats were wholly satisfactory to the administration, despite their independence of Republican principles. Although Lincoln had carried the state by landslide proportions and the Republicans had never lost a statewide election there, Maine had been throughout the 40s and the early 50s a Democratic stronghold, with a powerful pro-slavery faction dedicated to the interests of the South. As late as 1859 the Maine Democracy was anti-Douglas and pro-Lecompton, in which year a switch of only 4,471 votes would have been enough to knock the Republicans out of power. The Douglas-Breckinridge battle had hurt the state party badly, but the Bull Run defeat was supposed to have hurt the Republicans even more. The Maine Democracy of 1861 was vigorous and optimistic despite the absence of victory over the past seven years.

The Democratic State Convention of 1861, held in August, was the first large gathering of Democrats anywhere in the loyal states since the occasion of the Bull Run disaster. Symbolically, the convention fell to the control of the Peace faction, and resolutions condemning the war carried by a majority of one. Denouncing the vote, the War Democrats rose in a body and left the hall, whereupon the remaining delegates nominated John W. Dana for Governor. He was a Breckinridge leader, a former Governor, and an outspoken critic of the war.[25] Reconvening at another place, the War Democracy selected a ticket of their own headed by General Charles D. Jameson, serving currently under McClellan in the Army of the Potomac. He had been a Douglas delegate in the 1860 Charleston and Baltimore conventions. The War Democrat platform demanded preservation of the Union and quoted the famous line from Douglas' last Springfield speech: "There can be no neutrals in this war; there can be none but patriots and traitors." The platform recommended the appointment of Democrats to the Lincoln cabinet and repeal of all Personal Liberty laws.[26] Following the naming of the rival tickets, the Maine Democracy divided down the middle. Some local conventions announced for Jameson, some for Dana. The Democratic press also was divided, all over the state.[27] Delighted by the situation, the Republicans renominated Governor Israel Washburn, who was easily elected in September, receiving 52,000 votes against 37,000 for Jameson and Dana combined. War Democrat Jameson edged out Peace Democrat Dana for second place by a margin of 1,400 votes. Twelve Jameson backers running with a "War Democrat" designation were elected to the Assembly, three to the State Senate.[28]

In California, the September elections were spiced with the threat of treason. Although the state Breckinridge party proclaimed itself the friend of Peace, it was widely believed to be activley engaged in Secessionist operations. War Democrats in uniform, General Edwin V. Sumner and Captain Winfield Scott Hancock, were active in suppressing Secession sympathizers in advance of the election. Captain Hancock was particularly active in the Los Angeles area. General Sumner reported a large Secessionist faction operating openly in California, and ordered reinforcements sent from posts in Oregon.[29] The possibility of violence at the polls, victory of the Peace party, and/or Secessionist uprisings, was frightfully disturbing to Unionists all over the Pacific Coast.[30] On the eve of the California vote, Democratic Senator James W. Nesmith of Oregon wrote the following to a friend: "I am only speaking what I *know* when I say that an effort is being made by the (Breckinridge) party to revolutionize the state. . . . The disunionists, for the most part, are the most desperate men in the state, and are banding together in secret societies. They want to make California what Missouri is at this moment. If California swerves from her allegiance, the defection will doubtless extend throughout the entire western region of our country."[31]

The Douglas Democracy of California nominated a straight-out War ticket headed by Assemblyman John Conness, the candidate for Governor. He was an ardent Unionist who had fought the Antebellum Peace cause down to the wire. The Breckinridge candidate was John McConnell, a leader of the Peace faction, and the Republican candidate was Leland Stanford, who had made the race before without success in 1859. On that occasion Stanford had said he was regarded as nothing more than a political curiosity.[32] This time he was the favorite to win.

The Democratic division permitted the election of Stanford, with a plurality of 56,036; McConnell was second, with 32,750; Conness third, with 30,394.[33] In the two California congressional elections three tickets were again involved and in both elections the Republicans won—again with pluralities rather than majorities.[34] The War Democrats fared better in the legislative elections, winning a plurality in the Assembly and tying the Republicans in the State Senate.[35]

The Secession threat was stifled for the time being in the Far West and the Peace faction embarrassed by association with avowed Secessionists. In October, former Senator William M. Gwin, the leading Peace Democrat in California, sailed for Havana. His ship was stopped at sea on orders from Democratic General Sumner. Gwin was arrested, returned to shore, and imprisoned for a time in Ft. Lafayette. (Later released, he went to Mississippi, and then to France as a Confederate diplomat.)[36]

Another September state election occurred in Vermont where the Union party was once again in evidence. At the Democratic State Convention certain War Democrats protested against the presentation of a separate state ticket, recommending outright endorsement of the Republican candidates. The convention disagreed and a ticket was drawn up, headed by Douglas elector Paul Dillingham, candidate for Governor. Rejecting the decision, Independent War Democrats assisted in the calling of a Union convention. Equally dissatisfied, the Peace Democracy assembled on its own. War Democrat James T. Thurston, candidate for Treasurer on the Regular Democratic ticket, was nominated for the same office by the Union party and Benjamin H. Smalley was chosen as the Peace candidate for Governor.[37]

The Democratic party had been of small account in Vermont since the Free Soil Revolt of 1848, in which the anti-slavery faction left the Democratic fold never to return. In several other states the Free Soil defectors had experienced a change of heart, but not in Vermont. Instead, they worked thereafter in concert with the Whigs until the Republicans came along, whereupon they almost all became Republicans. Democratic prospects in Vermont in the 1861 campaign—already weakened by fragmentation of the party forces—were further weakened by the failure of War Democrat Paul Dillingham to campaign seriously for Governor. No surprises were forthcoming. Republican Frederick Holbrook was elected Governor, receiving 78 percent of the vote. The nonpartisan Union ticket obtained 5,722 votes out of 42,000 cast, Smalley and the Peace ticket receiving only 3,190.[38]

An outstanding 1861 election campaign took place in Confederate Tennessee, where the Union party triumphed once again—as in western Virginia, Kentucky, and Maryland earlier in the year. Elections to the Confederate Congress were held in August and, to the embarrassment of Confederate officials, the Union ticket swept the field in all of East Tennessee. War Democrats elected in congressional races included Andrew J. Clements and George W. Bridges (a Douglas elector), both of whom declared against Confederate authority and went to Washington, demanding seats in the U.S. Congress.[39]

*   *   *

In October, the War and Peace Democracies divided bitterly in Ohio and Pennsylvania, and the Republican organizations in both states joined in coalition with the War faction, agreeing in the process to abandon the Republican party name and drastically modify their principles along Conservative lines. The Democratic State Committee of Ohio was heavily influenced by the views of Congressman Clement L. Vallandigham, to the irritation of the War Democracy. When the Committee denounced the administration (in July) and turned its back upon proposals for a nonpartisan campaign, Democratic district leader G. Volney Dorsey appealed publicly for a merger of the War Democracy and the Republican party. The Democratic State Convention, held in August, declared in favor of the war but also came out vigorously in favor of peace negotiations, while at the same time denouncing the administration. Two leading Democratic newspapers, the Cleveland *Plain Dealer* and the Columbus *Capital City Fact,* criticized the Democratic platform and David Tod, twice the Democratic candidate for Governor, pronounced it a menace to the Union, attracting statewide attention in the process.[40] Seizing on the situation, the Republican State Central Committee agreed to the calling of a Union Convention, which gathered at Columbus in September. Radical Republicans opposed the merger for a time but finally agreed to it. The star of the convention was War Democrat David Tod, who was virtually assured the gubernatorial nomination before the delegates assembled.[41] He was an outstanding Negrophobe, having favored laws excluding Negroes from the state. When he campaigned for

Governor on the Democratic ticket in the 1840s the party slogan was "Vote for Tod and the Black Laws."[42]

The Union convention was decidedly conservative, rejecting even mild resolutions approving the policies of President Lincoln and the outgoing Governor. Also rejected was a pro-war resolution presented by a Radical delegate.[43] The party platform was based on the pro-slavery Crittenden Resolution.[44] Thomas Ewing, a former Whig Senator and a blazing Conservative on the slavery issue, gave his endorsement to the Union party as a genuine Conservative body, without "taint of abolition . . . sympathy."[45] In his letter of acceptance War Democrat Tod ignored the slavery issue altogether, concentrating solely on the question of the Union. In his opinion, a majority of southerners still were loyal to the federal authority, but there was no point in diplomatic dealings with their leaders, who had sold them out. He scorned all talk of compromise, pronouncing it laughable, and declared in favor of executing the Confederate leaders, as an example to incipient traitors.[46] Many well-known Democrats joined the Union party in Ohio. In addition to Tod, the Union Convention nominated Democrats for three state executive posts, giving them four out of seven places on the ticket.[47] War Democrat William H. Smith, former editor of the Columbus *Ohio Statesman* became Chairman of the Union State Committee.[48] Democrats attending the Union State Convention included Douglas electors Seraphim Myer, Chester D. Adams, and George F. Stayman, and Breckinridge elector John C. Carey (who spoke frequently). Luther Day of the Douglas State Central Committee was present, along with Thomas Sparrow, a Breckinridge candidate for Congress in the last campaign.[49] These were only the most prominent examples. Democratic delegates were numerous enough to render them the *dominant force*.[50] At the various Union district conventions many more Democrats played important roles, a large number securing Union nominations for the legislature and for county and municipal office. . . .[51] The Union party campaign went well in Ohio. War Democrat Tod was elected with a handsome majority of 55 thousand, and the Union party carried 14 Democratic counties, establishing a large majority in the legislature.[52]

Conservative control of the Union party was equally evident in Pennsylvania where a merger was effected by the followers of John W. Forney, editor of the War Democrat Philadelphia *Press,* and Republican Governor Andrew G. Curtin, elected in the Lincoln landslide. The Union party movement in Pennsylvania was inaugurated by Forney, July 3, at Washington, D.C., in remarks honoring the late Stephen A. Douglas. The eulogy amounted to a sharp attack on the Peace Democracy and a rallying cry for Union. Douglas always had regarded the Democracy as wise in its objectives, said Forney, but in the end his faith had failed, "When he saw the Southern leaders powerful enough, with the aid of this organization, to drive Mr. Buchanan from the path of duty into the path of depravity.'' If Douglas were still alive, Forney declared, "and could see the name of this powerful party flagrantly used as a cloak for treason, even in portions of the Free States, he would, in my opinion, feel that it was time to set aside a machine which has become so potent an engine of individual and general disaster."[53]

The Union party of Pennsylvania proved no great success in 1861. In Philadelphia, for instance, the Union Municipal Convention gave its endorsement to some Republican (People's party) candidates, but not to all. In every case in which endorsement was withheld, the Republican lost to a Peace Democrat.[54]

Prominent campaigners for the Union party in the city included Douglas leaders Forney, David Dougherty, and John Campbell, and Breckinridge leaders Nathaniel B. Browne, Benjamin H. Brewster, and Frederick C. Brewster (Chairman of the Union Municipal Convention). Elsewhere in the state the Union party movement was directed by Republican editor Alexander K. McClure of the Chambersburg *Franklin Repository* and Douglas leader John Cessna, a former Speaker of the Assembly, under whose Conservative guidance the War Democrats and Conservative Republicans combined forces in many Democratic districts in mutual support of Democratic Unionists. An outstanding example of such cooperation involved the nomination of District Judge Daniel Agnew, seeking reelection to a second ten-year term. Having won election as a Whig in 1851, he was renominated this year by the Democrats. Radical Republicans were not impressed by Agnew's Conservative record or by his non-Republican sympathies. But the Union party, without concern for Radical opinion, endorsed his nomination.[55]

The major issues of the 1861 campaign in Pennsylvania did not relate exclusively to the war. As elsewhere in the Union, economic conditions here were chaotic all year long and the voters were naturally alarmed. Ignoring public sensitivities, the Republican legislature repealed a law imposing heavy taxes on the Republican-controlled Pennsylvania Railroad and the Democrats declared that new taxes would now be necessary, at the expense of the little man. (As the property of Simon Cameron, Secretary of War, the Pennsylvania Railroad was at all times a hot political issue in Pennsylvania.) The anti-railroad attack was seemingly effective because Republican majorities in the western counties were dramatically reduced. As a result, the Democrats registered strong gains in both houses of the legislature, regaining control of the Assembly with a ten-seat majority.[56] Yet—for all their good fortune—the Regular Democrats were distinctly disappointed. They had expected a landslide, and this had been denied. Thirteen members elected as "Democratic Unionists" would constitute the balance of power in the next Assembly. Once again, it would appear that the War Democracy had shied away from voting for Democratic candidates clearly associated with the cause of Peace.

The Frontier States of Iowa and Minnesota also held elections in October. In Iowa, the Peace faction was operating in the open far in advance of the Bull Run defeat under the leadership of Henry Clay Dean, a Douglas-elector, and Dennis A. Mahony, editor of the influential Dubuque *Herald*. Together, they sought to seize control of the Democratic State Convention of July 24, in the name of the Peace. (Dean and Mahony of the *Herald* also had served as leaders of the Antebellum Peace crusade in Iowa,[57] and the *Herald* was the leading Democratic paper in the state.) In June, following the grand display of Democratic patriotism in answer to the presidential troop calls of April and May, Mahony published in the *Herald* the call for a Democratic State Convention. Included in the call were several standard Peace arguments, including an attack on Lincoln for exercising the executive war power.[58]

At the Democratic State Convention of July 24, Mahony delivered the keynote speech and was on this occasion attacked by Douglas-leader William W. Belknap of Keokuk, attending the convention as an observer. He was not a delegate, Belknap explained, because the Democrats of his county did not like the looks of the convention call. Invited to join the proceedings, he declined, announcing he had "no desire to train in such a crowd."[59] A platform was proposed and approved calling for a national Peace conference and criticizing the administration for exceeding the limits of the Constitution in the prosecution of the war.[60] A resolution offered by the War faction, approving the action of the Iowa Volunteers, was voted down by the majority.[61] Charles Mason, a former justice on the Iowa Territorial Supreme Court, was nominated for Governor and Judge Maturin L. Fisher for Lieutenant Governor. Both were in favor of the war and both declined the nominations,[62] at which point chaos overtook the Iowa Democracy.

Shortly following adjournment of the Democratic Convention a call went out for a non-Republican "Union" Convention, to be held at Des Moines, August 28. Peace Democrats attended in large numbers with the object of nominating one of their own for Governor: Le Grand Byington, Chairman of the Douglas State Central Committee. War Democrats also attended in force, and were successful in keeping the Peace men off the ticket. Instead of Byington, the Union party nominated Nathaniel B. Baker for Governor.[63] He was a War Democrat, a State Senator, and a former Governor of New Hampshire. (Ignoring the Union nomination, Baker announced for Kirkwood and the Republicans.[64]) Meanwhile, the Democtatic State Central Committee had selected a gubernatorial candidate to run in place of Judge Mason, who had withdrawn. The man selected was a soldier, Lieutenant Colonel William H. Merritt of the First Iowa Infantry, a veteran of Dug Springs and Wilson's Creek. Committee member Dennis A. Mahony protested in behalf of the Peace faction but was voted down.[65] Shortly afterward, Mahony accepted an independent nomination for Governor, on a Peace ticket, as did also Henry Clay Dean, on another Peace ticket. The Democratic cause was by this time a shambles. Having barely squeaked in two years before, Republican Governor Kirkwood was reelected in 1861 with a whopping majority of 65,265.[66]

In Minnesota, the Union party cause of 1861 operated under the name of "No Party"—a coalition organized by Early C. Goodrich, recently resigned as Chairman of the Democratic State Executive Committee. The No Party leadership offered a nonpartisan platform and ticket, headed by Conservative Republican William H. Dike, Major of the First Minnesota Infantry, and Douglas elector Christopher C. Andrews. Dike was the No Party candidate for Governor, Andrews the choice for Lieutenant Governor. The purpose of the No Party Campaign was to win the indorsement of one or both of the major parties, but the goal was not achieved. The Republicans nominated the incumbent Governor, Alexander Ramsey; the Regular Democrats selecting a pronounced War man, District Judge Edward O. Hamlin.

Two major spokesmen for the No Party cause in Minnesota were Breckinridge leader Wheeler H. Peckham and Douglas leader Napoleon J.T. Dana. Hoping to deflate the No Party movement by draining off its talent, the Democratic State Convention offered Peckham the nomination for Attorney General, and the offer was at once accepted. Working from the Republican side, Governor Ramsey recommended to the War Department a brigadier's commission for Colonel Willis A. Gorman, and this was agreed to. Gorman was then prevailed upon to write a letter to Major Dike, the No Party candidate for Governor, urging his withdrawal from the race.[67] In place of Gorman, as commanding officer of the First Minnesota Infantry, Governor Ramsey appointed Napoleon J.T. Dana, removing him from the center of the No Party experiment. Meanwhile, Christopher D. Andrews—the No Party candidate for Lieutenant Governor—was lured away from the political arena with an offer of employment on the staff of the St. Cloud *Union*.[68] In this manner the leaders of the No Party movement were scattered to the winds. After some deliberation, Major Dike withdrew his name from the gubernatorial contest, allowing the Republican campaigners to concentrate the full force of their fire on the Peace faction, which had forged to the front of the Democratic host, denouncing the President and the Union cause. With the issue boiled down to War versus Peace, the Republicans had little difficulty in reelecting Ramsey and maintaining their control of the Minnesota legislature. Although the Lincoln majority of nine thousand was cut in half and St. Paul went heavily Democratic, the farm areas remained firmly in Republican control and the Republicans were home free, with a majority of 5,800.[69] Despite the seeming likelihood of Democratic revival in all the October States, comparatively little was recorded. In some cases the Union party clearly was a factor in favor of the Republicans; in all cases the Peace faction clearly was a hindrance to the Regular Democracy.

Five states elected executive officers in November, and a large vote was cast in Kansas for a ticket later disqualified in court. Of the six contests, Union tickets were involved in five, and in the lone exception a Union ticket was seriously considered. As always, the New York state elections received national attention. The major Democratic politicians in the state canvass were Fernando Wood, Mayor of New York City; Daniel S. Dickinson, a former U.S. Senator and leader of the "Hard Shell" Hunkers, and a battery of "Soft Shell" leaders—Dean Richmond, Horatio Seymour, "Prince" John Van Buren, and George Bancroft. The Hard and Soft titles dated back to the 1850s in which the Softs—headed by Seymour—had sought reunion with the bolting Barnburners of 1848—headed by Van Buren—against the wishes of the Hards—headed by Dickinson.[70] The Hards were ardently pro-southern, pro-slavery, and hostile to all Democrats who disagreed with them on the slavery question. Dickinson epitomized their position on the matter, and no southern slaveholder was known to surpass him in his Antebellum worship of slave property rights. (At the 1860 Southern Rights Convention Dickinson finished second behind Breckinridge in the balloting for President.) Richmond and Wood starred in the 1860 state campaign—Richmond as Chairman of the Douglas State Committee, Wood as a major defector from the Hard Shell camp and the leading Douglas man in New York City.

In the Secession crisis, Dickinson, Wood, and every leader of the Albany Regency declared themselves for Peace on southern terms.[71] Describing the Republicans to a Conservative audience, Dickinson said that of all political competitors "a more graceless set . . . [has] never congregated They are desperate men from all parties—the lame, the halt, and the blind, gathered together, and what are they going to do? Going to help freedom! [yet] . . . their every effort jeopardizes freedom; . . . violating the Constitution, menacing the harmony and integrity of every bond of Union, rather than slavery should be extended."[72]

So spoke Dickinson in Antebellum times. Then came Sumter and the war, and everything was suddenly reversed. Throwing off years of pro-southern, pro-slavery fanaticism, he now declared himself in favor of the Union and the federal war policy, side by side with Republicans (many of whom were former Barnburners). And Seymour, for years the moderate, opposing the pro-slavery extremes of Dickinson and the Hards, became in wartime the champion of slavery. Explaining his wartime position in a letter to a friend, Dickinson wrote: "It is not Lincoln and the Republicans we are sustaining. They have nothing to do with it. It is the government of our fathers, worth just as much as it was administered by Andrew Jackson. There is but one side to it."[73]

In the manner of all War Democrats, Dickinson was ready to maintain his party loyalty when the war began; but the influence of the Peace faction was too strong for him to take, as it was for many others.

Following the battle of Bull Run the Republican State Committee contacted the Democratic State Committee, proposing creation of an uncontested Union ticket. There was only one Peace Democrat on the Democratic committee—Benjamin Wood—but he prevailed upon Committee Chairman Dean Richmond to reject the proposal, and Richmond agreed to his wishes. At the Democratic State Convention, shortly afterward, a ticket was assembled to the satisfaction of the War Democracy. But in the making of the platform a clause was included demanding no further censorship of the Peace press and restoration of the right of habeas corpus, both of which demands were offensive to the War faction. Lyman Tremain and Francis C. Brouck, candidates for Attorney General and Treasurer, denounced the platform and requested the removal of their names from the ticket.[74]

Unionists in general were harsh in criticism of the New York Democratic State Convention. Suspension of habeas corpus and the suppression of newspapers accused of disloyalty were simply not regarded in September 1861 as anything but reasonable precautions, and there developed in New York a mad rush in the opposite direction from the Democratic bandwagon. Mayor Wood of New York City started things off by rejecting both the ticket and the platform,[75] and the Tammany Leader criticized the "malignant and traitorous spirit" of the platform. In response to the furor, a "People's" convention was at once arranged, to consist entirely of Conservative Unionists equally hostile to the interests of the Peace Democrats and the Radical Republicans. When the delegates assembled, War Democrat Thomas A. Alvord was chosen to preside. He was a close friend of Mayor Wood and a member of Mozart Hall, best remembered as Speaker of the 1858 Assembly. The People's Convention was dominated by the oratory of the Breckinridge chieftain Daniel S. Dickinson, who was named to head the party ticket as candidate for Attorney General. Of nine nominations, the War Democrats received four, including all the most important. The People's platform came out for war, waiving political divisions and party traditions. There was nothing anti-slavery about it. When the convention adjourned, the Republican Convention adopted the People's platform and all but one member of the People's ticket, beneath the banner of the Union party.[76]

Heartily in favor of the war and totally devoid of anti-slavery principles, the New York Union party found friends in every Conservative sanctuary, including Democratic New York City. All the major metropolitan dailies gave it their endorsement, excepting only the Tammany *Leader.* Upstate, the campaign revived the Hard-Soft feud of Daniel S. Dickinson, speaking for the Union ticket, and Horatio Seymour, speaking for the Regular Democracy. Dickinson was everywhere, electrifying thousands. The Radical New York *Tribune,* which had hated him for years, now extolled him as a hero and a patriot.[77] Seymour was cited in Democratic papers all over the country for his eloquence and for his strong declaration of conditional support for the Union cause. Although praising the valor of the Union armies and urging them on to the victory, he came out vigorously against the censorship of Democratic newspapers and the possibility of anti-slavery legislation in Congress. Democrats might disagree about slavery, he said, but they all were wholly in agreement about Negroes. "We know that the people of the North would not consent that four million of free negroes should live in their midst." If ever the federal government were foolish enough to adopt Emancipation as a war aim, he said, the South would have a perfect right to secede.[78] Seymour had taken his stand. He was in favor of the war, on certain conditions. The moment federal guns threatened slavery, he was opposed to the federal guns. This was to become the basis of wartime thinking for a good one-third of the Democrats in Congress and elsewhere in the loyal states. And Seymour was to be their leader.

In the contest between individual politicians, War Democrat Daniel S. Dickinson defeated Conditional War Democrat Horatio Seymour on this occasion, because the Union party scored a ringing triumph in New York. Dickinson and the rest of the Union state ticket were elected with a majority of 100,000 and Republican and Union party candidates captured combined control of the legislature. If the War Democrats elected on the Union ticket voted solidly with Republicans, the Regular Democrats were outnumbered 26 to 6 in the Senate and 86 to 32 in the Assembly.[79]

In Maryland as in New York, a major feature of the fall campaign was the dramatic appearance of an organized Union party, to the utter consternation of the Regular Democracy. Having carried the state for Breckinridge the previous year, the Regular Democrats had relaxed in advance of the 1861 spring congressional elections, which they expected to win without difficulty. Instead, they were overwhelmed, losing every district but one to Independent Unionists campaigning without regular organization support.[80] Thoroughly humiliated, they had regrouped and reorganized in preparation for the November state elections; but in this respect the Unionists were matching them, step for step.

The newly organized Maryland Union party, meeting in the fall of 1861, nominated Augustus W. Bradford for Governor and Samuel S. Maffitt for Comptroller. Bradford was an Old-Line Whig, Maffitt a Douglas-elector.

Attorney Hugh North Martin, a Breckinridge Democrat, was nominated for the Superior Court. The rest of the Union ticket consisted of Know Nothings and Old-Line Whigs. (No Republicans were nominated. Having received less than three percent of the Maryland vote in the 1860 canvass, they were not a major factor in the political complexion of the state and were virtually ignored by Union party organizers.)[81] At the Democratic State Convention the gubernatorial nomination went to Benjamin C. Howard, an advocate of Peace. Angered by the actions of the convention, many Maryland Democrats took up the cause of the Union ticket.

The Regular Democrats attacked Bradford, the Union candidate, as a Republican, intent upon destroying slavery. War Democrat Francis Thomas delivered an address in Baltimore in Bradford's behalf, October 29, swearing to protect slavery wherever it existed.[82] Regular Democrats criticized the military arrest of civilians and sought to make a hero out of Secessionist Merryman, the object of the recent Supreme Court decision concerning his arrest. Congressman Thomas attacked both Merryman and the opinion of Justice Taney in *Ex parte Merryman*.[83] War Democrat Reverdy Johnson made only one speech during the campaign, denouncing Secessionists as rebels and traitors and calling on the people to vindicate the Constitution and the laws. Secessionist theories of state sovereignty were, he said, "obscure in principle and impracticable in practice."[84]

The military arrest of Judge Richard B. Carmichael and several members of the Maryland legislature at the height of the campaign, on the orders of Democratic General George B. McClellan, caused considerable excitement within the local Peace Democracy, as did also the action of the U.S. Post Office Department, barring several Democratic newspapers from the mails. Democratic General John A. Dix, commanding the Department of Maryland, was responsible for orders directing the U.S. Marshal at Baltimore to place under arrest all rebels returning home to vote,[85] for requiring voters to swear allegiance to the federal government, and for granting mass furloughs to Maryland troops, giving them the opportunity to vote.[86] A major occurrence of the campaign in Maryland was the dramatic reappearance of the recent presidential candidate, John C. Breckinridge of Kentucky. Having carried Baltimore in the last election, he took the stand there in 1861, to speak for Howard, but was rudely shouted down and compelled to retire without speaking.[87]

Instead of the close contest that was expected, the Maryland election amounted to a runaway victory for the Union party candidates. Bradford was easily elected, receiving 57 thousand votes against 26 thousand for Howard. Both houses of the legislature went Union and numerous Democrats were elected on the Union ticket. Of these, the best known were Reverdy Johnson and John A. J. Creswell, both of Baltimore. Peace Democrats protested that the presence of federal troops at the polls had decided the election by scaring off the Democrats, but there was evidence to the contrary. With troops on hand at St. Mary's county for example, the Peace faction came out ahead, 1,144 to 207. The Baltimore vote fell off 9,000 from 1860. Elsewhere, however, the volume for 1861 was very much the same as that of 1860.[88] Peace Democrats claimed that Union soldiers went around voting illegally, in every district, but the charge was not supported by evidence. The Peace faction also protested the use of the loyalty oath,[89] which in time would become an issue of importance in every loyal state. But the major obstacle to Democratic success in Maryland, in 1861, appeared to be the Union party movement, which had proved a great success.

The appearance of the Union party was again a matter of serious consequence in Wisconsin, where the Regular Democracy had expected victory in 1861 on the basis of economic troubles. As opposed to the nearby Frontier States of Iowa and Minnesota, which had gone heavily Republican in the most recent elections, Wisconsin was still closely divided between Democrats and Republicans. The Republican ticket had carried the state in five straight elections, but every victory was decided by a small margin, excepting only the Lincoln landslide, scored in a moment when the Democrats were terribly divided (Lincoln's majority: 21,000). The war had provided instant economic suffering to the farming communities of the Old Northwest, and Wisconsin was particularly hard-hit by this misfortune. The closing of the Mississippi River traffic was quickly followed by a sizeable increase in railroad freight rates, which Democratic spokesmen attributed to the wiles of New England capitalists, Republican state leaders, and the Lincoln administration. Sudden runs developed on scores of western banks, many of which could not stand the strain. In Wisconsin, from mid-January to mid-July, 1861, 38 bank failures were reported.[90]

Seeking to remove popular attention from this and other political embarrassments of the moment, a body of Conservative Republicans in Wisconsin began urging the creation of a Union party coalition and the calling of a Union state convention. Ignored by the Republican state leadership, the Union party advocates turned for assistance to the Democratic State Committee, which also rejected the proposal. Undaunted, the Union party men established a separate organization, announcing their intention to hold a state convention September 25, at Madison. (The same place and date as the Republican State Convention.) Acting on their own, without official support or standing, many Democratic leaders announced in favor of the Union party call.[91]

Upon assembling in convention at Madison, the Union delegates wrangled at length about slavery (until the Republicans surrendered) after which they drew up a state ticket including four Republicans and four War Democrats. Republican Louis Harvey was nominated for Governor, War Democrat Henry Palmer for Lieutenant Governor. When Palmer declined the nomination he was replaced on the ticket by War Democrat James T. Lewis, a former Secretary of State.[92]

On September 26 the Republican convention considered the Union party slate and accepted only part of it; mainly the Republican part. James T. Lewis, Union candidate for Lieutenant Governor, was named by the Republicans to run for Secretary of State, and Democrat W. H. Ramsey, overlooked by the Union convention, was selected for Bank Comptroller. (Ramsey was a member of the State Assembly. On the night of the Sumter attack he had led a group of Democrats into the Executive Rooms of the Assembly, where Republicans were meeting, and made a speech in favor of cooperation. The speech had a telling effect on the Republicans present.)[93] The rest of the Republican ticket consisted of Conservative Republicans, with Harvey the choice for governor.

The Democratic State Convention declared in favor of the war, apologetically, with a heavy reprimand for "the spirit of the North, which is attempting to force the Administration to make this war for the abolition of slavery." A plank in the Democratic platform called for the repudiation of all Personal Liberty laws, as proof of northern good intentions.[94] In the ensuing campaign the Regular Democracy appealed for party loyalty, to some effect. The leading warhawks in the state included Charles D. Robinson, editor of the War Democrat Green Bay *Advocate,* Democratic Mayor James S. Brown of Milwaukee, and Milwaukee Douglas leaders James H. Brodhead and Matthew H. Carpenter. (Brodhead was an early advocate of confiscation as a war measure and Carpenter had created a furor only recently, delivering an anti-slavery speech to an audience of Wisconsin soldiers.) The Union party people expected the support of all these men, but could not obtain it for all their effort. Most of the Democratic papers in Wisconsin came out in favor of the Regular Democratic candidates and the Union party appeared to be a failure. On voting day, however, the Republican-Union ticket was elected with a majority of 8,000 votes out of 100 thousand cast. Union party candidates, picking up 23 seats in the Assembly, obtained the balance of power in the legislature.[95]

Attempts to organize a "No Party" movement in Massachusetts in 1861 had the blessings of Democratic General Benjamin F. Butler, editor Benjamin F. Hallett of the Democratic Boston *Post,* and Breckinridge leader Caleb Cushing.[96] But the plan fell through. In the following election the Regular Democracy was badly beaten by the forces of Republican Governor John A. Andrew, in keeping with Massachusetts tradition. A Union party was organized in Kansas in 1861 under leadership of Radical Senator James H. Lane for the explicit purpose of ousting Governor Charles Robinson from office. Although the Union party triumphed in an uncontested election, the results were set aside by the courts and Robinson retained control of the state house.[97]

New Jersey was the site of an unusual event for 1861—the resurgence of Democratic power. Republicans, "Americans," Old-Line Whigs, and Douglas Democrats had coalesced in 1859 to insure the election of the "Opposition" ticket, at the expense of the Regular Democracy. But for all that the Democrats remained the traditional party of power in New Jersey. Following the death of the Lecompton dispute, at the outset of the war, and the return of the Douglas faction to Democratic Regularity, the New Jersey Democracy emerged once again as the dominant force. Trying furiously to stem the tide, the Union party of New Jersey solicited the backing of the War Democrats in the legislative elections of 1861, and in scores of Democratic districts War Democrats agreed to stand for election as Independents, against the Regular Democracy. On voting day, five of these attained election in normally Democratic districts;[98] but that was not enough. The State Senate went Democratic, 11–10, the Assembly 32–28,[99] and the trend was general. The outcome of the New Jersey campaign was cited as a good political lesson for all Republicans by Horace Greeley of the New York *Tribune*. The Union coalition in New Jersey was terribly Conservative. Why should Republicans expect to win on such a basis? "They have tried to overbear Pro-slavery Democracy with Pro-slavery Republicanism—a policy that never wins because it never ought to."[100]

With so little to cheer about, the Regular Democracy looked forward to the New York City municipal elections in December. Here was guaranteed victory, or so it appeared, for here the Democrats outnumbered the Republicans two to one. But once again the War Democrats bolted and once again the Union party triumphed.

An extraordinary development in New York City politics this year was the division of Mayor Fernando Wood and his brother, Benjamin, editor and publisher of the New York *News*. Having deserted the Peace cause when Sumter was attacked, Mayor Wood had engaged in the great New York City Union rally of April 20, called for creation of the "Mozart Regiment," and spoken at troop-raising ceremonies on numerous occasions. Editor Wood was meanwhile working openly against the war. Although the New York City Common Council was on record in favor of the war and the *News* was the official journal of the Council, the *News* was clearly out for Peace. Democratic Councilman Henry W. Genet was particularly disturbed by this arrangement, denouncing the *News* and demanding its rejection. In August the Council voted 17 to 3 in accord with Genet's demand.[101] A few days later, a grand jury in the U.S. District Court for the Southern District of New York pronounced the *News* and certain other New York papers abettors of treason for sympathizing and agreeing with the Confederacy. The postmaster of New York was ordered by the Postmaster General to bar the *News* from the mails.[102]

Seemingly disassociated from the political difficulties of brother Benjamin, Mayor Wood supported the New York Union ticket in the November state election, and secured renomination by Mozart Hall, running as a War Democrat.[103] In so doing he went against the public declarations of many Mozart leaders endorsing the policies of his brother and the defunct *News*.

The ensuing campaign brought forth many scandals, all at the expense of Mayor Wood, who was accused of selling nominations on the Mozart ticket and of handing over public contracts to the highest bidder, in defiance of the law.[104] Despite his pro-Union declarations, the Mayor was frequently assailed as a Peace Democrat both by Tammany and by the Republicans. Thoroughly infuriated, Wood wrote a letter to an old enemy, Secretary of State Seward in Washington, defending his loyalty and requesting an end to Republican attacks upon it.[105] Stepping up his own campaign propaganda, he delivered a rousing address to a German audience, condemning the Republicans as the "Abolition party," and warning that they wanted all the fighting done by others, such as German Democrats. Their only concern, he said, was achieving freedom for southern Negroes, whom they hoped to bring North to work in competition with the whites.[106] On election day, the vote was almost evenly divided in thirds but not quite. Opdyke, the Republican, was elected with 25,451; Gunther of Tammany was second with 24,644; Wood was third with 23,350. The deciding factor was the switch of several hundred votes in the several Democratic districts, to Republican advantage. Once again, War Democrats had determined to outcome of events.

In sharp contrast to the overall trend, a Democratic victory was scored in Illinois in the closing months of 1861, as a result of Republican failure to satisfy the War Democracy. Following the death in June of Senator Stephen A. Douglas, Illinois Democrats had expected the appointment of a Democrat to take his place, and Congressman John A. McClernand was regarded as the likely prospect.[107] Instead, Governor Yates selected a Republican attorney, Orville H. Browning. War Democrats were stunned by the decision and further irritated when Republicans in Washington proceeded with a mass housecleaning of federal appointees in Illinois, sweeping scores of Democrats out of office in the interest of Republican applicants. Democratic newspapers and speakers denounced Governor Yates for failing to practice the nonpartisan policy he was so fond of preaching, and the criticism took effect directly. The fall election deciding the makeup of the impending State Constitutional Convention resulted in a Democratic landslide. Out of 75 delegates elected only 20 were Republicans.[108]

Yet, this was clearly an exception to the rule. Generally speaking, the year 1861 had been disastrous for the Regular Democracy and a glorious time for Republicans and Unionists, despite the appearance of many factors seeming to benefit the Democrats, from military setbacks, to economic troubles, to controversies over slavery. All that was needed for a true

Democratic resurgence, it appeared, was adoption of a policy preventing the Peace faction from dominating Democratic gatherings; but that was seemingly impossible in many states. As a result, the Democratic party suffered badly, and the lesson was clear to history. It was a lesson the Democratic leadership would fail to understand, however, during the full course of the war.

NOTES

1. George H. Porter, p. 55.
2. Ibid., p. 72.
3. *Biographical Encyclopedia of Illinois,* p. 313.
4. Madison (Wisconsin) Weekly *Patriot,* April 6, 1861.
5. Sidney D. Brummer, p. 115.
6. *Tribune Almanac,* 1862.
7. The Democrats controlled California, Delaware, Kentucky, and Oregon. A coalition of Democrats and Constitutional Unionists controlled Rhode Island, Missouri, and the "Restored Government of Virginia."
8. A typical "Union" rally, favoring the Compromise of 1850 and aimed against actions and the policies of the "Wilmot Democrats" of Pennsylvania, was held at Philadelphia, November 21, 1850. Democrats attending the rally included many who later would fight and work for the Union cause, in company with the anti-slavery men they criticized on this occasion. Some typical examples were Robert Patterson, George C. Cadwalader, and Charles J. Biddle (all of Philadelphia), all of whom would serve as Union officers eleven years later; also John W. Forney, the father of Pennsylvania Union party movement of the Civil War years. Philadelphia Citizens, *Proceedings . . . 28th of November, 1850.*
   In New York, the Union party movement of 1851 was led by pro-slavery businessmen, both Democrat and Old-Line Whig. The pro-slavery Whigs of the 1850s were called in New York the "Silver-Greys." Their leaders were Francis Granger, William M. Evarts, Washington Hunt, Joshua J. Henry, and James W. Gerard. (By 1861, Hunt, Henry, and Gerard had joined the Democrats and campaigned for Breckinridge.) Another notable Union party leader in the 1851 campaign was the renowned pro-slavery Democrat Charles O'Conor. The New York Union party of 1851 solicited support among the businessmen of New York City by threatening to publicize the names of all who failed to join them, thereby ruining the southern trade of every dissident. The Union party campaign of 1851 was called the "Cotton Terror." Philip S. Foner, pp. 38–48.
9. A typical "Union" rally, favoring the execution of John Brown, was held five days later, December 7, 1859, at Philadelphia. Democrats attending the rally included many who later were to work and fight for the Union cause, in company with the anti-slavery men they criticized on this occasion. Some notable examples were Robert Patterson, George McCall, George C. Cadwalader, and Charles J. Biddle (soon to serve as Union officers) and James Campbell, Postmaster General under Pierce; also George Sharswood, George H. Boker, Benjamin H. Brewster, and Francis Wolgomuth, all of Philadelphia and all of whom would join the Union party cause in wartime. Philadelphia Union meeting, *Proceedings,* December 7, 1859. Another Union rally for the same purpose was held December 15, 1859, at the Academy of Music in New York City. Democratic leaders appearing on this occasion included

August Belmont, Alexander T. Stewart, Moses Taylor, Royal Phelps, Morris Ketchum, William B. Astor, John J. Astor, Jr., and Henry Grinnell. Philip S. Foner, p. 162.

10. A typical "Union" rally, favoring "compromise and conciliation," and critical of Republican party policy, was held at Albany, New York, January 31, 1861. Democrats attending the rally included many who later would fight and work for the Union cause, in company with the anti-slavery men they criticized on this occasion. Some notable examples were Dean Richmond, John Van Buren, and Horatio Seymour of the Albany Regency; "Grand Sachem" William D. Kennedy, Samuel J. Tilden, James T. Brady, John T. Hoffman, Peter B. Sweeney, and John Clancy of Tammany Hall; John Cochrane, Daniel E. Sickles, and Gilbert Dean of Mozart Hall; and business leaders Joshua J. Henry, August Belmont, and Edward Cooper. Sidney D. Brummer, p. 113.

11. In the 1860 Democratic campaign, David Turpie, Democratic candidate for Lieutenant Governor of Indiana, denounced the "New England merchants," in one speech after another, and Peter V. Deuster, editor of the Milwaukee *See-Bote* (a Democratic German weekly), attacked the "money power of New England." Western Democratic newspapers favoring secession of the Old Northwest, in 1861, blamed all sectional troubles on New England. When the war began, Democratic Captain Frederick W. Horn of the Wisconsin State Militia resigned his commission rather than engage in a war that was certain, in his estimation, to "plunder" in the Middle West "for the benefit of Pennsylvania iron mongers and New England manufacturers." In January, 1863, Democratic Congressman Clement L. Vallandigham of Ohio delivered an anti-war speech in the House, largely devoted to criticism of New England. Kenneth M. Stampp, *Indiana Politics,* p. 234. Frank L. Klement, *Wisconsin and the Civil War,* p. 26; *Congressional Globe* (37th Congress, 3rd session), Appendix, pp. 52–60.

12. William Lloyd Garrison, President of the American Anti-Slavery Society, attacked the Republican party in a speech delivered July 4, 1860. In his opinion, "The Republican party means to do nothing, can do nothing, for the abolition of slavery in the slave states. . . .The Republican party stands on a level with the Fugitive Slave Law. It has cursed all opposition to it. . . .And shall I vote that men who buy and sell and steal their fellow creatures shall have political power put into their hands? . . .No. . . ." Edith Ellen Ware, "Political Opinion in Massachusetts," p. 25.

   In October, 1860, Abolitionist leader Gerrit Smith of New York wrote a public letter, warning Abolitionists not to vote for Lincoln because he "is for a white man's party (and) is opposed to extending equal political rights to the black man." James M. McPherson, *The Struggle for Equality. Abolitionists and the Negro in the Civil War and Reconstruction* (Princeton: Princeton University Press, 1964), pp. 24–25.

13. Philip S. Foner, p. 150–201.

14. Baltimire *Republican,* June 14, 1861; Henderson (Kentucky) *Reporter,* June 20, July 18, 1861.

15. For Democrats accepting military commissions, see Appendix 2.

16. The great host of Republican office-seekers besieging Lincoln in the early months of 1861 had a negative effect on the attempt of the administration to establish a nonpartisan war machine. In trying to satisfy Republican demands at this time, President Lincoln agreed to the removal of many War Democrats from office, to the detriment of the nonpartisan spirit. A typical example was the case of Benjamin F. Watson, Postmaster of Lawrence, Massachusetts. A Breckinridge supporter, Watson was commissioned Major of the Sixth Massachusetts, and was involved in the Baltimore Riots of April 19, 1861. While serving in Washington, he was advised of his removal as Postmaster, and his replacement by a Republican. Benjamin F. Watson, pp. 15–16.

17. Charles C. Anderson, p. 33.
18. *Union Army*, II:295.
19. Walter C. Woodward, p. 173.
20. *Tribune Almanac*, 1862.
21. Thomas Speed, p. 90.
22. Ibid., p. 164.
23. E. Merton Coulter, p. 141.
24. Charles B. Clark, *Politics in Maryland during the Civil War* (Chestertown, Md., 1952), pp. 8, 9, 13, 26, 31, 63; *Union Army*, II:263.
25. Louis C. Hatch, II:440–41.
26. Ibid., II:242.
27. The Hancock and Waldo county conventions split in two. In Knox county the War Democrats merged with the Republicans. The Democratic organizations in Cumberland, Oxford, and Somerset counties announced for Dana and the Somerset delegates attacked the war as an Abolitionist crusade. The Penobscot and Aroostock conventions came out for Jameson. The Portland *Argus* supported Dana but not his platform; the Saco *Democrat*, Machias *Union*, North Anson *Advocate*, and Franklin *Patriot* announced for Dana. The Bath *Times*, Augusta *Age*, Belfast *Journal*, Lewiston *Advocate*, and Rockland *Democrat* announced for Jameson. Ibid., II:442.
28. Louis C. Hatch, II:436.
   The Bangor Republican caucus nominated for state representative S. H. Blake, a Douglas-leader. The Penobscot county Republican convention nominated two War Democrats: John A. Peters, for state senator, and Charles B. Stetson, for county attorney. The Cumberland county Republican convention left open the nomination of a county treasurer and a senator from Portland, inviting the Democratic organization to fill the nominations with choices of its own, subject to approval of the Republican convention and the Republican delegation from Portland. In Knox county a Union ticket was arranged and Ephraim K. Smart was nominated as a Unionist candidate for the State Senate. Smart was the Douglas candidate for Governor in 1860. Republicans in Augusta agreed to support War Democrat Samuel Cony for State Representative, expecting the Democrats to join them in the act. The Democrats rejected Cony, however, putting up another candidate. Ibid., II:437, 455. See also *Evening Journal Almanac*, 1862.
29. Elijah R. Kennedy, pp. 208, 211, 212.
30. Fearing collusion between the secessionists and Governor Whiteaker of Oregon, the War Department bypassed the Governor in the matter of troop-raising to deal instead with Unionists of solid reputation. Among several selected to serve in this capacity was Benjamin F. Harding, Democratic Speaker of the State Assembly. *Union Army*, IV:424-25.
31. San Francisco *Herald*, August 26, 1861.
32. William B. Hesseltine, p. 77.
33. The Douglas party received almost as many votes in 1861 as it had in 1859. The "Chivalry" Democracy received about thirty thousand less; the Republicans, about forty-six thousand more. *Evening Journal Almanac*, 1860, 1862.
34. Ibid., 1862.
35. *Evening Journal Almanac*, 1862.
36. Elijah R. Kennedy, pp. 227–28.
37. Burlington *Sentinel*, August 2, 1861. The other two Peace men running for state office in Vermont in 1861 were Erastus Plympton, candidate for Lieutenant Governor, and George Washburn, candidate for Treasurer, Both were delegates to the 1860 Douglas State Convention, as was also Benjamin H. Smalley, the Peace candidate for Governor. Burlington *Sentinel*, August 2, 1861.
38. *Tribune Almanac*, 1862.
39. Clifford R. Hall, pp. 13–14.

40. George H. Porter, p. 88.
41. Ibid., p. 88.
42. Benjamin P. Thomas, *Stanton,* p. 314.
43. George H. Porter, p. 89.
44. Edward C. Smith, p. 319.
45. Ibid., p. 88.
46. Ibid., p. 90.
47. War Democrats running on the Union state ticket included: David Tod, candidate for Governor, G. Volney Dorsey, Treasurer; J. H. Riley, Controller; John Torrence, Board of Public Works. Cleveland *Plain Dealer,* September 4, 1861.
48. Eugene H. Roseboom, *The Civil War Era. 1850–1873,* Volume Four of the History of the State of Ohio, 6 volumes (Columbus: Ohio State Archiological and Historical Society, 1944), p. 393.
49. Columbus *Ohio State Journal,* August 30, 1861. Thomas Sparrow was a Breckinridge candidate for Congress in 1860. He finished third behind the winner, Douglas Democrat Samuel S. Cox, and Republican Samuel Galloway. *Tribune Almanac,* 1861.
50. Democrats attending the Ohio Union Convention, in addition to those not listed previously, included Douglas leaders David Tod, G. Volney Dorsey, John Brough, Joseph Riley, and E. S. Flint; Breckinridge leaders John Geary, John A. Corwin, James M. Nash, and James B. Armstrong. Others: James M. Coffinbury, who served as Secretary; John C. Groom, George H. Safford, Alfred McVeigh, D. W. Stambaugh, Nicholas Bartlett, Octavius Waters, H. B. Smith, Judge Samuel Humphreville, Alexander G. McBurney, Dr. John McCook, K. Fritter, Lot L. Smith, James Warren, Henry G. Abbey, John W. Houx, R. B. Warden, Merrill Barlow, Franklin J. Dickman, D. W. Gage, and Dr. J. P. Robinson. Columbus *Ohio State Journal,* August 30, 1861.
51. Some typical examples of Democratic participation in the Union campaign: John C. Lee, Chairman, Seneca County Convention; former Congressman William S. Groesbeck, William S. Kennon, and W. R. Rankin, candidates for the Assembly; Franklin J. Dickman, R. B. Warden, and Dr. J. P. Robinson, candidates for the State Senate. Columbus *Ohio State Journal,* September 7, 16, 24, 1861.
52. *Evening Journal Almanac,* 1862.
53. John W. Forney, pp. 7–8.
54. Philadelphia *Press,* October 9, 1861.
55. *National Cyclopedia of American Biography,* IV:24.
56. Stanton Ling Davis, p. 207.
57. Ibid., pp. 71, 74. During the Secession period Mahony was opposed to federal capitulation, hoping to achieve some kind of compromise arrangement. When the war began, however, he came out flatly against the federal cause. Olynthus B. Clark, *The Politics of Iowa during the Civil War and Reconstruction* (Iowa City: Clio Press, 1911), p. 67.
58. Ibid., p. 107.
59. Ibid., p. 114.
60. Ibid., p. 115.
61. St. Paul (Minnesota) *Press,* September 10, 1861.
62. Olynthus B. Clark, p. 115.
63. Edward H. Stiles, *Recollections and Sketches of Notable Lawyers and Public Men of Iowa* (Des Moines: Homestead, 1916), p. 778.
64. Olynthus B. Clark, pp. 126–29; following the election Baker was appointed Adjutant General of Iowa.
65. Ibid., p. 131.
66. *Tribune Almanac,* 1862.
67. William J. Ryland, *Alexander Ramsey* (Philadelphia, 1951), p. 148; Theodore

C. Blegen, *Minnesota* (Minneapolis, 1963), p. 249; St. Paul *Press,* August 8, 1861; Ibid., September 10, 1861. Lieutenant Governor Ignatius Donnelly, a Radical Republican, criticized the actions of the Governor in seeking the backing of General Gorman. In Donnelly's opinion, the General was "without influence in the Democratic party and certainly without it in the Republican. It will be a question with you how long to hold on to a man of so little judgment as he has proven himself to be at all times and in all places." Ramsey papers, quoted in William J. Ryland, p. 147.

68. *Union army,* VIII:20.
69. *Tribune Almanac,* 1862; William J. Ryland, p. 150.
70. Allen Johnson and Dumas Malone, eds., XV:582. Some other Barnburners returning to the Regular Democracy, along with Richmond, included both Van Buren's, Samuel J. Tilden, John A. Dix, John Cochrane, and Sanford A. Church. Barnburners who did not come back included Preston King, David Dudley Field, James S. Wadsworth, and William Cullen Bryant, who remained Free Soilers until the Republican party was formed in 1854, at which point they became Republicans. De Alva Stanwood Alexander, II:p. 53, 126—69.
71. On January 18, 1861, Hards and Softs rallied together in New York City, in behalf of compromise proposals. Hard leaders included Benjamin Wood, James T. Brady, Gilbert Dean, and Congressmen Daniel E. Sickles and John Cochrane of Mozart Hall; Edwin Croswell, former editor of the Albany *Argus;* former Congressman Hiram Walbridge and the noted pro-slavery attorney, Charles O'Conor. Soft leaders included John Van Buren, Horatio Seymour, Congressman-elect Erastus Corning; Lyman Tremain, former Attorney General of New York; August Belmont. Financial Secretary, Douglas National Committee; William M. Tweed, Samuel J. Tilden, John T. Hoffman, Peter B. Sweeney, John Clancy, Elijah F. Purdy, and Richard B. Connelly of Tammany Hall. Sidney D. Brummer, p. 115.
72. Marvin Wheat, *The Progress and Intelligence of Americans; Proof of Slavery, from the First Chapter of Genesis.* . . (Kentucky, 1862), pp. 452–53.
73. John R. Dickinson, ed., *Speeches, Correspondence, etc., of the Late Daniel S. Dickinson of New York,* 2 vols. (New York: Putnam, 1867), II:550–51.
74. Ibid., III:24; Sidney D. Brummer, p. 105.
75. New York *Tribune* (Semi-Weekly), November 27, 1863.
76. De Alva Stanwood Alexander, III: pp. 21–24.
77. Ibid., III: p. 23.
78. Ibid., III:27–29.
79. *Evening Journal Almanac,* 1862.
80. Charles B. Clark, pp. 62–63.
81. During the 1860 election campaign, the Democratic St. Louis *Republican* carries a headline, for many days, reading: "The true issue (is) whether we shall be governed by a reign of negroarchy." The opinion reflected the prejudice of a large majority of the border slave-state electorate. St. Louis *Republican,* August 1, 1860.
82. Charles B. Clark, pp. 73–74.
83. Ibid., p. 74.
84. Ibid., p. 74.
85. Ibid., p. 76.
86. Ibid., p. 75.
87. Henry E. Shepherd, ed., *History of Baltimore, Maryland* (1893), p. 154.
88. Charles B. Clark, p. 80.
89. Ibid., p. 80. The major purpose of the troops at the polls, in the view of the military personnel involved, was not to scare off loyal voters of any political persuasion, but to stand guard against the threat of violence and disruption of the voting procedure. Democratic Colonel John W. Geary of the 28th Pennsylvania Infantry was stationed at Point of Rocks, Maryland, on election day,

and his troops were scattered about the various nearby towns. As a War Democrat, Geary was opposed to the Peace ticket and happy about the Union party majorities within his jurisdiction. His main satisfaction was professional, however; that "owing to the presence of the troops everything progressed quietly." Matthew P. Andrews, *History of Maryland: Province and State* (Garden City, Doubleday-Doran, 1929), p. 529.

90. Frank L. Klement, *The Copperheads of the Middle West* (Chicago: University of Chicago Press, 1960), p. 4.

91. A. M. Thomson, *A Political History of Wisconsin,* 2nd ed. (Milwaukee: Caspar, 1902 (1888)), p. 156.

92. Ibid., September 26, 1861.

93. E. B. Quiner, *The Military History of Wisconsin* (Chicago: Clarke, 1866), p. 45.

94. Milwaukee *Sentinel,* October 5, 1861.

95. *Evening Journal Almanac,* 1862.

96. For Butler's position, see Article from Lowell (Massachusetts) *Advertiser,* quoted in Rutland (Vermont) Weekly *Herald,* September 12, 1861; for Hallett's position, see Boston *Post,* September 14, 1861; for Cushing's position, see Boston *Advertiser,* September 19, 1861.

97. Albert Castel, *A Frontier State at War: Kansas, 1861–1865* (Ithaca: Cornell University Press (for American Historical Society), 1958), p. 95.

98. *Tribune Almanac,* 1860.

99. Daniel W. Wilder, p. 240. The vote to override was 30 to 8 in the House, 9 to 4 in the Council. Among the Democratic members voting to override, the most prominent was William R. Wagstaff, who would run for Governor in 1862. Others included Pascal S. Parks, Charles Sims, L. S. Cornwall, R. Sopris, and Frederick Brown.

100. *Tribune Almanac,* 1862.

101. St. Paul (Minnesota) *Press,* August 16, 1861.

102. Samuel A. Pleasants, *Fernando Wood of New York* (New York: Columbia University Press, 1948), p. 124.

103. New York *Tribune* (Semi-Weekly), November 17, 1863; Samuel A. Pleasants, pp. 128- 29.

104. Ibid., pp. 127-28.

105. Ibid., pp. 128-29.

106. Ibid., pp. 127.

107. Edward C. Smith, p. 315.

108. Springfield *Illinois State Journal*, January 7, 1862; *Tribune Almanac*, 1862.

8

Conservative Tradition at Bay: Slave Property Rights under Fire, 1862

Looking back on the chaos of the 1861 election campaign, the Democratic party leadership was able to discern one encouraging development: the "Conditional War" philosophy advanced by Horatio Seymour, former Governor of New York. When the Thirty-seventh Congress reconvened, December 2, 1861, a new faction was present in the form of the Conditional War Democrats, all of whom sounded like Seymour. The Conditionals were Unionists, but only on certain conditions. They doubted the integrity of the Republican leadership so far as slavery was concerned, calling upon the administration to guarantee the property rights of all slaveholders, loyal and disloyal. They were ready to revive the Antebellum campaign for Peace negotiations and were exceedingly hostile to anyone opposing such a move. Critical of mob attacks on Democratic newspaper offices and Democratic gatherings, the military arrest of civilians, and suspension of Democratic newspapers, the Conditionals called for preservation of free speech and assembly, as practiced by all persons opposing the party in power. Failure on the part of the administration to attend to these matters in the recommended manner would seriously diminish the Unionism of Democrats in general. So the administration was advised by the Conditionals, over and over again. "Conditionals" were not so designated at the

129

time and generally were classified as Peace Democrats; but this was misleading. The voting records of Democrats in Congress and in the several state legislatures reveal a sharp difference between the factions. Contrary to the Peace Democrats who voted against all war measures with a passionate consistency, the Conditionals were inclined to pick and choose, voting always for the war when they could do so without violating their special code. Contrary to the War Democrats, who frequently accepted as genuine the administration plea of wartime necessity, the Conditionals were inclined to regard all such pleas as basically deceptive.

A new note had been sounded. When Congress reconvened in December, the first fact in evidence was the defection of many War Democrats to the ranks of the Conditionals. Congressman William S. Holman of Indiana was a typical example. Severing his brief affiliation with the Union party, he returned to Washington to split his votes in Congress, some for War, some for Peace. Another backslider from Indiana was Congressman James A. Cravens. Ohio Congressman Samuel S. Cox, William Allen, Warren P. Noble, and James R. Morris followed the same course. Charles J. Biddle, a colonel in the Pennsylvania Reserves at the time of his election to Congress in July 1861, entered the House in December as a Conditional.[1] Senator Milton S. Latham of California, who had delivered one of the best pro-war speeches of the Special War Session, retreated in December to the ranks of the Conditionals. Some retreated even further. Colonel James E. Kerrigan of the disorganized and chaotic 25th New York Infantry, relinquished his commission to enter Congress in December 1861 as a Peace Democrat. He was joined in the Peace camp by Congressman Charles A. Wickliffe of Kentucky, Chairman of the Douglas National Committee and a former War Democrat.

The appearance of the Conditional War faction divided the Democrats in Congress almost evenly in thirds—for War, for Peace, and for War under certain conditions.[2] When Congressman John A. McClernand of Illinois resigned his seat to accept a brigadier general's commission, leadership of the War Democracy in the House fell to Hendrick B. Wright of Pennsylvania. He was the close friend and congressional agent of John W. Forney of the Philadelphia *Press,* holding much the same view of the war and arguing along much the same lines. Throughout their political careers in Pennsylvania, Wright and Forney had more or less agreed on most matters, and on the Kansas question they had wholly agreed. Wright was by nature a reformer in all areas except those involving slavery and race. His career began in the 1840s as a state legislator, opposing imprisonment for debt. It would end as a journalist, in the 1870s, fighting for the rights of coal miners. A strong Negrophobe, he had rejected the Republican "People's Party," when it first appeared in Pennsylvania, but supported some of its candidates in 1858, against the interests of the Lecompton Democracy (the same course followed by Forney and the *Press*). As Chairman of the Douglas State Executive Committee, he had utilized his influence, in cooperation with Forney, to shut the door to compromise with the Breckinridge Democracy, and when the war began he took the stump for the Union cause. The death of Republican Congressman George W. Scranton of Pennsylvania in the spring of 1861 was followed by a special election in which a coalition of Douglas Democrats and Republicans joined in backing Wright against Peace Democrat D. R. Randall, the Breckinridge candidate. Wright was easily elected.[3]

Conditional War Democrats in the House rejected Wright's leadership in favor of the less aggressive Unionism of Samuel S. Cox of Ohio and William S. Holman of Indiana. Again, as in the Special War Session, the Peace leader in the House was Clement L. Vallandigham of Ohio. (Although missing was his staunch lieutenant of the Special War Session, Henry C. Burnett of Kentucky, now serving as a member of the Confederate Congress.) The Senate had eight War Democrats, seven Peace Democrats, and two Conditionals.[4] McDougall of California remained the leader of the War faction. Senator Breckinridge of Kentucky having quit the Peace cause to serve in the Confederate army, his place among the Peace men was taken by his close friend, Lazarus W. Powell of Kentucky. Senator Saulsbury of Delaware, the advocate of a defensive war policy, led the Conditionals.

Of the first four major propositions considered in the second session of the Senate, three were resolutions calling for expulsion of Democratic members. The Peace Democrats had all along contended, and would continue to contend, that the Peace cause was neutral, and by no means pro-Confederate. But the Senate was missing the services of three members, all of whom were Peace Democrats in August 1861 and Confederates in December: John C. Breckinridge of Kentucky and Waldo P. Johnson and Trusten Polk of Missouri. All were expelled, without a single Democratic voice raised in their behalf.[5]

The first major House action in the Thirty-seventh Congress, Second Session, was a vote, December 4, on a motion by Holman of Indiana to redeclare the sentiment of the House in favor of the pro-slavery Crittenden Resolution. One of the conditions on which Holman was willing to support the federal war policy was adherence to all pro-slavery promises rendered by Republican officials. On July 22 the pro-slavery section of the Resolution had passed the House 117 to 2. On December 4 the Holman endorsement was ingloriously tabled, 71 to 65.[6] Times had changed and the Republicans were no longer willing to accept the pro-slavery dictation of Crittenden, Holman, and their kind.

Action in the Senate, December 9, and in the House, January 6, established the Joint Committee on the Conduct of War, "to inquire into the reason for the disasters that have attended public arms.'' In time the committee would become the target of abuse by Regular Democrats in all the loyal states. One Democrat voted for it in the Senate (McDougall of California), none in the House.[7] Senator Wade of Ohio was appointed Chairman of the Joint Committee, and two War Democrats were elected to serve under his direction: Senator Johnson of Tennessee and Congressman Odell of New York.[8] The Regular Democracy was suspicious of the Joint Committee from the moment it was born.

A significant fact about the Peace Democrats was that few of them were pacifists. Generally speaking, they had no objection to violence as a means of settling political problems. Many were veterans, even heroes, of the Black Hawk War and the War with Mexico. The only war they opposed was this one: the Civil War. On January 7, 1862, Congressman Vallandigham delivered a saber-rattling address, rebuking England for objecting to American conduct in the *Trent Affair*. He wanted to keep Mason and Slidell in prison and was not disturbed about the prospect of war with England. Radical Congressman Hutchins of Ohio chided him for adopting a warlike position and Vallandigham did not like being chided. If a man could not ''understand the differences between a civil war and a foreign war,'' Vallandigham said, ''I despair of enlightening him.'' Hutchins, in reply, accused Vallandigham of wanting war with England as a means of impeding the progress of the war with the Confederacy. In this he was supported by War Democrat Wright of Pennsylvania. Vallandigham held firm. Surrender to England, he said, would be ''a calamity tenfold more disastrous than a five years' war.'' Wright disagreed, urging the release of Mason and Slidell. He did not believe in fighting a war with England over a pair of ''rebel refugees.''[9]

Having quarreled with the Peace cause, in favor of the Union, War Democrat Wright changed front two weeks later to quarrel with the Radicals, in favor of slavery. The issue involved was a Radical proposal to extend the application of the Confiscation Act. Radical Bingham of Ohio favored something more along the lines of General Fremont's emancipation proclamation, but Wright objected to this on the ground that confiscation measures were certain of drastically reducing the Union sentiment in the border slave states, at the expense of many volunteer enlistments. He praised the President for carrying out a conservative policy on the slavery issue, declaring his intention to support the administration so long as it continued on its current course.

To illustrate the point, Wright came to the defense of the administration against the recent criticism of certain Democratic newspapers charging speculation on the part of federal officials and fraud in the drawing up of government contracts. There was no good point to this kind of talk, he said. ''There is but one great abiding and powerful issue today, the issue whether the country and the Constitution shall be saved, or whether it shall be utterly and entirely annihilated.''

According to the Peace philosophy, Republicans were fighting for the John Brown tradition, on the assumption that Negroes were as good as white men and deserved the same kind of rights and privileges. Everyone who assisted the Republican war effort was therefore favoring the interests of Old John Brown and Negro equality. Many War Democrats were deeply embarrassed by the contention, which Congressman Wright denied on this occasion, before concluding with a statement that he had no objection to confiscation as a war measure employed by the Army. What he was opposing was a set policy laid down by Congress, seeming to embrace the cause of Abolition, *per se.*[10]

Calming the suspicions of Conservative Unionists about slavery matters was a major objective of President Lincoln in the first year of hostilities, and the appointment of Breckinridge Democrat Edwin M. Stanton as Secretary of War was clearly undertaken with this issue in mind. It was easily the outstanding political development of January 1862, and was well received throughout the loyal states. The new Secretary had cabinet experience, and was a well-known Unionist with many friends in Conservative circles. As time passed it was becoming clear that the great bulk of general officers in the Union Army were Democrats. There appeared something logical about another Democrat handing them their orders. Many War Democrats had long objected to the absence of their kind in the wartime cabinet. The Stanton appointment provided a dramatic response, in behalf of the nonpartisan spirit.

From all accounts Edwin M. Stanton appeared as a most unusual man. It is often observed that he got along much better on the personal level with political Conservatives than he did with political reformers, who tended to annoy him. In the opinion of Conservative President Buchanan, he was unobtrusive, ingratiating, and overdiplomatic. The same opinion was held by Conservative Jeremiah S. Black, who served for several years as Stanton's immediate superior.[11] Abraham Lincoln had no such impression, however. In his eyes Stanton appeared in the nature of an angry whirlwind. Working with anti-slavery reformers in the Lincoln cabinet, he was known for his lack of diplomacy, his lack of tact, his brusqueness, and his bad manners, in total contrast to his reputation among the Conservatives of the Buchanan administration.[12]

It is generally agreed that the most chaotic executive performance of the Civil War was that of Stanton's predesessor, Simon Cameron. In Pennsylvania, where they had worked in political rivalry for several years, Cameron was regarded by all Democrats as a rascal and a thief, and Stanton accepted the opinion as fact. Personally involved with departmental reorganization, he appointed an investigating commission to examine all the recent business negotiations of Secretary Cameron with a view to uncovering chicanery in office. The commissioners were two—both Democrats—Joseph Holt of Kentucky and Robert Dale Owen of Indiana, who were called upon "to audit and adjust all contracts, orders, and claims on the War Department, in respect to ordnance, arms, and ammunition." Working rapidly, the commissioners submitted a report to Stanton on the first of July, calling Cameron to task for expenses unnecessarily incurred through faulty contractural agreements irregularly conceived. Resulting losses were estimated in the vicinity of $50 million. Rejecting certain contracts and drastically curtailing others, the commissioners shaved some $17 million from War Department expenditures. Cameron also was criticized for failing to follow the law requiring public advertisement of War Department contracts, and for permitting competitive bidding between state and federal purchasing agents.[13]

The appointment of Owen and Holt signaled the connection of the War Department, under Stanton's direction, with Democratic advisors all over the loyal-states and adoption of departmental policies more pleasing to Democratic prejudice. Reflecting Conservative nervousness about the military arrest and incarceration of certain opponents of the war, Stanton persuaded Lincoln to order the release of many such prisoners in the early months of 1862, and was widely praised, as a result, in the Democratic press.[14] Among Stanton's numerous advisers in his first year on the job were Edwards Pierrepont and Samuel J. Tilden of Tammany Hall and the Maryland railroad baron John W. Garrett, president of the Baltimore and Ohio.[15] A Breckinridge supporter in the 1860 campaign, Garrett had long identified himself with pro-slavery principles and when the war began he was regarded with distrust in Republican circles. Numbered among his worst enemies in the business world was Secretary of War Cameron who, as president of the Pennsylvania Railroad, hated Garrett for his competition and was unable, as a government official, to forgive and forget. The B & O was generally ignored by the War Department, poorly utilized by the government in 1861, and under-protected against enemy attack in western Virginia. When Cameron was replaced by Stanton in January 1862, Garrett was called to Washington for consultation, and a close rapport was finally established between the B & O and the federal authorities, to Garrett's satisfaction.[16] (Responding to the change in policy, the B & O directors ordered the display of the national flag at every station on the line, in keeping with federal proceedures.) When the road returned to normal operations in the West in March, the Louisville and Nashville Railroad was reactivated in Kentucky at the order of line president James Guthrie, a spokesman of the Antebellum Peace Democracy.[17]

Another War Democrat raised suddenly to prominence in 1862 was John B. Henderson, Douglas leader from Missouri, who entered the U.S. Senate about the same moment that Stanton was entering the War Department. Henderson was one of three new senators elected to replace departed Secessionists. A wealthy slaveholder and a native of Virginia, he had led the fight against Secession at the Missouri State Constitutional Convention of 1861, delivering a speech that was believed by many to have broken the back of Secession in the state.[18] He was, upon his arrival in Washington, staunchly Unionist and staunchly pro-slavery. As time passed, however, he was to alter his position on slavery from Conservative, to Moderate, to Liberal, to Radical. During his stay in Washington, Henderson became well acquainted with President Lincoln, who experienced an identical shift in political sentiment. When Lincoln agreed to enactment of the Thirteenth Amendment in 1865, the man who wrote the measure was John B. Henderson. When Lincoln had passed on, Henderson was also to compose the legislation leading to adoption of the Fifteenth Amendment.[19]

* * *

Having expelled three slave-state members in December 1861, the Senate next expelled a northerner—Jesse D. Bright, Democrat from Indiana. The basis for expulsion was a correspondence between Bright and Jefferson Davis in March 1861, concerning the supply of firearms to the Confederate authorities. War Democrats McDougall of California and Johnson of Tennessee branded Bright as a traitor, McDougall recommending capital punishment.[20] Johnson was critical of Peace Democrats in general, noting that they kept leaving the Senate to take commissions in the Confederate army.[21] The Senate voted 32 to 14 in favor of expulsion, and three Democrats were included among the majority.[22] With the Indiana State Legislature out of session, the job of picking a successor to Bright devolved upon Republican Governor Oliver P. Morton. Publicly dedicated to a nonpartisan war policy, the Governor was expected to select one of two likely candidates: War Democrats Robert Dale Owen and Joseph A. Wright. Having cooperated extensively with the Governor since the coming of the war, Owen had hopes of receiving the appointment and went so far as to request it in payment for his patriotic services. But he was outclassed, politically. Wright was the best Governor Indiana had had over a period of many years, and far more influential in Democratic circles. He was duly appointed and, as a consolation prize, Owen joined the Treasury Department as Assistant Secretary on the staff of Salmon P. Chase.[23]

* * *

The Union military operations of 1862 were under the direction of Democratic generals in every quarter of significance. George B. McClellan commanded the Army of the Potomac. Henry W. Halleck, commanding the Department of Missouri, directed operations on the Mississippi River and the invasion of West Tennessee. Ulysses S. Grant led the Army of the Mississippi under Halleck's overall command. Following the seizure of West Tennessee, direction of military matters in the state was passed along to General Don Carlos Buell. Troops engaged in land and naval assaults against North Carolina, South Carolina, and Louisiana were commanded by Generals Ambrose E. Burnside and Benjamin F. Butler. All were Democrats.

Burnside's North Carolina expedition was the first major Union military offensive of the year. The capture of Roanoke, February 7, rendered Burnside a national hero. Grant was soon afterward acclaimed an even greater hero for taking Fts. Henry and Donelson. Although not regarded as a clever man politically, Grant was never long in sensing the drift of political events. Of considerable significance was an order emanating from his headquarters February 26, over the name of Democratic Colonel Mortimer D. Leggett (Provost Marshal on the staff of General Grant), declaring that "Such slaves as were within the lines at the time of the capture of Ft. Donelson and such as have been used by the enemy in building the fortifications, or in any way hostile to the Government, will not be released nor permitted to return to their masters, but will be employed in the Quartermaster's Department for the benefit of the Government."[24] This was the first order issued in the West in keeping with the Contraband Policy of Democratic General Benjamin F. Butler. It also ran contrary to the principals of "General Order No. 2," isued the previous November by Grant's superior officer, Democratic General Henry W. Halleck, ending the military employment of Negro contrabands by Union forces in St. Louis.[25]

The first important Confederate attack of the year was carried out March 8, at Hampton Roads, by the Confederate ironclad *Virginia (nee Merrimac.)* Impregnable to Union shells, the *Merrimac* loomed for a moment as the deciding factor in the war and Washington was panicked by the possibility. Secretary of War Stanton was particularly upset, fearing disaster, and his performance in this moment of crisis hurt his reputation.[26] It so happened, however, that another War Democrat, John A. Griswold of Troy, New York, had provided the Union with a means of coping with the *Merrimac*. A former Mayor of Troy and a Democratic candidate for Congress in the 1860 campaign, Griswold also was an ironmonger of ability and a man of means. Contacted by John Ericcson, inventor of the *Monitor,* he had agreed to finance the building of the vessel, in the national behalf—and none too soon.[27] The *Monitor* met the *Merrimac* March 9, and held its own, destroying Confederate hopes of raising the Union blockade and ravishing the Northeast coast with an invincible monster. Buoyed by the success of his endeavors, John A. Griswold would soon return to politics as a formidable War Democrat.

When the Union Army of the Mississippi ground to a halt at Shiloh, in April, Democratic General Grant was blamed and removed from command. When the Union Army of the Potomac failed to get started, Democratic General McClellan was also criticized. Following his arrival at Washington, McClellan had made the acquaintance of many important people, not all of whom were in favor of the war. Congressman Moses F. Odell, a War Democrat from New York and a member of the controversial Joint Committee on the Conduct of the War, was a frequent visitor to McClellan's headquarters. According to his account, the General was surrounded much of the time by Democratic congressmen identified with the Peace cause.[28] When news of this got around, McClellan fell under suspicion in Unionist circles, and an anti-McClellan movement was soon in evidence.

Especially critical of McClellan's policies and suspicous of his purposes was the Joint Committee on the Conduct of the War. Alarmed by reports of growing anti-McClellan sentiment in Congress, McClellan wrote to Lincoln, in December, protesting against the possibility of congressional interference with his policies. Lincoln replied that the Committee was "in a perfectly good mood" and there was nothing for McClellan to worry about. No such mood was discernable, however, when the Committee assembled in conference with Lincoln, January 5, to discuss the lack of action in the East. The loudest voices raised in protest against the General on that occasion were not those of the Republicans present but of the two War Democrats, Senator Andrew Johnson of Tennessee and Congressman Moses F. Odell of New York, both of whom proposed the removal of McClellan, which advice was rejected by the President.[29] The removal was not to take place until McClellan had failed on the Peninsula and entered the political arena as author of the pro-slavery "Harrison's Landing Letter," at which point he was replaced, in July, by Republican General John Pope.

There were many critics of McClellan's performance on the Peninsula who doubted his sincerity, denying that he really wanted to win, and suggesting or openly declaring that his purposes were treasonable. Although defending the General against all charges of dishonorable intent, Secretary of War Stanton criticized his attitude. "This man has no heart for the cause," he was quoted as saying. "He is fighting for a boundary if he fights at all."[30] Throughout the entire Peninsula campaign, Stanton was in constant communication with McClellan, prodding him repeatedly and urging him to fight. Thereafter, McClellan regarded Stanton as an enemy.[31] It has also been observed that McClellan's performance on the Peninsula may well have made a Republican out of Stanton.[32]

Fired to enthusiasm by the Harrison's Landing Letter, the Regular Democracy came rushing to McClellan's defense, denouncing his dismissal. As it was the General's firm belief that Stanton had betrayed him to the Radicals and sabotaged his plans, the Secretary of War was at once transformed into the blackest of villains by order of the Democratic press (which only recently had praised him as a hero). It was Stanton, they said, who had prevented victory on the Peninsula by holding back the necessary men and materiel. Nelson Waterbury, Grand Sachem of Tammany Hall, so advised his followers in a Fourth of July address.[33] Many others said the same. Appearing at a Washington Union rally, in August, President Lincoln spoke in Stanton's behalf. "The Secretary of War," he said, "denied no one thing at any time in my power to give him. . . . I stand here . . . to take upon myself what has been charged to the Secretary of War. . . ."[34]

Repeatedly on future occasions, as on this one, Lincoln would defend the record and ability of Edwin M. Stanton against the criticism of every hostile faction. Conservatives would later say that Stanton had failed to return the loyalty of his chief, but no substantial evidence can be found in support of this damaging contention. The greatest sense of comraderie appears to have existed between the President and the Secretary of War, and no act or sign on Stanton's part would seem to suggest the betrayal of that personal relationship. At any hour of the day or night, we are told, the Secretary was inclined to visit the White House, and the President the War Department (where they were known to have worked together, side by side, for hours, in the telegraph office). "There grew between them," observed Nicolay and Hay, "an intimacy in which the mind and heart of each were given without reserve to the great work in which they bore such conspicuous parts."[35]

The Harrison's Landing Letter was not an attack on Stanton but an attack on Lincoln, placing McClellan at one pole and Lincoln at the other. Forced to choose between them, Stanton chose Lincoln. The resulting division between Stanton and McClellan came quickly to embrace the growing controversy over West Point Academy, which was regarded by Senator Wade of Ohio and certain other Radicals as a "school for traitors." In keeping with the testimony of Democratic Major N. Buell Eldredge of the Seventh Michigan Infantry (an eyewitness to the Union disaster at Ball's Bluff), the Joint Committee on the Conduct of the War had ordered the arrest of Democratic General Charles P. Stone on charges of criminal incompetence. Stone was a West Pointer and his incarceration was another black eye for West Point. As the principle defenders of West Point in the Senate, War Democrats Nesmith of Oregon and McDougall of California were called upon to speak in Stone's behalf, with McDougall leading the way. In line with recent attacks on Secretary Stanton, McDougall blamed him for the mistreatment of General Stone and for the humiliation of General McClellan. Speaking for the Joint Committee, Wade of Ohio undertook the castigation of Stone, West Point, and Senator McDougall. In the process of debating the issues he was caustic, brutal, and domineering.[36] (It may be significant that following the exchange McDougall was never again as active in support of the Union cause.)

So far as immediate congressional action was concerned, Senator Wade carried the day on this occasion. But five months later Stone was released from custody and restored to command. The case against him was wholly circumstantial and not handled with much concern for his civil liberties. In the year 1862, however, many soldiers were getting court-martialed and even shot for acting as Stone was said to have acted. Looking back upon the event 32 years later, a northern journalist and on-the-spot observer made the following statement concerning Stone's conduct as an officer: "I will say I was impressed by his soldierly bearing but found him so thoroughly a 'martinet' and so loud in his praise of Lee and other West Point (Southern) officers, that I was not surprised when he fell under suspicion after the Ball's Bluff disaster. Very likely he was treated unjustly, but his injudicious speech and manner certainly 'provoked injustice.' " It is interesting to note that in discussing his misfortunes, following his release, Stone was not primarily critical of Stanton and/or the Joint Committee on the Conduct of the War. His wrath was largely reserved for his former friend, McClellan, for failing to properly defend him.[37]

President Lincoln was not involved in the arrest of General Stone, being out of Washington at the time. Nor was he officially involved in the arrest of Democratic Generals Fitz John Porter and William B. Franklin, later in the year, on similar charges brought by Secretary of War Stanton. Accused of failing to follow orders on the battlefield, Generals Porter and Franklin were both suspended from command and Porter was court-martialed and cashiered, January 1, 1863. Because Porter, Stone, and Franklin were pro-slavery officers and close friends of General McClellan, the idol of the pro-slavery Unionists, it has been argued that Stanton and the Radical leaders of Congress were involved in a Radical conspiracy to persecute them, for political reasons.[38] It must be remembered, however, that President Lincoln was not altogether removed from connection with any of these matters, even if all of them were the product of Stanton's actions and decisions. For Lincoln was requested to to intervene in behalf of every one of the defendants, and in each case refused.

As a matter of record, Lincoln was in favor of a hard-fisted policy in cases of this kind. It was well known that General Stone had publicly discussed the political aspect of the war in strong terms (as did also General Porter, writing frequently to Manton Marble, Democratic editor of the Conservative Union party organ, the New York *World*).[39] Lincoln did not care for such behavior on the part of his officers, regardless of their political alignment. Major John J. Key, an outspoken Radical, was dismissed from service, December 27, 1862, for saying the adminstration was not truly concerned about defeating the Confederacy. All that was wanted, Major Key declared, was reunion with slavery intact.[40] Conservative General James G. Spears of Tennessee was dismissed from the service in 1864, on the order of President Lincoln, for criticizing federal anti-slavery policy.[41] If prejudice were an issue in the case of General Stone, it was a prejudice that easily extended past the Radicals to Lincoln, because Stone was acting in a way that Lincoln disliked intensely. By refusing to intervene in Stone's behalf, the President was setting his seal of approval on the imprisonment ordered by Stanton, and the initial action taken by the Joint Committee on the Conduct of the War.

A major development in 1862 was the appointment of military governments over reoccupied sections of the Confederacy. The seizure of West Tennessee by the armies of Democratic Generals Halleck and Grant presented the opportunity of establishing a Unionist as Military Governor, and a likely candidate was War Democrat Andrew Johnson, Senator from and a former Governor of Tennessee. On March 4, Secretary of War Stanton received a letter from Assistant Secretary of War Thomas A. Scott, postmarked Nashville. Having spent a while in Tennessee, and having talked with a large number of local Unionists, Scott had concluded that Johnson was not the proper man to serve in the capacity of Military Governor. Many Tennesseeans feared "that he would choose to be somewhat vindictive and persecute them," Scott reported. It was widely believed among Tennessee Unionists that the feeling against Johnson in the state was so bitter that he could very well be assassinated. A large number of Tennesseeans who might accept Union rule under another governor would never accept it under Johnson, Scott declared.[42] Stanton chose to ignore the warning, and Johnson was at once appointed Military Governor, with the rank of brigadier general, and the same day resigned from the Senate.[43]

Assuming office in March, Johnson inaugurated his administration with a proclamation explaining his position and indicating his policy, couched in the conservative phraseology of the Crittenden Resolution. It was the duty of the President, he said, to protect and defend the Constitution and the laws and to suppress insurrection. The sole purpose of the military government in Tennessee was to aid in the prompt restoration of the state to the Union. A number of Tennessee Unionists were selected to serve in the capacity of state officials, and a special proclamation was issued, requiring municipal officers to swear allegiance to the federal government. The oath was tendered March 27, and was promptly rejected by the Mayor of Nashville and all members of the city council. Governor Johnson thereupon declared vacant the offices of the Mayor and the city council members and filled them himself by appointment, pending an election. The new council imposed the loyalty oath on all municipal officers, including the members of the board of education and all school teachers. To finish up the matter, the Governor ordered the arrest and imprisonment of the recently deposed Mayor for disloyalty and the utterance of treasonable and seditious language. In the same vein, the Governor suspended publication of several Tennessee newspapers in April, and ordered the arrest of one editor. In June, six ministers were accused of preaching secession in Tennessee and were tendered the oath of allegiance. Upon refusing to take the oath, all were imprisoned and all but one were escorted South, beyond the Union lines.[44]

Another War Democrat assumed control of former Confederate territory on April 28, when the augmented Army of New England paraded into New Orleans, behind the leadership of General Benjamin F. Butler. The city had fallen to a naval assault, supplied by Flag Officer David G. Farragut, but the northern Unionist press was fond of Butler and praised him as the hero of the hour. (Showing some news reports to a friend, Admiral David Dixon Porter growled, sarcastically, "Butler did it all!")[45]

Back in Washington, pro-slavery Democrats supporting the federal war policy in Congress were shaken, in the early months of 1862, by signs of the dreaded anti-slavery crusade. As of February, President Lincoln had done nothing to harm the slavery cause. The only significant anti-slavery measure signed into law was the Confiscation Act of August 6, 1861, affecting only slaves engaged in hostile military service; and even this had not amounted to anything. Testifying before the Joint Committee on the Conduct of the War, Democratic General Daniel E. Sickles revealed that the Army had not as yet received orders from the President to implement the Act.[46] On the heels of this announcement, administration policy was drastically revised, and Congress came alive with anti-slavery proposals. Previously assuming that Conservative Unionists would quit the Union cause, *en masse,* if the federal authorities moved against slavery in the loyal states, the President now concluded otherwise. With his approval, a measure was introduced in the House, looking to the compensated emancipation of all slaves in the District of Columbia. While this was in the works, another plan was set in motion to free the slaves in all the loyal border slave states, with the approval of the several state legislatures. To pacify Conservative Unionists alarmed by the threat of interracial mingling, the President would recommend in both cases the colonization of all slaves freed by virtue of federal influence.

Acting independently of the President, the Radical congressional leaders introduced the Second Confiscation Act, declaring free the slaves of all residents of every state resisting the federal authority, and a separate measure emancipating *without* compensation *all* slaves residing in the territories. The Second Confiscation Act was so worded as to apply not only to Secessionists, but to Unionists and foreigners as well. A new Article of War was proposed, forbidding the use of Union troops in the return of fugitive slaves to owners in arms against the Union cause.[47] The Article of War was based on precedents established by Democratic Generals Benjamin F. Butler and John E. Wool, acting in defiance of the Fugitive Slave Law.[48] The most dramatic anti-slavery proposal advanced in 1862 was the "State Suicide" theory propounded by Radical Senator Sumner of Massachusetts.[49] Conservatives saw in this—and quite correctly—a move to authorize the death of slavery in every corner of the land. Radicals applauded the State Suicide theory while Conservative Unionists denounced it. President Lincoln adopted the Conservative position, insisting that the Union was still intact, that no states were out of it, and that Congress had no right to establish any conditions of reconstruction. In this, he was supported by all the War Democrats in Congress, in 1862. (Senator Henderson of Missouri attacked the State Suicide theory on April 8; Congressman Lehman of Pennsylvania attacked it April 23.)[50]

Abolition of slavery in the District of Columbia was opposed not only by Unionist slaveholders in the District, but by those in Maryland and northern Virginia who feared the reaction of their own slave property. War Democrat Richard Wallach, Acting Mayor of the District, criticized the plan, in company with a majority of his Board of Aldermen, most of whom were Democrats and several of whom were slaveowners. They sought a champion in Congress and found one in War Democrat Joseph A. Wright, Senator from Indiana (recently arrived as a replacement for Peace Democrat Jesse D. Bright). Hostile to Secession and all it stood for, Wright had won appointment to the Joint Committee on the Conduct of the War, to fill the place of Andrew Johnson. But he happened to belong to that breed of anti-slavery men who were also anti-Negro, and was very worried about the mixing of the races. With this in mind, he came out vigorously against the creation of a free-Negro colony in the District of Columbia—for that was what was coming, he warned the Senate, if the District Emancipation Bill were enacted into law.[51] "I am no apologist for slavery," he said. "I am opposed to it by prejudice and by education. It has destroyed the Democratic party and through its destruction has paved the way for the destruction of our Government itself." On the other hand, "We [in Indiana] intend to have in our State, as far as possible, a white population, and we do not intend to have our jails and penitentiaries filled with the free blacks."[52] To emphasize his feelings on the subject, Wright presented a memorial from Mayor Wallach and the Board of Aldermen of the City of Washington, D.C., requesting that no legislation be passed with the object of attracting Negroes to the city. The wording of the memorial was highly insulting to the Negro race.[53]

In January and February the Maryland legislature enacted pro-war, pro-slavery resolutions denouncing federal interference with every aspect of the right to property in slaves, and issued an appeal to Congress aimed against the passage of the District Emancipation Bill. (A moving force in the pro-slavery actions of the Maryland Assembly was War Democrat James A.J. Creswell of Baltimore. As a reward for his Conservative performance, Creswell was offered and accepted the position of Assistant Adjutant General, on the staff of Governor Bradford of Maryland.)[54]

On March 10, President Lincoln invited the congressional delegations of the several slave states to confer at the White House on the subject of the Gradual Emancipation Bill.[55] In advance of the conference, Horace Greeley of the New York *Tribune* sounded a warning to the border slave states, that they accept at once the moderate principles of Gradual Emancipation or suffer the Radical effects of the impending Second Confiscation Act. War Democrat Congressman Crisfield of Maryland protested to Lincoln, in behalf of the slaveholding Unionists of Maryland. He would not be bullied, he declared. Lincoln denied that he was trying to bully anybody, and had no intention of threatening the Unionist slaveholders of Maryland. That was all the work of the Radicals, and none of his. Would he make that statement public? Crisfield inquired. Lincoln said no, he would not, and Crisfield left the White House in a state of indignation.[56] War Democrat Senator McDougall of California came to the defense of Congressman Crisfield, on the Senate floor, and Lincoln wrote to him, attempting to change his mind, but without success.[57] So far as McDougall was concerned, Emancipation was unconstitutional, whether gradual or compensated, or neither or both. The same position was taken by the Peace Democracy, which attacked the proposal as an outright betrayal of all Republican promises on the slavery issue. Abolition was here at last!

On March 12, the District Emancipation Bill passed the House, 89 to 31, with five War Democrats voting in the majority. Considered by the Senate April 2, it again was passed 32 to 10, with one War Democrat voting in the majority.[58] Slavery was dead in the District. Thoroughly aroused, a group of Maryland slaveholders met in Montgomery County, on the outskirts of Washington, to draw up resolutions denying the constitutionality of the District Emancipation Act. War Democrat Reverdy Johnson, Senator-elect from Maryland, issued a statement supporting the slaveholder's position and suits were instituted with the object of testing the law in the courts. Several cases were expected to reach the U.S. Supreme Court and Johnson was prepared to handle them in behalf of the plaintiffs.[59]

Over the next few months, President Lincoln promoted the interests of Gradual Emancipation, seeking its adoption by the several border slave-state legislatures, while the Radicals continued pressing for passage of the Second Confiscation Act. Meanwhile, slavery was abolished in the territories, March 13, *without* compensation to slave owners. On March 25 War Democrat Senator Henderson of Missouri observed that the Republicans appeared certain, in their Radical zeal, to drive away the help offered by Unionists of every other kind.[60] The Gradual Emancipation Plan was enacted into law April 2 with the blessings of four Democratic Congressmen and one Democratic Senator.[61] But despite congressional approval the program was doomed, for without exception the several legislatures of the loyal border slave states declared against it. Delaware appeared exceptional for a moment, when a pair of Democratic legislators declared in favor of the plan; but with success apparently in sight, a Unionist legislator deserted the administration cause, and Gradual, Compensated Emancipation was defeated in Delaware. (The War Democrats favoring Emancipation on Lincoln's terms were Assemblyman Jacob Moore and State Senator Wilson S. Cannon, both of whom were read out of the Democratic Party for their action in defiance of Conservative tradition.)[62]

In the U.S. Senate the Second Confiscation Act was subjected to attack by several War Democrats, including Senator McDougall of California. The principles involved were harsh, he said, and certain to "subjugate the South." He pleaded with Republicans to abandon consideration of the measure, saying, "It has pained me whenever, since my arrival, I have heard these subjects discussed."[63] War Democrat Senator Henderson of Missouri criticized the Second Confiscation Act because it was designed to work against *all* southerners, Confederates and Unionists alike. He favored judicial review of every case involving confiscation of slave property on charges of disloyalty. Without this provision, he said, the measure was clearly dangerous to civil liberties. War Democrat Wright of Pennsylvania voiced the same protest in the House,[64] and War Democrat criticism of the Act came to center on this very issue, with the Radicals refusing to yield. Contrary to his Conservative position concerning slavery in the District, War Democrat Senator Wright of Indiana endorsed the Radical position in the matter of the Second Confiscation Act. It was a good proposal, he said, and was certain to accomplish more for the Union cause than "an army with banners."[65] Another Democrat in favor of the Act was Congressman Noell of Missouri, a member of the Select House Committee on Confiscation. Taking the floor May 20 and 26, he commended Confiscation as the best means of punishing disloyal slaveholders who otherwise could not be reached by law.[66]

The Second Confiscation Act passed both houses of Congress and (despite the reading of a veto message) was signed into law. By seeking in this manner to confuse the issue as to his own position on a controversial matter, Lincoln had taken a stand less Radical than that of War Democrats Wright of Indiana and Noell of Missouri, both of whom had risked their careers in supporting Radical policy.[67] Within the matter of several weeks, however, the same "Conservative" Lincoln was to permit the beginning of an ultra-Radical military move—the arming of the slaves—and to take a forceful stand against his own Conservative promise to leave the cause of slavery alone. In one case, as a mask for Radical operations, he would utilize the services of War Democrats in carrying out the act; in the other case he would take the advice of a War Democrat turned Radical overnight.

Seeking to slow the progress of the anti-slavery cause, the Regular Democracy was trumpeting the phrase, "The Union as it was, the Constitution as it is." In Congress the Radicals long since had rejected the appeal and Conservative Republicans were beginning to. The Conservative Republican position was best expressed in a letter from Lincoln to War Democrat August Belmont, Chairman of the Democratic National Committee, written in July 1862. The time for patience was past, Lincoln said. "This government cannot much longer play a game in which it stakes all, and its enemies stake nothing. Those enemies must understand that they cannot experiment for ten years trying to destroy the government, and if they fail still come back into the Union unhurt."[68]

Acting on the same doctrine, as the agent of the President, War Democrat Edwin M. Stanton, Secretary of War, inaugurated a powerful attack against the slavery institution in the spring and summer of 1862. At his directions, Democratic General David Hunter assumed command of the Department of the South, and with his knowledge an order was released by General Hunter, calling for enlistment of troops among the slaves of the Sea Islands. When the contents of the order became public knowledge, General Hunter was declared an outlaw by the Confederate government, for rejecting the "rules of civilized warfare," which honor also was bestowed upon Democratic Captain Charles G. Halpine, Adjutant General on the staff of General Hunter, for having co-signed the order.[69] In Congress the order was subjected to attack by Peace Democrats and pro-slavery Unionists. Responding to the protests, the President issued a statement to the press, criticizing General Hunter and appearing to order the disbanding of his Negro force. Problems of military emancipation, he said, "are questions which, under my responsibility, I reserve to myself."[70] In effect, Lincoln was repudiating the policy of Stanton, his Secretary of War. It is interesting, however, that he did not remove Stanton from the War Department (as he had removed Cameron earlier under very similar circumstances, and relieved Fremont in the West for acting without orders). It is also worth noting that he did not remove General Hunter from command, nor actually compel him to disband the force in question![71] All this would seem to suggest that Secretary Stanton was acting in full accord with the wishes of the President and taking the blame for all complaints on the subject, as a Democratic "whipping boy"—a standard method of operation so far as

Lincoln was concerned; e.g., Cadwalader at Baltimore *(ex parte Merryman)*, Butler at Fortress Monroe (Contraband Theory), and Wool at Fortress Monroe (rejection of the Fugutive Slave Law.)

Even assuming that Stanton was acting independently of Lincoln's knowledge in the matter of Negro troop-raising (and for reasons unknown was permitted to retain his post), his change of position from pro-slavery to anti-slavery in 1862 cannot be regarded as anything unusual, coinciding as it did with the speed of Lincoln's own opinion changes on the same question. Nor was it any faster than that of many other Democrats in 1862. Editor John W. Forney, for example, was veering toward a pronounced Radical position. In the case of Hunter's policy, he gave his approval to Lincoln's actions of repudiation, but stated the opinion that if South Carolina were to remain disloyal Hunter's policy would have to be adopted.[72] On July 30 Lincoln was criticized by Forney in the *Press* for failing to encourage slave insurrections. With the progress of the war, Forney was to favor the raising of Negro troops, paying them on equal terms with white troops, and abolishing slavery by means of a constitutional amendment.[73] Stanton was certainly no more of a Radical than Forney; and other War Democrats were altering their position in similar fashion. As of spring, 1862, Senator John B. Henderson of Missouri and Senator-elect Reverdy Johnson of Maryland were still on record against the passage of strong anti-slavery legislation by Congress; but they were changing their minds. In June, the Missouri Constitutional Convention took up consideration of a bill proposing gradual, compensated Emancipation.[74] In December, Henderson would introduce a bill in Congress, providing federal aid to Missouri in the matter of Emancipation.[75] Immediately following the abolition of slavery in the District of Columbia, by act of Congress, Senator-elect Johnson of Maryland had declared against the action and offered to take the matter to the federal courts.[76] In the Thirty-eighth Congress, he would be numbered among the anti-slavery forces. The Radical transformation of Democratic General Benjamin F. Butler became apparent about the same time. While Democratic General Hunter was creating a sensation with his Negro troop recruiting program in the Carolinas, Democratic General Butler was writing Secretary of War Stanton from New Orleans that Negroes could not be expected to make good soldiers and that he, Butler, had plans for the enlistment of Louisiana whites in the Union cause, and not Louisiana Negroes.[77] He was to change his mind on this question, however—and very soon. Before five months passes he had revised his policy, calling for enlistments among the free Negroes in his department.

Quite clearly, a lot of Democrats were changing their minds about slavery and Negroes in 1862. Secretary of War Stanton, much criticized for this particular change of mind, was merely following a growing trend among Democratic Unionists. To the extent that he was moving toward Radicalism in 1862 so was his superior officer, Abraham Lincoln, who on July 22 discussed with the cabinet the merits of issuing a proclamation declaring free the slaves of all rebels in arms against the goverment. The discussion occured only fifteen months following the Sumter attack, revealing the swiftness of Lincoln's conversion from a staunch defender of slave property rights in wartime. Yielding to the Conservative protestations of Secretary of State Seward on this occasion, he would abandon his proposal for the moment—but only for the moment. News of the Proclamation proposal escaped the White House immediately, becoming overnight the major topic of political discussion in the loyal states. Conservatives began demanding that the President abandon the proposal, and Radicals began calling for its implementation. Lincoln, who had started the controversy himself (by his statement to the cabinet) was rendered unhappy by the resulting furor—or so he said. To War Democrat Senator Henderson of Missouri he complained that Radical leaders were all the time after him about the Proclamation.[78] But that did not prevent him from continuing his forward surge along an anti-slavery course, with the help of as many War Democrats as he possibly could muster in the nature of a smoke screen.

Pro-slavery sentiment was no stronger anywhere in the Old Northwest than Indiana, which was largely populated by southern immigrants and their children. In January 1862 the Indiana Democratic State Convention adopted a pro-slavery platform, and when the Union State Convention met in June, the slavery issue was utterly ignored in its platform declarations. Moving in defiance of home-state opinion, War Democrat Robert Dale Owen of Indiana, Assistant Secretary of the Treasury, wrote to Secretary of War Stanton the day following the Proclamation proposal, declaring full support for the President. Not only was Emancipation legal under the circumstances, Owen insisted, but legally required by the Second Confiscation Act within 30 days of its adoption. The Owen Letter was published in the press, to the rage and astonishment of Conservatives in general, and a similar letter by the same author was received by the President August 19, warning of the need to implement the Second Confiscation Act.[79] Five weeks later (despite his ponderous rejection of Horace Greeley's "Prayer of Twenty Millions") the President presented to the country the preliminary Emancipation Proclamation, promising freedom to the slaves of every slaveowner in arms against the federal government as of January 1, 1863. Radicals might protest the limited nature of the preliminary Proclamation, which had no bearing on the loyal slave states or those sections of the Confederacy already occupied by Union arms, but a signal fact emerged—As of January 1, 1863 the progress of the Union army meant death to slavery wherever it occurred.

Significantly, the acceptance of Owen's anti-slavery argument by Lincoln, in 1862, was matched by disapprobation of Greeley's anti-slavery argument. Again it would appear that the public support of a well-known Democrat was preferable, from Lincoln's point of view, to that of a Republican.

The success of Democratic Generals Grant and Halleck in West Tennessee as far south as Shiloh, aroused the long-suppressed spirit of the Tennesee Unionist minority. Shortly following his arrival in March, Military Governor Andrew Johnson arranged some Union rallies, and many who had previously withheld their public support of the Union now declared it. Typical was a gala gathering at Nashville, presided over by William Campbell, an Old-Line Whig and for many years the bitter enemy of Johnson. On this occasion they were wholly in agreement, speaking from the same stand in company with several Douglas leaders including William H. Polk (brother of the late President Polk) and General Ebenezer Dumont of Indiana.[80]

When Grant was threatened by the Confederate counterattack at Shiloh, in West Tennessee, he had called in his reserves under Buell and Wallace, stationed previously in Central Tennessee, leaving Nashville open to the danger of recapture. Following the battle of Shiloh, messages were dispatched to Buell by Governor Johnson of Tennessee and another War Democrat, Governor James F. Robinson of Kentucky, imploring his return. Confederate raiding parties were streaking through the Union-occupied areas of both states, and a Confederate army under General Edmund Kirby-Smith was moving through western Kentucky in the direction of Cincinnati. Reacting to the crisis, Governor Robinson proclaimed the existence of a state of emergency, calling on the people of Kentucky "to rise up as a man and strike a blow for the defense of their native land, their property, and their homes. . . . To arms! And never lay them down till the Stars and Stripes float in triumph throughout Kentucky."[81]

The defense of Cincinnati fell to Democratic General Lewis Wallace of Indiana, recently embarrassed by a poor performance in the battle of Shiloh. Overcoming panic in the city streets, Wallace established martial law, suspended all business, and raised a makeshift army of 72,000, which proved formidable enough to intimidate Kirby-Smith and to restore the reputation of General Wallace.[82] Still vulnerable, however, was the Union stronghold at Nashville, rendering precarious the position of Military Governor Andrew Johnson. Throughout the summer and fall of 1862 the city was constantly in danger of capture. When the Confederates appeared in force at the close of July they were advised by Johnson that the first shot fired at their instigation would be a signal for the demolition of every residence belonging to a known Secessionist. The Confederates thereupon pulled back, Nashville was saved from capture , and so was the Governor.[83]

The performance of Andrew Johnson as Military Governor of Tennessee was highly satisfactory in the eyes of President Lincoln. In July 1862, another War Democrat was selected to serve in a similar capacity: John S. Phelps, Congressman from the Missouri, appointed Military Governor of Arkansas. He was the "Father of the House," a veteran of nine consecutive terms in Congress, and a highly regarded pro-slavery Unionist. At the head of "Phelps' Regiment" he had saved the city of Springfield, Missouri, from capture early in the war, and had fought with skill at Pea Ridge. He entered Helena, Arkansas, toward the end of July and took up the reins of government in the midst of a hostile population.[84]

One more War Democrat confronted and surrounded by the enemy for most of 1862—politically as well as militarily—was Democratic General Benjamin F. Butler, commanding the Department of the Gulf. Upon arriving at New Orleans in April, Butler was directed to establish unquestionable federal authority, to seize and hold all roads, railroad lines, and waterways leading to the city (including the Mississippi River north of Baton Rouge), and to cooperate with the Navy in forcing the reduction of Mobile, Galveston, and Pensacola. Every matter was attended to as directed except the reduction of Mobile and control of the Mississippi north of Baton Rouge, both of which projects were abandoned on the order of the Secretary of War for want of needed reinforcements.[85]

In his first military encounter at New Orleans, Butler drove the enemy from its fortified position at Manchac Pass. The Confederates returned under General Richard Taylor with an all-out assault, which was wholly unsuccessful. Democratic Captain John B. Hubbard of Maine was engaged in the action as Chief of Staff to Butler's favorite subordinate, General Godfrey Weitzel.[86] Democratic Colonel Stephen Thomas of Vermont was involved, at the head of a Negro regiment.[87] Not only was the enemy beaten off but driven back beyond Donaldsonville, 82 miles away.[88] Dissuaded from further assaults against New Orleans itself, the Confederates next engaged Butler at Baton Rouge, with Butler's former leader, General John C. Breckinridge, heading the attack. Repulsed repeatedly with considerable loss, Breckinridge withdrew.[89] From Richmond, many miles away, Confederate President Jefferson Davis declared Butler a felon, deserving of capital punishment.[90] Confederate leaders were infuriated by Butler's presence in the heart of the South and by his continued success in battle. Governor Thomos O. Moore of Mississippi wrote to Jefferson Davis, protesting that "the army of Butler is insignificant in numbers, and the fact makes our situation more humiliating. He has possession of New Orleans with troops not equaling in number an ordinary city mob."[91]

Another War Democrat became a Military Governor in 1862—General George F. Shepley of Maine, appointed Governor of Louisiana on the order of General Butler. Yet in most major matters Butler continued in the role of dictator, as Commander of the Department of the Gulf. As his first political act, he demanded respect for the national flag and for his officers and men. For failing to provide it one Confederate partisan was hanged, many more were jailed, numerous businesses were closed down, and the ladies of New Orleans were smitten with the "Woman Order." Sensing in advance of Walter Reed the cause of Yellow Fever, Butler was successful in cleaning up the city and checking the disease. In the process of running municipal affairs he antagonized the foreign consuls of several European powers, who complained to their ambassadors in Washington. Another antagonizing factor was the arrival at New Orleans of Andrew Jackson Butler, brother of the General, who overnight became a businessman of consequence. Butler was rumored to be involved in all kinds of shady commercial operations. To check on the rumors, emissaries were dispatched to New Orleans, both by Secretary of State Seward and Secretary of the Treasury Chase. Seward's emissary was War Democrat Reverdy Johnson, Senator-elect from Maryland, Attorney General under Zachary Taylor, and a bitter personal enemy of General Butler. His report to Seward amounted to reams of hearsay and nothing more, coupled with warnings about Butler's recent conversion to Radicalism and his policy of raising Negro troops, about which Johnson had many excited things to say. If the policy were not instantly abandoned, Johnson wrote, the Union cause would soon be dead in New Orleans. Advised of the warning, President Lincoln observed: "I distrust the wisdom if not the sincerity of friends who would hold my hands while my enemies stab me. This appeal of professed friends has paralyzed me more in this struggle than any one thing."[92] In so saying, Lincoln was rejecting the major Conservative demand of the hour and standing with the Radicals. As usual, however, public attention was not focused on the President in this moment of Radical frankness. Rather, it was centered on another War Democrat—Benjamin F. Butler—busily engaged in the process of putting Radical executive policy to work.

Suddenly and without explanation, Butler was replaced in mid-December as Commander of the Department of the Gulf. Upon returning to Washington he consulted with Lincoln, Stanton, and Halleck, demanding an explanation for his recall without receiving any. Everyone denied responsibility in the matter, or even knowlege of who was behind it. Secretary of the Navy Welles protested to Lincoln in Butler's behalf, without avail. The Treasury agent investigating the General's financial operations in New Orleans reported to Secretary Chase that the reason for his recall was unknown to anybody in the Department of the Gulf.[93] (It is perhaps significant that this same investigator, in company with Reverdy Johnson, investigator for the State Department, failed completely in the search for valid evidence of improper economic operations on Butler's part.)[94]

A major development in the loyal states in 1862 was the spreading influence of two rival organizations: the Knights of the Golden Circle and the Union Clubs. The Knights were a secret body of Peace Democrats, organized initially for the sake of self-defense against the violence of Unionist mobs. All chapters were devoted to opposing the federal war policy and supporting the political aspirations of the Peace Democracy.[95] Many chapters were said to exist in every section of the loyal states, with an especially strong network in the Old Northwest.[96] Fearing the power of the Knights, some western governors called for creation of a home guard trained to stifle civil insurrection. War Democrat Governor Tod of Ohio was highly in favor of the plan, regarding it as vital to loyal-state security.[97] All such talk was denounced in the Peace press as nothing but Republican-Abolitionist propaganda, designed to frighten Republicans and old ladies and confuse the thinking of loyal Democrats. It was nothing, they said, but a full-scale scare campaign. Yet many believed otherwise, including many Unionists and many Disunionists, numbering in the hundreds of thousands.[98]

On the other side of the issue, the first Union Club was established in Kentucky in 1861, involving Unionists of all political parties favoring a "vigorous prosecution of the war."[99] Club members conceived plans and policies designed to assist the Union troops in battle and the Union party at the polls. By 1862 there were Union Clubs in many of the loyal states and sections of the disloyal states reoccupied by Union arms. The first free state involved in the Union Club movement was Oregon, where the Peace faction was especially vigorous and hopeful of success. Stigmatized in the Peace press as mere agencies of the Republican administration, the Clubs were defended as truly nonpartisan by many War Democrats, of whom the most vociferous were editors Asahel Bush of the Salem *Oregon Statesman,* attorney Addison C. Gibbs (a U.S. Port Collector under Pierce), and George H. Williams, former Chief Justice of the Territorial Supreme Court.[100] In the Northeast, the first Union Club of consequence was formed in Philadelphia in 1862 at the home of Democratic financier George H. Boker. Many other Democrats were numbered among the founders of the group.[101] The Union Club of New York City had its genesis in the U.S. Sanitary Commission (a forerunner of the Red Cross.) An early Democratic joiner and promoter of the New York City Club was General John A. Dix. Another was George Bancroft, only recently a leader of the "Soft Shells."[102] In Boston, an important Democrat involved in the early operations of the local Union Club was George B. Loring, postmaster of Salem under Pierce, and a leader of the Breckinridge campaign. (At the Charleston Convention it was Loring who nominated Breckinridge for President.)[103] For every ounce of anti-war spirit generated by Peace Democrats operating within the Knights of the Golden Circle, an equal amount of patriotic response was provided by War Democrats working with the Union Clubs.

The Knights of the Golden Circle were believed by Unionists to be largely involved in seditious campaigns to encourage desertions from and discourage enlistments in the Union army, and to sow the seeds of discord by means of propaganda. To cope with these and all related problems, two additional branches of the War Department were established in 1862 under the direction of the War Democracy. The Bureau of the Provost Marshal General, organized in July, was designed to check desertions and organize recruiting. (When full-scale Conscription began, in 1863, the Bureau was to oversee enforcement of the process.) Selected to direct the unprecedented and highly controversial operations of the Bureau, with the title of Provost Marshal General, was Democratic Colonel James B. Fry of Illinois (recommended by Democratic General U.S. Grant).[104] In September, the Office of the Judge Advocate General was established, to apprehend and prosecute all persons accused of disloyal activities in the loyal states. To run the Office, as Judge Advocate General of the Army, Secretary Stanton appointed Joseph Holt of Kentucky, Postmaster General and Attorney General under President Buchanan.[105]

At the height of the 1862 election campaign, during the latter half of the year, none but Democrats were seriously considered for appointment to major military command. In this period Henry W. Halleck became General-in-Chief, John A. McClernand was briefly in charge of the Army of the Mississippi, and George B. McClellan was returned to his position of authority in the Army of the Potomac. Also under consideration for a time as possible Commanders in place of McClellan were Democratic Generals Ambrose E. Burnside, who rejected the opportunity of command on this occasion, and Isaac I. Stevens, who was killed in action before he could be contacted. Upon returning to command, McClellan was to rise to the peak of his controversial abilities in the battle of Antietam.

Release of the preliminary Emancipation Proclamation following Antietam was a logical climax to the anti-slavery campaign which had dominated Washington politics all year long. Although regarded as too mild by certain of the Radical leaders, it was strong enough to horrify a large number of pro-slavery Unionists. The Democratic Chicago *Times* which had supported the war previously, declared, "The President . . . has no constitutional power to issue this proclamation—none whatsoever."[106] Many War Democrat newspapers reacted the same way. The Cleveland *Plain Dealer* announced that Lincoln at last had surrendered to Abolition counsels. For the *Plain Dealer* "to remain silent longer would be to give ourselves up, body and soul, to the servile insurrectionists, in which name we greet all who would bid the slaves rise and indiscriminately butcher the people of the South."[107]

The Cincinnati *Enquirer* threatened to desert the war, together with the Detroit *Free Press*, the Columbus *Ohio Statesman*, the New Albany (Ind.)

Ledger, the Salem *Oregon Statesman,* and many others. Less dramatically and rather offhandedly, General McClellan contributed a comment on the Proclamation. From his headquarters in Maryland, an order came forth reminding his troops that they had no right to criticize the acts and orders of the President. Discontent could only be expressed at the polls. Implicit in the order was the impression that the army was raging against the Proclamation, as McClellan had warned it would be in the Harrison's Landing Letter of July 7.[108] In taking such a stand McClellan was joined by a large number of backsliding War Democrats, some of whom theretofore were numbered in the forefront of the Union cause.

Acting on opposite principles, a large number of War Democrats rejected the Conservative position. Former Senator Henry M. Rice of Minnesota, a Breckinridge leader in the 1860 campaign, came out firmly in the Proclamation's behalf.[109] So did Matthew H. Carpenter, a prominent Douglas leader in the Democratic stronghold of Milwaukee, Wisconsin.[110] Having insisted, from the moment Sumter was attacked, that slavery was the cause of all the national ills, Carpenter sent Lincoln an excited, enthusiastic telegram, declaring: "The great transaction's done. Your immortality will be co-existent with that of Jesus of Nazareth. Nothing but your decree of emancipation could have saved the Republic."[111] For taking such a stand, Carpenter was invited to engage in a giant Union rally at Chicago, September 30, hailing the virtues of the Proclamation. Other speakers at the rally included Illinois Democrats Ebon C. Ingersoll, Robert S. Blackwell, Usher F. Linder, Stephen A. Goodwin, Henry Greenbaum (a Douglas elector), and Colonel Timothy O'Meara of the 90th Illinois Infantry.[112]

Sympathy for the Proclamation was to be found in unexpected quarters such as slave-state Missouri, where War Democrat Charles D. Drake expressed his approval in the face of heated warnings of servile insurrection. Having been a Douglas-man in 1860 and a conservative "Conditional Unionist" during the Secession crisis, Drake was now affiliated with the Radical "Immediate Emancipation" branch of the Missouri Union party. In supporting the Proclamation, he said he would be sorry if he did, in fact, encourage slave revolts. Even in that event, however, "Let the responsibility rest where . . . it rightfully belongs—upon [the] Confederates whose reason creates the terrible necessity." All patriots were implored to support the presidential policies.[113]

Another surprising statement of support appeared in the Democratic Carbondale *Press,* published in the pro-slavery "Little Egypt" section of Illinois. "We are in favor of using all the means God and nature have placed in our power for the ending of this rebellion, The *Press* declared. "We are in favor of confiscating every inch of soil, every dollar's worth of personal property, and every 'nigger,' big, little, old or young, belonging to those in arms against the government. We shall stand [by] the government in all her struggles, and endeavor to sustain the arms of the brave boys who are dying in our defense. Such is our politics."[114]

War Democrat John Geary, editor of the Columbus (Ohio) *Capital City Fact,* approved the presidential policy and made the observation, October 8: "It is now over two weeks since President Lincoln issued the Proclamation of Emancipation . . . which, it was stated by the [Columbus] *Crisis,* [Columbus] *Statesman,* and papers of the ilk, would disorganize the country, and yet we hear no complaint from the people, everything works as smoothly and harmoniously as before. Will those papers advise their readers of the fact?"[115]

Also acting in behalf of the Proclamation was a conference of governors meeting at Altoona, Pennsylvania, September 24. War Democrats in attendance included William Sprague of Rhode Island and David Tod of Ohio. A resolution adopted by the conference (and signed by Sprague and Tod) had praise for both the Proclamation and its author. A message was dispatched by those assembled to all the other loyal-state governors, requesting their approval of the conference resolution. Five provided their approval, including War Democrat Addison C. Gibbs of Oregon; five withheld approval, including War Democrat James F. Robinson of Kentucky.[116]

Every major military engagement occurring toward the close of 1862 involved Democratic officers of importance. The battle of Perryville, October 8, ended the career of General Don Carlos Buell, to the immense satisfaction of his critics, chief of whom were War Democrats Andrew Johnson, Military Governor of Tennessee, and John Geary, editor of the Columbus (Ohio) *Capital City Fact.*[117] In the East, the Army of the Potomac—now under the command of Democratic General Ambrose E. Burnside—experienced the terrible Fredericksbug defeat of December 13 in which the total Union loss was over 12,000 men, the Confederate loss, 5,200. The Peace press called loudly for an end to the slaughter. On December 18, six days following Fredericksburg, the House of Representatives voted on a Military Appropriations Bill. Only two Democrats voted against it, but 28 abstained in protest. Fifteen War Democrats and Conditionals voted in the majority. The bill was passed 107 to 3.[118] In the face of great carnage and periodic catastrophe, a great many Democrats were still adhering to the Union cause.

NOTES

1. In November, 1861, Colonel Biddle attacked the Republicans for bringing on the war. Publisher John Campbell of Philadelphia, who had campaigned for Biddle in a special Congressional election five months earlier, denounced him

now for confusing the issues. Republicans were not responsible for starting the war, Campbell declared, "but the leaders of the Democracy—the leaders of your party and of mine." Biddle had implied that Democrats were doing all the fighting. Campbell cited the Republican heroes Nathaniel Lyon, Edward D. Baker, and Elmer E. Ellsworth, all of whom had died for the Union. Philadelphia *Press,* December 2, 1861.

2. In the House there now were 17 War Democrats (14 Regular Democrats, three Unionists), 18 Conditional War Democrats, and 19 Peace Democrats. See Appendix 1.
3. Allen Johnson and Dumas Malone, eds., XX:553–54.
4. See Appendix 1.
5. *Congressional Globe* (37th Congress, 2nd session), pp. 10, 263, and 264.
6. Ibid., p. 15.
7. Ibid., p. 198.
8. Ibid., pp. 110, 146.
9. Ibid., pp. 208–11.
10. Ibid., p. 405.
11. According to Black, Stanton never took issue with Buchanan at any time. Henry Wilson and Jeremiah S. Black, *A Contribution to History. Edwin M. Stanton: His character and Public Services on the Even of the Rebellion, as Presented in a Series of Papers* (Easton, Pa.: Cole, Morwitz, 1871), p. 26.
12. Don Piatt, *General George H. Thomas* (Cincinnati, 1893), pp. 436–37; Benjamin P. Thomas, *Stanton,* passim; Benjamin P. Thomas, *Abraham Lincoln* (New York: Knopf, 1942), p. 297.
13. Richard W. Leopold, *Robert Dale Owen* (Cambridge: Harvard University Press, 1940), pp. 349–50.
14. Benjamin P. Thomas, *Stanton,* p. 158.
15. Alexander C. Flick, p. 133; Benjamin P. Thomas, *Stanton,* p. 338; George E. Turner, *Victory Rode the Rails* (Indianapolis: Bobbs-Merrill, 1953), pp. 56–58.
16. Ibid., pp. 56–58.
17. Stanton clearly was devoted to the nonpartisan Union war policy. When Radical Senator Lane of Kansas protested the presence of Democratic General James W. Denver as commander of Ft. Leavenworth, in April, and called for his replacement, Stanton flatly rejected the demand. Roy P. Basler, V:180, n.
18. Describing himself as a genuine Conservative, Henderson declared, ". . .I have yet to cast a vote for a man claiming to be a Republican; and unless their views upon this slavery question shall be changed, so that they are no longer the party of the present day, I expect never to cast a vote for one. But, sir, I have my rights in this country, and if the Republican party are Union men, all I can say is that I will not abandon the Union because they cling to it." Missouri State Convention, March 1861, *Journal and Proceedings* (St. Louis: G. Knapp, 1861), p. 89.
19. William D. Foulke, *Life of Oliver P. Morton,* II:104.
20. *Congressional Globe* (37th Congress, 2nd session), pp. 582–85.
21. Ibid., p. 585.
22. War Democrats voting for expulsion: Johnson of Tennessee, McDougall of California, and Henderson of Missouri (Union party). Six Republicans joined eight Democrats in the minority, opposing expulsion.
23. Richard W. Leopold, pp. 351, 357; Allen Johnson and Dumas Malone, eds., XX:560.
24. James H. Wilson, p. 73.
25. W. A. Neale, p. 27.
26. Stanton's frantic response to news of the Merrimac's operations was widely publicized in the Peace press and severely damaged his reputation for a time. Benjamin P. Thomas, *Stanton,* p. 185.
27. Allen Johnson and Dumas Malone, ed., VIII:9.

28. T. Harry Williams, *Lincoln and the Radicals* (Madison: Universtiy of Wisconsin Press, 1941), p. 70.
29. David Donald, ed., *Inside Lincoln's Cabinet; The Civil War Diaries of Salmon P. Chase* (New York: Longmans, Green, 1954), p. 57.
30. Donn Piatt, *Memories,* p. 76.
31. Allen Johnson and Dumas Malone, eds., XVII:519.
32. Don Piatt, *Memories,* p. 76.
33. E. Vale Blake, *History of the Tammany Society* (New York, 1901), p. 78.
34. Roy P. Basler, ed., V:359. Stanton was not merely the object of criticism by Regular Democrats, but by certain Conservative Republicans as well. In the 1860 campaign Gideon Welles was the Radical Republican leader in Connecticut. By 1862 he was a leading Conservative member of the Lincoln cabinet, and a strong critic of the Radical Joint Committee on the Conduct of the War. When Stanton came in, one of the first things he did was to make friends with Radical Senator Wade of Ohio, Chairman of the Joint Committee, and Welles was disgusted. In his famous diary (written partially in wartime and partially much, much later), he suggested that Stanton was toadying to the Joint Committee, in the hope of covering up numerous shortcomings in his administration of War Department affairs. Benjamin P. Thomas, *Stanton,* p. 151.
35. Benjamin P. Thomas, *Abraham Lincoln,* p. 296.
36. *Congressional Globe* (37th Congress, 2nd session), pp. 1667–68, 1678–79, 1732–42.
37. Laura Stedman and James M. Gould, eds., *Life and Letters of Edmund Clarence Stedman,* 2 vols. (New York: Moffatt, Yard, 1910), I:225.
38. Otto Eisenschimmel, *The Celebrated Case of Fitz John Porter* (Indianapolis: Bobbs-Merril, 1950); Ulysses S. Grant, "An Undeserved Stigma," *North American Review, vol. 135 (December, 1882): pp. 536–46;* Mary R. Dearing, p. 12; T. Harry Williams, pp. 46–47; 95–104; 175–76; 224–25; 248.
39. Basil Leo Lee, p. 45.
40. There would be no real fight to the finish, according to Major Key, because slavery was certain to be saved. Found guilty of expressing these remarks, the Major was cashiered. Requested to intervene, Lincoln refused, saying, "In my view it is inadmissable for any gentleman holding a military commission from the United States to utter such sentiments as Major Key is. . .proved to have done." Roy P. Basler, ed., V:442.
41. Oliver P. Temple, *East Tennessee and the Civl War* (Cincinnati: Clarke, 1899). It is worth noting that of all three Democratic generals accused of wrong doing by the joint committee, only Porter was court-martialed. The other two were merely inconvenienced and embarrassed in a way that was not reserved for pro-slavery generals alone. In July, 1863, Democratic General Robert Milroy was the darling of the Radicals, having issued a proclamation, at Winchester, Virginia, guaranteeing freedom to all slaves escaping to his lines. Manchester (New Hampshire) *Democrat and American,* January 22, 29, 1863. But that did not save him from rough handling by the War Department. Overwhelmed at Winchester and his division destroyed, he was treated in the same manner as Generals Stone and Franklin until (as in the cases of Stone and Franklin) the charges against him were proven false and he was permitted to return to action. The War Department was not given to mistreating pro-slavery Union generals during the war, merely Union Generals suspected of failing the Union cause.
   It is notable that in none of these cases did Lincoln intervene, even when requested. If there was any kind of a conspiracy afoot, Lincoln would have to have been a party to it, and (we have it on the word of hundreds of Conservative historians) Lincoln was not a Radical by traditional standards.
   Another Democratic general cast aside by the War Department was Don Carlos Buell, Commander of the Department of the Ohio, 1862–1863. James

Ford Rhodes, *History of the Civil War, 1861–1865,* edited and with an introduction by E. B. Long (New York: Ungar, 1961), p. 178, portrays Buell as the victim of Radical persecution. Actually, Buell was in trouble from the start with Republican Governor Oliver P. Morton of Indiana, who was not a Radical, and War Democrat Governor Andrew Johnson of Tennessee, who was only a Radical by Tennessee standards and not by northern standards during the period in which he was dealing with Buell. Morton's favorite general was the violent Negrophobe Jefferson C. Davis, who was politically Conservative. Johnson had no favorite general. But they both despised Buell, and their position apparently was not politically inspired. For full account of Johnson's quarrels with General Buell, see Clifton R. Hall, pp. 38–64.

42. Ibid., pp. 30–31.
43. Ibid., p. 31.
44. Ibid., p. 43.
45. Robert S. Holzman, p. 65.
46. Ralph Korngold, *Thaddeus Stevens, A Being Darkly Wise and Rudely Great* (New York: Harcourt, Brace, 1955), p. 171.
47. James G. Randall, *Civil War and Reconstruction,* pp. 480–81. In the House, only one Democrat voted for the new Article of War: Moses F. Odell of New York. *Congressional Globe* (37th Congress, 2nd session), p. 959. In the Senate, two War Democrats voted for the Article: McDougall of California and Wright of Indiana. Ibid., p. 1143.
48. Robert S. Holzman, p. 42; Le Grande B. Cannon, pp. 52–53.
49. James G. Randall, *Civil War and Reconstruction,* p. 710.
50. *Congressional Globe* (37th Congress, 2nd session), pp. 1569–75; 1795–96.
51. As a Congressman from Indiana in the Twenty-eighth Congress, Wright voted in favor of John Quincy Adams' resolution repealing the pro-slavery "Gag Rule" in the House of Representatives. From there, Wright went on to become the leader of the Anti-Extensionist Democrats of Indiana, as opposed to the Pro-slavery faction, headed by Jesse D. Bright. Ibid., p. 1468; Allan Nevins, *Ordeal,* II:454.
52. *Congressional Globe* (37th Congress, 2nd session), p. 1468.
53. Ibid., (37th Congress, 2nd session), p. 1496.
54. Charles B. Clark, p. 164; Maryland, *House Journal,* 1862.
55. War Democrats involved in the White House Conference of March 10, 1862, included Congressmen Crisfield and Thomas of Maryland; Senator Henderson of Missouri; Representatives Phelps, Noell, Price and Hall of Missouri; Brown of Virginia, and Clements of Tennessee.
56. Charles B. Clark, p. 162.
57. Caroline T. Harnsberger, Comp., *The Lincoln Treasury* (Chicago: Wilcox and Follette, 1950), pp. 87–88.
58. *Congressional Globe* (37th Congress, 2nd session), pp. 1179, 1192. War Democrats voting in favor of the District Emancipation Bill in the House of Representatives included Brown of Virginia, Clements of Tennessee, Cobb of New Jersey, Haight of New York, and Lehman of Pennsylvania. Following the signing of the law, a presidential commission was established to determine the proper amount of compensation to provide slaveholders affected by the Gradual Emancipation program. War Democrat Horatio King of Maine (Acting Postmaster General under Buchanan, now engaged as a lawyer in Washington, D.C.) was appointed to serve on the commission. Allen Johnson and Dumas Malone, eds., X:392.
59. Charles B. Clark, pp. 163–64.
60. While the War Democracy was complaining about the Radical nature of administration war policy, Abolitionists and Radical Republicans were denouncing it on opposite grounds. The Gradual Emancipation program was described by Garrison in the *Liberator* as a "cowardly and criminal avoidance of the one great saving issue, namely, the immediate suppression of the slave sys-

tem." Edith Ellen Ware, "Political Opinion in Massachusetts during the Civil War and Reconstruction," *Columbia University Studies in History, Economics, and Public Law* LXXIV, no. 2 (1916): p. 96. Radical Majority Leader Stevens of Pennsylvania characterized the plan as "milk and water gruel." Ralph Korngold, *Thaddeus Stevens,* p. 180.

61. Brown of Virginia (Union party), Clements of Tennessee (Union party), Cobb of New Jersey, Haight of New York, and Lehman of Pennsylvania. *Congressional Globe* (37th Congress, 2nd session), pp. 1179, 1192.
   Ibid., p. 1496. The lone War Democrat voting for the bill was Senator Wright of Indiana.

62. Harold B. Hancock, *Delaware during the Civil War* (Wilmington: Historical Society of Delaware, 1961), p. 100.

63. *Congression Globe* (37th Congress, 2nd session), Appendix, p. 65.

64. Ibid., pp. 1575, 1884.

65. Ibid., p. 1876.

66. Ibid., Appendix, p. 93.

67. Despite his speech in favor of the Second Confiscation Act, in May, Noell was not brave enough to vote for it in July, at which point he abstained. Ibid., p. 3268.

68. Roy P. Basler, ed., V:350.

69. Charles G. Halpine, *The Poetical Works of Charles G. Halpine. (Miles O'Reilly). Consisting of Odes, Poems, Sonnets, Epics, and Lyrical Works,* edited by Robert B. Roosevelt (New York: Harper and Bros., 1869), p. X.

70. Roy P. Basler, ed., V:219.

71. Hunter's Negro troops became the First South Carolina Colored Regiment, which went into action in November, 1862, raiding into Florida. Dudley T. Cornish, *The Sable Arm* (New York: Longmans, Green, 1956), p. 85.

72. Elwyn B. Robinson, "The Press. . . ," p. 168.

73. Ibid., p. 169.

74. Howard L. Conard, ed., *Encyclopedia of the History of Missouri,* A Compendium of History and Biography for Ready Reference, 6 vols. (New York: Southern History, 1901), V:168.

75. *Congressional Globe* (37th Congress, 3rd session), p. 138.

76. Charles B. Clark, pp. 163–64.

77. Dudley T. Cornish, p. 59.

78. Ralph Korngold, *Thaddeus Stevens,* p. 181.

79. Richard W. Leopold, p. 355.

80. Clifton R. Hall, pp. 47–48.

81. Thomas Speed, p. 219.

82. Irving McKee, p. 61.

83. John Savage, *The Life and Public Services of Andrew Johnson, Seventeenth President of the United States* (New York: Durby and Miller, 1866), p. 271.

84. Phelps was familiar with Confederate vindictiveness from past experience in Missouri, where bushwhackers had been raiding his farm periodically ever since the war began. Jay Monoghan, *Civil War on the Western Border* (Boston: Little, Brown, 1955), p. 272.

85. James Parton, *General Butler in New Orleans. History of the Administration of the Department of the Gulf, In the Year 1862.* (New York: Mason Bros., 1864), pp. 551–52; H. C. Williams, ed., *Biographical Cyclopaedia of Maine of the 19th Century* (Boston, 1885), pp. 284–86.

86. Ibid., p. 295.

87. Walter H. Crockett, III:p. 530.

88. H. C. Williams, ed., p. 286.

89. Ibid., p. 100. Secretary of War Stanton had promised Butler reinforcements, to bolster his position at New Orleans and Baton Rouge, but the Union defeat in the Peninsula campaign and the threat of a Confederate counterattack in the East prevented the keeping of the promise. James Parton, p. 551.

Despairing of reinforcements, following the Union victory at Baton Rouge, Butler decided against continued occupation of the city, concentrating his entire force at New Orleans. Robert S. Holzman, p. 100.
90. Ibid., p. 102.
91. Kenneth P. Williams, IV:5.
92. Ibid., IV:16.
93. Ibid., IV:106–8; Noah H. Plympton, *The Patriotic Services of Benjamin F. Butler* (Boston, 1896), p. 19.
94. Robert S. Holzman, pp. 91–93.
95. The Knights of the Golden Circle were succeeded in 1863 by the Order of American Knights and in 1864 by the Sons of Liberty. All three organizations were officially dedicated to protecting the civil liberties of the Peace Democracy and many members of the Knights of the Golden Circle became members of the other two organizations. Frank L. Klement, *The Copperheads of the Middle West,* passim. Wood Gray, *The Hidden Civil War: The Story of the Copperheads* (New York: Viking, 1942), pp. 163–64. The Sons of Liberty entered into an agreement with Confederate officials looking to the success of the Confederate cause, and all the former members of the Knights of the Golden Circle who joined the Sons of Liberty were allied thereby to the Confederate cause. James D. Horan, p. 134.
96. Wood Gray, pp. 91, 216; Ibid., p. 92.
97. Ibid., p. 91.
98. Ibid., p. 92; Edward C. Smith, p. 327; Mayo Fessler, "Secret Political Societies in Indiana during the Civil War," *Indiana Magazine of History* XIV, no. 3 (September 1918): p. 189.
99. Thomas Speed, p. 165.
100. Addison C. Gibbs became "Grand President" of the "Union League of America for the State of Oregon," which was organized December 14, 1863. Ibid., p. 223. George H. Williams was a member of the "Grand Council" of the League. Walter C. Woodward, p. 225.
101. Included among the original members of the Union Club of Philadelphia were Democratic leaders such as General George Cadwalader, banker Andrew J. Antello, Dr. John F. Meigs (father of Montgomery Meigs, the U.S. Commissary General), and importer Adolph Borie; also Daniel Dougherty, Thomas A. Biddle, Frederick Fraley, William D. Lewis and J. B. Lippincott. Elias P. Oberholtzer, *Philadelphia, A History of a City and Its People, A Record of 225 Years,* 4 vols. (Philadelphia: Clarke, 1912), II:372.
102. Henry W. Bellows, *Historical Sketch of the Union League Club of New York, Its Organization and Work, 1863–1879* (New York: Club House, 1879), pp. 5, 38–39, 50. In Philadelphia, the U.S. Sanitary Commission also served as a first step for many War Democrats in their wartime departure from the Regular Democracy. The Commission Chairman was Democratic banker John Welsh, who later joined the Union party. Other notable members included lawyer Nathaniel B. Browne and businessmen Adolph E. Borie, Theodore Cuyler, John Robbins, Frederick Fraley, and Charles Macalester, who also deserted the Democracy before the war was over. E. P. Oberholtzer, p. 381.
103. Murat Halstead, *Caucuses of 1860. A history of the Nation's Political Conventions of the Current Presidential Campaign* (Columbus: Follett, Foster, 1860), p. 224.
104. *Union army,* VIII:93.
105. Successive acts of the wartime Congress had made specific provision that disloyal activity should be punished by the civil courts as opposed to military tribunals. Republican Senator Lyman Trumbull of Illinois was author of congressional policy in this regard, as opposed to President Lincoln, who did not trust the civil courts, which were largely controlled by Democratic judges. By securing congressional endorsement of the Office of the Judge Advocate General, Lincoln defeated Trumbull, and went along as in the past, securing

arrests without the difficulties involved in the standard civil procedure. Allen Johnson and Dumas Malone, eds., IX:182.
106. Chicago *Times,* September 23, 1862.
107. Archer H. Shaw, *The Plain Dealer* (New York: Knopf, 1942), p. 145.
108. Perry Belmont, *The Recollections of an American Democrat,* 2nd ed. (New York: Columbia University Press, 1941), p. 124.
109. William W. Folwell, *A History of Minnesota,* 4 vols. (St. Paul: Minnesota Historical Company, 1924), II:341.
110. Frank A. Flower, *Life of Matthew Hale Carpenter* (Madison: Atwood, 1883), p. 208.
111. Ibid., p. 209.
112. Springfield *Illinois State Journal,* September 30, 1862.
113. Charles D. Drake, ''The Proclamation of Emancipation,'' *Speech,* delivered at Turner's Hall, St. Louis, January 2, 1862.
114. Carbondale (Illinois) *Press,* quoted in Columbus (Ohio) *Capital City Fact,* October 4, 1862.
115. Ibid., October 8, 1862.
116. William B. Hesseltine, pp. 257–61.
117. Columbus (Ohio) *Capital City Fact,* October 28, 1862.
118. *Congressional Globe* (37th Congress, 3rd session), p. 130.

9

Lincoln Bows to the Radicals: Elections of 1862

Expecting victory in 1861, only to be beaten by a Union coalition composed in large part of their own kind, Democratic party leaders were hopeful of reestablishing "Democratic regularity" in 1862, with the help of a few well-chosen campaign issues. The military arrest of civilians, accepted as necessary in the early months of war, was no longer so regarded by a large number of Democrats who also objected to federal suspension of Democratic newspapers and mob attacks on Democratic newspaper offices (allegedly inspired by Republican propaganda). Some Democratic orators would talk about the tariff and its disadvantage to farmers. Others would talk about the wartime economic crisis, with special attention directed to rising railroad rates (said to be the product of Republican rule). But almost every Democrat would have a word to say about those two great issues: slavery and race.

Administration plans for Compensated Emancipation (made public in the spring) and rumors of a pending presidential Emancipation Proclamation (coming true in September) enflamed the minds of many Democratic spokesmen. Freedom for the slaves would mean a black invasion of the North, they said, and total disruption of the American economic system. The job of every white mill hand and miner and dock worker was now in danger. The blacks would work for less and wreck the northern labor market. Moreover, they were certain to go after the white females of the North. These were the major arguments of the Regular Democracy in the elections of 1862.

The campaign began in New Hampshire, where both parties held their state conventions in January, in preparation for general elections taking place in March. The leader of the Douglas Democracy in New Hampshire was Walter Harriman, editor of the Manchester *Union*. The leader of the Breckinridge Democracy was former President Franklin Pierce.[1] A vigorous, united Democratic campaign in 1859 had threatened the Republican control of New Hampshire, established initially in 1856. A shift of only 1,800 votes in 1859 would have returned the Democrats to power, and hope had revived to flood the hearts of Harriman and Pierce and all their followers. But party unity collapsed the following year when Pierce refused to work for Douglas. Thus divided, the New Hampshire Democracy was easily defeated by sizable majorities in the general elections of 1860 and 1861.[2]

When the war began, Pierce announced in favor of the Union[3] and the entire Breckinridge Democracy endorsed his position, in concert with Harriman and the Douglas faction. The unity lasted a little over two months, at which point a majority of the Democratic members of the state legislature declared against the "subjugation" of the South.[4] The Manchester *Union* expressed the dismay of War Democrat Harriman in whose opinion a vote for "no subjugation" amounted to a vote for the Confederacy and nothing less.[5] Speaking for the Peace cause, the Concord *Patriot* came out against "Mr. Lincoln's war for the subjugation of the South," condemning the President for "hurling our men upon certain defeat and death at Bull Run."[6] The Concord *Standard* (Breckinridge) also declared against the war. When Union troops returning from Virginia and defeat were subjected to ridicule in the pages of the *Standard*, a mob of Unionists assembled and stormed its offices, smashing the press and furniture and scattering the type.[7]

Embarrassed by expression of the Peace philosophy in the guise of Democratic party line, War Democrats in New Hampshire declared in favor of Militia General George Stark to head the state ticket in 1862. The Douglas candidate for Governor the year before and the principle organizer of New Hampshire's first volunteer regiments, Stark was easily the best-known War Democrat in the state. The Peace Democracy announced in behalf of John H. George, a former Chairman of the Democratic State Committee and a dedicated follower of Congressman Vallandigham. The Democratic State Convention was wholly in the control of the War faction and Stark was nominated on a platform hailing the pro-slavery Unionism of the Crittenden Resolution.[8] At the Republican convention, Radical Governor Nathaniel Berry was renominated for a second term, over the protests of the Conservative minority.[9] Rejecting both tickets, a coalition of War Democrats and Conservative Republicans staged a Union Convention at which Democratic Assemblyman Samuel M. Wheeler was nominated for Governor. The Union platform repeated, word for word, the Democratic plank concerning the Crittenden Resolution.

The Regular Democracy ran a strong campaign in New Hampshire and for a time it was believed they might carry the state on the strength of complaints about Union military reverses alone. This was seemingly prevented by the Union victories at Ft. Henry, Ft. Donelson, and Roanoke Island, which considerably reinforced the Republican position. As it turned out, the Republican state ticket squeaked in with a majority of less than 1,900 out of sixty-two thousand cast, War Democrat Wheeler getting only 1,709 votes running as a Union independent.[10] But the Wheeler candidacy was by no means unimportant. Had all the "Union" votes gone for Stark, the Regular Democrats would have finished close enough to call for a recount, to the distinct embarrassment of the Lincoln administration.

Of greater importance was the impact of the Union party movement on the Connecticut elections, taking place in April. Connecticut had not chosen a Democratic Governor since 1853.[11] But half the state delegation in Congress was Democratic, the usual Republican margin of victory was small,[12] and Republicans were decidedly worried about their chances of success in 1862. Especially alarming was the fact that Democratic victory in Connecticut was certain to be viewed as a mandate for Peace, since the most prominent Democrat around was Thomas H. Seymour who was openly against the war, having been so from the start. Seymour was the last Democrat to serve as Governor of Connecticut (1850–1854) and a first-class political organizer. In the 1860 presidential canvass, Breckinridge had done surprisingly well in Connecticut with Seymour running his campaign, receiving almost as many votes as Douglas and besting him in half the counties in the state.[13] The Breckinridge faction took control of the Democratic State Convention of 1861 and forced the selection of their candidate for Governor: James C. Loomis, a pro-slavery lawyer and a close friend of Seymour. He was defeated in the general election by only 2,000 votes.[14] As time approached for the 1862 campaign it was clear that Seymour still controlled the Democratic organization and still opposed the Union cause. War Democrats were powerless to alter this state of affairs from within the party organization itself. Accordingly, they turned their attention to plans for creation of a Union party.

On December 10, 1861, a political circular was dispatched to War Democrats throughout Connecticut by Douglas leader James T. Pratt, serving currently as Adjutant General on the staff of Republican Governor Buckingham. (Having run for Governor on the Democratic ticket in 1858 and 1859, and led the Douglas forces in the 1860 state campaign, "General" Pratt was a clear, unqualified spokesman of the Democratic faith.) His circular declared "the time has come when true friends of the Union should rally as one man, irrespective of past party lines . . . and to this end it is proposed to hold a Mass Convention of those favorable to a 'Union' organization."[15] It would appear that the circular was composed in cooperation with the Governor, who was a Radical; for, contrary to Radicals in most other states, those in Connecticut were inclined to favor the Union party proposal while the Conservative Republicans required a good deal of coaxing before agreeing to it.[16]

A Union party convention was held in Hartford, January 8, General Pratt was the presiding officer, and the Radical influence was heartily deemphasized. Of the two-hundred delegates in attendance not one was a well-known Radical. Douglas elector Frederick Croswell was an active participant, and War Democrats dominated the proceedings. A ticket was drawn up, including all the Republican incumbents except the Lieutenant Governor and Treasurer. For these positions the convention nominated a pair of Democrats: Roger Averill and Gabriel W. Coite. The Union party platform made no mention of slavery.[17] When the Republican convention assembled in Hartford the following week several delegates denounced the actions of the Union party. When the nominations were reported, however, they corresponded exactly to those on the Union slate.[18] At the Democratic State Convention the Peace faction proposed renomination of Breckinridge leader James C. Loomis, narrowly defeated in 1861. War Democrats in attendance favored Douglas leader John T. Waite. Loomis was chosen on the first ballot and Waite went over to the Union party, along with many of his followers.[19] To a very large extent the Connecticut campaign boiled down to a contest for the blessings of the War Democracy, which was easily captured by the Republican-Union coalition. In the vote for Governor, Buckingham received a majority of more than 9,000 votes, as opposed to only 2,000 the previous year.[20]

The April elections in Rhode Island also featured the appearance of a Union party label, but here the name had different connotations. Instead of meaning "anti-Peace," as in most other states, in Rhode Island the title stood for "anti-Radical." In 1855 the Know Nothings had carried the state and the following year, renamed "Americans," had formed a coalition with Republicans. The same arrangement prevailed through 1859 under Conservative leadership. When Radical control was established at the 1860 Republican State Convention the Conservatives bolted, throwing their support to Democrat William Sprague, the "Cotton King of New England," owner of numerous cotton mills and one of the richest men in the country. Sprague obtained the additional backing of a "Young Men's" convention opposing Radical policies. The Democrats seized upon the opportunity, nominating Sprague for Governor on a Fusion ticket including two other Democrats and two Republican-American incumbents. The 1860 Fusion ticket was easily elected.[21]

As Governor (1860–1862), Sprague had effected repeal of Rhode Island's Personal Liberty Law of 1848, supported Douglas for president,[22] endorsed the federal war policy, and secured an iron grip on the Rhode Island political situation. He was very young, rather short, and supposedly not very bright.[23] But he established a Democratic stronghold in New England for the first time since 1854, and it would prove impossible to knock him out of office. During the Secession crisis he ran for reelection on a "Constitutional Union" ticket identical to the Fusion ticket of 1860.[24] James Y. Smith, the Republican candidate for governor, was a Radical and a strong warhawk, but Sprague was a warhawk, too. On voting day, Sprague was reelected with a majority of 1600 votes out of 22,000 cast.[25]

The wartime policies of Governor Sprague delighted the Conservative Republicans and even satisfied the Radicals. In the 1862 gubernatorial campaign no Republican state ticket was named to run against him. War Democrats elected as "Conservatives' and "Sprague Unionists" established a 45–27 majority in the Assembly and a 17–15 majority in the State Senate.[26] When the legislature convened in May, Sprague was the Democratic candidate for U.S. senator and was elected to succeed James F. Simmons, Conservative Republican, whose term would expire in March, 1863. (Before the year was out Senator Simmons became embroiled in a war contracts scandal and decided to resign. He was replaced in August by Lieutenant Governor Samuel G. Arnold, a War Democrat and a veteran of the march to Washington's defense in April 1861.)[27]

A major political development occurred in June when the people of Illinois voted on five proposals advanced by the State Constitutional Convention of 1862. Thoroughly controlled by the Peace faction, the Convention had attempted to embarrass the Republican party by playing up the race issue whenever possible and emphasizing economic problems. Acting on precedent established by the Missouri State Constitutional Convention of 1861–1862, the Illinois Convention assumed in large degree the powers of a legislature. On this basis action was taken to ratify the pro-slavery Thirteenth Amendment enacted by the Thirty-sixth Congress, and a resolution was seriously considered to select a new Senator in place of Orville H. Browning, recently appointed by Republican Governor Yates. Extralegal orders and directives were issued by the Convention, criticizing the policies of the Governor, both civil and military.[28]

War Democrats in general were embarrassed by the Convention, which they assailed as the agent of anarchy and Confederate propaganda. Nathaniel Paschall of the War Democrat St. Louis *Missouri Republican* was especially critical, accusing the Convention of usurping the powers of the legislature. It was altogether different in Missouri, Paschall insisted, because Missouri had no regular form of government. But Illinois was not afflicted with any such problem, and had no need for extra-legal legislative policies.[29] Out of 75 delegates attending the Illinois Convention, 55 were Democrats, 39 of whom voted in approval of the pro-slavery Constitutional Amendment enacted by the Thirty-sixth Congress. The vote to ratify was carried, 39 to 23, but not without a protest by six War Democrats, who joined the Republicans in the minority, declaring that the only bodies entitled to decide on such matters were state legislatures, and conventions elected specifically for the purpose.[30]

During the critical period of April-May 1861, state funds were overextended by Illinois officials, and the action was seriously criticized by the 1862 Convention. Here again the War Democracy demurred. Editor James W. Sheehan of the Chicago *Post* observed that "We opposed Governor Yates' election; . . . but as party men . . . we should never venture to arraign him as false to his official obligations because he necessarily incurred liabilities to feed and clothe the troops of Illinois, when there was no one else to do so."[31]

Democratic officers of troops in the field were besieged with questionnaires signed by the Convention President, General James W. Singleton of the State Militia. Some of the officers were disturbed by the investigation and said so. In the view of Democratic Colonel Gilbert W. Cumming of the 51st Infantry, all inquiries of such nature were completely outside the powers of the delegates.[32] Democratic Major Quincy McNeil of the Second Cavalry replied, "Should I give you the information the resolution calls for, I should make as great an ass of myself as the convention has of you, by asking you to attend to that which is none of your business. . . . If I am rightly informed, you were elected to make a [constitution] for the state of Illinois. Why the hell don't you do it?"[33]

Setting forth the central argument of the Peace Democracy, the Convention passed a resolution absolving the South of all responsibility for the condition of the country and blaming the Republicans instead.[34] In keeping with standard political tradition, a giant gerrymander was arranged to the advantage of the Democratic party, together with a change of law requiring the election of a Governor every other year as opposed to every four. (The purpose here was clearly the removal of Governor Yates in November 1862.)[35] Economic difficulties of every kind were attributed to the state administration, from rising railroad freight rates[36] to the Bank Panic of 1861. (Out of 112 banks operating in Illinois in March 1861, only 17 survived the Panic.[37] In a burst of economic radicalism, the convention resolved against the chartering of any new banks ever in the future, under Illinois law.)[38] Seizing also on the race issue, the Peace faction proposed a constitutional change forbidding the entrance of free Negroes into Illinois, and another denying the franchise to Negroes already residing in the State.[39]

Of the several War Democrats attending the convention, the outstanding speakers were Norman Purple (a Breckinridge elector), Milton S. Bartley, and John W. Paddock.[40] When the convention adjourned, March 24, all three returned home to work against adoption of the new constitution and Paddock was especially active, speaking all over the state. Bartley staged a spirited campaign in his own district, denouncing the convention as an affront to the people of Illinois and declaring his conversion to the Union party.[41] Accepting the arguments of the War Democrats and other Unionist leaders, the people of Illinois voted down the proposed constitutional changes with the exception only of those aimed against the Negro (barring Negroes from the state and blocking Negro suffrage). The anti-bank proposal barely was defeated, by 2,000 votes out of 266,000 cast.[42]

Another vote was held in June in Oregon, where once again the Union party movement was effectively employed. Antebellum Oregon was a Democratic state in which Republicans were invariably outnumbered, two-to-one. As elsewhere the Lecompton issue had intervened in 1860, giving Oregon to Lincoln. In Pacific Coast tradition the Breckinridge party was strong in Oregon, under the leadership of General Joseph Lane, former Governor, former Congressman, and Vice Presidential candidate on the Breckinridge ticket, at whose direction an effective Democratic machine had been established in the 1850s with headquarters at Salem. It was known as the "Salem Clique," and all its officers held federal positions under Pierce and Buchanan.[43] During the Lecompton dispute, Lane came out in favor of Buchanan against the interests of Stephen A. Douglas. But the Salem Clique announced for Douglas and when Oregon became a state in 1859 slavery was outlawed by the constitutional convention, to the dismay of General Lane. The convention was controlled by the Douglas faction. When Lincoln carried Oregon in 1860, the Breckinridge-Lane forces blamed the outcome on the Douglas forces, calling them "Mullatoes," and accusing them of working secretly in Lincoln's behalf. (Actually, the problem was that the Breckinridge-Lane faction could not forgive the Douglas faction for past differences and by opposing all offers of compromise finally destroyed their own bargaining position. Two U.S. Senators were elected in Oregon in 1861. After many ballots the Douglas leaders [tiring of Breckinridge inflexibility] arranged an alliance with the hated Republicans, who agreed to run their most Conservative man: Edward D. Baker. The Douglas-Republican coalition unseated Senator Lane and one of his pro-slavery colleagues in favor of Baker and Douglas leader James W. Nesmith.)[44]

In Oregon as in California the Douglas faction came out quickly for the war, the Breckinridge faction playing possum for a few weeks, then coming out against it. Well in advance of Bull Run, Democratic Governor Whiteaker of Oregon was attacking the federal war policy[45] and the Peace press was urging him on. In Washington, Democratic Senator Nesmith voted steadily for the war while in Oregon the Douglas forces were aiding the formation of nonpartisan "Union Clubs" all over the state.[46] Pro-Union activity was sponsored by the Salem Clique and the War Democrat press, of which the leading examples were the Salem *Oregon Statesman,* the Portland *Times,* and the Jacksonville *Sentinel.*[47]

The Peace press of Oregon was unrestrained in its forthright condemnation of the wartime Union cause. So frankly pro-Confederate was the Albany *Democrat,* for example, that it was quickly barred from the mails by order of the Postmaster General.[48] Equally anti-Union was Breckinridge leader Benjamin Stark, a vocal proponent of Secession (for the South and Oregon as well). Following the death of Republican Senator Baker at Ball's Bluff in the fall of 1861, Stark was appointed his replacement on the order of Governor Whiteaker. Editor Asahel Bush of the War Democrat *Oregon Statesman* denounced the appointment as an outrage, describing Stark as "a Secessionist of the deepest dye and the craziest professions—a traitor as infamous as any that disgraces Northern soil."[49] Despairing of working with the Governor, Bush renounced affiliation with the Regular Democracy in October 1861, declaring in favor of a Union party coalition. In January 1862 a call went out for a Union state convention, signed by several important Republicans and equally important Democrats. The convention assembled at Eugene in April, and a coalition ticket was selected to stand upon a War platform devoid of anti-slavery principles. Democrat Addison C. Gibbs, a Port Collector under the Pierce administration, was nominated for Governor. Harvey Gorden, another Democrat, was nominated for State Printer. The nominations for Secretary of State, Treasurer, and Congressman-at-large were allotted to Republicans. War Democrat George H. Williams, former Chief Justice of the Territorial Supreme Court, declared privately that the Democrats came away from the convention with all the best offices.[50]

The Regular Democracy of Oregon ran a War Democrat for Congress and a Peace Democrat for Governor on a platform castigating the Democratic members of the Union party coalition, calling them "so-called Democrats" acting in collusion with "Abolitionists" who not only wanted to free the slaves but had hopes of giving them the vote.[51] The Union ticket had the strong backing in the following campaign of the Salem Clique and many other Douglas leaders, including George H. Williams and State Senator Luther Elkins. Among Breckinridge Democrats, some Union party converts were Matthew P. Deady, a recent candidate for the U.S. Senate and a former Chief Justice of the Territorial Supreme Court; also Justin Steinberger, a delegate to the Charleston and Baltimore Conventions.[52]

Lincoln's victory in Oregon was the result of a mere plurality but the Union ticket of 1862, headed by a Democrat, received a clear majority of 3,589 and captured control of the legislature.[53] Later in the year the new legislature rejected the services of U.S. Senator Benjamin Stark, previously appointed by Governor Whiteaker, in favor of War Democrat Benjamin F. Harding, Democratic Speaker of the Assembly, [54] elected with the backing of Douglas Democrats and Republicans combined.

Two more Unionist coalitions were heard from in the September elections of California and Vermont. On May 7 the Republican State Committee of California invited the Douglas State Committee to join in the call for a joint convention. The proposal was ignored by the Douglas State Committee but agreed to by a large number of Douglas Democrats acting on their own. Douglas leader Walter Van Dyke presided at the "Union Administration" Convention and William Higby, a member of the Douglas State Committee, was present as a delegate. A great many other Democrats were also in attendance, assisting in the nomination of a Republican candidate for Superintendent of Public Instruction.[55] When William Higby was expelled by the Douglas State Committee for working with Republicans, eight other committee members handed in their resignation, declaring their allegiance to the Union party cause.[56] With the strong support of many Douglas men, the Union ticket coasted home to victory in California with a majority of 14,000 votes. A Democratic majority in the legislature was transformed in this moment to a small minority.[57]

The outcome of the California elections finished the Senatorial career of one War Democrat—Breckinridge leader Milton S. Latham—while launching that of still another—John Conness, the Douglas candidate for Governor in 1861. The expiration of Latham's term in January 1863 led to an election involving Conness and three Republican opponents. The Union majority in the legislature was almost entirely Republican and when the voting for Senator began Conness was far behind. A deadlock developed, however, lasting for many weeks, and before it was over the Republican candidates had embarrassed each other through mutual recrimination. In this manner Conness was permitted to emerge as the leader in the struggle. As a final solution to the deadlock he was nominated by the Union caucus and elected by the Union majority.[58]

Irritated by the presence in Vermont of an anti-Republican Union party in the 1861 campaign, Republican leaders there decided to appropriate the "Union party" label in the hope of attracting the War Democracy. Throughout the summer of 1862 many War meetings were held in Vermont at one of which a call was issued in the name of the Republican State Committee for a Union convention, irrespective of party affiliations. The convention assembled under the chairmanship of a Breckinridge Democrat—Stoddard B. Colby—and a nonpartisan ticket was selected, featuring the incumbent Republican Governor Frederick Holbrook, with Douglas-elector Paul Dillingham the choice for Lieutenant Governor. As the Regular Democratic candidate for Governor the year before, Dillingham had devoted considerably more time to attacking the independent Peace ticket, headed by Benjamin H. Smalley, than he had to attacking the Republicans. At the 1862 Democratic state convention, attended mainly by the Peace faction, Smalley obtained the gubernatorial nomination without difficulty. Only three Democratic newspapers in Vermont supported the Regular Democratic ticket, the rest supporting Holbrook, Dillingham, and the Union slate which carried the state, 30,000 to 4,000.[59]

In Maine, as elsewhere in 1862, the Union party advocates consisted largely of the War Democrats and the Conservative Republicans, as opposed to the Peace Democrats and the Radical Republicans, who favored party regularity. Republican editor James G. Blaine of the Kennebek *Journal* and Democratic editor Ephraim K. Smart of the Rockport *Democrat* were hopeful of arranging a Union coalition, and both as journalists and as members of the legislature worked mightily with this object in mind.[60] They had expected to enlist the services of the Republican State Convention but were caught up short when a leading Radical, Abner Coburn, was chosen as the Republican candidate for Governor. Turning next to the Democrats, the Union party forces were once again discomfited. The Douglas State Convention of 1862—like that of 1861—erupted in a factional dispute between the War and Peace Democracies, and nothing could be done to effect a coalition with Conservative Republicans. Convention delegates John A. Peters and Albert G. Jewett delivered angry diatribes against the Peace Democrats and all candidates acceptable to them. The War faction proceeded then to steamroll the Peace faction. Jewett reported strong pro-war resolutions which were duly passed. McClellan was still engaged before Richmond and a resolution was adopted praising his performance. The Peace Democrats were cited in the same resolution as "wicked and scheming politicians who are endeavoring to undermine [McClellan] and weaken him and his army in their brave efforts for the vindication of the Union."[61] War Democrat John A. Peters moved the nomination of General Charles D. Jameson for Governor. The name of Bion Bradbury, a Conditional War Democrat and a major Douglas leader in Antebellum times, also came before the delegates; but Jameson was nominated, 166 to 106.[62]

At five Democratic congressional district conventions, the Peace faction prevailed in three, the War faction in two. Peace leaders were still interested in reestablishing party unity, but the War faction would not have it. In every district where a Peace man obtained the regular Democratic nomination, the War faction placed an Independent in the field.[63] Striking back, the Peace faction nominated a separate state ticket headed by Bion

Bradbury, a federal official under Pierce and Buchanan, and a major Douglas leader. The Peace platform called for compromise and Peace negotiations.[64] As in the case of the 1861 elections, the Democratic newspapers in Maine were divided.

But many more supported Bradbury than the number supporting Dana the year before.[65] The Union defeat at Second Bull Run, in August, the threat of conscription, and talk of proposed Emancipation measures dominated the Democratic campaign propaganda, and proved a highly effective combination. The Republicans won, but their 17,000 vote majority of 1861 was shaved to 6,000 and a Douglas supporter won a seat in Congress, defeating a Republican incumbent. The winner, War Democrat Lorenzo D. M. Sweat, was the first Democratic Congressman elected from Maine since 1854. In state contests, the Peace party registered a startling gain, receiving 32,000 votes against only 7,000 for the War Democracy. (The year before the War Democrats had come out ahead, 21,000 to 19,000.) The Republican majority in the legislature was reduced by several seats and Douglas leader John A. Peters was elected to the State Senate as one of twelve "War Democrat" Independents.[66]

Release of the preliminary Emancipation Proclamation, September 22, set the stage for the October and November elections and it would afterward be said that a great many voted then for outright repudiation of the federal war policy, in protest against the Proclamation. There is no real evidence supporting the contention and a great deal of evidence to the contrary. Seven states which had voted for Lincoln two years before went Democratic in October and November: Ohio, Indiana, and Pennsylvania (October); New York, Illinois, Wisconsin, and New Jersey (November). In no case, however, was the Peace cause triumphant. Nobody talked about repudiation of the war until *after* the votes were counted. Prior to that moment the War Democrats and Conditionals controlled the destinies of the Regular Democracy and it was their platform—a pro-war platform—that a large majority of anti-Administration voters supported in 1862.

What appears to have taken place in October was a breakdown in the forward motion of the Union party cause in Ohio, Indiana, and Pennsylvania, as a result of the Conservative Unionists' conviction that the Radicals were nothing but a nuisance, a hindrance, and a fifth wheel, and that they *were not needed*. On this basis Conservative Republicans and War Democrats attempted to junk the Radicals and carry on alone, with disastrous results. In November, the Radicals determined the selection of the New York Republican Union ticket, and the Conservatives refused to go along with it. Once again divided, the Unionists were once again defeated. In Illinois and Wisconsin the story was different. Yet here again it had nothing to do with the question of the prosecution of the war as such. In the Old Northwest the people were suffering severely from economic problems and the Regular Democrats prospered from the fact, as the party out of power. When New Jersey voted Democratic there was no cause for surprise because the state was Democratic by tradition and had voted Democratic the year before, the moment the Lecompton issue was submerged by the several major issues of the war. United once again, the New Jersey Democracy would surely prevail unless the New Jersey Union party proved successful, which it did not. There were many reasons for the Democratic resurgence of 1862 but none of them had anything to do with repudiation of the federal war policy.

In Ohio the Radicals had only one of their kind on the State Supreme Court and at the 1862 Union State Convention he was denied renomination. In Indiana, Governor Morton determined the selection of a Conservative ticket at the Union State Convention and sought to block renomination of the Radical leader, Congressman George W. Julian.[67] In Pennsylvania, where Conservative Republicans controlled the State Senate and had the power to fend off a Democratic gerrymander, nothing was done to prevent the destruction of the district belonging to Radical leader Galusha A. Grow, Speaker of the House. And when the Radicals carried two Pennsylvania Republican congressional district nominating conventions, by surprise, Conservative Republicans rejected the decision, putting up their own candidates (who were promptly endorsed by the Regular Democracy).[68]

In all three states—Ohio, Indiana, and Pennsylvania—War Democrats were named to head the Union ticket; Ohio: William S. Kennon, candidate for Secretary of State; Indiana: Delano E. Williamson, candidate for Attorney General; Pennsylvania: William S. Ross, candidate for Surveyor General. In the important Philadelphia elections War Democrat Frederick C. Brewster headed the National Union slate, running for Solicitor. Also in Philadelphia, Breckinridge leaders Benjamin H. Brewster and Nathaniel B. Browne campaigned for the Unionists, and Douglas leaders David Krause and Edward G. Webb accepted Union nominations for Congress. War Democrat Congressman William E. Lehman of Philadelphia was replaced on the Democratic ticket by a Peace candidate after which he declared for the National Union party.[69] Conservative Republicans were delighted with the backing of these and many other War Democrats, but the Radical Republicans were unmoved. For all their Unionism, the Conservative War Democrats represented the pro-slavery spirit of "the Union as it was, the Constitution as it is." Speaking for the Radicals, Congressman Stevens of Pennsylvania declared: "The Union as it was—and the Constitution as it is, God forbid it."[70]

While factionalism was wrecking the National Union organization in Pennsylvania, the Regular Democracy was pulling back together once again. Concluding from the 1861 election results that the Peace faction was incapable of carrying a single state election, the Regular War Democrats and Conditional War Democrats of the October States combined to keep the Peace men wholly in the background. In Ohio, Indiana, and Pennsylvania, War candidates and Conditionals walked away with all the major Democratic nominations, and in every case a War man was named to head the ticket: Ohio, William W. Armstrong; Indiana, James S. Anthon; Pennsylvania, James P. Barr.[71] None was identified with the Peace cause in the slightest degree.

Added to the other advantages enjoyed by the Democratic party in the fall elections of 1862 was the poor showing of the Army of the Potomac at Second Bull Run (under Pope) and Antietam (under McClellan), and Kirby-Smith's invasion of Kentucky, all on the eve of the elections. Fears about impending Emancipation were dwarfed by these developments, coupled with the threat of Conscription (haltingly inaugurated under the Militia Act of 1862) and the suppression of civil liberties. Defending the administration position on all these counts in the October States were the Philadelphia *Press,* the Cleveland *Plain Dealer,* the Columbus *Capital City Fact,* and (for a time) the New Albany (Indiana) *Ledger.* All were War Democrat and all endorsed the Union ticket until the *Ledger* broke away, denouncing the preliminary Emancipation Proclamation. The Union campaign in Ohio was directed by War Democrat William H. Smith, editor of the Cincinnati *Gazette* and Chairman of the Union State Committee. In Columbus, Editor John Geary of the War Democrat *Capital City Fact* worked hard against his former Breckinridge associate, Samuel Medary of the *Crisis,* and Medary's idol, Congressman Vallandigham, who was seeking reelection.

The War Democracy of Indiana was well represented on the Union ticket, supplying four of eight candidates for state executive office and four of eleven candidates for Congress.[72] The most popular and most effective of these was congressional candidate Ebenezer Dumont, a General of volunteers on leave from his duties with the Army of the Ohio. Two more outstanding Union party spokesmen were U.S. Senator Joseph A. Wright and Judge James Hughes of the U.S. Court of Claims. Dumont and Wright had supported Douglas in 1860, Hughes supporting Breckinridge. At the urging of Lincoln, Senator Wright came home to Terre Haute to speak against the spellbinding critic of Emancipation, Democratic Congressman Voorhees.[73] Also returned from Washington, Judge Hughes attracted statewide attention with the publication of a letter he had sent to Governor Morton, warning of the spread of the Knights of the Golden Circle who, he said, were rife in Indiana. Shortly afterward, Editor Joseph J. Bingham of the Indianapolis *State Sentinel,* supporting the Regular Democratic ticket, came out against *all* secret societies, including the Union Clubs and the Knights of the Golden Circle.[74]

The strong campaigning of Conservative Union party men was seriously offset by lack of concern on the part of many leading Radical Republicans, including George W. Julian and Michael C. Garber of Indiana, John A. Gurley and Joshua R. Giddings of Ohio, and Galusha A. Grow and Thaddeus Stevens of Pennsylvania, all of whom worked with limited enthusiasm. The preliminary Emancipation Proclamation came too late to make any difference in this regard. On voting day, the Regular Democrats carried Ohio by 6,000 votes, Indiana by 9,000 and Pennsylvania by 3,600.[75] Majority control of the legislatures and the congressional delegations of all three states was transferred from the Republican-Union coalition to the Regular Democracy. In Ohio, a Republican congressional majority of 13 to 8 was replaced by a Democratic majority of 14 to 5. Of the many War Democrats running for Congress on the Union ticket in all three states, the lone winner was General Ebenezer Dumont of Indiana. In carrying Philadelphia, the Union party elected War Democrat Frederick C. Brewster to the office of Solicitor, after "one of the bitterest contests in the history of the city."[76]

Another satisfactory result from the Union party viewpoint was the emphatic defeat of Congressman Clement L. Vallandigham of Ohio. The Peace press was properly shaken. According to the Peace-oriented Mt. Vernon (Ohio) *Banner,* news of the result was "greatly lamented by all good Union-loving Democrats." Speaking for the War Democracy, the Columbus *Capital City Fact* observed: "We want no better evidence . . . that the editor of the *Banner* is a rebel at heart, as are others who sympathize in Vallandigham's defeat."[77]

The legislatures elected in October 1862 determined the selection of five U.S. Senators in four states—Ohio, Minnesota, Indiana, and Pennsylvania. In each case the blessing of the War Democracy was regarded as a major factor by everyone concerned. Seeking reelection in Ohio, against the combined powers of the Regular Democracy and the Conservative Republicans, Senator Benjamin F. Wade secured the backing of War Democrat Edwin M. Stanton, Secretary of War and for 33 years a member of the Democratic party of Ohio. The Senator's defeat at this time, Stanton declared for publication, would be nothing less than a "national calamity."[78] Working for reelection by a Republican legislature, Democratic Senator Henry M. Rice of Minnesota called upon Wade for support and Wade responded with a letter calling Rice "one of my best friends."[79] Wade was reelected in Ohio, with Stanton's help, but the Conservative Republicans of Minnesota were determined on electing one of their own, and Rice was overwhelmed. Democratic capture of the Indiana state legislature in October revived the political hopes of Peace Democrat Jesse D. Bright, expelled from the Senate in February on charges of conspiracy. Hoping to regain control of his former seat, either for the seven-week remainder of his old term or the full six years of a new one, he wound up with nothing.

Elected on a Conditional War platform, the Democratic legislature bypassed Bright and the Peace cause, in favor of a pair of War Democrats, the
short-term going to David Turpie, the long-term to Thomas A. Hendricks.
Rejected by his party, Peace Democrat Jesse D. Bright retired to private
life.[80]

The Peace Democracy of Pennsylvania also went after a Senate seat in
1862, against the wishes of the War Democracy. The Peace candidate for
Senator was Francis W. Hughes, Chairman of the Breckinridge State
Committee, and author of a resolution (drawn up in 1861) calling for secession of Pennsylvania from the Union, in company with the cotton states.
Conspicuously involved in the 1862 Pennsylvania campaign, Hughes was
hailed as a hero by the Peace faction, when the Democrats won, and urged
upon the party leadership as a logical candidate for the U.S. Senate. Advised of this development and of the likelihood of Hughes' success was
Simon Cameron, U.S. Minister to Russia. Quitting his diplomatic respon-
sibilities, Cameron returned home to campaign against Hughes as the Republican nominee. He had some friends among the Democrats of Pennsylvania and, as a banker and businessman, had many Democrats in his debt.
He was talking Union all the way and visiting every Democratic legislator
he could find in Harrisburg, causing a sensation. Frightened by the force
of the Cameron campaign, the Democratic party of Pennsylvania abandoned Peace Democrat Hughes in favor of a War Democrat—Charles R.
Buckalew, U.S. Minister to Ecuador under Buchanan and a firm supporter
of the war.[81] Cameron was regarded as dishonest by his political opponents in Pennsylvania and was accused of having purchased his victories in
times past. Seeking to prevent a purchase on this occasion, and to intimidate pro-Cameron Democrats, a giant Democratic mob appeared at Harrisburg, threatening violence to any Democratic legislator with nerve enough
to vote for Cameron. Buckalew was duly elected, by one vote.[82]

It is often observed that Abraham Lincoln was bothered and disturbed by
the Radicals, and especially so during the war. We also are advised that he
got along well with the Conservatives, to a corresponding extent. It is interesting to note the role he played in the 1862 elections, insofar as the
division of Radicals and Conservatives was concerned. For in this case he
sided with the Radicals, all down the line. The point is germane to the
story of the War Democrats in that they tended to follow Lincoln's lead.
Trusting in his judgment, many of them were to go along with his
changes-of-mind, and if he went Radical, so would they; at least part of
the way.

In Pennsylvania, Indiana, and Ohio, the Union state conventions of 1862
were all held in advance of the release of the preliminary Emancipation
Proclamation. In every case, the Conservatives bested the Radicals, and
Lincoln was cognizant of the results. Had he been the Conservative he was

supposed to be he would have flatly endorsed the Conservative maneuvers, pushing the Radicals aside and hushing up the slavery issue. Instead, to the astonishment of the Conservatives, he accepted the arguments of a Radical War Democrat, Robert Dale Owen, and tore the campaign apart, releasing the preliminary Emancipation Proclamation, which was poorly received by his Conservative supporters everywhere.[83]

Despite all warnings that the loss of the October States was the direct result of his Radical experimentation, Lincoln proceeded directly down the Radical line without concern for Conservative advice. As a result, he was to lose the November states of New York and New Jersey, Wisconsin and his own Illinois. But he was to win in Michigan and Massachusetts (despite the defection of thousands upon thousands of Conservatives); he was to carry Missouri and Delaware (to the surprise of almost everybody), as well as Kansas. All this would be accomplished without the aid of numerous Conservative Republicans, who were clearly holding back. Offsetting their loss was the support of many War Democrats who were coming over to the President in droves, irrespective of his Radical designs—and his victories were largely traceable to this result.

In almost every state involved in the November elections, the picture of Conservative Unionists fighting hard against the Radicals was once again in evidence. In New York, the Conservative preference for the Republican-Union gubernatorial nomination was Democratic General John A. Dix. When Dix was beaten by a Radical—General James S. Wadsworth— the Conservatives refused to cooperate, and the Conservative leader, Thurlow Weed, did not come out for Wadsworth until the waning moments of the campaign when it was too late to matter.[84] In New York City a Conservative Republican was entered as an independent in the race for the House seat of Frederick A. Conkling, a leading Radical, thereby insuring his defeat and the election of a Democrat.[85]

In Michigan and Massachusetts, a large portion of the Conservative Republican faction merged with Democrats and Constitutional Unionists in anti-Radical coalitions. The only serious candidates for the Union gubernatorial nomination in New Jersey were a pair of Conservatives— Republican Marcus L. Ward and War Democrat Joseph T. Crowell. Ward received the nomination, the Radicals received no consideration, and on voting day the Radicals stayed home.[86] In Wisconsin, the Conservatives attempted to sabotage Radical Congressman John F. Potter by entering an Independent in the race for his seat. The plan was abandoned but the Conservatives worked hard against Potter, anyway, tearing the Republican campaign to shreds.[87] In Illinois, Conservative Republicans united with the Democrats against the reelection campaign of Radical Congressman Owen Lovejoy.[88] Wherever this kind of maneuvering occurred, the Radicals were infuriated and the Republican and Union parties buckled under the strain.

In New York, the Regular Democrats nominated Horatio Seymour for Governor in 1862 on his self-conceived Conditional War platform. Upon accepting the honor, Seymour delivered a speech very pro-war in some places, anti-war in others. According to Greeley of the *Tribune,* he had done his best to "shoot so as to hit it if it is a deer and miss if it is a calf."[89] The Democratic platform promised to support the federal authorities "by legitimate means" (meaning those means having nothing to do with slavery), while denouncing the censorship of speech and press and the military arrest of civilians.[90] The War Democrats of New York were largely impressed by Seymour's line of reasoning. Almost all the Democratic papers that had backed the Union party of 1861 returned to Democratic Regularity in 1862. And of 35 legislators elected as self-designated "War Democrats" and "Union Democrats" in 1861, almost all returned to the Regular Democracy in 1862. (Only three were reelected running on the Republican-Union ticket.)[91] Exceptions to the general trend included War Democrats Lyman Tremain, Attorney General Daniel S. Dickinson, General John Cochrane, State Senator J. McLeod Murphy, and former Congressman Hiram Walbridge. Tremain was a leading figure at the Republican-Union Convention and received the nomination for Lieutenant Governor; Dickinson and Cochrane spoke frequently at Republican-Union rallies, and Murphy and Walbridge ran for Congress in New York City. All were required, under the circumstances, to support the Emancipation Proclamation.[92]

Some outstanding features of the New York campaign included the sale and transfer of the New York *World* from the Union camp to the Democratic camp. War Democrat Manton Marble was managing editor of the *World.* He was a member of Mozart Hall, a close friend of Fernando Wood, and a strong supporter of Seymour.[93] Wood, who had campaigned for Mayor as a War Democrat in 1861, campaigned for Congress in 1862 as a Conditional.[94] James Gorden Bennett of the *Herald,* who had supported the Union ticket of 1861, declared for Seymour. A major feature of the Upstate canvass was a running debate between War Democrat Daniel S. Dickinson and Conditional War Democrat John Van Buren, stirring recollections of the Free Soil campaign of 1848. On that occasion. Van Buren had been for freedom, Dickinson for slavery. This time it was the other way around.[95] Without Conservative support, the Republican-Union ticket had no chance of victory in New York and Seymour's majority exceeded ten thousand. On the New York congressional delegation a 23–9 Republican majority was replaced by an 18–12 Democratic majority. In the state legislature the Republican-Union coalition retained an overall majority, but the Regular Democracy acquired equal standing in the Assembly.[96]

Having gone to pieces following First Bull Run, Horace Greeley of the

Tribune went to pieces once again at this juncture, declaring that the people of New York had wholly rejected the federal war policy.[97] There was no doubt about it, from his point of view. Acting on the same assumption, Congressman-elect James Brooks predicted that Seymour, as Governor, was certain to oppose the usurpations of federal authority, and could be counted on to use the state militia, if necessary, to enforce the writ of *habeas corpus* over presidential protests. Congressman-elect Fernando Wood was of the same opinion, declaring that Seymour would surely "stand up for the rights of his State against federal usurpation."[98]

A significant result of the New York campaign of 1862 was the unprecedented alignment of Radical Republicans and War Democrats in the same corner of the Republican-Union coalition. In the senatorial election of January 1863 the Radicals endorsed the nomination of War Democrat Daniel S. Dickinson as opposed to a Conservative Republican, former Governor Edwin D. Morgan. The Assembly was tied and no Speaker could be elected for many ballots. When finally the tie was broken, the winner was a War Democrat, Theophelus Callicott, who was at once accused by the Regular Democracy of trading his Senate vote to the Union party in exchange for the Speakership. As a Democratic mob had formed at Harrisburg a few weeks earlier, to prevent the election of Simon Cameron as U.S. Senator from Pennsylvania, another such mob appeared at Albany to block the election of Callicott and Dickinson. After long delay, Governor Seymour sent troops to the rescue, and order was restored. Seizing on the chaotic situation and cursing the Radicalism of Dickinson, the Conservative Republicans—in conjunction with the Democrats—shoved Dickinson aside, and saw to the election of former Governor Morgan.[99] (The only difference between Morgan and Dickinson was that Dickinson, of Democratic background, was in favor of the Emancipation Proclamation, while Morgan, an Old-Line Republican, was not.)

In Illinois, the other major November state, the Regular Democrats decided on a War ticket but rejected an unconditional War platform proposed by Colonel Walter B. Scates, favoring a vigorous prosecution of the war, "Whether slavery survives or perishes." (The Colonel was a member of the staff of Democratic General John A. McClernand. It was generally assumed that McClernand was author of the resolutions.)[100] Included therein was restatement of Douglas' dramatic last pronouncement: "There can be no neutrals in this war; only patriots and traitors", also an endorsement of the latest presidential troop call for 300,000 volunteers.[101] The so-called "Scates Resolutions" were put to a voice vote and declared not carried by the Chairman, although some observers believed they *had* carried.[102] The platform committee proposed and the convention adopted a much weaker platform, endorsing the Union cause only on certain Conservative conditions.[103] When the delegates adjourned, War Democrat Ebon C. Ingersoll of Peoria composed a letter to the press, denouncing Democratic party policy, and calling for a state convention of true, loyal Democrats, capable of drawing a distinction between Union and disunion, without an "if" or a "but." No such convention was forthcoming, but Ingersoll was invited to attend the State Republican-Union Convention, in company with a great many other War Democrats. All agreed to come, and their presence there was not merely for the sake of decoration. Out of 14 candidates for Congressman-at-large, five were War Democrats, including Ingersoll, who received the nomination. Out of 13 Republican-Union candidates for Congress, five were War Democrats.[104]

Following the defeat of so many sections of the Democratic state constitution in June, a sense of complacency had overcome the leaders of the Republican-Union cause in Illinois, there seeming little chance of a Democratic comeback in the fall campaign. But economic problems intervened, altering the public mood. The staple crop of Illinois was corn, which was not harvested until late in the summer. The harvest proved to be the worst in years and by the time the November elections arrived the state was confronted by economic disaster.[105] At the close of the campaign a decisive majority voted Democratic. The state legislature, in which the Republicans had controlled both houses with an overall majority of six seats, went Democratic by 28 seats. On the Illinois congressional delegation a one-seat Democratic advantage swelled to three.[106] All five War Democrats running for Congress on the Union ticket were beaten by Regular Democrats.[107] When the Illinois legislature convened in January the Democratic majority elected William A. Richardson to the Senate, as a replacement for Conservative Republican Orville H. Browning.[108] A War Democrat in 1861 and a Conditional in 1862, Richardson received the votes of many in both factions at the January Democratic caucus. But when he entered the Senate he at once declared as a Peace Democrat. In Richardson's opinion the 1862 returns were a mandate for Peace, and he would heed the mandate.

Wisconsin and New Jersey also voted Democratic in November. As in the case of the other Democratic victories this year, it would be said without justification that here again was an appeal for Peace. The leading Peace Democrat in Wisconsin in 1862 was Douglas elector Edmond G. Ryan, made famous by a Wisconsin Supreme Court decision in *Kemp* v. *Wisconsin,* involving the military arrest of civilians. Ryan had won the case against the state and entered the Democratic Convention as the Conservative hero of the moment.[109] Called upon to expound his views, he did so, taking the convention by storm. The "Ryan Address" attacked the anti-slavery cause, blaming the war on "Fanaticism at the North" and absolving the South of all blame. Republican denials of Abolitionist purposes were derided as political camouflage. Actually, the single Republican objective was freedom of the slave at the expense of white labor. Federal "crimes" against the people were criticized in the Address; such crimes including confiscation, suspension of *habeas corpus,* and interstate transportation of persons accused of criminal activity.[110]

The Ryan Address was adopted by a vote of 112 to 12, as the Democratic party platform of 1862.[111] The action was applauded by Democrats in general but criticized by some, including Charles D. Robinsin of the Green Bay *Advocate* and Marcus M. Pomeroy of the La Crosse *Democrat,* also George B. Smith and Jonathon E. Arnold, delegates attending the convention.[112] War Democrat Matthew H. Capenter, Ryan's former law partner, published a lengthy reply, describing the Address as the most unpatriotic declaration yet recorded by a northerner.[113] The nonpartisan Union party of Wisconsin, organized the previous year, nominated three candidates for Congress, opposing the Ryan Address and favoring the proslavery Crittenden Resolution. Two of the Union candidates were Democrats in uniform—General Edward S. Bragg and Colonel Joshua J. Guppey, both of whom received the endorsement of the Regular Democracy. In deference to Union party influence, not one Peace Democrat was nominated for Congress.

The preliminary Emancipation Proclamation evoked various responses from various Democrats in Wisconsin, but never once appeared as the major issue of the 1862 elections in the state. On voting day the Democracy scored a great comeback, obtaining a majority of the popular vote for the first time in ten years. Three out of six congressional races were decided in favor of the Democratic candidates, and a strong Democratic gain was recorded in the legislature. None of the Union party candidates was elected to Congress; but all three of the Democratic winners were on record in favor of the war.[114] Ignoring the facts of the matter, many Democratic newspapers hailed the outcome in Wisconsin as yet another mandate for Peace.

Much the same thing happened in New Jersey where the War Democrats carried everything only to have the Peace men claim the victory. The Democratic candidate for Governor of New Jersey was Joel Parker, a General of Militia who had helped to organize the state for war. He was a Douglas elector. Democrats in general supported Parker, War and Peace alike, and the Democratic ticket was easily elected. But the Peace Democracy was not a major factor in the contest. Only in Bergen county, where the War men were forced off the Democratic ballot and compelled to campaign as Independents, were the Peace Democrats truly powerful. Yet Parker's election was interpreted in the Peace press as another thumping Peace victory, and the claim had some effect on the senatorial election of January 1863, in which Peace Democrats James W. Wall and William Wright were elected for the short and full term, over the protests of the

War Democracy. (Wall was best known for serving time in a federal prison on charges of sedition).[115]

It was widely reported that the Democratic victories of 1862 in Pennsylvania, Indiana, New York, Illinois, Wisconsin, and New Jersey, amounted to a landslide rejection of administration war policy and anti-slavery principles in particular. None of this would appear to be true. There were 21 state elections held in 1862, in 15 of which the administration policy was overwhelmingly sustained.[116] When the 1862 campaign was over, the Regular Democracy was still the minority party in all important particulars.

As for the contention of the pro-slavery Democrats that the votes of Pennsylvania, Indiana, New York, Illinois, Wisconsin, and New Jersey were basically in protest against Emancipation, it is worth noting that the anti-slavery cause would further accelerate its activity as the war progressed without disturbing the voters in any of the states in question except, perhaps, New Jersey. It is probable that the Democratic gains of 1862 were not the result of pro-slavery protest, but pro-Union protest, against the failure to capture Richmond, and various and sundry other matters not involving slavery. Elsewhere in November, Union coalitions defeated the Regular Democracy in Delaware, Missouri, and Kansas, with War Democrats leading the way for the Union cause. Republicans, aided only by Independent Democrats, accomplished the same results in Michigan, Massachusetts, Iowa, and Minnesota.

The Delaware election story of 1862 was similar to that of several other border slave states in which a seemingly invincible Regular Democracy was cut down to size by a Union coalition hastily organized for the occasion. Delaware was traditionally Democratic, despite the Know Nothing victories of 1854 and 1856. For the past four years the Buchanan/Breckinridge Democracy had controlled the State House and the legislature, against the wishes of the "People's party" (representing the interests of Republicans, Know Nothings, and Douglas Democrats, working in conjunction. In Delaware, the Republicans were the strongest of the three factions out of power.) In the 1860 campaign, Breckinridge received more votes in Delaware than Lincoln, Bell, and Douglas combined.[117]

When the war began, the Breckinridge party divided, some for War, some for Peace. The War faction was headed by William Cannon, the Peace faction by Thomas F. Bayard. Both were members of the Breckinridge State Executive Committee.[118] Governor Burton of Delaware was uncommitted on the war and easily swayed by every expression of opinion. Unionist control of Delaware politics was never certain and always under fire. From First Bull Run to August 1862 the Peace faction appeared in charge of the Democratic party throughout the state, and at the Democratic State Convention of 1862 the Peace candidate, Samuel Jefferson, defeated the War candidate, Robert W. Reynolds, 76 to 67, and a clear-cut Peace platform was adopted. Rejecting the decision, a large body of War Democrats answered the call for a Union State Convention, issued by leaders of the People's party.[119] Breckinridge Unionists were the stars of the occasion and William Cannon of the Breckinridge State Committee was named to head the Union ticket, as candidate for Governor. He had attracted attention earlier in the year by working in behalf of Lincoln's Gradual Emancipation Plan, pending before the legislature. Denounced as a Radical for this endeavor, he had relied for protection on his Conservative past, including a term as State Treasurer, service in the Breckinridge campaign, and appointment to the Virginia Peace Conference of 1861. Several months preceding the 1862 Democratic State Convention he had established a newspaper, the Georgetown *Union,* to fight the Peace cause in southern Delaware. Also involved in the publication of the paper was another Breckinridge leader, Assemblyman Jacob Moore, who was largely responsible for securing Cannon's nomination at the Union State Convention. In the eyes of the Peace Democracy, Cannon and Moore were the basest villains in Delaware history, urging Abolition on the state, to the detriment of all.[120] Disturbed by the tone of Democratic campaign rhetoric and fearful of violence on voting day, Union party leaders requested the presence of federal troops at the polls and the troops were provided, to the dismay of the Regular Democracy.[121] When the vote was taken, War Democrat William Cannon defeated Peace Democrat Samuel Jefferson by 111 votes out of 16,200 cast. The Regular Democrats denounced the result, decrying the horrors of military despotism and the denial of the franchise to loyal men.[122]

The Union party of Missouri held power from April 1861 to January 1863 under the extra-legal authority of the State Constitutional Convention. The 1862 elections marked the return to legal political procedures in the state. As elsewhere, the Radical-Conservative division was present in Missouri—the Radicals coming to be known as "Charcoals," the Conservatives as "Claybanks." War Democrat Nathaniel Paschall of the St. Louis *Missouri Republican* was generally regarded as the founder of the Union party of Missouri and in 1861 was the leader of the Charcoal faction; but in 1862 he quit the Charcoals, denouncing them as Abolitionists intent upon establishing a despotism.[123] Taking his place at once was War Democrat Charles W. Drake, a former friend of slavery, now a firm member of the Charcoal cause. Having worked for Douglas and held to the Conservative "Conditional Unionist" position of the Antebellum period, Drake was quickly moving to the left. In the manner of War Democrat Senator John B. Henderson of Missouri, he was ready to accept Emancipation as a war aim. With the publication of the preliminary Emancipation Proclamation, Drake jumped the fence, coming out loudly for the Charcoal cause in the fall congressional campaign, and his leadership proved highly effective. Three War Democrats were nominated for Congress on the Charcoal ticket—incumbent John W. Noell and two members of the State Convention, Benjamin F. Loan and William W. McClurg. All had worked for Douglas in 1860, against Emancipation. All would run for Congress in 1862 as self-declared "Emancipationists." In the face of predictions of a Conservative, pro-slavery sweep by the Claybanks and the Democrats, the Charcoals picked up half of the eight congressional seats under contention. War Democrats Noell, Loan, and McClurg were all elected, and Drake became a member of the State Convention, where he at once assumed control as a Radical. Emancipationists (Charcoals and Claybanks combined) secured a majority in the first Missouri legislature elected since the 1860 campaign. In its initial action, the legislature endorsed the appointment to the Senate of War Democrat John B. Henderson. Opposed on this occasion by a Claybank candidate, Henderson transferred his allegiance to the Charcoals, declaring in behalf of the Emancipation Proclamation.[124]

By 1862 the Republican organizations in Kansas, Michigan, and Massachusetts had made no move to coalesce with other Unionists, leaving the way open for the non-Republicans to organize a Union coalition. In Kansas and in Michigan the Republican party was controlled by Radical Senators James H. Lane and (Zachary) Chandler, and the Conservative Republican machine in Massachusetts was reluctant to discard Senator Charles Sumner for fear of the Radical reaction. In all three states a large number of Conservative Republicans declared their independence of party regularity, establishing Union party coalitions with the War Democracy and the Constitutional Unionists. In Kansas the sole object of concern was control of the State House. In Michigan and Massachusetts there was the additional hope of capturing the legislature and bringing down both Chandler and Sumner, in behalf of Conservative tradition. In the organization of every anti-Radical Union party the Peace faction was left out in the cold and a War ticket was entered in the field. The Union candidate for Governor of Kansas was a War Democrat—William R. Wagstaff, well remembered for his anti-slavery stand against the wishes of Governor Medary in 1860.[125] The Union candidate for Governor of Michigan was a Conservative Republican; for Governor of Massachusetts, a Constitutional Unionist. All were defeated, as was also the Conservative plan for unhorsing Senators Chandler and Sumner.[126] The winner in Kansas was Thomas Carney, a former Douglas-man running as a Republican.[127]

The Peace faction, shut out in every other free-state in 1862, carried off the laurels at the Iowa Democratic State Convention, but having done so was at once deserted by the War Democracy. Chester C. Cole, an 1860 Democratic candidate for Congress, spoke at many Republican rallies, as did several Iowa Democrats in uniform, of whom the best known was

General Thomas Hart Benton, Jr.[128] The Regular Democracy improved its position by 30,000 votes over its showing in the previous campaign, but was badly beaten, nonetheless.[129]

Some special elections of consequence were held in 1862 in reoccupied sections of the Confederacy where once again War Democrats were very much in evidence. The military governors of Tennessee, Arkansas, and Louisiana—War Democrats Andrew Johnson, John S. Phelps, and George F. Shepley—were directed by Lincoln to register all qualified voters in preparation for return to civil government. Governor Johnson was the first to move, ordering the election of a Supreme Court Judge and the Mayor of Memphis. In both cases, a majority voted for Disunionists, to the embarrassment of the Governor. Fighting back as best he could, Johnson permitted the Supreme Court victor to receive his commission and on the same day ordered his arrest, appointing to his place the Unionist defeated at the polls. Clearly, the long awaited resurgence of Tennessee Unionism was not yet at hand.[130] Following release of the preliminary Emancipation Proclamation, federal commissioners were dispatched to Tennessee, Louisiana, and Arkansas to register the voters and urge the return of civil authority. Congressional elections were ordered by Governor Johnson for December 29, but a well-timed Confederate cavalry raid prevented them from taking place.[131]

By the summer of 1862, within a few weeks following the arrival of Union troops, a Union party existed in New Orleans. Most of its leaders were Old-Line Whigs and Americans, but some were Democrats, including Thomas J. Durant, Michael Hahn, and Joshua Baker, all of whom were involved in the congressional election campaign of 1862 culminating in December. A loyalty oath was employed (under the direction of Democratic General George F. Shepley, Military Governor of Louisiana), Secessionists were barred from the polls and two Unionists were elected, one of whom was War Democrat Michael Hahn.[132]

In New York City's December elections, the momentary dominance of the Republican party was splintered by the coalition of Tammany and Mozart Halls, and the choice of two War Democrats to head the municipal ticket—John E. Develan (Tammany) running for Comptroller, Matthew Brennan (Mozart), for Corporation Counsel. They were easily elected.[133] It is a notable fact that no Peace candidates received the slightest notice in the city-wide elections.

In looking back upon the 1862 congressional races, the pro-slavery Unionist Louisville *Democrat* listed as follows the "probable complexion of the next House of Representatives":[134]

	Democratic	Republican
Already Known	77	72
To elect	26	7
Total	103	79

The same view was held by many more observers, all of whom were wrong. Before the Thirty-eighth Congress assembled, in December 1863, Congressman would have to be elected from eight other states. It often is observed in this regard that the administration was able to recoup its losses in 1862 by placing "troops at the polls" in the 1863 border slave-states elections. All such statements are incorrect. Of the eight states electing Congressmen in 1863, only two were border slave states.[135]

Actually, the upstart Republican party and the makeshift Union party (which together had beaten the Regular Democracy in 1861) could well have been expected to lose in 1862. The Lecompton breakup was obviously healed over, to the great advantage of the Regular Democrats, and the end of the war was nowhere in sight, to the disadvantage of Republicans and Unionists. Suppression of civil liberties, once regarded as temporary, now appeared as permanent, providing grounds for endless Democratic campaign propaganda, pleading in behalf of the Bill of Rights. Wartime inflation was pressing in upon the average citizen and economic suffering was widespread. In addition to all this was the steady build-up of the Democratic anti-Negro campaign, centering on the threat of Negro immigration to the free-states and impending destruction of the white labor market. Yet, for all their advantages, the Regular Democrats were able merely to pull slightly ahead in the incomplete congressional count, by the close of 1862. Amazingly, a large number of voters were refusing to be stampeded by any of the Democratic warnings, threats, or battle cries. They were voting Union and Republican in large numbers, in all cases where the Peace men appeared as the leaders of the Democratic cause. The only real winners in the 1862 elections were the Conditional War Democrats, typified by Horatio Seymour of New York. By talking up the Union, preaching civil liberties, and frowning on Secession, Seymour was able to break the force of the Union party movement—setting the stage for a Democratic resurgence in 1863.

In such manner the Conditional War Democracy appeared for an instant in American political life, as the friends and arch protectors of both slavery and Union. Confronted by the force of this development, President Lincoln was expected to move to the right—to the Conservatives—in hopes of deflecting the pro-slavery counter-assault. As it worked out, he went the other way—appealing to the Radicals. Having tried the Conservative path, at the expense of his standing with the Radicals, and having gained nothing but the embarrassment of a rejected plan for Gradual Emancipation, he would henceforward follow the Radical lead. His pace of course was slow—much too slow for the Radicals themselves—but that was his direction, nonetheless.

In several of the first few contests with the Conditional War Democracy, Lincoln's new Radicalism was badly mauled. Victorious in these encounters, the Conditionals appeared capable of stalling the anti-slavery crusade. As always, the deciding element was the War Democrats, constituting the balance of power. If they agreed to go along with Lincoln and the Unconditionals, slavery was dead. If they agreed to go with Seymour and the Conditionals, slavery might yet prevail.

NOTES

1. Walter Harriman had the curious distinction of being closely associated with both the anti-slavery extension policies of David Wilmot, John P. Hale, and Stephen A. Douglas, and the pro-slavery policies of Franklin Pierce, Jefferson Davis, and Caleb Cushing. In January, 1848, he had electrified a Democratic Senatorial Convention by denouncing slavery as a moral wrong. The action rendered him the advocate of Radical John P. Hale, who had lost his seat in Congress two years earlier for favoring the Wilmot Proviso. In 1847 Hale was elected to the U.S. Senate, over the protestations of U.S. Senator Franklin Pierce of New Hampshire and the pro-slavery faction in the state. (The victory was long remembered as the "Hale-storm of 1847.") That same year Hale was nominated for President by the anti-slavery Liberty party, but the nomination was withdrawn in 1848 when the Liberty men merged in the Free Soil party, supporting Martin Van Buren. Despite his anti-slavery principles, Harriman rejected Free Soilism, finding it too radical for his tastes. In so doing, he wound up campaigning for Lewis Cass on a pro-slavery platform in company with Senator Pierce. From 1851 to 1857 Harriman supported Pierce at every turn, assisting his successful presidential campaign of 1852. Holding state office as Assemblyman, Senator, and Treasurer, and federal office under Pierce, working for the Indian Agency and the Pension Office, Harriman was now a strong Conservative and always pro-slavery. In 1856 he went to Michigan with Lewis Cass, to speak for James Buchanan. The Lecompton controversy altered his position once again, however, and from 1857 to 1862 he was the leader of the Douglas faction in New Hampshire, serving as chairman at the Democratic State Convention of 1859. In the 1860 canvass, he led the Douglas forces while Pierce and his lieutenants were working for Breckinridge, and Hale and his lieutenants for Lincoln.

   The most influential Douglas paper in New Hampshire was the Manchester *Democrat and Union,* edited by Harriman's close friend, James M. Campbell. When the war began, Harriman indorsed the Union cause but Campbell did not, coming out instead for Peace. War Democrats in Manchester stopped buying the *Democrat and Union,* in protest, and Campbell sought compromise, selling half-interest in the paper to Harriman, on the condition that Harriman determine all editorial policy. Upon taking charge, Harriman announced forcefully in favor of the federal war policy, and changed the paper's name to *Union*. Amos hadley, pp. 36–87; James D. Squires, IV:79.

2. *Tribune Almanac,* 1860, 1861, 1862.
3. James D. Squires, III:400.
4. New Hampshire, *Journal of the House,* June 28, 1862, pp. 164–65.
5. Manchester Weekly *Union,* July 9, 1861.
6. Concord *Patriot,* quoted in the St. Paul (Minnesota) *Press,* August 16, 1861. Preceding Bull Run, the *Patriot* had favored the war. In casting about for supporters, the Confederates claimed for a time the allegiance of Andrew Jackson Donelson, a hero of the War of 1812, who was alleged to have offered the services of a sword given him by Andrew Jackson. Advised of this, the *Patriot* denounced Donelson as "a double traitor." And when the New York *Atlas and Argus* announced in favor of the war in the name of self-interest, urging all Democrats to help the Union cause on that basis if not for the principles involved, the *Patriot* reprinted the statement and entered a similar plea. Concord *Patriot,* June 15, 22, 1861.
7. St. Paul (Minnesota) *Press,* August 16, 1861.
8. James O. Lyford, *Life of Edward H. Rollins. A Political Biography* (Boston: Estes, 1906), pp. 130–31.
9. Ibid., p. 130
10. Ibid., p. 132.
11. The last Democratic Governor elected in Connecticut was Thomas H. Seymour, who served two terms, in 1852 and 1853. A Democratic plurality was achieved in 1854 but a Whig-dominated legislature decided the election, seating the Whig candidate instead. *Tribune Almanac,* 1851–1861.
12. Republican majorities in 1857—546 votes; 1859—1,870 votes; 1860—542 votes. Ibid., 1858, 1860, 1861.
13. Ibid., 1861. Breckinridge vote exceeded Douglas vote in Hartford, New Haven, Middlesex, and Fairfield counties.
14. Ibid., 1862. Round figure.
15. Hartford *Courant,* December 13, 1861; *Commemorative Biographical Record of Hartford County, Connecticut* (Chicago, 1901).
16. Robert J. Lane, *A Political History of Connecticut during the Civil War* (District of Columbia: Catholic University, 1941), p. 182.
17. Hartford *Courant,* January 9, 1862.
18. Ibid., January 17, 1862.
19. Robert J. Lane, p. 154; Waite became an honored member of the Republican-Union coalition, and in 1864 was designated an elector on the national Union party ticket. *Evening Journal Almanac,* 1865.
20. *Tribune Almanac,* 1863.
21. Kenneth M. Stampp, *And the War Came,* p. 90. William B. Hesseltine, pp. 27–28; Democrats elected in company with Sprague included J. Russell Bullock, Lieutenant Governor, and Walter Burgess, Attorney General. *Evening Journal Almanac,* 1861.
22. *Union Army,* I:233; Henry W. Shoemaker, *The Last of the War Governors* (Altoona: Altoona Tribune, 1881), p. 8.
23. Journalist Henry Garrison Villard did not like Sprague, describing him as a man of "very little mental capacity (who) had reached political distinction at an early age through the influence of real or reputed great wealth." In comparison to his wife, Katherine Chase Sprague, Villard declared, "She was superior to him in every way, and married him for the enjoyment and power of his money." *Memoirs of Henry Garrison Villard* (Boston, Houghton, Mifflin, 1904), quoted in Ishbel Ross, *Proud Kate, Portrait of an Ambitious Woman* (New York: Harper, 1953), p. 125. John Hay, personal secretary to Lincoln, also was hostile to Sprague, whom he described as "a small, insig-

nificant youth who bought his place." Quoted in Ibid., p. 210. Radical Republicans insisted that Sprague spent $100 thousand purchasing votes in advance of the 1860 election. Ibid., p. 127. A similar charge was rendered by the Radicals, following the repeal of the Rhode Island Personal Liberty Law in 1861. William B. Hesseltine, p. 125.

24. Providence *Post,* March 21–31, 1861.
25. *Tribune Almanac,* 1862.
26. Ibid., 1863.
27. Allen Johnson and Dumas Malone, eds., I:372; *Biographical Congressional Directory, 1774 to 1911,* p. 445.
28. William B. Hesseltine, pp. 238–39; Edward C. Smith, p. 137; Springfield *Illinois State Register,* January 7, 1862.
29. St. Louis *Missouri Republican,* quoted in the Springfield *Illinois State Journal,* February 28, 1862.
30. Ibid., February 15, 1862.
31. Quoted in Ibid., February 11, 1862.
32. James G. Wilson, *Biographical Sketches of Illinois Officers Engaged in the War against the Rebellion of 1861* (Chicago: Barnet, 1862), p. 64.
33. Charles A. Church, Ibid., p. 87.
34. Ibid., p. 88; Edward C. Smith, p. 137; Springfield *Illinois State Journal,* January 7, 1862.
35. William B. Hesseltine, pp. 238–39.
36. Frank L. Klement, "Middle Western Copperheadism and the genesis of the Granger Movement," *Mississippi Valley Historical Review,* vol. XXXVIII, no. 4 (March 1952), p. 688.
37. Frank L. Klement, *The Copperheads in the Middle West,* p. 4.
38. Springfield *Illinois State Journal,* June 18, 1862.
39. William B. Hesseltine, p. 239.
40. The War Democrats first attracted notice at the convention by opposing ratification of the pro-slavery Thirteenth Amendment. Voting in this manner, along with the Republicans, were: Norman H. Purple, Milton S. Bartley, John W. Paddock, William M. Jackson, Jonathan Simpson, and Isaac L. Leith. Springfield *Illinois State Journal,* February 15, 1862.
41. Paddock's county voted heavily against the new constitution and shortly following the vote he was commissioned by Governor Yates Lieutenant Colonel of the 113th Illinois Infantry. Bartley became a major Union party leader in his district, receiving a congressional nomination in 1864. Breckinridge elector Norman Purple could play no further role, being very ill and on the verge of death. *Biographical Encyclopedia of Illinois,* p. 355; *Tribune Almanac,* 1865.
42. Springfield *Illinois State Journal,* June 18, 1862.
43. The "Salem Clique" was initially established when General Lane became Governor of Oregon Territory in 1853. Its members at the time included George H. Williams, Chief Justice of the Territorial Supreme Court; Matthew P. Deady and Cyrus Olney, Associate Justices, Territorial Secretary George L. Curry; Indian Superintendent Joel Palmer; U.S. Attorney Benjamin F. Harding; U.S. Marshal James W. Nesmith; Customs Collectors Addison C. Gibbs and John Adair; Postal Agent A. L. Lovejoy. George H. Williams, "Political History of Oregon," *The Quarterly of the Oregon Historical Society,* vol. II, no. 1 (March–December, 1901): p. 3. When the Lecompton dispute arose in 1857, most of these announced for Douglas and those in federal positions were relieved of authority.
44. Charles H. Carey, *History of Oregon* (Chicago: Pioneer Historical, 1922), p. 644. There was no truth to the claim that the Douglas forces worked for Lincoln's election in Oregon. This was merely a part of standard Breckinridge campaign propaganda, utilized repeatedly in many free-states. Here as elsewhere, the Douglas men were Negrophobic to the point of detesting Re-

publicans in general and could not easily agree to working with them. Instead, they earnestly attempted to reestablish Democratic party unity in the middle of the presidential campaign, proposing to divy up the two U.S. Senate seats, one for Douglas, one for Breckinridge, leaving the Republicans out in the cold. But the Douglas man they wanted was James W. Nesmith, whom the Breckinridge faction refused to accept. The seat at issue was occupied by Delazon Smith, a close ally of Senator Lane and editor of the pro-slavery Albany *Argus.* Denouncing the Salem Clique for seeking his defeat, Smith referred to Nesmith as "the vilest and most loathsome creature that wears a human form on the Pacific Coast." The Clique itself, was composed, he said, of "cut-throats, assassins, murderers, and their bastard vagabond allies." Quoted in Walter C. Woodward, p. 172. After many ballots, the Douglas leaders in the legislature tired of the game and entered an alliance with the hated Republicans, who agreed to run their most Conservative man: Edward D. Baker, a friend of Abraham Lincoln's, and a former Congressman from Illinois. Ibid., p. 183.

45. On May 28, 1861, Governor Whiteaker issued a long address, supposedly Unionist, but actually opposing flag-raisings and Union meetings on the grounds that they were inflammatory, and hostile to the hope of reconciliation. "These are not Union meetings," he said, "but are creating disunion directly in our midst. . . .In God's name, what good is this war to bring to the country? None; positively none." Ibid., p. 196.

46. Ibid., p. 194.

47. Ibid., p. 200.

48. Walter C. Woodward, p. 199.

49. Ibid., p. 198. War Democrats attacking Stark included Supreme Court Judge Reuben P. Boise, Lucien Heath, J.C. Peebles, Chester N. Terry, and Harvey Gordon.

50. Ibid., p. 208.

51. Ibid., p. 210.

52. Ibid., p. 213; Justin Steinberger also accepted a commission, as Colonel of the First Washington Territorial Infantry. *Union Army,* IV:448. Matthew P. Deady became a strong Unionist during the war and a Radical during the Reconstruction period. Walter C. Woodward, pp. 235, 254.

53. *Tribune, Almanac,* 1863.

54. *Evening Journal Almanac,* 1864.

55. Winfield J. Davis, p. 184.

56. Ibid., pp. 185–86.

57. *Tribune Almanac,* 1863.

58. Theodore H. Hittell, IV:337–38.

59. Walter H. Crockett, p. 547.

60. Hoping to sway Radical sentiment, Assemblyman Smart introduced a resolution early in the year, calling on the federal government to free the slaves of rebels, employ them in the army, and pay them the same as whites. A kind of colonization program was also recommended, for their postwar deployment. In both the Democratic and the Radical Republican press, Smart was attacked as a demagogue, and when a resolution passed the legislature recommending emancipation of the slaves it was not his but another, proposed by a Radical. Louis O. Hatch, pp. 443–45.

61. Louis C. Hatch, II:447.

62. Ibid., II:447.

63. *Tribune Almanac,* 1863.

64. Louis C. Hatch, II:447. Ibid., IV:400; *Biographical Directory of the American Congress, 1774–1942,* p. 1823.

65. R. H. Stanley and George O. Hall, p. 158. Louis C. Hatch, II:442.

66. *Evening Journal Almanac,* 1863. At the next meeting of the Maine legislature, Republican Senator Lot M. Morrill was reelected without difficulty, the

only fireworks involving a Douglas-Breckinridge battle for the Democratic nomination. State Senator William P. Haines, a Douglas leader, was chosen, to the great annoyance of the Breckinridge faction. He was then defeated by the large Republican majority. Louis C. Hatch, II:452.

67. Eugene Roseboom, p. 400; Patrick W. Riddleberger, *George W. Julian; A Study in Nineteenth Century Politics and Reform.* (Indianapolis: Indiana Historical Bureau, 1966), pp. 195–97.

68. The Conservative Republican "Independents" running with Democratic support were James T. Hale and Henry W. Tracy. *Tribune Almanac,* 1863; *Biographical Congressional Directory, 1774–1911,* pp. 693, 1062.

69. Benjamin H. Brewster spoke at many National Union party rallies in 1862. He would support Lincoln in 1864 and serve as Attorney General of Pennsylvania under a Republican administration in Reconstruction times, before accepting appointment as U.S. Attorney General under Republican President Arthur. N.B. Browne was, with Brewster, the outstanding Breckinridge campaigner in Philadelphia, in 1860, and had held federal office under both Pierce and Buchanan. In 1860 Edward G. Webb and David Krause had been leaders in the Douglas cause in Philadelphia. In 1862 they ran for Congress as Lincoln-men. When William E. Lehman failed of renomination by the Democrats of his district, he declared in favor of the National Union candidate, and was appointed in 1863 Provost Marshal for Philadelphia, under authority of the Lincoln administration.

70. Philadelphia *Age,* September 24, 1863.

71. Armstrong declared a War Democrat, as of 1862, in William H. Smith, p. 99; Anthon campaigned as a War Democrat in 1862. James P. Barr of Pennsylvania was editor of the Democratic Pittsburgh *Post,* which always supported the war.

72. War Democrats nominated on the Union ticket in 1861 included Delano E. Williamson, the candidate for Attorney General; William S. Smith, for Supreme Court Reporter; John I. Morrison for Superintendent of Public Instruction. Indianapolis *Journal,* October 1, 1862. Williamson was a former State Legislator, elected as a Democrat in 1850; ɪan again for the legislature in 1858 but was defeated by a Republican. In the 1860 campaign, he supported Douglas. Charles W. Taylor, *Biographical Sketches and Review of the Bench and Bar of Indiana* (Indianapolis: Bench and Bar, 1893), p. 700. William S. Smith was a Douglas elector in the 1860 campaign. Indianapolis *Journal,* October 1, 1860. John I. Morrison was a delegate to the Douglas State Convention, 1860. New Albany (Indiana) *Ledger,* January 13, 1860.

73. Roy P. Basler, ed., V:351–52.

74. Frank L. Klement, *The Copperheads of the Middle West,* pp. 147, 163; Indianapolis *State Sentinel,* June 24, 1862.

75. *Tribune Almanac,* 1863.

76. Allen Johnson and Dumas Malone, eds., III:27. War Democrats defeated for Congress in October, running on the Union ticket, were: William S. Groesbeck of Ohio; Allen May and James Gavin of Indiana; Edward G. Webb, David Krause, and Joel B. Wanner of Pennsylvania. *Tribune Almanac,* 1863.

77. Columbus (Ohio) *Capital City Fact,* October 21, 1862.

78. Benjamin P. Thomas, *Stanton,* p. 82.

79. William W. Folwell, II:76.

80. Allen Johnson and Dumas Malone, III:46.

81. Stanton Ling Davis, pp. 270-72.

82. Cameron's appeal for protection was delivered to the senior military officer in the vicinity, Alexander K. McClure, Assistant Adjutant General of the Army, on duty at Harrisburg. As a leader of the Conservative Republican faction, McClure had hopes of seeing Cameron defeated, and so refused to intervene in his behalf. The Democratic mob was permitted in this manner to decide the election. Stanton Ling Davis, pp. 272–73.

83. Stanton Ling Davis, p. 239. Allen Johnson and Dumas Malone, eds., III:176. In the absence of Thurlow Weed (who was in Europe on a bond-selling tour), Governor Morgan of New York was the leader of the Conservative Republicans of New York in the fall campaign of 1862. Invited to attend the Altoona Conference of September 24, he declined. Governor Olden, Conservative leader of the Union party of New Jersey, put in an appearance but when called upon to support Emancipation he steadfastly refused. William B. Hesseltine, pp. 257–61. J. Robert Lane, pp. 218–19.
84. Sidney D. Brummer, p. 250.
85. One of the outstanding Conservative Republicans in New York City was Orison Blunt who, in company with his mentor Thurlow Weed of Albany, was hostile to the Emancipation Proclamation. Frederick Conkling had one of the most Radical voting records of any Republican in Congress and was fully in favor of the Proclamation. By splitting the Republican vote, as an Independent candidate, Blunt disposed of Conkling. In the New York City mayorality election of 1863, Blunt was again the choice of the Conservatives and was successful in defeating the renomination bid of the Radical Mayor, George Opdyke.
86. Ward was spoken of at the Union State Convention as an Old-Line Henry Clay Whig. Charles M. Knapp, p. 70.
87. Frank Flower, pp. 207–8.
88. Lovejoy, who was used to winning by sizable majorities in a heavily Republican district, was barely reelected with a majority of 663 votes, over Conservative Republican Henderson.
89. New York *Tribune,* September 11, 1862.
90. De Alva Stanwood Alexander, III:40.
91. Statement based on a comparison of New York legislators listed in *Evening Journal Almanac* for 1862 and 1863.
92. Sidney D. Brummer, p. 234; *Tribune Almanac,* 1863.
93. Alan Johnson and Dumas Malone, eds., XII:267.
94. Samuel A. Pleasants, pp. 128–31.
95. De Alva Stanwood Alexander, III:49.
96. *Evening Journal Almanac,* 1862, 1863. War Democrats reelected on the Republican-Union ticket in 1862 included Albert Andrus, Francis B. Fisher, and Cornelius Church. They were joined by five others newly elected on this occasion: William Dewey, Ira Brockett, Horace Bemis, Byron Healey, and Francis B. Smith.
97. New York *Herald,* November 11, 1862.
98. Sidney D. Brummer, p. 256.
98-A. Some other Radical War Democrats in New York besides Dickinson were Lyman Tremain, former Attorney General of New York; Thomas G. Alvord, former Speaker of the State Assembly; Henry C. Page, former Chairman, Young Men's Democratic Club of New York City, and State Senator John Willard, President of the 1860 Douglas State Convention.
99. Ibid., p. 291.
100. Scates was a former Judge of the State Supreme Court. At the 1860 Douglas State Convention, he received 14 votes for the gubernatorial nomination. Chicago *Herald,* June 15, 1860.
101. Alexander Stevenson and Bernard Stuvé, *A Complete History of Illinois, from 1673 to 1884* (Springfield: Rokker, 1884), pp. 877–78.
102. Springfield *Illinois State Register,* October 13, 1862.
103. The Democratic State Convention also protested against Congress pledging the nation to pay for all slaves emancipated under the terms of the Gradual Emancipation program; condemned as tyrannical the recent wave of military arrests of civilians in the loyal states and their transportation beyond state lines, demanding their immediate restoration for trial at home; denounced federal interference with freedom of speech and freedom of the press; de-

nounced Republican extravagance; denounced federal taxation and reliance on the greenback; sustained the President in his recent declaration to "save the Union the shortest way under the Constitution;" requested the Republican state administration to implement the Negro-exclusion clause of the state constitution, ratified in June; and tendered their thanks to Illinois troops for services rendered in the war. Alexander Stevenson and Bernard Stuvé, p. 878.

104. Springfield *Illinois State Journal*, September 25, 1862. Democrats considered for the nomination of Congressman-at-Large included Ebon C. Ingersoll, Samuel W. Moulton, Cyrus Edwards, Henry W. Billings, and John A. McClernand.

105. Alexander Stevenson and Bernard Stuvé, p. 910.

106. *Evening Journal Almanac*, 1863.

107. Two War Democrats elected on the Democratic ticket in Illinois were Colonel William R. Morrison, a hero of the Union victory at Ft. Donelson, and James C. Allen, who beat the Union candidate, Ebon C. Ingersoll, campaigning as a Unionist and rejecting all the arguments of the Peace faction. Wood Gray, p. 105.

108. Browning was serving as an appointed replacement for the late War Democrat Senator Stephen A. Douglas.

109. Frank L. Klement, *Lincoln's Critics in Wisconsin*, p. 12.

110. Democratic party, Wisconsin, *Adress to the People of the Democracy of Wisconsin* (Milwaukee, September 3, 1862).

111. A. M. Thomson, *A Political History of Wisconsin*, 2nd ed. (Milwaukee: Caspar, 1902 (1893)).

112. E. Bruce Thompson, *Matthew Hale Carpenter, Webster of the West* (Madison: Wisconsin State Historical Society, 1954), pp. 71–73; Frank L. Klement, *Lincoln's Critics in Wisconsin*, p. 10; A. M. Thomson, p. 159.

113. Frank A. Flower, p. 212.

114. Eldridge was chairman of the Douglas State Convention of 1860. He also was a former Free Soiler. Frank A. Flower, p. 208; preceding his election to Congress, he had always spoken and acted in favor of the Union cause. James S. Brown was Attorney General of Wisconsin in 1848 and Mayor of Milwaukee in 1861. When the war began, he took a strong stand in favor of the Union. *Union Army*, IV:25. Ezra Wheeler was a county judge and a pronounced War Democrat, who would join the Union party in 1864 and work for Lincoln's reelection.

115. *National Cyclopedia of Biography*, VI:228. The Regular Democrats carried the district with a majority of 1100. Newark *Advertiser*, November 3, 1862. Charles M. Knapp, p. 81.

116. James Ford Rhodes offers the following extraordinary statement concerning the election results of 1862: "The Democrats made conspicuous gains in Congress and, *if they had had a majority in the other states,* would have controled the House of Representatives." (Italics added.) *History of the Civil War, 1861–1865,* edited by E. B. Long (New York: Ungar, 1961, p. 175. Later, referring back to the outcome of the 1862 campaign, Rhodes observes that "Lincoln had suffered a defeat at the ballot box." Ibid., p. 185.

117. Ibid., 1861. Breckinridge received 7,637 votes in Delaware; Bell, 3,864; Lincoln, 3,815; Douglas, 1,023. The only bright spot in the state, from the point of view of the anti-Breckinridge forces, was Wilmington, where the Douglas candidate for Mayor attracted enough Democratic votes to permit the Republican "People's party" candidate to win with a plurality, receiving 878 votes to 874 for the incumbent, Thomas Young (Breckinridge), and 87 for George Hagany (Douglas). Wilmington *Delaware Gazette*, September 7, 1860. Generally regarded as the man responsible for the result was Democratic City Councilman George Nebeker, who rallied the Douglas faction, urging complete rejection of Breckinridge and Southern Rights. Although the Douglas Democracy was badly beaten in the Wilmington elections, Nebeker was

reelected to the Council. Ibid., September 7, 1860. He later joined the Union party, supporting Lincoln in 1864.

118. Dover *Delawarean,* August 11, 1860.

119. Vice presidents of the Union State Convention included Dr. William Cummins, Chairman of the 1860 Douglas State Convention; Douglas electors Gideon B. Waples and Samuel P. Dixon; also James B. Anderson of the Breckinridge State Committee; Douglas supporters Thomas Scott and Isaac Price; Breckinridge supporters Jacob Moore, Wilson L. Cannon, and Andrew Eliason. Milford (Delaware) *News and Advertiser,* August 22, 1862.

120. Harold B. Hancock, p. 119.

121. William B. Hesseltine, p. 270.

122. Walter A. Powell, *A History of Delaware* (Boston: Christopher, 1928).

123. Springfield (Illinois) *State Journal,* November 11, 1862; Sceva B. Laughlin, pp. 103–4.

124. Considerable confusion prevailed concerning the 1862 Missouri election results. Nobody had expected the Charcoals to win, and could not understand how they had, in so many districts. The answer can be found in the actions of the State Constitutional Convention, dominated by the War Democrats, and the policy of Democratic General John M. Schofield, commanding the Department of Missouri from May through December, 1862.
   In June, the Constitutional Convention disfranchised all persons in arms against the state and federal authorities since a certain date. Many Conservatives formerly associated with the Secession cause were thereby removed from the voting rolls. (Regular Democrats were later to refer to this particular legislation as a glaring example of Radical Republican tyranny. It was adopted, however, before the Republicans emerged as a major force in Missouri, and was largely the work of the War Democrats, who clearly controlled the State Constitutional Convention.) During the first month of his command, General John M. Schofield issued "Order No. 19," threatening the execution of anyone convicted of guerilla operations, excepting only those who asked for amnesty and joined the state militia, at the same time surrendering the right to vote. The Order was exceedingly effective and many guerillas agreed to be disfranchised. As a result, thousands of Secession or "Peace" votes were lost to Claybank candidates running on the "Conservative" or Regular Democratic tickets. William E. Parrish, pp. 91–95.

125. Daniel Wilder, p. 240. Dissatisfied with the Union party platform, the Peace Democracy of Kansas held a separate convention and adopted a separate platform, but placed no ticket in the field. Albert Castel, p. 95.

126. The anti-Radical candidate for Governor of Michigan was Byron G. Stout, Republican president pro-tempore of the State Senate. Anti-Chandler Coservatives secured a ten-seat majority in the Michigan legislature as a result of the 1862 elections, but the War Democrats and Conservative Republicans—both of whom hated Chandler—could not agree upon a compromise candidate to put against him in the senatorial election of 1863, and he was therefore reelected. Charles Moore, pp. 423, 426.

127. The Republican party of Kansas was divided in 1862 between the Radical followers of U.S. Senator James H. Lane and the Conservative followers of Governor Charles Robinson. At Lane's instigation, Robinson was impeached early in the year on charges of malfeasance in office, but was found not guilty and retained in authority. He was ably defended in his impeachment trial by War Democrat William G. Wagstaff who, in 1862, received the gubernatorial nomination of the Anti-Lane forces, including the Conservative Republicans and the War Democrats. Many anti-Lane men were leaders in the Kansas business community. Wholly in control of the Republican State Convention, Lane confounded his opponents by arranging the nomination of Charles Carney, the richest man in Kansas, and a War Democrat. Siphoning off the blessings of many businessmen and many Democrats, Carney was eas-

ily elected over Wagstaff. Albert Castel, pp. 94–95.
128. Some other War Democrats in uniform supporting the Iowa Republican ticket of 1862 included Colonel Marcellus M. Crocker, Lieutenant Colonel William W. Belknap, and Lieutenant Colonel James A. Williamson, all of whom issued public statements on the subject, attacking the Peace Democracy. Olynthus B. Clark, p. 144.
129. Comparison of vote recorded in *Tribune Almanac* for 1862 and 1863.
130. Clifton R. Hall, p. 87.
131. Ibid., pp. 88–90.
132. Benjamin P. Thomas, *Abraham Lincoln*, pp. 356–58.
133. *Evening Journal Almanac*, 1863.
134. Louisville (Kentucky) *Democrat*, November 16, 1862.
135. William B. Hesseltine, p. 272.

10

Conservative Counterattack:
The Great Peace Crusade of 1863

The year 1862 closed in a state of political frenzy. Regular Democrats were claiming the greatest election victory in the history of the Union. Conservatives of every party were urging the President to abandon the Emancipation Proclamation, and Radicals were afraid that he would.[1] Yet nothing of the sort was forthcoming. With Conservative hopes and expectations at a zenith, Lincoln appealed in his Annual Message to the lame-duck session of the Thirty-seventh Congress, in December 1862, for funds in support of gradual, compensated Emancipation in the loyal border slave states.

Outraged by the Message and anxious to demonstrate his recent conversion to the Peace cause, Democratic Congressman Richardson of Illinois declared against the spirit and the purpose of the Gradual Emancipation plan. (As the 1860 campaign manager of the late Senator Douglas, Richardson retained the respect of Douglas men in the War camp, and was therefore influential.) The President, he said, was unconcerned about the fate of white Americans and interested only in the blacks; or so it appeared in the the Annual Message wherein "no page, no sentence, no line, no word is given to laud, or even mention the bravery, the gallantry, the good conduct of our soldiers . . . . No sorrow is expressed for the lamented

195

dead . . . . To feed, clothe, and buy, and colonize the negro we are to tax and mortgage the white man and his children. The white race is to be burdened to the earth for the benefit of the black race. . . ." The President was criticized for releasing the preliminary Emancipation Proclamation which had altered the purpose of the war. "The Army is being used for the benefit of the negro. This House is being used for his benefit," Richardson protested. "Every department of the government is being run for his benefit. . . .The people are sick and tired of this eternal talk upon the negro, and they have expressed their disgust unmistakably in the recent elections." It was time to set aside the Negro issue in favor of "compromise with white men."[2]

The Peace faction having fired the first salvo, an answer was supplied by a member of the War Democracy—Noell of Missouri—speaking in the President's behalf. Recently elected on the Union ticket, he here declared his fury for the Regular Democracy, expressing total disillusionment. Especially disturbing from his point of view was the Democratic policy of condemning the war as an "Abolitionist Crusade," which it was not. Through the constant employment of this policy, Noell declared, the Democratic party had forsaken the Union. It was now the "anti-war party," and basing its position on falsehood. Emancipation was wholly justifiable "as a means of successful prosecution of the war for the restoration of the Union." Democratic arguments to the contrary were meaningless and so was all the shouting about the tyranny of Lincoln. Defending the suspension of *habeas corpus,* Noell declared against the policies of pro-slavery judges, North and South, including Chief Justice Taney, who was singled out for his *Merryman* Decision of 1861. Not only was Confiscation legal, in Noell's opinion, but highly effective in the border slave states as punishment for treason—and far more practicable than mass-hanging, which the world would not condone. The Peace Democracy was saying that the war was too expensive and that the Treasury could not bear the strain. This, too, was anti-Union propaganda. As for a "compromise with white men" recommended by Richardson, Noell replied: "I am for compromise with no set of men who have undertaken to destroy this Government, short of absolute submission of their part."[3]

*   *   *

A strange interlude was provided at the opening of the lame-duck session by lame-duck Congressman Vallandigham of Ohio who, on December 5, came out in favor of the Union cause—for the first, last, and only time since the outbreak of the war. Presenting a long resolution aimed against the State Suicide Theory of Senator Sumner and the "dictatorship" of Lincoln, he also declared against division of the Union or foreign intervention, even for the sake of Peace. The Union must be preserved.[4] Opinions expressed on this occasion were far removed from anything Vallandigham had ever said before. Having led the Peace cause in Congress for a year, he had been punished at the polls. He was on the way out and as a last, strange sidestep, casually endorsed the war, as though he always had. Eight days later the Army of the Potomac was slaughtered at Fredericksburg and the great Peace campaign began, full force, whereupon Vallandigham went back to talking Peace at every turn. For one brief moment only he had spoken for the Union cause in wartime. He would do his best to erase the fact from memory in the months and years ahead.

*　　*　　*

The final Emancipation Proclamation of January 1, 1863 was not as Radical a document as certain Radicals had wanted it to be. It was Radical enough, however, to terrify Conservatives, North and South. The stage was now set for the freeing of the slaves wherever the Union army appeared, and nothing was said about sending anybody back to Africa. Abandoning colonization in this manner, the President was joining forces, at long last, with Garrison, Phillips, and the Abolitionists—the enemies of both slavery and colonization.[5] Another feature of the final Proclamation was the provision for raising Negro troops. Dismissed as unimportant in the spring of 1863, the Negro troops proposal would grow to gargantuan significance in the following year, to serve as a major feature of the presidential election campaign.

Bearing out some longstanding Conservative predictions, the Proclamation shocked and horrified many Conservative Unionists, including a large number of War Democrats. It was widely predicted that border slave-state Unionists no longer would fight for the Union cause now tarred with the brush of Abolition.[6] But the prediction proved false, in the general sense. When all was said and done the Union cause was no more badly damaged by the Proclamation in the border slave states than it was in the free states, and in both areas the number of defectors was not large enough to matter.

Border slave-state congressmen friendly to Emancipation were more in evidence in the lame-duck session of the Thirty-seventh Congress than in either of the preceding sessions. In December 1862 a number of War Democrats were ready and waiting to announce in behalf of Compensated Emancipation and anti-slavery principles in general. Included in the group were Congressmen Noell of Missouri, Thomas of Maryland, Brown of Virginia, and Clements of Tennessee, and Senator Henderson of Missouri, all of whom came forward with measures recommending gradual, Compensated Emancipation in their respective states.[7] (All were Union party

Democrats.) Speaking on the question, Henderson inquired, "Is the Proclamation of the President wrong? It may have been originally unwise in policy. I thought it was; but its withdrawal now will scarcely induce the rebels to lay down their arms." He urged Emancipation as the proper course in every state under federal control.[8] Noell, Thomas, Brown, Clements, and Henderson represented only one segment of loyal border slave-state opinion, but it was by no means insignificant. The West Virginia State Constitutional Convention, meeting in Wheeling, February 17, reflected the feelings of War Democrat Congressman Brown of West Virginia by striking down slavery with a vote of 54 to 0. When a popular vote was taken on the issue in April, the anti-slavery cause was sustained, 27,749 to 572.[9] Anti-slavery Unionists were no longer a rarity in the border slave states.

That is not to say, however, that pro-slavery Unionists were altogether out of business in the border slave states. Many of their kind were still around in 1863 to protest the presidential Proclamation and to curse the Union party. Democratic editors John H. Harney of the Louisville *Democrat;* Nathaniel Paschall, St. Louis *Missouri Republican;* and J. L. Walker, Paris (Kentucky) *Western Citizen,* followed such a course, as did many others. For the remainder of the war they would work for creation of a Unionist coalition free of pesky Emancipationists. Still despising and reviling the Peace cause, however, they would continue their support of the war.[10]

In short, it would seem that pro-slavery protests against Emancipation, which Conservative Republicans had feared so much and for so long, had failed to turn a sizable number of loyal-state Democrats against the war. It would prove possible in 1863 to rouse the Regular Democracy against some other administration policies, but the issues involved were the civil liberties of whites and not the property status of the Negro. A large number of Democratic Negrophobes in the loyal states would appear to have come around to accepting the propriety of Emancipation. To them, it no longer appeared as "another Santo Domingo": the signal for the murder of the white women and children of the South. In the heat of political combat, however, changes in popular sentiment are sometimes overlooked, and so it was in the case of this particular change. In every state in which the Democrats had scored big gains in the elections of 1862, the Peace faction sponsored in 1863, and the other Regular Democratic factions supported, protest campaigns against the freeing of the slaves.

*   *   *

War Democrats in uniform had much to do with the military operations of 1863 which broke the back of the Confederate resistance. Following considerable finagling, Democratic General Grant regained control of the Army of the Mississippi, at the expense of Democratic General McClernand, and proceeded to defeat the Confederates all over Mississippi. The Army of the Potomac, under Democratic General George G. Meade, defeated the Confederates at Gettysburg, July 4. The Army of the Cumberland, under Democratic General Rosecrans, defeated the Confederates at Stone's River on the first day of the year, and drove them into Georgia. The battle of Chickamauga ruined the career of Democratic General Rosecrans, but did little to improve the Confederate position. Torn to pieces by the forces of Democratic Generals George H. Thomas and James B. Steedman, the Confederate Army of the Tennessee was so badly damaged as to never win another battle of major significance for the remainder of the war. At the close of the year, Democratic General Grant led the Chatanooga campaign, which cleared the enemy from all of Tennessee.

But the military contributions of the War Democracy had no immediate effect upon the great Peace Campaign of 1863. Before the year was very far along the Peace Campaign was burning brightly in every corner of the loyal states, with the assistance of many Peace converts culled from disillusioned segments of the War Democracy.

In New York City, for example, the outstanding Peace Democrat of 1863 was Congressman-elect Fernando Wood of the Mozart Hall machine. Having supported the Union cause without conditions in 1861 and with conditions in 1862, he now declared against the war in its entirety and overnight became the leader of the Eastern Peace Democracy. When the New York *News* resumed publication in June 1863, Wood's brother Benjamin returned to the forefront of the propaganda struggle as a publisher of national importance, working for Peace.[11]

Hoping to break the force of the Peace buildup in New York, Lincoln wrote to Governor Seymour, March 23, requesting his support for the Union cause. In keeping with his general approach, Seymour replied, offering support on a Conditional basis. It was not an encouraging exchange so far as Lincoln was concerned.[12] Later in the year, another overture was made to Seymour by Secretary of War Stanton, very likely at Lincoln's request. Contacting his good friend Edwards Pierrepont of Tammany Hall, Stanton offered all the influence of the War Department in the matter of securing the 1864 Democratic presidential nomination, if Seymour would agree to announce in favor of the Union cause—without conditions.[13] The proposal came to nothing. For Seymour to work in harmony with Lincoln and Stanton, he would have to first repudiate the Peace Democracy, and the prospect of such a move had no appeal for him in 1863. The Peace cause was gaining strength in New York at this stage, and the administration losing popularity. Forced to choose between the two as a prospective ally, Seymour chose the Peace Democracy.

Another powerful Peace faction existed in Illinois, where the Democratic legislature of 1863 rejected the annual message of Republican Governor Yates, largely devoted to praise of the Emancipation Proclamation. As the first matter of business a resolution was considered calling for immediate withdrawal of the Proclamation in the interest of national unity. It failed of passage in the State Senate only because a Democratic member died.[14] The Democratic legislature of Indiana did not invite Republican Governor Morton to deliver the customary annual message in person, and it therefore appeared in printed form. A Peace Democrat proposed its flat rejection, but the motion was killed by Regular War Democrats and Conditionals voting against it, in company with the Unionist minority.[15] In both houses of the Indiana legislature the Peace Democracy railed against the Emancipation Proclamation, denouncing the war as an Abolitionist conspiracy, designed in part by Governor Morton. Widescale graft and corruption were attributed to the Governor, and special attention was called to the role of War Democrat Robert Dale Owen, Purchasing Agent for Indiana from April 1861 to February 1863. Military materiel obtained under Owen's authority had cost the state some $900,000, and the Regular Democrats wanted an accounting.[16] A resolution was offered, demanding removal of all war matters from the Governor's control and creation of a state military board, to govern the future expenditure of state war funds and oversee the conduct of the war. To stifle this proposal Union party members bolted the legislature, refusing to return.[17]

In Ohio, the Union party still controlled the legislature in 1863 and the Peace faction was powerless to force its policy on the state. Anti-administration proposals were offered in large number, nonetheless, and many Democratic leaders gave them their endorsement, including Hugh J. Jewett, Democratic candidate for governor, 1861. At a Jackson Day dinner in Columbus, January 8, Jewett said that had he been Governor when the presidential Proclamation was released, he would have replied with a proclamation of his own, countermanding the President's. Lyman R. Critchfield, the state's Attorney General, went further, coming out flatly against the further prosecution of the war. The Proclamation had altered everything, he said, changing the war for Union to a "nigger crusade."[18] These and other remarks of the same kind evoked a spirited response from the Ohio Union ranks—the most hostile answers coming from the War Democracy. In his Annual Address to the legislature, War Democrat Governor Tod declared in favor of a more forceful policy in dealing with the Peace Democracy. So far as he was concerned, the military arrest of civilians not only had the sanction of law but was absolutely necessary to preserve the Union cause. Every such arrest carried out in Ohio, the Governor said, could be properly regarded as his personal responsibility.[19]

Answering the Peace resolutions under consideration in the Illinois legislature, the Douglas Club of Vienna, Illinois, declared that "the errors of the administration. . .form no excuse for any loyal citizen to withhold his support from the government."[20] Among Illinois Democrats serving in the army, many had the same opinion. Democratic Generals Isham N. Haynie, Mason Brayman, and William P. Carlin of Illinois wrote public letters home, denouncing the Peace campaign.[21] Generals John A. McClernand and John A. Logan of Illinois announced their resignation from the Democratic party.[22] Anti-war measures in the Indiana legislature evoked a hostile reply from Democratic officers of Indiana troops serving currently in Arkansas. Colonel William E. McLean, 43rd Indiana Infantry, drew up an address to the People of Indiana, protesting that "The name Democrat, associated with all that is bright and glorious in the history of the past, is being sullied and disgraced by demagogues who are appealing to the lowest prejudices and passions of our people." The address was endorsed by General Alvin P. Hovey; Colonel William T. Spicely, 24th Indiana; Colonel George F. McGinnis, 11th Indiana; and Colonel James R. Slack, 47th Indiana. All were Democrats.[23]

Another War Democrat entering the Indiana controversy of 1863 was Robert Dale Owen, Assistant Secretary of the Treasury. While the Regular Democracy of Indiana was cursing the "dictatorial" policies of Governor Morton, in March, Owen was preparing and publishing a sixteen-page address, accusing the Peace faction of treasonable designs.[24] That the address received a hearty circulation in Democratic districts all over Indiana was a matter of importance. Sensing the drift of popular opinion (something of a rarity among the Regular Democrats of 1863), Thomas A. Hendricks of Indiana moved against the Peace campaign in the hope of sparing the Democracy from serious repurcussions. The recent breakup of the Indiana legislature was simply the result of a Union party bolt, and the Regular Democracy was not responsible for that. But a large majority of Indiana voters were sympathetic to the bolters for blocking the whirlwind Peace campaign. By voting Democratic in October 1862 the electorate had not declared against the Union cause, as the Peace faction was attempting to persuade the legislature to do. Whatever was intended by the vote, this was not it, Hendricks decided. Counting heads and asking questions, he determined that the War faction was numerous enough among the Democratic legislators to prevent the passage of any significant anti-Union legislation, and as the advocate of law and order he brought the message to the Union party bolters, requesting their return. Accepting Hendricks at his word, the Unionists resumed their seats, and the Peace resolutions were thereupon defeated.[25] (Legislative investigations into the wartime purchasing policies of Governor Morton and his special agent, War Democrat Robert Dale Owen, uncovered no evidence substantiating Democratic party charges of graft and corruption. Vast amounts of military materiel and the arsenal established to house it all were acquired at standard cost, without undue benefit to anyone involved. So the Regular Democracy was forced to concede.)[26]

In January 1863 War Democrat Joseph A. Wright of Indiana (Union party) was replaced in the Senate by War Democrat David Turpie (Regular). As a finai sally at the Peace Democracy in advance of his departure, Wright came to the defense of an administration policy hated by the Regular Democracy—the military arrest of civilians in wartime. "It is to be regretted," he said, "that, in an hour like this, men who profess to be loyal to the Government should seize upon questions of such a character and so discuss them as, notwithstanding their vaunted patriotism, to weaken the Government and the cause they profess to favor—the suppression of the rebellion." In Wright's opinion the War Democrats were the only true believers in Democratic party tradition. As a splendid example of true Democracy in action, he cited the policies of General William S. Rosecrans, Commander of the Army of the Cumberland, "one who is fighting for his country and not for the Presidency."[27] (The compliment also was intended as a jab at McClellan, already regarded as a major contender for the 1864 Democratic presidential nomination.)

The political importance of General Rosecrans was on the rise in 1863. As a War Democrat, he was alarmed about the Peace campaign to the point of arguing the matter in public. Especially disturbing, from his point of view, were Peace pronouncements emanating from the legislatures of Ohio (his home state) and nearby Indiana. Hoping to offset the Peace attack, he issued a statement from army headquarters at Murfreesboro, Tennessee, denouncing the Confederates and the Peace Democrats, at one and the same time.[28] Democratic Colonel John M. Connell of the 17th Ohio Infantry, fighting under Rosecrans, declared identical opinions for publication.[29]

In line with the resolutions and addresses emitting from the Murfreesboro battlefield, a mass meeting was held at Cincinnati February 23, under the chairmanship of War Democrat William S. Groesbeck, a former Congressman and Union party candidate for Congress in 1862. Speeches were delivered by Governor Tod of Ohio, and General Lewis Wallace and former Senator Wright of Indiana, all of whom were Democrats.[30] A similar meeting held in Columbus, March 3, featured an address by Andrew Johnson, Military Governor of Tennessee. According to Johnson he was still a Democrat, but a Democrat concerned for the Union. Those otherwise concerned he damned as traitors, including those who talked in terms of compromise. He was opposed, he said, to carrying out the war for the purpose of subjugation or the freeing of the slaves. If, however, freeing the slaves would help to win the war, he was in favor of that, too.[31]

Speaking from the Conditional side of the fence, Democratic Governor

Joel Parker of New Jersey delivered an inaugural address in 1863 calculated to please the War Democracy and Peace Democracy alike. The desired result was achieved and party unity established in New Jersey—for the moment. A War Democrat became Speaker of the Assembly,[32] a Peace Democrat Speaker of the Senate.[33] Encouraged by the compromise and lack of opposition within the Democratic party, the Peace Democracy of New Jersey went at once to work. As its first move, a resolution was advanced in the Assembly by Dr. Thomas Dunn English, declaring null and void the Emancipation Proclamation, while Senate resolutions were presented by Daniel Holsman, attacking the federal War policy as unconstitutional on many counts. The war itself was described as unnecessary, and a six-month armistice was recommended, together with a national Peace conference. Such policy, Holsman said, would properly reflect the wishes of the people of New Jersey and New Jersey soldiers in the field.[34]

The Holsman Resolutions were subjected to attack in the state Senate by War Democrat Joseph T. Crowell, who described them as "a libel on the people of New Jersey."[35] In the 1862 campaign the Democratic party and the Democratic candidate for Governor of New Jersey had campaigned on a pro-war platform, Crowell declared, and their victory could not be construed as a mandate for Peace. Indeed, it was the height of impudence for anti-war men to regard the "defeat of the administration as an approval of their Secessionism, or an indorsement of this. . .peace programme." In Crowell's opinion, the very mention of compromise by northerners in 1863 entitled the Confederates to assume that northerners "are all natural-born fools." The situation should by this time be clear to everyone; that the Confederates would not accept reunion even "if we would give them a blank sheet and let them dictate their own terms."[36]

Peace Democrat Holsman moved that Crowell be ruled out of order. The Speaker ruled otherwise but the Democratic majority overrode the decision of the chair, and Crowell was suppressed.[37] The struggle was renewed in the Assembly by Regular War Democrat Robert J. Chandler, who moved postponement of the Holsman Resolutions, and War Democrat James M. Scovel of the Union party, who delivered a long speech on the subject, explaining his conversion from Democratic Regularity to the support of Lincoln and the anti-slavery cause. Having followed the lead of Stephen A. Douglas (and "would to God his warning voice could reach his countrymen who have abandoned his teachings"), he could see no alternative to supporting the President and the federal war policy, as Douglas would surely have done. The actions of the President in the matters of the *habeas corpus* controversy and the Emancipation Proclamation, were wholly commendable, in Scovel's opinion, and Lincoln was not a tyrant but a savior.[38]

The Holsman resolutions were taken back and revised in caucus, in accordance with the views of the Regular War Democracy. As finally adopted they had little resemblance to the original, calling only for the visit of New Jersey commissioners to Richmond, with the power to inquire as to Confederate interest in Peace negotiations. Gone were all the implications of surrender and angry criticism of the Union cause.[39] But even this—the watered down version—was too strong for War Democrat Theodore F. Randolf, Majority Leader of the Assembly, who responded with an all-out attack on the Peace Democracy and a series of resolutions of his own declaring that the people of New Jersey would loyally support the enforcement of the federal law, seeking redress only in the courts and at the polls. The Rudolf Resolutions carried, together with a major War Loan bill.[40]

Similar events were transpiring in New York, where the Conditional War Democracy prevailed behind the leadership of Governor Seymour. Buoyed by the outcome of the 1862 elections and anxious to accelerate the battle with the anti-slavery opposition, the New York City Democratic leadership revived a propaganda agency dormant for many years—The Society for the Diffusion of Political Knowledge (War Democrat Samuel J. Tilden of Tammany Hall was largely instrumental in bringing this about).[41] By the close of February, the Society was in full operation. Another New York City Democratic journal, the *Old Guard*, began publication about the same time under the direction of C. Chauncy Burr, formerly of the Hackensack (New Jersey) *Bergen County Democrat*. The Society for the Diffusion of Political Knowledge would seek to represent the views of all the Regular Democratic factions, along the same lines as Governor Seymour. The *Old Guard*, which also claimed Seymour as a hero, was out-and-out for Peace and exceedingly hostile to the War Democracy. The *Old Guard*, and the Society for the Diffusion of Political Knowledge portrayed the Republican and the Union parties in the worst possible light, attacking as opportunists the Democratic members of the Union coalition. The same policy was adhered to by the Associated Press—the largest news-gathering agency in the United States, run by Democrats, for Democrats.[42] Against the propaganda power of the Regular Democracy the Union party leaders were to organize in 1863 the Loyal Publication Society, designed to furnish counter-propaganda. A major feature of the Unionist attack in this instance was the contribution of the War Democracy, represented by writers such as Robert Dale Owen, George Bancroft, and Peter Cooper.[43] Emphasized constantly in the arguments of the Loyal Publication Society was the overall importance of the War Democracy to the winning of the war. No other single issue would receive so much attention.[44]

Seeking to offset the great prestige of Governor Seymour, following the New York elections of 1862, a rally was held in New York City, January 5, at the Fifth Avenue Hotel, to sing the praises of Democratic General Benjamin F. Butler for his conduct as Commander of the Department of the Gulf. Numbered among the sponsors of the occasion were several leading Democrats.[45] Out of this evolved a public reception, April 2, 1863, at the Academy of Music, where Butler delivered a sensational speech.[46] Describing himself as an "Andrew Jackson Democrat", he said, "I am not for the Union as it was. . .I am not for the Union to be again as it was." Now that South Carolina had gone out of the Union, he said, "I shall take care that when she comes in again, she comes in better behaved, that she shall no longer be the fierbrand of the Union—aye, and that she shall enjoy what her people never yet have enjoyed—the blessings of a Republican form of Government.[47] Implicitely, the General not only approved of the Emancipation Proclamation but also of Sumner's "State Suicide" theory. A recent convert to the cause of anti-slavery reform, he was far ahead of many Republicans, including Abraham Lincoln.

To the same extent that General Butler fascinated the extremists in the War Democracy, so Congressman-elect Fernando Wood of Mozart Hall fascinated extremists in the Peace Democracy. And in all he said and did, Wood attempted to identify himself with Governor Horatio Seymour. Speaking in the Governor's behalf and without correction from any quarter, he predicted wholesale rejection of federal authority by the New York state government. Seymour would refuse to enforce all statutes of dubious constitutionality, Wood declared.[48] Tied in this way to the coattails of the most powerful Democratic politician in the East, Wood was once again regarded as a man of importance, and everything he said was aimed against the war.

At the Mozart Hall City Convention of March 24, a strong Peace speech was delivered by Wood in which he sought to read the War Democrats out of the Democratic party. "There is no such thing as a War Democrat," he said. "There cannot be War Democrats because that involves the necessity of supporting the policy of war; . . .any man who supports the policy in this administration cannot be a Democrat. The moment Democrats indorse the policy of the administration, they at once drop the characteristics of the Democratic party and merge into the Abolition party."[49] The audience responded with great excitement. A large element in Mozart Hall clearly had abandoned the war. Shortly following the convention, the Mozart Central Committee made plans for a giant Peace rally, to be held April 7, and a call went out, urging the attendance of all persons "opposed to the conscript act (pending in Congress), opposed to war for the negro, . . .(and) in favor of the rights of the poor." The rally was apparently a large success and resolutions were passed declaring "that the war, as conducted by this administration, has been a failure," and "Under these circumstances we declare for peace. This administration cannot conquer the South if they would—and would not if they could."

At the rally, Wood delivered a sensational address in which he said that Lincoln would be succeeded by a Democrat in 1865 and that peace would be secured through diplomacy. On this occasion, as often in the past, he referred with sadness to the 40th New York Infantry—the so-called "Mozart Regiment"—which he took credit for raising when the war was young. Those were the days when the war was for the Union, he said. Now the object of the war had changed to "unconstitutional" purposes and he could no longer be proud of his action, in the raising of the Mozart Regiment. Indeed, he wished the regiment were no longer in the field.[50]

From the front came a statement by Democratic Colonel Thomas W. Egan of the 40th New York. The Mozart Regiment was not the product of Wood's activity, Egan declared, but that of loyal citizens. Actually, Wood was not involved in the raising of a single man.[51] Egan was himself a product of Mozart Hall. Speaking for the regiment, he came out warmly for the war, repudiating the policies of Wood and all other Mozart leaders associated with the Peace campaign. He praised the speech of General Butler, recently delivered at the Academy of Music. Egan's declaration was endorsed by many Democratic officers serving in the 40th New York. (Nothing could more infuriate the Peace Democracy. Editor C. Chauncy Burr of the *Old Guard* depicted Colonel Egan as a contemptible opportunist, saying that he only was interested in becoming brigadier and that his officers had hopes of receiving regimental commands.)[52]

*   *   *

To break the force of the growing Peace campaign of 1863, the Unionists rallied the various independent Union Clubs throughout the loyal states and organized two major bodies of nonpartisan design—the Loyal National League and the Loyal Union League, supporting the war against the interests of the Peace Democracy. The Loyal Union League was founded at Cleveland in the spring of 1863; the Loyal National League at New York City, around the same time. A War Democrat, New York City businessman Prosper M. Wetmore, was called the originator of the Loyal National league, which was less Republican in composition than its rival.[53] War Democrats played a major part in the work of the Loyal National League, from first to last.[54] In addition to propaganda, a major purpose of both leagues was the raising of volunteers, white and Negro.[55]

The activities of the leagues and the declarations of their Democratic leaders thoroughly enraged the Peace Democracy. According to Chauncy Burr of the *Old Guard,* the Loyal National League was a grand collection of "fanatics, contractors, abolitionists, and fishy democrats. . .In one word, it is a new league of old-fashioned *federalism,* so long dead and buried in this country. It is really a disunion organization. Every man who joins it who is not a federalist and disunionist, is fooled and cheated. The national unity it talks about, means the destruction of the State Governments upon which the present Union rests for support. It is a revolutionary and treasonous organization which ought to be met in every township by a Constitutional League, to expose its revolutionary dangers."[56] Of the Democratic members of the Loyal National League, a prominent example was Daniel S. Dickinson, the former champion of Southern Rights, whom Burr called "niggerhead."[57] Among the Democratic members of the Loyal Union League, the best known were John Van Buren, James T. Brady, and Charles P. Daly, all of whom addressed a major rally on April 20, at Madison Square, honoring the great Union Square "uprising of the North," two years earlier. In Burr's estimation, the rally was nothing more nor less than a "Great Purchase and Sale of Damaged Democrats" and the man who paid the bill was President Lincoln, who "can buy the hide and tallow of thousands of fishy politicians."[58]

A disturbing aspect of the Unionist response to the great Peace campaign of 1863 was another flurry of violence against the editorial offices of the Peace Democracy.[59] Attracting national attention in March was the smashing of the presses of Samuel Medary's Columbus (Ohio) *Crisis.* The Peace faction was infuriated by the assault and especially critical of a couple of War Democrats—Military Governor Andrew Johnson of Tennessee and Joseph A. Wright of Indiana—for their association with it. Mutually involved in a patriotic speaking tour, Johnson and Wright appeared together for the first time at Columbus late in February. Condemning the Peace Democracy, they singled out the *Crisis* for special, lengthy criticism.[60] Many soldiers were on hand for the speeches and when the rally was over 200 of them broke into the *Crisis* office and tore the place apart. Later that evening the same mob visited the office of the *Ohio Statesman,* inflicting damage there as well. Editor Medary of the *Crisis* proclaimed himself the victim of an organized plot in which War Democrats Johnson and Wright were both deeply involved, having divested themselves of "the wildest political harangue before men could be found to engage in the dirty work." Out of town when the attack occurred, Medary was greeted by a brass band upon his return, carried to his carriage by a crowd of admirers, and escorted to his lodgings in a grand parade. A speech of tribute was provided by Allen G. Thurman, Conditional War Democrat. The sacking of the *Crisis* office had rendered Medary a hero of the national Democracy.[61]

Physical attacks on the Peace press had other unforeseen results, including the formation of a new secret society dedicated to Peace at any price: the Order of American Knights. Supporting the activities of the Knights of the Golden Circle, the new organization found many recruits in Missouri, Illinois and Indiana, drawing heavily on two main sources: libertarians concerned about the Bill of Rights, and pro-Confederates solely concerned with discouraging the Union cause. In many localities shooting brawls occurred in 1863 between soldiers and Peace extremists, and in every case the Unionist faction blamed the Order of American Knights.[62]

Seizing on reports of increased activity by disloyal northerners, War Democrats Andrew Johnson and Joseph A. Wright continued their speaking tour, and wherever they appeared the audience was seemingly electrified. In Pennsylvania, where the Regular Democracy controlled the legislature, Johnson and Wright created a disturbance by requesting an audience in the capitol building. A reply was offered by Democratic State Senator Heister Clymer, who regarded the request as shocking in purpose and brazen in detail. He was especially critical of War Democrat Andrew Johnson, who, he said, was not really Governor of anything at all, since there was no federal statute providing for the appointment of state governors, civil or military. In truth, Andrew Johnson was nothing more than "a mere hireling of patronage and power."[63] The Regular Democrats were called upon to stand together and to reject the request to transform the capitol building into a forum for Radical pronouncements. Ignoring the appeal, many Regular Democrats voted with the Unionists and Wright and Johnson were permitted the use of the hall.[64]

No such factious spirit was evident in the Illinois legislature, where the Peace Democracy failed by only one vote of enacting laws removing the state from the war. Seeking to prevent further attempts in this direction, Governor Yates of Illinois prorogued the legislature (June 10) after which the Republican and Union members returned to their homes. Democratic legislators denied the legality of the Governor's action but there was nothing they could do without a quorum, and after hanging around Springfield for several weeks they also went home. The matter came quickly to the attention of the State Supreme Court. Although finding that the Governor had no power to act as he had, the Court also found that dispersal of the legislature amounted to adjournment, *sine die*. Of the several Democratic judges on the Court, Pinkney H. Walker, and Sidney D. Breese were the most emphatic in declaring the backhanded victory of Republican Governor Yates.[65]

Similar to the questionable legality of Governor Yates' activity in 1863 was that of Governor Morton, blocking the actions of the Democratic legislature of Indiana. Departing Indianapolis in March, to take his seat in the U.S. Senate, War Democrat Thomas A. Hendricks abandoned control of the lcoal Democracy to the Peace faction, headed by Samuel H. Buskirk,

Speaker of the Assembly. Acting in unison, the Democratic majority bypassed Governor Morton's war appropriation bills and suddenly adjourned, leaving the Governor to operate as best he could, without funds. Confronted by the imminence of bankruptcy, Morton contacted the bipartisan Indianapolis law firm of English and New, requesting their assistance. The Democratic member of the partnership was former Congressman William H. English, famous for supporting the cause of slavery in Kansas, in 1858.[66] Subsequently, he had campaigned for Breckinridge, but in 1863 was a War Democrat and very hot against the Peace cause. With the assistance and personal guarantees of English and New, Governor Morton was able to negotiate a very large loan from a major banking firm in New York City. Practically on this amount alone he would manage to carry on the functions of the state authority without the assistance of the legislature, which was not directed to reconvene until the close of 1864.[67] The Democratic Indianapolis *State Sentinel* protested that "Indiana today is as completely under military rule as France, Russia, or Austria." Angered also by the failure of Peace propaganda to sway the War Democracy of Indiana, the *Sentinel* complained: "A large portion of the people are willingly bowing their necks to receive the yoke of despotism."[68]

A last exchange between the the leaders of the War and Peace Democracies of the Thirty-seventh Congress occurred in the House, January 14, 1863. Speaking for the Peace faction, Congressman Vallandigham of Ohio demanded once again surrender of the Union, and for so doing was criticized by Wright of Pennsylvania. The people were tired, Vallandigham declared, of never-ending taxation, and dreadfully tired of supporting the "war for the negro." They wanted Peace on any terms, he said—even at the cost of national unity. And they wanted the army drastically reduced in size. The 1862 election results had made this wholly clear.[69] Responding in behalf of the War Democracy, Wright denied the validity of Vallandigham's assertions. The recommendation for a smaller army in the midst of wartime was depicted as a "monstrous proposition," and the prospect of an armistice pronounced unthinkable, amounting merely to surrender. Nor was Vallandigham correct in the contention that the 1862 election results were a mandate for Peace. Indeed, "never was mortal man more mistaken on earth. The great change in public opinion as evidenced in these election results. . .(stems) from a want of confidence in the way in which the war has been conducted, and the blunders of the Administration." A strong supporter of General McClellan's unofficial campaign for President, Wright insisted that "the people of the country have not abandoned the idea of saving their country, but they *have* adopted the idea of changing their rulers."[70] Vallandigham and other Peace Democrats were constantly referring to the Confederates as "our brothers." Wright did not approve of the term. "They are not 'my brothers, in the cant phrase of the northern (Secession) sympathizers. They are rebels. It is only loyal men who are my brothers." Vallandigham had criticized New England as an Abolitionist stronghold. Wright defended New England, denouncing those who sought to drive a wedge between the loyal Union people of the East and West. The Peace Democrats, he said, were "demagogues. . .attempting to corrupt the people."[71]

The presidential policy of pampering and reassuring the Conservative Unionists on the slavery issue was never really abandoned at any time. But by 1863 it was little more than verbiage. Having introduced the radical Emancipation Proclamation, Lincoln soon afterwards was ready for another radical step—the arming of the slaves. He would not admit to such a plan, however, until it was well under way; and even then, he would do his best to make it seem that somebody else was the plan-maker. In the arming of the slaves, as in the case of so many other radical actions, he would call to the forefront one of several War Democrats who, it would appear, were the authors of Radical policy unparalleled in nature.

As an alleged Conservative, Lincoln was confronted in September 1862 by a group of Radicals from Chicago, urging upon him the arming of the slaves. Lincoln was cold to the idea. "If we were to arm them," he said, "I fear that in a few weeks the arms would be in the hands of the rebels."[72] But Radical Republicans were not alone in urging the employment of Negro troops. Democratic Generals David Hunter and Benjamin F. Butler were on record in favor of the policy, in company with Democratic Governor Sprague of Rhode Island and Democratic editors John Forney and Nathaniel Paschall (Philadelphia *Press*, Washington *Chronicle*, and St. Louis *Republican*).[73] Thus encouraged, administration leaders introduced a measure in Congress authorizing the enlistment of Negro recruits in the Regular Army and the Navy (the Negro Troops Bill of 1863). Before the bill was out of committee, a Negro troop-raising campaign already was in progress in Louisiana. Lincoln had wanted the services of Democratic General Benjamin F. Butler in this instance, and had offered him the opportunity of going back to New Orleans on a grand troop-raising tour (which offer Butler had declined.[74]) Democratic blessings were nonetheless obtained shortly afterward in the form of public statements by Montgomery C. Meigs, Quartermaster General of the Army, and Andrew Johnson, Military Governor of Tennessee. (In short time a vigorous Negro troop-raising program was in full swing in all of Tennessee reoccupied by Union arms.)[75]

Meanwhile, Congress had taken up consideration of the Negro Troops Bill, and Conservatives were having a field day attacking it. The Negro was basically a coward, they said, and could not be expected to win against Confederate bravery and manliness. The Negro was ignorant and stupid, they said, and could not learn to operate machinery as complex as a musket or a rifle. And, finally, the Negro was vicious and brutal, and his presence in the army was certain of producing "another Santo Domingo," at the expense of the white women and children of the South. (This last contention was basically repetitious of the Confederate position, branding as outlaws all persons associated with the arming of the Negroes.) Peace Democrat May of Maryland delivered a speech in the House of Representatives declaring unqualified opposition to the Negro Troops Bill. It was, in his estimation, "simply preposterous" as a manifestation of military strength, and "imminently disgraceful" as an evidence of national policy. Further, he declared that the "amiable disposition, inert nature, slovenly habits, clumsiness, (and) want of vigilance" of the Negro rendered him incapable of worthwhile military service.[76] The Congressman's remarks represented the opinion of thousands of observers, North and South. Other Democrats in Congress made speeches to the same effect. War Democrat Wright of Pennsylvania pleaded with the Radicals to change their minds. "Introduce the negro into your Army," he said, "and you demoralize that Army and destroy its usefulness."[77] Democratic Congressman Lazear of Pennsylvania, theretofore in favor of the war, attacked the arming of the Negroes and quit the Union cause, announcing in favor of "peace by just measures and dignified conciliation."[78] Never again would he cast his vote in favor of the war.

The previous May, Democratic General Benjamin F. Butler had written the War Department, opposing the arming of Negroes in the Department of the Gulf. In his opinion, as of that moment, the average Negro was afraid of firearms and utterly unable to defend himself in a shooting engagement.[79] Believing otherwise, Secretary of War Stanton continued to press for the raising of Negro volunteers, on a state basis, while the Radicals in Congress were ramming home the Negro Troops Bill which passed the House, February 3, 1863, by a vote of 83 to 54. Two War Democrats voted in the majority (Brown of Virginia and Noell of Missouri.) Thirteen War Democrats voted in the minority.[80] Upon its passage in the Senate, the bill was signed into law by Lincoln and quickly became a major factor in the war.

Dealing as he was with political dynamite, the President determined on using as many Democrats of Conservative reputation as he possibly could in the mustering of Negro troops and sending them against Secession. War Democrats prominently involved in the raising of the first federal Negro regiments (as opposed to state contingents) included General Silas Casey of Rhode Island and Colonel Hiram Scofield of Iowa. Casey was a veteran of the Peninsula Campaign and a bitter critic of McClellan and all other proslavery officers, against whom he had testified before the Joint Committee on the Conduct of the War. In the latter half of 1863 he was appointed president of a selecting board charged with the responsibility of finding officers for federal Negro regiments.[81] Scofield was a veteran of Ft. Donelson, Shiloh, Corinth, and Hatchie, Mississippi. In May he was promoted from captain, to colonel of the 47th U.S. Colored Infantry which was to do all its fighting in Louisiana.[82]

Among the first to organize Negro troops on the state level were the Governors of Kansas, Wisconsin, and Ohio, and the Military Governor of Arkansas—War Democrats Thomas Carney, James T. Lewis, David Tod, and General John S. Phelps.[83] War Democrat Governor William Sprague of Rhode Island was also authorized to raise a Negro regiment, but his term was expiring and he abandoned the idea.[84] War Democrats prominently identified with the battlefield performance of Negro state units included Generals Benjamin F. Butler, Ambrose E. Burnside, and Edward Ferrero, and Colonels William B. Wooster and John F. Appleton.[85] All were engaged in the Virginia campaigns of 1863 through 1865, under Democratic Generals Meade and Grant, with the lone exception of Colonel Appleton who served with General Banks in the Department of the Gulf. Negroes engaged in battle under the Democratic officers in question did not bear out the dire predictions of the anti-Negro zealots. In May 1863 (three months following Congressman May's diatribe against the Negro character, in the House of Representatives) the First Kansas Colored Infantry entered combat at Center Creek, Missouri, the Second Arkansas Colored near Island No. 65, on the Mississippi. They were the product of troop-raising efforts by War Democrat Governors Carney and Phelps, and both were impressive, to the distinct satisfaction of their sponsors. Additional Negro troops were called upon in the defense of southern Kansas against the depredations of Confederate raiding parties. In mid-July, 1863, the Leavenworth *Conservative* announced, "All reports from the lower country are to the effect that we have to rely mainly upon colored soldiers."[86]

On May 27, the Negro regiments organized under Democratic General Butler in the Department of the Gulf fought well at Port Hudson, Louisiana, under General Banks. Democratic Colonel John F. Appleton was engaged at the head of a Negro regiment. (He was the son of John Appleton, Democratic Chief Justice of the Maine State Supreme Court).[87] A small battle involving Negro troops occurred June 7, at Milliken's Bend, Louisiana. Taken by surprise by a Texas regiment the Negroes fled but regrouped and drove the Texans from the field. A witness to the battle was Democratic Colonel John C. Black of the 37th Illinois, who declared in a letter home: "How humiliating (to the Confederates) and how convincing a proof of the wisdom of the administration."[88] At Ft. Wagner, off the coast of South Carolina, Democratic General Truman Seymour directed an assault, July 10–11, with the help of Negro troops. Seymour was wounded and the attack was beaten off, but to all accounts the Negroes fought bravely and effectively, contrary to the expectations of Democrats in general.[89]

Wholly committed to the further use of Negroes in the war, President Lincoln and Secretary of War Stanton were very tough in their dealings with army officers hostile to the policy. Shortly following their refusal to raise Negro volunteers, Democratic Generals Don Carlos Buell and Henry M. Naglee were relieved of their commands. When Buell requested a court-martial he received instead a private hearing, the results of which were never made public.[90] General Grant was suspected for a time of not really trying to find Negro volunteers, but he assured the War Department that his officers were doing all they could in this regard.[91]

Once decided on a sweeping Emancipation policy and the arming of the Negroes, Lincoln next endeavored to establish an effective federal program to equip the Negro freedmen with a system of survival in a free society. At the order of War Democrat Edwin M. Stanton, a three-man "American Freedmen's Inquiry Commission" was appointed "to investigate the condition of the colored population emancipated by acts of Congress and the President's proclamation (and) to report what measures will best contribute to their protection and improvement, so that they may defend and support themselves; and also how they can most successfully be employed in the service of the government in the suppression of the Rebellion." Selected as Chairman of the Commission was War Democrat Robert Dale Owen of Indiana.

The Freedmen's Commission conducted extensive investigations and submitted three reports, the first of which was written by the Chairman and published June 30, 1863. It was a Radical document, both in spirit and detail, urging the adoption of a federal policy of encouraging slave escapes for the remainder of the war, and a "plan of provisional organization for the improvement, protection and employment of refugee freedmen," requiring division of the southern seaboard in three military departments, following the war, to insure protection of emancipated Negroes in their new freedom. Radicals praised the Commission's preliminary report and Regular Democrats condemned it. Democratic Senator Hendricks of Indiana denounced it as plain old Abolitionist propaganda, while leading the attack against it. (Only twelve years earlier, Hendricks and Robert Dale Owen had cooperated in obtaining passage of the anti-Negro "Black Laws" of Indiana.[92] Once again it would appear that Lincoln had succeeded in stealing away an outstanding Conservative Democrat, in the interest of antislavery reform.)

Another drastic measure recommended by the President in 1863 was troop conscription as a means of filling the depleted Union ranks. Cited by the Peace faction as another example of unprecedented Republican tyranny, the Conscription Law actually was something less than that. It was not unprecedented, having been utilized previously (on a state basis) in the War of 1812. Nor could it be said to be the product of Republican theorists alone. An early advocate of Conscription was August Belmont, Chairman of the Democratic National Committee. Another was Roman Catholic Archbishop Hughes of the New York Diocese.[93] The Conscription law had a major shortcoming, however—the so-called ''Commutation Clause''—which was strictly the work of the administration. Under the terms of the Commutation Clause, a conscript could pay a substitute to take his place. A leading congressional critic of Commutation was Conditional War Democrat Holman of Indiana, who attacked it as a favor to the bankers and the men of commerce. (Both the father and son of Congressman Holman were serving in the army at the time.) An amendment to the Conscription Act was offered by Holman, striking down the cause, and there were many who agreed with the amendment, including some who did not say so publicly. One of these was Secretary of War Stanton who, as Lincoln's advisor, could not persuade him to abandon Commutation, and as Lincoln's supporter could not quarrel with him openly. Without Republican votes the Holman Amendment failed of adoption, 67 to 87.[94]

Peace Democrats attacked the Conscription Act on many counts, describing it as one more example of despotic Republican rule. Democratic Congressmen Voorhees of Indiana, C. A. White of Ohio, and Biddle of Pennsylvania were especially vocal in their opposition. But the measure passed the House, 145 to 48, and overcame a motion in the Senate for indefinite postponement. Five War Democrats supported Conscription in the House, three in the Senate.[95]

Enforcement of Conscription was largely the business of the Bureau of the Provost Marshal General, commanded by Democratic Colonel James B. Fry of Illinois.[96] In every state, commissioners, provost marshals, and staff doctors were appointed to serve at Fry's command. A great many War Democrats were among those so designated.[97] But from the moment the bill became law, it was clear that a great many people accepted the principle argument of the Peace Democracy: that Conscription was an out-and-out transgression against long-established personal rights, and in full defiance of the Constitution. The argument was highly inflammatory, and a good one for stirring up the voters. Peace extremists recommended civil disobedience and the total rejection of Conscription. Peace moderates counseled legal protest. A group of Peace moderates in Illinois addressed a letter to Democratic Judge John D. Caton of the State Supreme Court, declaring opposition to the purpose and the spirit of the law and asking his opinion. Caton replied that the courts must decide on all questions of constitutionality; and that the only proper course in the meantime was the peaceful acceptance of standard legal procedures. Violent protest against Conscription would not do for Democrats, Judge Caton wrote, for that was the way of the Abolitionists. "Let us not follow their wicked teachings."[98]

Dramatically involved in the enforcement of the Conscription Law was Democratic General Ambrose E. Burnside. Removed from command of the Army of the Potomac following his terrible defeat at Fredericksburg, Burnside was reassigned in April 1863 to the Department of the Ohio, embracing Kentucky and the Old Northwest. Upon arriving in April at Cincinnati, he was confronted by the great and growing Peace Campaign, centering now around Conscription. Disturbed by anti-Union hyperbole, and fearful of military action by the newly formed Order of American Knights, Burnside moved to quiet things down with a show of force. This was the purpose of General Order No. 38, announcing that "the habit of declaring sympathy for the enemy will no longer be tolerated in this Department. Persons committing such offense will be at once arrested with a view to being tried (in military court) or sent beyond our lines into the lines of their friends."[99] The order proved obnoxious to a vast majority of Regular Democrats. In Ohio, for example, it brought together for the first time War Democrat George E. Pugh, Conditional War Democrat Samuel S. Cox, and Peace Democrat Clement L. Vallandigham. They still did not agree about the overall issue of the war itself, but stood united on the matters of Conscription and federal censorship of political expression, both of which they denounced as illegal abridgement of American rights. Especially furious was Vallandigham, who on May 4 delivered an attack on Order No. 38 and General Burnside, in the presence of federal agents, at Mt. Vernon, Ohio. For so doing he was arrested on a charge of disloyalty, at the order of Democratic General Burnside, and became at once a martyr—to the total embarrassment of the Union cause. A great many eastern Republican newspapers were critical of Burnside for acting as he had, and doubted that the courts would back him up. The fact was noted with high satisfaction by Samuel Medary in the Peace Democrat Columbus *Crisis*.[100] It was noted with irritation by War Democrat William H. Smith of the Cincinnati *Gazette*, who protested that, "Our eastern contemporaries, who have commented on this arrest as unnecessary, do not appreciate the entire situation."[101]

With a choice of trial or transportation at his disposal, General Burnside decided in favor of a trial.[102] The Provost Marshal selected to represent the government was a War Democrat on Burnside's staff, Colonel J. Madison Cutts, Jr., brother-in-law of the late Stephen A. Douglas. Democratic Colonel Daniel T. Van Buren, a cousin of the late Martin Van Buren, was a member of the Commission. Following the hearing—at which Vallandigham refused to enter any plea—the Commission found against him, and he was sentenced to close confinement for the remainder of the war. When the court adjourned, Vallandigham applied through his lawyer, George E. Pugh, for a writ of *habeas corpus*, and the matter went before District

Judge Humphrey H. Leavitt of Cincinnati, an appointee of Andrew Jackson and a lifelong Democrat. When last heard from in a major case, several years earlier, Leavitt had sustained the constitutionality of the Fugitive Slave Law of 1850, to the outrage of the anti-slavery cause. In this case, however, he was decidedly hostile to Conservative tradition. Following the usual procedure, he would have issued a writ of *habeas corpus,* and permitted General Burnside to offer a reply. Instead—to the defendant's disadvantage—he invited Burnside to present a statement in advance, and then refused the writ upon the grounds that the arrest was legal. According to the argument of lawyer Pugh, a law recently enacted by Congress, relating to *habeas corpus* and regulating judicial proceedings in certain cases, disallowed the action of the government in this instance. Judge Leavitt ruled otherwise, declaring that the government had no proper course of action other than the course pursued by General Burnside. The court opinion described the Peace Democracy as "a class of mischievous politicians (who) had succeeded in poisoning the minds of a portion of the community with the rankest feelings of disloyalty," and "Artful politicians, disguising their latent treason under hollow pretensions of devotion to the Union." Vallandigham's arrest "was virtually the act of the Executive Department under the power vested in the President by the Constitution."[103]

The decision was completely unexpected and Leavitt was subjected to attack by the Peace Democracy as a total incompetent.[104] By the same token he overnight became a hero of the Union cause. In the opinion of President Lincoln, the Vallandigham decision was worth three victories in the field.[105] Peace Democrat Samuel Medary of the Columbus (Ohio) *Crisis* was frankly astonished by the actions of all the War Democrats involved excepting only the defense counsel. Why Burnside, a Democrat, should have arrested Vallandigham in the first place, was bewildering in itself. Why Leavitt, a Democrat, should refuse to turn him loose, was equally bewildering.[106] From his "military bastile" in Cincinnati Vallandigham issued an appeal to the Democracy of Ohio, declaring, "I am for liberty—this is my only crime."[107]

Bothered by the presence of a *cause celebre* in the loyal states, Lincoln set aside the Commission decision rendered against Vallandighan, and directed that the prisoner be transported beyond the Union lines. The action was disturbing to Burnside, who protested, and to Radicals in general, but the President was adamant.[108] Following a very brief stay in the Confederacy, Vallandigham boarded ship, ran the Union blockade, and sailed to Canada, where he established headquarters at Windsor, just across the line from Detroit.[109] . . .President Lincoln had mixed feelings about the Vallandigham arrest. When the eastern Republican press criticized the action, he was deeply upset, regarding Burnside as in error. When Judge Leavitt found in favor of the government he was jubilant, assuring the General that no matter what others might think, he the President was wholly in favor of the Burnside policy.[110]

*   *   *

The trial and banishment of Vallandigham had a powerful impact on the Regular Democracy. Personal liberty was the main issue involved, the Peace men said; Freedom of speech, freedom of assembly, and overall freedom of dissent were in danger of extinction. The question of supporting or not supporting the war was no longer paramount. War Democrats and Conditionals were urged to unite with the Peace faction in behalf of the personal liberty of all Americans.[111] What happened in response to this particular appeal was the virtual dissolution of the Conditional War faction, so recently successful in the 1862 election campaign. As a participant in the Vallandigham trial, Congressman Cox of Ohio regarded himself as very personally involved. Having held back, since April 1861, avoiding association with Vallandigham and Peace, and having altered that policy only recently to protest against Conscription, he now went all the way, seemingly rejecting the war. Vallandigham's counsel, George E. Pugh, previously devoted to the Union cause, also declared for Peace. Congressmen Noble and Nugen of Ohio did the same.[112]

Conversely, a large number of Conditional War Democrats reacted the other way. As the Conditional faction began to fall apart, they joined the straight-out War faction, with whom they would affiliate for the remainder of the war. Ohio Congressman Allen not only became a War Democrat but also joined the Union party.[113] So did Thomas Sparrow of Ohio, 1860 Breckinridge candidate for Congress, and County Judge Philip Mallon of Ohio, all of whom would serve as leading figures at a War Democrat convention held at Columbus later in the year.[114] The Conditional War faction dissolved at this point not only in Ohio but almost everywhere else.[115] Only in New York state did it actually survive in force, behind the leadership of Governor Seymour who continued to support the war in his own extraordinary, Conditional way.

*   *   *

Undeterred by the Peace campaign of 1863, War Democrats in uniform continued to perform with great enthusiasm and occasionally with considerable skill. Democratic General Joseph Hooker was defeated by General Lee at Chancellorsville and his Democratic successor, General George G. Meade, was the winner at Gettysburg. Democratic General Daniel E. Sickles won fame and criticism for his unorthodox fighting at Gettysburg, and following the battle New York City erupted in the Draft Riot of 1863, resulting in the ruin of the city and the massacre of many hundreds of Negro citizens.

War Democrats working for law and order in the midst of the riots included General John E. Wool, Commander of the Department of the East; General Edward R.S. Canby, Commander of the New York City District; Colonel Robert Nugent, Assistant Provost Marshal General for New York City; Colonel H. F. O'Brien of the 11th Infantry, New York Militia; Justice George C. Barnard of the State Supreme Court; and Samuel L. M. Barlow, the well-known financier. John Archbishop Hughes of the New York City Diocese—spiritual leader of many thousands of Irish Democrats—did what he could to pacify the situation, and, after considerable delay, so did Governor Seymour. During the first two or three hours of rioting the mobs routed every detachment of police and military encountered in the streets. Buildings were burned, stores looted, and Negroes butchered with impunity. A mob surrounded the house of Republican Mayor Opdyke, but was dissuaded from burning it down by the arguments of Democratic Judge Barnard of the State Supreme Court.[116] Colonel Nugent was active in organizing troops for use against the mobs.[117] Colonel O'Brien commanded a detachment of 200 policemen and members of the Invalid Corps, on the second day of the riot, beating off a mob of 2,000. Later on, he was recognized walking alone, by members of the mob who stoned, kicked, and clubbed him to death.[118]

On the morning the riots began, Seymour was not to be found. It was believed he could calm the rioters but nobody knew where he was. It was widely believed he was in hiding to avoid taking action, and the suspicion was not held by Republicans alone. War Democrat Samuel L. M. Barlow of New York City, a close friend of Seymour's, wrote to War Democrat Samuel J. Tilden, also of New York City, observing that the riot could not be ended without the use of force, that the Governor should employ the force required, immediately, "and no one but yourself can influence him to do this."[119] Finally located in northern New Jersey, July 14, Seymour hurried to New York City and issued an appeal, asking all citizens to enroll for the draft, in the name of law and order.[120] A second Seymour proclamation, dated July 14, declared New York City in a state of insurrection and promised punishment of all the riot leaders. But for all its firm, decisive tone, the second proclamation meant nothing. Incorrectly dated, for political effect, it was not actually released until July 16 after news had arrived that troops from Gettysburg were on their way to the rescue.[121] Small draft riots were reported in many other communities, including Boston, Milwaukee, Cleveland, Portsmouth, Green Bay, and Rutland, Vermont; and Peace extremists were responsible for the murder of several federal Enrolling Officers.[122]

The scapegoat of the New York City Draft Riots was Democratic General John E. Wool, Commander of the Department of the East, who was relieved of command, July 18, retired from the service, and replaced by another Democrat: General John A. Dix, formerly Commander of the Maryland Department. When last observed, in the fall of 1862, Dix was working in the interest of Horatio Seymour, then candidate for Governor. Immediately upon his arrival he was besieged by Seymour with appeals for suspension of the draft in New York City, until order was restored. A similar appeal was dispatched to Washington by way of War Democrat Samuel J. Tilden of Tammany Hall and a rumor started circulating that Seymour's wishes would be granted—that the second draft call for New York, scheduled for August 19, would not be issued. It was rumored that Seymour was preparing to take New York out of the Union and that Lincoln was trying to appease him by promising withdrawal of the Emancipation Proclamation and the disbanding of all Negro regiments. Advised of the rumors, Secretary of War Stanton responded with an order *speeding up* enlistment of Negro troops. Also advised of the rumors, General Dix put pressure on Seymour to take a public stand for compliance with the draft call of August 19. Seymour did so, and the draft proceeded peacefully in New York City.[123]

It was noted by Unionists that almost all the city courts were controlled by Democratic judges and could not be expected to find the rioters guilty of anything at all. Despite that likelihood, numerous suspects were taken into custody on charges of rioting and looting, and the City Recorder's Office began preparing cases against them. John T. Hoffman of Tammany was the Recorder (presiding officer of the principal city court). With a vigor and a diligence astonishing to everyone familiar with his politics, Hoffman prosecuted the accused, a jury found them guilty, and they received prison terms.[124]

*   *   *

Considering the power of the Peace faction in nearby New Jersey, the chance of rioting there was instantly apparent following the outbreak in New York City. That no such rioting occurred was due, in large part, to the groundwork laid by Democratic Governor Parker.[125] There has been a tendency over the years to regard New Jersey of Civil War times as the tail to the New York kite, and Governor Parker as a little brother to Governor Seymour. There is not much to be said for this interpretation. All the time that Seymour was consulting with Wood, Vallandigham, and other Peace leaders, attending their functions, and talking their jargon, in 1863, Parker was avoiding association with the New Jersey Peace faction, dodging their meetings, and talking up the war.[126] Although Parker was opposed to conscription on constitutional grounds, to the same extent as Seymour, he handled the matter in a wholly different way. In early summer 1863, preceding the first draft call, he contacted Washington, requesting one more chance of obtaining the New Jersey quota through volunteer enlistments. Permission was granted, the volunteers were raised, and trouble was averted.[127] So clearly in favor of the war was Parker that by November 1863 he was the target of furious criticism by the New Jersey Peace faction, which deserted him completely.[128]

Another War Democrat deeply involved with the problems of the draft was Governor Tod of Ohio. Through the dispensation of liberal bounties, in 1863, he was able to inveigle four-fifths of the militia into enlisting as three-year volunteers. But for all that, he was still required to call upon the draft. In certain Democratic counties, Ohio provost marshals were driven off in the process of enforcing the enrollment act, whereupon militia regiments were dispatched to the trouble spots on Tod's orders, and the draft proceeded under armed guard.[129] . . .When mobs started forming in the streets of Boston in July, the Massachusetts State Militia was ordered into readiness by Democratic Major and Brigade Inspector Charles W. Wilder. Upon the restoration of order Wilder was commended by Republican Governor Andrew.[130]

Legal proceedings were brought against the Conscription Act in several states in 1863, with varying degrees of success. In Pennsylvania, for example, the State Supreme Court declared against the act by a vote of 3 to 2. (War Democrat William Strong dissenting.)[131] In the case of *Kemp* V. *Wisconsin* (1862) the Supreme Court of Wisconsin rendered the law inoperable within the state; and yet in all cases tried before the U.S. circuit courts in Pennsylvania and Illinois it was upheld.[132]

*   *   *

Some Union heroes of the battlefield in 1863 included Democratic General T. Lyle Dickey, commander of the cavalry under Grant and the author of "Grierson's Raid," carried out in April, from La Grange, Mississippi to Baton Rouge.[133] The Confederates responded with "Morgan's Raid," carried out in July, and culminating in the capture of General Morgan. The hero of the affair was Democratic General Edward H. Hobson of Kentucky. Democratic General Ambrose E. Burnside won slight recognition in the Knoxville campaign of November 1863, while battering the army of Confederate General Longstreet. When the War Department moved to the defense of Chatanooga, following the battle of Chickamauga, an avalanche of railroad cars was rushed to the scene with the vital assistance of War Democrat John Garrett, president of the Baltimore and Ohio. Twenty-three thousand men entrained for Chatanooga and made the trip in seven days.[134]

By the close of 1863 numerous War Democrats of prominence were retired to the sidelines, while others were achieving new stature, both as soldiers and civilians. The outstanding civil appointment of the year was accorded by Lincoln to War Democrat Stephen J. Field of California, who in March became a member of the U.S. Supreme Court. In the 1860 campaign Field had been a member of the Breckinridge party. He was now an anti-slavery man.[135] Breckinridge leader Stoddard B. Colby of Vermont accepted a position as Register of the Treasury, tendered by Secretary Salmon P. Chase, and moved at once to Washington.[136] Very busy much of the year promoting the Union cause in Europe, were War Democrats August Belmont, Chairman of the Democratic National Committee, and Robert J. Walker of Mississippi. Walker was responsible for the sale of $250,000,000 worth of federal government bonds.[137]

General Benjamin F. Butler, unemployed for more than a year, was appointed in November to command the Department of Virginia and North Carolina.[138] Defeated by Grant in the struggle for command of the Army of the Mississippi, and dismissed from service under Grant, Democratic General John A. McClernand was no longer a figure of military importance. General Lewis Wallace, also on the outs with Grant, was actively in search of a command all year long, and was frequently a visitor to Washington. General Daniel E. Sickles, having lost a leg at Gettysburg, remained in uniform but did no more fighting, and General John Cochrane, never prominent in battle, retired from the service. (Sickles and Cochrane would return to politics—Cochrane in 1863, Sickles the following year—as members of the New York Union party.) War Democrat John S. Phelps of Missouri, Military Governor of Arkansas, was felled by a serious illness in 1863 and forced to retire from command before the year was out.

On December 8, 1863, President Lincoln issued his Proclamation of Amnesty and Reconstruction, providing pardons, with certain exceptions, to former Confederates who agreed to take an oath to support the Constitution and the Union. The "Ten Percent" Plan was now brought forward, promising presidential recognition to the government of any state in which the number of oath-takers equaled one-tenth the number of voters in the 1860 elections.[139] For the remainder of the war, Radical and Conservative Republicans and Unionists would divide over this document, the Radicals opposing, Conservatives supporting it. War Democrats would stand on both sides of the question.

NOTES

1. During a conversation with Edward Stanly, Military Governor of North Carolina, President Lincoln reportedly said that the Radicals would probably stop supporting the further prosecution of the war unless the Proclamation went into effect. The remark was passed along by Stanly to Editor James C. Welling of the Washington (D.C.) *National Intelligencer,* who recorded it in his diary September 27, 1862. Ralph Korngold, *Thaddeus Stevens,* p. 292. Among the War Democrats of Lincoln's close acquaintance, a strong opponent of the Emancipation Proclamation, in advance of its release, was General John A. McClernand of Illinois. At the last moment (December 29, 1862) Lincoln received a letter from McClernand, explaining the supposed advantages of Confederate surrender with slavery intact. Such an arrangement was still conceivable, McClernand declared, but Lincoln wrote back, ruling out all such possibilities. The Proclamation was now a part of the federal war policy; "And being made, it must stand." Roy P. Basler, ed., VI:49. McClernand accepted the decision and publicly declared in favor of the Proclamation, serving as Permanent Chairman of the Conference Convention of the War Democracy of the Northwest, meeting in Chicago, November 25, 1863. The Convention declared in favor of the freeing of the slaves. Chicago *Tribune,* November 26, 1863.
2. *Congressional Globe* (37th Congress, 3rd session), Appendix, pp. 39–40.
3. Ibid., pp. 112–14.
4. Ibid., p. 15.
5. William Lloyd Garrison and Wendell Phillips had previously criticized the President for his conservative anti-slavery policy. Garrison had cursed the *preliminary* Proclamation and both denounced the Gradual Emancipation Plan. Both endorsed the *final* Proclamation, however, and thereafter supported the Union cause without conditions. Phillips remained suspicious of the President but Garrison was a changed man, becoming overnight a Lincoln Republican. Ralph Korngold, *Two Friends of Man,* pp. 307, 324–25.
6. When advised of the emancipation proclamation issued in Missouri by General Fremont, August 30, 1861, a company of Kentucky troops reportedly threw down their arms. Richard Hofstadter, pp. 126–27. Much more of the same thing was expected by Conservatives in the event that Lincoln should issue such a proclamation.
7. *Congressional Globe* (37th Congress, 3rd session), p. 283 (Thomas); p. 91 (Noell); p. 283 (Brown); p. 138 (Henderson).
8. Ibid., p. 356. While Congress was debating the pros and cons of Emancipation in the border slave states, in 1863, a Unionist convention at Wheeling, Virginia was considering the prospect of establishing the state of West Virginia, devoid of Negro slavery. On hand at Wheeling was U.S. Senator Waitman T. Willey of Virginia, working for a free-state constitution. In Washington, working with the same basic purpose in mind, was War Democrat Congressman William G. Brown of Virginia, sponsor of a House bill providing funds for the compensated Emancipation of all Unionist slaveholders in his state, Charles H. Ambler, *Waitman T. Willey, Orator, Churchman, Humanitarian* (Huntington, W. Va.: Standard, 1954), pp. 84, 89; *Congressional Globe* (37th Congress, 3rd session), p. 283.
   John W. Noell, War Democrat from Missouri, offered a resolution in the House favoring compensated Emancipation in Missouri. The principle was warmly endorsed by Andrew J. Clements, War Democrat from Tennessee (Clements favoring a sweeping national policy, rather than the piece-meal method, state by state). Ibid., pp. 207–9.
   On January 12, the House voted 50 to 85 against the tabling of a resolution to approve, ratify, and confirm the Emancipation Proclamation. War Democrat

Noell of Missouri voted in the Majority. Although a number of War Democrats voted to the contrary, several others abstained. Ibid., p. 281. War Democrats who abstained from voting on the resolution included Thomas of Maryland, Brown of Virginia, Haight of New York, Lehman of Pennsylvania, and English of Connecticut.

9. Charles H. Ambler and Festus P. Summers, *West Virginia, The Mountain State* (Englewood Cliffs, N.J.: Prentice-Hall, 1958), pp. 242–47.

10. Although supporting the Regular Democratic ticket in the state elections of 1863 and 1864, in company with many Peace Democrats, the Louisville *Democrat,* Paris *Western Citizen,* and St. Louis *Mirrouri Republican,* retained all the qualifications of War Democrat newspapers. They still applauded Union victories and lamented Union defeats. They still referred to "our men" and "our troops," meaning Union troops, and continued calling the Confederates "rebels" and "the enemy." (The members of the Peace press went far out of their way to avoid any such phrases.) The failure of these and many other War Democrat journals in the border slave-states to abandon the Union cause, following release of the Emancipation Proclamation, has received very little attention from the great mass of Civil War historians. It was one more example of the great contempt of many pro-slavery War Democrats for the arguments of the Peace Democarcy. Hating the anti-slavery cause, they still refused to work in league with pro-slavery men espousing Peace on pro-Confederate terms. The fact of this went largely unnoticed, even at the time of its occurrence. Hence, Secretary of the Treasury Chase was denouncing the Louisville *Democrat* as a "Copperhead" paper in the fall of 1862, and a year later the Springfield *Illinois State Journal* (Republican) was applying the same nickname to the St. Louis *Missouri Republican,* despite the fact that the *Republican* favored the Radical campaign for the enlistment of Negro troops. E. Merton Coulter, p. 160; Springfield *Illinois State Journal,* December 5, 1863.

11. Robert S. Harper, p. 117.

12. Roy P. Basler, VI:146.

13. Benjamin P. Thomas, *Stanton,* p. 259. In his later years, Thurlow Weed said that Lincoln once commissioned him to act as a messenger between Seymour and himself, with authority to offer Seymour the 1864 Union presidential nomination if he only would agree to support the Union cause. Robert S. Mitchell, *Horatio Seymour of New York* (Cambridge: Harvard University Press, 1938), p. 273. Stanton's biograpapher, Benjamin P. Thomas, questions the validity of the story. Benjamin P. Thomas, *Stanton,* p. 259.

14. Edward C. Smith, pp. 338–39.

15. Regular War Democrats and Conditionals in the Indiana legislature followed the leadership of former Governor Paris C. Dunning, President of the State Senate. They held the balance of power and could block any Peace vote they chose to. They also acted in concert with numerous War Democrats elected on the Union ticket, who refused to go along with the Emancipation Proclamation or the military arrest of civilians. Indiana, State *Journal of the Senate,* 42nd session. Indiana, State *Journal of the House of Representatives,* 42 session.

16. Richard W. Leopold, p. 348.

17. Francis M. Trissal, *Public Men of Indiana* (Hammond, Indiana: Conkey, 1922), p. 36.

18. George H. Porter, p. 150.

19. For taking such a stand, Tod received the compliments of Secretary of War Stanton. It was observed by Secretary of the Navy Welles that none of the other loyal-state governors had spoken so forcefully as Tod since Fredericksburg. Later that year, Tod was arrested in his office on charges brought against him by Peace Democrat Edson B. Olds, jailed in 1862 on Tod's orders for rendering "treasonable utterances." Tod was accused by Olds of

kidnapping and when a grand jury found in favor of the charge Tod appealed the decision. The case ultimately was dropped, without a satisfactory decision being rendered. William B. Hesseltine, pp. 310, 263–64; 329–30.

20. *Union Army*, III:229.
21. Ibid., p. 230.
22. Edward C. Smith, p. 340.
23. Francis M. Trissal, p. 38.
24. Richard W. Leopold, p. 358.
25. Francis M. Trissal, p. 38.
26. Richard W. Leopold, p. 348.
27. Bright was expelled February 5, 1862; Republican Governor Morton appointed Wright to take his place, March 3, 1862; the Democratic legislature elected Turpie to replace Wright, January 22, 1863, and Hendricks to replace Turpie, for a full six-year term, March 4, 1863. *Biographical Congressional Directory, 1771 to 1911,* pp. 499, 720, 1068, 1131. Turpie was a War Democrat preceding his arrival in the Senate, after which he acted with the Peace faction.
28. Loyal Publication Society, ''The patriot soldier and hero: General Rosecrans to the legislatures of Ohio and Indiana,'' *Pamphlet No. 4* (February, 1863): p. 7.
29. William S. Rosecrans, *Letters from. . .to the Democracy of Indiana. Action of the Ohio regiments at Murfreesboro, Regarding the Copperheads* (Philadelphia, 1863).
30. George H. Porter, p. 116.
31. Columbus *Ohio State Journal,* March 4, 1863.
32. New Jersey, *Minutes of the Assembly* (Hackensack, 1863): p. 8.
33. New Jersey, *Minutes of the Senate* (Hackensack, 1863): p. 8.
34. Joseph T. Crowell, *Speech, in the Senate of New Jersey, January 22, 1863, on the Motion to Postpone Indefinitely the Anti-War Resolutions Offered by Hon. Daniel Holsman,* p. 2.
35. Ibid., p. 2.
36. Ibid., p. 3.
37. Ibid., p. 5.
38. Charles M. Knapp, pp. 85–90; James M. Scovel, pp. 11–31.
39. Charles M. Knapp, p. 88.
40. Ibid., p. 90.
41. Alexander C. Flick, p. 140, credits Tilden with reorganizing the Society for the Diffusion of Political Knowledge, in the hope of counteracting the effect of the Union Clubs and the Loyal Publication Society. The revival was arranged in February, 1863, at a gathering of Democratic leaders in Delmonico's Restaurant. Ibid., p. 140. In a counter move, the Union League was organized in March 1863. As opposed to the local Union Clubs, the League had chapters in every loyal state. Sidney D. Brummer, p. 295. Although originally independent, the Loyal Publication Society was taken over, in 1863, as spokesman for the Union League.
42. T. Harry Williams, p. 232.
43. James McKaye credited with forming the Loyal Publication Society in Richard W. Leopold, p. 361. See also: Frank Friedel, ''The Loyal Publication Society: A Pro-Union Propaganda Agency,'' *Mississippi Valley Historical Review* XXVI, no. 3 (December 1939): 360, 362, 373. President Charles King of Columbia became president of the Loyal Publication Society in 1863, at which time McKaye was appointed chairman of the publications committee. A large contributor to the Society from 1863 to 1865 was dry goods merchant Alexander T. Stewart, a leading New York City Democrat; Ibid., p. 371.
44. Loyal Publication Society, *Papers,* 1863–1865.

45. Prominent Democrats among the signers included William F. Havemeier, Tammany candidate for Mayor, 1859; John J. Cisco, Assistant U.S. Treasurer under Buchanan; Prosper M. Wetmore, dry goods shipping merchant; and Peter Cooper, munitions manufacturer. Loyal Publication Society, "Character and Result of the War. How to Prosecute and How to End It. A Thrilling and Eloquent Speech by General B. F. Butler," Reported by A. F. Warburton (New York, 1863).
46. Another War Democrat attending the rally at the Academy of Music was General John E. Wool. Ibid., p. 10.
47. Ibid., p. 10.
48. Sidney D. Brummer, p. 256.
49. New York *Herald*, March 25, 1863.
50. New York *Herald*, April 8, 1863. Wood supplied a list of eleven types of people who supported the war: 1. banking interests. 2. New England commercial interests. 3. railroad interests. 4. debtor class, hoping to profit by inflation. 5. abolitionists. 6. office-holders, contractors, and government employees. 7. administration members, hoping to perpetuate their political control. 8. Republican partisans. 9. War Democrats, hoping to share in spoils. 10. some honest patriots. 11. the army.
51. Colonel Egan was correct in the statement that Wood had never raised a single soldier for the Mozart Regiment. When the regiment was formed in Yonkers, in 1861, the organizing force was the Union Defense Committee of New York City and not Mozart Hall. It first was named the "United States Constitution Guard," but later was renamed, at the solicitation of the Mozart Hall Committee. Frederick Phisterer, p. 403.
52. *The Old Guard,* vol. I, no. 5. (May 1863): 118.
53. Loyal National League of New York, *Proceedings* (Cooper Institute, March 20, 1863), p. 6. There was no apparent difference between the policies of the two leagues. The Albany *Atlas and Argus* reported that the Loyal National League was the creation of War Democrat John W. Forney of Philadelphia. The New York *Herald* declared that the Loyal National League was dominated by Salmon P. Chase of Ohio and that the Loyal Union League was a machine in the interests of William H. Seward of New York. According to the New York *Tribune,* the two leagues had about as much connection with Chase and Seward as they had with "the man in the moon." New York *Tribune,* May 29, 1863.
54. There were two great gatherings of the Loyal National League of New York in the spring of 1863. War Democrats were paramount at both occasions. The March rally at Cooper Institute was chaired by Democratic General John Cochrane and the principle speaker was Democratic General Andrew J. Hamlton (a former Congressman from Texas.) A Council of Twenty-five was named, including numerous War Democrats, of whom the best known were businessmen Alexander T. Stewart, Moses Taylor, Francis B. Cutting, and John J. Cisco. An Executive Committee was formed, including numerous War Democrats, of whom the best known were businessmen Robert B. Minturn, Jr. and James A. Roosevelt, U.S. District Attorney for Southern New York under Buchanan.
    Vice Presidents included War Democrats Jacob S. Westervelt, John Slosson, John D. Townsend, Augustus Schell, Richard Schell, Francis B. Cutting, Royal Phelps, Alexander T. Stewart, William F. Havemeier, Moses Taylor, Edwards Pierrepont, G. C. Verplanck, Samuel Wetmore, Henry G. Stebbins, Isaac Bell, Stephen Cambreleng, Cyrus W. Field, Benjamin H. Field, William B. Astor, George Bancroft. John J. Cisco, Shepherd Knapp, Samuel Sloan, John Jacob Astor, Jr., Peter Cooper, James B. Murray, Matthew T. Brennan, James R. Whiting, Lloyd Aspinwall, William H. Aspinwall, Joseph Lee, Cornelius Vanderbilt, John A. Lott, and William Allen Butler. Letters of approval were received from Democratic Generals Irvin McDowell,

Henry W. Halleck, and Daniel E. Sickles; also from War Democrats Horatio Ballard, Secretary of State for New York, and Henry Morris of the state legislature. Loyal National League, *Proceedings,* March 6, 1863.

On April 20, the Loyal National League served as sponsor to a giant rally at Madison Square, commemorating the "great uprising of the North" exactly two years earlier, in Union Square. War Democrat Prosper M. Wetmore called the gathering to order and War Democrat Jacob A. Westervelt was named as one of three Acting Presidents, overseeing proceedings at one of three separate stands. Vice Presidents included many War Democrats of whom the best known were August Belmont, Moses Taylor, Charles H. Russell, Francis B. Cutting, Moses H. Grinell, John J. Cisco, William B. Astor, John J. Astor, Jr., Robert B. Minturn, Robert B. Minturn, Jr., Isaac Bell, Alexander T. Stewart, Samuel Sloan, William F. Havemeier, Edwards Pierrepont, Abraham M. Cozzens, James A. Roosevelt, Peter Cooper, Cyrus W. Field, Lloyd Aspinwall, Richard Busteed, and John C. Green. Speeches were delivered by War Democrats Daniel S. Dickinson, General John Cochrane, Chancellor Samuel M. Harrington of Delaware, George Bancroft, John Van Buren, Edward N. Dickerson, and David S. Coddington. Loyal League of Union Citizens, *Commemoration. Anniversary Celebration of the Great Uprising of the North.* Held in Madison Square, New York, April 20, 1863.

An outstanding Union Club entering the Union League at this point was one from Philadelphia organized in November, 1862. Democratic members included financial leader George H. Boker, the Club President; General George A. Cadwalader, Dr. John F. Meigs, and lawyers Daniel Dougherty, William D. Lewis, Frederick Fraley, and J. B. Lippincott. Elias P. Oberholtzer, II:322.

55. Henry W. Bellows, p. 54.
56. *The Old Guard,* vol. I, no. 4 (April 1863): p. 96.
57. Ibid., vol. I, no. 5 (May 1863): p. 118.
58. Ibid., vol. I, no. 4 (April 1863): p. 95.
59. The following Democratic papers were attacked by Unionist mobs in 1863, according to: Robert S. Harper, passim:

Illinois:	Belleville *Volksblatt,* March.
	Olney *Herald,* August 30.
Indiana:	Richmond *Jeffersonian,* March 15.
	Rockport *Democrat,* late January.
Iowa:	Keokuk *Constitution,* February 19.
Kansas:	Leavenworth *Enquirer,* February 11.
	Leavenworth *Western Sentinel,* August 27.
	Marysville *Constitutional Gazeteer,* August 20.
Ohio:	Cadiz *Sentinel,* September.
	Columbus *Crisis,* March.
	Jackson *Express,* July.
	Marietta *Republican,* March.
Pensylvania:	Huntington *Monitor,* May 20.
	Kittaning *Monitor,* May 13.

60. Ibid., p. 338.
61. Ibid., p. 338; George H. Porter, p. 156.
62. Wood Gray, pp. 164–65, lists the following clashes, in 1863 and 1864, between Unionists and suspected members of the Order of American Knights and its successor organization, the Sons of Liberty: "Skunk River War," in Keokuk county, Iowa, August, 1863; Canton, Ohio, March, 1864; also in March, 1864, Union Soldiers broke up a Peace demonstration at Paris, Illinois. A few days later, at Charleston, Illinois, a Peace mob invaded a Union rally, with arms concealed, and started shooting.
63. *Record of Heister Clymer,* p. 6.
64. Pennsylvania, *Journal of the Senate,* March 6, 1863, p. 300.

65. David W. Lusk, *Politics and Politicians: A Succinct History of the Politics of Illinois from 1856 to 1864.* (Springfield, 1884), pp. 159–62. John D. Caton, another Democratic member of the Illinois Supreme Court, did not vote on this matter. Judges Walker and Breese wrote separate opinions, but were basically agreed. See also W. B. Hesseltine, p. 318.

66. During the first year of controversy over the Lecompton Constitution of 1857, Congressman William H. English was affiliated with the Anti-Lecompton faction, headed by Senator Douglas. In the summer of 1858, he changed sides, introducing the "English Bill," offering to Kansas some millions of acres of public lands providing she agreed to ratify the Lecompton Constitution. On August 21, 1858, by a vote of 11,300 to 1,788, Kansas rejected the proposal. English was reelected to Congress in October, 1858, running as a Buchanan Democrat. Failing of renomination in 1860, he had stumped his district for the Breckinridge national ticket.

67. Francis M. Trissal, p. 77

68. Indianapolis *State Sentinel,* May 21, 1863.

69. *Congressional Globe* (37th Congress, 3rd session), pp. 104, 313–14.

70. Ibid., pp. 313–14; 318–21.

71. Ibid., p. 318.

72. John G. Nicolay and John Hay, eds., *Abraham Lincoln. Complete Works,* 10 vols. (New York: Century, 1914), VIII:32.

73. Elwyn B. Robinson, p. 69; St. Louis *Missouri Republican* reported coming out in favor of Negro troop enlistments by Springfield *Illinois State Sentinel,* December 5, 1863. *National Cyclopedia of American Biography,* VI:27.

74. Benjamin F. Butler, p. 550. Following Butler's refusal to return to New Orleans, Lincoln contacted Colonel Daniel Ulman of the 78th New York Infantry (Know Nothing candidate for Governor of New York, 1854.) He was commissioned general and sent to New Orleans, to raise a full Negro brigade. Dudley T. Cornish, p. 101.

75. For Meigs on Negro troops, see Manchester (New Hampshire) *Democrat and American,* January 29, 1863; for Lincoln's letter to Andrew Johnson, concerning the need for Negro troop-raising in Tennessee: Roy P. Basler, ed., VI:149–50.

76. *Congressional Globe* (37th Congress, 3rd session), p. 688.

77. Ibid., Appendix, p. 76.

78. Ibid., Appendix, pp. 159–61.

79. Benjamin F. Butler, *Private and Official Correspondence of. . .during the Period of the Civil War,* 5 vols. (Norwood, Mass.: Plimpton, 1917), I:519.

80. *Congressional Globe,* (37th Congress, 3rd session), p. 690.

81. *Union Army,* VIII:53.

82. *U.S. Biographical Directory and Portrait Gallery of Eminent and Self-Made Men, Iowa Volume* (Chicago, 1878), p. 621.

83. Dudley T. Cornish, pp. 176, 241 (Arkansas: Phelps), 241 (Kansas: Carney); William B. Hesseltine, p. 289 (Ohio: Tod); E. B. Quiner, p. 197.

84. William B. Hesseltine, p. 188.

85. Butler's Democratic affiliations are well known. Burnside was a Democratic candidate for Congress in 1857. Ferrero was a member of Tammany Hall, Wooster was a Democratic member of the Connecticut legislature, and Appleton the son of a Democratic Chief Justice of the state of Maine.

86. Leavenworth *Conservative,* July 17, 1863.

87. Dudley T. Cornish, p. 142; H.C. Williamson, ed., pp. 152–57; Allen Johnson and Dumas Malone, eds., I:328–29.

88. Quincy (Illinois) *Herald,* September 12, 1863.

89. Dudley T. Cornish, p. 242.

90. Roy P. Basler, ed., VI:483; *Union Army,* VIII:40–41.

91. Benjamin P. Thomas, *Edwin M. Stanton,* p. 266.

92. Richard W. Leopold, pp. 362–63.

93. Perry Belmont, pp. 77–82; Basil Leo Lee, p. 105. Stevens of Pennsylvania, the Radical House leader, defended the Commutation Clause as a means of raising revenue. The amount raised in such manner was insignificant, however, considering the daily cost of the war.

94. *Congressional Globe* (37th Congress, 3rd session), p. 1292; Basil Leo Lee, p. 91.

95. Ibid., Appendix, pp. 173, 3089.

96. Fry was from southern Illinois. He was the son of Jacob Fry, Collector of the Port of Chicago under Buchanan until he was removed for supporting Douglas in the Lecompton controversy. Jacob Fry was a prominent Douglas leader in the 1860 campaign. St. Louis *Republican,* August 5, 1860; Joseph Kirkland, *History of Chicago, Illinois,* 2 vols. (Chicago: Dibble, 1892–1894), I:148; James B. Fry was also a Douglas Democrat. As a soldier he served as an artilleryman in the Mexican War and as Chief of Staff to General Irwin McDowell at First Bull Run; transferred west, he also served as Chief of Staff to General Don Carlos Buell during the siege of Corinth. *Union army,* VIII:93. He was praised by both McDowell and Buell for conduct under fire, and General Grant recommended his promotion to Provost Marshal General. Allen Johnson and Dumas Malone, eds., VII:47.

97. The Provost Marshal General had an Assistant Provost Marshal General stationed in the capital city of every loyal state. In New York, Assistants also were stationed at Elmira and New York City. For every congressional district there was appointed a provost marshal, a commissioner, and a surgeon. Robert S. Mitchell, pp. 311–12. Some notable Democrats working for the Office of the Provost Marshal General are listed below: Assistant Provost Marshal General for New York (New York City): Robert Nugent; Provost Marshals: John Duffy and William F. Rogers, New York; William E. Lehman, Pennsylvania; J. Madison Cutts, Jr., Ohio; Charles W. Noell and Abram Comingo, Missouri. Commissioners: Dexter R. Wright, Connecticut; James M. Scovel, New Jersey; Samuel W. Moulton, John E. Detrich, and Andrew J. Kuykendall, Illinois; Levi B. Vilas, Wisconsin; William J. Hobson, Kentucky. Medical Examiners: Daniel Brainard, Illinois; James R. McCormick, Missouri.

98. Frank L. Klement, *The Copperheads of the Middle West,* p. 81.

99. Allen Johnson and Dumas Malone, eds., III:311–12.

100. The Columbus *Crisis,* May 20, 1863. Unionist papers critical of Vallandigham's arrest included the New York *Tribune,* the New York Evening *Post,* New York *Commercial Advertiser,* Albany *Statesman,* Boston *Advertiser,* Boston *Traveler,* and Springfield *Republican.* All in this category were regarded as outstanding examples of the Unionist press, and all supported Lincoln in the 1860 campaign. Robert S. Harper, p. 245.

101. Cincinnati *Gazette,* May 19, 1863.

102. Allen Johnson and Dumas Malone, eds. III:312.

103. Union League of Pennsylvania, *Decision of Judge Leavitt of Ohio in the Vallandigham Habeas Corpus Case* (Philadelphia, 1863).

104. Editor William W. Seaton of the pro-slavery Washington, D.C. *National Intelligencer* accused Leavitt of being ignorant of the law. Robert S. Harper, p. 245. At the Ohio Democratic State Convention of 1863 attorney George E. Pugh delivered an address calling for the impeachment of Leavitt. Society for the Diffusion of Political Knowledge, *Papers* (New York, 1868), pamphlet no. 9, p. 137. According to George H. Porter, p. 166, a federal statute enacted March 3, 1863, superceded Lincoln's proclamation suspending *habeas corpus,* and the law required Vallandigham to be delivered over to the civil courts. In Porter's opinion Leavitt ignored this particular law. Ibid., p. 165. Porter also declares that Burnside's action of resorting to martial law, based on the recent presence in Kentucky of Confederate troops, was unjustified, because the civil courts were still in operation in Ohio. Ibid., p. 166. Judge Leavitt held that the writ of *habeas corpus* was not grantable as of

right, but only on sufficient showing that it ought to issue, and that its refusal would be justified if the court were satisfied that the petitioner would not be discharged upon a hearing after its return. He held that the court could not go into the question of the jurisdiction of a military commission and hence could not discharge the prisoner. Since Burnside had acted as the agent of the President and since the powers of the President as Commander-in-Chief of the Army were not defined by the Constitution, Judge Leavitt declared that the matter was not reviewable by the courts. Union League of Pennsylvania, passim.

105. Robert S. Harper, p. 243.
106. Ibid., p. 340.
107. James G. Randall, *Civil War and Reconstruction,* p. 897.
108. Frank L. Klement, *The Limits of Dissent; Clement L. Vallandigham and the Civil War* (Lexington: University Press of Kentucky, 1970), p. 177.
109. Eugene H. Roseboom, p. 414.
110. George H. Porter, p. 36.
111. New York *Herald,* May 21, 1863. In many states the initial Peace appeal was apparently approved by all Democrats excepting only the ones aligned to the Union party. In the Connecticut Assembly, for instance, Peace leader William W. Eaton introduced the so-called "Vallandigham Resolutions" of May 6, 1863, affirming the right of the states to resist the federal government whenever it was adjudged to have overstepped its authority. Eaton led the fight for the resolutions, supported by every Regular Democratic member of the Assembly. War Democrat Dexter R. Wright, a member of the Union party, led the opposition, which sank the resolutions, 127 to 94. W.A. Croffutt and John M. Morris, p. 329.
112. George E. Pugh delivered an address at the 1863 Ohio Democratic State Convention in which he bitterly assailed the administration. George H. Porter, p. 171. Thereafter, he never supported the Union cause. Congressman Noble and Nugen stopped voting for war measures. See Appendix 1. George W. Manypenny steered the Columbus *Ohio State Sentinel* into the Peace camp, where it remained for the rest of the war years. See Columbus *Ohio State Sentinel,* May, 1863–April, 1865.
113. U.S. Congress, *Biographical Directory of the American Congress, 1774–1961,* p. 473.
114. Columbus *Ohio State Journal,* September 23, 1863.
115. The leading Conditional War Democrat in Indiana was Congressman William S. Holman. When the Conditional faction broke up, Holman joined the unconditional War Democracy. Other Conditionals in Indiana included Congressmen James A. Cravens and John Law, former U.S. Senator David Turpie, and Horace Heffren, editor of the Salem *Washington Democrat.* All of these came out for Peace. Congressman Charles A. Wickliffe of Kentucky, Chairman of the Douglas National Committee, swung from Conditional to Peace. In Pennsylvania, former Secretary of State Jeremiah S. Black and Congressman Sydenham E. Ancona swung from Conditional to Peace. So did Congressman William G. Steele of New Jersey and former Governor Peter D. Vroom of New Jersey, E. St. Julian Cox of Minnesota, and Martin Van Buren Bennett of Iowa, to name only a few.
116. Ibid., pp. 251–52.
117. Basil Leo Lee, pp. 104–5. Colonel Nugent became a target of special abuse by the mobs who burned his house to the ground. Ibid., pp. 104–5.
118. Dennis T. Lynch, pp. 262–64.
119. Alexander C. Flick, p. 142.
120. Ibid., p. 143.
121. Dennis T. Lynch, p. 260–66.
122. James Truslow Adams, ed., II:164.
123. One concession was accorded Seymour, in answer to his protest that the draft

was unfair, bearing more heavily on Democratic districts than Republican ones. A three-man board of inquiry, established to investigate the matter, found in favor of Seymour's contention and the New York quotas were changed, erasing the inequity. Benjamin P. Thomas, *Stanton*, p. 282; William B. Hesseltine, pp. 301–4. A pair of Democratic members on the board of Inquiry were William F. Allen of New York, Judge of the State Supreme Court, and John Love, Inspector General of the Indiana State Militia. Roy P. Basler, ed., VII:211.

124. Allen Johnson and Dumas Malone, eds., IX:113.

125. Newark, New Jersey, had an anti-draft "demonstration," but not a riot. The home of Provost Marshal Miller was attacked and the office of the Newark *Mercury* was stoned (the *Mercury* representing the Union party.) A proclamation issued by Democratic Governor Parker had a considerable calming effect, and order was quickly restored. Charles M. Knapp, p. 96.

126. Ibid., p. 98.

127. William S. Myers, ed., *The Story of New Jersey*, 5 vols. (New York: Lewis, 1945), I:231.

128. Charles M. Knapp, pp. 100–1.

129. William B. Hesseltine, p. 293.

130. H. C. Williams, ed., *Biographical Encyclopedia of Massachusetts of the 19th Century*, 2 vols. (Boston: Metropolitan, 1883), II: pp. 254–55.

131. Harrisburg (Pennsylvania) *Patriot and Union*, November 12, 1863.

132. Robert S. Mitchell, p. 314.

133. James G. Randall, *Civil War and Reconstruction*, p. 533.

134. George E. Turner, p. 289.

135. Allen Johnson and Dumas Malone, eds., VI:373.

136. A. M. Hemenway. *The Vermont Historical Gazeteer, 5 vols.* (Burlington, 1891), IV:469.

137. Allen Johnson and Dumas Malone, eds., II:169–70; XIX:357.

138. Richard S. West, p. 219.

139. Roy P. Basler, ed., VII:53–56; James G. Randall, *Civil War and Reconstruction*, p. 690.

11

Lincoln and the War Democrats Smash the Peace Crusade: Elections of 1863

According to one respected historian, the 1862 election results "showed clearly that the people of the North were opposed to the Emancipation Proclamation, opposed to governmental encroachment on individual rights, and opposed to conscription."[1] The statement is highly debatable to say the least. Yet the same view was held and acted upon by the Peace Democracy in the election campaign of the following year, which got under way at the New Hampshire Democratic state convention, November 20, 1862. Here, for the first time in New Hampshire since the war began, the Peace faction outnumbered the War faction at a statewide Democratic gathering. In the winter of 1862–1863 the Peace Democrats had increased the clamor of their protests, reaching a crescendo on the day of the convention. Many members of the old Pierce machine were openly for Peace, and though Pierce himself had not yet come out against the war he was generally regarded in that light.[2] Among the Douglas Democrats of New Hampshire, the leading Peace men were Douglas elector John G. Sinclair and Supreme Court Judge Ira A. Eastman. Amid great enthusiasm, Eastman was nominated for Governor, against the opposition of the War Democracy. His acceptance speech amounted to a diatribe against the war and President Lincoln, whom he described as a potential dictator.[3] In all three Democratic congressional district conventions the Peace candidates defeated candidates speaking for the war.

New Hampshire Republicans convened January 1, obviously shaken by the Peace Campaign. Only two persons received serious consideration for the gubernatorial nomination and both were Conservative: Republican Joseph Gilmore and War Democrat Walter Harriman. Gilmore was a member of the State Senate and Harriman Colonel of the 11th New Hampshire Infantry, formerly editor of the Manchester *Union,* and a Douglas champion three years earlier. The Radical faction, favoring neither candidate, swung to Gilmore in preference to Harriman and Gilmore won the nomination.[4]

From stump and press, the Peace men criticized the President, congressional war measures, and anti-slavery legislation, without reserve and with open contempt for the patriotic protestations of Republican campaigners. John H. George, Democratic candidate for Congress, declared: "If the South need any assistance, *I will go out and assist them. . . .I won't do a thing* to sustain the President, the Administration, Congress, or any of the piratical crew that have control of this Government. *I won't do anything that can be interpreted as in any way supporting this war."* George referred to Lincoln as a *"knave,* an *imbecile,* a *usurper,* and a *tyrant,* who *curses* the country with his administration." According to Josiah Minot, the Abolitionists were more insidious and more dangerous than the Confederates, and were responsible for bringing on the war. Minot was in favor of an armistice, followed by a convention looking to a peace arranged "by mutual compromise." Judge Eastman also warned against the Abolitionists. William Burns, candidate for Congress, declared for slavery, first, last, and always. "Rather than that the Emancipation Proclamation should be enforced, and slavery be abolished, I would prefer that the Government should be destroyed."[5]

The Proclamation and the Conscription Act (debated and passed in February 1863) were central targets of the Peace Campaign. Thomas J. Whipple, formerly Colonel of the Second New Hampshire Infantry, denounced the war and campaigned for the Peace candidates.[6] Democratic Colonel Michael T. Donohue of the 10th New Hampshire Infantry (a veteran of the Fredericksburg campaign) returned home to take a stand in favor of the war.[7] Whipple and Donahue were longtime Democrats-in-arms and once the closest of associates; but the bond was broken totally in 1863.

Hoping for further division in the Democratic ranks, Secretary of War Stanton contacted Colonel Walter Harriman of the 11th New Hampshire Infantry, stationed at Newport News, Virginia. Things were looking bad for the Union cause in New Hampshire, Stanton explained. What was needed was an uprising of the War Democracy against the Peace Democracy. Would Harriman consent to run for Governor as an Independent War Democrat with the object of inciting such an uprising? Harriman agreed, whereupon Stanton sent word to Douglas elector William C. Clarke, who issued a call for a "Union convention" to be held at Manchester, February 17, with the object of attracting the backing of the War Democracy.

Harriman was not friendly to the Republican state leadership at this point in his career. He had stood by the Democratic party during the Free Soil Revolt of 1848 and the Compromise of 1850, the Kansas-Nebraska Act, the Lecompton controversy, and the Sumter attack. Had the Regular Democrats nominated anyone except an out-and-out Peace man in 1863, he would have remained a Democrat. But Ira Eastman and the Peace campaign drove him from the Regular Democracy.[8]

The Peace press attacked the Union party call as Republican subterfuge, but the sizable body of delegates attending the Union convention were bonafide Democras. War Democrat William C. Clarke presided and Democratic Colonel Walter Harriman of the Eleventh New Hampshire Infantry was nominated for governor, War Democrat John Coughlin, Lieutenant Colonel of the Tenth New Hampshire Infantry, for Railroad Commissioner. Harriman was denounced in the Peace press as an opportunist who had joined the Republicans on the promise of receiving a brigadier's commission. Harriman denied the charge.[9]

Democratic expectations of victory in New Hampshire rendered the election of national importance and the state campaign was hotter than any held in recent years. Numerous Democrats of national reputation arrived, to speak for all the candidates. General Benjamin F. Butler of Massachusetts addressed the Republicans, Congressman William A. Richardson of Illinois addressed the Democrats, and General Andrew J. Hamilton of Texas regaled the Union party.[10] On voting day, for the first time in history, the New Hampshire Republicans failed of obtaining majority support. Peace Democrat Eastman finished first, with almost 33,000 votes, Republican Gilmore second with almost 29,000. The number of votes separating them was 3,889. War Democrat Walter Harriman, running on the Union ticket, received 4,446 votes, denying a majority to Eastman and throwing the election to the legislature, where the Republicans still retained control. Gilmore was therefore installed in the Governor's Mansion and the Peace campaign was foiled in New Hampshire. According to the Republican State Chairman, the true hero of the occasion was Secretary of War Stanton, for persuading Harriman to run. "But for your aid," the Chairman declared, "the rebel yell of victory would have been heard along the white hills of New Hampshire."[11]

In keeping with the anti-Radical campaign of 1862, the Conservative Republicans of New Hampshire not only determined the party choice for

Governor but prevented the renomination of Radical Congressman Gilman Marston. He was replaced on the ticket by a Conservative, and when the vote was held in March the Conservative lost. In this manner the first Democrat was elected to Congress from New Hampshire since 1853.

*   *   *

In Michigan as in New Hampshire, the Regular Democracy passed from the control of the War faction in 1863. Release of the Emancipation Proclamation had reversed the position of the powerful Detroit *Free Press,* from War to Peace, and the Democratic comeback in Wisconsin the year before was generally regarded as an anti-war development. The Michigan Democracy was deeply effected by this interpretation. Credit for the change in Wisconsin opinion was bestowed upon lawyer Edward G. Ryan, author of the Peace-tinted "Ryan Address." Seeking something of the same nature for Michigan, in 1863, the Democratic State Central Committee contacted Breckinridge leader William V. Morrison, the outstanding Peace man in the state, requesting a strong statement of party policy. The request was granted in the form of a long denunciation of the Union cause, closely resembling the Ryan Address. According to Morrison, the major issue of the war was the choice between freedom and despotism, with President Lincoln representing the latter. The Morrision Opinion was adopted, without changes, as the Democratic platform for 1863. Speaking in approval of the platform at the February Democratic State Convention, delegate George W. Peck denounced the President as "the despot of Washington, the tool of the usurpers."[12] The initial result of the Michigan campaign was disintegration of the anti-Radical Union party coalition organized the year before. Infuriated by the Morrison platform, certain War Democrats went over to the Radicals, without reservations. Of these, the best known were Lewis Cass, Secretary of State under Buchanan; Major N. Buell Eldredge; Robert McClelland, Secretary of the Interior under Pierce; and General Orlando B. Wilcox of Detroit.[13]

In the midst of the Michigan campaign, on March 6, a lynch mob stormed a jail in Detroit, attempting to remove from custody a Negro convicted of raping a white girl. Driven off by the provost guard, the mob turned on the Negro section of the city, burning down 35 houses and destroying other property. The Republican state legislature proposed that the city pay the victims for losses incurred, but the Democratic City Council rejected the proposal. Peace spokesmen condemned the action of the legislature, denouncing the Republicans for sympathizing with Negroes while at the same time ignoring the suffering of whites.[14] Despite appeals to race prejudice, war weariness, and economic instability—the standard line of the 1863 Peace campaign—the Regular Democracy was swept aside in

Michigan by a vote of 69,000 to 61,000[15] (about the same results as 1862.) The Peace experiment in Michigan could not be construed as a success.

$$*\qquad*\qquad*$$

April elections in Connecticut featured the appearance of a mixed ticket of Regular Democrats, War and Peace, against the nonpartisan Republican-Union state administration of Governor Buckingham. As in New Hampshire and Michigan, the Peace faction determined the outcome of every major decision at the Democratic state convention. Peace leader Alfred E. Burr, editor of the Hartford *Times*, managed the gubernatorial nomination of Peace leader Thomas H. Seymour, and William W. Eaton, Chairman of the Breckinridge State Executive Committee, reported a solid, unequivocal Peace platform.[16] The War faction resisted, and almost blocked the Seymour nomination. Out of 453 votes cast in an informal poll the majority for Seymour was only 16. That was enough, however, and he was duly nominated (after which the action was widely reported as sweeping and unanimous).[17]

The Peace Democracy of Connecticut was exceedingly confident of victory in 1863. As recently as September and November 1862, strong Democratic gains had been registered in municipal elections all over the state. (Milford went Democratic for the second time in history, and the first time in 50 years. New Haven and Hartford went Democratic by large majorities.) Following that came Fredericksburg. When the Republican-Union party assembled in convention at New Haven, January 8, there was a small attendance and the leading speaker, Conservative Republican Senator James Dixon, created havoc, delivering an attack on the Emancipation Proclamation. Radicals were furious, denouncing the Senator as the enemy of Governor Buckingham.[18] They made no move to break the non-partisan Buckingham ticket, however, and all of its members won renomination, including War Democrats Roger Averill, Lieutenant Governor, and Gabriel W. Coite, Treasurer, both of whom were opposed in the ensuing campaign by members of the Peace Democracy. In congressional races, the Republican-Union party nominated three Republicans and one Democrat: Henry C. Deming, former State Senator and Acting Speaker of the Assembly; Colonel, 12th Connecticut Infantry, and Mayor of New Orleans under martial law. A major feature of the campaign was Deming's race against Alvin P. Hyde, a former War Democrat now running as a self-styled "Copperhead."[19] War Democrats William E. English and George C. Woodruff stood for reelection to Congress as Regular Democrats, ignoring the Peace platform and campaigning on their pro-war voting records.

The Regular Democrats' Peace campaign emphasized the threat of Negro immigration (posed by release of the Emancipation Proclamation), the threat of Conscription (currently under consideration by Congress), and the supposed invincibility of the Confederacy. Delighted by the pro-slavery nature of McClellan's "Harrison's Landing letter," in the summer of 1862, many Peace leaders in Connecticut had come out briefly in favor of the war. Thomas H. Seymour and Alfred E. Burr of the Hartford *Times* were notable examples. The dismissal of McClellan destroyed all their Unionism, however, and they were back on the Peace bandwagon in time for the 1863 campaign.[20] The Union party of Connecticut retained its allegiance to the Republican-Union coalition, as did several Democratic papers. The Democratic New London *Star* declared that "Thousands of true Democrats will stand where we stand and will care nothing for the edicts of (Alfred E. Burr, the Hartford *Times,* and) the Hartford Junta." The *Times* and the rest of the Peace press attacked the *Star* and all other War Democrat newspapers as Republican propaganda organs, working in disguise.[21]

As in New Hampshire, the Regular Democracy registered strong gains in Connecticut in 1863, reducing the Republican-Union margin in the legislature from 142 seats to 52. But Seymour and the Democratic State ticket were defeated by 2600 votes, and of the four Regular Democrats running for Congress three were beaten, including an incumbent. War Democrat Henry C. Deming was just barely elected to Congress on the Republican-Union ticket over Peace Democrat Alvin P. Hyde with a majority of 335 votes out of 21,000 cast.[22]

The Confederate Richmond (Virginia) *Dispatch* reported: "The Connecticut elections have gone against the Democrats. Gold has fallen on the strength of Republican success, obtained, no doubt, by bribery, and the hopes which rested on the triumphs of Seymour have fallen to the ground. The importance of this to the Democracy cannot well be exaggerated: for if the result had been otherwise, *the Northwest would have risen, the Peace party would have been* organized on a permanent basis; the next meeting of Congress would have been followed by a summary abrogation of the imperial powers bestowed upon Lincoln by the Abolition Congress just ended, and a cessation of hostilities might have been confidently looked for, at or before the close of 1863."[23]

The Rhode Island April elections of 1863 centered on the political transformation of War Democrat William Sprague, who resigned as Governor in March to enter the U.S. Senate. During the first two years of the war, Sprague had been absent from the state much of the time, consulting with officials in Washington, reviewing Rhode Island troops in the field, and attending to his cotton enterprises. On trips to Washington he had become acquainted with Katherine Chase, daughter of Salmon P. Chase, Secretary of the Treasury, and was frequently a visitor at the Chase household. Under the influence of either Katherine or the Secretary, or both, the Governor became a convert to Republican principles. He therefore decided to transfer Rhode Island from the Democratic column (where he had placed it in 1860) to the Republican column.

Upon returning home, Sprague established a close rapport with certain Republican state leaders and began working for coalition of the several pro-war factions into an all-embracing Union party (as opposed to the anti-Radical Union party of 1861–1862). In his nonpartisan endeavors, Sprague was supported by numerous Democratic district leaders and minor officials.[24] But every Rhode Island Democrat of consequence turned away.

Especially hostile were the Senator's brother, Amasa Sprague, and William C. Cozzens, President of the State Senate, sometime Acting Governor, and a strong Conservative on the slavery issue. Instead of agreeing to the inclusion of Radicals in their ranks, they announced in favor of return to the Democratic standard and abandonment of the Union party principle. Sprague had been defeated, beyond question. He was not down for long, however, for in the same way that he had tipped the scales in 1860, depriving the Republican-American coalition of just enough votes to oust it from control, he tipped them back again in 1863 at the expense of the Regular Democracy.

The ticket selected at the Rhode Island Democratic State Convention of 1863 was composed exclusively of War men, with Cozzens the candidate for Governor. The Democratic platform came out in favor of the war, claiming only that Democrats could run it better and without resorting to Emancipation.[25] The Republican ticket was headed by Radical James Y. Smith whom Sprague had defeated in 1861. War Democrat Abraham Payne accepted the Republican nomination for Attorney General. Incumbent Congressman George H. Browne (Colonel, 12th Rhode Island Infantry) was renominated by the Regular Democrats, War Democrat Charles S. Bradley receiving the other party nomination for Congress.[26]

Sprague announced in favor of the Republicans, and campaigned for Smith. Following three straight years of Democratic success, Smith, Republican, was elected over Cozzens, Democrat, by 3,291 votes, in company with the entire Republican state ticket. Both of Rhode Island's congressional seats were taken by Republicans, and the complexion of the legislature was altered from an anti-Republican "Union" party majority of 62–42 to a Republican majority of 76–30.[27] The outcome amounted to a roaring personal triumph for War Democrat William Sprague.

The 1863 campaign included, for the first time, the West Virginia free state, admitted to the Union in June. Preceding congressional recognition of statehood an election of state officials was held in May, and Union men rallied to the anti-slavery, non-Republican Union party banner. War

Democrat Abraham D. Soper (Chairman of the State Constitutional Convention, held in February) was offered the Union nomination for Governor, but declined on account of age. At his recommendation, the honor was offered to and accepted by Arthur I. Boreman, an Old-Line Whig. The remainder of the Union ticket was half composed of Douglas Democrats, half of Whigs.[28] Congressional nominations were accorded two Whigs and one War Democrat—William G. Brown, serving at the moment as a member of Congress from Virginia. The Union party of West Virginia was committed to the Union and the anti-slavery cause, endorsing the Radical provisions of the free-state constitution adopted in February.[29] Pro-slavery forces in West Virginia were disorganized by the force of the free-state campaign and failed to wage an effective battle of their own. As a result, the Union party captured control of every state executive office but one, without forceful opposition from any quarter, and established control of the legislature, with a giant majority.

In nearby Tennessee the Union party organization broke apart in 1863 under the impact of Emancipation. In its place appeared a Radical Free-State movement, headed by War Democrat Governor Andrew Johnson, and a pro-slavery Conservative party headed by a pair of Old-Line Whigs: Emerson Etheridge, Clerk of the House of Representatives, and former Governor William B. Campbell. Radical "Union Clubs", organized in Tennessee, endorsed the Governor, declaring in favor of Emancipation. Since Tennessee was not included under the terms of the Emancipation Proclamation, the Radicals urged the calling of an anti-slavery state convention, to accomplish for Tennessee what the Proclamation was designed to accomplish for the other former Confederate states. The Radicals favored disfranchisement of all disloyal persons for as long a probation period as that required of "unbiased and unprejudiced foreigners."[30] The proposal received the firm endorsement of Judge Samuel Milligan of the State Supreme Court, formerly aligned to the Breckinridge Democracy.[31] It was angrily denounced, however, by former Governor William B. Campbell, who severed his relations with Military Governor Johnson and the Union party cause. Seizing on the situation, Tennessee Conservatives called a wild-cat election, to be held in August, with Campbell the Conservative candidate for Governor. He was elected—without opposition—to the great embarassement of Governor Johnson. In Washington, Emerson Etheridge labored long and hard in the frantic attempt to persuade Lincoln to recognize the election, but Lincoln refused. Instead, he wired off a message to Johnson, warning that "The whole struggle for Tennessee will have been profitless to both state and nation if it so ends that Governor Johnson is put down and (Confederate) Governor Harris is put up. It must not be so. You must have it otherwise. Let the reconstruction be the work of such men only as can be trusted for the Union. Exclude all others. . . . Get emancipation into your new state government-constitution. . . .''[32] (It is interesting to note the low regard held by Lincoln for the pro-slavery Unionists of Tennessee. The election of Campbell was comparable, in his estimation, to the election of a rank Confederate.) Replying to the President, Johnson explained that if *ever* he was going to secure a bonafide Union government for Tennessee, he would require considerably more executive authority at his disposal. The requested authority was instantly supplied.

In preparation for congressional elections long postponed in Tennessee (and now rescheduled for September) Union rallies were staged in every district reclaimed from Confederate control and Union party candidates began stumping their respective districts. The Confederate victory at Chickamauga altered the situation completely, however, and the election had to be postponed again.[33] Even so, the Tennessee election campaign of 1863 had great significance, establishing Governor Johnson as an unqualified Radical determined to effect Emancipation in Tennessee in accordance with the wishes of President Lincoln.

In Kentucky as in Tennessee the Union party organization fell apart following release of the Emancipation Proclamation. Kentucky Unionists, theretofore allied as "Union Democrats," now were divided in four distinct categories: Conservative, Radical, Peace, and Southern Rights. A majority of Conservative Unionists retained allegiance to the Union-Democratic party, supporting both slavery and Union. But the failure of the party to criticize (to the satisfaction of some Conservatives) the military arrest of civilians, suspension of civil guarantees, abrogation of states' rights, and organization of Negro troops, led to the desertion of a great body of voters, some of whom attended a "Southern Rights" Convention, held at Frankfort in February.[34] For failing to endorse the Emancipation Proclamation the Union Democrats also lost the backing of the Radicals, who established the "Union Administration" ticket of 1863, running candidates for Congress on an anti-slavery platform in four of Kentucky's nine congressional districts. Three of the Radical candidates were War Democrats—Green Clay Smith, Lucian Anderson, and Brutus J. Clay. Smith was a Douglas elector, Anderson a Douglas supporter in a district formerly dominated by Secession sentiment. Congressman John J. Crittenden, who quit the Conservatives in the final moments of his life to run for Congress as a Radical, died in the midst of the campaign. He was replaced on the ticket by War Democrat Brutus J. Clay.[35]

Although officially in favor of the war, the Regular Democrats drew heavily on the language of the Peace faction, attracting in the process disloyal elements in Kentucky and neighboring Tennessee. Union Democrats and the Administration-Union candidates were hopeful of preventing the disloyal from voting, and called for federal assistance to effect this result.

Their wishes were agreed to by the War Department. As Commander of the Department of Ohio, embracing Kentucky, Democratic General Ambrose E. Burnside saw to the appointment of election judges, the requirement of a loyalty oath as a prerequisite for voting, and the presence of troops at the polls. The actions were immediately assailed by the Regular Democracy as a Republican plot to intimidate the voters, as was also the arrest of a Democratic candidate for Congress on charges of disloyalty.[36]

The Union Democratic party of Kentucky overwhelmed the Regular Democracy, receiving 68,000 votes out of about 87,000 cast. In four districts Administration-Union candidates were elected to Congress (including War Democrats Greene Clay Smith, Lucian Anderson, and Brutus J. Clay). In five districts the Union Democratic candidates prevailed. In all districts the Regular Democrats were defeated. Both branches of the legislature went Union-Democrat almost completely.[37]

Because 145,000 Kentuckians voted in the 1860 elections and only 85,000 voted in 1863, it has been argued that the Union party victory of 1863 was the direct result of military orders and threats of perscution for voting the Democratic ticket.[38] The argument is rendered meaningless by the fact that only 87,000 Kentuckians voted in the 1864 elections, which resulted in a Democratic victory, notwithstanding the presence of the Union military in the state.[39] It is probable that the 1863 results represented the true feelings of Kentucky Unionists who were voting then in favor of the war, against the arguments provided by the Peace campaign. A year later, voting for a War Democrat—General George B. McClellan—they would support a different ticket but with the same object in mind.

*   *   *

Another Union party organization came into existence in 1863, in the State of Maine. Here, the Regular Democracy had divided, War and Peace, in 1861 and 1862. But the War faction was badly shaken by release of the Emancipation Proclamation, and many who had once espoused the war now fell silent. Congressman-elect James G. Blaine, Chairman of the Republican State Committee, moved against reunification of the Democrats by issuing a call for a Union convention, to meet in Bangor, July 1, 1863. Ephraim K. Smart, editor of the War Democrat Rockland *Democrat,* gave his endorsement to the call. "Every loyal Democrat is invited to participate" in the convention, Smart declared, "and if Republicans carry away the honors it will be because loyal Democrats allow them to do it by refraining to act in the primary meetings." He urged the abandonment of Radical Governor Coburn and reserved the right to enter the Union convention as a Democrat.[40]

Radicals were angered by the action of State Chairman Blaine and criticized the Union party plan. There was nothing they could do about it, however, except surrender. When the Union convention assembled, Blaine was in the chair and a coalition of Conservative Republicans and War Democrats constituted a majority.[41] The coalition favorite was Samuel Cony, a Douglas Democrat well remembered for service to the Union cause early in the war in the capacity of Assistant Paymaster. One of the wealthiest businessmen in Maine, he had loaned his money freely in the interest of the Union cause. With strong Conservative support, Cony swept aside the forces of Radical Governor Coburn, and was nominated by a vote of 899 to 66.[42] The Union party platform avoided the slavery issue but did come out in favor of military arrest for civilians in wartime, denouncing the arguments of the Peace press as Confederate propaganda.[43]

The Democratic party convened at Portland August 6, with a Quaker presiding and Bion Bradbury, a Conditional War Democrat, the predetermined choice for Governor. The convention was postponed to provide additional time in which the more extreme Peace leaders were lectured on the matter of party unity. The Lincoln administration was attacked in the Democratic platform for destroying the government through Abolition, Conscription, the military arrest of civilians, and censorship of the press. All these were assailed, and a letter from Bradbury was read to the delegates, one of whom attacked it for not being sufficiently critical of the war. But when the voting came, Bradbury was nominated.[44]

The Union party campaign was directed by Blaine, who staked his career on its success. Cony campaigned in company with many other War Democrats standing on the Union platform.

On the Democratic side, the platform was conditionally in favor of the war, but criticized every forceful federal war policy as a threat to American liberties. Large crowds turned out to hear the Democratic speakers, and the Peace press stood by Bradbury despite his mild approval of the war. It was hinted that the Maine shipping interests were for peace, in behalf of sea commerce, and Democratic hopes were high. But the Union ticket triumphed, with a majority of almost 18,000 out of 119,000 cast (the 1862 Republican majority, 6,000).[45]

At the Vermont Republican State Convention the Radicals came forward with a semi-Abolitionist, John Gregory Smith, as their candidate for Governor. Denouncing Smith as unacceptable, Conservative Republicans rallied to the Lieutenant Governor, War Democrat Paul Dillingham. A stormy contest ensued in which Smith, the Radical, emerged victorious, with Dillingham returning to his old spot as second on the ticket. The Regular Democrats in convention declared forcefully for Peace. Breckinridge leader Timothy P. Redfield, a strong opponent of the war, was nominated for Governor and a bitter campaign ensued. Although the Peace vote exceeded that of the year before by 8,200, the Union ticket was easily elected in September with a margin of 17,000 votes.[46]

The California elections, also held in September, highlighted the campaign activity of War Democrat John Conness. Following election to the U.S. Senate in January, Conness had toured the state, organizing Union Clubs everywhere, and making many friends. At the Union State Convention, held in June, the major contenders for the gubernatorial nomination were the Conservative incumbent, Leland Stanford, and the Radical challenger, businessman Frederick F. Low. As a War Democrat, Conness was expected to throw in with Stanford, the Conservative. Instead he gave his blessings to Low, who won the nomination with the strong support of War Democrats in attendance. A War Democrat and a close friend of Senator Conness was the former Mayor of Sacramento, Benjamin B. Redding, who received the nomination for Lieutenant Governor. The rest of the state ticket consisted of Republicans. The convention also decided the choice of three candidates for Congress, two of whom were War Democrats—Douglas leader William Higby (expelled from the Regular Democracy for attending the Union convention of 1862) and Douglas leader Thomas B. Shannon. Both were lieutenants of Senator Conness and both were nominated without opposition. The party platform endorsed the Emancipation Proclamation.[47]

To meet the Union party challenge of 1863, the Douglas and Breckinridge Democracies united in one swift action. Ignoring the call for a Union-Democratic convention, scheduled for June 24, the Douglas men abandoned independence to join the Fusion Democratic State Convention, two weeks later at Sacramento. Resolutions were passed on this occasion condemning the Emancipation Proclamation, Soft Money, and the suppression of free speech. The Union cause was nonetheless supported, and a strong War speech delivered by Colonel F. L. Hatch.[48] The platform declared against secret organizations of every kind, Union and Peace alike, and the military arrest of civilians was pronounced unconstitutional. The party platform approved "The Constitution as it is and the Union as it was." Former Governor John G. Downey, a Conditional, was nominated for governor. Colonel Hatch sought the nomination for lieutenant governor but was defeated by the Peace faction.[49]

The moderate tone of the Democratic campaign was disrupted by an angry Peace speech delivered shortly following the convention by Charles L. Weller, Chairman of the Democratic State Committee. The general commanding Union forces in California at the moment was War Democrat Irvin McDowell. Advised of Weller's remarks, McDowell ordered his arrest and pandemonium broke loose. Tyranny was charged by the Peace faction, and many speakers threatened armed revolt.[50] In this atmosphere the campaign was carried out. Abandonment of Conservative Governor Stanford and the charge of Radicalism, hurled against the Union candidate, Frederick F. Low, gave great hopes to the Regular Democrats, who had ruled the state for so long before the war. The hopes proved false, however. With War Democrats leading the way for the Union campaign, and the Peace men heading up the Democratic cause, Low defeated Downey, 63,000 to 43,000. War Democrats Redding, Higby, and Shannon were easily elected, running on the Union ticket, Redding receiving more votes than any other candidate for state office.[51]

*   *   *

The Ohio elections, taking place in October, once again involved a joust between the War and Peace Democracies. Before his arrest in May, 1863, Clement L. Vallandigham had declared himself a candidate for the Democratic gubernatorial nomination. He was opposed, for a time, by the Cleveland *Plain Dealer,* the Columbus *Ohio Statesman,* and the Cincinnati *Enquirer,* which denied his chance of winning, under any circumstances. The War candidate favored by them all was Hugh J. Jewett, the party choice for Governor in 1861. But following the arrest, banishment, and martyrdom of Vallandigham, there was no stopping him. Jewett withdrew from the race, and the Democratic Convention went for Vallandigham, by acclamation. Still in Canada, in exile, Vallandigham accepted the nomination through former Senator George H. Pugh, defense counsel in his military trial. Peace Democrat Edson B. Olds was the preconvention choice for Lieutenant Governor, but Pugh's address had rendered him a figure of importance and the nomination went instead to him.[52] (A War Democrat preceding the arrest of Vallandigham, Pugh was from that point forward a leader of the Peace cause, all down the line.) Peace men were selected to fill out the rest of the Democratic ticket, but the party platform (surprisingly) did not come out for Peace. Allen G. Thurman, a Conditional War Democrat and former Chief Justice of the State Supreme Court, was author of the platform, which was based on the Conditional War philosophy rejected by Vallandigham. For all its protesting about military arrests and other matters almost incidental, it declared at last in favor of the war. Stunned by this development, some Peace extremists (Alexander Long and William Cory) attacked the platform as wholly inappropriate, proposing another of their own, praising the Confederates and offering surrender. It was flatly rejected by a large majority. From Canada, Vallandigham declared his approval of the War platform.[53]

At the Union State Convention, the War Democracy was wholly in command. A letter was read from Democratic Colonels Ferdinand Vander Veer, George P. Este, and Durbin Ward of the 15th, 14th, and 17th Ohio Infantry, declaring the Vallandigham nomination an insult to Democratic party traditions.[54] The only serious candidates for the gubernatorial nomination were all War Democrats—incumbent David Tod, Judge Stanley Matthews of the State Supreme Court, and John Brough, a railroad president and former Auditor. The best speaker of the three was Brough, and Governor Tod had made a host of enemies among Republicans in the Union coalition by appointing only Democrats to office and by dragging his feet about Emancipation. John Brough, on the other hand, was ardently in favor of Emancipation, and for so being had the backing of many Republican newspapers throughout the state. Governor Tod carried his fight for renomination to the convention floor (having strong support from delegates elected before Brough entered the race). But on the first ballot, Brough received the nomination.[55] Radical influence was thoroughly hidden from the public. The platform said nothing about slavery and the Radical choice for Supreme Court Judge was beaten down in favor of a Conservative.[56] Aside from War Democrats Brough and G. Volney Dorsey (seeking reelection as Treasurer), the ticket was otherwise Conservative Republican. But the major point was this—that Tod, who was mild on Emancipation—was out of the picture; and Brough—who had embraced Emancipation—was in.

The Ohio canvass of 1863 was perhaps the most exciting of the war, serving as a climax to the great Peace campaign of that year. The battle began with a surprising statement in Vallandigham's acceptance speech, that following the overthrow of the Confederacy the Democrats would best be suited to handle the problems of postwar Reconstruction.[57] The statement ignored all past denials on the part of the speaker that the Confederates ever could be beaten. Little attention was paid to the message, however. Clinging to the old line, Peace orators and newspapers demanded peace immediately, minimizing Union victories, and belittling the chances of federal success.

Colonel John C. Groom, formerly of the 100th Ohio, and Colonel Newton Schleich, formerly of the 61st Ohio, declared themselves Peace converts and campaigned for Vallandigham.[58] A great many Ohio Democrats stood back, however, refusing to endorse the Democratic ticket. Among these were all the Union party Democrats together with numerous Regulars of note, including Judge Rufus P. Ranney of the State Supreme Court; Hugh J. Jewett, candidate for governor, 1861; and Henry B. Payne, candidate for governor, 1857, all of whom declined to speak for Peace.[59] The Unionists relied largely on War Democrats Brough and Tod who, as well known Negrophobes, did much of the replying to the constant barrage of anti-Negro propaganda supplied by the Regular Democracy.

Editor Murat Halstead of the Conservative Republican Cincinnati *Commercial* wrote to Secretary of the Treasury Chase, in August, that the Union party stood a chance in his district only if there could be a few moments quiet on the Negro question. But he feared that Ohio in general preferred Vallandigham's view of slavery to Lincoln's, exemplified by his "foolish and hopelessly impracticable proclamation."[60]

In so believing, Halstead misread the picure in Ohio, in every detail. As an example of what was actually going on, the "Convention of the War Democracy of Ohio" assembled at Columbus, September 22, with 150 delegates in attendance. Everyone present favored the election of War Democrat Brough as opposed to Peace Democrat Vallandigham. Colonel Barnabus Burns of the 86th Ohio Infantry (Democratic candidate for Congress, 1860) chaired the meeting. Numerous other army officers were present, the most conspicuous being Colonel Stephen J. McGroarty of the 61st Ohio Infantry, who took the occasion to attack former comrades-in-arms currently campaigning for Vallandigham. Of these the worst, he said, was Colonel Schleich, who had been dismissed from the service for cowardice in battle.[61] The War Democrats declared against peace on any terms except submission to the federal Constitution and the laws of the land. The nomination of Vallandigham was described as a terrible mistake which, if sanctioned by the people of Ohio, would seriously endanger the safety of the government.[62] Democratic General William H. Lytle of Ohio, speaking in Bridgeport, Alabama, provided copy for the Union press back home, attacking the Peace cause in general and truce proposals in particular. A ten years' war would be better than peace by diplomacy, without the defeat of Confederate arms.[63] Democratic Colonel Mortimer D. Leggett of the 78th Ohio Infantry defended the Lincoln administration, urging all Democrats to do the same. "No blunder or mistakes upon the part of the President," he said, "can justify me in withdrawing from the army, while the enemies of the government are in arms against it."[64]

The fierce campaign brought a record number of Ohio voters to the polls. Peace Democrat Vallandigham received more votes than any Democratic candidate for Governor in the history of the state as of that time, but War Democrat Brough attracted even more—roughly 101,000, of which 62,000 were provided by civilians. Brough was elected with a walloping majority and when the news was in, received a wire from Washington, reading: "Glory to God in the highest. Ohio has saved the Nation. A. Lincoln."[65]

The War and Peace Democracies were again the major factors in October elections taking place in Pennsylvania. At the National Union State Convention, the Conservative Republicans united with the War Democracy, insuring the renomination of Governor Andrew G. Curtin. The War Democrat leaders were John W. Forney, editor of the Philadelphia *Press*. Frederick C. Brewster, Solicitor for Philadelphia (a recent winner in a federal case involving the legality of Lincoln's Soft-Money policies), and Judge Daniel Agnew of the State Circuit Court. Brewster was among the several candidates for Governor defeated by Curtin, and Agnew was nominated for a place on the State Supreme Court.[66] The Democratic State Convention involved a long struggle between the War Democracy, favoring former Congressman William H. Witte for Governor, and the Peace Democracy, favoring State Senator Heister Clymer. The matter was finally decided by selection of a compromise candidate, Conditional War Democrat George W. Woodward of the State Supreme Court. A platform was adopted favoring the war, but denouncing Conscription and the military arrest of civilians.[67]

Woodward was a Democrat of Conservative connections going back to the days of the Free Soil Campaign. As a member of the State Supreme Court he had supported numerous war measures enacted by Congress, but had come to the attention of the Peace faction for his vote against Conscription. Despite his alleged moderation on the issues of the war, he was savagely attacked by War Democrats supporting the National Union cause, and furiously defended by the Peace Democracy. Nathaniel B. Browne, a Breckinridge supporter in 1860 and a Lincoln-man in 1863, denounced the Judge as the friend of Secession, having heard him often on the subject during the 1860 campaign.[68] The Democratic Philadelphia *City Item*, which had supported the Democracy in 1861 and 1862, announced against the Woodward ticket, declaring it the agency of out-and-out surrender.[69] The Union League of Philadelphia took an identical position, with the blessings of the League president, War Democrat George H. Boker. A well-publicized gathering of the Philadelphia League, September 15, was chaired by Boker and attended by War Democrats John W. Forney, John C. Knox, Nathaniel B. Browne, Benjamin H. Brewster and Daniel Dougherty, all of whom announced for Curtin, Agnew, and the National Union party, observing that the main hope of the Confederacy "lies in the selection of such men in northern States as Clement L. Vallandigham, of Ohio, and George Woodward of Pennsylvania, and nowhere is there to-day such anxiety felt for their success as at Richmond and Charleston. It is a wise saying, 'that we should always avoid doing what our enemies wish us to do.' "[70]

Despite all protestations of Unionist sympathy by leaders of the Pennsylvania Democracy, the Peace theme seemed to be their song. According to Charles J. Biddle, State Chairman of the Democratic party, the federal Emancipation policy had come to justify the claims of the Secessionists. According to Surveyor General James P. Barr, the Emancipation Proclamation was a "disunion edict," certain of preventing reunion of the sections. Seeking to sound pro-slavery only, they came off sounding anti-war. As editor of the Pittsburgh *Post*, Barr denounced the Union cause in every vital respect. As editor of the Philadelphia *Age*, Biddle did the same. If Woodward were elected, said Heister Clymer, he would join with Vallandigham and Seymour of New York and Parker of New Jersey to "compel" the administration to abandon its anti-slavery policies.[71] Late in the campaign, when Woodward was under attack as an enemy of the Union, a letter was published over the name of General George B. McClellan, stating the belief that Woodward was a loyal man. But many were convinced otherwise. As in Ohio, the 1863 election results in Pennsylvania reversed the edict of the preceding year. Curtin was reelected over Woodward by about 15,000 votes; War Democrat Daniel Agnew was elected to the State Supreme Court; and the National Union party won control of the legislature.[72] Following the vote, former President James Buchanan came out publicly in favor of Conscription, urging Judge Woodward to give it his support.[73] The advice was ignored. On November 9 the State Supreme Court declared against the law, three-to-two, with Woodward casting the deciding vote. (War Democrat William Strong dissented, in favor of the law.)[74] When War Democrat Daniel Agnew joined the Court the following year the balance of power shifted dramatically and on January 16, 1864 the Court reversed itself, in favor of Conscription.[75]

Of less moment, the October elections in Minnesota received scant attention, even in the western press. Involved in the battle was a straight-out gubernatorial contest between Radical Republicans and War Democrats—a repetition of the 1861 campaign. On this occasion, however, the Democratic forces collapsed completely under the impact of the race issue. When the New York City Draft riots broke out in July, the War Democracy of Minnesota declared against the rioters without reservation. John E. Warren, the Democratic Mayor of St. Paul, called for law and order and devotion to the Union cause.[76] In Minneapolis, Democratic district leader Henry T. Welles lamented the murder of New York City Negroes. A former schoolteacher, he had taught Negro children, and was outraged by the beastial behavior of New York City Democrats.[77] The Democratic State Convention selected Welles as the candidate for Governor, and came out firmly in support of the war, whereupon the Peace Democracy withdrew from the campaign.[78] Without the backing of the Peace faction Welles was overwhelmed by a Republican majority three times that of 1861.[79]

For the fall campaign in Indiana, involving only country and municipal offices, Republican Governor Morton called for the enthusiastic support of all War Democrats in the Union party organization. Outstanding performances were rendered by Union State party chairman Joseph A. Wright; General Lewis Wallace; Judge David S. Gooding; Judge Joseph S. Buckles; Robert Dale Owen, Chairman of the American Freedmen's Inquiry Commission; Douglas Leaders Thomas B. McCarty, J. T. Eliot, Delano E. Williamson, John I. Morrison, and Dr. Albert G. Porter. Democratic General John A. McClernand of Illinois also campaigned for the Indiana Union party. Speaking at Indianapolis in September, the General attacked the Peace Democracy, saying that "The man or party that hesitates or halts in this great business must be ground into atoms and scattered to the winds."[80] Letters received from General Robert H. Milroy and Colonel Cyrus L. Dunham (both Democrats), condemning Peace propaganda, were reprinted and widely circulated by the Union campaign managers.[81] Despite the fact that no elections were held in one-quarter of the counties in the state, the Indiana Union party picked up an additional 15,000 votes over the number received the year before, amounting to an impressive majority.[82]

*   *   *

The New York state campaign began in May, concluding in November. Vallandigham's arrest aroused the Peace Democrats to great activity all over the state, but did not place them in command of the Regular Democracy. Anson Herrick, Congressman-elect, Conditional War Democrat, and editor of the New York *Atlas,* reminded his readers that the Peace faction had named the ticket in the recent Connecticut and New Hampshire elections, and in both cases "the 'copperhead' experiment was an egregious blunder." Democratic victories of 1862 were not the product of Peace propaganda, Herrick said, but of a loyal, Unionist campaign.[83] These were also the opinions of Governor Horatio Seymour and the Albany Regency.[84] The Democratic State Committee, controlled by the Regency, refused to work for Peace, adopting instead a Conditional War platform.[85] The following month a similar platform was adopted by the Tammany General Committee.[86] Alone among the Democratic factions in New York, Mozart Hall campaigned for Peace in 1863.

Shortly following the Chancellorsville defeat, in May, Mozart called a "Peace and Reunion" convention to meet in New York City, June 3, with the object of adopting measures looking to a speedy settlement of the war. An address was drawn up, insisting that "the professed democrat. . .who is deliberately for the war, is not a democrat in fact, but an abolitionist of the most radical, violent and destructive kind." The Peace platform was certain of success, Mozart Hall declared. "The great body of the people are tired of war and demand peace. . . .the war cannot succeed. We have been beaten. We cannot conquer the South."[87] The New York *News* (recently revived) announced that if the Albany Regency were to oppose the nomination of Peace candidates at the forthcoming Democratic state convention, the Peace Democracy would call a separate convention and name their own ticket.[88]

Democratic victory in New York had been achieved in 1862 with the help of the Constitutional Union party, whose leader at the time was James Brooks, and Brooks was for Peace. There also was a War faction within the Constitutional Union party, headed by Daniel B. St. John. In 1863 the two-party alliance was maintained, but on this occasion St. John was named to head the ticket, as the candidate for Secretary of State. War Democrats Sanford Church and William B. Lewis were nominated for Comptroller and Treasurer. No Peace men were nominated for any state office, and Governor Seymour addressed the convention without expressing approval of the Peace Campaign.[89] Clearly, the Governor was more concerned about regaining the allegiance of War Democrats operating with the Union party than he was about the threats of Mozart Hall, Fernando Wood, and the New York *News*. But the plan did not work. In failing to satisfy Fernando Wood, Seymour also failed to repudiate him, and this proved disastrous. The transformation of Wood from War to Peace had horrified many leading New York Democrats, who had worked for Seymour in 1862. And the Seymour-Wood alliance had horrified them further. By April 1863, James T. Brady was touring the East, speaking for the Union ticket.[90] Responding to Seymour's convention speech, Bennett of the *Herald* observed that "Governor Seymour can talk more without saying anything, than any other man we know. . . .We consider Seymour not much of a man and no Governor at all."[91] John Van Buren, who had led the Seymour bandwagon a short time previously, renounced his leadership and joined the Union League.[92]

The Radicals having lost the New York elections of 1862, control of the Republican-Union organization passed to the Conservatives who conceived a ticket devoid of Radicals and a platform almost devoid of ideas. Conscription received no mention, one way or the other (the convention taking place on the heels of the Draft riots.) Also ignored in the initial platform draft was the Emancipation Proclamation, which Conservative Republicans abhored. But the Radicals protested, and the Proclamation was accorded a nod of approval.[93] The leading Radical at the Republican-Union Convention was War Democrat Daniel S. Dickinson, rendered prominent in the summer of 1863 by a running fight with Governor Seymour. At issue was the federal Conscription law, which Seymour had declared unconstitutional, only to be countered by Dickinson—his own Attorney General —who issued an opinion to the contrary, full of legal precedents. Having battled Seymour in such manner, Dickinson was outraged by the Conservative nature of the Republican-Union State Convention, regarding it as outright surrender to the Governor. He therefore declined renomination as Attorney General, and his place on the ticket was accorded to War Democrat General John Cochrane, formerly of Mozart Hall.[94] The only Radical note sounded at the Republican-Union Convention was a message from President Lincoln, defending the Emancipation Proclamation and the use of Negroes in the army and the navy. Comparing Negro troops to Peace Democrats, Lincoln observed, "there will be some black men who can remember that, with silent tongue, and clenched teeth, and steady eye, and well poised bayonet, they have helped mankind on this great consumation, while I fear there will be some white ones unable to forget that with malignant heart and deceitful speech they have striven to hinder it.'' Radicals were highly pleased by these remarks. All year it had been rumored that Lincoln was planning on retracting the Proclamation. But that was impossible, he now declared. Indeed, ''the emancipation proclamation could not be retracted any more than the dead could be brought to life.''[95] Following this Radical declaration, War Democrats Henry G. Foster, E. Darwin Smith, and Josiah G. Sutherland accepted Union nominations for the State Supreme Court,[96] and in so doing identified themselves with the use of Negro troops.

Seymour delivered four speeches during the 1863 campaign, contending that repeated military failure had led the country into bankruptcy, that the ill-advised actions of administration subordinates had sapped the liberties of the people, and that base motives inspired the policies of the government.[97] The Draft Riots served as a major target of Union party propaganda and Seymour was accused not only of failing to suppress the rioters but of encouraging them in their murderous ways. War Democrat Lyman Tremain, referring to Seymour's conciliatory speech of July 14, declared: ''Here was a scene for the painter! The Governor of this powerful State standing before a mob whose hands were red with the blood of their murdered victims, alarmed at the storm which had been raised, promising to do what he could to give them a victory over law—.''[98]

Democratic General Thomas F. Meagher of New York, founder of the Irish Brigade, became a Union party spokesman in 1863. At the height of the state campaign he wrote the editors of two Dublin newspapers, praising the anti-slavery position. His remarks were reprinted and distributed in the Irish districts of New York City.[99] Another Union party convert in 1863 was the millionaire munitions manufacturer Peter Cooper, an old friend of Governor Seymour and a generous benefactor of many Democratic campaigns. Writing the Governor in September, Cooper expressed abhorrence for all Democratic propaganda concerning state sovereignty. In his estimation, the national sovereignty was paramount and should be so recognized by everyone. He recommended Democratic surrender on the slavery issue. Northern opinion could not abide the pro-slavery arguments any longer, he said, because the anti-slavery cause was obviously damaging the enemy. Captured Confederate officers were said to have admitted that the Emancipation Proclamation ''played hell with them'' through its effect on the slaves. In conclusion, Seymour was urged to take a firm and clear position in favor of suppressing the rebellion. All of the advice was ignored, and Cooper responded by publishing his letter and coming out in favor of the Union ticket.[100]

On October 17 President Lincoln called for three hundred thousand additional volunteers. If the quotas were not quickly filled on a voluntary basis, a draft would have to be arranged to secure the necessary remainder. Seymour criticized the call as cruel and unfair.[101] On the eve of the elections, Secretary of War Stanton granted furloughs to more than 16,000 New York troops and the Regular Democrats protested.[102] The Union ticket carried the New York elections with a majority of almost 30,000. War Democrat John Cochrane was elected attorney general and War Democrats Josiah Sutherland, E. Darwin Smith, and Henry G. Foster were elected to the State Supreme Court bench, all with the backing of the Union party.[103]

* * *

Of the several other November state elections, War Democrats were most conspicuously engaged in Wisconsin, Illinois, Maryland, Missouri, and New Jersey. The story in Wisconsin hinged upon approval of the so-called "Ryan Address," delivered at the 1862 Democratic State Convention by Douglas elector Edward G. Ryan. Although purportedly Conservative in nature, the Address was basically for Peace and utterly enraged the War faction. When the Democrats convened in 1863, the Peace men were firmly in control and a platform was adopted including the Address and other resolutions even more extreme.[104] Hoping to pacify the War Democracy, the party managers agreed to a pro-war state ticket headed by attorney Henry L. Palmer, who in turn agreed to embrace the Ryan Address. George B. Smith, a convention delegate and a firm supporter of the war, was wholly disgusted. According to his account, Ryan escorted Palmer to the speaker's stand, telling him, quietly, "Now, Palmer, endorse the address; and endorse it *damned strong*," and Palmer "like a docile child in his great father's arms," did so.[105]

In defiance of Palmer and the Ryan Address, the War Democracy of Wisconsin convened separately at Janesville, September 17. Jonathan Arnold, 1860 Democratic candidate for Congress, was chosen to preside and a series of resolutions were offered by Matthew T. Carpenter of Milwaukee, who had signed the convention call and was generally regarded as the guiding spirit of the occasion. The Carpenter Resolutions were harsh in their criticism of the Ryan Address and the Madison platform, and fully in favor of the war. Judge Levi Hubbell, General John A. McClernand, General Edward S. Bragg, and James C. Allen delivered brief speeches and Judge MacArthur delivered a long one, attacking the Peace leaders for their "singular abuse of the term, . . . 'Democratic party'. . . . The last object of (their) concern," he said, "is the vigorous chastisement of the rebellion, and the primary one is to spread the firebrands of doubt, apprehension, and the wildest alienation from our own government." The cautious phraseology of the Ryan Address did not appease MacArthur, who saw it as mere camoflage—"some patriotic commonplaces as a mask to their real designs."[106] True War Democrats could not endorse the Ryan Address, the Madison platform, or the Regular Democratic ticket.[107]

Momentarily elated by division in the Democratic ranks, Wisconsin Republicans became suddenly alarmed at the prospect of an independent War Democracy which well could split the Unionists. Calling in the War Democrat leaders for consultation, the Republicans agreed to a merger, with a War Democrat in command. The Republican party was officially dissolved in favor of the Union party and, in a very close race, Republican Governor Salomon was defeated for renomination by War Democrat James T. Lewis, Secretary of State under the Solomon administration.[108] Out of six candidates for executive office on the Union ticket, three were Democrats: Lewis for Governor, Lucius Fairchild for Secretary of State, and Winfield Smith for Attorney General.[109]

A central issue of the Wisconsin campaign was the *Kemp* decision of the State Supreme Court, denying the military the right to the arrest of civilians in wartime. In this manner the Conscription law was rendered unenforcible in Wisconsin, in keeping with the arguments of the Ryan Address and the Madison platform.[110] A number of leading War Democrats supporting the Union party in Wisconsin contacted Democratic General John A. Dix, requesting his opinion on the matter and Dix replied, defending the Act against all criticism. As a veteran of the War of 1812, he recalled that Democratic President Madison had then proposed conscription, with the full backing of the Democratic party. The Federalists had worked against conscription, he said, before it was adopted as a war measure on a state basis. But once it had become law in certain areas they accepted the decision and did not seek to turn the people against their elected leaders, in the manner of the Peace Democracy. As a Democrat, he now endorsed Conscription and urged all other Democrats to do the same. As a Democrat, he promised to do anything in his power to rescue his party from the Peace faction.[111] With the full force of the Wisconsin War Democracy aimed against the Regular Democratic ticket, the Union party carried the day. War Democrat James T. Lewis was elected by the largest majority ever obtained by a gubernatorial candidate as of that time, and the Unionist majority in the legislature was dramatically increased.[112]

Wholly rejecting the Peace Democracy in the spring of 1863, the people of Illinois turned for leadership to War Democrat Francis C. Sherman, Mayor of Chicago. Standing for reelection in April and seeking once again the Conservative Republican vote, Sherman urged the Union on to victory, while at the same time assailing the anti-slavery cause. He was barely reelected, with a majority of 550 votes out of 29,000 cast.[113] But following the arrest of Vallandigham in May and the suspension of the Chicago

Times by General Burnside in June, the Illinois Peace faction sought once again to seize control of the Democratic state machine.

When Governor Yates prorogued the Illinois legislature, and before the legislature had dispersed, the Regular Democracy held a mass meeting at Springfield, June 17, attended by a crowd of 40,000. Everybody present was for Peace. U.S. Senator Richardson presided and speeches were delivered by Congressmen Voorhees of Indiana and Cox of Ohio, criticizing the Governor for the suspension of popular government, General Burnside for suspension of the *Times,* and President Lincoln for the Vallandigham arrest. Sympathy was expressed for Union troops and $47 thousand was pledged to aid in the care of sick and wounded Illinois volunteers. The war itself was roundly condemned.[114] In answer to the challenge, a Union party mass meeting was held at Springfield, and patriotic speeches were delivered by many political leaders, including Democratic Generals John A. McClernand and Isham N. Haynie.[115] Democratic General John A. Logan was furloughed home to speak at several Union rallies, receiving a wild reception wherever he appeared.[116]

On voting day, the Illinois Union party swept to victory, returning Unionists to power in county and municipal offices all over the state. Exceptional were Chicago and Springfield where the Regular Democratic candidates were War men, and won with the backing of the War Democracy. Wherever Peace Democrats prevailed in conventions and Peace candidates nominated for state office, the Democratic party was defeated. Statewide, the Union majority was 30,000.[117]

In Maryland, as in Kentucky and Tennessee, the 1863 campaign involved the breakup of the Union party and the sudden appearance of a Radical anti-slavery party, opposing Conservative tradition. And once again, the Radical leader turned out to be a War Democrat. In preference to the Peace Democracy, in 1861, the Radicals of Maryland had rallied to the leadership of the pro-slavery Whig Governor Augustus W. Bradford, who did everything possible to play down the slavery question, opposing anti-slavery measures of every kind. Requested by Lincoln to assist in the promotion of Compensated Emancipation, he simply had refused.[118] At the Union State Convention of May 1862 Bradford's lieutenants had declared against the mere discussion of slavery, *per se,*[119] and at the Altoona Governors' Conference of September 1862 Bradford stood alone against Lincoln's Emancipation policy. Tired of such leadership, the Radical members of the Maryland Union party broke ranks with the Conservatives in 1863, coming out in favor of the Gradual Emancipation plan and denouncing the legislature for coming out against it. The leading Radicals in Maryland were former Congressman Henry Winter Davis and State Senator Henry H. Goldsborough. Davis was an "American" and a former Congressman from Baltimore. Goldsborough was a Breckinridge Democrat and a State Senator from a heavy slaveholding district in the southern section of the state. Both were now for Lincoln and for Emancipation, and when they made their feelings known to the Union State Committee the reaction was decidedly negative.[120] Riding headlong into the Conservative Unionist opposition, Davis captured the Union congressional convention in his district, and won the party nomination, while Goldsborough began the organization of a separate Radical party that was to overthrow the Bradford regime. The Goldsborough forces came before the public as the "Unconditional Union" party, with Goldsborough the choice for State Comptroller, against the Conservative Union candidate, Samuel S. Maffitt.[121] War Democrat John A. J. Creswell, Assistant Adjutant General on the Governor's staff, joined the Unconditionals to run for Congress in a Conservative Baltimore district. Preceding release of the Emancipation Proclamation, Creswell had led the fight against it as a member of the State Assembly. But Lincoln had convinced him of the error of his ways and Creswell now was working with the Radicals.

A major issue of the 1863 Maryland campaign was Conscription and a Conservative demand for application of the law in such manner as to benefit wealthy slaveholders, at the expense of non-slaveholders. The drafting of free Negroes and the undraftability of slaves decreased the cash value of the non-slaveholders' crops, to the benefit of their slaveholding rivals. Non-slaveholders protested, urging the drafting of slaves, to reestablish economic equilibrium, and the Unconditional Union party seized upon the issue, protesting to the government in Washington. The protest proved highly disturbing to the slaveholding minority in the state, but was favorably received by the non-slaveholding majority.[122] The day of the Cavalier was over, so far as Maryland politics were concerned, and anti-slavery sentiment was suddenly respectable.

War Democrat Congressman Thomas of Maryland, supporting the Conservative Union ticket, wrote to Governor Bradford warning of the change in public opinion and urging the Governor to abandon his pro-slavery position, in the interest of the Union party. Bradford agreed, and reversed himself on the slavery question, declaring in favor of compensated Emancipation. But that was not enough for the Unconditionals, who now announced in favor of the use of Negro troops, and on that basis pressed their election drive in every corner of the state. Startled by the power of the Radical campaign, the Governor abandoned the Conservative Union candidates, as did also Lincoln's Conservative ally, Postmaster General Montgomery Blair, (Jr.)[123]

A great confusion arose in Maryland in 1863 concerning "federal interference at the polls." On July 28, the Conservative Unionists, under Bradford, appealed to Lincoln for the presence of troops at the polls on voting day, and the troops arrived in answer to the call. But the Radicals carried the election, to the amazement of the Conservatives, and for the following year the Conservatives did little but talk about the outrage of "federal interference at the polls." Under the direction of the army, many ballots were disallowed, and when the vote count was completed the Radical majority was 20,376. War Democrat Henry H. Goldsborough was elected comptroller. In the congressional races the Union party captured three seats, the Unconditionals one, and the Democrats one. War Democrat Francis Thomas was reelected as a Unionist; War Democrat John A. J. Creswell was elected as an Unconditional. Most startling of all, the Unconditionals captured control of the legislature.[124]

Angered by the election results, Governor Bradford and War Democrat Reverdy Johnson, Senator-elect, denounced the actions of the army, claiming federal interference at the polls. Replying to the complaint, President Lincoln said that Bradford was elected in 1861 with the help of "federal interference at the polls," and so was the legislature that later sent Johnson to the Senate. Responsibility for federal intervention in Maryland affairs fell, he said, on Maryland, for failing to enact a loyalty oath of its own, which action would have negated the need for federal interference at the polls.[125]

*   *   *

Politics in Missouri in 1863 pitted two War Democrats against each other in the persons of General John M. Schofield of Illinois, Commander of the Department of Missouri, and Charles D. Drake, a member of the Missouri State Convention. Schofield was a professional soldier, a scholar, and a former instructor at West Point. In the early days of the war he had left his position as guest-instructor at St. Louis University to help organize the Union forces in Missouri. He was present at Wilson's Creek as Chief of Staff to General Lyon; also directing organization of the Missouri Militia, and performing brilliant service in the field, both in Missouri and Arkansas. In May 1863, he had received the Missouri command.

As a political Conservative, Schofield was at one point in tune with Drake, who had entered the war as a friend of slavery. But as Drake went Radical, Schofield had come to regard him as a troublemaker. Reelected to the State Constitutional Convention in 1863, Drake began to organize a move to rid the state of its pro-slavery Governor Hamilton R. Gamble. By lining up a Charcoal (Radical) slate of candidates for the State Supreme Court, he hoped to dominate the Court and secure a decision removing the Governor from office. (Gamble never having been elected, a majority of the Court could declare him a usurper, vacate the State House, and call for an election.) Schofield sided with the Governor and sought to block the Charcoals. The Charcoals, in turn, demanded the removal of Schofield from command and his replacement with a Radical, such as Benjamin F. Butler. Pressing the issue to the full extent, Drake took his argument to Lincoln, presenting evidence of misconduct by Schofield (all of which Schofield insisted was false and misleading.)[126]

When Drake was finished talking in Washington, Schofield was finished as commander in Missouri, but not immediately. He remained in charge until the state elections were over, and his continued presence in Missouri affected the election results. Out of 93,000 votes cast, the Charcoal candidates received a majority of about 1,700. But county clerks out of sympathy with the Charcoals rejected 3,000 soldier ballots, tipping the scales in favor of the Claybanks. When the Charcoals protested to Schofield, he refused to intercede in their behalf, the Claybanks were declared elected, and Governor Gamble retained his authority.[127]

Immediately following the general elections the Missouri legislature was required to select two U.S. Senators. Incumbent War Democrat John B. Henderson was supposedly a Claybank, having entered Congress in 1862 as one of the richest slaveholders in Missouri. But his closeness to Lincoln, gradual Emancipation, the Proclamation, and the arming of the Negroes had rendered him a Charcoal by 1864. The Claybank candidate for his seat was War Democrat John S. Phelps, recently retired as Military Governor of Arkansas. Henderson defeated Phelps, 84 to 21, and was returned to the Senate.[128] The other Senate seat went to a Republican, B. Gratz Brown.

Of all the November states, conservative, pro-southern New Jersey appeared the most in tune with the Great Peace Campaign of 1863. But even here the Peace men bungled their attack, to the point of breaking up the Democratic party. Following the Vallandigham arrest, great Peace rallies were held throughout the state in May, June, and July, featuring speeches by C. Chauncy Burr, David Naar, Albert R. Speer, Daniel Holsman, Dr. Thomas Dunn English and Andrew J. Rogers. While the protests were in progress, Governor Joel Parker and his lieutenants were conscientiously avoiding all contact with the Peace faction. Invited to a Vallandigham rally in Newark, May 30, Parker declined, saying he agreed that the question of arbitrary arrests was worthy of discussion, but objected to being associated in the public mind with Vallandigham's principles.[129] . . .The major elections in New Jersey determined control of the legislature, and the Peace faction was mainly responsible for the nature of the Democratic campaign. War Democrats seeking Democratic nominations were opposed by the Peace faction in every district and many were defeated at the party nominating conventions, including some incumbents. (Prime targets of the Peace assault were Democratic Assemblyman Jacob Vanatta, who barely scraped through, and Democratic State Senator Joseph T. Crowell, who failed of renomination.) The Peace men worked against the nomination of

War Democrat Theodore Runyon for Mayor of Newark, but without success.[130] C. Chauncy Burr, formerly of the Hackensack *Bergen County Democrat,* declared against the War Democrats, reading them out of the party. "Are these men Democrats," he asked, "after they have sold themselves, and betrayed their party and their country? No. There are no War Democrats. . . .No honest Democrat would ever support a war that is waged in violation of every principle of democracy and liberty. Hence we say they are not Democrats. They are not Christians. They are disciples of old John Brown."[131]

The Democratic campaign was heavily laden down with Peace dogma, which distinctly limited the participation of Governor Parker. Finally, at the peak of the campaign, he stated his opinion, directly contrary to the Peace Democracy, announcing in favor of the latest presidential troop call as a matter of national necessity. "Our armies should be largely reinforced," he said. "A crushing blow at the armed power of the rebellion, if allowed by wise, just and conciliatory councils, will open the door to that peace which we so much desire and has thus far eluded us."[132] Not only was the Peace faction infuriated by the Governor's attitude, but by that of his good friend, Theodore Runyon, running for mayor of Newark. In the legislative races, the Democrats gained one Senate seat, losing five in the Assembly. But most of the losses were charged against the War faction and most Peace incumbents were successful of achieving reelection. Totally deserted by the Peace Democracy, War Democrat Runyon was barely elected mayor, by fewer than a thousand votes.[133] The moment the election was over, the Peace faction declared the result a mandate for Peace and launched an attack against the Governor.

*   *   *

By the time the 1863 campaign had gotten under way in Massachusetts, the failure of the Great Peace Crusade was clear to everybody and the War faction prevailed at the Democratic State Convention. War Democrat Henry W. Paine was nominated for Governor and War Democrat Thomas F. Plunkett for lieutenant governor. The party platform supported the Union cause although criticizing Emancipation, and other "unconstitutional acts of the party in power." Payne spoke frequently, in company with War Democrats George B. Loring, Josiah G. Abbott, and Edwin C. Bailey. The Republican cause needed little help from the War Democracy, relying mainly on Radical speakers of the Republican school. Exceptional were War Democrats Caleb Cushing and Solomon Parsons, who campaigned hard for Governor Andrew, berating the Peace cause and talking up Emancipation.[134] Dissolution of the People's party of 1862 brought a host of Conservative Unionists back to the Republican fold. Confronted by

Democrats alone, without the help of Constitutional Unionists and dissident Republicans, the Republican party was once again supreme, endorsing the Andrew administration, with a 14,000 vote majority, and regaining most of the legislative seats lost in 1862.[135]

In Delaware, the major issue of the November elections was the policy of War Democrat Governor William Cannon, in calling for the presence of troops at the polls. Charles Brown, the Regular Democratic candidate for Congress, attacked the Governor as a despot, but the War Democrat Georgetown *Union* supported him, declaring that ". . .every vote for Brown is in the indorsement of treason and will gladden the heart of Jefferson Davis."[136] General Schenck, as Commander of the Maryland Department, further agitated the situation by requiring an oath of allegiance on the part of all prospective voters. The Regular Democrats protested and proceeded to boycott the vote, whereupon the Union candidate was elected without opposition.[137]

The Kansas elections involved control of the legislature and the State Supreme Court, and in both cases the candidates were all Radical—anti-Lincoln Radicals versus pro-Lincoln Radicals. The longstanding leader of Kansas Radicalism was U.S. Senator James H. Lane, but Lane was now allied to Lincoln in Washington. Anti-Lincoln Radicals in Kansas were taking orders from their other Senator, Samuel C. Pomeroy, who was soon to declare against the reelection of the President. Lane's Senate term was about to expire (in Pomeroy's opinion) and a War Democrat—Governor Thomas Carney—was Pomeroy's choice for Lane's successor. According to Lane's interpretation of the Kansas state constiution, his term extended into 1865. But Pomeroy believed otherwise—that it was over in 1864 and that Carney was free to run for U.S. Senator at the meeting of the next legislature. With Pomeroy's blessings, Carney was elected; but when he got to Washington he could not obtain a hearing and was told to go home. Friendly to Lane and suspicious of Pomeroy, Lincoln had thrown his influence in Lane's direction, at Carney's expense. (When Pomeroy came out against Lincoln's renomination in 1864, Lincoln was to to turn on Carney, once again, denouncing him as an incompetent.[138])

At the Iowa Democratic State Convention of 1863 a compromise was arranged, with the Peace faction deciding the platform and the War faction naming the ticket. The plan collapsed when the candidate for Governor, Maturin L. Fisher, denounced the platform and declined to run, at which time the nomination was bestowed on General James M. Tuttle, a hero of the recent Vicksburgh campaign. Tuttle accepted the nomination, but in the process of doing so threw away the platform. He was wholly in favor of the war.[139]

Seeking to corral the War Democracy again, as in 1861 and 1862, the Iowa Republicans proclaimed themselves "the party of the Union," and sought the speaking talents of as many War Democrats as they could find. At the first big party rally of 1863 at Oskaloosa, February 13, and Ottuma, the next day, War Democrat Chester C. Cole was the featured speaker. At the second such rally, Democratic Judge David Rorer "skinned the copperheads alive."[140] Cole continued speaking for the Republicans all year long, in company with War Democrats Henry Beekman, George Crane, and Hugh Phelps.[141] Much was said by the Regular Democracy about the questionable constitutionality of the Soldier Vote Law and the possibility of its gross misapplication, to Republican advantage. In answer to the charge, Democratic General Ulysses S. Grant advised the Democratic State Central Committee of Iowa that nobody coerced the soldiers in his command, on voting day or in advance of voting day, and that "No power on earth shall prevent them from voting the ticket of their choice."[142] The Republican-Union trend held firm in Iowa where General Tuttle was defeated by Republican Colonel William M. Stone by 30,000 votes.[143]

* * *

As a postlude to the state campaigns of 1863, a "Consulting Convention of the Northwestern States" was held at Chicago and resolutions were adopted setting forth again the principles of Peace.[144] This was matched by a "Conference Convention of the War Democracy of the Northwest," meeting in Chicago in November. The War Democrats were called to order by Colonel Barnabas Burns of the 86th Ohio Infantry, and General John A. McClernand of Illinois served as permanent chairman. Breckinridge leader J. W. Taylor of St. Paul, Minnesota, drew up resolutions demanding that the Democratic party separate itself from all sympathy with the pro-slavery cause. Another resolution proposed creation of a Negro community, to be established on the sea coast lands of South Carolina, Georgia, and Florida. The Community could be utilized, on a voluntary basis, as an alternative to a racially integrated society. The resolutions further declared that Congress had the right to impose whatever conditions it preferred upon the seceded states, following the war, insofar as the issue of voting rights were concerned.[145]

Despite the appeal for racial segregation, this was a Radical position to assume on a vital issue; a total repudiation of the traditional Democratic demand for "the Union as it was and the Constitution as it is," and the wholesale acceptance of Radical Senator Charles Sumner's "State Suicide" theory (granting Congress the privilege of bestowing the franchise on the Negro freedman). On December 8 President Lincoln issued his Amnesty and Reconstruction Proclamation, containing the so-called "Ten Percent" provision, returning the seceded states to the Union without modification of their voting laws (thereby denying the franchise to the Negro freedman). The "Conference Convention of the War Democracy of the Northwest" was clearly established on extreme ground, far to the political left of President Lincoln.

*   *   *

The New York City municipal elections, held in December, featured once again the War and Peace Democracies in mutual combat. Earlier in the year, preceding the Draft Riots, the Peace factions in Tammany Hall and Mozart Hall had controlled the destinies of both outfits, under the personal direction of William M. Tweed and Fernando Wood.[146] But by election time that was no longer the state of affairs. Public reaction to the riots was enough to drive both leaders from authority, with the War Democrats assuming control over both machines. At Tammany, Peter B. Sweeney succeeded Tweed. At Mozart, Manton Marble of the New York *World* replaced Fernando Wood. To insure the election of a War Democrat for Mayor in 1863, Sweeney and Marble declared for the same candidate—Alderman Francis I. A. Boole of Tammany—at which point the new York City Union party deserted George Opdyke, the Radical Mayor, in favor of Orison Blunt, Conservative.[147] Boole was a War Democrat. He appeared the likely winner, with the blessings of Marble of the *World*, Clancy of the Tammany *Leader*, and James Gorden Bennett of the *Herald*. But the injection of the Negro troops issue into the November state campaign, by Lincoln himself, had revived the Peace Democracy of New York City which came out fighting on an anti-Negro platform. For failing to follow suit, War Democrat Boole was declared a "nigger lover" and a Peace ticket—the "McKeon Democracy"—entered the campaign, behind the leadership of John McKeon and Godfrey C. Gunther of Tammany and Oswald Ottendorffer of the German-language *Staats Zeitung*. Gunther was the candidate for Mayor.[148]

War Democrats in general supported Boole. Samuel J. Tilden, Henry C. Murphy, Luke F. Cozzens, A. Oaky Hall, Elijah Ward, Henry L. Clinton, Colonel Spencer W. Cone, and Gilbert Dean all campaigned in his behalf. Marble of the *World* predicted a forty thousand vote majority for Boole,[149] but in this he was sorely mistaken. A great swarm of Tammany and Mozart men had quit their party regularity to work for Gunther and for Peace. Their loss proved fatal to the Boole campaign.

The Negro vote was very slight in New York City, hampered as it was by property qualifications. The Irish vote, with no such qualifications, was of course considerable. Anti-Negro Irish voters were advised that Boole was after the Negro vote and was doing everything he could to obtain it. The charge worked wonders and the Irish deserted Tammany in large numbers.[150] On voting day, Gunther was elected over Boole with a plurality of six thousand. Union candidate Blunt finished a very poor third, receiving only 17 percent of the vote.[151] In reporting the result, The *Herald* observed that "from the general tenor of conversation (around Tammany headquarters following the news of Boole's defeat) it really appeared that there was no regret. . . .On the whole, it really seemed as if Gunther, not Boole, was the Tammany candidate."[152] Manton Marble of Mozart and the *World* concluded the brief alliance of Tammany and Mozart by declaring that the sordid reputation of Tammany had clearly scared away the voters.[153]

Partially offsetting the New York City results was the outcome of the municipal elections in Brooklyn, where the Peace faction had controlled everything for the past year. At the 1863 Union borough convention, the nomination for Mayor was accorded to War Democrat Alfred M. Wood, former President of the New York Common Council, former Colonel of the 84th New York Infantry, currently a Collector of Internal Revenue. Wounded and captured at First Bull Run, Wood was exchanged late in 1861 and upon returning to his home declared himself a convert to the Union party cause. Mayor Martin Kalbfleisch of Brooklyn, a defiant Peace partisan, was renominated by the Regular Democracy. Wood and Kalbfleisch were political allies of many years standing, but they fought each other sharply in this campaign from which Wood emerged the victor, receiving about twelve thousand votes against eight thousand for the Peace ticket.[154]

* * * * * * * *

On November 19 President Lincoln delivered the Gettysburg Address, in which he utilized again the inflamatory Jeffersonian contention that "all men are created equal," and otherwise disturbed the feelings of the Peace Democracy. It was made clear in the Address that war weariness was not going to undermine the federal war policy, if the President had anything to say about it; that is, the Union armies were not going to stop fighting until the enemy was ready to surrender. The Gettysburg Address was one more blow to the joint cause of Peace and Conservative tradition, which had entered the year with high hopes of success, only to be buffeted unmercifully by Lincoln's nonpartisan coalition, in the interest of the Union.

NOTES

1. William B. Hesseltine, p. 265.
2. The Pierce machine included Harry Bingham, Edmund Burk, and John B. Palmer. Bingham was the outstanding spokesman for every major Peace proposal yet considered by the legislature. Burk's Concord *Standard* and Palmer's Concord *Patriot* were easily the leading Peace papers in the state. See St. Paul (Minnesota) *Press,* August 16, 1861. The *Patriot* was regarded as the mouthpiece of former President Pierce. Ibid., August 16, 1861. Pierce went on record against the war in a speech delivered on the Fourth of July, 1863. James D. Squires, III:400. Editor Edmund Burk of the *Standard* was a former Congressman and Commissioner of Patents under Polk; also an outstanding lawyer and stump speaker. Everett S. Stackpole, III:314; IV:192. Following First Bull Run, the *Standard* and the *Patriot* were both disposed to blame the Republicans for bringing on the war. A *Patriot* editorial described the war as "Mr. Lincoln's war for the subjugation of the South." It blamed the President for "hurling our men upon certain defeat and death at Bull Run." Quoted *in* St. Paul (Minnesota *Press,* August 16, 1861.
3. Loyal Publication Society, Pamphlet 9 (New York, 1863).
4. Amos Hadley, p. 144.
5. Loyal Publication Society, Pamphlet 9 (New York, 1863).
6. Manchester (New Hampshire) *Democrat and American,* February 19, 1863.
7. Ibid., February 19, 1863.
8. Benjamin P. Thomas, *Stanton,* p. 278; James O. Lyford, p. 154; Manchester (New Hampshire) *Democrat and American,* February 18, 1863; Amos Hadley, p. 145.
9. Ibid., p. 151.
10. William B. Hesseltine, p. 319. While addressing a Union rally in New Hampshire, General Butler was reminded by a Democrat in the audience that he had worked for Breckinridge in the 1860 campaign. Butler acknowledged the truth of the remark, but said that he had changed his mind. Judas Iscariot was once regarded as an admirable man, he pointed out. As "a true follower of his master, he was no doubt a worthy example to be followed." It was not reasonable to assume, however, "that a man to preserve his consistency must continue to follow Judas after he had betrayed the Lord." Manchester *Union,* September 3, 1863, quoting from a Philadelphia *Press* story early in the year.
11. *Tribune Almanac,* 1864; Benjamin P. Thomas, *Edwin M. Stanton,* p. 278.
12. John P. Pritchett, "Michigan Democracy in the Civil War," *Michigan History Magazine,* vol. XI, no. 1 (January 1927): pp. 92–109.
13. The Michigan Democratic ticket was not entirely composed of Peace men, despite the Peace platform. War Democrats accepting nominations included Benjamin F. H. Witherell, candidate for Circuit Court Judge, and William A. Moore and Nathaniel A. Balch, candidates for the Board of Regents.
14. *A thrilling Narrative from the Lips of the Sufferers of the Late Detroit Riot, March 6, 1863, . . .and Destruction of Colored Men's Property, Not Less than $15,000* (Detroit, 1863).
15. *Evening Journal Almanac,* 1864.
16. W. A. Croffutt and John M. Morris, p. 323.
17. Robert J. Lane, p. 224.
18. Ibid., pp. 215, 218, 219.
19. *Evening Journal Almanac,* 1864.
20. John Niven, *Connecticut for the Union; The Role of the State in the Civil War* (New Haven: Yale University Press, 1965), p. 81.
21. Robert J. Lane, p. 223.
22. *Evening Journal Almanac,* 1864.

23. Loyal League of Union Citizens, p. 78.
24. Some Democrats who followed Sprague in merging with the Republicans: Duncan C. Pell, candidate for Lieutenant Governor, 1856; the Reverand John Tillinghast, a former member of the legislature; Abraham Payne, delegate to the 1860 Douglas State Convention.
25. See Providence *Post,* February 1863 (all editions).
26. Charles S. Bradley was not only a strong pro-Union man but furiouisly anti-slavery and hostile to the South, even in Antebellum times. Following the Brooks-Sumner altercation of 1854, he delivered an address denouncing Brooks and warning the South that if Brooks were applauded for his conduct by pro-slavery men, the sentiment would lead in time to civil war. *Biographical Cyclopedia of Representative Men of Rhode Island,* p. 154.
27. *Evening Journal Almanac,* 1864.
28. Charles H. Ambler and Festus P. Summers, p. 249.
29. *Evening Journal Almanac,* 1864.
30. Oliver P. Temple, p. 47.
31. Ibid., p. 47.
32. Clifton R. Hall, pp. 100, 106, 107; U.S. War Department, *Official Records of the War of the Rebellion,* Series III, vol. III, p. 709.
33. E. Merton Coulter, p. 173.
34. Ibid., p. 171.
35. Ibid., p. 176.
36. Ibid., p. 177.
37. *Evening Journal Almanac,* 1864.
38. E. Merton Coulter, p. 178.
39. *Evening Journal Almanac,* 1865.
40. Louis C. Hatch, ed., II:453.
41. Ibid., II:453.
42. Ibid., II:454.
43. Ibid., II:455.
44. Ibid., II:455.
45. *Evening Journal Almanac,* 1864, 1863.
46. Walter H. Crockett, p. 569.
47. Winfield J. Davis, p. 194. The Chairman of Organization at the 1863 California Union State Convention was War Democrat W. L. Dudley, and one of the vice presidents of the gathering was John Bidwell, a Douglas leader at the 1860 Charleston Convention. Some other prominent Democrats in attendance included J. B. Frisbie, George S. Evans, J. J. Gardiner and James Green. Gardner was nominated for Surveyor General, but lost out to a Republican nominee; Green was nominated for Clerk of Court, but also was defeated by a Republican. War Democrat Bidwell was named a member of the Union State Committee. Ibid., pp. 194–95; Rockwell D. Hunt, *John Bidwell, Prince of California Pioneers* (Caldwell: Idaho, 1942), p. 182.
48. Winfield J. Davis, pp. 197.
49. Ibid., pp. 197–200.
50. Ibid., p. 203.
51. *Evening Journal Almanac,* 1864.
52. Pugh's acceptance speech was violent. Addressing his remarks to General Burnside, he said, "I scorn your Order No. 38. I spurn, I execrate, I trample under foot the order of any military officer defining treason and prescribing liberty. Come what will, come imprisonment, exile, stripes, hard labor, death, I defy Order Number 38." He warned the audience that if the Democrats should lose the next election they would be better off emigrating to another land where freedom was possible, for they would not get it here. Ibid., p. 171.
53. Ibid., p. 177.

54. Whitelaw Read, *Ohio in the War,* 2 vols. (Columbus, 1893), I:168.
55. George H. Porter, pp. 119–20.
56. Ibid., p. 121.
57. Wood Gray, p. 150.
58. Columbus *Ohio State Journal,* September 23, 1863.
59. George H. Porter, p. 179.
60. Ibid., p. 180.
61. Columbus *Ohio State Journal,* September 23, 1863. Some other war veterans attending the Convention of the War Democracy of Ohio included: General John Bates of the State Militia; Colonel J. W. Bourke, 10th Ohio Infantry; Colonel James A. Jones and Lieutenant Colonel William P. Richardson, 25th Ohio Infantry; Lieutenant Colonel Benjamin F. Potts, 32d Ohio Infantry; Lieutenant Colonel James Laughlin, Fifth Ohio Cavalry; and Lieutenant Jacob A. Egley, 108th Ohio Infantry.
62. Ibid., September 23, 1863.
63. Rutland (Vermont) Weekly *Herald,* September 3, 1863.
64. Loyal Publication Society, "Voices from the army!" Pamphlet 5 (New York, 1863).
65. George H. Porter, p. 183; William B. Hesseltine, p. 335.
66. Agnew was elected on the Whig ticket in 1851 to a ten-year term as President Judge of the Pennsylvania District Court, and reelected as a Democrat in 1861.
67. Stanton Ling Davis, pp. 297–98; Harrisburg (Pennsylvania) *Patriot and Union,* June 25, 1863.
68. Francis L. Conlin, "The Democratic Party in Pennsylvania from 1856 to 1865," American Catholic Historical Society of Philadelphia, *Records,* vol. XLVII, no. 1 (March 1936): 169.
69. Philadelphia *City Item,* September 1863—all editions.
70. Union League of Philadelphia. *Addresses and resolutions.* September 16, 1863.
71. Heister Clymer, pp. 7–8.
72. *Evening Journal Almanac,* 1864; *National Cyclopedia,* IV:24.
73. Stanton Ling Davis, p. 312.
74. Harrisburg (Pennsylvania) *Patriot and Union,* November 12, 1863.
75. *Encyclopedia of Contemporary Biography of Pennsylvania,* 2 vols. (New York: Atlantic, 1869), I:59. Robert S. Mitchell, p. 314.
76. Christopher C. Andrews, p. 130.
77. Charles E. Flandreau. Encyclopedia of biography of Minnesota. History of Minnesota. 2 vols. (Chicago: Century, 1900). I:147.
78. The Peace press tended to ignore the Welles campaign.
79. *Evening Journal Almanac.* 1864.
80. Loyal Publication Society. Publication No. 5. *Voices from the Army.*
81. Ibid.
82. *Evening Journal Almanac,* 1864.
83. New York *Atlas,* quoted in New York *Herald,* May 26, 1863. The *Atlas* also cited as "Copperhead" the 1863 Democratic ticket in Rhode Island, but that was a mistake. It actually was War Democrat.
84. The New York *Atlas* was an organ of the Albany Regency. Sidney D. Brummer, p. 315.
85. Ibid., p. 316.
86. Ibid., p. 316.
87. New York *Herald,* May 21, 1863.
88. New York *News,* quoted in the Albany *atlas and Argus,* June 9, 1863.
89. New York *Herald,* September 11, 1863.
90. Loyal League of Union Citizens, *Commemoration,* p. 64. The remarks of Lyman Tremain would indicate that Thomas J. Brady engaged in the Connecticut election campaign of 1863, in behalf of the Union candidates.

91. New York *Herald,* September 11, 1863.
92. Loyal League of Union Citizens, p. 16.
93. De Alva Stanwood Alexander, III:76–77.
94. Alan Johnson and Dumas Malone, eds., V:295.
95. New York *Herald,* September 3, 1863.
96. *Evening Journal Almanac,* 1864.
97. De Alva Stanwood Alexander, III:81.
98. Sidney D. Brummer, p. 347.
99. Robert G. Athearn, p. 134.
100. Loyal Publication Society, Pamphlet No. 28, *The Death of Slavery,* Letter from Peter Cooper to Governor Seymour (New York, 1863). (Written September 22, 1863).
101. Thomas M. Cook and Thomas W. Knox, eds., *Public Record of Horatio Seymour: Including Speeches, Messages, Proclamations, Official Correspondences and Other Public Utterances, from the Campaign of 1856 to the Present Time,* with an Appendix (England, 1868), pp. 168–76.
102. William B. Hesseltine, p. 337.
103. *Evening Journal Almanac,* 1864.
104. Frank A. Flower, p. 231.
105. E. Bruce Thompson, p. 73.
106. Janesville (Wisconsin) Convention, *Resolutions,* September 17, 1863.
107. Janesville (Wisconsin) Convention, *Resolutions,* September 17, 1863.
108. Parker M. Reed, *Bench and Bar of Wisconsin* (Milwaukee, 1882), p. 121.
109. Although an ardent Democrat before and during the first year of the war, Lucius Fairchild began saying complimentary things about the Republicans while serving in the army and his change of heart aroused suspicion in certain quarters. Upon reading a letter he had written to a friend, praising the Lincoln administration, a Democratic partisan declared, "Lushe wants to be a Brigadier General that's what ails him." Quoted in Mary Dearing, p. 13. On the other hand, maybe not. Upon accepting the Union party nomination for Secretary of State, in 1863, Fairchild attacked the Peace Democracy, concluding, "I cannot believe any discouragement to the government can help to put down the rebellion." Rutland (Vermont) *Herald,* September 3, 1863.
110. E. Bruce Thompson, pp. 75–78.
111. Morgan Dix, II:347–52. The Democrats speaking for the "War Democracy of Wisconsin" were Matthew H. Carpenter, Levi Hubbell, and Charles D. Robinson, all of whom supported Douglas in 1860. E. Bruce Thompson, p. 160.
112. *Evening Journal Almanac,* 1864.
113. Frederick Rex, *The Mayors of Chicago, from March 4, 1837 to April 13, 1933 (Biography–History)* (Chicago: Municipal Reference Library, 1934 (?)), pp. 40, 43.
114. Edward C. Smith, p. 339; John Moses, II:688.
115. John Moses, II: 689; *Union Army.* III: 235.
116. *Union Army,* III:235;
117. *Evening Journal Almanac,* 1864.
118. William B. Hesseltine, p. 259.
119. Charles B. Clark, p. 160.
120. Ibid., p. 97.
121. William L. W. Seabrook, *Maryland's Great Part in Saving the Union; The Loyalty of Her Governor, Thomas Holliday Hicks, and a Majority of Her People* (Westminster, Md.: American Sentinel, 1913), p. 43.
122. Charles B. Clark, p. 181.
123. Ibid., p. 101.
124. Charles B. Clark, pp. 99–112; Bernard C. Steiner, p. 64.

125. Charles B. Clark, pp. 106–7.
126. Galusha Anderson, *The Story of a Border City during the Civil War* (Boston: Little, Brown, 1908), pp. 284–87; Albert Castel, p. 151.
127. William E. Parrish, pp. 171–72.
128. Missorui *Senate Journal,* November 13, 1863.
129. Charles M. Knapp, p. 98.
130. Ibid., p. 100.
131. *The Old Guard,* vol. II, no. 8 (August 1863): "War Democrats and Their Crimes," p. 204.
132. Trenton *True American,* October 23, 1863.
133. Charles M. Knapp, p. 100.
134. Ibid., pp. 133–34; Parsons was among the most active War Democrats in the state. He would attend the Jacksonian Democrat Convention of 1864, as a delegate from Massachusetts.
135. *Evening Journal Almanac,* 1864.
136. Georgetown (Delaware) *Union,* November 13, 1863.
137. Henry C. Conrad, p. 211.
138. Albert Castel, pp. 169, 170, 174; Roy P. Basler, ed., VII:340–41.
139. Charles B. Clark, pp. 187–90; Cyrenus Cole, p. 364.
140. Ibid., p. 177. Quoted from Des Moines *Iowa State Register,* March 3, 1863.
141. Beekman, Crane, and Phelps were now committed to the Emancipation principle. They would serve as delegates to the 1864 "Jacksonian Democrat" convention, which supported the Republican-Union coalition. Cole would head the Iowa Union ticket of 1864, as candidate for a place on the State Supreme Court.
142. *Union Army,* IV.
143. *Evening Journal Almanc,* 1864.
144. Wood Gray, pp. 158–59.
145. Chicago *Tribune,* November 26, 1863.
146. Sidney D. Brummer, pp. 353.
147. New York *Herald,* October 13, 1863.
148. Ottendorffer's Support of Gunther Reported in the New York *Herald,* November 17, 1863.
149. Ibid., November 25, 1863.
150. Basil Leo Lee, p. 163. Author Lee repeats the McKeon-Gunther accusation as a fact, that Boole appealed directly for the Negro vote. We have found no evidence to sustain the contention, nor is any evidence cited by Lee.
151. The vote for Gunther, 29,121; Boole, 22,597; Blunt, 19,393. Ibid., p. 163.
152. New York *Herald,* December 2, 1863.
153. New York *World,* December 2, 1863.
154. Henry R. Stiles, II:437–38.

12

Conservative Tradition
Beaten in the Field: 1864

The Thirty-eighth Congress included members elected both in 1862 (the year of the Regular Democracy's Great Victory) and 1863 (the year of the Regular Democracy's Great Repudiation). In the Senate, the Republican-Union coalition retained its powerful majority. Nor was there cause for alarm by administration leaders concerning control of the House. Democratic victories in the 1862 congressional races were sufficiently offset by Republican-Union victories in 1863 to insure the maintenance of administration policy in the Thirty-eighth Congress. The only Republican losers of consequences were the Radicals and in deference to this, Conservative Republican Schuyler Colfax of Indiana was chosen Speaker in place of Radical Galusha A. Grow of Pennsylvania, defeated in 1862. The vote was not close: 100 for Colfax, 42 for Samuel S. Cox of Ohio, a recent convert to the Peace cause.[1] There were 35 War Democrats in the House (24 Regular, eleven Union) as opposed to 50 Peace Democrats, and nine War Democrats in the Senate (Five Regular, Four Union) as opposed to six Peace Democrats and two Conditionals.[2]

War Democrat leadership in Congress changed hands again in December 1863, owing to the backsliding of Senator James A. McDougall of California and the gerrymandering of Congressman Hendrick B. Wright of

Pennsylvania. Bewildered and disturbed by the build-up of the anti-slavery campaign, McDougall no longer was willing to take the lead in promoting military appropriation bills in the Senate. (The role was therefore passed along to War Democrat John B. Henderson of Missouri, who was now a confidant of Lincoln.) In the House, the new leader of the War Democracy was General Green Clay Smith of Kentucky.

As wartime converts to the anti-slavery cause, Henderson and Smith had much in common. As southerners and slaveholders they had pro-slavery family traditions extending back for generations. Both had campaigned against Lincoln in the 1860 campaign, as Douglas electors, and both had risen to prominence in the Secession period, as opponents of Disunion. By the time Smith arrived to take his seat in Congress, in December 1863, Henderson was already established as a symbol of southern Unionism—but Smith was soon to equal his performance. Having proven himself in battle, as Colonel of the Fourth Kentucky Cavalry, he was to prove himself in politics as well, as a fierce opponent of Conservative tradition. Accepting and defending the Emancipation Proclamation in 1863, he had come to the attention of the Radical faction in Kentucky and was nominated for Congress on the "Administration-Union" ticket against incumbent John W. Menzies, a critic of the Proclamation.[3] Following a hard-fought campaign, Smith defeated Menzies, surprising almost everybody, and upon arriving at Washington assumed command of the War Democracy in the House of Representatives. Regular Democrats working often in conjunction with Congressman Smith in the Thirty-eighth Congress included two New Yorkers—John A. Griswold, promoter of the ironclad *Monitor* and a former Mayor of Troy, and Henry G. Stebbins, one of New York City's leading bankers. Two Regular Democrats working often in conjunction with Senator Henderson in the Thirty-eighth Congress included James W. Nesmith of Oregon and Thomas A. Hendricks of Indiana.[4] The presence of Hendricks in the Senate coincided with the absence of War Democrat Joseph A. Wright of Indiana, unseated by authority of the Indiana legislature. As a member of the Joint Committee on the Conduct of the War, Wright had served for several months as its most Conservative influence, beyond question. He was replaced in the Thirty-eighth Congress, by two more War Democrats of Conservative bent—Benjamin F. Harding of Oregon (Union) and (later) William A. Buckalew of Pennsylvania (Regular.) Both were Negrophobes, alarmed about Emancipation. When Republican Congressman Covode of Pennsylvania left the Joint Committee he was replaced in January 1864 by War Democrat Congressman Benjamin F. Loan of Missouri (Union), an uncompromising Radical.

The Thirty-eighth Congress opened with the reading of the President's Annual Address, explaining the nature of the "Ten Percent Reconstruction program." Generally speaking, the Conservatives favored the proposal, from the start, while the Radicals were coming out against it or saying nothing. Of the ten War Democrats in the Senate, eight were Conservative, two Radical. Of 37 War Democrats in the House, 30 were Conservative, seven Radical.[5] And yet, aside from Reconstruction issues, the War Democracy remained in this Congress solidly against the Peace Democracy and wholly in favor of the Union cause. In answer to a call for a national Peace conference (proposed by Fernando Wood, December 14) the House voted negative, 98 to 59, with 18 War Democrats numbered in the majority.[6] On the same day, War Democrat Holman of Indiana tried again (for the third time in two years) to get the House to redeclare support for the pro-slavery Crittenden Resolution of August 1861. The motion was tabled by a vote of 88-66, twelve War Democrats voting in the majority.[7] On December 17, a Peace Democrat presented a resolution forbidding the military arrest of civilians in the loyal states. The resolution was lost, 67 to 90, nine War Democrats helping to defeat it.[8]

Shortly before Congress reassembled in December 1863, Negro troops under Republican General Stephen A. Hurlburt routed a Confederate force at Wolf River Bridge near Moscow, Tennessee, and the victory was widely publicized in the loyal states.[9] Conservatives were bothered by the tone of the public reaction to the news. On December 21, Peace Democrat Harding of Kentucky offered an amendment to the House Deficiency Bill, providing that no part of the appropriation be "applied to the raising, arming, equiping, or paying of Negro soldiers." The amendment was lost, 41 to 85, with 23 War Democrats voting in the majority (twelve Unionists, eleven Regulars).[10] A Radical trend on the part of the War Democrats was apparent in both houses, on every major vote.

Two of the most Radical and easily the most controversial War Democrats in the Thiry-eighth Congress were Representatives John A. J. Creswell of Maryland and Lucian Anderson of Kentucky. Both were Douglas Democrats in 1860, both were anti-slavery extremists in 1864, and both were elected on the Union ticket in 1863 with federal troops stationed at the polls. Both were also from districts which the Regular Democrats had expected to carry in 1863. When the districts instead went Union, the Regular Democrats cried foul. They were convinced that the presence of the troops had scared away Democratic voters and that Creswell and Anderson were virtually elected by force of arms.[11]

A major critic of the federal policy of maintaining "troops at the polls" in the border slave-state elections, was War Democrat Reverdy Johnson of Maryland, who had taken his arguments to the White House in 1863, without results, and therefore brought them to the Senate floor in 1864, describing the election of Creswell as a fraud against the country and the Congress. A Radical colleague of Creswell's—concerned for the fate of the Unconditional Union party in the face of this attack—wrote the Congressman, urging him to answer Johnson. "Endorse everything done (in the election) and the people will sustain you," he declared. "If you don't fight we are ruined."[12]

Much the same kind of criticism was directed against War Democrat Congressman Anderson of Kentucky. In January, a speech was delivered in the House by William J. Allen of Illinois, denouncing all federal appointees holding office in former Confederate territory. War Democrat Andrew Johnson, Military Governor of Tennessee, was cited as the prime example of a man trading principles for power. Another example: War Democrat Andrew J. Hamilton, Provisional Governor of Texas; others: Horace Maynard and William G. Brownlow of Tennessee. All were federal appointees and all were despicable, in Allen's opinion. They did not have the backing of the people in their states. Congressman Anderson was equally open to criticism, holding his position merely as "one of the President's military appointees from Kentucky."[13]

Replying to Congressman Allen, Anderson denounced his arguments as "false and slanderous, without any foundation in fact. . .I was elected by as true, unflinching, sturdy Union men as breathe upon the continent of America, not professed Union men, but Union men who have been tried by the fires of persecution, . . .without the smell of treason about them, Union men who have been robbed and plundered, who have been imprisoned, Union men who have been hunted with hell-hound ferocity by the rebels in arms against this Government and who seem to have an apologist upon this floor today in the person of the gentleman from Illinois." Taking up the arguments of Congressman Allen, one by one, Anderson observed, "He makes the declaration that he is an unconditional Union man. If it had not been for that declaration, made over and over again by the gentleman in his speech, I would have thought that it was one made in the so-called Confederate Congress at Richmond. He denounces the (Amnesty) proclamation of the President of the United States of 8th December last, as applicable to Union men. Do you find any Union men in the border-states denouncing the President of the United States for that proclamation? No, sir. . .Not satisfied. . . ,he goes further, and denounces men like Andrew Johnson, Brownlow, and Maynard, of Tennessee, and Hamilton, of Texas. Why, sir, they stand in patriotism and in loyalty as far above the gentleman from Illinois as heaven is above hell. Their acts will live in the memory of the American people when the gentleman's name will go down to posterity 'unwept, unhonored, and unsung.' "[14]

As the war progressed, there would be more exchanges of this kind, between anti-slavery southern Unionists and pro-slavery northern Copperheads, tending further to confuse the picture of a war between the "anti-slavery North" and the "pro-slavery South." Another case in point in Congress was provided by the actions of Peace Democrat Rogers of

New Jersey and War Democrat Smith of Kentucky. A resolution introduced by Rogers, January 7, favored the calling of a Peace convention including only delegates from the loyal states, to draw up Peace conditions guaranteeing the continued existence of slavery in the South and reunion without punishment of the seceded states, excepting only punishments stipulated in the Constitution and laws pursuant thereof. The resolution was tabled by a vote of 78 to 42, with 13 War Democrates voting in the majority.[15] On the same day a resolution was introduced denouncing the policy of proposing Peace conventions, as tending to subvert the spirit of the Union cause. It was carried, 88–24, with 21 War Democrats voting in the majority.[16]

According to another resolution introduced January 18 by War Democrat Smith of Kentucky, a policy in support of the war was "the political, civil, moral, and sacred duty of the people." Peace Democrat James C. Allen of Illinois moved the House adjourn, but the motion was lost, 33–98. The Smith resolution then carried, 112 to 16, with 34 Democrats voting in the majority.[17]

In the middle of debate on the House Deficiency Appropriations Bill, January 25, Peace Democrat Brooks of New York belittled the Emancipation Proclamation, describing it as feeble competition for Confederate guns. The issue was at once taken up by War Democrat Smith of Kentucky, speaking for Emancipation. Offering a resolution of his own, embodying the main clauses of the Proclamation, Smith declared, "I say it here as a Kentuckian and as a southern man, always having been identified with the institution of slavery, and believing that as a citizen of Kentucky I had a right to it, and so believing still—that whenever you sap the foundation of this accursed rebellion and tear from under the rebels that which has given them strength and power, you destroy the rebellion, and your artillery is effective."[18]

The remark created pandemonium on the floor and in the gallery, and Smith became at once the target of abuse by Regular Democrats in general. Had he not broken his word to the voters? he was asked. Had he not campaigned as an anti-Emancipation candidate? Had he not promised to vote for a War Democrat for Speaker? And had he not, in Washington, endorsed Emancipation and voted for Colfax? Smith replied that when the Democrats nominated Cox, he had to vote for someone who was certain of beating him, because Cox was for Vallandigham and he (Smith) would never vote for such a man. Accused of entering the Republican caucus, Smith replied, "No, Sir I went into a Union, an unconditional Union caucus." (Other Unionists chimed in, "Good!" "Good!") Nor had he tried to find a War Democrat worth voting for in the Regular Democratic caucus, Smith explained, "because I smelt the atmosphere and discovered its character before I got in."[19] For speaking in this manner, Smith was villified by several advocates of Peace. According to one Democratic editor, it now appeared that he was "bought up by the Abolitionists."[20]

*   *   *

In the Senate, the outstanding new member of the Thirty-eighth Congress was War Democrat Reverdy Johnson of Maryland, who established himself on a nonpartisan basis the moment he arrived. In his maiden speech, delivered December 17, 1863, he came to the defense of Republican Senator Hale of New Hampshire, accused of accepting a bribe in the guise of a legal retainer.[21] Shortly afterward, he spoke in behalf of Senator Davis of Kentucky, a Peace Democrat threatened with expulsion for recent criticisms of the President.[22]

The question of Conscription was again brought forward in 1864, and the major voice of protest on this occasion was War Democrat Senator Nesmith of Oregon. As a member of the Committee on Military Affairs and the Militia, Nesmith was in favor of outright repeal of the controversial Commutation Clause in the Conscription Act. "The reduction of patriotism to a financial standard may fill your coffers," he said, "but it will certainly deplete your ranks." A large army was desperately needed, but the working men of the country still were holding back and refusing to volunteer, resentful of a law so terribly unfair as the Conscription Act. Criticizing the administration for failing to have secured the troops necessary for so great an undertaking, Nesmith said, "We have raised armies just in proportion as we supposed the rebels had power to resist them, and our successes have been quite as attributable to the mismanagement of our enemy as to our own exhibition of strength, or forethought." If the current policy were maintained, Nesmith warned, it would be possible, some day, to "write upon the tombstone of the nation: " 'Died of Commutation.' " The Senate disagreed, and the anti-Commutation resolution was lost, 15 to 24.[23] Although defeated on this count, Nesmith agreed to endorse the Conscription Bill Report, which was adopted by the Senate, 25 to 16, with five War Democrats voting in the majority.[24]

During House debate on the Enrollment Bill, Radical leader Stevens of Pennsylvania proposed an amendment calling for enrollment of all ablebodied Negroes in the Union between the ages of 20 and 45. Military service would free the slave from bondage and loyal slaveholders would be compensated for property loss to the extent of $300 per slave. War Democrat Clay of Kentucky protested against drafting the slaves of Unionists. Secessionists had always prophesied that this would happen, he said, and southern Union men had constantly denied it. If the Stevens amendment were adopted, the Secessionists would be proven right, to the embarrassment of southern Unionists. Ignoring the argument, War Democrat Creswell of Maryland (Union) criticized the Stevens proposal as over-generous, and suggested that the freedom-price be lowered from $300 to $25. Unionist Davis of Maryland agreed with Creswell, denouncing the Stevens resolution as over-generous. Thoroughly astonished, Peace Democrat Harris of Maryland declared: ". . .I will say I look more for justice to the gentleman from Pennsylvania (Stevens) than I do to (Creswell and Davis.)" Stevens being the leading Radical in the House and the bitterest foe of the pro-slavery cause, Creswell had no objection to Harris' implied acceptance of his judgment. "I am willing to unite with the gentleman (Harris). . .and to submit the whole question to the tender mercies and grim justice of the gentleman from Pennsylvania (Stevens)," Creswell declared.[25] Seldom was the Radical zeal of Thaddeus Stevens overshadowed by that of anybody else. In this case, the honors went to Creswell, a slave-state Douglas-man.

Repudiation of the Peace Democracy in the 1863 elections made way for consideration of the revolutionary Thirteenth Amendment to the federal Constitution, abolishing slavery in the Union. It is noteworthy that the original joint resolution proposing such amendment was not the work of a Radical Republican nor any kind of Republican, but that of a War Democrat: U.S. Senator John B. Henderson of Missouri (Union). The joint resolution was introduced January 11, 1864, and referred to the Senate Judiciary Committee.[26]

A large number of War Democrats were adopting opinions similar to Henderson's in 1864. On January 12, Senator Johnson of Maryland (Union) delivered an address approving the Emancipation Proclamation.[27] In February, War Democrat Carolan O'Brien Bryant (Independent) of the New York Assembly introduced a resolution favoring passage of an anti-slavery Constitutional Amendment.[28] On February 11, Peace Democrat Harding of Kentucky declared in Congress that proposed Emancipation legislation made a mockery of declarations in the Republican platform of 1860, promising no such legislation. War Democrat Higby of California (Union) replied, "When slavery fired on Sumter it left the Republican party without a platform. That is the answer to the gentleman's speech."[29] On April 5, War Democrat Senator Johnson of Maryland endorsed the anti-slavery amendment to the Constitution proposed by fellow War Democrat Senator Henderson of Missouri.[30]

On the other side of the issue stood War Democrat Senator Hendricks of Indiana, who criticized the same proposed Amendment as a direct repudiation of the Crittenden Resolutions of 1861.[31] Replying to the charge, War Democrat Henderson of Missouri declared the need to "say something in order that gentlemen from non-slaveholding states. . .may better understand the position that we of the border slaveholding states now occupy." Rejecting his Democratic party background and his own slave-holding traditions, Henderson praised "The earnest men of the anti-slavery party who stuck to the one idea of their faith, and demanded its recognition in political platforms, as well as in religious creeds, though hounded as zealots, Abolitionists, disturbers of the public peace, yet stood upon the one truth, and challenged its denial. If the truth had been acknowledged and acted upon by the other side, we should have had no war." So long as toleration of slavery had helped in preserving the peace, said Henderson, he had stood for toleration. When it failed to preserve the peace, he had decided against all further toleration. He believed (mistakenly) that once slavery was dead the Radicals would abandon the State Suicide theory, to which he was opposed. Dramatically, he noted that his anti-slavery sentiments could not be said to "spring from hatred of slaveholders, for, whether in honor or shame, I am a slaveholder, today."[32]

Doubting public approval of the Anti-slavery Amendment, President Lincoln did not take the lead in openly espousing it throughout the course of the 1864 campaign. For some time the measure appeared as wholly the creature of War Democrat Senator Henderson of Missouri. On April 8, 1864, the Amendment passed the Senate by a vote of 38 to 6, with six War Democrats voting in the majority.[33] But that, for the moment, was as far as it could possibly proceed. Upon reaching the House, June 15, it was subjected to opposition from all the Peace Democrats, half the War Democrats, some border slave-state Whigs and "Americans", and a handful of Conservative Republicans. Unexpected support was supplied by fourteen War Democrats, one of whom—Ezra Wheeler of Wisconsin—delivered a powerful speech in its behalf, belaboring the pro-slavery arguments of the Peace faction as hostile to the interests of the Union. The vote on the Amendment was 93–65, in favor of adoption—12 votes shy of the necessary two-thirds majority.[34]

Another Radical development in the spring of 1864 was provided by the American Freedman's Inquiry Commission, chaired by War Democrat Robert Dale Owen of Indiana. In its final report of May 15, 1864, the Commission came out in favor of full civil and political rights for the Negro freedman, "in order that he might stand on his own feet without being a burden to the government." Following publication of the report, work was begun in Congress for creation of a national Freedman's Bureau.[35]

*   *   *   *   *

The Unionist spirit ran high during most of the year, even in the early months when Union victories were scarce. It was generally believed in Union circles that the Confederacy was verging on defeat. In this atmosphere a banquet was held in New York City, January 16, for members of the Irish Brigade at home on leave. The principal speaker of the occasion was Democratic General Thomas F. Meagher, who delivered a political address. In the eyes of loyal men, said Meagher, there no longer existed a Democratic party, nor a Republican party, nor a Know Nothing party. So long as the war continued and the Union remained in danger, the only proper place for patriotic citizens was in the Union party. The Irish veterans applauded the remark.[36]

Missing from the gathering was Democratic General Michael Corcoran, Commander of the famed "Corcoran Legion," killed in a riding accident a few weeks earlier.[37] Present was Major Charles B. Halpine, formerly of the Democratic New York *Leader;* also, formerly Adjutant on the Staff of Democratic General David Hunter, and a former member of the Irish Brigade. Currently engaged as a member of the staff of Democratic General John A. Dix, Halpine was now involved in running down bounty-jumpers in New York City. Called upon for a literary offering, he contributed a song for the occasion, concerning the arming of the Negroes. Nowhere in the loyal states was the enrollment of Negro troops less popular than the Irish districts. But Halpine favored Negro troops, and so did the song which the Irish veterans sang with great enthusiasm, upholding the sentiment expressed in the title: "Sambo's Right to be Kilt". Although spoofing "Sambo" in traditional Irish-American terms, the song in fact endorsed the Negro soldier, declaring:

> The men who object to Sambo
> Should take his place and fight;
> And its better to have a naggur's hue
> Than a liver that's wake and white.
> Though Sambo's black as the ace of Spades,
> His finger a thrigger can pull,
> And his eye runs straight on the barrel sights
> From under its thatch of wool.[38]

The song became popular quickly, especially with the Irish, many of whom had previously opposed Negro troop enlistments. It was not popular, however, with the Democratic New York *Irish-American,* which denounced the preceedings at the banquet hall as Republican propaganda.

$$* \qquad * \qquad *$$

The rumored spread of underground Peace socieites in 1864 was matched by the appointment of War Democrats to military command in vital areas across the country, with the object of suppressing all signs of treasonable activity. At the close of January, Democratic General William

S. Rosecrans became commander of the Department of the Missouri, with headquarters at St. Louis.[39] At the close of March, Democratic General Lewis Wallace became commander of the Middle Department, with headquarters at Baltimore.[40] On July 1, Democratic General (Irwin) McDowell was appointed commander of the Department of the Pacific.[41]

Aside from the "March to the Sea" by Republican General William T. Sherman, the major Union military operations of 1864 were all in the hands of Democratic Generals. When the Confederate army of the West was shattered at Chickamauga, the work was performed by Democratic General George H. Thomas. When the same Confederate army was beaten at Lookout Mountain and Missionary Ridge, the man responsible was Democratic General Ulysses S. Grant. Overall command of operations in Virginia in 1864 again was the responsibility of Grant. The Union disaster at Petersburg, in the Battle of the Crater, was blamed on Democratic Generals Ambrose E. Burnside, Orlando B. Wilcox, and Eward Ferrero, and the Union failure at Bermuda Hundred tarnished the name of Democratic General Benjamin F. Butler. The unsuccessful Red River Expedition of 1864, looking to the reoccupation of Texas, was initially the business of Democratic General John A. McClernand but sickness prevented his participation, and the dismal results did not redound to his disadvantage. Democratic General Lewis Wallace, commanding the Middle Department, met the Confederates at the Monocacy River (with an army of amateurs, invalid troops, and boys, outnumbered almost 3 to 1). Although defeated, he stalled the enemy long enough to prevent the destruction of Washington, D.C. The return of the Confederates to Tennessee, following the fall of Atlanta, was halted by Democratic General George H. Thomas, in the battle of Nashville. The promotion of Democratic General Grant to the rank of Lieutenant General, in 1864, had the effect of demoting Democratic General Henry W. Halleck from command of the armies, to the great satisfaction of certain Radicals who regarded Halleck as a champion of slavery. Having voted for the Grant promotion, War Democrat Reverdy Johnson of Maryland delivered a declaration in the Senate, praising Halleck, and insisting that the purpose of the vote was to injure no one.[42]

* * * *

While feuding constantly over Reconstruction matters, Radical Unionists and Conservative Unionists in Congress remained united on the issues of the war. On February 29, Peace Democrat Long of Ohio proposed appointment of a presidential peace commission, to be composed of former Presidents Pierce and Fillmore, together with Thomas Ewing of Ohio and anyone else the Presidnet might care to include, to treat with the Confederates. The propsoal was denounced as an insult to the Union cause and failed of adoption by a vote of 22 to 96. More Democrats voted against it than for it.[43] (It is worth recalling in this connection that this was the Congress largely elected in the great "Peace Landslide of 1862.") Hoping to pull in the strays, a Peace leader proposed a resolution denouncing the arrest of Vallandigham as unconstitutional. This also was easily defeated, 84–33, with eleven War Democrats voting in the majority.[44] Peace Democrat Fernando Wood of New York was fond of saying that he once had supported the war, but only on the basis of the Crittenden Resolution. The Republicans having turned their backs on that noble declaration, he now felt free to turn his back on the war. War Democrat Dumont of Indiana (Union) replied that when the Peace men talked that way, he doubted their veracity. "Trace them up and run them back," he said, "and as sure as God lives it will be discovered that if at any time they have seemed to be yielding a hearty support to the war it was a deception, and that the brindle hide of the wolf that is now worn without a blush might any time have been discovered, if the robe of hypocrisy had been torn away." Congressman Wood was himself a perfect example, Dumont declared. He didn't tell the truth. While claiming to support the Crittenden Resolution, he simultaneously recommended the acceptance of negotiated peace. "How can one who favors such a peace be for the Crittenden propositions, which are in utter antagonism to such a disgraceful surrender?"[45]

Congressman Voorhees of Indiana delivered a strong Peace speech, March 5, declaring that the war was the product of Republican designs and was kept alive only at Republican insistence. Peace negotiations were not proferred to the Confederacy, he said, because the administration knew they would be accepted and the war would come to a close before the budding Republican dictatorship was fully established.[46] Peace Democrat Long of Ohio delivered a similar address, blaming the war on the Republicans,[47] and Peace Democrat Fernando Wood of New York presented to the Clerk's desk copies of several fiery Antebellum speeches by Radical Republicans. These, he said, were the reasons for the war.[48]

War Democrat Smith of Kentucky (Union) replied, speaking in behalf of the Unionist coalition. The Regular Democracy was at fault, he said, for failing to support the war every inch of the way, in the manner of the Unionists. Douglas was quoted as saying, "there are but two parties in the country today—patriots and traitors." The galleries applauded. Peace Democrat Cox of Ohio (another Douglas man) questioned the likelihood that Douglas would have disagreed with him about the war. How was it, he asked, that Smith could commune with the spirit of Douglas and he could not? Perhaps, said Smith, there is a separation between good and bad things, and on that basis Cox was out of touch with Douglas. Announcing that he was in favor of Emancipation, Smith again was applauded by the galleries. In conclusion, he delivered a ringing declaration, in total contempt of the policy of Peace negotiations. The Confederates had rejected negotiations in advance, he said, and to plead with them now would be degrading and disgraceful.[49] War Democrat Anderson of Kentucky (Union) concurred, announcing that "the rebels, from the highest to the lowest, have declared time and time again, upon every occasion, that they would agree to nothing save the acknowledging of their independence. Every act and declaration of those in rebellion is to this effect. Then why talk about compromises, unless you are willing to compromise on that basis?"[50]

On April 8, Peace Democrat Long of Ohio addressed the House for an hour in favor of peace negotiations. In his opinion, the law was on the side of the Confederates and the Union cause was wholly indefensible. When the hammer fell, ending the hour, Radical Washburne of Illinois proposed that Long be allowed to continue, because "the speech of the gentleman from Ohio is the key-note of the Democratic party in the coming election. . .It means recognition of the Confederacy by foreign powers, and peace upon terms of disunion."[51] Continuing his remarks, Long observed that, "I now believe there are but two alternatives, and they are either the acknowledgment of the independence of the South as an independent nation, or their complete subjugation and extermination as a people; and of these alternatives, I prefer the former."[52] When the speech was over, Long was berated as a traitor by Radical Republican Garfield of Ohio.[53]

On the following day, Speaker Colfax relinquished the chair to present a resolution expelling Long from the House for favoring recognition of the Confederacy. There followed a spirited debate, involving Peace Democrats Cox of Ohio, Fernando Wood of New York, and Harris of Maryland, opposing War Democrats Winfield of New York, Smith of Kentucky (Union), and Rollins of Missouri. According to Wood, "There can be no such thing as a War Democrat because when a man is in favor of the war, he must be in favor of the policies of the war as it is prosecuted by the party in power, with its unavoidable tendency to destroy the Constitution and the Union. He cannot be a Democrat and a disunionist also."[54] The statement was challenged by Winfield of New York. ". . .There is (and) always has been (and always will be) such a thing as a War Democrat," Winfield replied. "There will be a War Democrat whenever the honor of the country is in danger. . .When our national honor, our national integrity, or national flag has been assailed in all the past, it has been the boast of the party that has sustained (Congressman Wood) that it is always on the side of the country and in favor of maintaining its honor and dignity by arms to the extent of the last dollar and the last available resources of the nation. Such I believe to be its position now." The Peace Democracy was wrong in declaring that the war had the backing only of Republicans, for in so doing they ignored the patriotic actions of thousands and thousands of perfectly good Democrats. "We have claimed (all along) that our Army has been largely filled up by War Democrats, and that every call made by the President was largely and gloriously responded to by the generous Union-loving Democracy of the land; and it is too late to say or insinuate that all men who advocate the prosecution of this war by Constitutional means or for Constitutional purposes have forfeited their allegiance to the Democratic party." Having supported the war himself, he said, ". . .you cannot wonder, sir, that I felt startled to hear myself read out of the party for believing with General (Andrew) Jackson that when citizens defied the laws to compel submission was an obvious duty." The war must go on until a Union victory was attained. Although denouncing the Radicals for classing all Democrats as traitors, and defending Governor Seymour against all charges of encouraging race riots in New York City, Winfield warned the Regular Democrats against accepting the leadership of the Peace faction. If they did so in the 1864 campaign, he said, they were sure of being beaten.[55]

War Democrat Smith of Kentucky (Union) denied the Regular Democracy the right to work against the war. Peace Democrat Pendleton of Ohio replied, accusing Smith of seeking the extermination of all the people in the South (little children specifically included). Echoing Long of Ohio, Pendleton announced for "peace in this country; peace, peace, if I can have it, rather than the extermination of these people who are struggling in a cause which they believe to be right." Pendleton also complained about the contemplated "subjugation" of the South. Smith replied that "the word subjugation, as I understand it, only means to bring within the power of the Government, by force, those who are in rebellion. Why, sir, under the laws of your States and municipalities, you bring to the gallows a man for the commission of murder. Shall you not bring him to the same sentence and judgment for the commission of treason? For in the commission of treason he commits many murders, and should be punished."[56]

War Democrat Rollins of Missouri said he would not vote for Long's expulsion because he believed that his speech fell within the bounds of free discussion. (The same position was adopted earlier by War Democrat Winfield of New York.) However, said Rollins, he disagreed with Long, *"toto coelo"* because Long was for disunion and surrender, while he was for Union and victory. The struggle should not be abandoned until the last dollar in the country was expended, the last able bodied citizen inducted into the army, the national credit ruined, patriotism rotted away, and all respect gone. Only then would it be time to stop fighting. The Confederacy was wholly unjustified in all its arguments, Rollins declared.[57]

The defenders of Congressman Long emphasized that he had done nothing but talk, which they said could not properly be regarded as treason.

Speaking for the other side, War Democrat Dumont of Indiana (Union) declared: "It is mere words, it is said. . .The letter of (Benedict) Arnold, whereby his treason was discovered, was mere words, too. . . ."[58] For saying, in defense of Long, that he hoped the Union forces failed to subjugate the South, Harris was censured by a vote of 93–18, 24 War Democrats voting in the majority. By a vote of 80 to 69, Long was then declared "an unworthy member of the House of Representatives."[59]

*   *   *   *   *

Outside of Congress, the Union war policy was ably assisted in 1864 by the vigorous activity and contagious enthusiasm of Negro troops, ably led by Democrats in uniform. It has been observed that in the process of training for the disastrous battle of the Crater, at Petersburg, Negroes in the Fourth Division of the Army of the Potomac sang a song entitled "We Looks Like Men A' Marchin' On; We Looks Like Men o' War"—and that following the battle, the survivors sang no more.[60] The observation is misleading. The battle of the Crater was not the last but the first significant appearance of Negro troops in Grant's Virginia campaign. In August, September, and October, Negroes fighting under Democratic generals Ambrose E. Burnside and Benjamin F. Butler were engaged in major battles at Deep Bottom, New Market Heights, and Darbytown Road, near Petersburg. Following the Chaffin's Farm campaign of September–October, 1864, Congressional Medals of Honor were bestowed on 37 Union troops, 14 of whom were Negroes. At New Market Heights, in the Chaffin's Farm campaign, Butler's Negro division broke the Petersburg defenses six months before Grant accomplished the same trick, at the very close of the war.[61] (Also at New Market Heights and at Deep Bottom, a major Union force involved was the 29th Connecticut Colored Infantry, commanded by Democratic Colonel William B. Wooster.[62]) Instead of fading out, following the Battle of the Crater, the Negro troops were extensively used, especially in Virginia.[63] It must be assumed in this regard that General Grant was able to overcome the traditional contempt of the Democratic partisan for the fighting potential of the Negro soldier.

It is a remarkable fact that the man who directed the raising of the Negro troops and saw to their implementation once they were ready for combat—War Democrat Edwin M. Stanton, Secretary of War—was not himself a Radical. Having carried out the orders of President Lincoln in matters concerning the organization of Negro troops, he was prominently involved in their Radical venture. On his own, however, Stanton was clearly not Radical at all. It was he who established the separate pay scales for white and Negro troops, to the advantage of the whites, and in short time the Negroes were protesting the inequity.[64] Nor did Stanton's respect for Radical innovation on the race issue extend even to the matter of medical facilities. As Secretary of War, he determined the number of doctors required, and there was no provision for the employment of Negro doctors. This Conservative oversight, together with the fact that white doctors were reluctant to serve with Negro units, left the Negro troops without satisfactory medical attention. As a result, the Negro death rate in battle was far in excess of the white rate,[65] and the man to blame was Stanton. (Not Stanton the Radical, but Stanton the Conservative.)

* * *

Some major executive appointments were offered to and accepted by certain War Democrats in 1864. When Salmon P. Chase resigned as Secretary of the Treasury in July, the post was tendered to War Democrat David Tod, former Governor of Ohio, but he declined.[66] When Edward Bates resigned as U.S. Attorney General in September, President Lincoln sought the services of War Democrat Joseph Holt of Kentucky, Judge Advocate General of the Army. Holt also declined, recommending instead another War Democrat: James Speed of Kentucky. Acting on the recommendation, Lincoln contacted Speed, who accepted the appointment and joined the cabinet in Washington.[67] On the state level, War Democrats John T. Peters of Maine, Jacob Moore of Delaware, and Thomas T. Crittenden of Missouri were rewarded for service to the Union party in their respective states by appointment to the office of Attorney General. On the national level, with no fanfare at all, President Lincoln inaugurated the "Carpetbagger" movement in the South, appointing War Democrat Richard Busteed of New York City to serve as a Federal District Judge in Alabama.[68]

The death in October of Roger B. Taney, Chief Justice of the United States, brought about a major contest, behind the scenes, to determine his successor. The Radical choice was Salmon P. Chase, former Secretary of the Treasury; the leading Conservative contender, Montgomery Blair, recently resigned as Postmaster General. Also in contention was Edwin M. Stanton, Secretary of War, who had hopes of obtaining the appointment on the basis of his strong performance in the cabinet, his close relationship with Lincoln, and his detachment from the Radical–Conservative controversy within the Union coalition. A major supporter of Stanton in this instance was War Democrat Robert C. Grier, of Pennsylvania, Associate Justice on the U.S. Supreme Court.[69] Trusting neither Stanton nor Blair to vote against the Conservative pro-slavery tradition with any degree of consistency, Lincoln turned once again to the Radicals, appointing Chase to the exalted office of Chief Justice. Conservatives would shake their heads in sadness, regretting the decision of the President to surrender to the

Radicals in the interest of "political expediency." The presidential record for the year was Radical, however—Radical all the way—and Lincoln was ready now to slay the dragon of slavery without further delay, without qualification, and with the full approval of many War Democrats who, a month or a year earlier, would have cursed the proposal as a villainous attack upon the basic framework of the Union.

NOTES

1. From 1854 to 1861 Colfax had acted as a leader of the Conservative faction in Republican party circles. While Radical Republicans were working against the Lincoln nomination, in 1860, on the grounds that Lincoln was too Conservative, Colfax was opposing him for being too Radical. In advance of the 1860 Republican National Convention, Colfax favored the presidential aspirations of Edward Bates, the ultra-Conservative Republican leader from Missouri. Kenneth M. Stampp, *Indiana politics,* p. 35. In the Thirty-sixth Congress, Colfax voted in favor of Charles Francis Adams' and John Corwin's pro-slavery Thirteenth Amendment. *Congressional Globe* (36th Congress, 2nd session), p. 1285. In the Thirty-seventh Congress, he voted in favor of the pro-slavery section of the Crittenden Resolution. Ibid. (37th Congress, 1st session), p. 223. He was never a Radical on the slavery issue until the war was fully under way.
2. Out of 20 War Democrats elected to the Thirty-seventh House, only seven were reelected to the Thirty-eighth: Francis Thomas of Maryland (Union); William G. Brown of West Virginia (Union); Joseph Baily and Jesse Lazear of Pennsylvania; William E. English of Connecticut; and John B. Steele and Moses F. Odell of New York.
3. War Democrats were well treated in the matter of assignments to standing House Committees. John A. Griswold of New York and James S. Rollins of Missouri, Naval Affairs. (Having run for office as an Independent Unionist, in Missouri, Rollins joined the Democrats, upon his arrival in Washington.) Moses F. Odell of New York, Archibald McAllister of Pennsylvania, Benjamin F. Loan of Missouri (Union), and Henry C. Deming of Connecticut (Union), Military Affairs; Henry G. Stebbins of New York, Ways and Means; Francis Thomas of Maryland (Union), Francis Kernan of New York, and Austin A. King of Missouri, Judiciary; Ezra Wheeler of Wisconsin, District of Columbia; and Green Clay Smith of Kentucky (Union), Militia. *Congressional Globe,* (38th Congress, 1st session), p. 18.
  In doling out the Senate committee posts, the Republican-Union leadership rewarded the War Democrats as follows: Reverdy Johnson of Maryland (Union) and James A. McDougall of California, Foreign Affairs; William Sprague of Rhode Island (Union), Commerce and Military Affairs and the Militia; James W. Nesmith of Oregon, Military Affairs and the Militia; John B. Henderson of Missouri (Union), District of Columbia (important because of the existence of slavery in the District.) Ibid., pp. 8, 16.
4. Benjamin P. Thomas, *Stanton,* p. 308.
5. For the Radical reaction, in opposition to the Reconstruction program proposed by Lincoln in December, 1863, see Ralph Korngold, *Thaddeus Stevens,* pp. 235–45. For the Conservative reaction, in opposition to the same program at the same time, see *The Old Guard,* vol. II, no. 1 (January 1864): pp. 15–16.
6. Select committees were appointed in both houses to consider the proposals of

the President concerning postwar Reconstruction. The Select House Committee on the Rebellious States included two War Democrats: Holman of Indiana and English of Connecticut. The Select House Committee on Emancipation also included two War Democrats: Middleton of New Jersey and Anderson of Kentucky (Union). *Congressional Globe* (38th Congress, 1st session), p. 37.

7. War Democrats voting to table Holman's motion to redeclare support for the Crittenden Resolution of August, 1861 included: Creswell of Maryland (Union), Dumont of Indiana (Union), Higby of California (Union), Loan of Missouri (Union), McClurg of Missouri, (Union), Marvin of New York (Union), Rollins of Missouri (Union), Shannon of California (Union), Smith of Kentucky (Union), Clay of Kentucky (Union), and Thomas of Maryland (Union). Ibid., p. 22.

8. War Democrats giving their approval to the military arrest of civilians in the loyal states included: Creswell of Maryland (Union), Dumont of Indiana (Union), Higby of California (Union), Loan of Missouri (Union), McClurg of Missouri (Union), Marvin of New York (Union), Shannon of California (Union), and Smith of Kentucky (Union). Ibid., p. 45.

9. Dudley T. Cornish, p. 258.

10. Regular Democrats voting for Negro troops: Baily of Pennsylvania, English of Connecticut, and Ganson, Kernan, Odell, Radford, Stebbins, Steele, Ward and Winfield of New York; also (mysteriously) Fernando Wood of New York. Union Democrats voting for Negro troops: Andersen of Kentucky, Brown of West Virginia, Creswell of Maryland, Deming of Connecticut, Dumont of Indiana, Higby of California, Marvin of New York, McClurg of Missouri, Shannon of California, Smith of Kentucky, and Thomas of Maryland. *Congressional Globe* (38th Congress, 1st session), p. 75.

11. Irritated by Creswell's repeated assertion that he was out of order, Peace Democrat James Brooks of New York declared on one occasion: "I cannot yield to the Member from Maryland again. He is not a Member of the House by election but by force. He is only the representative of the bayonet. He has no moral or constitutional right to be heard here at all." Ibid., p. 1968.

12. Quoted in Charles B. Clark, p. 115.

13. *Congressional Globe,* (38th Congress, 1st session), p. 456.

14. Ibid., pp. 456–59.

15. War Democrats voting in favor of tabling the Rogers Peace Resolution included: Anderson of Kentucky, Brown of West Virginia, Creswell and Thomas of Maryland, Deming of Connecticut, Higby and Shannon of California, Loan, Marvin and McClurg of Missouri, Odell and Stebbins of New York, and Smith of Kentucky. Ibid., pp. 127–28. War Democrat Griswold of New York voted for the Rogers Peace Resolution, but four days later apologized for doing so, explaining that he had acted hastily without a full understanding of the matter. The resolution, as he now understood it, was "unpatriotic, unwise, and only pernicious in its tendency." Ibid., p. 150.

16. War Democrats voting in favor of the Smith Resolution, denouncing Peace conventions, included: Anderson of Kentucky (Union), Baldwin of Michigan, Baily of Pennsylvania (Union), Brown of Wisconsin, Brown of West Virginia (Union), Creswell of Maryland (Union), Deming of Connecticut (Union), Griswold of New York, Higby of California (Union), Holman of Indiana, Kernan of New York, King of Missouri, Loan of Missouri (Union), McClurg of Missouri (Union), Marvin of New York (Union), Middleton of New Jersey, Odell of New York, Shannon of California (Union), Smith of Kentucky (Union), Stebbins of New York, and Sweat of Maine. Ibid., p. 127.

17. War Democrats voting in favor of the Senate Resolution, demanding the support of the war as a "sacred duty," included: Baldwin of Michigan, Baily of Pennsylvania (Union), Brown of Wisconsin, Brown of West Virginia (Union), Clay of Kentucky (Union), Cravens of Indiana, Creswell of Mary-

land (Union), Deming of Connecticut, Ganson of New York, Griswold of New York, Harding of Kentucky (Union), Higby of California (Union), Holman of Indiana, Johnson of Ohio, Kernan of New York, Loan of Missouri (Union), McClurg of Missouri (Union), Marvin of New York (Union), Middleton of New Jersey, Nelson of New York, Odell of New York, Radford of New York, Rogers of New Jersey, Rollins of Missouri, Shannon of California (Union), Smith of Kentucky (Union), Stebbins of New York, Strouse of Pennsylvania, Stuart of Illinois, Sweat of Maine, Wheeler of Wisconsin, and Winfield of New York. Ibid., p. 261.

18. Ibid., p. 338.
19. Ibid., p. 340.
20. *The Old Guard,* vol. 2, no. 2 (February 1864): p. 46.
21. Hale was accused of accepting a fee, as a lawyer, from a client concerned in the passage of federal legislation. According to Senator Johnson, bribery could not be proven in a case of this nature. Moreover, a Senator had a perfect right to continue his law practice and was entitled to accept fees from any client at any time. As a member of the Senate, Johnson declared that he would not hesitate to act as Hale had acted in this instance. Bribery was not in any way involved. The argument convinced the Senate and the charges against Hale were abandoned. Bernard C. Steiner, pp. 65–66.
22. Ibid., pp. 69–70.
23. *Congressional Globe* (38th Congress, 1st session), pp. 226–27. The anti-commutation fight was not exclusively a Democratic concern. On February 1, Radical Republican James F. Wilson of Iowa proposed a House resolution killing the commutation clause. The resolution was opposed by War Democrat Ganson of New York, who said that some had used the clause to their advantage and that others deserved an equal opportunity. War Democrat Deming of Connecticut [Union] had another protest about exemptions from the draft. Petitions for exemption had been received, he said, from the Quakers, Shakers, Dunkers, Mennonites, Rogerenes, and Peace Democrats. He was opposed to exempting anybody. Ibid., pp. 433, 575.
24. War Democrats voting for the Conscription Bill Report included: Harding of Oregon (Union), Henderson of Missouri (Union), Nesmith of Oregon, and Sprague of Rhode Island (Union). Ibid., 38th Congress. 1st session. p. 756.
25. Ibid., pp. 598, 600.
26. Ibid., p. 145.
27. Ibid., p. 161.
28. New York Assembly, *Journal,* 1864, p. 737.
29. *Congressional Globe,* (38th Congress, 1st session), p. 602.
30. Ibid., pp. 1421–24.
31. Ibid., pp. 1456–59.
32. Ibid., pp. 1459–63.
33. Ibid., p. 1490. War Democrats voting for the Thirteenth Amendment included: Conness of California (Union), Harding of Oregon (Union), Henderson of Missouri (Union), Johnson of Maryland (Union), Nesmith of Oregon, and Sprague of Rhode Island (Union).
34. War Democrats voting for the Amendment in the House included Anderson of Kentucky (Union), Baily of Pennsylvania (Union), Creswell of Maryland (Union), Deming of Connecticut (Union), Griswold of New York, Higby of California (Union), Ingersoll of Illinois (Union), Loan of Missouri (Union), Marvin of New York (Union), McClurg of Missouri (Union), Odell of New York, Shannon of California (Union), Smith of Kentucky (Union), Thomas of Maryland (Union), and Wheeler of Wisconsin. *Congressional Globe* (38th Congress, 1st session), p. 2295. Wheeler's speech: Ibid., Appendix, pp. 124–26.
35. Richard W. Leopold, pp. 362–63.
36. Robert G. Athearn, p. 132.

37. *Union Army*, VIII:60.
38. The rest of the lyrics are recorded below:

> Some tell us 'tis a burnin' shame
>   To make the naggurs fight
> An' that the thrade o' bein' kilt
>   belongs but to the white;
> But as for me, upon my soul!
>   So liberal are we here,
> I'll let Sambo be murthered instead of myself
>   On every day in the year.
> On every day in the year, boys,
>   And in every hour of the day;
> The right to be kilt I'll divide wid 'im
>   And divil a word I'll say.
> In battle's wild commotion
>   I shouldn't at all object
> If Sambo's body should stop a ball
>   That was comin' for me direct;
> And the prod of a Southern bayonet,
>   So ginerous are we here,
> I'll resign and let Sambo take it
>   On every day of the year.
> On every day of the year, boys
>   And wid none o' your nasty pride,
> All my right in a Southern bayonet prod
>   Wid Sambo I'll divide!
> The men who object to Sambo
>   Should take his place and fight;
> And it's better to have a naggur's hide
>   Than a liver that's wake and white.
> Though Sambo's black as the ace of spades,
>   His finger a thrigger can pull
> And his eye runs straight on the barrel-sights
>   From under its thatch of wool.
> Dudley T. Cornish, pp. 229–30.

39. *Union Army*, VIII:216.
40. Ibid., VIII:289.
41. Ibid., VIII: passim.
42. *Congressional Globe* (38th Congress, 1st session), p. 792.
43. War Democrats voting against Long's Peace Commission proposal included Anderson of Kentucky (Union), Baldwin of Michigan, Brown of West Virginia (Union), Creswell of Maryland (Union), Deming of Connecticut (Union), Dumont of Indiana (Union), Ganson of New York, Griswold of New York, Higby of California (Union), Holman of Indiana, Hutchins of Ohio, Kernan of New York, King of Missouri (Union), Loan of Missouri (Union), Nelson of New York, Radford of New York, Shannon of California (Union), Smith of Kentucky (Union), Stebbins of New York, Steele of New York, Thomas of Maryland (Union), Winfield of New York. Ibid., p. 878
44. Anderson of Kentucky (Union), Baily of Pennsylvania (Union), Creswell of Maryland (Union), Deming of Connecticut (Union), Dumont of Indiana (Union), Higby of California (Union), Loan of Missouri (Union), McClurg of Missouri (Union), Marvin of New York (Union), Shannon of California (Union), and Thomas of Maryland (Union). Ibid., p. 879.
45. Ibid., pp. 1070–71.
46. According to Voorhees, the Republicans were a "baleful brood of political

distructionists [who] do not want public tranquility. They invoked the storm which has since rained blood upon the land. They courted the whirlwind which has prostrated the progress of a century in ruins. They danced with a hellish glee around the bubbling caldron of civil war, and welcomed with ferocious joy every hurtful mischief which flickered in its lurid and infernal flames." Ibid., Appendix, pp. 74–76.

47. Speech cited in Ibid., p. 1581.
48. Wood's action cited in Ibid., p. 1581.
49. Ibid., pp. 1581–84.
50. Ibid., Appendix, p. 103.
51. Ibid., p. 1503.
52. Ibid., p. 1503.
53. Ibid., p. 1503.
54. Ibid., p. 1537.
55. Ibid., pp. 1596–97.
56. Ibid., pp. 1584, 1632.
57. Ibid., pp. 1602–6.
58. Ibid., p. 1556.
59. Ibid., p. 1519. War Democrats voting in favor of censuring Harris included. Ganson, Kernan, Marvin (Union), Nelson, Odell, and J.B. Steele of New York; Holman and Dumont (Union) of Indiana; Higby (Union) and Shannon (Union) of California; Anderson (Union) of Kentucky; Baily and McAllister of Pennsylvania; Baldwin of Michigan; Cox of Ohio; English of Connecticut; Loan of Missouri (Union) and McClurg of Missouri (Union); Middleton of New Jersey; W. G. Steele of New Jersey; and Thomas of Maryland (Union).
60. Bruce Catton, *A Stillness at Appomattox* (Garden City: Doubleday, 1953), p. 252.
61. Dudley T. Cornish, pp. 266, 279–80. The Confederate position at Newmarket Heights was taken with bayonets, at the order of General Butler, with the object of proving Negro courage in battle. Nine infantry and one dismounted cavalry regiments were involved, and 1,000 Negroes were killed or wounded. Ibid., pp. 279–80. Failure to follow up the victory permitted the Confederates to regain control of the heights at the close of the day, and the great loss of life was rendered meaningless, excpet in terms of propaganda value.
62. *Union Army,* I:300.
63. In the battles before Petersburg, Virginia, in 1864–1865, twenty-two Negro regiments were frequently engaged. Dudley T. Cornish, p. 226.
64. James H. McPherson, *The Struggle for Equality,* pp. 213–19.
65. Herbert M. Morais, *The History of the Negro in Medicine* (New York: Publishers, 1967), p. 36.
66. Allen Johnson and Dumas Malone, XVIII:568.
67. Ibid., XVII:440.
68. Richard Busteed was a leader of the Protestant Irish in New York City and Corporation Council of New York City, 1856–1859. He was a strong pro-slavery spokesman and a Douglas leader in the 1860 campaign. For services at Yorktown in the Peninsula campaign of 1862 he was commissioned brigadier, but resigned before the action was confirmed by the Senate, on the assumption that confirmation was impossible, for political reasons. *Union Army,* VIII:46.
69. Benjamin P. Thomas, *Stanton,* pp. 336–37.

13

Conservative Tradition Beaten at the Polls: Elections of 1864

A major feature of the 1864 election campaign was the continuing Radical drift of President Lincoln. It was not discernable to all—certainly not to the majority and not to those Radicals who had determined on painting Lincoln as a Conservative no matter what he did. But there were many who saw it for what it was. Thurlow Weed, 1860 Chairman of the New York Republican State Committee, would quit the party in 1864, protesting this development.[1] Henry H. Haight, 1860 Chairman of the California Republican State Committee, would do the same.[2] Hoping to promote a Conservative stampede, at the expense of the administration, the Cairo (Illinois) *Democrat* observed of Lincoln, "He is as good an Abolitionist as the best of them, but the great trouble is, he is always six months behind in acting the thing out."[3]

Hoping against hope that this interpretation was not correct (but fearing that it was), Conservative Unionists had been urging repudiation of the Emancipation Proclamation since January 1863, and the Radical critics of the President were convinced that he would yield to these wheedlings, some day—with doleful consequences. Such thinking was increased by the pocket veto of the Radical Wade-Davis Reconstruction bill, July 2, 1863, but laid to rest at last by presidential policy enunciated in the Pardon and Amnesty Proclamation of December 8, 1863, committing the President to enforcement of the Emancipation Proclamation for the remainder of the war. It was a very Radical stand and surely would have been pleasing to the Radical leadership had it not been coupled with rejection of Sumner's "State Suicide" theory. The resulting contest between Lincoln and the Wade-Davis Radicals was to attract the national attention at the time, and has received a thorough treatment by historians. But the great mass of Radical leaders stood by Lincoln all the way—from Garrison and Wilson of Massachusetts, to Dennison and Riddle of Ohio, Arnold, Lovejoy, and Washburne of Illinois, Cameron of Pennsylvania, Roscoe Conkling of New York, and Lane of Kansas—even Thaddeus Stevens of Pennsylvania (who declared for Lincoln in May, while anti-Lincoln Radicals were working hard for Chase and John Charles Fremont).[4] Also regarded by many as a Radical in 1864 was War Democrat Edwin M. Stanton, Secretary of War. He, too, came out for Lincoln, in opposition to Chase and Fremont, as did many other leaders of the War Democracy, each of whom was hotly pursued by all the presidential candidates and would-be candidates in this election year.

It was not the defection of Radicals that Lincoln had cause to fear in 1864 but the defection of Conservatives. Republican victories from 1854 to 1860, and Republican and Union party victories from 1861 to 1863 were all the result of strong Conservative support; and if the Conservatives were to quit the Union cause in 1864, Lincoln was doomed. With this in mind, he was especially concerned about War Democrat reaction to his Radical change of policy. It was the War Democrats who had carried him through to victory in 1861 and 1863, and prevented disaster in 1862. Their defection now—either to anti-Lincoln Radicals or anti-Lincoln Conservatives—well could ruin him. Already apparent was the failure to hold the Constitutional Unionists, in many areas, and the Conservative Republicans in many others, and no more losses could be borne.[5]

Comparatively few War Democrats were numbered among the backers of Lincoln's chief Union party challengers in 1864, Secretary of the Treasury Chase and General Fremont. Exceptional were Governor John Brough of Ohio, Union party Chairman William H. Smith of Ohio, and Senator William Sprague of Rhode Island, all of whom declared for Chase, and General John Cochrane of New York, who chaired the so-called "Radical" Convention at Cleveland (attended by Radicals and Conservatives combined) and was the candidate for Vice President of the Fremont ticket (the so-called "Radical Democracy"). Some War Democrats in the anti-Lincoln camp preceding the Union National Convention of 1864 were General Benjamin F. Butler of Massachusetts and Daniel S. Dickinson and

Lyman Tremain of New York. All were courted by the Chase and Fremont forces, and Chase wanted Butler as his running mate. But nothing came of the courtships, and when the campaign began Butler, Dickinson, and Tremain were foremost in the pro-Lincoln ranks.[6]

In the 1864 political campaign the first elections of importance were held in territory recaptured from Confederate control—Arkansas, Louisiana, and Tennessee. In every case War Democrats figured prominently in the contests, either as candidates or as directors of the elective process. State constitutional conventions in all three states declared Secession null and void. In Arkansas, the star of the convention was Isaac Murphy, an Antebellum Democrat, a former Assemblyman, and the leading Unionist in Arkansas from 1861 to 1864. He was elected Provisional Governor by the 1864 convention and Governor by the people, in the March elections.[7] On Reconstruction issues Murphy was Conservative and his election was a blow to the small Radical faction in the state which was hopeful of Radical reform, including the establishment of Negro voting rights. Radicals in Louisiana had the same object in mind. Their leader was War Democrat Thomas J. Durant of New Orleans, who appealed to the authorities to let the Negroes engage in the 1864 campaign. In this he was opposed by the Conservative candidate for Governor, War Democrat Michael Hahn of New Orleans. Democratic General George F. Shepley, Military Governor of Louisiana, sided with Hahn against Durant, President Lincoln did not intervene, the Conservatives carried Louisiana in a landslide, and War Democrat Michael Hahn was elected Governor.[8]

In Tennessee, it was all the other way around, with the Conservative Unionists getting short shrift from War Democrat Governor Andrew Johnson, who was wholly dedicated to Radical reform. With Lincoln's approval, Johnson established as a prerequisite to voting an oath of loyalty, to be followed by a six-month waiting period.[9] In this manner everyone in Tennessee was denied the franchise in the March county elections of 1864 excepting only those who had resisted Confederate authority from the start of the war, and were able to prove it. The Johnson Radical forces carried the March elections against virtually no opposition at all. Addressing an audience largely comprised of Negroes, Johnson declared himself for Negro political rights and the suppression of Conservatives opposing them.[10]

$$* \qquad * \qquad *$$

The first loyal-state elections of 1864 took place in March in New Hampshire, where one year earlier the Peace Democracy had almost scored a signal triumph. Rescuing the Republicans on that occasion were War Democrats voting for the independent Union ticket. Gathering the import of the 1863 results, the Republican State Central Committee issued a call for a Convention open to all supporters of the Union cause.[11]

Absent from the convention was Democratic Colonel Walter Harriman of the Eleventh New Hampshire Infantry, Union party candidate for governor the year before. Captured in the battle of the Wilderness, he was still a prisoner of the Confederacy and not available for political service. But most of his supporters of 1863 supported the Republicans in 1864. Conservative Republican Joseph Gilmore was renominated for Governor, with the backing of Radicals and War Democrats combined. (Douglas electors Henry P. Rolfe and William C. Clarke were now among the strongest supporters of the Governor, Rolfe as an Assemblyman, Clarke as State's Attorney General.[12]) The state party platform, reported by the Radicals, had words of praise for Secretary Chase and failed to mention Lincoln, but the convention overrode the platform committee, declaring for the President.[13]

The Democratic State Convention was exclusively the playground of the Peace forces. William H. Duncan presided and delivered an impassioned address against the war, and Ira A. Eastman (who had received the popular plurality in 1863) was once again declared the candidate for Governor. The Democratic platform attacked the Thirteenth Amendment (currently under congressional consideration) as "unwise, impolitic, cruel and unworthy of the support of civilized people." The Regular Democrats had the backing of former President Franklin Pierce, who had abandoned the Union cause in a speech delivered the previous Fourth of July. Support was also provided by out-of-state Copperheads William W. Eaton and James Gallagher of Connecticut, A. Oaky Hall of New York, and William D. Northend of Massachusetts. For Gilmore and the Union ticket the War Democracy supplied a battery of speakers, local and from out of state, who campaigned furiously in all the Democratic districts. General Richard Busteed of New York appeared at several rallies, as did Lieutenant Governor Paul Dillingham of Vermont, and Lewis Barker of Maine.[14] New Hampshire election results revealed a major shift in political sentiment, from a three thousand Democratic plurality in 1863 to a six thousand Republican-Union majority in 1864. The legislature went heavily Republican-Union in both houses, with Radical majorities.

The April elections in Connecticut and Rhode Island featured once again the intra-party battles of the Regular Democracy, to the benefit of the Union party coalition. The loss of the War Democrat vote had cost the Regular Democracy of Connecticut severely in three straight wartime elections. The small War faction within the Regular Democracy was therefore able to enlist the support of the Conditionals in advance of the 1864 Democratic State Convention, with the object of naming a War ticket. In place of Thomas H. Seymour, the Copperhead candidate for Governor the year before, the Regular Democracy selected his cousin, Judge Origen S.

Seymour of the State Supreme Court. A War Democrat, Judge Seymour had supported the Union cause at many rallies and troop-raising ceremonies. He was acceptable to the Peace faction because he had declared against the legality of Conscription, and because he was willing to stand upon the Democratic State Platform of the previous year, with all its anti-war trappings.[15] At the Republican-Union State Convention, Governor William A. Buckingham was renominated, together with the coaltion ticket of 1861–1863, including War Democrats Roger Averill, Lieutenant Governor, and Gabriel Coite, Treasurer. Ignoring the record and the declarations of the Democratic standard-bearer, Judge Seymour, the Unionists attacked his party platform and shot him down, securing a majority of 5,700.[16]

The party-jumping of War Democrat Senator William Sprague of Rhode Island in 1863, and the resulting collapse of Democratic fortunes in the state, produced monumental chaos in the Democratic state campaign of 1864. When the Peace faction seized control of the nominations committee at the Democratic State Convention, the War faction rejected the proposed ticket, calling for the naming of another by the Democratic State Committee.[17] In the struggle for control of the Republican-Union State Convention, the Chase faction, headed by War Democrat Senator William Sprague, came out in favor of a second term for Radical Governor James Y. Smith. Pro-Lincoln Radicals, following the lead of Senator Henry B. Anthony, deserted Smith in favor of an Aboltionist—Amos C. Barstow. With two Radical candidates in the field the Democratic State Committee named a ticket of its own choosing, totally in favor of the war. The candidate for Governor was George H. Browne, a member of the Thirty-seventh congress and Colonel of the Twelfth Rhode Island Infantry.[18]

The War Democrats of Rhode Island, formerly in line with the dictates of Senator William Sprague, deserted him in droves in 1864 to work and vote for his opponents. The Senator even had to suffer the embarrassment of seeing his own brother—Amasa Sprague—take the stump for Browne and the Regular Democrats. Daniel Rodman, brother of the martyred General Isaac P. Rodman, also spoke for Browne, in company with William C. Cozzens, Walter W. Burges, Henry H. Cooke, and J. Russell Bullock, all of whom had served in Sprague's administrations while he was Governor. Still a millionaire and still a very talented politician, Sprague pulled every string he knew, in the face of a furious campaign by the Regular Democracy; and, once again, emerged triumphant. Colonel Browne, Democrat, received 7,302 votes, and Barstow, Independent Republican-Union, 1,329. Eking out ahead, Governor Smith polled 8,836, a bare majority.[19]

The Rhode Island results were the first and last encouraging development in the Chase campaign for the Union party presidential nomination.

Exposure of the Pomeroy Circular, in February 1864, ruined Chase and damaged the reputation of his son-in-law, War Democrat Senator Sprague. Under attack by Congressman Blair of Missouri, for daring to oppose Lincoln, Chase resigned his cabinet post in June. Sprague was also criticized by Blair for the alleged purchase of Confederate cotton, under questionable circumstances. (The charge, repeated in detail by a Texas cotton planter later in the year, was investigated by the War Department but shortly afterward dismissed for want of corroborative evidence.[20])

June 1864 was the occasion of congressional and legislative elections in Oregon, where the War Democracy had run the Union party from 1861 to 1863, but now was in the process of breaking up. The leaders of the party in 1862 had been Asahel Bush, editor of the War Democrat Salem *Oregon Statesman,* and George H. Williams, former Chief Justice of the Oregon Territory. But Bush endorsed McClellan and the Harrison's Landing Letter, in 1862, while Williams was embracing the Emancipation Proclamation. In 1863, Williams joined the Union League and stumped the state, declaring for Emancipation. In 1864 he was named Chairman of the Union State Executive Committee, and his appointment was the signal that the Radicals were in command. Meanwhile, Bush had sold his interest in the *Statesman* and retired from politics, while others of his kind were searching for a home, somewhere between the Peace cause and the Radicals.[21] Former Congressmen Andrew J. Thayer and Lafayette Grover were involved in this endeavor, as were also U.S. Senator Benjamin F. Harding and Luther Elkins, president of the Union State Convention of 1862. But the Democratic party made no move to win them back. The state party platform of 1864 went overboard for Peace, and the Regular War Democrats had no choice but to retire to the sidelines and watch the Peace men fight the Radicals.[22]

Despite the rash of War Democrat defections in 1864, the Union party campaign in Oregon was largely directed by members of the War Democracy. Governor Addison C. Gibbs and Party Chairman George H. Williams (both War Democrats) spoke frequently, and the Union League (under the control of Williams and his lieutenants) worked overtime, stirring up the Union party vote. Democratic General Joseph Hooker sent word from the front, giving his endorsement to every Union candidate.[23] The outcome of the campaign was a landslide for the Union ticket, which carried almost everything in sight (taking every legislative contest but seven). When the legislature met later in the year, War Democrat George H. Williams was elected to a seat in the U.S. Senate, replacing the War Democrat incumbent, Benjamin F. Harding, who was knocked out of politics.[24]

The Radical trend in Union party policy put a great strain on party leaders in the border slave states in all of which the party divided in half during the 1864 campaign. Radical members of the Union-Democratic party of Kentucky broke away from the Conservatives at the "Slave State Freedom Convention," held in Louisville, February 22–24. The delegates announced in favor of Emancipation, Negro troops, and the Wade-Davis Reconstruction plan. Conservatives assembled at Louisville, May 25, under the banner of the Union-Democratic party, and delegates were elected to attend the Democratic National Convention.[25] War Democrats were in the forefront of the battle on both sides of the issue in Kentucky. The major campaigners for the Conservative "Union Democracy" were Governor Thomas E. Bramlette and Attorney General John M. Harlan. Speaking for the Union party and Emancipation was a great array of Democrats turned Radical, including Douglas leaders James Speed and Joshua Speed, Lucian Anderson, Green Clay Smith, George T. Wood, Samuel L. Lusk, and T.S. Goodloe, and Breckinridge leader James Prall. (Lusk and Anderson were delegates-at-large to the 1864 Union National Convention; Prall, James Speed, Smith, and Goodloe were district delegates.) Most of the Conservative leaders were former Whigs.[26] Exceptional were Conservatives James Guthrie, James F. Robinson, Colonel Frank Wolford, and Lieutenant Governor Richard T. Jacob, all of whom were Antebellum Democrats.

In convention, the Conservatives condemned the Wade-Davis Reconstruction plan and various "usurpations" of power by the federal authorities. The war should be fought to protect the Union, the Conservatives insisted, not to tear apart the Constitution. The raising of Negro troops was declared "degrading to our armies, humiliating to the nation, and contrary to the ways of civilized warfare." For failing to repudiate the war, the Union-Democratic party lost the backing of the Peace faction, which denounced the Union-Democratic ticket and called its own convention.[27]

The Kentucky state elections, held in August, were disrupted by the action of the Office of the Judge Advocate General, headed by War Democrat Joseph Holt of Kentucky. Acting on intelligence that the Democratic-Union candidate for Supreme Court judge was a member of the Order of American Knights, Holt ordered the arrest of the candidate, who fled the state at once.[28] He was replaced on the ticket and the campaign continued without him, while everywhere protests were raised against "federal tyranny" and "military despotism." As the campaign proceeded, so proceeded the work of the Office of the Judge Advocate General. Among a large number of persons arrested for belonging to disloyal organizations, the best known was the Chief Justice of the Kentucky State Supreme Court. Again the cry of federal tyranny was raised,[29] and the voters went along with it. On voting day, the Union-Democrats derailed the Union party, capturing all the state executive posts under contention, and winning control of the legislature.[30] Peace leaders elsewhere claimed victory in Kentucky, but the claim was false. When the newly elected legislature assembled, its first action was the outright rejection of Peace Democrat

Senator Lazarus W. Powell and his replacement by War Democrat James Guthrie.[31]

*　　*　　*　　*

Failure of the Chase presidential boom in the spring of 1864 did not guarantee the renomination of Abraham Lincoln. By working over toward the Radical position on the slavery issue, the President had guaranteed the loss of many of his Conservative supporters. And by adopting a Conservative position in the matter of Reconstruction policy, he had obviously disturbed a host of Radicals. The Radical Cleveland Convention of May 31 was called to satisfy anti-Lincoln Radicals, but actually accomplished something else. So many non-Radicals were present as delegates, supporting the likes of General McClellan, the darling of Conservatives, and War Democrat General Grant, who was also a Conservative, that the myth of rampaging, overpowering anti-Lincolnism in the Radical ranks was largely discredited.[32]

The outstanding War Democrat in attendance at Cleveland was General John Cochrane, who served as Permanent Chairman. His preference for the presidential nomination was General Grant.[33] Having campaigned for the New York Union tickets of 1862 and 1863, he now denounced the Union party as "a medley of trading, scurvy politicians, which never represented War Democrats." Seizing on an issue long identified with the Peace Democracy, he upbraided the wartime censorship policies of the Lincoln administration.[34]

Much attention was given the Cleveland convention by Democratic newspapers hostile to the Union party, but the Radical press lost interest quickly. Fremont was nominated for President and War Democrat Cochrane for Vice President on a platform mixing Radical proposals, Copperhead slogans, and traditional Democratic party dogma. Radicals were pleased by one resolution calling for the end of slavery and one declaring for the Wade-Davis Reconstruction plan. But they were not pleased by many other planks of many other kinds resembling in some cases the standard anti-Lincoln propaganda of the Peace school.[35]

The Union National Convention gathered at Baltimore June 7, and was well attended by the War Democracy. Two days before the delegates assembled, a mass meeting was held at New York City, ostensibly for the purpose of praising the military accomplishments of War Democrat Ulysses S. Grant—actually to promote him as a rival to Lincoln for the Union presidential nomination.[36] But there was no stopping Lincoln at Baltimore. He had the Radicals wrapped up, as well as the Conservatives. Symbollically, a Radical and a Conservative fought for the right to present his name to the convention. Symbollically, the Radical won the contest. The Conservative was Thompson Campbell of California. He was a former neighbor of Lincoln's in Illinois, where he had served the cause of Breckinridge four years earlier, as a presidential elector. To him was accorded the official honor of nominating Lincoln. But before he could act upon his authority in the matter, Campbell was upstaged by Radical Simon Cameron of Pennsylvania, who delivered a message of praise in Lincoln's behalf that developed unexpectedly into a nomination speech.[37] There being no organized opposition, Lincoln won renomination without a fight.

In the battle for the Vice Presidential nomination, the Republican incumbent, Hannibal Hamlin, was the favorite to win. But Union party tradition was tied to the War Democracy, and Hamlin did not fit. At Lincoln's suggestion, War Democrat General Benjamin F. Butler was contacted in advance of the convention, to determine his interest in the Vice Presidency. Having spurned it once before, when offered by the Chase faction, Butler spurned it once again.[38] Of a different turn of mind were War Democrats Daniel S. Dickinson of New York and Andrew Johnson of Tennessee. Both courted the nomination at the Union National Convention, and when the voting began they were the featured contestants. On the first ballot, Johnson was selected over Dickinson, 200 to 108.[39]

The Democratic National Convention, meeting in Chicago, August 29, was attended by a clear majority of War Democrats and Conditionals, inexpertly led, and a minority of Peace Democrats. No struggle seemed likely concerning the party platform. Nor was there serious doubt concerning the nature of the Democratic presidential nomination. Of the two possibilities at the beginning of the year, General McClellan and Governor Seymour of New York, only McClellan remained. Despite apparent certainty of his nomination, and despite the presence at Chicago of a War Democrat majority, the outstanding delegate in attendance was Clement L. Vallandigham, Supreme Commander of the Sons of Liberty, recently returned from exile. War Democrats controlling the Ohio Democratic state convention, held in March, had prevented his election as a delegate-at-large. But he had overcome their purposes, reentering the country from Canada to stand for election as a district delegate, at the risk of being once again arrested by the military. Creating a sensation upon his return, he was easily elected.[40]

War Democrats determined the choice of a permanent chairman at Chicago, and all other convention officials. They also determined the makeup of all committees, including the Resolutions Committee. Fully in control, they had the power to hold in check the power of Vallandigham and seemed intent on doing so. But the Peace faction fought back, with remarkable success. As a member of the Resolutions Committee, Vallandigham was opposed by the arguments of Committee Chairman James Guthrie of Kentucky and Samuel J. Tilden and Peter Cagger of New York, all of whom were War Democrats. Thirteen committee members were supposed War men, as against eleven who were out for Peace. But Vallandigham prevailed anyway, against the odds, ramming through a long and vaguely worded resolution, calling for a national Peace conference, and admitting the failure of the war.[41] (The curse of the "Failure of the War" resolution was to follow Samuel J. Tilden into the presidential campaign of 1876, in which he was accused of helping Vallandigham to win on this occasion.) McClellan was nominated for President and a Peace Democrat, Congressman George H. Pendleton of Ohio, for Vice President. Since the Special War Session of 1861 Pendleton had not once voted for the war.

Immediately following the national conventions a struggle began, between the War and Peace factions, concerning the presidential candidate's traditional letter of acceptance. War Democrats supporting McClellan wanted him to say that no armistice would go into effect until the Confederate states agreed to reenter the Union. Peace Democrats wanted him to recommend an armistice as a prelude to diplomatic negotiations. McClellan wanted to go along with the Peace faction. He had been warned by Vallandigham and others that failure to do so would result in their mass desertion. Moreover, he believed that if negotiations failed, the armistice could end and the war could recommence without difficulty. Writing and rewriting his letter of acceptance, he sought to patch together something satisfactory to both sides, without success. Before the letter was fully composed, he received a message from August Belmont, Chairman of the Democratic National Committee, restating the War Democrat position: no armistice until the Confederate states agreed to reenter the Union. Reversing his stand, McClellan adopted Belmont's position as his own, and his letter of acceptance went forth as a virtual repudiation of the Peace plank.[42] The Peace Democracy was stunned; the Regular War Democracy was jubilant. The party as a whole was thoroughly split.

Much the same could be said for the national Union party. Following Lincoln's nomination there still were many Unionists thoroughly convinced that of all possible candidates he was the least likely to win. Word of this was rampant in Washington, where it was picked up by James Shaffer, Chief of Staff to General Benjamin F. Butler, and relayed to Butler in the field. According to Shaffer's informants, many War Democrats were anxious to abandon the Union ticket in Butler's favor, providing the General was interested in any such arrangement. From Cincinnati came word that Fremonters and War Democrats were uniting for similar purposes.[43] War Democrat John W. Forney, editor of the Washington *Chronicle* (who heretofore had stood by Lincoln without reservation) offered now to back another Unionist if it appeared he had a better chance of winning.[44] The same sentiment was expressed by Greeley of the New York *Tribune,* in company with War Democrats Daniel S. Dickinson of New York, and William H. Smith of Ohio, editorial voice of the Radical Cincinnati *Gazette*. (Smith also headed the Ohio Union ticket as candidate for Secretary of State.) Editorially, he recommended the withdrawal of both Lincoln and Fremont and their replacement by Chase.[45] A secret call for a second Union National Convention, to be held September 28, went forth from New York City. It was hotly denounced by many, including Radical leader Roscoe Conkling of New York, and was subsequently withdrawn.[46]

In the middle of the frenzied proposals that Lincoln leave the scene, in the interest of the Union party, a letter arrived at the White House from War Democrat Benjamin H. Brewster of Pennsylvania, summing up the strong opinions of the Lincoln Radicals on this particular question. In Brewster's estimation, the only members of the party opposing the President's renomination were "the unsteady, the unfaithful and the timid. . . .For God's sake—disregard these clamors and outcryes."[47]

In time, the rumors and manipulations subsided, and as the national campaign developed, Radical and Conservative Unionists alike rallied to the President. In September Mongomery Blair retired from the cabinet and Fremont withdrew from the presidential contest.

$$* \quad * \quad * \quad * \quad *$$

McClellan's nomination was expected to weaken the nonpartisan Union coalitions in the several states. No evidence of this was visible, however, in the September elections, in which the War Democracy was very much in evidence in the Union party camp. Although the Peace faction was voted down at the Democratic state convention and a Conditional—Judge Joseph Howard—received the party nomination for Governor, the War Democracy of Maine was evidently unimpressed. At the Union State Convention War Democrat Governor Samuel Cony was renominated by acclamation, and numerous War Democrats were to stump the state in his behalf, the best known being Colonel Walter Harriman of New Hampshire, recently returned from a Confederate prison, full of fury for the Confederacy and the Democratic party.[48] War Democrat Cony was reelected Governor by a majority of almost 16,000—about the same as that of 1863. Substantial Union majorities were retained in both houses of the legislature, and all five congressional seats went to Unionists, the Regular Democrats losing the only one they had carried in 1862. A Soldier Vote Amendment to the state constitution was ratified by a majority of more than three to one.[49]

In Vermont, for the second straight year, the Regular Democrats nominated Timothy P. Redfield on a Peace platform.[50] At the Union State Convention, War Democrat Paul Dillingham was renominated for Lieutenant Governor, and a Union district convention elected a War Democrat, Bradley Barlow, to attend the National Union Convention.[51] Prominent campaigners for the Union ticket included State Senators Roderick Richardson and Addison W. Peck, War Democrats elected as Unionists in 1861.[52] Following Republican tradition, the Vermont Union ticket coasted to victory in 1864, with a giant majority of 19,000.[53]

*   *   *   *

That Lincoln had no clear Reconstruction policy in the waning days of the war is rendered clear by comparison of Louisiana's fall elections of 1864 to those of Tennessee. The man in charge of the voting process in Louisiana was War Democrat Governor George F. Shepley, who worked within the confines of Louisiana's Antebellum laws. In consequence of this, the legislature elected in 1864 was terribly Conservative and the U.S. Senators elected by the legislature were anti-Lincoln Secessionists of the deepest dye. The Senate would reject them, out of hand. In Tennessee, under the authority of War Democrat Governor Andrew Johnson, things came out very differently in 1864, for there the law books were simply set aside in favor of political expediency. At the order of Governor Johnson a convention assembled September 5, at Nashville, to further implement the Radical policies of the Governor. More than forty counties were represented, but the delegates had not been regularly chosen, and in some case had not been chosen at all but came on their own responsibility. A large majority were Johnson Radicals and in short time the Conservatives were hooted from the hall.

For the first time since Johnson had returned in 1862 there now existed in Tennessee a convention agreeable to anti-slavery reform, and Johnson was gratified. That the delegates were not elected properly, in many instances, was a matter of indifference to him. They could serve the Union cause, and that was enough. At the behest of the convention, voting laws were enacted of the most stringent nature, preventing the election of any but the most unfaltering of Union men. Union party candidates and Union party policies received a full endorsement, as did also the Governor, and a resolution was adopted approving the passage of an anti-slavery Amendment to the Constitution. When the delegates adjourned, a proclamation was issued by the Governor, lauding the work of the convention and calling an election for President and Vice President, to be held November 8. Voting was to be carried out, the Governor declared, under terms prescribed by the convention, denying the franchise to anyone favoring negotiated peace. The national Democratic platform having favored negotiated peace, a vote for McClellan thereby was proclaimed illegal. Regular Democrats denounced the voting laws and called upon Lincoln to strike them down. But Lincoln stood by Johnson and the Radical approach to Reconstruction, and refused to intervene.[54]

In all the October States the Regular Democracy devoted its attention to a full-scale attack against Conscription and the "barbaric" use of Negro troops. The October campaign in Pennsylvania involved elections for Congress and the legislature. Twelve out of 24 Pennsylvania members in the Thirty-eighth Congress belonged to the Regular Democracy. Of these, only two (Archibald McAllister and Joseph Baily) had voted in favor of the War and neither was renominated by the Democratic party in 1864. Baily was offered and accepted a Union party nomination and ran for reelection against a Peace Democrat. War Democrat William M. Heister was nominated for Congress by the Union party, to challenge the authority of the Peace incumbent Sydenham E. Ancona.[55]

In 1861 and 1862 the Union party campaign had been directed in Pennsylvania by War Democrat John W. Forney and Conservative Republican Alexander K. McClure. The 1861 election results were disappointing from the Union party point of view, and the 1862 results even more so. In 1863 War Democrat Forney teamed up with Radical Republican Simon Cameron, and the Union party staged a comeback. The same combination, Forney and Cameron, worked well together once again in 1864.[56] (As the victim of the most scurrilous newspaper attacks of the Civil War era, Cameron was deeply grateful to Forney, who defended him on many occasions in the Philadelphia *Press* and the Washington *Chronicle*.)

Cameron was a leading Lincoln Radical from the start of the 1864 campaign and Forney announced for Lincoln's renomination in January, 1864. Both were hostile to the Cleveland Radical Convention. The Regular Democrats could not wholeheartedly support the federal forces in the field, Forney said, because "the great and pressing want of the McClellan Democracy. . .was a sweeping defeat of the armies of the Union."[57] The absence of Forney, in Washington, much of the time in 1864, directed attention in Pennsylvania to the spirited campaign work of Union party leader Thomas Fitzgerald, editor of the War Democrat Philadelphia *City Item*.[58] Douglas leader Thomas Cunningham was named as a Lincoln elector, and Democratic Generals George G. Meade, Andrew J. Smith, and Samuel P. Heintzelman, all of Pennsylvania, all announced for Lincoln.[59]

In Ohio, the Union State Convention named the State party Chairman, War Democrat William H. Smith, to head the ticket as the candidate for Secretary of State. Although a leading Chase supporter, he campaigned vigorously for Lincoln following the departure of Chase from the presidential picture. War Democrat Colonel W. P. Richardson of the 25th Ohio Infantry was nominated for Attorney General; Luther Day of the Douglas State Central Committee was a Union candidate for the State Supreme Court. The Regular Democracy nominated a mixed bag of War and Peace candidates, with the Peace men comprising a large majority.[60]

War Democrat David Tod, who had failed of renomination for Governor at the 1863 Union State Convention, was grieved by the experience, and it was feared for a time he would abandon the Union party. When Salmon P. Chase resigned as Secretary of the Treasury in June, the position was offered to Tod, who turned it down. But the tribute was nonetheless appreciated. In 1864 the former Governor attended the Union State Convention as a delegate-at-large, and spoke for Lincoln throughout the state.

Repudiation of the Peace platform by General McClellan knocked the heart out of the campaign for many Regular Democrats, including a large number in Ohio. When Congressman Cox continued to speak in McClellan's behalf, he was attacked in the pages of the Columbus Crisis.[61] Dissident Peace Democrats nominated Congressman Alexander Long of Ohio for President, on an anti-war, pro-slavery platform, but Long declined the honor and the movement collapsed.[62]

The Union party of Ohio, with a state ticket loaded down with War Democrats, overwhelmed the Regular Democracy, with a majority of 55,000. In congressional races the Union party captured all but two of Ohio's nineteen seats. Every War Democrat running as a Unionist was elected, every War Democrat running as a Regular defeated.[63]

The other big October state was Indiana, where the Regular Democracy had surged to power in 1862, and the Union party was determined to reassume control in 1864 (with the assistance of the War Democracy, or at least a large portion of it). Directing the Union campaign throughout the year was War Democrat Joseph A. Wright, Chairman of the Union State Committee. At the 1864 Union State Convention, Republican Governor Oliver P. Morton was renominated on a state ticket bristling with War Democrats: for Auditor, Thomas B. McCarty; Treasurer, James I. Morrison; Attorney General, Delano E. Williamson; Supreme Court Judge, J. T. Elliot. In 1860 all had worked for Douglas, as had also Lincoln's 1864 electors for Indiana, Joseph A. Wright, David S. Gooding, and James C. Denny. War Democrat Ebenezer Dumont stood for reelection to Congress on the Union ticket and War Democrat Thomas N. Stilwell (an army veteran and a former Douglas leader) was nominated for Congress in a Democratic district, to run against a Peace incumbent. A pair of War Democrats seeking no office, but actively engaged in the Union party campaign in Indiana were Robert Dale Owen, Chairman of the American Freedmen's Inquiry Commission, and Andrew Johnson, Military Governor of Tennessee.[64]

In State Convention, the Regular Democracy of Indiana rejected the Peace faction. Party leadership was instead accorded to War Democrat Senator Thomas A. Hendricks, and a state ticket was selected along Conditional lines, headed by Joseph E. McDonald, candidate for Governor, and General Mahlon D. Manson, running for Secretary of State. The Peace faction fought back in southern Indiana, defeating War Democrat Congressman Holman in his bid for renomination.[65]

Investigations by the Office of the Judge Advocate General, under War Democrat Joseph Holt—which had shaken the Kentucky campaign earlier in the year—collided also with the Indiana campaign. At the order of Judge Holt, a number of Indiana's Democratic leaders were arrested by troops commanded by Democratic General Alvin P. Hovey.[66] As in the case of the Democrats arrested in Kentucky, those in Indiana were accused of belonging to a subversive organization and of planning to disorganize and frustrate the Union cause. None of the members of the Democratic state ticket were accused of such associations, but the State Party Chairman, Joseph J. Bingham, was taken into custody, along with Horace Heffren (a Union army veteran) and several others. Three of the accused turned states evidence, revealing the activities of the entire group. Testimony at the trial, held in October, exposed Clement L. Vallandigham as National Commander of the Sons of Liberty. Testimony also implicated Congressman Voorhees of Indiana in the purchase of 20,000 rifles for use by members of the Sons of Liberty. Another report (later substantiated by the writings of a member of the Confederate Commission in Canada) brought to light the plans for a northern insurrection in the event of Vallandigham's seizure by the military.[67]

The arrest of Democratic leaders in Indiana was denounced by Regular Democrats in all the loyal states. It was a hoax, they said; an Abolitionist plot, and a threat to constitutional liberty. The voters of Kentucky having recoiled in shock as a result of such protests, those of Indiana reacted the other way, applauding the action as eminently proper. Governor Morton was reelected in October with a majority of 22 thousand, all the Union candidates for state executive office receiving similar majorities. The state legislature, in which the Democrats had held an edge of 30 seats, went Union by 10 seats. In Congress, where the Democrats had held a 7 to 4 advantage, Union candidates captured 10 of 12 seats.[68]

The total failure of the anti-Lincoln Radicals at the Cleveland Convention of 1864, and the strong alliance of Lincoln and a large number of Radical leaders was reflected in the November State elections, in all of which the Union party appeared at long last united. In New York, preceding the Cleveland Convention, War Democrat Lyman Tremain was widely regarded as the Wade-Davis candidate for the Union gubernatorial nomination, as opposed to War Democrat John A. Dix, the so-called Lincoln candidate. But following the Cleveland Convention both War Democrats were set aside—Conservative and Radical—in favor of a compromise choice, Republican Congressman Reuben E. Fenton. War Democrats were represented on the Union ticket by Thomas G. Alvord, formerly of Mozart Hall, the candidate for Lieutenant Governor.[69] In congressional races the Union party nominated three War Democrats of whom the best known was incumbent John A. Griswold, sponsor of the *Monitor* and a leading minority member on the House Committee on Naval Affairs. Elected as a Regular Democrat in 1862, Griswold had voted so often in favor of the war that he was no longer welcome in the Democratic councils. Another New York Democrat rejected by the Regular Democracy in 1864 was Congressman Moses F. Odell of Brooklyn, an energetic member of the Joint Committee on the Conduct of the War. Having favored the removal of McClellan from command and having voted for the Thirteenth Amendment, he was no longer regarded as a Democrat by many of his former supporters, and was replaced on the ticket by an advocate of Peace.

The New York State Democratic Convention of 1864 was wholly the creature of Governor Horatio Seymour, who won renomination without serious opposition of any kind. His leading convention supporter was Peace Democrat John A. Green, Chairman of the Democratic State Committee.[70] But when the campaign began Green was shoved aside in favor of the War Democracy. In New York City, the Peace men controlled the McKeon machine, which controlled City Hall, while Tammany and Mozart Halls remained in favor of the war. Despite the recent triumph of McKeon, Seymour courted Tammany and Mozart, seeking the War vote. In so doing he regained the support of War Democrats John Van Buren, Charles P. Daly, and J. McLeod Murphy, all of whom had worked against the Democratic ticket of 1863. Van Buren campaigned in 1864 as the arch-opponent of Negro troops. For sending Negroes against the white men of the South, Lincoln was denounced by Van Buren as a "twenty-second rate man."[71] Democratic soldiers supporting the Regular Democratic ticket organized the McClellan Legion. It had many members in New York City. Colonels Henry I. Liebenau of the Seymour Light Cavalry and George B. Hall of the 71st New York Infantry played a prominent part in all the Legion's operations.[72]

A new War Democrat in the fold of the Regular Democracy in 1864 was Thurlow Weed, former Chairman of the New York State Republican Committee. Having lost his faith in Lincoln for going Radical, Weed declared against his reelection and joined the Democratic cause.[73] Generally speaking, however, the trend was all the other way. Some former members of Tammany Hall campaigning for Lincoln in 1864 included Daniel E. Sickles, David Coddington, Edwards Pierrepont, and Francis R. Tillou. Some former members of Mozart Hall campaigning for Lincoln included Alvord, the candidate for Lieutenant Governor, John Cochrane, and Thomas W. Egan. A self-styled "New York State Committee of War Democrats," meeting in Syracuse, declared for Lincoln in advance of his renomination. Douglas leader George A. Brandreth chaired the gathering and Henry C. Page served as Secretary. Page was a former Chairman of the Young Democrats of New York City, who had worked for Douglas in company with Brandreth. Another pair of New York City Democrats to join the Lincoln cause in 1864 were Generals Richard Busteed and Thomas F. Meagher. Both were Irish, Busteed representing the Protestant element, Meagher the Catholic. Both spoke frequently in the Irish districts.[74] Although defeated in his bid for the Vice Presidential nomination at the Union National Convention, War Democrat Daniel S. Dickinson campaigned vigorously for Lincoln, all over the state.

At the end of October a call was issued from New York City for a convention of "Jacksonian Democrats" opposing the McClellan ticket. John A. Dix, Edwards Pierrepont, Alexander T. Stewart, Peter Cooper, Robert B. Roosevelt, and Moses Taylor were listed as sponsors. The convention was held, November 1, at Cooper Union with James Worrell of Pennsylvania chairing the occasion. (Four years previously Worrell had campaigned for Congress as a Democrat.[75]) Speeches were delivered by Pierrepont of Tammany, former Congressman Hiram Walbridge, Generals Sickles and Dix, and others. Editor Edwin C. Bailey of the Boston *Herald* and recently Chairman of the Massachusetts Democratic State Committee, was named chairman of the National Committee of the War Democracy. Great excitement prevailed.[76]

A major development in New York City Union party campaign was the editorial position assumed by James Gorden Bennett of the War Democrat New York *Herald*. Starting off neutral and critical of everybody, the *Herald* veered slowly toward the Union party as the campaign progressed, finally embracing Lincoln with enthusiasm.[77]

In Illinois—the other major "November state"—a matter of symbolic import was the death in 1864 of Radical Congressman Owen Lovejoy and his replacement in Congress by War Democrat Ebon C. Ingersoll, elected on the Union ticket. At the Illinois Union State Convention, War Democrat Samuel W. Moulton was named to run for Congressman-at-Large. Having offered to support Democratic General John A. Logan for Congress in 1862 (which offer was declined), the Union party turned in 1864 to his Democratic associate of many years, Colonel Andrew J. Kuykendall, who accepted.[78]

Discord in the Democratic camp insured Union victory in Illinois. At the Democratic state convention called for the selection of delegates to the national convention, the Peace faction prevailed. The victory was followed by a giant Peace rally in Peoria, and when the Regular War Democracy gathered at Springfield to offer a reply, the Peace faction invaded the gathering. The Democratic convention held in August, to name a state ticket, was another example of the Peace faction in high gear, without concern for compromise.[79] In consequence of these developments, the War Democracy of Illinois went over to the Union party, lock, stock, and barrel. (It was recalled that the leading Democratic figures in the 1860 Illinois campaign were Robert G. Ingersoll, John A. Logan, John A. Rawlins,

John A. McClernand, Green B. Raum, William A. Richardson, and William R. Merrick.[80] In 1864, all but Merrick and Richardson were on the other side.) Breckinridge leaders John Dougherty and Thomas Snell campaigned for the Union nominees, and Democratic General John A. Logan came home on furlough from Georgia to speak in their behalf.[81] Some other War Democrats in uniform working for the Union party cause included Generals Isham N. Haynie and Mason Brayman,[82] and Colonels Walter B. Scates and Stephen G. Hicks. (Scates would represent Illinois at the Jacksonian Democrat Convention, in New York City.[83])

The Democratic candidate for Governor of Illinois was Congressman James C. Robinson; the candidate for Lieutenant Governor, S. Corning Judd. Both were ardently for Peace and both were subjected to merciless campaign criticism. In confessions made public at the Indiana "Treason Trials" of 1864, Judd was revealed as an officer in the Illinois chapter of the Sons of Liberty. It also was revealed that Confederate agents in Canada had offered to finance a large share of Robinson's gubernatorial campaign and that the offer was accepted in Robinson's behalf by Clement L. Vallandigham, as National Commander of the Sons of Liberty. Witnesses contended that Robinson had promised, in the event of his election, to relinquish control of the Illinois State Militia to the Sons of Liberty, with the object of negating its usefulness as an instrument of war.[84]

The Union party of New Jersey sought to exploit the rift between the Regular War Democrats, led by Governor Joel Parker, and the Peace faction, led by State Senator Thomas Dunn English. The Governor was an ardent supporter of McClellan for the Democratic presidential nomination, and as the 1864 campaign progressed he became more of a War man and more the enemy of Peace. Yet he remained the defender of slavery, and on this ground was sharply criticized by War Democrats in the Union party, of whom the most vocal were State Senator James M. Scovel, former State Senator Joseph T. Crowell, and former Congressman George T. Cobb, all of whom had led the Douglas parade only four years before as "northern men with southern priciples."[85] In Massachusetts, War Democrats Benjamin F. Butler, Caleb Cushing, George B. Loring, Whiting Griswold, and Edwin C. Bailey took the stump for Lincoln and Emancipation.[86]

In Wisconsin, the Union party organization was wholly dependent for success on the backing of the War Democracy, and the leading party figure of 1864 was War Democrat Governor James T. Lewis. The Governor's election the year before had been largely the work of Charles D. Robinson, editor of the War Democrat Green Bay *Advocate*. In 1864, Robinson declared for McClellan, but many other War Democrats in Wisconsin rejected his advice, and took their stand by Lincoln. The best known of these were Matthew Carpenter, father of the Janesville Convention, and backbone of the Union party in the state; Judge Arthur Mac Arthur; General John C. Starkweather; General Lucius Fairchild, and Congressman Ezra A. Wheeler. (Having voted for the Thirteenth Amendment, Wheeler was of course denied renomination by the Regular Democracy.[87])

In Kansas, the Union party divided, Conservative and Radical, in 1864. The Conservative leader was War Democrat Governor Thomas Carney; the Radical leader, U.S. Senator James H. Lane. In keeping with his overall policy in every election campaign since 1861, President Lincoln gave his blessings to the Kansas Radicals at the expense of Governor Carney, who retaliated by declaring in favor of the Cleveland Convention and the Fremont-Cochrane ticket.[88] At the Union National Convention, Lane was a major supporter of Lincoln's renomination bid, and upon returning home took with him the presidential favor. Making matters worse for himself at every opportunity, Carney accepted the backing of the Regular Democracy, and denounced as scare stories the warnings of Senator Lane concerning the approach of "Price's Army." When Price invaded Kansas, in keeping with the prophesies of Lane, Carney's political career was ended in advance of the election.[89]

Another new Union party organization came into being in 1864 in Iowa, where the War Democracy was praised in profusion at the Union State Convention. War Democrat Chester C. Cole was selected to head the Union state ticket in November as candidate for Judge of the State Supreme Court.[90]

Having all along controlled the Democracy of Minnesota, the War faction continued in control in 1864. At the Democratic state convention, three men were nominated for the State Supreme Court: O.C. Chatfield for Chief Justice, and Eli T. Wilder and former Governor Edward O. Hamlin for Associate Justices. Following the Democratic National Convention, Hamlin denounced the national party platform, coming out for Lincoln, in company with Henry M. Rice, leader of the Minnesota Breckinridge Democracy. Democratic State Senator Daniel S. Norton did the same.[91]

In California, the Union party continued to emphasize the importance of the War Democrats at the Sacramento State Convention of 1864. J. G. McCallum, War Democrat, chaired the gathering. Walter Van Dyke, War Democrat, served as a Vice President. James J. Green, War Democrat, was appointed to the Resolutions Committee which reported in favor of an anti-slavery Amendment to the Constitution. The delegates nominated three congressional candidates, one of whom was incumbent War Democrat William Higby. War Democrat Thomas B. Shannon failed of renomonation but was replaced on the ticket by War Democrat John Bidwell. (On Reconstruction issues Bidwell was Radical, Shannon Conservative.) War Democrat J. A. McCallum was named as an elector on the Lincoln-Johnson ticket.[92]

As in New York the 1864 Radicalism of Lincoln had cost him the support of Thurlow Weed, former Chairman of the Republican State Committee, so in California it cost the support of Henry H. Haight, former Chairman of the Republican State Committee. At the Democratic State Convention Haight was chosen to head the ticket as candidate for Judge of the State Supreme Court. But in California, as in New York, the Conservative Republican bolt was more than offset by the War Democrat bolt, and the Union party appeared ready to sweep the state.

As in all the border slave states, the Union party of Missouri broke apart in 1864. Conservative control of party policy, maintained under the authority of Governor Gamble and Democratic General Schofield, collapsed immediately upon the death of Gamble in January 1864, and the departure of Schofield shortly afterwards. The new Governor—Willard P. Hall—was also a Conservative, but he lacked the power to keep the Radical "Charcoal" faction in check. Rival delegations—Charcoal and Claybank—were named to represent Missouri at the Union National Convention, in Baltimore. The Conservative leader at Baltimore was War Democrat Thomas L. Price; the Radical leader, War Democrat Charles D. Drake. At the Slave State Freedom Convention, held at Louisville in February, Drake had blocked a move to abandon the Union party in favor of an independent Radical organization.[93] For this he was upbraided by the Wade-Davis Radicals, who sent a delegation to the Cleveland Radical Convention, on their own. When the Missouri Conservatives, under War Democrat Price, were unseated at the Union National Convention by the Missouri Radicals, under War Democrat Drake, the glory went to Drake. Buoyed by the victory at Baltimore, Drake turned with vigor to the question of Reconstruction in Missouri. To the same extent as War Democrats Andrew Johnson of Tennessee and Thomas J. Durant of Louisiana, he was determined that none but loyal men should be allowed a voice in the process of Reconstruction (in keeping with the advice provided Andrew Johnson by no less an authority than Lincoln himself, in 1863: "Let the reconstruction be the work of such men only as can be trusted for the Union. Exclude all others. . .").[94]

The breakup of the Union party in Missouri placed War Democrat Charles D. Drake on the same side as War Democrat Senator John B. Henderson, in favor of Emancipation and the use of Negro troops, in company with many other Missouri Conservatives of yesterday turned Radical today. War Democrats nominated for Congress on the Republican Union ticket in Missouri included Joseph W. McClurg, Benjamin F. Loan, Robert T. Van Horn, and John F. Benjamin. All were Union veterans and all were anxious for the end of slavery.

In Maryland, too, the Union party foundered on slavery and race in 1864; and, as usual, War Democrats were called upon to save the situation. Maryland had two important elections to attend to, one deciding the makeup of the State Constitutional Convention of 1865, the other for state and national officials. Overseeing both elections, as Commander of the Middle Department, was Democratic General Lewis Wallace. Upon assuming command in March, he was advised by Secretary of War Stanton that his job included the abolition of slavery in Maryland and a pro-Lincoln vote by the Maryland majority. To guarantee the accomplishment of both purposes, the franchise was denied by judging boards to two-thirds of the voters in the state and three-quarters of the voters in Baltimore county.[95] On this basis, 61 Emancipationists were elected to serve in the convention, as against 35 opponents of Emancipation.[96] The Maryland election procedures of course had the approval of President Lincoln, who otherwise would have used the executive power to overrule General Wallace, in the name of free elections. The State Convention assembled at Annapolis April 27 and was still in session six weeks later when the Union National Convention assembled at Baltimore. The right to hold slaves as property was outlawed by the State Convention, June 24, by a vote of 53 to 21. To assist in the election of Union party candidates, in November, an oath of loyalty was established by the State Convention as a prerequisite to voting, and the franchise was extended to Maryland soldiers in the field.[97] A popular vote on all proposed changes in the state constitution was scheduled for October 29.

Uniting in the face of the anti-slavery crusade, pro-slavery Unionists and Disunionists organized a ticket, with Ezekiel F. Chambers the candidate for Governor. He had served in the War of 1812, and was well remembered for his opposition to coercion of the South in 1861. He was an Old-Line Whig. Against him, the Radical faction sought to send a lifelong Democrat, Comptroller Henry H. Goldsborough, recently elected as an anti-slavery man. But that proved impossible. The Radicals having decided the nature of the Union party platform at the State Convention, the Conservatives claimed the right to name the ticket and this was agreed to. Thomas Swann, an Old-Line Whig, was the Union candidate for Governor. He had little to do with the anti-slavery revolution sweeping Maryland in 1864, but that, perhaps, was his strongest selling point.

The outstanding campaigner for the Union party in the 1864 Maryland campaign was War Democrat John A. J. Creswell, running for reelection to Congress. The outstanding campaigner for the Maryland Democracy was War Democrat Senator Reverdy Johnson. In addition to Creswell, War Democrats selected by the Union party forces included Francis Thomas and Charles E. Phelps, two nominees for Congress. Thomas was an incumbent, Phelps a veteran of the 1864 Virginia campaign, under Grant.

In speaking for the Regular Democracy in 1864, Senator Johnson was turning his back on a year's worth of anti-slavery talk in Congress. His main concern, he said, was not the fate of slavery but the fate of civil liberty in Maryland. The Loyalty Oath imposed upon the voters of the state was unconstitutional, and should be instantly retracted. For so saying, Johnson was denounced by former allies in the Union party ranks, and the Oath was utilized, to dramatic effect. On October 29 the Maryland electorate (or that part of it designated loyal by General Wallace and his vast array of election judges) ratified the anti-slavery state constitution by a vote of 30,174 to 29,799.[98]

The Regular Democracy of Maryland railed against the vote as a fraud upon the state. Of civilian voters, a majority had opposed the constitution, and only the soldier vote had carried it to victory. Regular Democrats insisted that the soldier vote had been doctored by Republican agents. Senator Johnson consulted with Governor Bradford, requesting that he utilize his influence with Lincoln and General Wallace in the interest of "free elections." Governor Bradford was a Conservative and long the close ally of Senator Johnson, but he did not trust the Regular Democrats and when Johnson rejoined them Bradford felt differently about taking his advice. Despite all protests, the Governor proclaimed the transformation of Maryland from slave-state to free.[99] President Lincoln was accused by Senator Johnson of denying the freedom of elections in Maryland. If he should try doing so again in November, said Johnson, the people of Maryland were to rise in protest and "not submit to tyranny."[100]

The states of Delaware, West Virginia, and Nevada also held elections in November. War Democrat Governor William Cannon of Delaware attracted notice by calling for the presence of troops at the polls, to the rage of the Regular Democracy. Although the same request was granted in the case of New York City (where an army arrived on voting day with War Democrat Benjamin F. Butler leading the parade), no troops were provided in the case of Delaware.[101]

The November states provided the final touch to the sweeping Union party victory of 1864. In Iowa, War Democrat Chester C. Cole led the Unionists to victory, capturing a seat on the State Supreme Court.[102] The Illinois legislature, in which the Democrats had held a majority of 27, went Union by 20 seats. Of all the November states, only Delaware and New Jersey voted Democratic. Fifteen War Democrats were elected to Congress in November, running on the Union ticket. Only one was defeated—John A. J. Creswell of Maryland, overwhelmed in a Conservative Democratic district, despite the presence of troops at the polls. Fighting back in his behalf, the Maryland legislature was to appoint Creswell to the U.S. Senate in December.

In the national elections, the Lincoln-Johnson ticket carried every state in the Union but three—Kentucky, New Jersey, and Delaware. The popular majority of the Union party was 400,000; the electoral count, 212 to 21.[103] "Seldom in history," wrote Ralph Waldo Emerson about the 1864 elections, "was so much staked upon a popular vote. I suppose never in history."[104] There is no doubt that the outcome of the vote was determined by the loyal War Democracy.

In this, the crowning year of the wartime Union party, it is worth considering some notable facts about the true nature of the party hierarchy and the accusation of Conservatives that the Union party was merely "the Republican party under a different name." Andrew Johnson, the Union candidate for Vice President, was a War Democrat. In the States of Maine, Ohio, and Iowa, War Democrats received the Union nomination for the highest state executive position under consideration by the voters. In New York, Vermont, Ohio, and Connecticut, War Democrats received the Union nomination for the second-highest state executive position. In Indiana, four Union nominations for major state executive office were accorded War Democrats; in Ohio and Connecticut the number was three. In congressional races, the Union party nominated seventeen War Democrats. In California, a majority of the Union nominees for Congress were War Democrats.[105] In Ohio, Indiana, Oregon and New Jersey the Union State party chairmen were War Democrats.[106] On the Union State Central Committee of Connecticut, ten of 23 members were War Democrats.[107] And so on, *ad infinitum.* . .It must be asked of the Conservative historians: If this kind of non-partisan display was *not enough* to establish the Union party as a truly nonpartisan body, what then was required? In fact, it would appear that the Union party was all it claimed to be; and much of the credit belongs to Abraham Lincoln, whose gentle hammering proved devastating to the Conservative principles of the Democratic party.

NOTES

1. Weed declared against the reelection of Lincoln in a letter published in the Albany Evening *Journal,* October 14, 1864.
2. Haight headed the Democratic state ticket in 1864 as candidate for a place on the State Supreme Court. *Evening Journal Almanac,* 1865.
3. Cairo (Illinois) *Democrat,* January 3, 1864.
4. Cameron nominated Lincoln for President at the Union National Convention of 1864. William F. Zornow, *Lincoln and the Party Divided* (Norman: University of Oklahoma Press, 1954), p. 98. Washburne was a major advisor to Henry J. Raymond, Chairman of the Republican National Committee and a pronounced Lincoln-man. Ibid., p. 113. Lovejoy declared at the height of the Fremont boom, "that if [Lincoln] is not the best conceivable President, he is the best possible." Ibid., p. 74. Arnold was Lincoln's strongest supporter in the House. Ralph Korngold, *Thaddeus Stevens,* p. 222. Garrison broke with Wendell Phillips early in the year, declaring in favor of Lincoln's renomination. Ralph Korngold, *Two Friends of Man,* p. 324. Francis Leiber declined to serve as a leader of a Fremont Club in New York City, coming out instead for Lincoln. William F. Zornow, p. 74. When anti-Lincoln forces in New

York proposed a Radical convention, following Lincoln's nomination, Roscoe Conkling protested furiously and the idea was abandoned. De Alva Stanwood Alexander, III:104. James H. Lane was opposed by the Pomeroy forces in Kansas and attended the 1864 National Union Convention as a Lincoln man. Albert Castel, p. 176. (The Anti-Lincoln "Radicals" of Kansas, working under Senator Pomeroy, received the blessings and support of the Regular Democrats, which shows how "Radical" they were. Ibid., p. 180.) Former Governor Dennison of Ohio opposed the Chase boom from the start. William F. Zornow, p. 41. Congressman Riddle of Ohio had the most Radical voting record of anybody in Congress, having provided one of the two Nay votes against the pro-slavery section of the Crittendon Resolution when it first appeared, in 1861. *Congressional Globe* (37th Congress, 1st session), p. 223. From first to last he was Radical and from first to last he was a Lincoln-man. Albert G. Riddle, *Recollections of War Times* (New York: Putnam's, 1895), p. 218, n. Senator Anthony of Rhode Island led the Lincoln forces against the Chase forces dominated by Senator Sprague. Providence *Press*, March 22, 1864.

5. The Constitutional Unionists of New York and New Jersey had gone in coalition with the Democrats in 1862, and were regarded as partially responsible for the Democratic victories in both states that year. Their coalition with the Democrats in Massachusetts, in 1862, had resulted in great gains for the anti-Republican cause, as had the same coalition in Michigan. In Michigan and Massachusetts, in 1862 and 1863, and in Rhode Island, in 1863 and 1864, the Conservative Republicans had deserted to the Democratic cause in great number. The same thing occurred in Kansas in 1862.

6. For Butler's lack of interest in the Chase and Fremont campaigns and the advances of the Chase faction, see William F. Zornow, p. 146. Dickinson was reportedly favorable to the calling of a new Republican national convention and the selection of a new candidate, other than Lincoln—as a gesture of Radical defiance of the Conservative Union party leaders. In this he was supported by Horace Greeley and (probably) by War Democrat Lyman Tremain, who tended to agree with Dickinson about everything. But the Lincoln nomination won the backing of an Old-Line Radical, former Congressman Roscoe Conkling of New York, who threatened and cajoled the anti-Lincoln Radicals into abandoning their talk about conventions; and from that point forward Dickinson and Tremain were firmly in the Lincoln camp. De Alva Stanwood Alexander, III:104.

7. David Y. Thomas, ed., *Arkansas and Its People,* 4 vols. (New York: American Historical Society, 1930), I:136–37.

8. John R. Ficklin, "History of Reconstruction in Louisiana (through 1868)," *Johns Hopkins University Studies in Historical and Political Science,* series XXVIII, no. 1 (1910): p. 83.

9. Clifton R. Hall, p. 119.

10. Ibid., p. 155.

11. State ticket called "Republican" in elections of 1861 through 1863. In 1864, ticket is listed as "Republican-Union" and "Union-Republican" in Manchester *Mirror and American,* March 8, and "Union Republican" in Concord *Independent Democrat,* August 18.

12. Rolfe listed as a member of the State Assembly in New Hampshire (State) *Journal of the House,* 1864. Clarke listed as Attorney General in *Evening Journal Almanac,* 1865.

13. James O. Lyford, pp. 166–67.

14. Ibid., p. 167; James D. Squires, III:400. Some prominent War Democrats supporting the New Hampshire Republican-Union ticket of 1864 included most of the local Union party men of 1863, plus Francis Cogswell, former president of the Boston and Maine Railroad; Thomas Cogswell, former

county judge; State Senator Warren F. Daniell; Sugar River businessman Dexter Richards; and Nathaniel Upham, Superintendent of the Concord Railroad.

15. New Haven *Palladium,* March 10, 1864; W. A. Croffut and John W. Morris, p. 234; Hartford *Courant,* April 1, 1864.

16. *Evening Journal Almanac,* 1865.

17. Newport (Rhode Island) *Advertiser,* March 22, 1864.

18. The Conditional War ticket initially selected at the Democratic State Convention, March 21, 1864, included: For Governor, Elisha B. Potter (unsuccessful candidate, 1855, 1856); Lieutenant Governor, Thomas A. Reynolds; Secretary of State, Josiah Titus; Attorney General, Nicholas Van Slyk; Treasurer, Henry H. Cook. Providence *Press,* March 22, 1864; nominated by order of the State Central Committee: George H. Browne, Governor; Henry Butler, Lieutenant Governor; Union party incumbent John R. Bartlett, Secretary of State; Walter Burgess, Attorney General, and Henry H. Cook, Treasurer. Ibid., April 3, 1864. As a delegate to the Virginia Peace Conference, Browne espoused compromise in Antebellum times. As a member of the 37th Congress, he acted with the Conditional War Democracy. Failing of reelection in 1863, he accepted a commission tendered by Acting Governor William C. Cozzens. John R. Bartlett, *Memoirs of Rhode Island Officers, Who Were Engaged in the Service of Their Country during the Great Rebellion of the South* (Providence: Riker, 1867), pp. 426–28; *U.S. Congress, Biographical Directory of the American Congress, 1774–*1911, p. 506.

19. *Evening Journal Almanac,* 1865.

20. Thomas G. Belden and Marva R. Belden, *So Fell the Angels* (Boston: Little, Brown, 1956), passim. The various and sundry charges of Harris Hoyt are accepted as truth by the authors, and the entire work is dedicated to the contention that War Democrat William Sprague traded thousands of dollars worth of military materiel to Confederate representatives, in exchange for Texas cotton with which to run his mills. Unsupported by any other testimony, the charges appear as flimsy today as they did in 1865 when they first were voiced by Hoyt, a federal prisoner fearing for his life, and anxious to bargain with his captors.

21. Walter C. Woodward, pp. 223–24; Sidney Teiser, "Life of George H. Williams: almost Chief Justice," *Oregon Historical Quarterly* XLVII, no. 3 (September 1946): p. 268. Purchased from Bush by a Democratic journalist, the *Statesman* came out for Peace and started losing subscribers at a rapid rate. In November, 1863, the paper once again was sold, and this time the purchasers were Unionists. The new owners, collectively known as the Oregon Printing and Publishing Company, included War Democrats Rufus Mallory and Chester N. Terry. Walter C. Woodward, pp. 219–20.

22. Ibid., p. 231.

23. Philadelphia Enquirer, November 2, 1864. 24. *Biographical Congressional Directory, 1774–1911.*

24. *Biographical Congressional Directory, 1774–1911.*

25. E. Merton Coulter, p. 182.

26. Former Whigs involved in the Union-Democratic state campaign of 1864 included Governor Bramlette and Attorney General Harlan, Auditor W. T. Samuels and Registrar James A. Dawson, Congressmen Aaron Harding, Robert Mallory, George H. Yeaman, and William H. Wadsworth.

27. Louisville *Journal,* May 26, 1864.

28. S. Merton Coulter, p. 185.

29. Ibid., p. 185.

30. *Evening Journal Almanac.* 1865.

31. *Biographical Congressional Directory, 1774–1911,* pp. 691, 933. Commenting on Guthrie's appearance in the Senate in 1865, Peace Democrat Chauncy

C. Burr declared approval of his placement at the tail end of the Finance Committee, "for Guthrie has placed himself at the tail end of all society by his unnatural support of the abolition war." *The Old Guard,* vol. III, no. 5 (May 1865): p. 237.

32. William F. Zornow, p. 281. William Lloyd Garrison, a true Radical, said that never in history had there been a more ludicrous nor abortive gathering. Ibid., p. 84.

33. Ibid., p. 82.

34. Edward McPherson, *History of the United States during the Great Rebellion* (Washington: Solomon and Chapman, 1876), p. 411.

35. Included in the platform of the Radical Democracy were demands for a free press and the right to *habeas corpus,* in terms made familiar by three years of Peace propaganda. Political integrity and economy also were demanded, together with enforcement of the Monroe Doctrine, to drive the French out of Mexico. William F. Zornow, pp. 79–80.

36. De Alva Stanwood Alexander, III:93.

37. William F. Zornow, p. 98. Campbell was a Breckinridge elector in Illinois in 1860, moving to California immediately following the election.

38. Robert S. Holzman, p. 139.

39. Edward McPherson, p. 407.

40. George H. Porter, pp. 195–96.

41. De Alva Stanwood Alexander, III:110.

42. Charles R. Wilson, "McClellan's Changing Views on the Peace Plank," *American Historical Review,* vol. XXXVIII, no. 3 (April 1933): pp. 498–505.

43. William F. Zornow, p. 111.

44. Ibid., p. 114.

45. De Alva Stanwood Alexander, III:104; Eugene H. Roseboom, pp. 431–32.

46. De Alva Stanwood Alexander, III:104.

47. Roy P. Basler, ed., VII:524.

48. Other War Democrats campaigning for the Union party in Maine in 1864 included: John A. Peters, Attorney General for Maine; Albert G. Jewett, Mayor of Belfast; and lawyer Lewis Barker, a candidate for the legislature. The Lewiston *Democratic Advocate,* edited by Douglas leader Charles P. Stetson, came out for Lincoln and the Union party and the passage of an anti-slavery Amendment to the Constitution.

49. *Evening Journal Almanac,* 1865.

50. Ibid., 1865.

51. Ibid., 1865; *The first three Republican Conventions, 1854, 1860, 1864,* p. 248.

52. Abbey M. Hemenway, IV:14, 546.

53. *Evening Journal Almanac,* 1865.

54. Clifton R. Hall, pp. 140–53.

55. Heister supported Douglas in 1860; cited in the press as a member of pro-Douglas rallies and conventions.

56. For full account of McClure's failure as manager of the Union party campaign of 1862, *see:* Stanton Ling Davis, pp. 242, 263. Cameron served as Chairman of the Republican State Committee in 1864. Wayland F. Dunaway, *A History of Pennsylvania* (New York: Prentice-Hall, 1948), p. 429.

57. Philadelphia *Press,* September 23, 1864.

58. Having supported the Regular Democracy in 1861 and 1862, Fitzgerald was driven off by the Peace Campaign of 1863, coming out vigorously for the Union party in that year, and for Lincoln in 1864.

59. For Union electors, see Philadelphia *Press,* October 1, 1864; for sentiments of Meade, Smith, and Heintzelman, see Milwaukee *Sentinel,* October 13, 1864.

60. Columbus *Ohio State Journal,* October 1, 1864.

61. Madison (Wisconsin) *State Journal,* August 20, 1864.
62. Eugene H. Roseboom, p. 434.
63. War Democrats elected on the Union ticket in Ohio included: William H. Smith, Secretary of State; William P. Richardson, Attorney General; Luther Day, Supreme Court. War Democrats defeated, running as Regular Democrats, included: William W. Armstrong, incumbent Secretary of State, Congressman Wells A. Hutchins, and congressional candidates Americus V. Rice and George E. Pugh.
64. Willard H. Smith, *Schuyler Colfax: The Changing Fortunes of a Political Idol* (Indianapolis: Indiana Historical Bureau, 1932), pp. 200–201; Richard W. Leopold, p. 365.
65. Israel G. Blake, *The Holmans of Veraestau* (Oxford: Mississippi Valley Press, 1943), p. 127.
66. James G. Randall, *Civil War and Reconstruction,* p. 399.
67. James D. Horan, pp. 89–90. Following trial before a military commission, in October 1864, Harrison H. Dodd and three of the other defendents were sentenced to be hanged, and Lambdin P. Milligan was sentenced to life imprisonment. (Democratic Colonel William E. McLean of the 43d Indiana Infantry was a member of the Commission handing down the sentences.) The prisoners were not punished as the commission directed. Dodd escaped from custody and was never recaptured. All the death sentences were appealed and all were commuted to life, and the original life sentence was reduced to something resembling house arrest. Following the war the actions of the commission were ruled illegal by the U.S. Supreme Court, which held that the army had no jurisdiction over civilians in matters of this kind. Kenneth M. Stampp, *Indiana Politics,* p. 253; Francis M. Trissal, p. 39; Wood Gray, p. 297.
68. *Evening Journal Almanac,* 1865.
69. Ibid., 1865.
70. Sidney D. Brummer, pp. 418–19.
71. New York *Herald,* November 5, 1864.
72. Mary R. Dearing, p. 129; New York *Journal of Commerce,* November 7, 1864.
73. Albany Evening *Journal,* October 14, 1864.
74. New York *Herald,* May 26, 1864; *Union Army,* VIII:46; Robert A. Athearn, p. 134.
75. *Tribune Almanac,* 1861.
76. New York *Herald,* November 2, 1864.
77. Robert S. Harper, pp. 320–21.
78. David W. Lusk, pp. 166, 176.
79. John Moses, II:704–8.
80. Charles A. Church, p. 80.
81. Arthur C. Cole, p. 328.
82. John Moses, II:708; James G. Wilson, p. 30.
83. New York *Herald,* November 2, 1864.
84. Wood Gray, pp. 168–69; 197–98.
85. Scovel and Crowell were delegates-at-large to the Union National Convention, and Cobb campaigned for Union candidates. In 1865 Cobb was elected to the State Senate on the Union ticket.
86. For Cushing: Claude M. Fuess, p. 279; for Butler: "What genuine Democrats think of the rebellion." (Letter from Butler to Simon Cameron). Collection of the Library of Congress; for Loring: Boston *Advertiser,* October 20, 1864; for Bailey: Rutland (Vermont) *Herald,* September 4, 1864; Concord (New Hampshire) *Statesman,* October 28, 1864.
87. Wheeler declared for Lincoln; see Philadelphia *Enquirer,* November 2, 1864. Fairchild endorsed the Union party campaign of 1862 and never returned to the Regular Democracy. Mary R. Dearing, p. 13. Starkweather declared for

Lincoln in 1864. Milwaukee *Wisconsin State Sentinel,* October 31, 1864.
88. Albert Castel, p. 180.
89. William E. Connelley, *A Standard History of Kansas and Kansans,* 5 vols. (Chicago: Lewis, 1918), II:754.
90. *Evening Journal Almanac,* 1865.
91. Lucius F. Hubbard and Return I. Holcomb, III:99.
92. California State Library, "History of Political Conventions. . . ," pp. 209–11.
93. Sceva B. Laughlin, "Missouri politics. . . ." p. 265.
94. Clifton R. Hall, p. 106; U.S. War Department, *Official Records of the War of the Rebellion,* Series III, III:p. 289.
95. Irving McKee, p. 68.
96. Charles B. Clark, pp. 115–16.
97. Ibid., pp. 115–16.
98. Ibid., pp. 191–92.
99. Ibid., pp. 192–93; Frederick *Maryland Union,* November 3, 1864.
100. William E. Smith, II:294, footnote.
101. William B. Hesseltine, p. 383.
102. *Evening Journal Almanac,* 1865.
103. Ibid., 1865.
104. Godfrey R. B. Charnwood, p. 426.
105. Of three Union candidates for Congress, one was William Higby, the lone Douglas delegate from California attending the 1860 Charleston National Convention; the other, Douglas leader John Bidwell.
106. War Democrats serving as Union party chairmen: Ohio, William H. Smith; Indiana, Joseph A. Wright; Oregon, George H. Williams; New Jersey, Joseph C. Potts.
107. War Democrats on the Union State Central Committee of Connecticut included: John J. Jacques, James T. Pratt, W.H. Chollar, F.S. Wildman, D.S. Ruddock, O.S. Williams, Abijah Catlin, William R. Smith, William Dorrance, and J.T.P. Ladd, all of whom had served as delegates to the War Democrat Union Convention of 1863. New Haven *Palladium,* March 1864 (every edition).

14

John Wilkes Booth: Avenging Angel of Conservative Tradition

The 1864 election results ushered in the Reconstruction period, without a moment's pause. And as Commander of the Middle Department, bordering on Washington, War Democrat General Lewis Wallace of Indiana became at once a leading figure in the Reconstruction drama. While the Maryland Free-State Constitution was under consideration by the 1864 State Constitutional Convention, certain Maryland slaveholders in consultation decided in favor of a policy designed to nullify the anti-slavery aspects of the constitution, in the event of its adoption, by means of an "apprenticeship" labor system similar to Russian serfdom. (The system would become famous later in other states, under the name of the "Black Codes.") As Commander of the Middle Department, General Wallace was advised of the apprenticeship plan, which he regarded merely as a legal maneuver to reestablish slavery under a different name. On the day following the Maryland elections, he therefore issued General Order No. 112 granting military protection to all Negro freedmen residing in the Middle Department, until the Maryland legislature convened in January 1865. The same order created the Bureau of Freedmen's Affairs, for the state of Maryland, and specifically outlawed the "apprenticeship" labor system. Wallace's policy was in line with the spirit of the Emancipation Proclamation, and was hailed by Maryland Radicals as the only acceptable basis of operation. Conservatives objected on the ground that the Emancipation Proclamation did not apply to Maryland.[1] Wallace bore the brunt of all such criticism, but he was not an independent policy-maker. As the agent of the War Department, he carried out the dictates of Secretary of War Stanton, and none of Stanton's policies regarding slavery contradicted those of President Lincoln. The Radical anti-slavery program forced upon Maryland, in 1864–1865, must be regarded as Lincoln's handiwork; and once again, the policy-enforcer was a War Democrat. The Freedman's Bureau established in Maryland by General Wallace was a forerunner to the national Freedman's Bureau, established by Congress March 3, 1865, at the urging of the American Freedmen's Inquiry Commission, appointed by War Democrat Edwin M. Stanton and chaired by War Democrat Robert Dale Owen.[2]

The major Democrat in uniform in 1865 was General Ulysses S. Grant, assaulting the Confederate defenses at Petersburg, Virginia. His only remaining rivals for acclaim by this time were Republican General William T. Sherman, involved in the March to the Sea, and Democratic General Benjamin F. Butler, engaging in an all-out assault against Ft. Fisher, the Confederate stronghold at Wilmington, North Carolina. Repulsed at Ft. Fisher under embarrassing conditions, Butler was presented with a presidential order relieving him of command.[3] Few Democrats in uniform were as thoroughly hated by the pro-slavery forces, at this stage, as General Butler. His name was anathema to them and they prayed for his comeuppance. News of the Ft. Fisher fiasco was hailed as a blessing in pro-slavery circles throughout the loyal states.[4]

In the same manner as Rosecrans at Chickamauga, Burnside at Fredericksburg, and Hooker at Chancellorsville, Butler had failed as an army commander in his last major undertaking. And in the same manner as the others, he would be classified, historically, as a military incompetent.

*   *   *

Another War Democrat in the news in the early months of 1865, was James Speed of Kentucky, who entered the cabinet as Attorney General at the close of 1864. A Douglas Democrat in the 1860 campaign, in company with Judge Advocate General Joseph Holt and Congressmen Green Clay Smith and Lucian Anderson of Kentucky, Speed had followed the same course as they, from mild Conservative to angry Radical. As a replacement for the Conservative Edward Bates of Missouri, he changed the balance in the cabinet from moderate to Radical, and his opinion, as a border slave-state man and a former Democrat, was of consequence to Lincoln.

*   *   *

When the third and "lame duck" session of the Thirty-eighth Congress assembled in December 1864, the first issue for consideration was the annual presidential message proposing adoption of an anti-slavery Amendment to the Constitution. Although defeated twice previously, in 1864, for lack of Conservative Unionist support, the measure at last appeared likely of passage. Not only was it now endorsed by Lincoln, but by many other Conservative Unionists deeply impressed by the 1864 election results.

Ashley of Ohio, a Lincoln Radical, had charge of the Amendment, and the first to defend it were members of the same faction. The first War Democrat to speak in their support was a lame-duck Unionist, Creswell of Maryland. Slavery, he said, was a curse that almost had destroyed the glory of his state which, by rights, should rank among the wealthiest in the Union. With two great ports and an abundance of farmland and industrial talent, Maryland initially had challenged the commercial leaders of the Northeast. But slavery had changed all that, degrading labor, scaring away northern capital, and driving the small farmer from the land. It also had dehumanized the Negro, Creswell said, although it now appeared the Negro was ready to reclaim his manhood in every regard. The war had shown that the Negro was not what slave-holders had always said he was. Where were the Negro insurrections that slaveholders had warned the North about for years? They had not taken place, despite the opportunity. And had the Negro proved a coward in battle, as he was supposed to be? On the contrary; even now the Confederates were making plans to incorporate their own Negroes in the front lines, having witnessed the bravery of Negro troops in the Union army. The clamor for compensated Emancipation, got up by slaveholders in the loyal states, was unworthy of recognition, because slavery and the rebellion walked hand-in-hand. If one died, they both should die, and without compensation.[5] Peace Democrats Brooks of New York, Bliss of Ohio, and Rogers of New Jersey denounced Creswell's arguments in the name of the federal Constitution which, they said, denied to Congress the right to free a single slave. Rogers said further that slavery had not brought on the war. It was all the fault of the Abolitionists, he said. War Democrat William Higby of California (Union party) joined with Republicans in denying Rogers' statement.[6]

War Democrat Odell of Brooklyn, who had voted for the Amendment in June 1864 and subsequently failed of renomination by the Regular Democracy, delivered a strong speech, attacking all Democrats opposing the Amendment. "The South," he said, "by rebellion has absolved the Democratic party at the North from all obligation to stand up longer for the defense of its 'cornerstone.' " Confederate plans to free their slaves and use them in the lines, against the Union, made an absolute mockery of the Union's past policy of protecting the slavery institution. The Democratic party had been wrecked by slavery, Odell declared, and so had the Union, and so had the independent, slaveless farmers of the South. All would benefit by the Amendment. He realized that most of his Democratic colleagues disagreed with him on the slavery question, but, "I yield to none of them in my attachment to the party with which I have ever acted. . . .I believe this thing of slavery has lifted its hydra head above the Government of my country. It has been for years a dead weight upon our party. And the time. . .has now come when we as a party ought to unloose ourselves from this dead body. . .The times now favor, and the way is open for the great Democratic part to turn its back upon the dark past and its eyes upon the bright future."[7]

The pro-slavery advocates fired back with warnings of political doom and social chaos. If enacted, the proposed Amendment would ruin the country, they said. It would alter "the organic law of the Constitution," prevent reunion of North and South, and/or establish an "aristocracy" of anti-slavery states. It was impossible to amend the Constitution without the presence and support of two-thirds of the members electable under the Constitution, and the absence of so many southern members prevented the possibility of such a vote. Socially, miscegenation was bound to result. War Democrats speaking for the pro-slavery cause included Townsend and Ward of New York, Clay of Kentucky, and Holman of Indiana. Peace Democrats joining in the attack included Fernando Wood of New York and Pendleton of Ohio.[8] Some time later it would be said that Cox of Ohio had worked mightily for passage of the Amendment, behind the scenes. Even publicly, he now attacked Negro slavery as "the most repugnant of all human institutions," but sorrowfully opined that the Congress was powerless to kill it.[9]

On January 13 the pro-Amendment forces brought out the first of several surprise witnesses, a few of whom were Regular Democrats who had campaigned for McClellan, in 1864. Rollins of Missouri announced a total change of heart. "I am proud that a man has a right to change," he said. "I am gratified that I am not too obstinate to change." When the Declaration of Independence observed that "All men are created equal," it meant that every man was "created in the image of his Maker. . .without regard to race, color, or any other accidental circumstances by which he may be surrounded." His own state of Missouri would be far better off today, he said, if slavery had been outlawed the moment the war began.[10]

When the House debate on the Amendment was just beginning, Peace negotiations were inaugurated between Washington and Richmond, with Francis P. Blair, Sr., serving as the agent of the federal government. Blair returned in mid-January without result. (Something more would later come of this undertaking, but it was not yet apparent.) Disgusted by the obstinacy of the Confederates, War Democrat McAllister of Pennsylvania presented a statement in the House, reversing his position on the Amendment. Although voting against it the previous June, he said, the Confederates had made him change his mind. Slavery, was indeed the "cornerstone of the Confederacy," and therefore must be smashed.[11]

Unexpectedly, Peace Democrat Coffroth of Pennsylvania came forward to agree with McAllister's remarks. The proposed Amendment was not unconstitutional, nor even sectional, because it could not become law without the ratification of several southern states. As a man of Peace, he now had decided that the end of slavery meant the end of the war.[12] The statement came as a great shock to Peace Democrat Miller of Pennsylvania, who disputed the logic of it, blaming the anti-slavery conversion of his good friend, Coffroth, on the influence of their congressional colleague, War Democrat Baily of Pennsylvania.[13] (Coffrath and Baily had argued the slavery issue for years, and Baily apparently had been the most convincing.)

Herrick of New York was the next Regular Democrat to reverse himself. The recent election results had made clear, he said, that the people of the loyal states wanted slavery abolished, and he was in favor of following the wishes of the people. If the present Congress did not pass the Amendment, with Democratic support, the next Congress (already elected, and with a monumental Unionist majority) was certain to do so, without Democratic support. In Herrick's opinion, the approaching vote on the Amendment presented "a desirable opportunity for the Democracy to rid itself at once and forever of the incubus of slavery, and to banish its perplexing issues beyond the pale of party politics. . . ." The Democratic party was ruining itself by driving away the anti-slavery men, "until our once powerful organization has trailed its standard in the dust and sunk into a hopeless minority in nearly every State in the Union; and every year and every day we are growing weaker and weaker in popular favor, while our opponents are strengthening, because we will not venture to cut loose from the dead carcass of negro slavery." Why should northern Democrats support the slavery institution when southern ones, such as John A. Rollins and Austin A. King of Missouri, were ready to abandon it? The state of New York was certain to go Democratic again, Herrick said, once slavery was out of the picture. But if the Democratic party were ever to regain its former grandeur, "it must now let slavery slide."[14]

The vote followed, shortly afterward. The House galleries were filled for the occasion and there was grave doubt that a two-thirds majority could be attained. The first surprise came when a Peace Democrat, Baldwin of Michigan, voted for the measure. The next was the 'aye' vote of Regular Democrat English of Connecticut.[15] A flurry of applause came from the

Union side of the House. It was repeated when Regular Democrat Ganson of New York also voted 'aye.' Speaker Colfax rapped for order, admonishing the House members. The vote continued. Regular Democrats Hall of Missouri and Herrick of New York voted 'aye.' So did Regular Democrats King of Missouri, McAllister of Pennsylvania, and Nelson, Odell, and Radford of New York, Steele of New Jersey, and Wheeler of Wisconsin. Every War Democrat in the Union party coalition voted for the Amendment, including the border slave-state members: Anderson and Smith of Kentucky, Brown of West Virginia, Loan and McClurg of Missouri, and Thomas of Maryland. (The free-state members were Baily of Pennsylvania, Ingersoll of Illinois, Marvin of New York, and Shannon and Higby of California.) When the House Clerk had finished calling the roll, Speaker Colfax directed that his name also be called, which was done, and Colfax voted 'aye.' He then announced that the measure had passed, with the necessary two-thirds majority, and the galleries responded with wild enthusiasm. Members on the Unionist side of the House sprang to their feet and, without regard for rules or decorum, cheered and applauded. Male spectators in the crowded galleries waved their hats and ladies their handkerchiefs, adding to the excitement. When the chamber quieted down War Democrat Ingersoll of Illinois moved that the House adjourn in honor of the occasion. Peace Democrat Harris of Maryland demanded a call of the roll, but Ingersoll's motion carried, 121 to 24.[16] When the Amendment was dispatched to the several states, to be considered by the state legislatures, it was supported by all of the War Democrat governors elected on the Union ticket: Brough of Ohio, Cony of Maine, Cannon of Delaware, Carney of Kansas, Lewis of Wisconsin, Gibbs of Oregon, Hall of Missouri, Hahn of Louisiana, Murphy of Arkansas, and even Bramlette of Kentucky, who had campaigned for McClellan.[17]

While the House was in the process of considering universal Emancipation, the states of Delaware, Tennessee, and Missouri were grappling with the same problem. In his annual address to the state legislature in January 1865, War Democrat Governor Cannon of Delaware recommenced an anti-slavery amendment to the state constitution. In Tennessee, War Democrat Governor Andrew Johnson made the same recommendation to the assembled state constitutional convention, despite the irregular nature of the action (the convention having been called for another purpose). There being very few lawyers present and many Union soldiers, the Governor's arguments were readily accepted. Johnson wanted slavery abolished and he also wanted loyal men to rule in Tennessee. The delegates agreed and the work was begun.[18]

Emancipation was now the ruling force in Missouri politics. In his farewell address, War Democrat Governor Hall declared that, "Slavery will be abolished, with the almost unanimous approval of the people of

Missouri.'' The State Constitutional Convention assembled, to attend to the matter, January 6. As in Tennessee, few lawyers were present and Union Army veterans were very vocal. The Radical leader, War Democrat Charles D. Drake, was in charge of matters from the start. His purposes were identical to those of War Democrat Governor Andrew Johnson: not only to abolish slavery, but to guarantee the rule of loyal Union men. To this end he recommended the adoption of a stringent voting oath, similar to that employed in Tennessee, with the object of denying the franchise to the disloyal. The recommendation was approved and enacted by the convention.[19]

The Delaware legislature rejected the anti-slavery proposal of Governor Cannon, who was hampered in his operations by the fact that he was sick and in the process of dying. The legislature voted down Emancipation, only to have Congress override the action within a matter of days. Governor Cannon passed away March 1, 1865, and his passing symbolized the end of a political era. He was replaced by a Peace man, elected by the legislature.[20] In this manner Delaware became the first border slave state to repudiate the Union party tradition.

The star of the Tennessee State Constitutional Convention was Governor Andrew Johnson, who addressed the delegates frankly concerning the extra-legal nature of their undertaking. How would history regard them? he asked. ''Suppose you do violate the law, if by so doing you restore the law and the constitution, your consciences will approve your course, and all the people will say, Amen! You are without law and without a constitution, and it is your duty to get it back for the people.'' It was important to kill slavery and reestablish civil government to once. The convention should do so, without concern for legal technicalities.[21] Acting on the Governor's advice, the delegates drew up resolutions proposing several constitutional amendments to be voted on by the people in February 1865, abolishing slavery, disfranchising many whites, and enfranchising many Negroes.[22]

Although the Missouri State Convention did not agree to the Negro vote, War Democrat Charles D. Drake of Missouri sought the same two goals as Andrew Johnson of Tennessee—abolition of slavery and the guaranteed ascendency of loyal Union men in the Reconstruction process. (Seeking the election of *all* state officials under the terms of the stringent voting oath of 1865, the Missouri Convention required the resignation of every state official currently in office. All complied except two Supreme Court justices who had to be removed by force, in June, 1865.[23])

The so-called ''Johnson Constitution'' of Tennessee was ratified by the voters, 25,293 to 48.[24] The so-called ''Drake Constitution'' of Missouri was ratified by a vote of 43,000 to 41,000.[25] In both cases, the result was described as a fraud by the Regular Democracy, on the contention that the loyalty oath had scared away the voters. Radical Governor Fletcher of Missouri was disturbed by the stringent oath, as were War Democrats John B. Henderson and Francis P. Blair, Jr. of Missouri. But Drake was very persuasive and managed to convince both Fletcher and Henderson that the oath was necessary to the Union cause.[26]

When Andrew Johnson of Tennessee resigned his commission as Military Governor to take up his vice presidential duties, in Washington, he was replaced in Tennessee by a civil Governor: William G. Brownlow, elected in March under the stringent voting laws recommended and approved by Johnson.[27]

*　　*　　*

On March 3 the Thirty-eighth Congress adjourned. On March 13 Lincoln was inaugurated President for the second time and War Democrat Andrew Johnson was sworn in as Vice President. The outstanding feature of the occasion was an unprecedented address delivered by the Vice President immediately following the swearing-in ceremony. Although later denied by his supporters, it was generally believed at the time that Johnson was drunk. On April 2 Confederate General Lee ordered the evacuation of Petersburg and the city was occupied by Union forces the following day. Shortly afterwards, peace negotiations were inaugurated between Grant and Lee, with Grant, as always, looking to his Chief of Staff, Democratic General John A. Rawlins, for council and advice. Although Lee proposed the discussion of political issues touching on the "restoration of peace," the suggestion was denounced by Rawlins as a trick. "He wants to entrap you into making a treaty of peace," Rawlins protested to Grant. No treaties or political discussions were in order. All that was in order was Confederate surrender. Anything else was out of Grant's authority; so Rawlins advised.[28] On that basis, the peace negotiations were resumed, leading to the surrender of General Lee at Appomatox, April 9, 1865.

On the night of April 14, 1865 the coalition of Lincoln and the War Democrats was destroyed by the assassination of Lincoln, at Ford's Theater in Washington. Appropriately, the assassin was a Peace Democrat, John Wilkes Booth of Maryland. Personally speaking, Unionists in general were grief-stricken by the assassination. Politically, they were outraged and all semblance of respectability fell suddenly from the Peace Democracy. In every loyal state, leading Peace Democrats stood in danger of physical attack.[29] Moderation was a dead letter in the loyal states for the time being. Fury was suddenly in style, and thousands upon thousands of Unionists expressed their thanks that Andrew Johnson, the fierce, angry, and uncompromising dictator of Tennessee, had been selected by stern Providence to succeed to the mantle of the gentle martyr. Certainly no more forceful, no less sentimental, no more vindictive Unionist could have been found for the task, if one were to judge from the evidence at hand. Lincoln's close ally, War Democrat John W. Forney, observed in the Philadelphia *Press,* "The loss we have sustained—the loss of Abraham Lincoln, that great and good man—is one which had been determined on by God. It is—we say this with reverence, but unhesitatingly—to God's purpose that he has been taken from us. A sterner and less gentle hand may at this juncture have been required to take hold of the reins of Government."[30] A new era was approaching for the War Democracy; an era devoted to a thorough suppression of the remnants of rebellion, at the direction of the tigerlike Andrew Johnson, Grand Captain of the War Democracy, General-in-Chief of the Union party, and President of the United States.

Or so it seemed in mid-April, 1865

NOTES

1. Charles B. Clark, pp. 197–98.
2. According to Senator Charles Sumner of Massachusetts, President Lincoln had announced the intention of naming Robert Dale Owen to head the federal Freedman's Bureau. The death of Lincoln led to the appointment of another man, General Oliver Otis Howard by President Johnson. Richard W. Leopold, p. 365.
3. Richard S. West, Jr., pp. 272–92.
4. Carl Sandburg, *Abraham Lincoln: The War Years,* 4 vols. (New York: Harcourt, Brace, 1939), IV:24.
5. *Congressional Globe* (38th Congress, 2nd Session), pp. 120–24.
6. Ibid., pp. 155–56.
7. Ibid., pp. 174–75.
8. Ibid., pp. 221–25; 238.
9. At this moment, Cox was very hopeful of arranging meaningful peace negotiations between Washington and Richmond. He was tired of defending slavery and said so, but he would not endorse the Amendment, because he feared that the Amendment would wreck the negotiations. He therefore contented himself with a sudden, unexpected attack on Peace Democrat Brooks of New York, an ardent pro-slavery man. "Speaking for myself," said Cox, "Slavery is to me the most repugnant of all human institutions. No man alive should hold me in slavery; and if it is my business no man, with my consent, shall hold another. This I voted in 1851, in Ohio, with my party, which made the new constitution of my own State. I have never defended slavery; nor has my party." As a former Whig, Peace Democrat Brooks "did not profess to speak for the Democratic party. . . , nor does (he) . . . commit any Democrat to his moral convictions." *Congressional Globe* (38th Congress, 2nd Session), January 12, 1865; reprinted in Loyal Publication Society, pamphlet 80, *America for the Free Working Man* (New York, 1865). In 1868, William H. Seward would maintain that the Amendment owed its passage to the backstage labors of Cox, notwithstanding his vote against it. William V. Cox and Milton H. Northrup, *Life of Samuel Sullivan Cox* (Syracuse, 1899), p. 95.
10. *Congressional Globe* (38th Congress, 2nd Session), pp. 258–62.

11. Ibid., p. 523.
12. Ibid., p. 523.
13. Ibid., p. 524.
14. Ibid., pp. 525–26.
15. A War Democrat in the Thirty-seventh Congress, English was a Conditional in the Thirty-eighth. He always had stood by slavery in the past but he took great satisfaction in voting against it on this occasion, regarding it as the most important vote he ever cast in his life. *Representative Men of Connecticut, 1861-1894.* (Everett, Mass.: Massachusetts Publishing, 1894), p. 359.
16. *Congressional Globe* (38th Congress, 2nd Session), p. 531.
17. Allen Johnson and Dumas Malone, eds., II:596.
18. Henry C. Conrad, I:213; Sceva B. Laughlin, "Missouri Politics. . . ," vol. XXIV, no. 2 (January, 1930): p. 275. Clifton R. Hall, p. 168; Galusha Anderson, p. 342.
19. Henry C. Conrad, I:213.
20. William B. Hesseltine, p. 388.
21. Clifton R. Hall, p. 168.
22. Ibid., pp. 165, 169–70.
23. William E. Smith, II:347.
24. Clifton R. Hall, p. 173.
25. William E. Smith, II:347.
26. Sceva B. Laughlin, "Missouri politics. . . ," vol. XXIV, no. 2 (January 1930):p. 274.
27. Clifton R. Hall, p. 173.
28. James H. Wilson, pp. 318–19.
29. Louis C. Hatch, II:469; *Union Army,* IV:408.
30. Quoted in Robert S. Harper, p. 355.

15

War Democrats without Lincoln: 1865 and After

War Democrat Andrew Johnson of Tennessee was inaugurated President April 15, 1865. As his first major executive act, he rejected the Durham Station surrender terms accepted by General William T. Sherman. It was Johnson's intention that Sherman be spared the humiliation of public censure, but his views were so badly stated as to utterly confuse two of his subordinates—Edwin M. Stanton, Secretary of War, and Henry W. Halleck, Army Chief of Staff. Sherman was therefore criticized publicly by his superiors, and humiliated. In matters concerning slavery and race, Sherman was Conservative—Republican, but Conservative; and by 1865 War Democrat Stanton was, in many respects, acting with the Radicals. In pondering the fact of his diplomatic failure and subsequent embarrassment, Sherman concluded (in the same manner as McClellan, following the Peninsula Campaign) that Stanton had been out to get him—that he had sought to hurt the standing of a Conservative, for the purpose of pleasing the Radicals.[1] But Sherman's opinion was not necessarily correct, and there are grounds for regarding it as altogether wrong. Stanton the Radical was not the only person who had misunderstood the President, to the detriment of Sherman. Halleck the Conservative was equally confused. Responsibility for the misunderstanding would appear to have rested with Johnson.

A second surrender by Confederate General Johnston, without political reservations, proved satisfactory to the President and the cabinet, and the war at last was over. Meanwhile, the frenzied search for Lincoln's murderer was receiving the full attention of the country, and several War Democrats were prominently engaged in the chase. Preceding and following the inauguration of President Johnson, Secretary of War Stanton directed the wandering operations of the *posse comitus* seeking the whereabouts of John Wilkes Booth.[2] Soldiers involved in the search, in company with civilian police, took orders from Democratic General Winfield Scott Hancock, Military Commander of the District of Columbia.[3] The death of the fugitive was followed, soon afterwards, by the arrest of eight Peace Democrats accused of complicity in the assassination plot. They were remanded to the custody of the Office of the Judge Advocate General and brought to trial on a charge of conspiring with Jefferson Davis and the Confederate Commissioners in Canada to murder the President of the United States.[4] On May 10, 1865, a military commission assembled at Washington, D.C., under the presidency of General David Hunter, and the most famous of American murder trials began. War Democrats involved included Hunter; Judge Advocate General Joseph Holt, Chief Prosecutor; General Lewis Wallace, Commission member; and Senator Reveredy Johnson of Maryland, one of several attorneys for the defense. Doubting the integrity of the Commission, Johnson became discouraged. As the trial wore on, he appeared less and less frequently and his final argument was read by a junior associate, denying the jurisdiction of the court and the legality of military commissions in the United States. The Commission found against the defendants, four of whom were sentenced to be hanged. The verdict and sentences imposed aroused little protest at the time, although one of the prisoners executed was a woman—Mrs. Mary Surratt.[5]

War Democrats Holt and Wallace were major figures once again in the military trial of Henry Wirz, superintendant of Andersonville prison camp, in Georgia. (Another member of the Commission was Democratic General Gershom Mott.[6]) The close of hostilities had brought home thousands of Union prisoners of war, full of horror stories about life in Confederate prisons. Unionist reaction to the pitiful condition of many of the former prisoners was one of considerable political importance, stamping out the traditional American tendency to "live and let live" with defeated enemies. The reaction fell hardest on Superintendant Wirz, under whose authority some 13,000 prisoners had died in confinement. The President of the Commission which heard the case was General Wallace, and War Democrat James Hughes of Indiana began the trial as one of several defense attorneys, in opposition to Judge Holt, who again appeared in person as Chief Prosecutor. Accusing the Commission of gross irregularities, to the detriment of the defense, War Democrat Hughes withdrew from the case before the trial was over.[7] Wirz was found guilty and executed in November 1865.

At the urging of Judge Advocate General Holt and with the full approval of President Johnson, an attempt was made to bring Jefferson Davis to trial before a military commission. The move was prevented only by a Supreme Court decision denying the legality of military trials for civilians in peacetime.[8] The decision came too late to save Mrs. Surratt, but did save her son, John Surratt. Arrested two years later, he was tried in a Maryland civil court at the peak of the Reconstruction controversy, before a jury selected without the requirement of a loyalty oath. Several of the jurors were well-known Secessionists and Lincoln-haters.[9] When the jury deadlocked, John Surratt went free.[10]

In coping with the problems of Reconstruction in 1865, President Johnson was besieged with advice from Radicals and Conservatives alike. It was Johnson who had said, almost before anyone else (in December 1860) that all states seceding from the Union would revert automatically to the condition of territories[11]—the same argument now espoused by Sumner and the "ultra" Wade-Davis faction. The stage apparently was set for the implementation of Radical policy without restraint. But suddenly, within a matter of weeks following his inauguration, Johnson changed his mind about the State Suicide theory, coming out against it.[12] He was to hold thereafter—as had Lincoln—that the President and not the Congress had the power to reconstruct the Union. In this contention he was supported, initially, by all the members of his cabinet, including War Democrats Stanton and Speed. In their opinion, as in his, the President was wholly capable of punishing treason and rewarding loyalty on his own, without congressional assistance. So Lincoln had believed. So Johnson now believed, and the cabinet sustained him, not excepting Stanton and not excepting Speed.[13] War Democrats in general agreed with the cabinet that the President was right in his interpretation of the law. Editors John W. Forney and James Gorden Bennett were loud in praise of the Presidential policy in the early aftermath of war, as were Senators James W. Nesmith of Oregon and Reverdy Johnson of Maryland, Chairman Joseph A. Wright of the Indiana Union State Committee, General John A. Dix of New York, and Congressman Andrew J. Kuykendall of Illinois, to name only a few. Senators Foster and Dixon of Connecticut and former Congressman Blair of Missouri—elected as Republicans, now acting with the Democrats —announced emphatically for the Johnson policy, as did Conservative Republicans in general.[14]

In the summer of 1865 the State Suicide theory of Senator Sumner was restated by Sumner at the Massachusetts Republican-Union State Convention, and by Congressman Stevens of Pennsylvania in the middle of the Pennsylvania state campaign. The generosity of the Presidential Amnesty and Pardoning policy was allowing all but a small number of Secessionists to regain their citizenship and their places of authority. In the estimation of Sumner and Stevens, the policy was lunatic, returning to power the very people who so recently had sought the wrecking of the Union. Of the same turn of mind was War Democrat Robert Dale Owen of Indiana, Chairman of the American Freedman Inquiry Commission, who issued a statement questioning the logic and propriety of increasing southern representation in the Congress on the basis of Negro citizenship, without granting the franchise to the Negro.[15] Similar remarks were uttered in the Wisconsin campaign by War Democrat Matthew Carpenter, speaking for the Republican-Union ticket, and in New Jersey by War Democrat H. Judson Kilpatrick, recently a hero in the March to the Sea.[16] But these were the exceptions. Almost everybody else of consequence was on Johnson's side, in early 1865. At Republican state conventions from coast to coast pro-Johnson men were nominated over anti-Johnson men virtually in every instance. At Democratic gatherings, the pro-Johnson spirit was equally in evidence. In Ohio, the outstanding speaker of the 1865 campaign was Clement L. Vallandigham, the "King of the Copperheads," who created a sensation by extolling his old enemy, War Democrat Andrew Johnson, as the friend of Conservative tradition. Slavery was indeed dead, Vallandigham lamented, and nothing could be done to bring it back. As the next best thing, he urged his wartime followers to rally to the cause of Presidential Reconstruction. Accept the free status of the Negro, and agree to let him pay taxes and serve on juries. The big issue, Vallndigham declared, was Negro voting rights, which must be denied. And the best way to attend to that was to work in concert with the President.[17]

In Iowa, the pro-Johnson Democrats organized a new party with the frank title of "Anti-Negro Suffrage," headed by General Thomas Hart Benton, Jr.[18] In Ohio, Pennsylvania, and Minnesota, no new organization was created but the Regular Democrats campaigned on the contention that the major issue of the moment was one of racial supremacy. All white men concerned for the future of western civilization were called upon to support the Democratic cause, and in every instance War Democrats were named to head the Democratic ticket. Wherever pro-Johnson Unionists confronted pro-Johnson Democrats, the Unionists won—but wherever the issue of Negro suffrage came up for a vote, Conservative Unionists sided with the Democrats, and suffrage was denied. In California, the anti-Negro spirit was extended to the Orientals in 1865, breaking the Union party in half. Conservative Republicans (called Short Hairs) formed a coalition with the Regular Democracy, and a leading War Democrat—U.S. Senator John Conness—jumped the Union party to join the coalition. Following a furious campaign, the Short Hairs were defeated by the regular Republican-Union organization (called Long Hairs), and Conness was destroyed.[19] (He had returned too soon to the embraces of Conservative tradition. In the very next election the Regular Democracy was to regain control of California, running on an anti-Oriental platform.). . .Wherever elections were held in 1865 the Radicals were cursed as lovers of the Negro and challenged to deny it. Seeking a Conservative image, to counteract the Democratic accusations, Union party men turned once again to the War Democracy for leadership. In the 1865 campaign War Democrats headed four Union state tickets, and in every case the candidates ignored the race issue, refusing to discuss it.[20] War Democrat Lucius Fairchild, Republican-Union candidate for Governor of Wisconsin, maintained a fierce silence on the question, despite the demands of his opponents that he state his position, clearly and without equivocation. "I am paying no attention to them," he wrote. "They can all go to hell."[21]

Despite exceptions to the rule, it was apparent by December 1865 that the pro-Johnson forces controlled the Republican-Union party machinery in almost every loyal state. So the election results suggested and so the President was informed by his supporters, right and left. The Presidential Reconstruction policy retained the backing of the major Republican-Union newspapers in every section. It had the powerful blessings of Wall Street.[22] Although it later would be claimed that northern businessmen had urged the Radical politicians along and/or acted in concert with them, against the Conservative Reconstruction policy of President Johnson,[23] that was simply not the case. The businessmen favored the Presidential Reconstruction policy in 1865. Only after it was dead were they ready to declare in favor of the Radicals. Also in favor of the Presidential Policy, in 1865, was a grand assemblage of vocal war heroes, including Democratic Generals Grant, George H. Thomas, Logan, Sheridan, Meade, Hancock, Steedman, Schofield, Custer, Slocum, George W. Morgan, Runyon, Thomas Hart Benton, Jr., Hamilton, Hobart, and Couch, to name only a few.[24]

Outnumbered, out-influenced, out-publicized, out-financed, and opposed by a popular prejudice of the greatest magnitude (the Negro race issue), the Radicals had seemingly very little chance of victory, when Congress reassembled in December 1865. The race issue was clearly the most important political matter of the moment and the loyal states were obviously Conservative along this line. Everything was pointing to Conservative success and Radical failure. But the Johnson Reconstruction policy had a way of working against itself. When the South Carolina State Constitutional Convention called an election for October, the voters bypassed every Unionist and neutralist nominee in contention, in favor of well-known Confederate heroes. The action was typical of the course to be followed by the Conservative southern majority during the entire period of Presidential

Reconstruction.[25] Out of the conventions came Conservative legislatures and the "Black Codes," seeking creation of a new kind of slavery.

In the process of establishing Presidential Reconstruction policy, Johnson had selected several commanders for the Union military forces occupying former Confederate territory. Most of them were War Democrats, of whom the best known was General Daniel E. Sickles, the "Hero of Gettysburg," commanding the Department of South Carolina. A Tammanyman in Antebellum times, Sickles had converted to anti-slavery during the war, in company with thousands of other War Democrats, but he was definitely Conservative in the matter of Reconstruction until December 1865, when the South Carolina Black Codes went into effect.[26] Astonished by the nature of the Codes, Sickles responded with a general order, issued January 1, 1866, declaring null and void every law specifically designed to harm the Negroes in the state. Henceforward, he declared, "All laws shall be applicable alike to all inhabitants." Sickles also was distressed by violence on the part of Conservatives against the homes and property of freedmen and of federal facilities designed for their benefit, especially schools. If such violence continued, he warned, he would move all freedmen from the area where they were under attack, and provide for their safety at the expense of their former masters.[27] Violence was increasing in South Carolina, under Sickles' command, and the more it increased, the more Radical he became. When several of his troops were murdered, he arrested some suspects, tried them before a military commission, and when called upon to release them, by a federal judge, ignored the order of the court. (The precedent here was laid down by Lincoln in the Merryman case of 1861.[28])

Continued violence in the former Confederacy against freedmen, occupation troops, federal officials, and Union veterans of both races were altering the political attitudes of many who had initially endorsed the Johnson Reconstruction policy. One of these was Andrew J. Hamilton, Provisional Governor of Texas; another, Senator-elect Michael Hahn of Louisiana; another, Judge Samuel Milligan of Tennessee. All were War Democrats and all had once held high hopes for the Johnson Reconstruction policy. Seeing it in operation, they were losing their enthusiasm for it.

The same response was apparent in Congress, in December 1865. President Johnson's Annual Congressional Address, setting forth the Presidential Reconstruction policy, received applause from many quarters, but had little effect on Congress itself.[29] Despite the extraordinary election campaign of 1865, in which almost everybody endorsed the presidential policy, the anti-Johnson forces fared very well when Congress assembled in December, securing an even break in chairmanships, major committee assignments, and other influential positions. Impressed by Radical organization and dismayed by Conservative confusion and the pro-Johnson declarations of many wartime Copperheads, a large number of freshmen Unionists trooped into the Radical camp, in company with numerous veteran campaigners previously regarded as Conservative.

Accepting the leadership of Radical Congressman Stevens of Pennsylvania, the Thirty-ninth Congress refused to seat the senators and representatives elected under the Presidential Reconstruction policy. The Republican-Union majority voted for creation of a Joint Committee on Reconstruction, with fifteen members, authorized to examine the whole Reconstruction question and render proposals for Congressional action. In the House, eleven War Democrats voted for the bill. In the Senate the number was four. (All were members of the Republican-Union party.[30]) War Democrats appointed to serve on the committee included Senators Reverdy Johnson of Maryland and George H. Williams of Oregon.[31] Johnson was a devoted admirer of Presidential Reconstruction; Williams one of its severest critics.

President Johnson was infuriated by creation of the Joint Committee, and as time passed and his policy continued to be criticized in Congress his fury increased. Responding to this development, the Peace Democracy began to rally to the Presidential cause, whereupon some leading War Democrats decided to desert it without delay. As of New Year's Day 1866, eastern Conservatives included in their number War Democrats John W. Forney and James Gorden Bennett, editors of the influential New York *Herald,* Philadelphia *Press,* and Washington *Chronicle.* Bennett of the *Herald* was intrigued by the growing conflict within the Union party and urged the President along, calling for the sacking of the Radicals. But Forney of the *Press* and *Chronicle* was appalled by the sudden alliance of Johnson and the Copperheads, and withdrew his blessings from the Presidential policy. In his extraordinary Washington's Birthday Address of 1866 (in which he questioned the loyalty of Sumner and called for the hanging of Stevens), the President went out of his way to characterize War Democrat Forney as a "dead duck." Despite the unprecedented nature of the speech, the President retained the backing of many influential Conservatives, of whom a notable example was War Democrat Bennett of the *Herald,* who came out in favor of the sentiments contained in the Washington's Birthday Address, urging the President to drop the Radicals at the earliest opportunity.[32]

Reports of violence in the former Confederate States were regarded by Conservatives as Radical propaganda, designed to discredit the Presidential Reconstruction policy. But the Radicals believed the reports and called for law and order. Civil courts established under the Johnson state governments were said to be working to the total disadvantage of the Negro freedmen, who reportedly could not obtain justice from any but the most exceptional civil magistrate. Johnson supporters denied these claims as well, but the Radicals believed them. In keeping with the Radical viewpoint, the Joint Committee on Reconstruction reported out a bill indefinitely extending the life of the Freedmen's Bureau, with the object of further protecting the freedmen from intimidation, assault, and general mistreatment. One of the main features of the bill was a provision permitting the trial of civilians by military commissions in all cases involving the alleged abridgement of the freedmen's rights. The bill was vetoed by President Johnson on the grounds that the states affected by it had not been represented in Congress when it was passed, and that the provision for the military trial of civilians violated the Constitution.[33]

Many Lincoln Radicals looked upon the veto as wholly justified. War Democrats in this category included Secretary of War Stanton and Attorney General Speed; Senators Henderson of Missouri and Conness of California; Congressmen Griswold of New York and Thomas of Maryland. They also believed that another piece of legislation—The Civil Rights Bill—would accomplish all the goals of the Freedmen's Bureau Bill, without stepping on the Constitution.[34] The Civil Rights Bill conferred citizenship on the Negro, assuring him equality of treatment before the law. To the surprise and chagrin of the Lincoln Radicals, President Johnson vetoed the Civil Rights Bill, declaring it clearly in defiance of states' rights, and certain to revive the spirit of rebellion. The veto lost the President the backing of many Lincoln Radicals in Congress and was promptly overridden by a sizeable majority. Only seven members of the President's own party in the House voted to sustain him.[35] Stunned by the action of Congress, the President fought back through the patronage system, removing 2,500 federal office holders identified with the Radical cause. In their places went Conservatives, meaning in most cases War Democrats and Conservative Republicans, although sometimes Peace Democrats were also appointed.[36] In addition, the President utilized the veto power, with devastating effect. Two bills defeated in this manner sought the admission to the Union of Nebraska and Colorado. If enacted, they would have provided the Radicals with six more votes in Congress; four in the Senate and two in the House. Another veto defeated the new Freedmen's Bureau Bill. There were enough Radical votes to override the last of these vetoes but the other two were sustained, as were some earlier ones. An impasse was at hand.

In this situation, the Radicals were by no means united. Many Radicals now were Negrophiles, and wanted Negroes to have the vote, on equal terms with whites. Many other Radicals were *not* Negrophiles, and were very much aware of anti-Negro feeling in the North. Anxious to prevent the return of southern Conservatives to power, they dared not utilize the Negro vote in seeking that result, for fear of a Conservative reaction by their own constituents.

To break the logjam caused by division in the Radical ranks, Congressman Stevens came forward with a proposal to amend the Constitution in such manner as to permit the establishment of Negro voting rights in the South, without requiring their establishment in the North. The author of the plan was a War Democrat—Robert Dale Owen, Chairman of the American Freedman Inquiry Commission. Under the proposed Amendment, the Negro would receive the vote in every state in which the legislature agreed to the plan, and every such agreement would result in an increase in congressional representation. Northern states were in this manner free to kill the Negro vote, as were also southern states. But if the southern states killed it, they also killed the chance of increasing their political power in Washington. The plan was not to give the Negro anything in the way of political power, merely to keep him from serving as a silent pawn for his enemies in the South. Conservative newspapers, which had been gloating over the prospect of increased southern representation in the Congress, were outraged by the Owen Plan, and sharply critical of its author. James Gorden Bennett of the War Democrat New York *Herald* was especially vitriolic in his references to Owen's past.[37]

Yet the Owen Plan was nothing as compared to another Amendment proposal offered in the Senate by War Democrat John B. Henderson of Missouri, demanding Negro voting rights in North and South alike. As author of the Thirteenth Amendment and as a known friend of the martyred Lincoln, Henderson was not without prestige at this point. But his proposal was too much for the Radicals to swallow. Many northern states had just gotten through voting on the Negro franchise, and all which had done so were against it. Northerners had no objection to Negroes voting in the South, as Owen's plan would permit them to do; but Negores voting in the North was quite a different matter. Ignoring northern prejudice, Henderson insisted on a universal suffrage, North and South. As a southerner, he said, he could not stand by and watch while the North imposed a system on the South which was itself abhorent to northerners.[38] Nobody argued with Henderson, but nobody voted with him either. His amendment proposal was set aside, in favor of Owen's which (although itself amended) was in essence enacted in June 1866 as the Fourteenth Amendment to the Constitution, and dispatched to the states for final consideration.[39] The President declared against the proposed Amendment, and called upon the voters to sustain him. In breaking completely with the Radicals at this juncture, he was urged along by Conservative advisors who assured him that the people were certain of rejecting the Radical demands. Everywhere it seemed, War Democrats associated with the wartime Union party were returning to the Democratic party. In April 1866, the Union party of Connecticut (headed by War Democrat James T. Pratt) pulled free from the Republican-Union coalition, declaring for the Regular Democracy. A War Democrat—James E. English—was the Democratic candidate for Governor, and the party platform was a ringing endorsement of Presidential Reconstruction. Conservative Republicans in Rhode Island bypassed the Radicals to nominate War Democrat Ambrose E. Burnside for Governor, and everything possible was done to avoid association with Radical purposes in Washington. On this noncommital basis, Burnside was elected and the Republican-Union party retained control of the state. War Democrat English was defeated in Connecticut, but by very little.[40] The Republican-Union cause was clearly in a perilous condition there and elsewhere in New England.

The return of congressional representation to the former Confederate states was expected to deliver the last crushing blow to the Radical cause in 1865, and the Radicals in Congress were said to be desperate. All over the country, War Democrats were declaring for the President and warning the Radicals that Presidential Reconstruction must be permitted to proceed, without congressional interference. War Democrat John A. McClernand of Illinois, who had joined the Radicals in wartime, now announced against them. He was quoted as saying that southerners elected to Congress under the Johnson state governments should come to Washington and occupy their seats, "peacefully if they could, forcibly if they must."[41] Montgomery Blair of Maryland, now acting with the Democrats, declared a willingness to work against the Radicals with the aid of the "Rebels or anyone else."[42] In Ohio, the outstanding Johnson-man was Clement L. Vallandigham; in New York, it was Fernando Wood. The Presidential forces included members of all the wartime factions, excepting only the Radicals.

Creation of the conservative National Union party in 1866 was supposed to merge these forces to the total dismay of the Radicals in Congress. But many War Democrats and many Conservative Republicans had come to recognize the weakness of the Presidential Reconstruction policy and the growing power of the Peace Democracy in the pro-Johnson camp. For all their irritation with the Radicals, they had no interest in a giant Peace parade, which apparently was in the process of formation with Johnson in the lead, accompanied by Vallandigham, Wood, and the rest of the Peace establishment. Strongly opposed to the call for a National Union Convention were the War Democrats in the Johnson cabinet—James Speed, U.S. Attorney General, and Edwin M. Stanton, Secretary of War. Speed resigned in protest, July 17, but Stanton did not resign. He had considered doing so several months earlier, before the outbreak of the war between President and Congress, but had been persuaded not to by several of his friends, including Governor Morton of Indiana and War Democrats Samuel Cony, Governor of Maine, and John W. Forney of the Philadelphia *Press* and Washington *Chronicle*. None of the advisors was hostile to the President at the time (indeed Morton and Forney were two of his strongest supporters), but all of them were wary of Conservative influence in the cabinet, especially that of Seward. Stanton should remain in office, they insisted, to properly advise the President. In a sense, the war was not yet over and Stanton could not yet be spared. Accepting these arguments, Stanton abandoned his retirement plans for the moment,[43] and as time passed, and as the President did in fact adopt a position out of keeping with Stanton's notions of reason and good sense, retirement was utterly forgotten. A special aspect of Stanton's importance was his power over the movements of U.S. military forces. For as the controversy increased between the President and Congress, both sides became disturbed about the possibility of military assault by the other; and in both cases it was feared the assault would be engineered by the Union Army itself.[44] In line with these fears, the Johnson forces were especially alarmed by creation of a veterans' association, the Grand Army of the Republic, in which the leaders were identified with the Radical cause. The founder of the group was War Democrat John A. Logan of Illinois, and a leading organizer in Illinois was War Democrat Robert G. Ingersoll. In Antebellum times they had led the Conservatives in Little Egypt, but both were now Radical—especially Ingersoll, who was going around talking like an Abolitionist. In Massachusetts, the leading member of the G.A.R. was War Democrat Benjamin F. Butler, another Radical.[45]

While plans for the pro-Johnson National Union Convention were being acted upon throughout the North, trouble was developing in certain sections of the former Confederacy supposedly pacified by the Presidential Reconstruction policy. In every such case, Radical Unionists claimed persecution at the hands of the Conservatives, without the vaguest possibility of obtaining justice from the Johnson state governments. In every such case, the answer to the problems of the Unionists was clear: that the only way of keeping the Conservatives out of power was to ratify the Fourteenth Amendment, now pending in the counsels of the several state legislatures. In Louisiana, Radical War Democrat Thomas J. Durant was now joined by War Democrat Michael Hahn, Senator-elect and former leader of the Conservative Unionists. Despairing of justice under Presidential Reconstruction, Hahn came out in favor of the Fourteenth Amendment, supporting Durant in the campaign to reconvoke the State Constitutional Convention of 1864. Johnson Conservatives denounced the proposed convention as illegal. If ever it should actually assemble, they said, violence was certain to result. The convention *was* called, violence *did* result, and the Conservative cause was ruined as a consequence. (Over 200 Negroes and Radical whites were killed in the New Orleans riot, and many more were wounded. One of the wounded was War Democrat Michael Hahn, who was shot in the leg and crippled for life.)[46]

The National Union Convention met in the shadow of the riot, from which it never was able to escape. Its strongest point was the presence of so many well-established War Democrats, including General Dix of New York, Tilden and Church of New York; former Governor Parker of New Jersey; former Congressman English of Connecticut; Senators Johnson of Maryland and Stockton of New Jersey; former Congressman Packer of Pennsylvania and Winthrop and Abbott of Massachusetts. But for all their contributions, they could not overcome the stain of New Orleans and the unrequested blessings of Vallandigham, Wood, and the entire Peace Democracy, not to mention those of some Confederate veterans. The highlight of the National Union campaign was President Johnson's ill-starred "Swing Around the Circle," which proved almost as disastrous to his cause as the butchery at New Orleans.[47]

The Loyal Union Convention, called by the Radicals in response to the Conservative gathering, was far more impressive, and the contribution of the War Democracy considerably more dramatic. The keynote speaker was War Democrat James Speed of Kentucky and the outstanding delegate War Democrat Benjamin F. Butler of Massachusetts. Others in attendance included War Democrats John W. Forney of Pennsylvania, Governor Burnside of Rhode Island, Governor Cony of Maine, Governor Fairchild of Wisconsin, Senator Williams of Oregon, Senator Creswell and Congressman Thomas of Maryland, Congressman Van Horn of Missouri, Thomas J. Durant and former Governor Hahn of Louisiana, former Governor Hamilton of Texas, and Daniel H. Hoge of Virginia. Butler of Massachusetts was a leading supporter of the Fourteenth Amendment, among the delegates, as were also Williams of Oregon and Hamilton of Texas. When the convention adjourned, War Democrats Hamilton of Texas and Butler of Massachusetts set off on a tour of their own, to rival the President in his Swing Around the Circle. The War Democrat New York *Herald,* still supporting Johnson, described the Hamilton-Butler performance as the "journey of the negrophiles and the miscegenes."[48]

Counting on the Conservative nature of military tradition, and hopeful of combatting the Radical influence of the Grand Army of the Republic, the Johnson forces sought to mobilize the great mass of Union veterans against the interests of Radical Reform. The Soldiers and Sailors Convention at Cleveland, September 17, amounted to an all-out assault on the Fourteenth Amendment by 3,000 veterans, most of whom were Democrats. General George P. Este of Ohio was temporary chairman; General John E. Wool of New York, permanent chairman. Both had been members of the wartime Union party and both had worked for Lincoln in 1864. Addressing the convention, Wool condemned the Radicals as Abolitionists. In wartime, he had himself opposed the cause of slavery by impeding enforcement of the Fugitive Slave Law in his department. But that was all forgotten. The "Abolitionists" must now be stopped, he said. They were a menace to the country—"a body of revengeful partisans with a raging thirst for blood and plunder." On hand for the occasion was Democratic General John A. McClernand of Illinois, a Lincoln supporter in 1864. Also, present were Democratic Generals James W. Denver of California, Willis A. Gorman of Minnesota, Alexander McD McCook of Ohio, Edward S. Bragg and Harrison C. Hobart of Wisconsin, Thomas E. Bramlette of Kentucky, Herman H. Heath of Nebraska (formerly of Iowa), Charles E. Phelps of Maryland, and many more.[49] Chief targets of the numerous speakers were the Fourteenth Amendment and Secretary of War Edwin M. Stanton (who was harshly condemned in a round robin signed by many of the delegates).[50]

Meeting the Conservative challenge once again, Radical supporters of the Fourteenth Amendment sent out a call for their own Soldiers and Sailors Convention, which assembled at Pittsburgh, September 25. War Democrat John A. Logan of Illinois was chosen to preside, but replaced by another at his own request. The best-known War Democrats in attendance included Logan, Benjamin F. Butler of Massachusetts, Ambrose E. Burnside of Rhode Island, John W. Geary and John S. Negley of Pennsylvania, John Cochrane of New York, William D. Leggett of Ohio, Thomas S. Allen of Wisconsin, John McNeil of Missouri, and Edmund G. Davis of Texas.[51]

The delegates denounced the President for "his attempt to fasten his scheme of Reconstruction upon the country", describing it "as dangerous as it is unwise." Presidential Reconstruction policies were said to have "retarded the restoration and unity, . . .converted conquered rebels into impudent claimants to rights which they have forfeited and to places which they have desecrated. If the President's scheme be consumated it would render the sacrifice of the Nation useless, the loss of her buried comrades vain, and the war in which we have so gloriously triumphed a failure, as it was declared to be by President Johnson's present associates in the Democratic National Convention of 1864."[52] The driving force of the Pittsburgh convention was said to be War Democrat Benjamin F. Butler; the most eloquent delegate, War Democrat John Cochrane, who said of the Fourteenth Amendment that "a more complete, just, and righteous platform for a whole people to occupy has never before been presented to the National sense."[53]

It must be concluded that of the four great national conventions staged in 1866, the two Radical ones made the greatest impression.[54] By mid-October, the number of Old-Line Republicans supporting the President had dwindled to a handful.[55] Among the War Democrats, editor James Gorden Bennett of the New York *Herald* swung over to the Radicals in time to influence the New York elections.[56]

Eighteen loyal states elected Congressmen following the national conventions, two in September, four in October, and twelve in November. If the National Union party were to win control of Congress, it was required to unseat 25 Radicals incumbents. From that vantage point it would be possible, with the seating of the southern delegations elected under Johnson rule, for the National Unionists to organize the House. But none of this transpired. In the Republican-Union district conventions, not one National Unionist was nominated for Congress, and of the National Unionists nominated by the Regular Democracy only six were elected.[57] All in all, the Congressional Reconstruction forces elected 128 House members to the House; the Presidential Reconstruction forces, 34.[58] The Radical arguments had carried the day.

To the extent that thousands of War Democrats appeared to vote against the War Democrat President in 1866 and in favor of his enemies, it can be observed that all of them had supported either Stephen A. Douglas or James Buchanan in Antebellum times. All had abandoned those idols in favor of Lincoln, and Johnson was not at all like Lincoln. He was part Douglas, part Buchanan. Douglas had been tied to the Popular Sovereignty principle, which was a beautiful theory but simply did not work. Transfering their support from Douglas to Lincoln in wartime, many War Democrats had come to appreciate the extraordinary political abilities of Lincoln, who never stood still, whose policies were always changing, from one minute to another, and who managed, in the meantime, to lead the Union on to victory. Of the two men—Douglas and Lincoln—President Johnson much more closely resembled Douglas. Deciding on a policy, he was determined to see it through, even if the policy failed to work and even if it meant he must destroy his party in the process. Like Popular Sovereignty, the Johnson Reconstruction policy was a grand design without practical application. Yet Johnson could not back away from it, even when he saw it driving off the Unionists and bringing in the Copperheads. There was also a touch of Buchanan in the Johnson Reconstruction policy and the echo of Ft. Sumter—We must yield to the South, regardless of the outcome, because the Constitution can be construed by Conservative lawyers as saying that we must. A great many War Democrats were terribly hostile to that kind of reasoning, in company with a great many Old-Line Republicans. They had been through this whole thing before, back in 1861, and they were not anxious to experience it again.

It has been written and rewritten a thousand times or more that Andrew Johnson attempted to enforce "Lincoln's Reconstruction policy."[59] But there is something not quite right about the statement. In the first place, Lincoln specifically declared that he had no set Reconstruction policy.[60] And in trying to determine what policy he might have decided upon had he lived, it is worth recalling his letter of advice to Governor Andrew Johnson of Tennessee in the summer of 1863. "Let the reconstruction be the work of such men only as can be trusted for the Union," he wrote. "Exclude all others."[61] The firmness of this position was later weakened by the intention of granting a general amnesty, but the amnesty was conceived only as a balance to another intention—to establish "the principle of civil and political equality of both races." So Lincoln declared in a letter to General James S. Wadsworth, in the early weeks of 1864.[62] The Reconstruction policy of President Johnson bore no relation whatever to Lincoln's declarations to Governor Johnson and General Wadsworth.

A large number of Lincoln-men—War Democrats and Old-Line Republicans alike—decided finally, in 1866, that the Presidential Reconstruction policy was not really "Lincoln's Reconstruction policy," after all. If it was truly Lincoln's policy, why was it supported by Vallandigham and Fernando Wood? Why was it supported by every Copperhead in the loyal states and every well-known Confederate in the South? Why was it opposed by the great mass of Conservative Republicans who had supported Lincoln all the way? Lincoln would never have accepted the kind of allies who proved acceptable to Johnson. The very idea was unthinkable. So believing, a large number of War Democrats voted for the Radicals in 1866, and their decision settled the election results.

Campaigning for the Republicans in the following Presidential election, War Democrat Walter Harriman of New Hampshire expressed the opinion of many thousands of his kind, declaring: "perish forever from this green earth, and from the memory of man, a party having for its dearest shibboleth the constitutionality of the rebellion, and the unconstitutionality of putting it down."[63] When the Copperheads came forward to support the constitutional protestations of the President, in 1866, the sentiment so expressed by Harriman appeared to flood the loyal states, at the expense of Presidential Reconstruction.

It often is observed by persons favoring the Presidential Reconstruction policy of 1865–1866, that the political record of War Democrat Andrew Johnson was consistent, clear, and easy to understand from the moment the war began. According to Howard K. Beale: "The truth was that the development of his (Reconstruction) policy had been steady and logical from beginnings under Lincoln and his own experiments in Tennessee to its final form late in 1865."[64] Nothing would seem to be further from the truth. Johnson's policy as Military Governor of Tennessee was Radical, extra-constitutional, and devoted to one cardinal principle: That loyal men and they alone should hold the reins of state government in the former Confederacy. It is a notable fact that Johnson argued frequently with Lincoln about the moderate nature of wartime Reconstruction policy, and sought to make it increasingly Radical, insofar as it applied to Tennessee.[65] As Military Governor, Johnson revealed an extraordinary lack of concern for legal technicalities, and when Tennessee rejoined the Union on July 24, 1866, she did so on the strength of actions taken by the totally irregular Nashville State Constitutional Convention of September 1864. As Governor, Johnson took full responsibility for those irregularities.[66] As President, however, he became at once a man obsessed with legal technicalities, to such an extent that he abandoned the principle he had preached consistently since 1861: that loyal men and they alone should govern. For the sake of legal technicalities and conservative interpretation of the Constitution, he suddenly agreed to the existence of state governments managed by men convicted of disloyalty, at the expense of the political freedom of men who had risked their lives in the national behalf. For reversing himself in this vital moment President Johnson lost, virtually overnight, the support of many thousands of Unionists who had been willing, only one year earlier, to serve as his allies.

The outcome of the 1866 campaign not only finished off the power of the first War Democrat President, but demolished the War Democrats as a political entity. In 1867, the Republican-Union party would shorten its name to Republican and the last shadow of the wartime Union party disappeared. War Democrats affiliated with the Republicans thereafter would merely be known as "Republicans," and nothing more. Let us, however, retain the name "War Democrat" a little longer, in order to follow the wandering of the various and sundry War Democrats of the war years, throughout the remainder of the postwar period. The Radical-dominated Thirty-ninth Congress reconvened in December 1866, and began at once dismantling the Presidential Reconstruction policy. One of the major figures in the dismantling process was a War Democrat—Senator George H. Williams of Oregon. The Radical Reconstruction plan, as finally adopted, orignated in a resolution introduced by Williams,[67] who also introduced the Tenure of Office Act.

As principal beneficiary of the Tenure of Office Act, Secretary of War Edwin M. Stanton has been harshly judged for his connection with it; perhaps too harshly judged. In sympathizing with the Radical side of the Reconstruction controversy he of course was acting for partisan purposes in failing to leave the War Department at the President's demand. But Stanton also was a lawyer and a "letter of the law" man, in the manner of many other War Democrats. As such, he had supported the Missouri Compromise, under Van Buren, Harrison, and Polk, and its repudiation under Pierce; as such, he had supported the Fugitive Slave Law of 1850 and the Lecompton Constitution, adopted under Pierce. As such, he had interpreted the Federal Constitution as guaranteeing the slave property rights of southerners in the antebellum period. He had supported the federal authority against the onslaughts of the Confederacy. In breaking with legal tradition repeatedly throughout the course of the war, he did so only as the agent of the President, acting on the basis of executive war power conferred by the Constitution. If anybody in the war was *consistent* it was Edwin M. Stanton. As a letter-of-the-law man, he might regard the Tenure of Office Act as unacceptable in the estimation of the courts, but he would not himself assail the law until directed to do so by the courts. So far as he was concerned, the Tenure of Office Act was the law of the land, and he would support it on that basis.

In the resulting crisis the War Democracy fragmented once again, some supporting Johnson, some supporting Stanton. The G.A.R., headed by War Democrats John A. Logan and Lewis Wallace, offered military aid to Stanton, and "Andrew Johnson Veteran Volunteers Clubs" came into existence in the East. Conservative veterans in the West rallied to the call of the "White Boys in Blue."[68] In the end the matter went to court, and talk of violence subsided. Out of the controversy came the Impeachment Trial of President Johnson, in which War Democrats served as the starring attorneys for both sides—Benjamin F. Butler of Massachusetts for the prosecution, William S. Groesbeck of Ohio for the defense. To remove the President from office required the vote of 36 senators. The prosecution failed by one vote of securing the required majority. It was generally agreed that Butler, who was seldom outclassed as a trial lawyer, was decidedly outclassed on this occasion by War Democrat William S. Groesbeck.[69]

Four War Democrats voted for removal of the President and seven against.[70] Much attention has been paid to the negative vote of Old-Line Republican Senator Edmond G. Ross of Kansas, which was designated the deciding factor in the outcome of the case. But a one-vote victory renders vital *every* vote. It is interesting to consider the negative vote of War Democrat Senator Daniel S. Norton of Minnesota. Elected to the State Senate with Republican support in the 1860 campaign, Norton also had the backing of the "Railroad" faction, and on that basis won the additional endorsement of the Breckinridge Democracy. Relected without Republican support in 1863, he acted with the Democratic party until the Democrats drew up the Vallandigham Peace platform in 1864, whereupon he entered the Union caucus.[71] When the Radical and Conservative Republicans fought each other to a standstill in the Senate election of 1865, the Radical candidate was incumbent Morton S. Wilkinson, and the Conservatives could not beat him with any of their own established leaders. War Democrats Norton and Henry M. Rice therefore entered the race, seeking the support of War Democrats and Conservative Republicans in the Union coalition.[72] Norton won the nomination and easily defeated the Regular Democratic candidate. So it evolved that Daniel S. Norton never once was elected without approval of a Democratic faction and was, to all intents and purposes, a War Democrat. Upon arriving in Washington, he became a Johnson-man, and when the showdown arrived and Johnson was fighting for his political life, Norton voted for him, as a fellow War Democrat unable to accept the program of the Radicals.

Andrew Johnson was not considered as a presidential nominee by either party in 1868, but the outstanding candidate, courted by both sides, was another War Democrat; Ulysses S. Grant. Republican Congressman Elihu B. Washburne warned his colleagues that "if the Republicans don't nominate Grant, the Democrats will."[73] Grant was offered and accepted the Republican nomination and was duly elected over the Democratic nominee, Conditional War Democrat Horatio Seymour of New York. War Democrat Francis P. Blair, Jr., of Missouri, was Seymour's running mate. The Democratic platform featured the inflationary "Soft Money" proposals of Peace Democrat George H. Pendleton of Ohio.

The currency problems of the postbellum period would produce a great many "friends of the little man," favoring inflation and Soft Money. Pendleton was one of them. Another one, with a far more consistent record on currency matters, was War Democrat Benjamin F. Butler of Massachusetts, who would quit the Republicans in 1883, cursing their desertion of the wartime Greenback and the economic interests of labor and the debtor class. Having entered politics initially as the friend of labor and the ten-hour day, Butler was the logical leader of the Soft-Money cause favored by the working man, opposed by Wall Street. During the controversy over the Soft-Money policies of Secretary Chase, he had sustained the Secretary while Pendleton was opposing him as a dangerous innovator.[74] Of the two men—Butler and Pendleton—the Soft Money faction preferred Butler, who received the presidential nomination of the Greenback party, in 1884. Pendleton was still around at the time, but the Greenbackers wanted Butler.

Because the Reconstruction period was so lengthy and the issues of the period so complex, we have no intention of attempting to analyze it all in one brief chapter. Reference must be made, however, to several of the major Reconstruction issues in which War Democrats were dramatically involved. The two presidential administrations of War Democrat Ulysses S. Grant covered the vital period of Congressional Reconstruction, and the failure of the Congressional program can be partially attributed to the inability of Grant to cope effectivly with the many problems besetting the country at the time. Never an effective politician on his own, Grant initially attempted to obtain the services of those who, in his opinion, could best guide him through political crises; but when influential Republicans denounced his first cabinet selections, he yielded to their opinions and in so doing threw away his lone chance for political effectiveness. As a general, Grant had broken all the rules. One of the first examples in this regard was the selection of a mere politician, War Democrat John A. Rawlins, to serve as Chief of Staff. Upon becoming President, he endeavored to follow the same unconventional pattern, naming Rawlins Secretary of War, War Democrat Adolf Borie of Pennsylvania Secretary of the Navy, and Radical Congressman Elihu B. Washburne of Illinois Secretary of State. None was a political power in the Republican party, but all were friends and acquaintances of Grant's, and each was highly effective in his own field. With such advisors Grant would have been comfortable as an executive, and his decisions might well have been entirely different; but that was not to be. By 1869, the postwar period of industrial expansion already was in full swing, and the business wing of the Republican party already was involved in the full scaie purchase of political influence, which would lead in time to political disgrace. Elihu B. Washburne, whom Grant wanted for Secretary of State, was known as the most honest man in Congress; his nickname: "The Watchdog of the Treasury."[75] At a moment when Wall Street and Congress were preparing to parcel out the public funds among themselves and their friends, it would not do for "The Watchdog of the Treasury" to be on hand in Washington as Secretary of State. In the matter of international commerce, the same business coalition was looking forward to cutting off foreign competition by means of high tariff barriers. A docile cabinet unconcerned with foreign trade was required to permit this maneuver, and War Democrat Adolf Borie of Pennsylvania was not a docile man. As a leader of the War Democracy, in 1862, he had helped to wrench the city of Philadelphia from the control of the Regular Democracy and establish the formidable Union party coalition.[76] Moreover, Borie was an importer and one of the wealthiest in the country and could not be expected to approve a high tariff policy.[77] The business interests insisted on his removal, along with that of Washburne, and Grant agreed to the demand. Ill health compelled Rawlins to retire from the War Department within the matter of a few months. He was replaced by another War Democrat—General William W. Belknap of Iowa, a hero at Shiloh and an able lieutenant of General Sherman in the March to the Sea. (Succumbing to the call of the boodle, Belknap was soon to become involved in the sale of federal offices and was later impeached for malfeasance in office.[78])

The outstanding accomplishment of the two Grant administrations was passage of the Fifteenth Amendment, in 1869, establishing universal suffrage in the Union. The author of the Fifteenth Amendment was the redoubtable War Democrat Senator John B. Henderson of Missouri, previously cited as author of the Thirteenth Amendment and would-be author of the Fourteenth Amendment.[79] Having voted against the removal of President Johnson from office, Henderson had lost favor with his Radical associates in Missouri, and failed of reelection to the Senate. But for all that he remained the voice of ultra-Radical reform—universal male suffrage without racial qualifications, in defiance of Conservative tradition and the strong prejudice of the white majority. The Fifteenth Amendment passed Congress in 1869, was ratified, and went into effect the following year. It was to serve as a major bone of political contention for the next hundred years—perhaps even the next six hundred.

It is noteworthy that John B. Henderson, author of the Fifteenth

Amendment, was a principle member of the War Democracy in Washington. He was beyond question the standout example of Abraham Lincoln's converts from the Democratic party dogma of latter-day origins to the true teachings of Jefferson. A slave-holder and an arch-Conservative on many counts, in 1861, Henderson had crossed over the line—at Lincoln's urging—to stand above the rest as the legislative father of both universal freedom and universal suffrage. Step by step, he had followed Lincoln's leadership, accepting every Lincoln change of mind and Lincoln change of heart—from Confiscation to Gradual, Compensated Emancipation, the Emancipation Proclamation, the use of Negro troops, and—finally —uncompensated Emancipation. It is especially interesting that in the final quarrel between Lincoln and the Radical leadership, over Reconstruction policy, Henderson had sided with Lincoln—and yet when Andrew Johnson sought to associate Lincoln's name with his own brand of arch-Conservative politicking, Henderson refused to go along. It is a fact that Andrew Johnson was not the *only* politician attempting to unravel the riddle of "What would Lincoln have done, had he lived?" There were many others in Washington and Henderson was one of them. In his opinion, Lincoln would have rejected Andrew Johnson's Conservative approach, and gambled once again on the Jeffersonian contention that in matters political, "All men are created equal."

$$* \quad * \quad * \quad * \quad * \quad *$$

Rejecting the Fifteenth Amendment in 1872, the Conservative branch of the Republican party (disguised as "Liberal Republicans") deserted the Radicals again, in favor of eccentric Horace Greeley and the principle of white supremacy. War Democrat Ulysses S. Grant was reelected President by the Regular Republicans, but the Regulars were scared. Hoping to regain Conservative support, they sponsored the Amnesty Act of 1873, returning the voting rights of all former Confederates previously disfranchised for disloyalty. War Democrat Benjamin F. Butler of Massachusetts- —generally regarded as the symbol of Radical vindictiveness—introduced the Amnesty measure in the House.[80] Its passage returned control of the former Confederacy to the Conservative forces opposing the cause of Radical Reconstruction.

The Panic of 1873, continued violence in the South, effective Democratic propaganda concerning "Black Rule" in the South, and southern economic instability, severely damaged the standing of the second Grant administration, to the peril of the cause of Negro civil rights. War Democrats prominently engaged in the battle for Negro civil rights in Reconstruction times included General Daniel E. Sickles of New York; Andrew J. Hamilton, Morgan C. Hamilton, Edmund J. Davis, and Elisha M. Pease of

Texas; Powell Clayton of Kansas; William B. Woods of Ohio; and Walter Harriman of New Hampshire. War Democrats opposing Negro civil rights in Reconstruction times were legion; but the two best known were Andrew Johnson and General Winfield Scott Hancock. General Sickles attracted considerable attention at the outset of Congressional Reconstruction by defending the Negroes of North Carolina against a fantastic whipping orgy sponsored by Conservative whites. Under North Carolina law a man who had been whipped for a crime could not vote. Fearing the result of Negro political power, Conservatives in Sickles' district began arresting Negro freedmen, right and left, and whipping them on any pretext. Sickles outlawed the practice, to the indignation of the Conservative leadership, especially President Johnson, who denounced the General for breaking the law.[81]

Deserting the Presidential Reconstruction policy, War Democrats Andrew J. and Morgan C. Hamilton of Texas campaigned for the Radicals in 1866, and the following year supported the appointment of War Democrat Elisha M. Pease to the office of Provisional Governor, at the order of Democratic General Philip Sheridan, Commander of the Department of Texas and Louisiana. When civil government was restored in Texas in 1870, the first elected Governor was *another* War Democrat: Colonel Edmund J. Davis of the First Texas (Union) Cavalry. Throughout the full period of Congressional Reconstruction, the leader of the Radical Republicans in Texas was War Democrat Morgan C. Hamilton, U.S. Senator, 1870–1877.[82] In Arkansas, the second Republican Governor elected under Congressional Reconstruction, in 1868, was General Powell Clayton, formerly of Kansas and a War Democrat.[83]

William B. Woods was Democratic Minority Leader of the Ohio Assembly in 1861. He entered the army, rose to the rank of major general and when the war was over settled in Alabama, establishing a law practice. Appointed to the bench of the U.S. Circuit Court in 1870, he moved to Atlanta and ten years later was appointed by President Hayes to the U.S. Supreme Court.[84] Walter Harriman, elected Governor of New Hampshire as a Republican in 1867 and 1868, came South in 1872 as a Carpetbagger, to work for the Republicans of North Carolina.[85] Powell Clayton of Kansas came south to Arkansas and served as Governor from 1868 to 1873.[86]

General Winfield Scott Hancock received command in 1867 of the Military District of Louisiana and Texas, in which capacity he declared against trials by military tribunals and so became a hero of the national Democratic party. He was a prominent candidate for the Democratic presidential nomination in 1868, 1872, and 1876, and was finally nominated in 1880. In the ensuing presidential campaign Hancock received almost as many popular votes as the Republican candidate, James A. Garfield, but was badly defeated by electoral votes.[87]

In 1870, one year following his retirement from the White House, War Democrat Andrew Johnson sought reelection as Senator from Tennessee running as an Independent. He was defeated by the votes of East Tennessee Radicals who once had worshipped his name. In 1872, he ran for Congressman-at-Large as an Independent and was again defeated by the votes of his former admirers. In 1875, he received the support of the Regular Democracy and was reelected to the U.S. Senate, largely on the strength of support supplied by former Confederates.[88]

A major aspect of the Reconstruction period was the Conservative campaign to overthrow Radical legislation in the courts, in which endeavor a number of War Democrats were featured on both sides of the issue. Speaking for the Conservatives, the outstanding voice was that of Jeremiah S. Black of Pennsylvania. Speaking for the Radicals, the best was Matthew H. Carpenter of Wisconsin.[89]

The failure of Radical Reconstruction has been laid to many causes, from the alleged ignorance and dishonesty of southern Negro state officials to the scare tactics of the Ku Klux Klan, to the desertion of the Carpetbaggers by northern business interests. Without arguing the point at any great length, we conclude that the major force that killed off the Radical Reconstruction program was the U.S. Supreme Court, which struck down every vital part of the Radical civil rights legislation enacted during the 1860s and 1870s, leaving the southern Negro minority, the Carpetbaggers, and the Scalawags at the mercy of the Conservative southern white majority. War Democrats involved in the several significant court decisions included Stephen J. Field of California (appointed by Lincoln), William Strong of Pennsylvania (appointed by Grant), William B. Woods of Ohio and Georgia, and John M. Harlan of Kentucky (appointed by Hayes), and Stanley Matthews of Ohio (appointed by Arthur.) Of these a large majority assisted in the Court's demolition of the Radical Reconstruction program. Exceptional was War Democrat John M. Harlan of Kentucky who, in the manner of many Conservative Unionists of Antebellum times, regarded with alarm the Conservative destruction of civil rights, at the expense of the southern Negro population.

As Attorney General of Kentucky in 1864, Harlan had campaigned in favor of McClellan and against adoption of the Thirteenth Amendment. Upon passage of the Amendment he had opposed its ratification, siding with Conservatives at every turn. But when he saw the results of Johnson Reconstruction in the former Confederate states and the return of Secessionists to power, he reversed himself, announcing in favor of the Thirteenth Amendment and urging adoption of the Fourteenth. The Democrats swept Kentucky in 1866, and many Unionists deserted the Republicans there to reap the glories of Democratic ascendency; but Harlan quit the Democrats, announcing in favor of the Fifteenth Amendment. He campaigned for Grant in 1868 and ran for Governor in 1871 and 1875 on the Republican ticket, without victory. In 1877 he was appointed to the U.S. Supreme Court, over the angry protestations of southern Democrats, and served for 34 years, in which period he fought for the Radical Reconstruction program and Negro civil rights, without let-up, becoming known as the "Great Dissenter". Retreating from the race issue, the Court declared, in the Civil Rights Cases of 1883, that Congress had no power under the Fourteenth Amendment to protect the Negro against discrimination practiced by individuals. Dissenting with all the vigor of an old-time Abolitionist (which he was not), Harlan insisted that the Court majority had utterly ignored the purpose of the Congress, at the expense of human rights. (Of all his 316 dissenting opinions, he regarded this the most important.) He also objected lengthily to the Court's decisions that the Guarantees of the Federal Bill of Rights are not among the privileges and immunities protected by the Fourteenth Amendment. Nor could he accept as constitutional the racial segregation laws abridging Negro civil rights, since they denied to Negroes the right to equal protection under the law (supposedly guaranteed by the Fourteenth Amendment). His dissents were often furious in tone and charged with emotion. When the Negro was driven from an equal status in the public schools (*Plessy v. Ferguson*, 1896), Harlan's dissenting opinion was a rebuke to the Court unparalleled in judicial history. Defeated all along the line in his fight for Negro civil rights, John M. Harlan was nonetheless a giant among the War Democrats of a later year.[90]

The War Democrats defied party traditions and in many cases changed parties during the war. What was their motivation? It is customary among a certain school of political historians to imply or to frankly declare the belief that the many politicians who transferred from the Conservative column in 1860 to the Radical column in wartime or in the postwar years were acting in the interest of political expediency. This interpretation places the political conversion of War Democrats Edwin M. Stanton, Benjamin F. Butler, and all the rest, in the worst possible light. It is worth noting, however, that the same historians arrive at no such conclusion concerning the motivation of those politicians who went the other way, from Radical in 1860 to Conservative in the postwar years. They were also numerous. Francis P. Blair, Jr., and Montgomery Blair, Jr., were outstanding examples in this regard. So was Horace Greeley. So were Orville H. Browning of Illinois; Salmon P. Chase, and William H. Seward. So were Lafayette S. Foster and James Dixon of Connecticut, Henry Haight of California, Lucius Robinson of New York, Henry W. Slocum of New York, Fitz Henry Warren of Iowa, Gideon Welles of Connecticut, Thurlow Weed of New York, James R. Doolittle of Wisconsin, and many more. They also altered their political convictions during the Civil War period and there is no reason to assume that they did so for the sake of political expediency, any more than there is for assuming that Stanton, Butler, Sickles, Logan, or any of the other War Democrats changed their beliefs merely to get on the winning side. To suggest such a thing without something resembling supporting evidence is to betray the cause of history.[91]

It would not be proper to finish the story of the War Democrats without a special word of defense for those most maligned on the flimiest grounds: Edwin M. Stanton of Pennsylvania, Benjamin F. Butler of Massachusetts, and William Sprague of Rhode Island. Stanton is described in volume after volume as a betrayer of Presidents. It is said that he put the knife to Buchanan, Lincoln, and Johnson, all in the same way; by pretending to agree with them, while all the time conspiring with the Radicals. What is the actual case against him? In his dealings with Buchanan, Stanton followed the same policy as all the proto-War Democrats, attempting in every way possible to prepare the loyal states for war, in the face of Confederate aggression bolstered by Buchanan's overwhelming tendency to feebleness. If in opposing the Confederates in this period Stanton cooperated with the Radicals, there was nothing traitorous in that. The villain of the piece was not Stanton, but Buchanan. To say that Stanton either should have followed Buchanan's lead or else have resigned from the cabinet is to ignore the nature of the whole Secession story and Buchanan's part in it. So far as the Unionists were concerned, Buchanan was on the verge of throwing away the Union, which act he had no right as President to perform. All who interfered, all who obstructed Buchanan in this attempt (Stanton, Dix, Black, Holt, Sickles, and the rest) were worthy of the highest commendation. And *all* of them, at one time or another, worked without Buchanan's knowledge. It was *he* who could not be trusted, in the struggle to preserve the Union, not they.

In the case of Lincoln, Stanton can hardly be accused of duplicitous behavior. He was constantly at Lincoln's side, and Lincoln was not inclined to overlook personal disloyalty. As Secretary of War, Stanton issued hundreds of orders, all of which must have had Lincoln's approval. Had they not, Stanton would have been removed, at once, in the manner of Fremont and Cameron who acted on their own, as anti-slavery men, without consulting Lincoln. We have the word of David H. Bates, manager of the telegraph office at the War Department, that Lincoln and Stanton worked constantly together.[92] That Stanton was capable of fooling Lincoln at such close range for so long a period of time seems highly unlikely. As for Stanton's policy of listening to an argument, nodding and expressing a sense of understanding, but acting afterward against the argument advanced, it may be noted that Lincoln had the same policy. So have many people. It is a confusing and frequently disturbing policy, but does not constitute deceit or wickedness.

In the case of Johnson, Stanton was in agreement with the early phases of Presidential Reconstruction, and when he began to disagree he held his post in what he regarded as the national interest. As Buchanan had seemed to him ready to throw away the Union in 1861, so Johnson seemed ready to do much the same thing in 1866. Why leave at such a time? What is government all about? Is it a matter of not hurting the feelings of a President? Surely, Stanton did hurt the feelings of President Johnson, but that is hardly a matter of political importance. As in 1861 he had exerted his influence against Conservatives working in the political interest of the Secessionists, so in 1866 he did the same. Personal loyalty is the foggiest and least consequential aspect of political life and does not compare with the national interest. In choosing the interests of the Union over personal loyalty to Buchanan and Johnson, Stanton was acting as a statesman.

Next to Stanton, the most vilified War Democrat is perhaps Benjamin F. Butler. The fact that Butler voted for Jefferson Davis at the Charleston convention and supported Breckinridge in the 1860 presidential campaign, only to become a Union general in 1861 and a leading Radical in 1864, seems to flabbergast the average American historian. The fact that hundreds and hundreds of other Breckinridge Democrats followed exactly the same course has apparently escaped their notice altogether. Ben Butler is branded as an opportunist, without proof and without the benefit of mind reading. Those who so denounce him do not know if Butler was sincere or not. They only say that they know. Having read his mind in this regard, they read it again in every other regard, proclaiming him a charletan at every turn. When his underlings fail him in battle (as at Big Bethel) they say it was his fault. (When General Lee's underlings fail him in battle, as at Philippi, Antietam, and Gettysburg, it is customary to blame the underlings. But General Butler has no special rules of that kind to protect him from historical attack.) As a man who had known many gentlemanly southern Democrats in Antebellum times and virtually no Negroes whatever, Butler was a strong Conservative on the Negro race issue when the war began. Upon witnessing the wartime behavior of southern Democrats in general and serving as commander of effective and courageous Negro troops, it is entirely possible that he *really did* change his opinion on the race issue. He just may not have been pretending. (His postwar position on Negro rights is really much easier to understand than that of many other War Democrats, including General James B. Steedman of Ohio, who fought side-by-side with Negroes at Nashville and praised their courage, yet once the war was over did all he could to deny them access to political responsibility and authority.)

Wherever Butler went during his lifetime, sensational rumors followed, and he made it a practice never to deny them. But that does not mean that all of them were true. In New Orleans, he was investigated by hostile federal agents who had nothing to report, afterward, except rumors. Why was nothing found? Why no evidence of wrong-doing? Perhaps it was because Benjamin F. Butler was an honest man; *perhaps even the most honest in the Union!* Until evidence to the contrary is presented there are grounds for believing nothing else.

William Sprague of Rhode Island deserves defense against the charge of insignificance, unimportance, and stupidity. As the husband of Kate Chase, he may have been something less than a smashing success. As a politician, however, he was utterly magnificent. Elected Governor of Rhode Island in 1860, as a Democrat, he broke the hold of the Republican-Know Nothing coalition, which had run the state for six straight years. While the rest of New England remained Republican, from 1860 to 1863, Sprague was able to beat off all Republican assaults, and to establish a sizeable Democratic majority in the legislature. And when he himself converted to coalition with Republicanism in 1863, he was capable of taking the state with him, influencing the change of just enough votes to knock the Democrats out of power and wholly reversing the political situation, virtually singlehanded. It has been written that Sprague was ignorant, and the statement has been often repeated,[93] but there is nothing in his political record to support the contention.

In defending the War Democrats, one comes to wonder about the recent popularity of their rivals, the Peace Democrats. We would hazard a surmise in this regard. During the period when the Negro was a negligible factor in American political life (from 1900 until the Supreme Court school desegregation decision of 1954) a majority of Americans came to disregard the historical significance of the Negro, and a strange alliance came into existence in the field of American political history: The Marxists and the Southern Sentimentalists marching hand-in-hand. Under their guidance we were led to believe that the Republican party was and always had been the party of Wall Street and Big Business and therefore was evil, and all its enemies were therefore good: from Robert E. Lee to Clement L. Vallandigham to William Jennings Bryan to Woodrow Wilson to Franklin D. Roosevelt. The Populist movement also was good, because it was anti-Big Business (which pleased the Marxists) and anti-Negro (which pleased the Southern Sentimentalists.) Out of this agreement arose the notion that the Populists were the forerunners of the New Deal, on the one hand, and successors to the Peace Democrats, on the other (it having been observed that the Peace Democrats had taken a stand in favor of certain economic reforms—notably federal regulation of the banks and the railroads—and were full of bluster about the "Money Power of the Northeast"). Here, we were told, in the Peace Movement of the Civil War period, were the true Liberals of the 1860s; the grand reformers of a bygone day. Carried away on the strains of that refrain, historian Wilfred E. Binkley proclaimed Clement L. Vallandigham the "John the Baptist of Populism."[94]

There is nothing much to be said in favor of this reasoning, excepting that Populism was strong in the South for awhile and the southern Populists did, in fact, promise economic reform in the interest of the local political majority, while at the same time advocating persecution of a local political minority. In that respect the Peace Democracy and the Populists were identical. (In that respect they also were identical to the National Socialist Party of Germany, in the 1932 campaign.) Upon close examination, it would appear that the Peace faction of the Civil War period had nothing whatever to do with political reform. In all respects, it was a negative political force in the manner of the Know Nothings. It was anti-Lincoln administration and therefore anti-anything else that could possibly be tied to the administration by any stretch of consciousness. The railroads, it said, were agents of the administration, overcharging the farmers in the interest of Wall Street, which was also the agent of the administration. The charge was absurd. The banks were the agents of the administration, milking the farmers for the sake of Lincoln and his party. The charge was absurd. Abolitionists were from the Northeast, and so were the business interests, so the war was a plot, arranged to make Abolitionist businessmen rich. So ran the arguments of Clement L. Vallandigham, more properly entitled "John the Baptist of Wonderland." In the same manner ran the arguments of Congressman George H. Pendleton of Ohio. Did the administration favor soft money to help the Union cause? Pendleton was against it, and so were all his Democratic farmer-followers from the Old Northwest. A few years later, in 1868, Pendleton was campaigning for the presidency as a soft-money candidate, with the blessings of his Democratic farmer-followers from the Old Northwest. Was it wrong to use force to sustain the federal authority? Vallandigham thought so, and Pendleton thought so too, from 1861 to 1865. But when the possibility arose that a Conservative President (Johnson) might win control of the army, in his battle with a Radical Congress, Vallandigham was all in favor of the President restoring order by force, at the expense of what?—of democratic government. When the war began, Vallandigham was in favor of Congress running the show, as opposed to Lincoln. His argument was based, he said, on constitutional grounds. When the war was over, Vallandigham was in favor of the President running the show instead of Congress. His argument was based, he said, on constitutional grounds.

To read the speeches and pronouncements of the Peace Democrats is to read the prating of persons obsessed by one thing—the Negro race issue—and that alone. For that they were willing to give up everything else; and because the War Democracy felt otherwise, they came to hate the War Democracy and their hatred has proven infectious, so far as American historians are concerned.

As a result, the War Democrats have been treated very badly by history. In his interesting work, *Damaged Souls,* William Gamaliel Bradford undertakes the worthy enterprise of defending several prominent Americans victimized by history, and one of the defendants is Benjamin F. Butler. Truly, Butler is a Damaged Soul. But he is only one of many, so far as the War Democrats are concerned. Having deserted the most important of Conservative American traditions—the pro-slavery, anti-Negro cause—in 1861, *all* War Democrats were heartily detested by true-blue Conservatives, as of 1865. And those who remained in the battle against anti-Negro tradition during the Reconstruction period were stigmatized, by the same traditionalists, one and all, as adventurers, opportunists, and out-and-out rascals. It was this particular action—the endorsement and assistance of Radical Reconstruction policy by certain members of the War Democracy—that so terribly antagonized Conservatives in general. For acting as they did in this regard, the Radical War Democrats have been castigated in a manner having nothing to do with reason or reality. Historians who will quietly and calmly explain the conduct of Benedict Arnold, and the pro's and con's of Indian massacres, will rant and rave on the subject of Benjamin F. Butler and Edwin M. Stanton. It is quite remarkable. And it is quite respectable, too. To this day, many highly respected historians still are hanging Butler and Stanton without benefit of evidence or judge or jury or anthing other than the gift of hyperbole.

The major crime of the War Democrats who went Radical in the Reconstruction period—of all their variouis alleged crimes—would appear to have been their stand on the subject of Negro Civil Rights. One of the most detested for a time was Robert G. Ingersoll of Illinois, a Douglas Democrat turned Unionist in wartime. At the height of the Reconstruction controversy, Ingersoll had the temerity to say, "I am the inferior of any man whose rights I trample under foot. Men are not superior by reason of the accidents of race or color. They are superior who have the best heart—the best brain."[95] Talk of that nature was the kind that scorched and seared the Conservative tradition of the period. It is the same kind that scorches and sears the Conservative tradition of today; and the man who stirred it all into existence was Abraham Lincoln, the prince of turbulent reform. Conservative historians would have it otherwise, telling weird and terrible stories of the Reconstruction period—of Negro ignorance and Carpetbagger trickery—at the expense of many good War Democrats turned Radical. But what does it all mean? As John Steinbeck has aptly observed, Conservative historians reporting Reconstruction matters are unfortunately inclined to "lie or forget or both."[96]

It has been necessary to speak for the War Democrats in such detail because so much has been said against them. Clearly they baffle many historians. Comfortable historical patterns are arranged, and most of the Civil War factions fit the patterns. But the War Democrats do not. Why should this be? It is our assumption that the War Democrats were basically frustrated reformers. Born to a political faith—the Democratic Party—which quoted from Jefferson and Madison, trumpted about the Rights of Man, serenaded the principles of freedom, and congratulated itself repeatedly for improving the lot of humanity on earth, they had all been forced to wonder, periodically, about the evils of Negro slavery. How did that fit into their philosophy? All had concluded—from Jefferson to Douglas, year in, year out—that the Union was so constructed, under the terms of the Constitution, that it could not survive without slavery. The "South" wanted slavery; the "North" agreed to let her have it in 1787, and that was that. But Democrats have consciences, and consciences cannot always live with easy and foolish answers.

In advance of the Civil War, Abraham Lincoln began appealing to the conscience of the Democrats. He pleaded, he wheedled, he haggled, and he pounded. In the Douglas debates he laughed at Douglas and his arguments and ridiculed the Democratic shibboleths. He stirred the Democratic conscience. Slavery was *not* more important than the Union, he said. Slavery was vile. Slavery was worthless; and every Democrat alive should know it.

In pleading his cause with increasing intensity, from 1832 to 1865, Lincoln wrenched and tore and wrecked a major aspect of Conservative American tradition, and if justice and history went hand-in-hand, he would since have served as the target of Conservative wrath. But Lincoln was a winner and a hero, who had saved the Union, and his power was too great, especially in death, to leave him vulnerable to any such attack. Other targets, less well armored, were needed for the work, and the War Democrats were instantly selected. Having deserted their Conservative principles of the Antebellum past, in the interest of the Union, to follow Lincoln and to endorse his reforms, they were denounced as impure and driven from their patriotic pedestals by politicians and historians anxious to contend that consistency alone is virtuous. On this assumption, Jefferson Davis, Robert E. Lee, and Clement L. Vallandigham all can be hailed as symbols of purity (providing nobody looks too closely), while Edwin M. Stanton, Benjamin F. Butler, Ulysses S. Grant, Joseph Holt, John A. Logan, John B. Henderson, and others of their kind must all be classified as evil power-hungry men, devoid of principle.

As a great speaker and a great politician, Abraham Lincoln did not direct his most profound arguments to those who agreed with him. Instead, he spoke to those who disagreed, most of whom were Democrats. On this basis, he swung the elections of 1860 and 1864. On this basis, he rallied the troops in April 1861. On this basis, he gathered support for the Emancipation Proclamation, the arming of the slaves, and the Thirteenth Amendment. Talking constantly to Democrats, he worried those Radical Republicans who feared he would yield to Conservative tradition. But all such worries were groundless. Lincoln could no more yield to Conservative tradition than water is capable of yielding to the flame. The Democrats were in effect his flock, whom he sought to instruct, and with remarkable success.

Where Jefferson had failed, where Garrison and Phillips had failed, where Greeley had failed, Abraham Lincoln succeeded, in convincing a large portion of the Democratic party in the loyal states that slavery must die that the Union might live. And as the teacher of War Democrat John B. Henderson, U.S. Senator from Missouri and author of the Fifteenth Amendment, he set the stage for an even greater political revolution which has shaken the country for a century since his death, and shakes it still.

NOTES

1. As a general of California Militia, in 1856, Sherman was called upon to undertake diplomatic measures in the hope of replacing vigilante law with official law and order. He bungled the job. An observer declared: "Sherman was a better soldier than diplomatist. He seems to have been a signal failure whenever he attempted the office of intermediary." Gertrude Atherton, p. 194.
2. Otto Eisenschiml, *Why Was Lincoln Murdered?* (Boston: Little, Brown, 1937), presents the argument that Lincoln was assassinated at the order of the Radicals, and that the search for the murderer, directed by Stanton, was purposely meandering and chaotic to prevent anybody from being captured. The argument is not impressive to anyone familiar with police work, which often begins with a search in the wrong direction.
3. As Military Commander of the District of Columbia, Democratic General Hancock issued a special appeal to the Negro residents of the District, declaring: "He has fallen by the assassin, and without a moment's warning, simply and solely because he was your friend and the friend of our country. Had he been unfaithful to you and to the great cause of human freedom, he might have lived. . . .You can do much. . . .You will hunt down this cowardly assassin of your best friend as you would the murderer of your own father." B.F. Morris, *Memorial Record of the Nation's Tribute to Abraham Lincoln* (Washington: Morrison, 1867), p. 117.
4. The attempt of Judge Advocate Genral Holt to implicate the Confederate government in the assassination of Lincoln has been severely criticized by many historians. The theory behind the charge was perfectly reasonable, however. Investigations by Holt's office had brought to light the many seditious operations of the Sons of Liberty as well as the financial relationship between the Sons of Liberty and the Confederate Mission to Canada, which was of course directed from afar by Jefferson Davis. The Confederate Mission had conspired with members of the Sons of Liberty in several instances, for the purpose of aiding the Confederate cause. Morgan's Raid; the planned insurrection in protest against Vallandigham's expected rearrest, in 1864; the planned takeover of the Illinois State Militia, by the Sons of Liberty; the planned capture of Fort Douglas, Illinois, in 1864, and the release of Confederate prisoners there. Could not Booth have been the agent of the Sons of Liberty on the night of the assassination? Judge Advocate General Holt came to believe he had a strong enough case to prove the charge. He was mistaken; but the charge was not absurd; it was perfectly believable.

5. Irving McKee, pp. 78–81.
6. *Union Army*, VIII:183.
7. Irving McKee, pp. 83–89.
8. Allen Johnson and Dumas Malone, eds., IX:183; Howard K. Beale, p. 34. President Johnson wrote a letter to a friend, declaring, "I shall go to my grave with the firm belief that Davis, Cobb, Toombs, and a few others of the arch-conspirators and traitors should have been tried, convicted, and hanged for treason. . . .If it was the last act of my life I'd hang Jeff Davis as an example." Johnson to B.C. Truman, August 3, 1868, *Century Magazine,* LXXXVI (1913): p. 438; quoted in Ibid., p. 34.
9. At the close of the trial, the jury was deadlocked, nine-to-nine. General Thomas M. Harris, a member of the commission that had previously convicted Mrs. Surratt, was disgusted by the Supreme Court decision in the case of *Ex parte Milligan,* preventing further use of the commission system and requiring a return to civil court procedures. When Surratt went free, Harris observed that, "No government could protect itself under such a construction of the Constitution, because no government could ever convict an assassin (of the President) before a jury made up of its enemies as well as its friends." Thomas M. Harris, *Assassination of Lincoln: A History of the great conspiracy* (Boston: American Citizen, 1897), p. 233.
10. Sympathy for Mrs. Surratt grew rapidly in conservative circles, during the Reconstruction period. A Roman Catholic, she appeared as a martyr to many others of her faith, and as a strong conservative, her memory was revered by many former Confederates and Peace Democrats. Civil libertarians, opposing any form of military intervention in civil governmental proceedures, also championed her cause. In time, Judge Advocate General Holt would be accused of killing off Mrs. Surratt for political purposes. The charge was terribly upsetting to Holt, who spent the final years of his life defending his position in the case.
    In the later stages of the controversy the chief witness against Judge Holt was former President Johnson who, in 1865, had failed to act in accordance with a recommendation for clemency signed by five members of the military tribunal. According to Johnson, the recommendation was concealed from him by Holt, until it was too late to act upon. Holt denied the charge, insisting he had shown the recommendation to Johnson, as directed by the tribunal, at a cabinet meeting attended by Stanton, Seward, and James Speed. By the time the public dispute began, Stanton and Seward both were dead, and Speed was refusing to discuss the matter, on the ground that the action in question was cabinet business and therefore private business: so far as he was concerned. (Speed was politically opposed to Holt, at this point, having returned to the Democratic party, and was under no requirement to assist a Republican in difficulty.) Holt therefore turned to former Congressman Horace Maynard of Tennessee, who cast some doubt upon the recollections of former President Johnson. In 1872, Johnson, Maynard, and a third candidate had staged a series of joint debates in a contest for election to the House of Representatives. On several occasions, Johnson was interograted concerning his part in the execution of Mrs. Suratt. "His defense was manly and statesmanlike," Maynard recalled; "nothing apologetic or deprecatory. She had been fairly tried, convicted of a dreadful crime, and sentenced by a constitutional tribunal, and he had seen no such circumstances of palliation as would justify executive interposition." According to Maynard, Johnson never once "excused himself on the ground that the recommendation for clemency signed by five members of the tribunal had been withheld from him, or that in any aspect he had not fully comprehended the case. "Had he urged such defense," said Maynard, "it would surely have attracted my attention, and I could hardly have forgotten it."
    Speaking in his own behalf, Holt inquired of Johnson why he had failed to

bring his charges to bear sooner, when he was President, at which time he could have called on Seward and Stanton for substantiation, and prosecuted Holt for the commission of a terrible crime. The answer was clear, said Holt. Johnson wanted to wait until Seward and Stanton had passed away, in order to make his accusations without fear of contradiction. *Rejoinder of Joseph Holt, Judge Advocate General, to Ex-President Johnson's Reply to His Vindication of 26th August Last* (1873).

At the civil trial of John Surratt, Holt was accused of suppressing important evidence in the military trial of Mrs. Suratt, notably the diary of John Wilkes Booth, and charges were hurled against him and all the members of the military commission for accepting with regretable credulousness certain testimony which was now denied by other witnesses. Allen Johnson and Dumas Malone, eds., IX:182–83.

Democratic General Lewis Wallace, who voted for the conviction of Mrs. Surratt and therefore was also a party to her execution, was not nearly so disturbed about the matter as Judge Holt. In Wallace's opinion, looking back upon the case, the trial of Mrs. Surratt by the military tribunal had been a bad mistake. But the war had caused many people to make many bad mistakes, he said. This was only one of them, and he refused to regard it as a major one. Irving McKee, p. 89.

11. Speech cited in Kenneth M. Stampp, *And the War Came*, p. 37.
12. Frank Moore, comp., *Speeches of Andrew Johnson* (Boston: Little, Brown, 1866), pp. 483–84.
13. Howard K. Beale, p. 35.
14. Ibid., passim.
15. Richard W. Leopold, p. 366.
16. Kilpatrick was active in New Jersey politics in the 1850s as a supporter of Democratic Congressman George Vaile, who sponsored him as a candidate for West Point. James W. Moore, *Kilpatrick and Our Cavalry* (New York: Widdleton, 1865). In 1865, campaigned for Union party candidates in New Jersey, against Governor Joel Parker, who supported both the Democratic ticket and Presidential Reconstruction. Opposing Parker and Presidential Reconstruction, Kilpatrick declared: "I am not willing to see the rebels of the South, whose hands are yet red with the blood of our fallen braves, restored to all their rights and privileges; and that, too, before they have shed one penentential tear for the great crimes they have committed." Charles M. Knapp, p. 151.
17. George H. Porter, p. 204.
18. Cyrenus Cole, pp. 378–79.
19. Theodore H. Hittel, pp. 393–404.
20. War Democrats campaigning for Governor on the Republican-Union ticket in 1865 included: incumbant Samuel Cony of Maine, General Lucius Fairchild of Wisconsin, and Paul Dillingham of Vermont. All were elected.
21. Mary B. Dearing, p. 66.
22. Governor Oliver P. Morton of Indiana wrote President Johnson, December 7, 1865, that he had the full support of the "financial and commercial departments of business" in New York City. Howard K. Beale, *The Critical Year. A Study of Andrew Johnson and Reconstruction*, p. 49. Among political leaders of the Reconstruction period, those most closely identified with the commercial interests were War Democrat John A. Dix of New York and Conservative Republicans Edward Evarts and Hamilton Fish of New York, all of whom supported Johnson, in company with the New York *Journal of Commerce* and all other such publications associated with Wall Street.
23. Matthew Josephson, *The Politicos, 1865–1896* (New York: Harcourt, Brace, 1938), pp. 13–19; Claude G. Bowers, *The Tragic Era: The Revolution after Lincoln* (New York: Houghton, Mifflin, 1920), pp. 115–18; 146.
24. Generals Slocum, George W. Morgan, Thomas Hart Benton, Jr., Runyon,

Hobart, and Couch were all candidates for Governor on the Democratic ticket in 1865. Grant, George H. Thomas, Cochrane, Dix, Halleck, Sheridan, Meade, Hancock, Steedman, Custer, and Schofield declared in favor of the Presidential policy. *Tribune Almanac,* 1866; Howard K. Beale, pp. 48, 49, 110, 119; Robert W. Winston, *Andrew Johnson, Plebian and Patriot* (New York: Holt, 1928), p. 340.

25. Howard K. Beale, p. 37.
26. At the New York Republican-Union State Convention of 1865 the paramount issue was the Presidential Reconstruction policy, and in the balloting for Secretary of State General Sickles was the choice of the Conservative faction. De Alva Stanwood Alexander, III:129–30.
27. Francis B. Simkins and Robert H. Woody. *South Carolina during Reconstruction* (Chapel Hill: University of North Carolina Press, 1932), p. 57.
28. Ibid., p. 57.
29. Following the Presidential Address to Congress, War Democrats George Bancroft and John A. Dix publicly declared for the Presidential Reconstruction policy. So did Massachusetts Republican James Russell Lowell and Charles Francis Adams. Howard K. Beale, p. 49.
30. *Congressional Globe* (39th Congress, 1st session), pp. 6, 30.
31. Ibid., pp. 57, 106.
32. Howard K. Beale, p. 87.
33. Robert W. Winston, pp. 348–49.
34. Howard K. Beale, pp. 85, 87.
35. Ibid., p. 92.
36. *The Nation,* September 6, 1866, p. 191; September 27, 1866, p. 241. For partial list of federal officials appointed by Johnson during the great purge of Radical office holders in 1866, see *Evening Journal Almanac,* 1867, pp. 24–25.
37. Richard W. Leopold, p. 321.
38. *Congressional Globe* (39th Congress).
39. Ralph Korngold, *Thaddeus Stevens,* p. 339.
40. War Democrat James T. Pratt, founder of the Union party in Connecticut, declared for the Johnson policy in December 1865 and ended all connections with the Radicals of the wartime Buckingham administration. Howard K. Beale, p. 49. George W. Peet, a member of the Douglas Executive Committee in the 1860 campaign and a prominent Lincoln supporter in 1864, declared for Johnson. He would run for Congress on the Democratic ticket in 1884. Richard D. Hubbard, a Democratic candidate for Congress in 1857 and a Union party man in wartime, declared for Johnson and at once assumed command of the Democratic organization in the state. He would serve as a Democratic Governor in 1876–1877.
41. Edmund Whipple, "The Johnson Party," *Atlantic Monthly* (September 1866): reprint, p. 7.
42. Ibid., p. 7.
43. Howard K. Beale, p. 103.
44. Edmund P. Whipple, pp. 7–8; Mary R. Dearing, pp. 105–8.
45. Mary R. Dearing, pp. 59, 82.
46. John R. Ficklin, "History of Reconstruction in Louisiana (through 1868)," *Johns Hopkins University Studies in Historical and Political Science,* series XXVIII, no. 1 (1910): pp. 162–68; Allen Johnson and Dumas Malone, eds., VIII:88.
47. Howard K. Beale, pp. 362–69.
48. Robert W. Winston, p. 369.
49. National Convention of Union Soldiers and Sailors. . . , Cleveland, 1864.
50. Ibid., p. 5.
51. Philadelphia *North American and State Gazette,* September 27, 1866; James G. Blaine, II:231.

52. Ibid., II:232.
53. Ibid., II:232.
54. II:232–33.
55. De Alva Stanwood Alexander, III:159, 163; George H. Porter, p. 283; New York *Tribune,* October 16, 1866; New York *Times,* October 2,5, 1866; Howard K. Beale, p. 107.
56. Ibid., p. 109.
57. War Democrats elected to Congress in 1866 with the backing of the National Union party included Morgan and Mungen of Ohio, Holman of Indiana, Haight of New Jersey, Noell of Missouri, and Phelps of Maryland. Among War Democrats running for Congress on the Republican-Union ticket, for the first time, eleven were elected over Democrats supported by the National Union party. The winners were: Butler of Massachusetts; Ingersoll, Raum, and Logan of Illinois; Peters of Maine; Robinson of New York; and Mullins of Tennessee.
58. *Biographical Congressional Directory,* 1774 to 1911.
59. Charles H. McCarthy, *Lincoln's Plan of Reconstruction* (New York: McClure, Phillips, 1901).
60. In his last public address, Lincoln said: "In the Annual Message of December, 1863 and accompanying Proclamation, I presented a plan of reconstruction (as the saying goes). . . .I distinctly stated that this was not the only plan which might be acceptable; and I also distinctly protested that the Executive claimed no right to say when, or whether members should be admitted to seats in Congress from such States." Roy P. Basler, ed., VIII:401–2.
61. U.S. War Department, *Official records.* . . series III, vol. III, p. 789; quoted in Clifton R. Hall, p. 106.
62. John G. Nicolay and John Hay, eds., XI:131; quoted in Archer H. Shaw, *Lincoln Encyclopedia,* p. 272.
63. Amos Hadley, p. 275.
64. Howard K. Beale, p. 36.
65. Clifton R. Hall, pp. 74, 114, 119, 131.
66. Ibid., pp. 147, 167, 168. Addressing the delegates of the Nashville Constitutional Convention of 1864, Johnson had said: "Suppose you do violate law, if by so doing you restore the law and the constitution, your conscience will approve your course, and all the people will say, amen!"
67. Allen Johnson and Dumas Malone, eds., XX:262.
68. Mary R. Dearing, pp. 138–42.
69. The main burden of the prosecution argument was expected to fall on Thaddeus Stevens of Pennsylvania, who had intended to emphasize that President Johnson was, in the opinion of the House, politically dangerous to the Union, as a result of his policies in general, not merely because he had broken a single law. Stevens was dying, however, and was thereby prevented from directing the prosecution's case. Upon taking Stevens' place, General Butler did not see fit to follow Stevens' plan of action. Instead he attempted to convince the Senate that the breaking of a law was good enough grounds for removing the President from office. Ralph Korngold, *Thaddeus Stevens,* pp. 417–18. Adolphus B. Miller, *Thaddeus Stevens* (New York: Harper, 1939), p. 350. According to Butler, the Presidential right to pass upon the constitutionality of the Tenure of Office Act was exhausted by his veto. Thereafter, he was bound to respect the action of the Congress, whose action had nullified the veto. To act in any other way "would in effect be for him to execute his veto and leave the law unexecuted." That was a course he could follow "at his peril;" but that peril was impeachment. David M. De Witt, *The Impeachment Trial of Andrew Johnson* (New York: MacMillan, 1903), p. 413. Speaking for the President, War Democrat Groesbeck denied that any kind of

actual law was ever really broken, because whenever "an act of Congress be unconstitutional it is no law; it never was a law; it never had a particle of validity, although it went through the forms of congressional enactment; from the beginning *ab initio* it was null and void, and to execute it is to violate that higher law, the Constitution of the United States, which declares that to be no law which is in conflict with its provision." Ibid., p. 474.

Following the vote against the removal of the President from office, Congressman Stevens of Pennsylvania, the Radical leader, was exceedingly disturbed. He nonetheless paid tribute to Groesbeck, saying, in the House, that "the gentleman. . .implored the sympathy of the Senate with all the elegance and pathos of a Roman senator pleading for virtue; and it is to be feared that his grace and eloquence turned the attention of the Senate upon the orator rather than upon the accused." Quoted in Ibid., p. 481.

70. War Democrats voting in favor of removing the President from office included the following (all Republican-Union): John Conness of California, Charles D. Drake of Missouri, William Sprague of Rhode Island, and George H. Williams of Oregon; those opposed (total, seven: Regular Democrat, four; Republican-Union, three): Charles R. Buckalew of Pennsylvania, Thomas A. Hendricks of Indiana, Reverdy Johnson of Maryland, and George Vickers of Maryland (Regular Democrat), James A. Dixon of Connecticut, John B. Henderson of Missouri, and Daniel S. Norton of Minnesota (Republican-Union). *Tribune Almanac*, 1869.

71. Winona (Minnesota) *Democrat*, October 20, 1860; Harlan P. Hall, *H. P. Hall's Observations from 1849 to 1904* (St. Paul, 1905), pp. 65–66.

72. Ibid., pp. 65–66; Lucius F. Hubbard and Return I. Holcombe, III:111; William D. Folwell, II:343.

73. Harriette Dille, p. 90, fn.

74. When the House passed the National Currency Bill, February 20, 1862, establishing a Soft Money policy, for the sake of an inflationary wartime economy, Pendleton voted in the negative. So did several others who supported the "Pendleton Plan" (Soft Money) in 1868 (e.g., Samuel S. Cox of Ohio, William S. Holman of Indiana, Clement L. Vallandigham of Ohio, and James C. Robinson of Illinois. *Congressional Globe* (37th Congress, 2nd Session), p. 1148.

75. Allen Johnson and Dumas Malone, eds., XIX:505.

76. Although supporting the war from the start, Borie rejected all appeals to assist the People's (Republican) party in 1861, instead campaigning actively for the Democratic ticket. Philadelphia *Fitzgerald's City Item*. October 12, 1861. By 1864, he had joined the Union party, supporting Lincoln for reelection.

77. Allen Johnson and Dumas Malone, eds., II:464.

78. Ibid., II:148.

79. William D. Foulke, II:103–4.

80. Robert S. Holzman, p. 209.

81. Fawn M. Brody, *Thaddeus Stevens, Scourge of the South* (New York: W. W. Norton, 1959), p. 301.

82. Charles W. Ramsdell, "Reconstruction in Texas," pp. 176–256.

83. *National Cyclopedia of American Biography*, X-80; *Union Army*, VIII:56.

84. Allen Johnson and Dumas Malone, eds., XX:205.

85. Amos Hadley, pp. 224–28; 273–75; 307.

86. *Union Army*, VIII:56–57.

87. *Tribune Almanac*, 1881. Garfield's popular majority over Hancock was only seven thousand votes out of nine million cast.

88. *Biographical Directory of the American Congress. 1774–1911*, p. 761. The Republican party lost control of the Tennessee legislature in 1870 and the requirement of the loyalty oath was instantly removed, permitting the election

of former Confederates to office. Stanley J. Folmsbee, Robert E. Corlew, and Enoch L. Mitchell, *Tennessee. A Short History* (Knoxville: University of Tennessee Press, 1969), pp. 370–72.

89. In addition to Carpenter, War Democrats working in the courts for the Radicals included John B. Henderson and Charles D. Drake of Missouri, Benjamin F. Butler of Massachusetts, and James Hughes of Indiana. In addition to Black, War Democrats working in the courts for the Conservatives included Reverdy Johnson of Maryland and Thomas C. Durant of Louisiana. (In the early years of Reconstruction, the Conservatives also had the services of Carpenter, before he changed sides). One of the earliest of the several Reconstruction trials of national importance involved a Missouri law requiring the swearing of a loyalty oath by every minister of the gospel. When the war was over a Catholic priest, Father Cummings, brought suit against the state, denying the constitutionality of the law. War Democrat Senator Reverdy Johnson of Maryland came out to Missouri to speak in behalf of Father Cummings, against the arguments of War Democrat Senator John B. Henderson of Missouri. The Republican party of Missouri, to which Henderson now belonged, was fighting the combined forces of the loyal Democrats and returning Confederates and was therefore hopeful of retaining the power of the oath, to prevent the ex-Confederates from voting. If disloyal ministers could preach again, they reasoned, it was very likely that disloyal voters would soon be voting again. The decision of the federal court, handed down in 1866, gave the victory to Johnson and the Conservatives over Henderson and the Radicals. William E. Smith, II:350–53; Harold E. Hyman, *Era of the Oath; Northern Loyalty Tests during the Civil War and Reconstruction* (Philadelphia: University of Pennsylvania Press, 1954), pp. 110–13.
Reverdy Johnson also accepted another important case, involving the disputed right of a former Confederate to practice law before the U.S. Supreme Court. This was *Ex parte Garland* (1867) in which War Democrat Matthew H. Carpenter of Wisconsin was also employed by the Conservatives. At issue was an act passed in January, 1865, disbarring southern attorneys from Federal court unless they subscribed to an oath that they had never voluntarily borne arms against the government or given counsel to anyone engaged in armed hostility thereto. Speaking against the law, Johnson and Carpenter denounced it as *ex post facto* and a violation of the constitutional prohibition against bills of attainder. They also argued that their client had received a presidential pardon which could not be set aside in this manner. As in the case of Father Cummings, the Court declared again against the oath. E. Bruce Thompson, p. 89.
Another case decided by the Supreme Court in 1867 was *Ex parte Milligan*, arrising out of the Indiana "Treason Trials" of 1864. Representing the government in this instance was War Democrat James Speed, U.S. Attorney General, assisted by General Benjamin F. Butler. Milligan's attorney was War Democrat Jeremiah S. Black. To the shock of Radicals in general, the Court declared against the the functioning of military tribunals in the North, and Black was proclaimed a hero of the Conservative cause. William N. Brigance, pp. 150–56. Still another case in the works at that moment was *Ex parte McCardle*, involving the military arrest of a Mississippi editor for denouncing the presence of the army in the South. If the Court should hold in this instance as it had in *Ex parte Garland*, military arrests would be illegal in the South and Congressional Reconstruction would come to a halt (since the Southern civil courts were largely dominated by former Confederates and could not be expected to serve the interests of justice in behalf of Negro freedman and southern Unionists) War Democrats were hired as counsel by both sides to argue the matter. Having previously resigned as Attorney General, in protest against the Presidential Reconstruction policy, War Democrat James Speed was no longer on hand to represent the government,

and his successor, Henry Stanbery, refused to serve in the case, having already come out aginst the Reconstruction Acts as unconstitutional, in accordance with the views of President Johnson. The choice of government counsel fell to Secretary of War Stanton who selected Lyman Trumbull, Republican Senator from Illinois, directing him to engage the assistance of War Democrat Matthew H. Carpenter (who had done so well working for the Conservatives, in *Ex parte Garland*). Another pair of War Democrats involved in the proceedings were James Hughes of Indiana, hired by the government, and Robert J. Walker of Mississippi, hired by McCardle. On January 31, 1868, Carpenter and Hughes moved to dismiss the case on grounds of non-jurisdiction, and Black opposed the move. The Court agreed with Black. (At this point, Congress began work on legislation requiring a two-thirds majority vote for the Court to set aside a federal law.) Carpenter then prepared and delivered an argument not based on the congressional war power but on the simple right to protect the interests of the government in peacetime. It was an able statement which was generally believed to have decided the case. The Court agreed to the contention that it had no jurisdiction in the matter, and Carpenter was declared the saviour of Radical Reconstruction. Ibid., pp. 89—92.

Black and Carpenter met again in 1868, in *Georgia v. Grant,* involving the validity of the Military Reconstruction Acts in Georgia. Black was especially eloquent on this occasion, chewing tobacco throughout the length of his delivery. Turning to Secretary Stanton, Carpenter whispered, "They've got us. Black has filled one spittoon and sent for another." Ibid., p. 97. But for all Black's brillance, Carpenter was better. When he sat down, Stanton seized his arm and said, "Carpenter, you have saved us." Even the judges congratulated him, and Black frankly proclaimed him "the first Constitutional lawyer in the country." Ibid., p. 98.

When the butchers of New Orleans attempted to turn the Fourteenth Amendment against the Louisiana Legislature in the Slaughterhouse cases of 1869, Carpenter represented the Legislature and Black represented the butchers, in cooperation with War Democrat Thomas C. Durant of Louisiana. Once again, Carpenter was brilliant, portraying the Amendment as a measure designed exclusively for Negro civil rights, as opposed to a spreadagel economic interpretation, for the benefit of businessmen. Ibid., pp. 100–102. So long as Military Reconstruction continued to survive, through 1875, Carpenter could take considerable credit for the fact. On the strength of the McCardle Case decision he was elected in 1869 as a Republican to the U.S. Senate, where he served with distinction as a champion of the Radical cause, supporting Grant for reelection in 1872 against the wishes of Conservative Republicans (calling themselves "Liberals" and working with the Democrats against the Reconstruction program and Negro civil rights). An all-around reformer, Carpenter also came to grips with the Conservative Republicans of Wisconsin by advocating federal controls for railroads, in the matter of interstate commerce. For taking such a stand, he was opposed by the business interests back home and failed of reelection in 1875. The following year, in his absence, Radical Reconstruction was set upon and torn apart in Washington by Democrats and Conservative Republicans, Allen Johnson and Dumas Malone, eds., III:512.

Another major scandal of the 1870s was the exposure of corrupt operations by the Democratic "Tweed Ring" of New York City. In this instance, the chief villain was a Peace Democrat, "Boss" William M. Tweed; but his able lieutenants, also implicated in the scandal, consisted of a trio of War Democrats: Peter B. Sweeney, Richard B. Connelly, and A. Oaky Hall. M.R.Werner, p. 112. Another scandal, the "Whiskey Ring" exposure of 1875, involved a huge conspiracy by which hundreds of distillers, in collusion with Treasury officials, evaded the internal revenue tax and defrauded the government. The federal prosecutor, who tried the case and brought to light the culprits, many of whom were convicted, was War Democrat John B. Henderson, former Senator from Missouri. *National Cyclopedia of American Biography,* XIII:50.

Another major court battle over Reconstruction was *Blair v. Missouri* (1870), in which War Democrat Charles D. Drake of Missouri defended the Radical position and won the case. He was serving at the time as U.S. Senator from Missouri, but following the decision he resigned to become Chief Justice of the U.S. Court of Claims. William E. Smith, II:354; Howard L. Conard, ed., II:313.

When the scandals of the Reconstruction period began to appear, the War Democrats were once again conspicuous on both sides of the issues involved. The "Black Friday" financial embroglio of 1869 was especially embarrassing to President Grant, who had befriended the speculators responsible for it. A bitter outcome of the friendship was economic chaos on a nationwide scale, extending through the national elections of 1872. Of a different nature but equally embarrassing to the Grant administration was the so-called "Salary Grab" of 1873, in which the salary of Congressmen was increased dramatically at a moment when much of the public was struggling to stave off bankruptcy and starvation. The author of the ill-conceived measure was War Democrat Benjamin F. Butler of Massachusetts. James G. Randall, *Civil War and Reconstruction,* pp. 819–20. War Democrats personally involved in the scandals of the 1870s included William W. Belknap of Iowa, Secretary of War under Grant, and George H. Williams of Oregon, U.S. Attorney General under Grant. Accused of accepting bribes from a trader at an Indian post, Belknap resigned under fire and was impeached for malfeasance in office. Williams, while serving as Attorney General under Grant, in 1875, was nominated for Chief Justice of the U.S. Supreme Court. His name was later withdrawn from consideration, following the revelation that as Attorney General he had removed from office a U.S. District Attorney for insisting on the prosecution of influential persons accused of engaging in election frauds. Ibid., p. 281; Allen Johnson and Dumas Malone, eds., XX:262.

90. Ibid., VIII:271.

91. So far as the charge of opportunism is concerned, it is worthwhile considering the cases of certain War Democrats who deserted the Regular Democracy in favor of the wartime Union party under circumstances having no apparent connection with political advantage. One such man was Matthew P. Deady of Oregon, onetime Judge of the Oregon Territorial Supreme Court, Antebellum advocate of slavery in Oregon, Southern Rights delegate to the 1860 Charleston National Convention, and Breckinridge supporter in the 1860 campaign. In the manner of Benjamin F. Butler and Edwin M. Stanton, Deady was converted to the anti-slavery cause during the war years. (The conversion is incidentally but unmistakably described in Walter C. Woodward, passim.) Yet Deady was no longer an active politician when he swung over to the anti-slavery cause, having already returned—once and for all—to his private law practice. In changing from the ranks of the pro-slavery forces to the anti-slavery forces, he was not securing favors, nor wealth, fame, or position. He was simply exercising a *change of of opinion*. Consider also the cases of Daniel E. Sickles and John Cochrane, Antebellum Congressmen from Democratic New York City. What possible political advantage was there in quitting the Democratic party in wartime, so far as they were concerned? None whatever, because the city was a Democratic stronghold. There were no local offices open to non-Democrats, nor had there been for many years (with rare exceptions.) And by the time that either Cochrane or Sickles had returned, full time, to politics—in 1863—the Regular Democracy was in control of the State House, under Seymour, and all appointive state offices were out of reach of Union party men.

92. David H. Bates, *Lincoln and the Telegraph Office* (New York: Century, 1907), passim.
93. Henry Garrison Villard, *Memoirs.* Quoted in Ishbell Ross, p. 125.
94. Wilfred E. Binkley, *American Political Parties* (New York: Knopf, 1945), p. 265.
95. John Bartlett, Ibid., p. 662.
96. Washington *Post,* March 2, 1961.

Appendix 1

DEMOCRATIC CONGRESSMEN AND SENATORS, 1861–1865

Democratic Congressmen and Senators are here classified as War Democrats, Conditional War Democrats, and Peace Democrats on the basis of their votes on a number of vital war measures, cited below. Since many self-declared War Democrats regarded slavery as an issue apart from the war, and therefore insisted on the right to vote against anti-slavery bills advanced as war measures by administration leaders, we have not counted the pro-slavery votes of Democrats as anti-war votes. On the other hand, we have counted the anti-slavery votes of Democrats as pro-war votes. The following were war measures, and were not aimed against the slavery institution, *per se:*

House.   37th Congress.

1. To coerce seceded states into paying federal revenue. July 10, 1861.
2. To enact the Loan Bill. July 10, 1861.
3. To expel Congressman John B. Clark of Missouri, for supporting the Confederate cause. July 13, 1861.
4. To table a proposal for a peace conference with Confederate officials. July 15, 1861.
5. To enact the Conspiracy Bill. July 15, 1861.

6. To adopt the pro-war section of the Crittenden Resolution. July 22, 1861.
7. To enact the Supplemental Loan Bill. July 25, 1861.
8. To table a proposal for a peace conference with Confederate officials. July 29, 1861.
9. To adopt the Majority Committee Report on the Supplemental Loan Bill. August 1, 1861.
10. To retain a section in the Soldiers' Pay Bill indemnifying federal officials against civil suits occasioned by the military arrest of civilians. August 7, 1861.
11. To table a motion overruling the presidential suspension of *habeas corpus* in wartime. December 10, 1861.
12. To table a motion threatening war with England over the "Trent Affair." December 16, 1861.
13. To enact the Army Deficiency Bill. April 16, 1862.
14. To enact a bill taxing citizens in insurrectionary districts recaptured by Union arms. May 28, 1862.
15. To enact the Army Appropriation Bill. December 18, 1862.
16. To enact the Currency Bill. February 20, 1863.
17. To enact the Conscription Bill. February 25, 1863.
18. To enact the Indemnity Bill. March 2, 1863.

Senate. 37th Congress.

1. To enact the Volunteer Bill. July 10, 1861.
2. To establish certain duties on imports. July 12, 1861.
3. To defeat a motion denying seats to Unionist Senators from Virginia. July 13, 1861.
4. To enact a bill providing pay for military police in Baltimore. July 24, 1861.
5. To pass a motion favoring the supremacy of the federal government. July 26, 1861.
6. To pass a motion to reconsider passage of the Supplemental Loan Bill. August 2, 1861.
7. To defeat pro-slavery Constitutional Amendments designed to placate the Confederate authorities, in the interest of reunion. August 3, 1861.
8. To retain a section in the Soldiers' Pay Bill indemnifying federal officials against civil suits occasioned by the military arrest of civilians.
9. To expel Senator John C. Breckinridge of Kentucky for supporting the Confederate cause. December 4, 1861.

10. To defeat a motion criticizing the presidential suspension of *habeas corpus* in wartime. December 16, 1861.
11. To expel Senator Waldo P. Johnson of Missouri for supporting the Confederate cause. January 10, 1862.
12. To expel Senator Trusten Polk of Missouri for supporting the Confederate cause. January 10, 1862.
13. To expel Senator Jesse D. Bright of Indiana for having, in a letter to Jefferson Davis, recognized him as the "President of the Confederate States."
14. To defeat a motion postponing indefinitely consideration of the Conscription Bill. February 28, 1863.
15. To defeat a motion to reconsider passage of the bill indemnifying federal officials against civil suits occasioned by the military arrest of civilians. March 3, 1863.
16. To pass a motion against foreign intervention. March 3, 1863.

House. 38th Congress.

1. To table a proposal for a peace conference with Confederate officials. December 14, 1863.
2. To defeat a motion declaring illegal the military arrest of civilians in wartime. December 17, 1863.
3. To pass a resolution denouncing all proposals for peace conferences with Confederate officials. January 7, 1864.
4. To table a proposal for a peace conference with Confederate officials. January 7, 1864.
5. To pass a resolution calling for the crushing of the rebellion. January 18, 1864.
6. To enact a bill permitting the enlistment of Union troops in areas retaken from the Confederates. February 26, 1864.
7. To table a proposal for a peace conference with Confederate officials. February 29, 1864.
8. To table a motion denouncing as unconstitutional the arrest and banishment of Clement L. Vallandigham. February 29, 1864.
9. To enact a bill providing for the speedy punishment of guerillas apprehended by the Union forces. June 6, 1864.
10. To approve the majority report on the Army Appropriation Bill. June 13, 1864.
11. To table a proposal for a peace conference with Confederate officials. January 16, 1865.
12. To enact the Enrollment Bill. February 27, 1865.
13. To reward the heroes of the U.S.S. *Kearsarge* for the sinking of the Confederate battleship *Alabama*.

Senate. 38th Congress.

1. To accept the Majority Report on the Conscription Bill. February 19, 1864.
2. To enact the Army Appropriation Bill. April 22, 1864.
3. To amend the Conscription Bill. June 23, 1864.
4. To accept the Majority Report on the Conscription Bill. July 2, 1864.

* * *

The War Democrats voted more often for than against the measures listed above. Conditional War Democrats voted equally for and against, or less often for than against, but nonetheless *did* vote for them a sizable percentage of the time. The Peace Democrats seldom voted for any of them.

A full list of War Democrats, Conditional War Democrats and Peace Democrats in the Thirty-Seventh and Thirty-Eighth Congresses appears below.

House. 37th Congress.

War Democrats (20)
Baily, Joseph, of Pennsylvania
Brown, William G., of Virginia (Union party)
Cobb, George T., of New Jersey
Cooper, Thomas B., of Pennsylvania[1]
Crisfield, John W., of Maryland (Union party)
English, William E., of Connecticut
Haight, Edward, of New York
Lazear, Jesse, of Pennsylvania
Lehman, Edward H., of Pennsylvania
McClernand, John A., of Illinois[2]
Noell, John W., of Missouri
Odell, Moses F., of New York
Phelps, John S., of Missouri
Smith, Edward H., of New York
Steele, John B., of New York
Thayer, Andrew J., of Oregon[3]
Thomas, Francis, of Maryland (Union party)
Vibbard, Chauncy, of New York
Woodruff, George C., of Connecticut
Wright, Hendrick B., of Pennsylvania (Union party)

Conditional War Democrats (20)
Allen, William, of Ohio
Allen, William J., of Illinois[4]
Ancona, Sydenham E., of Pennsylvania
Biddle, Charles J., of Pennsylvania[5]
Browne, George H., of Rhode Island
Cox, Samuel S., of Ohio
Cravens, James A., of Indiana
Fouke, Philip B., of Illinois
Hall, William A., of Missouri[6]
Holman, William S., of Indiana
Knapp, Anthony L., of Illinois[7]
Law, John, of Indiana
Logan, John A., of Illinois[8]
Morris, James R., of Ohio
Noble, Warren P., of Ohio
Nugen, Robert H., of Ohio
Price, Thomas L., of Missouri[9]
Steele, William G., of New Jersey
Ward, Elijah, of New York
White, Chilton A., of Ohio

Peace Democrats (17)
Burnett, Henry C., of Kentucky[10]
Corning, Erastus, of New York
Johnson, Philip, of Pennsylvania
Kerrigan, James E., of New York
May, Henry, of Maryland (Union party)
Norton, Elijah H., of Missouri
Pendleton, George H., of Ohio
Perry, Nehemiah, of New Jersey
Randall, Samuel J., of Pennsylvania
Reid, John W., of Missouri
Robinson, James C., of Illinois
Shiel, George K., of Oregon[11]
Stiles, John D., of Pennsylvania[12]
Vallandigham, Clement L., of Ohio
Voorhees, Daniel W., of Indiana
Wickliffe, Charles A., of Kentucky (Union party)
Wood, Benjamin, of New York

NOTES

1. Died April 4, 1862.
2. Resigned October 28, 1861.
3. Served until July 30, 1861; succeeded by George K. Shiel who contested his election.
4. Elected to fill a vacancy caused by the resignation of John A. Logan, and took his seat June 2, 1862.
5. Elected to fill a vacancy caused by the resignation of E. Joy Morris, and took his seat December 2, 1861.
6. Elected to fill a vacancy caused by expulsion of John B. Clark, and took his seat December 1, 1862.
7. Elected to fill a vacancy caused by resignation of John A. McClernand, and took his seat December 12, 1861.
8. Resigned April 2, 1862.
9. Elected to fill a vacancy caused by expulsion of John W. Reid, and took his seat January 21, 1862.
10. Expelled by resolution of December 3, 1861.
11. Successfully contested the election of Andrew J. Thayer, and took his seat July 30, 1861.
12. Elected to fill a vacancy caused by the death of Thomas B. Cooper, and took his seat June 3, 1862.

Senate.   37th Congress.

War Democrats (10)
Arnold, Samuel G., of Rhode Island[1]
Harding, Benjamin F., of Oregon (Union party)[2]
Henderson, John B., of Missouri (Union party)[3]
Johnson, Andrew, of Tennessee[4]
Latham, Milton S., of California
McDougall, James A., of California
Nesmith, James W., of Oregon
Rice, Henry M., of Minnesota
Thomson, John R., of New Jersey[5]
Wright, Joseph A., of Indiana (Union party)[6]

Conditional War Democrats (2)
Saulsbury, Willard, of Delaware
Carlile, John S., of Virginia (Union party)

Peace Democrats (10)
Bayard, James A., of Delaware
Breckinridge, John C., of Kentucky[7]
Bright, Jesse D., of Indiana[8]
Johnson, Waldo P., of Missouri[9]
Pearce, James A., of Maryland[10]
Polk, Trusten, of Missouri[11]

Powell, Lazarus W., of Kentucky
Richardson, William A., of Illinois
Turpie, David, of Indiana
Wall, James W., of New Jersey

NOTES

1. Elected to fill a vacancy caused by the resignation of James F. Simmons, and took his seat December 1, 1862.
2. Elected to fill a vacancy caused by the death of Edward D. Baker, and took his seat December 1, 1862, replacing Benjamin Stark who had served by appointment since February 27, 1862.
3. Appointed to fill a vacancy caused by the expulsion of Trusten Polk, and took his seat January 29, 1862.
4. Resigned March 4, 1862, to become Military Governor of Tennessee.
5. Died September 12, 1862.
6. Appointed to fill a vacancy caused by expulsion of Jesse D. Bright, and took his seat March 3, 1862.
7. Expelled by resolution of September 4, 1861.
8. Expelled February 5, 1862.
9. Expelled by resolution of January 10, 1862.
10. Died December 20, 1862.
11. Expelled by resolution of January 10, 1862.

House. 38th Congress.

War Democrats (35)
Anderson, Lucien, of Kentucky (Union party)
Baily, Joseph, of Pennsylvania[1]
Baldwin, Augustus C., of Michigan[2]
Brown, James S., of Wisconsin
Brown, William G., of West Virginia (Union party)
Coffroth, Alexander H., of Pennsylvania[3]
Creswell, John A.J., of Maryland (Union party)
Deming, Henry C., of Connecticut (Union party)
Dumont, Ebenezer, of Indiana (Union party)
English, William E., of Connecticut
Ganson, John, of New York
Griswold, John A., of New York
Herrick, Anson, of New York
Higby, William, of California (Union party)
Holman, William S., of Indiana
Hutchins, Wells, of Ohio
Ingersoll, Ebon C., of Illinois (Union party)[4]

Kernan, Francis, of New York[5]
King, Austin A., of Missouri[6]
McAllister, Archibald, of Pennsylvania
Middleton, George, of New Jersey
Nelson, Homer A., of New York
Odell, Moses F., of New York
Price, Thomas A., of Missouri
Radford, William, of New York
Rollins, James S., of Missouri[7]
Shannon, Thomas B., of California (Union party)
Smith, Green Clay, of Kentucky (Union party)
Stebbins, Henry G., of New York[8]
Steele, John B., of New York
Sweat, Lorenzo, D.M., of Maine[9]
Thomas, Francis, of Maryland (Union party)
Ward, Elijah, of New York
Wheeler, Ezra, of Wisconsin
Winfield, Charles H., of New York

Peace Democrats (46)
Allen, James C., of Illinois
Allen, William J., of Illinois
Ancona, Sydenham E., of Pennsylvania
Bliss, George, of Ohio
Brooks, James, of New York
Chanler, John W., of New York
Cox, Samuel S., of Ohio
Cravens, James A., of Indiana
Denison, Charles, of Pennsylvania
Eden, John R., of Illinois
Edgerton, Joseph K., of Indiana
Eldridge, Charles A., of Wisconsin
Finck, William E., of Ohio
Hall, William A., of Missouri
Harding, Aaron, of Kentucky
Harrington, Henry W., of Indiana
Harris, Benjamin G., of Maryland
Harris, Charles M., of Illinois
Kalbfleisch, Martin, of New York
Knapp, Anthony L., of Illinois
Law, John, of Indiana
LeBlond, Francis C., of Ohio
Long, Alexander, of Ohio

McDowell, James F., of Indiana
Mallory, Robert, of Kentucky
Marcy, Daniel, of New Hampshire
Miller, William H., of Pennsylvania
Morrison, William R., of Illinois
Noble, Warren P., of Ohio
O'Neil, John, of Ohio
Pendleton, George H., of Ohio
Randall, Samuel J., of Pennsylvania
Robinson, James C., of Illinois
Rogers, Andrew J., of New Jersey
Ross, Lewis, of Illinois
Scott, John G., of Missouri[10]
Steele, William G., of New Jersey
Stiles, John D., of Pennsylvania
Strouse, Myer, of Pennsylvania
Stuart, John T., of Illinois
Townsend, Dwight, of New York[11]
Voorhees, Daniel W., of Indiana
White, Chilton A., of Ohio
White, Joseph W., of Ohio
Wood, Benjamin, of New York
Wood, Fernando, of New York

NOTES

1. Elected as a Regular Democrat in 1862, but stood for reelection as a Unionist in 1864.
2. Voted seldom for war measures, but voted to repudiate Peace negotiations with Confederate officials.
3. Voted seldom for war measures, but voted in favor of Thirteenth Amendment.
4. Elected to a vacancy caused by the death of Owen Lovejoy, and took his seat May 20, 1864.
5. Voted seldom for war measures, but voted to repudiate all Peace negotiations.
6. Voted seldom for war measures, but voted to repudiate all Peace negotiations.
7. Elected as a Unionist in 1862, but stood for reelection in 1864 as a Regular Democrat.
8. Elected as a Regular Democrat in 1862, but stood for reelection in 1864 as a Unionist.
9. Voted seldom for war measures, but voted to repudiate all Peace negotiations.
10. Elected to fill a vacancy caused by the death of John W. Noell, and took his seat December 7, 1863.
11. Elected to fill a vacancy caused by the resignation of Henry G. Stebbins, and took his seat December 5, 1864.

Senate. 38th Congress.

War Democrats (8)
Buckalew, Charles R., of Pennsylvania
Conness, John, of California (Union party)
Harding, Benjamin F., of Oregon (Union party)
Henderson, John B., of Missouri (Union party)
Johnson, Reverdy, of Maryland (Union party)
McDougall, James A., of California
Nesmith, James W., of Oregon
Sprague, William, of Rhode Island (Union party)

Conditional War Democrats (3)
Carlile, John S., of Virginia (Union party)
Hendricks, Thomas A., of Indiana
Wright, William, of New Jersey

Peace Democrats (5)
Bayard, James A., of Delaware
Davis, Garrett, of Kentucky (Union party)
Powell, Lazarus W., of Kentucky
Richardson, William A., of Illinois
Riddle, George R., of Delaware

Appendix 2

SOME OUTSTANDING DEMOCRATS IN THE MILITARY SERVICE

GENERALS

Abbott, Henry L.
> Son of Josiah G. Abbott, Breckinridge leader in Massachusetts.

Andrews, Christopher C.
> Douglas elector for Minnesota, 1860.

Bayard, George D.
> Called a Democrat by Congressman George W. Julian of Indiana. *Congressional Globe* (37th Congress, 3rd session), p. 1068.

Belknap, William W.
> Democratic member, Iowa Assembly, 1857-1858; supported Douglas, 1860.

Berry, Hiram G.
> Former Mayor of Rockport, Maine; supported Breckinridge, 1860. Edward K. Gould, *Major General Hiram G. Berry* (Rockland: Maine, 1899).

Blair, Francis P., Jr.
> Joined Democrats in 1865; Democratic candidate for Vice President, 1868.

Blenker, Louis
Called a Democrat in T. Harry Williams, *Lincoln and Radicals* (Madison: Wisconsin, 1941), p. 119.

Bragg, Edward S.
Douglas delegate to Charleston and Baltimore Conventions, 1860.

Bramlette, Thomas E.
Old-line Whig at outset of the war; supported McClellan in 1864. Source: James R. Robertson, "Sectionalism in Kentucky from 1855 to 1865," *Mississippi Valley Historical Review,* vol. IV, no. 1 (June 1917): p. 61.

Brayman, Mason
Called a Democrat in James G. Wilson, *Biographical Sketches of Illinois Officers* (Chicago, 1862), p. 30.

Buell, Don Carlos
Called a Democrat in Benjamin P. Thomas, *Stanton: The Life and Times of Lincoln's Secretary of War* (New York, 1962), p. 260.

Buford, John
Brother of Democrat Napoleon B. Buford.

Buford, Napoleon B.
Called a Democrat by John A. Rawlins. James H. (Williams,) *Life of John A. Rawlins* (New York, 1916), p. 65.

Burnside, Ambrose E.
Democratic candidate for Congress, 1857.

Bussey, Cyrus
Douglas delegate to Charleston and Baltimore Conventions, 1860.

Busteed, Richard
Supported Douglas, 1860. *Union Army,* VIII:46.

Butler, Benjamin F.
Breckinridge candidate for Governor of Massachusetts, 1860.

Cadwalader, George C.
Called a Democrat by Congressman William A. Richardson of Illinois. *Congressional Globe* (37th Congress, 2nd session), p. 24.

Campbell, William B.
Former Governor of Tennessee; supported Bell, 1860; campaigned for McClellan, 1864.

Canby, Edward R.S.
Son of Israel T. Canby, Democratic leader in Indiana and a candidate for Governor of Indiana, 1828.

Carlin, William P.
Son of Thomas Carlin, Democratic Governor of Illinois, 1838–1842; called a Democrat in Roy P. Basler, ed., *The Collected Works of Abraham Lincoln,* 8 vols. (New Brunswick, 1953), p. 117, fn.

Casey, Silas
Called a Democrat in Milwaukee *Sentinel,* October 13, 1864.

Champlin, Stephen G.
Called a Douglas Democrat in *American Biographical History of Eminent and Self-Made Men, Michigan Volume* (Cincinnati, 1878), part V, p. 17.

Clayton, Powell
Delegate to 1860 Kansas Democratic Territorial Convention.

Cochrane, John
Democratic Congressman, 1860–1861; supported Douglas, 1860.

Cook, John
Elected Mayor of Springfield, Illinois, as a Democrat, 1855; elected Sheriff of Sangamon County, Illinois, as a Democrat, 1856. (Sangamon went democratic by a wide margin. *Tribune Almanac*, 1857.)

Corcoran, Michael
Called a Democrat in Florence E. Gibson, *The Attitude of the New York Irish toward State and National Affairs, 1848–1892* (New York, 1951), p. 115.

Corse, John M.
Democratic candidate for Lieutenant Governor of Iowa, 1860.

Couch, Darius N.
Democratic candidate for Governor of Massahcusetts, 1865.

Craig, James
Democratic Congressman from Missouri, 1860–1861; member, Douglas National Executive Committee, 1860.

Crocker, Marcellus M.
Called a Democrat in Olynthus B. Clark, *The Politics of Iowa during the Civil War and Reconstruction* (Iowa City, 1911), p. 144.

Curtis, N. Martin
Democratic candidate for New York Assembly, 1860.

Custer, George A.
Called a Democrat in Thomas E. Powell, ed., *The Democratic Party of the State of Ohio,* 2 vols. (Columbus, 1913), I:170.

Dana, Napoleon J.T.
Opposed Republican ticket in Minnesota, 1861, as a leading supporter of No Party ticket; federal appointee under Democratic President Grover Cleveland.

Davis, Edmund J.
Elected Judge of the District Court, Rio Grande district of Texas, in 1854, running as a Democrat; held office through 1861; supported Douglas, 1860.

Dennis, Elias S.
Called a Democrat in James A. Wilson, *Biographical Sketches of Illinois Officers* (Chicago, 1862).

Denver, James W.
Governor of Kansas Territory and Commissioner of Indian Affairs

under Buchanan; supported Douglas 1860; candidate for Democratic nomination for U.S. Senator from California, 1861.

Dix, John A.

Democratic Senator from New York, 1845–1849; Free Soil candidate for Governor, 1848; Assistant Treasurer of the U.S. under Pierce, 1853; Postmaster of New York City under Buchanan, 1860; Breckinridge candidate for Governor of New York, 1860.

Dumont, Ebenezer

Democratic elector for Indiana, 1852; elected to state legislature, 1852, running as a Democrat; supported Douglas, 1860.

Duryee, Abram

Democratic delegate to anti-Republican Fusion party rally, New York City, October, 1860.

Duval, Isaac H

Federal appointee under Polk.

Egan, Thomas W.

Member of Mozart Hall; recommended to Governor Morgan by Mayor Fernando Wood of New York City, leader of Mozart Hall.

Este, George P.

Declared self a Democrat in a letter to the Union State Convention of Ohio, 1863.

Fairchild, Lucius

Son of Jairus C. Fairchild, Democratic Treasurer of Wisconsin, 1848–1852, and Douglas elector, 1860.

Ferrero, Edward

Member, Tammany Hall. Allen Johnson and Dumas Malone, eds., *Dictionary of American Biography,* VI:339.

Franklin, William B.

Called a Democrat in T. Harry Williams, *Lincoln and the Radicals* (Madison, 1941), p. 119.

Fry, James B.

Son of Jacob Fry, Chairman, Douglas Convention, Greene County, Illinois. St. Louis *Missouri Republican,* August 5, 1860; Newton Bateman, ed., *Historical Encyclopedia of Illinois,* 2 vols. (Chicago, 1907), I:178.

Garrard, Kenner

Brother of James A. Garrard, Kentucky Breckinridge leader and Attorney General of Kentucky, and Theophilus T. Garrard, Douglas elector for Kentucky.

Garrard, Theophilus T.

Douglas elector for Kentucky.

Geary, John W.

Governor of Kansas Territory under Pierce and Buchanan; regarded as a Democrat throughout the war. Harry M. Tinkcom, *John White Geary, Soldier-Statesman* (Philadelphia, 1945).

Gorman, Willis A.

Douglas elector for Minnesota; Governor of Minnesota Territory under Pierce.

Grant, Ulysses S.

Called a Democrat by Adjutant General John A. Rawlins. James H. Williams, *Life of John A. Rawlins* (New York, 1916), p. 66.

Halleck, Henry W.

Called a Democrat in Allen Johnson and Dumas Malone, eds., *Dictionary of American Biography,* VIII:151; Wood Gray, *The Hidden Civil War, The Story of the Copperheads* (New York, 1942), p. 62.

Hamilton, Charles S.

Called a Democrat in Milwaukee *Sentinel,* October 19, 1861.

Hancock, Winfield S.

Democratic candidate for President, 1880.

Hartranft, John F.

Called a Democrat in William N. Ashman, *The Life and Services of John F. Hartranft, Address,* Pennsylvania Club Lectures, Course of 1889–1890 (Philadelphia, 1890).

Haynie, Isham N.

Douglas elector for Illinois.

Heintzelman, Samuel P.

Called a Democrat in Milwaukee *Sentinel,* October 13, 1864.

Hobson, Edward H.

President, Kentucky Douglas State Convention, 1860.

Hooker, Joseph

Superintendent of Federal Roads in Oregon under Buchanan. Called a Douglas Democrat in Walter E. Hebert, *Fighting Joe Hooker* (Indianapolis, 1944), pp. 42–44.

Hovey, Alvin P.

U.S. District Attorney for Indiana under Buchanan, defeated for Congress in 1858, running as a Douglas Democrat; supported Douglas, 1860.

Hunter, David

Called a Democrat by Congressman George W. Julian of Indiana. *Congressional Globe* (37 Congress, 3rd session), p. 1067.

Jameson, Charles D.

Douglas delegate to Charleston and Baltimore Conventions, 1860.

Johnson, Richard W.

Declared himself a Breckinridge Democrat. Richard W. Johnson, *A*

Soldier's Reminiscenses (Philadelphia, 1886), p. 163; delegate, Charleston Convention, 1860.

Kearny, Philip

Called a Democrat in Irving Werstein, *Kearny the Magnificent* (New York, 1962), p. 158.

Kiernan, James L.

Called a Breckinridge Democrat in New York *Journal of Commerce,* September 26, 1860.

Kilpatrick, H. Judson

Democratic campaign speaker in New Jersey Congressional elections of 1854. James W. Moore, *Kilpatrick and Our Cavalry* (New York, 1865).

Leggett, Mortimer D.

Elected Superintendent of Public Schools, Zanesville, Ohio, on the Democratic ticket, 1857.

Logan, John A.

Elected as a Democrat to Congress from Illinois, 1860; supported Douglas, 1860.

Lytle, Thomas H.

Democratic candidate for Governor of Ohio, 1857.

McCall, George A.

Democratic candidate for Congress in Pennsylvania, 1862.

McCandless, William

Democratic candidate for Congress in Pennsylvania, 1856.

McClellan, George B.

Democratic candidate for President, election of 1864.

McClernand, John A.

Democratic Congressman from Illinois, 1861.

McCook, Alexander McD.

Called a Democrat in Allen Johnson and Dumas Malone, eds., *Dictionary of American Biography,* 20 vols. (New York, 1933), XI:601.

McCook, Daniel

Called a Democrat in Allen Johnson and Dumas Malone, eds., *Dictionary of American Biography,* 20 vols. (New York, 1933), XI:601.

McCook, Edward M.

Called a Democrat in Allen Johnson and Dumas Malone, eds., *Dictionary of American Biography,* 20 vols. (New York, 1933), XI:601.

McCook, Robert L.

Called a Democrat in Allen Johnson and Dumas Malone, eds., *Dictionary of American Biography* 20 vols. (New York, 1933), XI:601.

McDowell, Irvin

Called a Democrat in Benjamin P. Thomas, *Stanton: The Life and Time of Lincoln's Secretary of War* (New York, 1962), p. 260.

McGinnis, George F.

Called a Democrat in Francis M. Trissal, *Public Men of Indiana* (Hammond, Ind., 1922), p. 38.

McPherson, James B.

Evidently favored Buchanan, 1856–1860; opposed Republicans, 1860. Elizabeth J. Whaley, *Forgotten Hero: General James B. McPherson* (New York, 1955), pp. 100–104.

Manson, Mahlon D.

Democratic candidate for Lieutenant Governor of Indiana, 1864.

Marcy, Randolph B.

Father-in-law of Democratic General George B. McClellan; supported McClellan, 1864.

Meade, George G.

Called a Democrat in Milwaukee *Sentinel,* October 13, 1864.

Meagher, Thomas F.

In election of 1856 supported Buchanan; in election of 1859 supported Tammany candidate William F. Havemeir for Mayor of New York City. New York *Irish News,* purporting to represent his views, announced for Douglas, 1860. Robert G. Athearn, *Thomas Francis Meagher: an Irish Revolutionary in America* (Boulder, Colo.: University of Colorado Studies, Series in History No. 1, December, 1949), pp. 85, 89.

Meigs, Montgomery C.

Called a Douglas Democrat in Russell F. Weigley, *Quartermaster General of the Union Army* (New York, 1959), p. 15.

Milroy, Robert H.

Called a Democrat in Loyal Publication Society Pamphlet No. 5 (1863), "Voices of the Army," p. 2.

Mitchell, John G.

Called a Democrat in Samuel J. Crawford, *Kansas of the Sixties* (Chicago, 1911), p. 192.

Mitchell, Ormsby M.

Called a Democrat in Samuel J. Crawford, *Kansas of the Sixties.* (Chicago, 1911), p. 192.

Mitchell, Robert B.

Delegate from Kansas to Charleston and Baltimore Conventions. 1860.

Morgan, George W.

Minister to Portugal under Buchanan; supported Douglas, 1860.

Mott, Gershom

Old-Line Whig when the war began; supported McClellan in 1864.

Naglee, Henry M.
  Called a Democrat in Milwaukee *Sentinel,* October 13, 1864.
Negley, James S.
  Called a Democrat in T. Harry Williams, *Lincoln and the Radicals*
  (Madison, 1941), p. 119.
Nelson, William
  Called a Democrat by Congressman George W. Julian of Indiana,
  Congressional Globe (37th Congress, 3rd session), p. 1066.
Newton, John
  Son of a Democratic Congressman from Virginia.
Ord, Edward O.C.
  Called a Democrat in Bernarr Cresap, *The Career of General Edward
  O.C. Ord to 1864* (Nashville, 1951), p. 19.
Patrick, Marsena R.
  Called a Democrat in Benjamin P. Thomas, *Stanton: The Life and Times*
  of Lincoln's Secretary of War (New York, 1962), p. 378.
Patterson, Francis E.
  Son of Democratic General Robert Patterson.
Patterson, Robert
  Called a Democrat in Allen Johnson and Dumas Malone, eds.,
  Dictionary of American Biography, XIV:306.
Phelps, John S.
  Democratic Congressman from Missouri, 37th Congress and several
  preceding Congresses.
Porter, Andrew
  Called a Democrat in T. Harry Williams, *Lincoln and the Radicals*
  (Madison, 1941), p. 119.
Porter, Fitz John
  Called a Democrat in T. Harry Williams, *Lincoln and the Radicals*
  (Madison, 1941), p. 119.
Potts, Benjamin F.
  Attended the "Convention of the War Democracy of Ohio," at Col-
  umbus, September 22, 1863. Columbus *Ohio State Journal,*
  September 23, 1863.
Powell, William H.
  Called a Democrat in Thomas E. Powell, *The Democratic Party of the
  State of Ohio,* 2 vols. (Columbus, 1911), I:271.
Raum, Green B.
  Called a Douglas Democrat in Allen Johnson and Dumas Malone,
  eds., *Dictionary of American Biography,* XV:392.
Rawlins, John A.
  Douglas elector for Illinois, 1860.
Reynolds, John F.
  Called a Democrat in Edward J. Nichols, *Toward Gettysburg, A Biog-*

raphy of John F. Reynolds (Pennsylvania State University Press, 1958), pp. 73, 161.

Rice, Americus V.

Elected as a Democrat to Congress, from Ohio, 1874.

Rodman, Isaac P.

Democratic member, Rhode Island State Senate, 1861.

Rosecrans, William S.

Called a Democrat in Wood Gray, *The Hidden Civil War, The Story of the Copperheads* (New York, 1942), p. 62.

Ross, Leonard F.

Called a Democrat in James G. Wilson, *Biographical Sketches of Illinois officers* (Chicago, 1862), p. 110.

Schofield, John M.

Called a Democrat in Milwaukee *Sentinel,* October 13, 1864.

Scofield, Hiram

Called a Democrat in *U.S. Biographies Directory and Portrait Gallery of Eminent and Self-Made Men, Iowa Volume* (Chicago, 1878), p. 621.

Seymour, Truman

Called a Democrat in *Milwaukee Sentinel,* October 13, 1864.

Shepley, George F.

Douglas delegate from Maine, Charleston and Baltimore conventions, 1860.

Sheridan, Philip H.

Called a Democrat in Samuel J. Crawford, *Kansas of the Sixties* (Chicago, 1911), p. 192.

Sherman, Francis T.

Son of Francis C. Sherman, Democratic Mayor of Chicago, 1862–1864.

Shields, James

Democratic Senator from Illinois, 1849–1855; Democratic Senator from Minnesota, 1858–1859; supported Douglas, 1860.

Sibley, Henry H.

Democratic Governor of Minnesota, 1858–1860. Supported Douglas.

Sickles, Daniel E.

Democratic Congressman from New York, 1860–1861.

Slack, James R.

Democratic member, Indiana State Senate, 1861.

Slocum, Henry W.

Became a Democrat during the war; Democratic candidate for Secretary of State for New York, election of 1865.

Slough, John P.

Delegate to the Kansas Democratic Territorial Convention of 1860.

Smith, Andrew J.

Called a Democrat in Milwaukee *Sentinel,* October 18, 1864; National Union Executive Committee, *What Genuine Democrats Think of the Rebellion* (NY, 1864).

Smith, Charles F.
Called a Democrat in T. Harry Williams, *Lincoln and the Radicals* (Madison, 1941), p. 119.

Smith, Green Clay
Douglas Elector for Kentucky.

Smith, Thomas Kilby
Called a Douglas Democrat in Walter G. Smith, *Life and Letters of Thomas Kilby Smith* (New York, 1898), p. 10.

Smith, William F.
Called a Democrat in T. Harry Williams, *Lincoln and the Radicals* (Madison, 1941), p. 119.

Spears, James G.
Called a Douglas Democrat in Oliver P. Temple, *Notable Men of Tennessee* (New York, 1912), p. 187.

Spinola, Francis B.
Delegate to the Charleston and Baltimore Conventions, 1860.

Starkweather, John C.
Called a Democrat in Milwaukee *Sentinel,* October 13, 1864.

Stevens, Isaac I.
Chairman, Breckinridge National Committee, 1860.

Stone, Charles P.
Called a Democrat in T. Harry Williams, *Lincoln and the Radicals* (Madison, 1941), p. 119.

Stoneman, George
Democratic Governor of California, 1883–1887.

Stoughton, Edwin H.
Delegate from Vermont attending the Charleston, Baltimore, and Richmond National Conventions, 1860; Temporary Chairman, Vermont Breckinridge State Convention, 1860; member, Breckinridge State Committee.

Stuart, David
Called a Democrat in James G. Wilson, *Biographical Sketches of Illinois Officers* (Chicago, 1862), pp. 113–14.

Sumner, Edwin V.
Called a Democrat in Milwaukee *Sentinel,* October 13, 1864.

Taylor, George W.
Called a Democrat at New Jersey Democratic State Convention, 1862.

Taylor, Joseph P.
Called a Democrat by Congressman Henry L. Dawes of Mas-

sachusetts. *Congressional Globe* (37th Congress, 2nd session), p. 2386.

Taylor, Nelson

Elected to Congress in 1862 as a Democratic member from New York.

Thomas, George H.

Called a Democrat in Donn Piatt, *Memories of the Men Who Saved the Union* (New York, 1887), p. 75.

Thomas, Stephen

Democratic candidate for Lieutenant Governor of Vermont, 1860.

Todd, John B.S.

Elected as a Democratic Delegate to Congress from Dakota Territory, 1860.

Tuttle, James M.

Elected County Recorder on the Democratic ticket, 1859; supported Douglas, 1860; Democratic candidate for Governor, 1863.

Van Derveer, Ferdinand

Member, Douglas State Central Committee of Ohio, 1860.

Viele, Egbert L.

Son of Henry K. Viele, Breckinridge candidate for Lieutenant Governor of New York, 1860; elected to Congress on the Democratic ticket, 1884.

Wallace, Lewis

Called a Democrat in Allen Johnson and Dumas Malone, eds., *Dictionary of American Biography,* XIX:375.

Ward, John H. Hobart

Supported McClellan, 1864.

Warner, Adroniam J.

Elected as a Democrat to Congress several times following war; first time: 1878.

Warren, Fitz Henry

Became a Democrat during the war. Democrat candidate for Congress, 1866.

Wilcox, Orlando B.

President, Young Men's Douglas Club of Detroit. Detroit *Free Press,* October 13, 1860.

Williams, Alpheus

Called a Democrat in Harriette M. Dill, *The Politics of Michigan, 1865–1878* (New York, 1912), p. 64.

Williamson, James A.

Member, Douglas State Executive Committee of Iowa, 1860.

Woods, Charles R.

Brother of William B. Woods Democratic Minority Leader, Ohio Assembly, 1861.

Woods, William B.
Democratic Minority Leader, Ohio State Assembly, 1861.

Wool, John E.
Called a Democrat in Rutland (Vermont) Weekly *Herald,* October 13, 1864.

Bibliography

Adams, James Truslow, ed. *Dictionary of American history*. 5 volumes. New York: Scribner's, 1951.

Alexander, De Alva Stanwood. *A Political History of the State of New York*. 3 volumes. New York: Holt, 1906–9.

Ambler, Charles H. *Waitman Thomas Willey; Orator, Churchman, Humanitarian*. Huntington, West Virginia: Standard, 1954.

Ambler, Charles H., and Festus P. Summers. *West Virginia, the Mountain State*. Englewood Cliffs, New Jersey: Prentice-Hall, 1958.

American Biographical History of Eminent and Self-Made Men. Michigan Volume. Cincinnati: Western Biographical, 1878.

Anderson, Charles C. *Fighting by Southern Federals*. New York: Neale, 1912.

Anderson, Galusha. *The Story of a Border City during the Civil War*. Boston: Little, Brown, 1908.

Andrews, Christopher C. *History of St. Paul, Minnesota*. Syracuse, 1890.

Andrews, Matthew P. *History of Maryland, Province and State*. Garden City: Doubleday-Doran, 1929.

Athearn, Robert G. "Thomas Francis Meagher: an Irish Revolutionary in America," *University of Colorado Studies in History*, no. 1 (December, 1949).

Atherton, Gertrude F. *California, An Intimate History*. New York: Boni and Liveright, 1927.

Bartlett, John R. *Memoirs of Rhode Island Officers, Who Were Engaged in the Service of Their Country during the Great Rebellion of the South*. Providence: Riker, 1867.

Basler, Roy P., ed. *The Collected Works of Abraham Lincoln*. 8 volumes. New Brunswick, 1953.

Bates, David H. *Lincoln and the Telegraph Office*. New York: Century, 1907.

387

Beale, Howard K. *The Critical Year; A Study of Andrew Johnson and Reconstruction*. New York: Harcourt, Brace, 1930.

Belden, Thomas G., and Marva R. Belden. *So Fell the Angels*. Boston: Little, Brown, 1956.

Bellows, Henry W. *Historical Sketch of the Union League Club of New York, Its Organization and Work, 1863–1879*. New York: Club House, 1879.

Belmont, Perry. *The Recollections of an American Democrat*. 2d edition. New York: Columbia University Press, 1941.

Binkley, Wilfred E. *American Political Parties. Their Natural History*. 2d edition. New York: Knopf. 1954. p. 267.

Biographical Cyclopedia of Representative Men of Maryland and the District of Columbia. Baltimore: National Biography, 1879.

Biographical Cyclopedia of Representative Men of Rhode Island. Providence: National Biographical, 1881.

Biographical Encyclopedia of Illinois. Philadelphia, 1875.

Biographical Encyclopaedia of Maine of the 19th Century. Boston, 1885.

Black, Chauncy F. *Essays and Speeches of Jeremiah S. Black*. New York: Appleton, 1895.

Blake, E. Vale. *History of the Tammany Society, from its Organization to the Present Time*. New York: Souvenir, 1901.

Blake, Israel G. *The Holmans of Veraestau*. Oxford: Mississippi Valley Press, 1943.

Blegan, Theodore C. *Minnesota. A History of a State*. Minneapolis: University of Minnesota Press, 1963.

Brigance, William N. *Jeremiah Sullivan Black, A Defender of the Constitution and the Ten Commandments*. Philadelphia: University of Pennsylvania Press, 1934.

Brody, Fawn M. *Thaddeus Stevens, Scourge of the South*. New York: Norton, 1959.

Brummer, Sidney D. *Political History of New York during the Period of the Civil War*. New York: Columbia University, 1911.

Bryan, Wilhelmus B. *A History of the National Capital*. 2 volumes. New York: Macmillan, 1916.

Buckingham, Samuel G. *The Life of William A. Buckingham*. Springfield: Adams, 1894.

Butler, Benjamin F. *Butler's Book*. Boston: Thayer, 1892.

———. *Private and Official Correspondence of . . . during the Period of the Civil War*. 5 volumes. Norwood, Massachusetts, 1917.

Campbell, Henry C. *Wisconsin in Three Centuries, 1634–1905*. 4 volumes. New York: Century History, 1906.

Campbell, John. *Unionists versus Traitors: or The Nominees that Ought to be Elected in 1861*. Philadelphia, 1861.

Cannon, Le Grande B. *Personal Reminiscences of the Rebellion, 1861–1866*. New York, 1895.

Capers, Gerald M. *Stephen A. Douglas, Defender of the Union*. Boston: Little, Brown, 1959.

Carey, Charles H. *History of Oregon*. Chicago: Pioneer Historical, 1922.

Castel, Albert. *A Frontier State at War: Kansas, 1861–1865*. Ithaca: Cornell University Press, 1958.

Catton, Bruce. *A Stillness at Appomattox*. Garden City, New York: Doubleday, 1953.

Charnwood, Godfrey R.B. *Abraham Lincoln*. Garden City, New York: Garden City, 1917.

Chittenden, Lucius E. *Debates of the Peace Conference Convention*. New York: Appleton, 1864.

Church, Charles A. *History of the Republican Party of Illinois, with a Review of the Aggressions of the Slave Power*. Rockford: Wilson, 1912.

Clark, Charles Branch. *Politics in Maryland during the Civil War*. Chestertown, Maryland, 1952.

Clark, Olynthus B. *The Politics of Iowa during the Civil War and Reconstruction*. Iowa City: Clio Press, 1911.

Clymer, Heister. *Record of . . . and Historical Parallel between Him and Major General John W. Geary, Also Official Returns of Election on Constitutional Amendments Allowing Soldiers the Right to Vote*. Philadelphia: T. K. Collins, 1866.

Cole, Arthur C. *The Era of the Civil War*. Springfield: Illinios Centennial Commission, 1919.

Cole, Cyrenus. *A History of the People of Iowa*, Cedar Rapids: Torch Press, 1921.

Collins, Herman L. *Philadelphia, A Story of Progress*. 4 volumes. New York: Lewis, 1941.

Commemorative Biographical Record of Hartford County, Connecticut. Chicago, 1901.

Conard, Howard L., ed. *Encyclopedia of the History of Missouri, A Compendium of History and Biography for Ready Reference*. 6 volumes. New York: Southern History, 1901.

Congressional Globe. See U.S. Congress. *Congressional Globe*.

Conlin, Francis Loretto. "The Democratic Party in Pennsylvania from 56-to-65." American Catholic Historical Society of Philadelphia. *Records*. Vol. XLVII. (March 1936) No. 1.

Connelley, William E. *A Standard History of Kansas and Kansans*. 5 volumes. Chicago: Lewis, 1918.

Conrad, Henry C. *History of the State of Delaware*. 3 volumes. Wilmington, 1903.

Cook, Frederick F. *Bygone Days in Chicago*. Chicago: McClurg, 1910.

Cook, Thomas M., and Thomas W. Knox, eds. *Public Record of Horatio Seymour: Including Speeches, Messages, Proclamations, Official Correspondence, and Other Public Utterances, from the Campaign of 1856 to the Present Time*. With an Appendix. New York: England, 1868.

Cornell, William M. *The History of Pennsylvania*. Philadelphia: Quaker City, 1876.

Cornish, Dudley T. *The Sable Arm*. New York: Longmans, Green, 1956.

Coulter, E. Merton. *The Civil War and Readjustment in Kentucky*. Chapel Hill: University of North Carolina Press, 1926.

Cox, William V., and Milton H. Northrup. *Life of Samuel Sullivan Cox*. Syracuse: Northrup, 1899.

Crockett, Walter H. *Vermont, the Green Mountain State*. 5 volumes. New York: Century History, 1921.

Croffutt, W.A., and John M. Morris, *The Military and Civil History of Connecticut*. New York: Ledyard Bill, 1869.

Crowell, Joseph T. *Speech, in the Senate of New Jersey, January 22,*

1863, on the motion to postpone indefinitely the anti-war resolutions offered by Honorable Daniel Holsman.

Curtis, George Tichnor. *Life of James Buchanan, Fifteenth President of the United States.* 2 volumes. New York: Harper & Brothers, 1883.

Davis, Stanton Ling. *Pennsylvania Politics, 1860–1863.* Cleveland: Western Reserve University, 1935.

Davis, Winfield J. "History of Political Conventions in California. 1849–1872." California State Library. *Publications.* Sacramento, 1893.

Dearing, Mary R. *Veterans in Politics.* Baton Rouge: Louisiana State University Press, 1952.

Democratic party. Wisconsin. *Address to the People of the Democracy of Wisconsin.* Milwaukee. September 3, 1862.

DeWitt, David M. *The Assassination of Lincoln and Its Explanation.* New York: Macmillan, 1909.

Dickinson, John R., ed. *Speeches, Correspondence, Etc., of the Late Daniel S. Dickinson of New York.* 2 vols. New York: Putnam, 1867.

Dix, Morgan, ed. *Memoirs of John Adams Dix.* 2 vols. New York: Harper and Brothers, 1883.

Donald, David, ed. *Inside Lincoln's Cabinet: The Civil War Diaries of Salmon P. Chase.* New York: Longmans, Green, 1954.

Drake, Charles D. "The Proclamation of Emancipation." Speech . . . delivered at Turner's Hall, St. Louis, January 2, 1862.

Eddy, Thomas M. *Patriotism of Illinois.* 2 vols. Chicago, 1865.

Eisenschiml, Otto. *The Celebrated Case of Fitz John Porter.* Indianapolis: Bobbs-Merrill, 1950.

———. *Why Was Lincoln Murdered?* Boston: Little, Brown, 1937.

Encyclopaedia Britannica. 14th ed. 24 vols. London, 1929.

Encyclopedia of Contemporary Biography of Pennsylvania. 2 vols. New York: Atlantic, 1889.

Evening Journal Almanac. 1859–1869.

Federal Writers' Project. New Jersey. *Bergen County Panorama.* (American Guide Series.) Hackensack, 1941.

Fesler, Mayo. "Secret Political Societies in Indiana during the Civil War." *Indiana Magazine of History.* Vol. XIV (September 1918) No. 3.

Ficklin, John R. "History of Reconstruction in Louisiana (through 1868)." *Johns Hopkins University Studies in Historical and Political Science.* Series XXVIII. No. 1. Baltimore: The Johns Hopkins Press, 1910.

Fite, Emerson D. *The Presidential Campaign of 1860.* New York: Macmillan, 1911.

Flandrau, Charles W. *Encyclopedia of Biography of Minnesota.* Chicago: Century, 1900.

Flick, Alexander C. *Samuel J. Tilden, A Study in Political Sagacity.* Port Washington, N.Y.: Kennikat Press, 1964 (1939).

Flower, Frank A. *Life of Matthew Hale Carpenter.* Madison: Atwood, 1883.

Folmsbee, Robert E.C., and Enoch L. Mitchell. *Tennessee, a Short History.* Knoxville: University of Tennessee Press, 1969.

Folwell, William W. *A History of Minnesota.* 4 vols. St. Paul: Minnesota Historical, 1924.

Foner, Philip S. *Business and Slavery*. Chapel Hill: University of North Carolina Press, 1941.

Forney, John W. *Eulogy upon Hon. Stephen A. Douglas, Delivered at the Smithsonian Insitute, Washington, D.C., July 3, 1861*. Philadelphia, 1861.

Foulke, William D. *Life of Oliver P. Morton*. 2 vols. Indianapolis: Bowen-Merrill, 1899.

Friedel, Frank. "The Loyal Publication Society: A Pro-Union Propaganda Agency." *Mississippi Valley Historical Review*. Vol. XXVI (December 1939) No. 3.

Fryer, Benjamin A. *Congressional History of Berks County*. Reading: Historical Society of Berks County, 1939.

Fuess, Claude M. *The Life of Caleb Cushing*. Hamden, Conn.: Archon Books, 1951.

Fuller, Hubert B. The Speakers of the House. Boston: Little, Brown, 1909.

Gara, Larry. *The Liberty Line. The Legend of the Underground Railroad*. Lexington: University of Kentucky Press, 1961.

Gibson, Florence E. *The Attitude of the New York Irish toward State and National Affairs, 1848–1892*. New York: Columbia University, 1951.

Going, Charles B. *David Wilmot. Free Soiler*. New York: Appleton, 1924.

Goodloe, William C. *Kentucky Unionists of 1861*. Read before the Society of Ex-Army and Navy Officers in Cincinnati, Ohio. April 10, 1884.

Gray, Wood. *The Hidden Civil War. The Story of the Copperheads*. New York: Viking, 1942.

Hadley, Amos. *Life of Walter Harriman*. Boston: Houghton, Mifflin, 1888.

Hall, Clifton R. *Andrew Johnson, Military Governor of Tennessee*. Princeton: Princeton University Press, 1919.

Hall, Harlan P. *H. P. Hall's Observations, from 1849 to 1904*. St. Paul: 1904.

Halpine, Charles G. *The Poetical Works of Charles G. Halpine (Miles O'Reilly). Consisting of Odes, Poems, Sonnets, Epics, and Lyrical Works*. Edited by Robert B. Roosevelt. New York: Harper, 1869.

Halstead, Murat. *Caucuses of 1860. A History of the Nation's Political Conventions of the Current Campaign*. Columbus: Follett, Foster, 1860.

Hancock, Harold B. *Delaware during the Civil War*. Wilmington: Historical Society of Delaware, 1961

Harlow, S. R., and S. C. Hutchins. *Life Sketches of State Officers and Members of the Assembly of the State of New York in 1868*. Albany, 1868.

Harper, Robert S. *Lincoln and the Press*. New York: McGraw-Hill, 1951.

Harshberger, Caroline T., comp. *The Lincoln Treasury*. Chicago: Wilcox and Follette, 1950.

Hatch, Louis C., ed., *Maine. A History*. Centennial Ed. 6 volumes. New York: American Historical Society, 1919.

Hemenway, Abby M., ed. *The Vermont Historical Gazeteer*. 5 volumes. Burlington, 1891.

Hesseltine, William B. *Lincoln and the War Governors*. New York: Knopf, 1955.

Hittel, Theodore H. *History of California*. 4 volumes. San Francisco: Stine, 1879.

Hofstadter, Richard. *The American Political Tradition, and the Men Who Made It*. New York: Knopf, 1948.

Holliday, John H. "Idianapolis in the Civil War." Indiana Historical Society. *Publications*. Vol. IV (1911) No. 9.

Holt, Joseph. *The Fallacy of Neutrality*. Address delivered at Louisville, July 13, 1861. New York: Gregory, 1861.

———. *Rejoinder of . . . , Judge Advocate General, to Ex-President Johnson's Reply to His Vindication of 26th August Last*. 1873.

Holzman, Robert S. *Stormy Ben Butler*. New York: Macmillan, 1954.

Horan, James D. *Confederate Agent, A Discovery in History*. New York: Crown, 1954.

Hubbard, Lucius F., and Return I. Holcombe. *Minnesota as a State, 1858–1870. Volume 3 of Minnesota in Three Centuries, 1655–1908*. 4 vols. Edited by Lucius F. Hubbard. New York: Publishing Society of Minnesota, 1908.

Hughes, Langston, and Milton Meltzer. *A Pictorial History of the Negro in America*. New York: Crown, 1956.

Hulbart, Henry C. *The Older Middle-West, 1840–1880*. New York: Appleton, 1936.

Humes, Thomas W. *The Loyal Mountaineers of Tennessee*. Knoxville: Ogden, 1880.

Hunt, Rockwell D. *John Bidwell, Prince of Carpetbaggers*. Caldwell: Idaho, 1942.

Hunter, David. *Report on the Military Services of . . . , U.S.A., during the War of the Rebellion, Made to the War Department, 1873*. New York: Van Nostrand, 1873.

Hyde, William, and Howard L. Conard. *Encyclopedia of the History of St. Louis*. 4 vols. Southern History, 1899.

Hyman, Harold M. *Era of the Oath: Northern Loyalty Tests during the Civil War and Reconstruction*. Philadelphia: University of Pennsylvania Press, 1954.

Indiana State. *Journal of the Senate*. Special Session. 1861.

———. *Journal of the House of Representatives*. 42nd session.

———. *Journal of the Senate*. 42nd session.

Janesville (Wisconsin) Convention. *Resolutions*. September 17, 1863.

Johannsen, Robert W. *The Letters of Stephen A. Douglas*. Urbana: University of Illinois Press, 1961.

Johnson, Allen, and Dumas Malone, eds. *Dictionary of American Biography*. 20 vols. New York: Scribners, 1930.

Josephson, Matthew. *The Politicos, 1865–1896*. New York: Harcourt, Brace, 1938.

Julian, George W. *The Life of Joshua R. Giddings*. Chicago: McClurg, 1882.

Kennedy, Elijah . R. *The Contest for California in 1861*. Boston: Houghton-Mifflin, 1912.

Kettleborough, Charles. "Indiana on the Eve of the Civil War." Indiana Historical Society. *Publications*. Vol. VI (1919) No. 1.

Kirkland, Joseph. *History of Chicago, Illinois*. 2 vols. Chicago: Dibble, 1892–1894.

Klement, Frank L. *The Copperheads of the Middle West*. Chicago: University of Chicago Press, 1960.

———. *The Limits of Dissent; Clement L. Vallandigham and the Civil War*. Lexington, University Press of Kentucky, 1970.

———. *Lincoln's Critics in Wisconsin*. Address at annual meeting of the Lincoln Fellowship of Wisconsin. Madison, February 14, 1955.

———. "Middle Western Copperheadism and the Genesis of the Granger Movement." *Mississippi Valley Historical Review*. XXXVIII (March 1952)

———. *Wisconsin in the Civil War*. Madison, State Historical Society of Wisconsin, for the Wisconsin Civil War Centennial Commission, 1963.

Knapp, Charles M. *New Jersey Politics during the Period of the Civil War and Reconstruction*. New York: Columbia University, 1924.

Korngold, Ralph. *Thaddeus Stevens. A Being Darkly Wise and Rudely Great*. New York: Harcourt, Brace, 1955.

———. *Two Friends of Man. The Story of William Lloyd Garrison and Wendell Phillips and Their Relationship to Abraham Lincoln*. Boston: Little, Brown, 1950.

Lane, Robert J. *A Political History of Connecticut during the Civil War*. Washington, D.C.: Catholic University Press, 1941.

Laughlin, Sceva B. "Missouri Politics during the Civil War." *Missouri Historical Review*. Vol. XXIII (October 1928) No. 1.

Lee, Basil Lee. *Discontent in New York City, 1861–1865*. Washington, D.C.: Catholic University Press, 1943.

Leopold, Richard W. *Robert Dale Owen*. Cambridge: Harvard University Press, 1940.

Levin, H. *Lawyers and Lawmakers of Kentucky*. Chicago: Lewis, 1874.

Logan, John A. *The Great Conspiracy*. New York: Hart, 1886.

Lord, John K. *A History of Dartmouth College*. Concord: Rumford, 1913.

Loyal League of Union Citizens. *Commemoration*. Anniversary celebration of the great uprising of the North, held in Madison Square, April 20, 1863.

Loyal National League of New York. *Proceedings*. Cooper Institute, March 20, 1863.

Loyal Publication Society. *Character and Result of the War*. "How to prosecute it and how to end it." A thrilling and eloquent speech by General Benjamin F. Butler. Reported by A.F. Warburton. New York: 1863.

———. *America for the Free Working Man*. New York, 1865. (Pamphlet 80.)

———. *The Death of Slavery*. Letter from Peter Cooper to Governor Seymour. Written September 22, 1863. (Pamphlet 28.)

———. *The Patriot Soldier and Hero: General Rosecrans to the Legislatures of Ohio and Indiana*. February 1863. (Pamphlet 4.)

———. *Voices from the Army*. 1863. (Pamphlet 5.)

Lusk, David W. *Politics and Politicians: A Succinct History of the Politics of Illinois from 1856 to 1864*. Springfield, 1884.

Lyford, James O. *Life of Edward H. Rollins, A Political Biography*. Boston: Estes, 1906.

Lynch, Dennis T. *"Boss" Tweed. The Story of a Grim Generation*. New York: Boni and Liveright, 1927.

Macartney, Clarence E. N. *Little Mac*. Philadelphia: Dorrance, 1940.

McKee, Irving. *"Ben Hur" Wallace. The Life of Lew Wallace*. Berkeley: University of California Press, 1947.

McPherson, Edward. *Political History of the United States of America during the Great Rebellion.* Washington, D.C.: Solomon and Chapman, 1876.

McPherson, James M. *The Struggle for Equality. Abolitionists and the Negro in the Civil War and Reconstruction.* Princeton: Princeton University Press, 1964.

Manakee, Harold R. *Maryland in the Civil War.* Baltimore: Maryland Historical Society, 1961.

Maryland. State. *House Journal.* 1862.

Mellvane, Mabel, ed. *Reminiscences of Chicago during the Civil War.* Chicago, 1914.

Milton, George Fort. *The Eve of Conflict; Stephen A. Douglas and the Needless War.* Boston: Houghton, Mifflin, 1934.

Missouri State Convention. March 1861. *Journal and proceedings.* St. Louis: Knapp, 1861.

Mitchell, Robert S. *Horatio Seymour of New York.* Cambridge: Harvard University Press, 1938.

Monoghan, Jay. *Civil War on the Western Border.* Boston: Little, Brown, 1955.

Moore, Charles. *History of Michigan.* 4 volumes. Chicago: Lewis, 1915.

Moore, Frank, comp. *Speeches of Andrew Johnson.* Boston: Little, Brown, 1866.

Moore, James W. *Kilpatrick and Our Cavalry.* New York: Widdleton, 1865.

Morais, Herbert M. *The History of the Negro in Medicine.* New York: Publishers, 1967.

Morris, B. F. *Memorial Record of the Nation's Tribute to Abraham Lincoln.* Washington, D.C.: Morrison, 1867.

Moses, John. *Illinois Historical and Statistical, Comprising the Essential Facts of Its Planting and Growth as a Province, Territory, and State.* 2 vols. Chicago: Fergus, 1889–1892.

Myers, William S., ed., *The Story of New Jersey.* 5 volumes. New York: Lewis, 1945.

National Cyclopedia of American Biography. New York: White. 1898.

Neale, William A. *An Illustrated History of the First Missouri Engineer and 25th Infantry Regiments.* Chicago: Donohoe and Henneberry, 1889.

Nevins, Allan. *Emergence of Lincoln.* New York: Scribner's, 1950.

———. *Ordeal of the Union.* 2 volumes. New York: Scribner's, 1947.

Niven, John. *Connecticut for the Union; The Role of the State in the Civil War.* New Haven: Yale University Press, 1965.

Nicolay, John G., and John Hay, eds. *Abraham Lincoln. Complete Works.* 10 vols. New York: Century, 1914.

North, James W. *The History of Augusta.* Augusta: Clapp and North, 1870.

Oberholtzer, Elias P. *Philadelphia. A History of a City and Its People; A Record of 225 Years.* 4 vols. Philadelphia: Clarke, 1912.

Old Guard, The. New York, 1863–1865. Vols. I–III.

Packard, Roy D. *The Lincoln of the Thirtieth Congress.* Boston: Christopher, 1950.

Parrish, William E. *Turbulent Partnership. Missouri and the Union,*

1861–1865. Columbia: University of Missouri Press, 1963.

Parton, James. *General Butler in New Orleans. History of the Administration of the Department of the Gulf in the Year 1862.* New York: Mason, 1864.

Patterson, Robert. *A Narrative of the Campaign in the Valley of the Shenandoah, in 1861.* Philadelphia: Campbell, 1865.

Pennsylvania. State. *Adjutant General Annual Report.* 1866.

Perkins, Howard C., ed. *Northern Editorials on Secession.* 2 volumes. New York: Appleton-Century, 1942.

Philadelphia Citizens. *Proceedings of the great Union meeting, held in the large saloon of the Chinese Museum, Philadelphia, on the 21st of November, 1850.*

Phisterer, Frederick. *New York in the War of the Rebellion, 1861–1865.* 2nd ed. New York: Weed, Parsons, 1890.

Piatt, Donn. *General George H. Thomas. A Critical Biography.* Cincinnati: Clark, 1893.

———. *Memories of the Men Who Saved the Union.* New York: Belford, Clarke, 1887.

Pinchon, Edgcum. *Dan Sickles, Hero of Gettysburg and "Yankee King of Spain."* Garden City: Doubleday, Doran, 1945.

Pleasants, Samuel A. *Fernando Wood of New York.* New York: Columbia University, 1948.

Plympton, Noah H. *The Patriotic Services of Benjamin F. Butler.* Boston, 1896.

Porter, George H. *Ohio Politics during the Civil War.* New York: Columbia University, 1911.

Powell, Walter A. *History of Delaware.* Boston: Christopher, 1928.

Pratt, Fletcher. *Stanton, Lincoln's Secretary of War.* New York: Norton, 1953.

Pritchett, John P. "Michigan Democracy in the Civil War." *Michigan Historical Magazine.* Vol. XI (January 1927) No. 1.

Quiner, E.B. *The Military History of Wisconsin.* Chicago: Clarke, 1866.

Ramsdell, Charles W. "Reconstruction in Texas." *Studies in History, Economics and Public Law.* New York: Columbia University, 1910.

Randall, James G. *Civil War and Reconstruction.* Boston: Heath, 1953 (1937).

———. *Lincoln the President.* 4 vols. New York: Dodd, Mead, 1945–1955.

Reid, Whitelaw. *Ohio in the War. Her Statesmen, Her Generals, and Soldiers.* 2 vols. Cincinnati: Moore, Wilstach, and Baldwin, 1868.

Record of Heister Clymer. See Clymer, Heister. *Record of. . . .*

Reed, Parker M. *Bench and Bar of Wisconsin. History and Biography.* Milwaukee: Reed, 1882.

Representative Men of Connecticut, 1861–1894. Everett, Mass.: Massachusetts Publishing Company, 1884.

Rex, Frederick. *The Mayors of Chicago, from March 4, 1837 to April 13, 1933. Biography and History.* Chicago: Municipal Reference Library, 1934 (?).

Rhodes, James Ford. *History of the Civil War. 1861–1865.* Edited and with an introduction by E. B. Long. New York: Ungar, 1961.

Riddle, Albert G. *Recollections of War Times.* New York: Putnam's,

1895.

Robinson, Elwyn D. "The Press: President Lincoln's Philadelphia Organ." *Pennsylvania Magazine.* Vol. LXV (January 1941) No. 1.

Roseboom, Eugene H. *The Civil War Era. 1850–1873.* Volume 4 of *The History of the State of Ohio.* 6 vols. Edited by Carl Wittke. Columbus: Ohio State Archeological and Historical Society, 1944.

Rosecrans, William S. *Letters from . . . to the Democracy of Indiana.* Action of the Ohio regiments at Murfreesboro regarding the Copperheads. Philadelphia, 1863.

Ross, Ishbell. *Proud Kate. Portrait of an Ambitious Woman.* New York: Harper, 1953.

Ryland, William J. *Alexander Ramsey.* Philadelphia: Harris and Partridge, 1941.

Sandburg, Carl. *Abraham Lincoln: The Prairie Years and the War Years.* One volume ed. New York: Harcourt, Brace, 1954 (1925).

Savage, John. *The Life and Public Services of Andrew Johnson, Sixteenth President of the United States.* New York: Durby and Miller, 1866.

Scovel, James M. *Three Speeches. . . , delivered in the Senate and the House of Representatives of New Jersey.* With an introduction. (1. New Jersey for the war. 2. New Jersey for the Union. 3. New Jersey for Enfranchisement.) Camden: Dick, 1870.

Seabrook, William L. W. *Maryland's Great Part in Saving the Union; The Loyalty of her Governor, Thomas Holliday Hicks, and a Majority of Her People. . . .* Westminster, Md.: Sentinel, 1913.

Shaw, Archer H. *The Lincoln Encyclopedia.* New York: Macmillan, 1950.

———. *The Plain Dealer.* New York: Knopf, 1942.

Shepherd, Henry E., ed. *History of Baltimore, Maryland.* 1893.

Shoemaker, Henry W. *The Last of the War Governors.* Altoona, Pa.: *Altoona Tribune,* 1916.

Smith, Edward C. *The Borderland in the Civil War.* New York: Macmillan, 1927.

Smith, Willard H. *Schuyler Colfax; The Changing Fortunes of a Political Idol.* Indianapolis: Indiana Historical Bureau, 1952.

Smith, William E. *The Francis P. Blair Family in Politics.* 2 vols. New York: Macmillan, 1933.

Smith, William H. *A Political History of Slavery.* 2 vols. New York: Putnam's, 1903.

Speed, Thomas. *The Union Cause in Kentucky.* New York: Putnam's Sons, 1907.

Squires, James D. *The Granite State of the United States.* New York: American History, 1956.

Stackpole, Everett S. *History of New Hampshire.* 4 vols. New York: American History Society, 1916.

Stampp, Kenneth M. *And the War Came: the North and the Secession Crisis, 1860–1861.* Baton Rouge: Louisiana State University Press, 1950.

——— *Indiana Politics during the Civil War.* Indianapolis: Indiana Historical Bureau, 1949.

Stanley, R. H., and George O. Hall. *Eastern Maine and the Rebellion.* Bangor: Stanley, 1887.

Stedman, Laura, and James M. Gould, eds. *Life and Letters of Edmund*

Clarence Stedman. 2 vols. New York: Moffatt, Yard, 1910.

Steiner, Bernard C. *Life of Reverdy Johnson.* Baltimore: Remington, 1914.

Stevens, Hazard. *The Life of Isaac Ingalls Stevens.* 2 vols. Boston: Houghton, Mifflin, 1900.

Stevens, Walter B. *Missouri, the Centre State.* 2 vols. Chicago: Clarke, 1915.

Stevenson, Alexander, and Bernard Stuvé. *A Complete History of Illinois, from 1673 to 1884.* Springfield: Rokker, 1884.

Stiles, Edward H. *Recollections and Sketches of Notable Lawyers and Public Men of Iowa.* Des Moines: Homestead, 1916.

Swanberg, W. *Sickles the Incredible.* New York: Scribner's, 1956.

Tarrant, Eastham. *The Wild Riders of the First Kentucky Cavalry.* Louisville: Carothers, 1894.

Taylor, Charles W. *Biographical Sketches and Review of the Bench and Bar of Indiana.* Indiana Bench and Bar, 1895.

Teiser, Sidney. "Life of George H. Williams: Almost Chief Justice." *Oregon Historical Quarterly.* Vol. XLVII (September 1946) No. 3.

Temple, Oliver P. *East Tennessee and the Civil War.* Cincinnati: Clarke, 1899.

————. *Notable Men of Tennessee, from 1833 to 1875. Their Times and Their Contemporaries.* New York: Cosmopolitan, 1912.

Thomas, Benjamin F. *Abraham Lincoln.* New York: Knopf, 1942.

————. *Stanton; the Life and Times of Lincoln's Secretary of War.* New York: Knopf, 1962.

Thompson, E. Bruce. *Matthew Hale Carpenter, Webster of the West.* Madison: State Historical Society of Wisconsin, 1954.

Thomson, Alexander M. *A Political History of Wisconsin.* 2nd ed. Milwaukee: Caspar, 1902 (1898).

A Thrilling Narrative from the Lips of the Sufferers of the Late Detroit Riot. March 6, 1863.

Tribune Almanac. New York, 1840–1870.

Trissal, Francis M. *Public Men of Indiana.* Hammond: Conkey, 1922.

Turner, George E. *Victory Rode the Rails.* Indianapolis: Bobbs-Merrill, 1953.

Tuttle, Charles R. *General History of the State of Michigan.* Detroit: Tyler, 1873.

Union Army, The. 8 volumes. Madison: Wisconsin, Federal, 1908.

Union League of Pennsylvania. *Decision of Judge Leavitt of Ohio in the Vallandigham Habeas Corpus Case.* Philadelphia, 1863.

Union League of Philadelphia, Pennsylvania. *Address and Resolutions.* September 16, 1863.

U.S. Biographical Directory and Portrait Gallery of Eminent and Self-Made Men. Iowa Volume. Chicago, American Biographical, 1878.

U.S. Congress. *Biographical Congressional Directory. 1774–1911.* Washington, 1913.

U.S. Official Register, 1859.

U.S. War Department. *Official Records of the War of the Rebellion.* 1st Series. XXIV. Part 2.

Vallandigham, James L. *Life of Clement L. Vallandigham.* Baltimore: Turnbull, 1872.

Villard, Henry Garrison. *Memoirs.* Boston: Houghton, Mifflin, 1904.

Ware, Edith Ellen. "Political Opinion in Massachusetts during the Civil War and Reconstruction." Columbia University Studies in History, Economics, and Public Law. LXXIV (1916) No. 2.

Watson, Benjamin F. "Abraham Lincoln as Seen by a Life-long Democrat." *The Magazine of History.* Volume 50 (1935) No. I. Extra No. 197.

West, Richard S., Jr. *Lincoln's Scapegoat General; A Life of Benjamin F. Butler. 1818–1893.* Boston: Houghton, Mifflin, 1955.

Western Reserve Historical Society. *Collections.* Cleveland, 1918.

Wheat, Marvin. *The Progress and Intelligence of Americans: Proof of Slavery, from the First Chapter of Genesis.* Kentucky, 1862.

Whipple, Edmund P. "The Johnson Party." *Atlantic Monthly.* September 1866. Reprint.

Wilder, Daniel. *The Annals of Kansas.* Topeka: Martin, 1875.

Williams, George H. "Political History of Oregon. 1853–65." *The Quarterly of the Oregon Historical Society.* Vol. II (March–December, 1901) No. 1.

Williams, Henry C., ed. *Biographical Cyclopedia of Maine of the Nineteenth Century.* Boston: Metropolitan, 1885.

————, ed. *Biographical Cyclopoedia of Massachusetts of the Nineteenth Century.* 2 vols. Boston: Metropolitan, 1885.

————, ed. *Biographical Cyclopoedia of Vermont of the Nineteenth Century.* Boston: Metropolitan, 1885.

Williams, Kenneth P. *Lincoln Finds a General.* 5 volumes. New York: Macmillan, 1949–1959.

Williams, T. Harry. *Lincoln and the Radicals.* Madison: University of Wisconsin Press, 1941.

Wilson, Charles R. "McClellan's Changing Views on the Peace Plank." *American Historical Review.* XXXVIII (April 1933) No. 3.

Wilson, Henry, and Jeremiah S. Black. *A Contribution to History. Edwin M. Stanton: His Character and Public Services on the Eve of the Rebellion, as Presented in a Series of Papers.* Easton, Pa.: Cole, Morwitz, 1871.

Wilson, James G. *The Memorial History of the City of New York.* 4 vols. New York: New York Historical, 1893.

————. *Biographical Sketches of Illinois Officers Engaged against the Rebellion of 1861.* Chicago: Barnet, 1862.

Wilson, James H. *The Life of John A. Rawlins.* New York: Neale, 1916.

Winston, Robert W. *Andrew Johnson, Plebian President.* New York: Holt, 1928.

Woodward, Walter C. *Political Parties in Oregon, 1843–1868.* Portland: Gill, 1913.

Zornow, William F. *Lincoln and the Party Divided.* Norman: University of Oklahoma Press, 1954.

Index

Abbreviations

WD:	War Democrat
PD:	Peace Democrat
CWD:	Conditional War Democrat
R:	Republican
CU:	Constitutional Unionist
KN:	Know Nothing
AM:	"American"
UW:	Union Whig
AB:	Abolitionist
ABD:	Antebellum Democrat
ABR:	Antebellum Republican
ABW:	Antebellum Whig
ABPD:	Antebellum Peace Democrat
pWD:	proto-War Democrat

Congress, 43, 50

Agnew, Daniel (WD, Pennsylvania): renominated for District Judge by Union convention, 112: National Union candidate for State Supreme Court, 246; elected, 247; swings Court in favor of Conscription, 247; mentioned, 264

Albany Regency (N.Y.): reaction of, to Secession crisis, 115; in election of 1863, 248; mentioned, 103

Allen, James C. (PD, Illinois: Douglas), 192

Allen, James C. (WD, Wisconsin): addresses War Democrat Janesville Convention, 251

Allen, Thomas S. (WD, Wisconsin): delegate, Pittsburgh Soldiers and Sailors Convention, 337

Allen, William (WD / CWD, Ohio: Douglas): as proto-War Democrat, 50; pro-war resolution of, 77; quits War faction, 130; joins Union party, 217; mentioned, 82

Allen, William F. (WD, New York: Douglas): member, Commission to Investigate New York Draft Quotas, 230

Allen, William J. (CWD / PD, Illinois: Douglas), 192

Altoona Governors' Conference, 154, 191, 253

Alvord, Thomas G. (WD, New York: Breckinridge): joins Radicals, 191; Union candidate for Lieutenant Governor (1864), 301, 302

American Freedmen's Inquiry Commission, 213, 316

American party: members of, 17, 18, 52, 81, 99, 107

Amnesty Act (1873), 344

Amnesty, Proclamation of . . . and Reconstruction (1863), 259, 270

Ancona, Sydenham E. (PD, Pennsylvania: Breckinridge), 229

Anderson, Hugh J. (WD, Maine/District of Columbia), 99

Anderson, James B. (WD, Delaware: Breckinridge): delegate, Union State Convention (1862), 193

Anderson, Lucian (WD, Kentucky:

Douglas): "Union Administration" candidate for Congress (1863), 239, 240; Conservatives enraged by victory of, 269; denounced by W. J. Allen; replies, 270; declares against Peace negotiations, 278; member, Select House Committee on Emancipation, 283; some War votes in 38th Congress, 284, 285, 286; votes for Thirteenth Amendment, 284; and state campaign (1864), 320; delegate-at-large, Union National Convention (1864), 320; supports Thirteenth Amendment (1865), 320; mentioned, 21, 316

Anderson, Robert (apolitical, Kentucky), 36, 40, 43, 44, 51, 55

Andrew, John A. (R, Massachusetts), 93, 120, 220, 257

"Andrew Johnson Veterans Clubs," 341

Andrews, Christopher C. (WD, Minnesota: Douglas): "No Party" candidate for Lieutenant Governor of Minnesota (1861), 114; joins staff of St. Cloud (Minn.) *Union,* 114. *See also* Appendix 2

Andrus, Albert (WD, New York), 191

Antello, Andrew J. (WD, Pennsylvania: Douglas); member, Union Club of Philadelphia, 159; mentioned, 48

Anthon, James S. (WD / PD, Indiana): Democratic candidate for Secretary of State (1862), 174; elected on a War platform, 174

Anthony, Henry B. (R, Rhode Island), 310

"Anti-Negro Suffrage" party (Iowa), 328

Antietam (Maryland) Campaign (1862), 152, 173

Appleton, John (WD, Maine), 212

Appleton, John F. (WD, Maine), 212, 227

Appomattox, Va.: Confederate surrender at, 322

"Arbitrary" Arrests. *See* Military Arrest of Civilians

Arkansas, 149, 184, 221, 289

Armstrong, James B. (WD, Ohio: Breckinridge): delegate, Union State

Douglas), 229

Benton, Elbert J. (historian): description of Union party, 21

Benton, Thomas Hart, Jr. (WD, Iowa): supports Republican ticket (1862), 184; leads "Anti-Negro Suffrage" party, 328; early supporter of Johnson Reconstruction policy, 329; "Anti-Negro Suffrage" candidate for Governor (1865), 356

Bermuda Hundred, Va.: campaign (1864), 276

Berrett, James G. (PD, District of Columbia: Breckinridge), 88

Berry, Hiram G. (WD, Maine: Breckinridge). *See* Appendix 2

Berry, Nathaniel (R, New Hampshire), 163

Biddle, Charles J. (WD / CWD / PD, Pennsylvania: Breckinridge): deserts War cause, becomes Conditional, 130; attacks Republicans in Congress, 154; criticized by publicist J. Campbell, 154-55; and state campaign of 1863, 246; mentioned, 81, 123, 214

Biddle, Thomas A. (WD, Pennsylvania: Breckinridge): member, Union Club of Philadelphia, 159

Bidwell, John (WD, California: Douglas): vice president, Union State Convention (1863), 263; member, Union State Committee (1863), 263; Union candidate for Congress (1864), 305; Radical on Reconstruction matters, 305

Bigler, William (PD, Pennsylvania: Breckinridge), 47

Billings, Henry W. (WD, Illinois), 192

Bingham, Harry (PD, New Hampshire), 262

Bingham, John A. (R, Ohio), 132

Bingham, Joseph J. (CWD / PD / Indiana), 173, 301

Binkley, Wilfred E. (historian): opinion of Clement L. Vallandigham, 350

Black, Jeremiah S. (pWD / CWD / PD, Pennsylvania: Breckinridge): as leading proto-War Democrat in Buchanan cabinet, 35-36; on E. M. Stanton and Buchanan, 155; nominated

for U.S. Supreme Court, 36; joins Peace cause, 229; and Reconstruction court cases, 346, 360, 361; mentioned, 49, 53, 348

Black, John C. (WD, Illinois: Douglas): on Negro troops, 312

"Black Codes": in Maryland, 315; throughout South, 330

"Black Friday," 362

Blackwell, Robert S. (WD, Illinois): addresses Emancipation Proclamation rally (1862), 153

Blaine, James G. (R, Maine), 170, 240-41

Blair, Francis P., Jr. (R / WD, Missouri), 97, 292, 322, 342, 247. *See also* Appendix 2

Blair, Francis P., Sr. (R, Maryland), 318-19

Blair, Montgomery, Jr. (R, Maryland), 65, 254, 281, 297, 334, 347

Blaisdell, Albert (WD, New Hampshire), 69

Blenker, Louis (WD, New York). *See* Appendix 2

Blood, Isaiah (WD, New York: Douglas): attends Governor's War Council (1861), 72

Blunt, Orrison E. (R, New York), 191, 260

Boise, Reuben P. (WD, Oregon), 189

Boker, George H. (WD, Pennsylvania: Douglas): promoter, Union Club of Philadelphia, 1851, 226; member, Union League, 226; denounces Democratic state ticket (1863), 246; mentioned, 123

Boole, Francis I. A. (WD, New York: Douglas): Tammany-Mozart candidate for Mayor of New York City, 1863, campaigning on a War platform, 260-61; defeated, 261; accused of entertaining pro-Negro sentiments, 260-61, 266

Boone, William P. (WD, Kentucky: Douglas): elected to legislature on Union ticket (1861), 107; mentioned, 106

Booth, John Wilkes (PD, Maryland), 322, 326, 354

Border Slave-State Convention (1861),

shire): campaigns for Lincoln (1864), 311

Richardson, Roderick (WD, Vermont): delegate, Union National Convention (1864), 298

Richardson, William A. (WD/PD, Illinois: Douglas): identified with Antebellum Peace cause, 57; deserts Peace cause, 59, 71; elected to U. S. Senate (1863), 179; returns to Peace cause, 179

Richardson, William P. (WD, Ohio): delegate, Convention of the War Democracy of Ohio (1863), 264; Union candidate for Attorney General (1864), 313; elected, 299-300, 313

Richmond, Dean (WD / CWD, New York: Douglas), 115, 116, 124, 127

Richmond, Van Rensalear (WD, New York): member, Governor's War Council (1861), in capacity of State Engineer, 72

Riddle, Albert G. (R, Ohio), 288, 310

Riggs, George W. (WD, District of Columbia: Breckinridge): Financial Secretary, Breckinridge National Committee, 99; declares for wartime Union cause, 99

Riley, Joseph H. (WD, Ohio: Douglas): delegate, Union State Convention, 1861, 126; nominated for Controller, 126

Riots. *See* Draft Riot; Baltimore Riot; Detroit Riot; New Orleans Riot

Robbins, John (WD, Pennsylvania: Douglas): member, U.S. Sanitary Commission, 159

Robinson, Charles (R, Kansas), 120, 193

Robinson, Charles D. (WD, Wisconsin: Douglas): declares for wartime Union cause (1861), 120; supports Democratic ticket (1861), 120; criticizes "Ryan Address" (1862), 180; signs appeal to General J. A. Dix concerning Conscription, 252, 265; campaigns for McClellan (1864), 304

Robinson, J. P. (WD, Ohio): Union candidate for State Senate (1861), 126

Robinson, James C. (PD, Illinois), 57, 304, 359

Robinson, James F. (WD, Kentucky: Breckinridge): appeals for federal troops to assist in repelling Confederate raiders (1862), 148; proclaims state of emergency, 148; denounces Confederates, 148; refuses endorsement to preliminary Emancipation Proclamation, 154; and 1864 campaign, 293; mentioned, 21

Robinson, Lucius (R, New York), 347

Robinson, William E. (WD, New York): elected to Congress as National Union candidate (1866), 358

Rodman, Daniel (WD, Rhode Island): campaigns for Democratic state ticket (1864), 290

Rodman, Isaac P. (WD, Rhode Island): Union general, killed in the war, 291. *See also* Appendix 2

Rogers, Andrew J. (PD, New Jersey): War vote, 38th Congress, 284; mentioned, 256, 271, 283, 317

Rogers, William F. (WD, New York): Provost Marshal for New York, 228

Rolfe, Henry P. (WD, New Hampshire: Douglas): Republican-Union Assemblyman (1864), 290; campaigns for Lincoln's reelection, 290

Rollins, James S. (WD, Missouri: Bell/McClellan): defends War Democrat position against criticism of Peace faction, in Congress (1864), 179; member, House Committee on Naval Affairs, 38th Congress, 282; some War votes, 38th Congress, 283, 284; speaks for Thirteenth Amendment (1865), 318; anti-slavery action of, cited by A. Herrick in House speech in behalf of Thirteenth Amendment, 319

Roosevelt, James A. (WD, New York: Breckinridge): member, Loyal Union League (1863), 225; officiates at League rally (1863), 226

Roosevelt, Robert B. (WD, New York: Douglas): campaigns for Lincoln, 303

Rorer, David (WD, Iowa): campaigns for Republican state ticket (1863),

Speed, Joshua F. (WD, Kentucky: Douglas): campaigns for Union cause in Kentucky in wartime, 89; assists in arming of Kentucky Unionists (1861), 90; and state campaign in 1864; supports Lincoln and Emancipation, 293

Speer, Albert R. (PD, New Jersey: Breckinridge), 256

Spicely, William T. (WD, Indiana: Breckinridge): denounces Peace Campaign of 1863, 201

Spinola, Francis B. (WD, New York: Douglas): supports passage of New York War Bill (1861), 62; attends Union rally (spring of 1861), 68. See also Appendix 2

Sprague, Amasa (WD, Rhode Island; Douglas): campaigns for Democratic ticket (1864), 290

Sprague, William (WD, Rhode Island: Douglas): and Antebellum Peace cause, 40; organizes Rhode Island troops (1861), 54; attends Altoona Governors' Conference (1862), 154; endorses preliminary Emancipation Proclamation, 154; elected Governor (1860), 164-65; reelected (1861), 165; unopposed, 1862, 165; elected to U.S. Senate as a Democrat (1862), 165; and Katherine Chase Sprague, 187; criticism of, by H. G. Villard, 187-88, by Radicals, 188; and Negro troops, 210, 212; resigns as Governor (1863), 236; endorses Republican-Union state ticket (1863), 237; leads it to victory, 37; member, Senate Committee on Commerce, and Committee on Military Affairs and the Militia, 38th Congress, 282; supports Conscription, 284; votes for Thirteenth Amendment, 284; supports Chase boom (1864), 281; and Pomeroy Circular, 292; accused by historians of illegal, unpatriotic activity, 311; charge dismissed, 311; record defended, 350; votes for removal of Johnson from office, 359

Stambaugh, D. W. (WD, Ohio: Douglas): delegate, Union State Convention (1861), 126

Stampp, Kenneth M. (historian): description of Union party, 22

Stanbery, Henry (WD, Ohio): and Reconstruction court cases, 361

Stanford, Leland (R, California), 109, 242

Stanly, Edward (R, North Carolina), 222

Stanton, Edwin M. (WD, Pennsylvania: Breckinridge): as a leading proto-War Democrat in Buchanan cabinet, 42, 43, 44, 49; counsels S. Cameron to promote the arming of the slaves, 96; appointed Secretary of War, 96, 133-35; Buchanan's opinion of, 133; J. S. Black's opinion of, 133; attitude of, toward S. Cameron, 133-34; close relationship of, with other Democrats, 134; and release of political prisoners (1862), 134; praised in Democratic press, 134; frantic reaction to Merrimac attack, 136, 155; and G. B. McClellan, 137-38; and Negro Troop Order of General D. Hunter (1862), 145; service as a "whipping boy" for Lincoln, 145; Radical tendencies of (1862), 146; and change of mind on Negro race issue, 146-47; supports Democratic General J. W. Denver against Republican demands, 155; befriends B. Wade, 156; antagonizes G. Welles, 156; relieves General R. Milroy of command, 156; campaigns for B. Wade (1862), 174; and raising of Negro troops, 211; and American Freedmen's Inquiry Commission, 213; critic of Conscription Act, 214; election campaign of 1863 and, 232, 233; and medical facilities for Negro troops, 280-81; seeks appointment as U.S. Chief Justice (1864), 281; supports Lincoln's renomination (1864), 288; and Maryland elections of 1864, 307; and Reconstruction policy in Maryland, 316; relationship to Lincoln, 316; and Durham Station surrender terms, 325-26; early supporter of Johnson Reconstruction policy, 329, 332; opposes call for